I0003523

Customary Law of the Internet

In the Search for a Supranational Cyberspace Law

For other titles in the Series see p. 413

INFORMATION TECHNOLOGY & LAW SERIES 13

CUSTOMARY LAW OF THE INTERNET

In the Search for a Supranational Cyberspace Law

by

Dr. Przemysław Paul Polański

T•M•C•ASSER PRESS
The Hague

The *Information Technology & Law Series* is published
by T·M·C·ASSER PRESS
P.O. Box 16163, 2500 BD The Hague, The Netherlands
<www.asserpress.nl>

T·M·C·ASSER PRESS English language books are distributed exclusively by:

Cambridge University Press, The Edinburgh Building, Shaftesbury Road,
Cambridge CB2 2RU, UK,
or
for customers in the USA, Canada and Mexico:
Cambridge University Press, 100 Brook Hill Drive, West Nyack, NY 10994-2133, USA

<www.cambridge.org>

The *Information Technology & Law Series* is an initiative of IT*e*R, the National Programme for Information Technology and Law, which is a research programme set up by the Dutch government and the Netherlands Organisation for Scientific Research (NWO) in The Hague. Since 1995 IT*e*R has published all of its research results in its own book series. In 2002 IT*e*R launched the present internationally orientated and English language *Information Technology & Law Series*. This series deals with the implications of information technology for legal systems and institutions. It is not restricted to publishing IT*e*R's research results. Hence, authors are invited and encouraged to submit their manuscripts for inclusion. Manuscripts and related correspondence can be sent to the Series' Editorial Office, which will also gladly provide more information concerning editorial standards and procedures.

Editorial Office
eLaw@Leiden, Centre for Law in the Information Society
Leiden University
P.O. Box 9520
2300 RA Leiden, The Netherlands
Tel. +31(0)715277846
E-mail: <ital@law.leidenuniv.nl>
Web site: <www.nwo.nl/iter>

Single copies or Standing Order
The books in the *Information Technology & Law Series* can either be purchased as single copies or through a standing order. For ordering information see the information on top of this page or visit the publisher's web site at <www.asserpress.nl/cata/itlaw11/fra.htm>.

ISBN 10: 90-6704-230-7
ISBN 13: 978-90-6704-230-7
ISSN 1570-2782

Cover and lay-out: Oasis Productions, Nieuwerkerk a/d IJssel, The Netherlands

To my grandmother Klementyna
for her love and patience

PREFACE

In January 2006, InternetWorldStats.com announced that the number of Internet users exceeded one billion worldwide.[1] This means that 15.7 per cent of the world population has access to the Internet. Even more important is the growth of Internet usage. In the first five years of this millennium the average growth of Internet users exceeded 180 per cent worldwide.[2] As far as the number of websites is concerned, Google – the most popular Internet search engine – has indexed more than eight billion web pages.[3] These figures clearly show that the Internet has become a fundamental tool in global communication and trade and is the symbol of the Information Age.

At the same time, two important events in global Internet regulation have taken place. First, the second World Summit on Information Society (WSIS), which was held in November 2005 in Tunis, gathered nearly 20,000 participants from all over the world to discuss important issues ranging from the need for internationalisation of the Domain Name System to the need to close the digital divide between the industrialised world and developing countries. However, the Summit did not bring any major changes with respect to the management of the Domain Name System, which was retained with the US government.

Second, on 23 November 2005 the United Nations General Assembly adopted the new Convention on the Use of Electronic Communications in International Contracting. This Convention was prepared by UNCITRAL and will be open for signature by all states at United Nations Headquarters in New York from 16 January 2006 to 16 January 2008. This is a very important development as the Convention is the first international treaty drafted specifically for international electronic commerce.

However, despite these developments, transnational electronic commerce remains largely unregulated. At the time of writing the new Convention has not yet become a binding law. Furthermore, the Convention to a large extent repeats the general provisions of the UNCITRAL Model Law on Electronic Commerce, which means that many specific problems were not addressed. On the other hand, although many states have adopted comprehensive legislation with respect to electronic commerce, legal recognition of international transactions remains uncertain. This is because of the lack of unified and flexible legal regulation in this regard.

---

1 1,018,057,389users. See <http://www.internetworldstats.com/stats.htm>, last visited: 24/01/2006.

2 *Ibidem.*

3 8,168,684,336 web pages. See <http://www.google.com>, last visited: 16/08/2005.

The present book is the outcome of several years of both empirical and theoretical research on international Internet commerce. Having both a legal and a technical background I was given a unique opportunity to combine both areas in a multidisciplinary research supervised by two faculties of the University of Melbourne in Australia: the Department of Information Systems in the Faculty of Science and the Faculty of Law. The present volume is partly based on my doctoral dissertation 'Custom as a source of supranational Internet commerce law' written at the University of Melbourne between 2000 and 2003. A rather rigid structure and language of the book as well as citation practice and glossary were dictated by the need to find a compromise between a traditional way of presenting arguments in the legal profession and the modern way of writing in the information science field.[4]

However, I have made significant additions and changes to the original manuscript. The most important changes include four new chapters: one on recent discussion on Internet governance, one on international e-commerce law, which discusses the most important developments in international e-commerce law, and the last two chapters of the book, which discuss the examples of potential Internet customs that have emerged in the last decade and the concept of autonomous Internet law. The new chapter on international regulation also provides the first analysis of the new Convention on electronic contracting. In addition, introductory chapters have been completely rewritten to make them less formal and more reader-friendly. Remaining chapters have been revised.

This book is about international Internet law, but it is not a typical one. It does not present the Internet law from a given state-law perspective, as virtually all books do. Instead, it attempts to find a new way of establishing global rights and obligations in cyberspace beyond parties' contractual self-regulation and national or regional legislation. The overriding argument of this book is that the Internet community has already developed norms that could be utilised by international organisations, local governments, arbitrators and judges to settle disputes in cyberspace as well as to draft better, harmonised laws.

The present book covers many areas of law and technology. It examines the history of the Internet and electronic commerce and issues raised by the phenomena of open networks. It also looks at the problem of the lack of Internet government and the lack of globally binding laws by discussing the most important international developments in e-commerce law. However, the major focus is on the idea of customary practices of the Internet community and their potential legal value.

The present book proposes the idea of custom as a source of Internet law. It brings together various concepts of custom ranging from the notion of international custom in international public law, through commercial usage to various ideas on custom in Western and non-Western legal cultures. These concepts are analysed in order to

---

[4] For a detailed discussion of these issues see section 1.6 Implications of the multidisciplinary approach in Polanski, P.P. (July 2003), *Custom as a Source of Supranational Internet Commerce Law (PhD Thesis)*, p. 15.

offer the notion of Internet commerce custom that could be acceptable to various cultures in cyberspace. To make the concept practically viable the book proposes a methodology for evidencing customary practices on the Internet and applies the theory and the methodology in two case studies, which rely on two very important Internet customs: strong encryption of financial transactions and immediate transaction confirmation. Emerging customs are discussed in the last part of the book.

The present study is addressed both to national and international governments, judges and arbitrators as well as to online merchants, researchers and the Internet community as a whole. It is especially addressed to international organisations and national governments dealing with the Internet regulation to help them with drafting better, harmonised laws. In this respect, this book should be of particular interest to organisations such UNCITRAL or UNIDROIT. Furthermore, it might be also of interest to the Member States of the European Union, who, according to the EU Directive on Electronic Commerce, should exchange information on practices and customs of online merchants.

This book is dedicated to arbitrators of Internet disputes as they are given greater freedom than national judges with respect to norms and legal systems to rely on in settling commercial disputes. However, it is to be hoped that national judges will be interested in learning about e-mercantile customs, as both civil law tradition and common law culture permits the supplementing of express contractual terms with norms of trade customs and usages. Also, in most or all legal cultures, contracts are interpreted with a reference to customary understanding of a given term.

Furthermore, this book might be of interest to academic and practising lawyers interested in cyberspace regulation, as no book has so far examined the non-written sources of Internet law. Almost every book devoted to this subject area treat Internet law from a national perspective. This book attempts to present a radically different approach, one that focuses on supranational commonalities rather than local peculiarities.

Finally, it is hoped that this will be of interest to the Information Technology community, especially researchers, online entrepreneurs and IT managers, who might greatly benefit from learning what the value of common practices is, what the current common practices are, and what might happen to them if they do not follow the established practice.

Melbourne/Utrecht/Salzburg/Poznań/Warsaw Paul P. POLAŃSKI
August 1999 – January 2006

ACKNOWLEDGMENTS

Since this book is largely based on my research conducted at the University of Melbourne between 2000 and 2003 I would like again to express my indebtedness to Associate Professor Robert B. Johnston for his enormous support and unwavering encouragement. His excellent theoretical capabilities, constant search for weaknesses in my reasoning and a profound understanding of the evolution of technology gave me a unique opportunity to learn from a man who spent last 25 years working in the industry as an IT specialist. At the same time, I would like to thank Professor Gillian Triggs, who kindly agreed to co-supervise my research, for her invaluable advice, modesty, support and courage in taking on such a difficult project. The work of my supervisors was particularly difficult as their research interests represent two unrelated fields of knowledge: the science of information systems and the science of law. In addition, I would like to express my gratitude to Associate Professor Frank Dignum from the University of Utrecht, the Netherlands whom I visited thanks to a 2002 Melbourne Postgraduate Award Scholarship. I would also like to Dr Marco Wiering for stimulating discussions about artificial intelligence.

I would also like to thank everyone I visited during my stay in Europe, as well as the staff of the Department of Information Systems and the Faculty of Law at the University of Melbourne. A special thanks goes to the French Department of the University of Melbourne for allowing me to improve my language skills necessary for the successful completion of this book. I would also like to thank the staff of the Legal Resource Centre of the University of Melbourne for their enormous help in obtaining materials often not available in the library, in particular Dr Caitlin Stone, Mrs Elisa Quattrocelli and Mrs Sofia Kosmidis.

After my return to Poland, I had to introduce numerous changes to the manuscript. Invaluable comments were offered by Professor Corien Prins and Professor Rob van Esch, who turned out to be the examiners of my thesis. I would also like to thank Professor Aernout Schmidt, the editor-in-chief of the Series, for his critical remarks about my book. I am indebted to Professor Filip de Ly for interesting debates about the current state and future of *lex mercatoria.*

The completion of this book would be difficult without the encouragement of Professor Witold Bielecki from the Faculty of Information Systems of the Leon Kozminski Academy of Enterpreneurship and Management as well as Professor Eugeniusz Piontek, Professor Jerzy Poczobut, Professor Marek Safjan and Professor Tadeusz Tomaszewski from the Faculty of Law of the University of Warsaw, who gave me strong support in not always easy moments following my return to Poland.

Finally, I would like to especially thank my fiancée Anna Dombek, my very close friends in Australia, especially Alicja and Wojtek Allery, Marek Gąsiorowski and

Stefan Mrowiński, as well as my family in Poland. This book would not have been completed without them. Their continuous support was the key factor in the daily process of writing this challenging, multidisciplinary dissertation.

TABLE OF CONTENTS

LIST OF TABLES AND FIGURES

Chapter I
INTRODUCTION

1. The idea of the book

The topic of this book might at first seem self-contradictory. To connect the largely forgotten phenomenon of custom with modern Internet technology has to bring some disorientation. One evokes tradition, conservative values, inflexibility and slowness. The other evokes innovation, an enormous pace of change and disregard for old ways of thinking. The two ideas just do not seem to hold together. But this is only a first impression.

The Internet has brought a revolution. But this revolution, which enables instantaneous, transnational presence and communication, has been the child of humanity. And humans are social creatures, Aristotelian 'political animals' living and acting in accordance with a prevailing trend. The 'life' of the Internet is therefore no different. It is subject to norms arising out of dominant practices, and standards of behaviour which dictate what is good and expected, or bad and unwelcome. But the fact that the Internet is deprived of a central authority, global written laws, traditional mechanisms of enforcement or an easy way of identifying its users does not necessarily make it a lawless phenomenon. It only makes it a phenomenon more difficult to govern. This, in turn, does not mean that disputes arising on the Internet cannot be solved according to some principles, developed by a community in accordance with the nature of the Internet. To learn these principles one has to study how the Internet community actually behaves.

The topic of this book is the notion of custom as a potential source of global Internet law. Custom is the oldest source of law, known to all legal orders across space and time. It continues to govern our relationships unconsciously despite the apparent monopolisation of legal norms in written instruments. The amount of statutory law and judicial decisions, as well as the speed of change, renders it impossible to even familiarise oneself with binding law. Therefore people continue to live by following what others do. This is the most important reason why custom should still be respected as a source of general binding law. Its nature teaches us this.

Although custom has been marginalised by written law in modern Western domestic legal systems, it remains a very important source of legal norms in numerous indigenous legal cultures, non-Western traditions and supranational legal orders. In particular, ancient and medieval merchants developed their own transnational and flexible customary Law Merchant, independent of formalistic laws of the land

and applicable only to mercantile disputes. The notion of international customary law of merchants has been revived in the modern doctrine of *lex mercatoria*. The emergence of Internet commerce and customs of online merchants has been argued to constitute a venue for the development of a new *lex mercatoria* – the Internet Law Merchant.

Custom is also a fundamental source of international law, and it is in this area where it has been most deeply analysed. The doctrine of international custom provides the best starting point to discuss what transnational custom as a source of law really is. However, the approach of international lawyers is not flawless. The widely accepted theory of international custom requires not only proof of general practice but also evidence of its acceptance as law. The last requirement, as will be shown, creates logical contradictions that are impossible to resolve. The International Court of Justice has often reaffirmed this theory, but has never satisfactorily applied it in practice.

The central argument of this book is that given the lack of supranationally binding written Internet laws, one may discover and resort to the universal principles enshrined in customs of the Internet. Internet customary practices evolve in a borderless space that spans the whole world, and which enables very rapid communication. They are created unconsciously by the community itself and enforced by software, which mechanically imposes certain practices. Internet norms can develop very quickly, within a few years, months or even within a couple of hours in case of widespread subscription to automatic online update facilities. Their growth can be subjected to research that can be performed manually or automatically by software agents. The last part of this book will demonstrate a number of customs in the area of intellectual property, electronic contracting and Internet security.

The idea of custom has additional advantages. It is a very flexible source of norms, as it reflects changes in the practices of participants and it does so as soon as a change takes place. Its norms are not enacted: they are simply there. It can be said that it is a source of already enforced norms in a given community, since it reflects what a majority does anyway. Moreover, those practices are known to the majority of the community. Its advantages over statutory regulation are clearly visible in this respect, since a promulgation of a given law by a national agency is rarely known by the citizens of a given state, and it takes a long time before citizens learn what is expected of them and conform their behaviour to what a statute says. As a result of a flood of written regulations, most written statutory laws will remain unknown to the average citizen of a modern state.

From the legal perspective, the concept of custom plays a very important role in the interpretation and filling gaps in statutory and conventional laws. Custom can also provide an invaluable tool in the interpretation and filling in of gaps left by parties to a contract. Furthermore, customary norms can override contrary statutory or conventional norms, which are no longer adhered to through the process of disuse (*desuetude*).

Custom in the context of the Internet offers an additional and profound advantage. The Internet enables a revolutionary way of establishing regularities in the behaviour of the participants of electronic commerce transactions. In consequence, electronic commerce practices can be established much more easily than in the traditional paper-based world. Both a human expert, as well as software, could be used for the purpose of identifying and tracking electronic commerce practices. Traditional custom does not possess qualities that can be so easily identified and recorded.

Custom also has some disadvantages. From the perspective of the regulatory power of custom, it seems to possess very limited proactive power. It is a very modest instrument of social engineering. By reflecting what is already happening in a society, it is not a good candidate tool for promoting certain behaviour. Written law seems much better able to fulfil this role.

The mechanism of custom formation is very poorly understood. Existing theories of international custom have not so far successfully explained this very complex phenomenon. There is also a great deal of dispute as to what constitutes a custom. Legal theory and practice is divided in its understanding of this problem. Moreover, traditional customary practice is very difficult to evidence. No legal work has attempted to prescribe a methodology for evidencing customary norms. For example, most customary norms discussed in cases of the International Court of Justice are *declared*, rather than *induced*, from empirical observation. Those that are allegedly induced are insufficiently supported by material evidence.

But the Internet enables us to overcome some of these traditional issues associated with the concept of custom as a source of law. The unique features of the Internet enable a new approach to the concept of common practices and their legal value. This change in the perspective on custom can give us new insights into the traditional concept of custom and lead us to a better understanding of this fascinating social phenomenon.

There are two major benefits of the notion of Internet custom that might greatly affect both Internet legislation and jurisdiction. First, customary practices of Internet users could be used by governments to harmonise relevant national legislation. Adoption of customary norms in national legislations would not only help to standardise, modernise and interpret Internet-related laws in various jurisdictions but would also give them more credibility, because the new laws would reflect what the majority does anyway. In this way, a vigilant legislator could lessen or even avoid a serious issue of enforcement of Internet-related laws.

The same approach could be taken by international, intergovernmental and regional organisations interested in the development of international Internet law. To create a useful framework for global Internet commerce it is of vital importance to understand what cyberspace users have already achieved and what needs to be addressed further. There is nothing worse than, after long and difficult negotiations, to adopt an international treaty for Internet commerce, which will not be understood or regarded as necessary by the Internet community.

The second major benefit of e-commerce customary norms is that they could be used by judges and arbitrators to settle disputes involving international Internet commerce. In most modern legal systems, contractual relationships can be enriched with terms implied by usage or custom that parties ought to have known. Such a mechanism, under various names, is certainly available in common law jurisdictions as well as in continental law systems. Therefore, the awareness of current customary practices might be of great help in settling disputes for which there is no specific written provision or relevant contractual provision.

Thus, Internet customary law offers a solution to international Internet and electronic commerce disputes in cases where there is no rule of law. Online trade usages can also become a source of supplementary norms, especially in cases where the rules at hand are too vague, as indeed might well be the case with the new Convention on electronic contracting. Similarly to how merchants traded in the past, by being subject to differing customs of various fairs and marketplaces, modern Internet merchants would have to comply with what is generally done on the Web. Internet custom, as in ancient times, can create new laws, abolish existing written laws and be the best interpreter of written law. This book will demonstrate that there is a 'bridge' that links customs of various cultures, across different epochs, with those observed on the Internet.

This judicial aspect of customary norms could be taken even further. Taking into account the development of the modern notion of *lex mercatoria* one could argue that customary norms could form the basis of an supranational legal framework for cyberspace (Internet *lex mercatoria*). Coupled with the international domain name dispute resolution system (as well as important developments in international commercial law such as the new Convention on the Use of Electronic Communications in International Contracting and 2004 UNIDROIT Principles, relevant arbitrary awards and standard contract terms and conditions), one could envisage the development of a truly supranational legal order for Internet commerce. Therefore, similarly to what is actually happening in offline international commerce, Internet *lex mercatoria* could be chosen by cyberspace merchants as a law applicable to their contractual obligations and be applied by arbitrators in the absence of the law governing a contractual relationship.

2. Aim and Scope of the Book

The aim of this book is twofold: to propose the concept of custom as a potential source of supranational Internet law in order to provide adjudicators with a source of norms on which to settle a dispute, and to help governments and international organisations to draft better Internet-related laws. In addition, this book aims to provide a methodology that an adjudicator or an expert witness could follow in order to test whether a given practice is of a customary nature or not.

This book will primarily relate to the commercial sphere of the Internet, despite its direct applicability in non-commercial areas. There are three reasons for the choice of the commercial sphere of the Internet. Firstly, unlike the non-commercial Internet, there are important international legal developments in this field. Secondly, from a technical perspective, electronic commerce is more standardised than the non-commercial Internet, which, as will be shown, greatly facilitates the evidencing of e-commerce customary practices. Thirdly, the practical importance of e-commerce disputes is usually greater than in the non-commercial Internet. On the other hand, the choice of international e-commerce was made to exemplify better problems of transnational Internet trade and the inadequacies of a national approach to regulate it.

From the perspective of actors engaged in electronic commerce this study will focus on business-to-business (B2B) and business-to-consumer (B2C) transactions. A distinction between treatment of businesses and consumers is important in national legal systems and international commercial law, because consumers are given a much greater level of mandatory protection than professional traders. However, the distinction between B2B and B2C e-commerce is often difficult to make and justify because businesses and consumers frequently buy goods and services from the same websites. Furthermore, many consumers are better educated in Internet intricacies than 'offline' professionals. In addition, both professionals and consumers should have a right to demand the conformance of a given website to a common practice of trading. For these reasons, both B2B and B2C international e-commerce will be taken into account, although the primary focus will be on the former, because of the weaker legal protection of professional parties.

The book will focus on web-based commerce. In other words, it will investigate only commercial websites utilising HyperText Transfer Protocol (HTTP) or HTTP Over Secure Sockets Layer (HTTP/S) protocols to exchange data. E-mail and peer-to-peer networks will be given less extensive treatment. Other electronic commerce technologies, such as instant messaging, mobile devices (m-commerce), old Electronic Data Interchange private networks, Automatic Teller Machine (ATM) networks, and so on, will not be covered, although many of the findings of this study could potentially find application in these fields. These technologies were excluded because web commerce is the most important example of Internet commerce and other technologies are both too old and publicly inaccessible (such as EDI), or still too young (such as mobile commerce) or they are used primarily in non-commercial settings (such as instant messaging). Thus, this research will be limited to publicly accessible websites, thus excluding private networks such as intranets or extranets, virtual marketplaces, and so on. This research will focus on goods and services, both in a tangible as well as intangible form. The concept of intellectual property introduces additional complications and will be mentioned in the text only by explicit reference.

Legal developments in the field of electronic commerce and Internet law will be analysed from the international perspective. This approach is consistent with the aim of the book to study Internet commerce law from a global rather than national perspective. Resort to national legislation or case law involving Internet or electronic commerce will be an exception only made to illustrate certain important points.

With respect to the main topic of the book, special attention will be paid to the concept of international custom. Again, this study will focus on various theories of international, rather than domestic, custom. There are numerous interesting theories of custom, particularly created by German[5] and French[6] scholars, but these formulations mostly look at custom from a single state or a single nation perspective. Consequently they will not be discussed because the idea is to describe transnational phenomenon using transnational theories.

Furthermore, the concept of custom in international electronic commerce will be examined from the legal perspective. This will focus on developments in international public law, despite the fact that the concept of custom has been a matter of interest to many other fields of knowledge including history, anthropology, sociology, psychology, linguistics, economy, law and the natural sciences. The reason for the choice of international public law is that this is the only universally recognised international system of law, existing independently of domestic legal systems. As will be shown later, international commercial law or *lex mercatoria*, although thematically more related to the concept of online commerce, has not yet achieved a status of universally accepted international regime of law, independent of national legal systems. Moreover, there is no single and deeply analysed theory of commercial custom as a source of law that transcends national boundaries. The concept of custom has been much more deeply analysed in the international law doctrine, and for this reason it is a much richer source of ideas to draw from. For these reasons, the concept of international custom, as defined in international public law, will be used. However, the role of treaties, as well as the interrelation between custom and treaties or contracts, will not be the main subject of analysis here. Also, enforcement of customary norms, although crucial to their effective functioning, will remain outside the interests of this study.

3. Methodology

In order to achieve its goal this study has to link two divergent and somewhat incompatible subjects: legal science and information systems science. This is not an easy task. These two fields of knowledge have not only different subject-matters,

[5] For instance, the works of Puchta, Brie, Ihering, Oertmann, Ehrlich, Stein, Titz, Bierling, Stammler, Mayer, Dniestrzański, Windscheid, Enneccerus, Thöl, Zitelman, Tilsch, Jellinek, Rümelin, Somlo, Danz, Biermann. For a discussion of these theories see, for example, Studnicki, F. (1949), *Działanie zwyczaju handlowego w zakresie zobowiązań z umowy*

[6] For instance, the works of Gény, Colin-Capitant, Lyon-Caën-Renault, Josserand, Thaller, Kahn, Lagarde, Lebrun, Laezmarie, Houin, Kassis.

but different research methodologies, different ways of presenting arguments and different ways of citing the works of other authors. Law has traditionally relied on a deductive methodology whereas information systems science has favoured an inductive methodology. These different approaches towards gaining knowledge have had considerable impact on the organisation of this research, its data collection process, and the presentation of its results.

Part of this book is based on an analysis of the available literature. Information systems literature, and the vast amount of material available on the Internet, will be used to analyse the Internet and electronic commerce. Legal developments in electronic commerce will be analysed on the basis of legal literature and the work of various international organisations. A primary focus will be on international legal developments attempting to impose some restrictions on Internet-based commerce.

The analysis of the concept of custom as a potential source of electronic commerce law will be based on both theoretical works as well as empirical data. The theoretical foundation of this part of the research will be legal literature and case law. The primary focus will be on legal literature on international law, as well as relevant cases of the International Court of Justice and domestic case law. In addition, international trade law literature, as well as legal anthropology and legal history, will be examined when needed.

The practical basis of this work will be examples of established web practices identified on the Internet, based on empirical observation of a number of websites and reports of practices provided by Internet companies specialising in web analysis. The capabilities of certain software packages will also be examined. These practices will serve as the building blocks for the development of a methodology for evidencing Internet commerce custom. The proposal will aim at the development of a set of methods that are practical and consistent with the theory of electronic commerce custom. Throughout this entire book two hypothetical case studies will be used to examine the usefulness of current developments in international Internet law and to test the theory of electronic commerce custom as well as the methodology for evidencing it. The last part will identify several emerging customary practices.

4. Organisation of the Book

This book is divided into four parts. Part I focuses on current international legal framework for Internet-based commerce. Chapter II discusses the basic concepts behind the Internet and electronic commerce. After a brief introduction to the Internet and electronic commerce, an overview of problems posed by the Internet is discussed in detail. Chapter III discusses the concept of Internet governance. Chapter IV analyses current developments in international e-commerce law. This analysis focuses on the Vienna Convention for the International Sale of Goods and the new United Nations Convention on the Use of Electronic Communications in International Contracting, as well as UNCITRAL model laws, 2004 UNIDROIT Principles and various European e-commerce directives. In addition, Internet-related instruments are discussed, such as the Convention on Cybercrime and WIPO Internet Treaties. Hypothetical case studies show the inadequacy of the current approach.

Part II discusses the general concept of custom, as well as the concept of international custom. Chapter V includes a brief presentation of the history and importance of the concept of custom from ancient to modern times, followed by a concise analysis of the role of custom in Western and non-Western legal traditions. The process of custom codification and its marginalisation is outlined. The importance of custom in modern international commercial law is then presented. In Chapter VI the analysis turns to the notion of international custom. Various definitions and approaches to capture the meaning of international custom are presented. This part then discusses at length the most important issues associated with international custom, and presents solutions from the literature as well as from cases of the International Court of Justice. Finally, three recent cases are presented to illustrate the practice of evidencing international custom by the International Court of Justice. Chapter VII then proposes the concept of electronic commerce custom based on the previous analysis of international custom and its issues. It explains why the concept of international custom cannot be directly applied to electronic commerce. A novel approach to understanding characteristics of Internet custom, such as the rejection of the time factor, then follows. The new concept is discussed using hypothetical case studies.

Part III succinctly outlines problems with evidencing custom in jurisprudential practice. Chapter VIII offers a new methodology for evidencing customary practices on the Internet. First, the general question of sampling a large population is studied. Then new ways of establishing web custom, using manual and automated data collection methods, is presented. A three-step framework for evidencing Internet customary norms is presented and applied to the hypothetical case studies.

Part IV is a new development. Chapter IX presents emerging customary practices in electronic commerce, particularly those related to online property, web-based contracting online advertising and Internet security, as well as some general customary principles of e-commerce. The list of potential Internet customs might serve as a starting point for the development of an supranational Internet *lex mercatoria* that is then discussed in Chapter X.

5. Important definitions

(a) **Internet**

The Federal Networking Council (FNC) proposed the following definition of *the Internet* in its resolution passed unanimously on 24 October 1995:

'"Internet" refers to the global information system that — (i) is logically linked together by a globally unique address space based on the Internet Protocol (IP) or its subsequent extensions/follow-ons; (ii) is able to support communications using the Transmission Control Protocol/Internet Protocol (TCP/IP) suite or its subsequent extensions/follow-ons, and/or other IP-compatible protocols; and (iii) provides, uses or makes accessible, either publicly or privately, high level services layered on the communications and related infrastructure described herein.'[7]

(b) **Electronic commerce**

is defined as:

'technology-mediated exchanges between parties (individuals or organization) as well as the electronically based intra- or inter-organizational activities that facilitate such exchanges.'[8]

(c) **Custom**

The Oxford English Dictionary provides the following two meanings of the term *custom*:

'1. A habitual or usual practice; common way of acting; usage, fashion, habit (either of an individual or of a community)
2. Law. An established usage which by long continuance has acquired the force of a law or right esp. the established usage of a particular locality, trade, society, or the like.'[9]

(d) **International custom**

Article 38 of the Statute of International Court of Justice defines *international custom* as:

'evidence of general practice accepted as law.'[10]

(e) **Electronic commerce custom**

Electronic commerce custom (or *e-custom*) will be defined as the legally relevant practice of trading on the Internet, which is sufficiently widespread so as to justify the expectation that it will be observed.

---

[7] Resolution passed by FNC on 24/10/1995, see also Leiner, B.M., et al. *A Brief History of the Internet*

[8] Rayport, J.F. and Jaworski, B.J. (2002), *Introduction to e-Commerce*, p. 4.

[9] Simpson, J.A. and Weiner, E.S.C. (eds.) (1989), *The Oxford English Dictionary*.

[10] United Nations Conference on International Organization at San Francisco (26 June 1945), *Statute of the International Court of Justice*.

This term will be used interchangeably with terms such as Internet custom, Internet commerce custom, e-custom, common practice, widespread practice, online custom, digital usage, and so on, unless the context dictates a different interpretation of a given term. Note that the justification of this definition is a major part of this book.

(f) **Methodology**

Methodology will be defined as the structured set of directives designed to solve a particular problem.

6. Hypothetical Case Studies

This section presents two hypothetical case studies that will be used throughout the book to illustrate the weaknesses of the current approaches to regulating electronic commerce and to show how web-based customary practices could be used to solve these problems. The two examples provide an example of how custom can affect both the norms governing the formation of a contract, as well as the content of a contract. The first example shows how the web customary practice of *immediate confirmation of practice* has changed the idea of electronic contract formation. The second example shows how the common practice among financial institutions of *providing high encryption* might affect the content of the contract.

Part I of this book searches for solutions to these hypothetical cases offered by current developments in international electronic commerce law. Part II presents a solution to these cases using the concept of Internet commerce custom as a source of law. Part III shows how to prove the customary norms that are used to solve the hypothetical cases.

6.1 **Transaction confirmation case**

A website operator does not include an order confirmation screen in his or her online ordering system. An international client purchases a number of items from this site, and uses a credit card to make the payment. After filling in all the necessary details, the client clicks an 'order' button. However, an order confirmation screen does not appear. Also, no e-mail confirmation is received. Instead, the client is redirected to the homepage of the international supplier. The client, being unsure about the status of the transaction, requests the credit card issuer to cancel the unconfirmed transaction, and purchases the desired items from another website. Two weeks later the items from the first supplier are delivered. The client refuses to accept them and refuses to pay for the delivery, claiming that it is now customary to immediately provide an order confirmation screen after ordering the goods. Is this claim justified?

6.2 Strong encryption case

A software development company produces an electronic system for sending sensitive trading data and transactions between a large international bank and its global clients. It uses client-server technology and the Internet as the message transport medium. The issue of message encryption was not explicitly discussed in the system specification stage between the bank and the developer. Also, the software licence agreement between the client and the bank does not address the issue of transaction encryption. In this system, messages are unencrypted or weakly encrypted, due to the inability of the bank's web server to support strong encryption, and even though clients' web browsers support strong encryption. As a consequence, a message from the international client is intercepted and, due to this breach of security, a loss of business value occurs. Negotiations with the bank do not give results and the client initiates arbitral proceedings. Can the client successfully sue the bank for damages based on the breach of the custom of providing strong encryption in financial transactions?

Part I
THE INTERNET AND THE LAW

Chapter II
INTERNET ARCHITECTURE AND ITS IMPLICATIONS

1. Introduction

This chapter presents a brief introduction of the history of the Internet in order to provide the necessary background information about its technical architecture. Furthermore, the history of electronic commerce will be outlined in order to demonstrate the difference between modern open Internet-based electronic commerce and earlier closed private networks. Then the impact of Internet architecture on the laws of various countries will be presented. Legal issues will be dealt with in a rather general manner, in order to give only an outline of problems created by the Internet.

2. Brief History of the Internet

On 1 January 1983 the ARPANET network, the predecessor of today's Internet, started to speak one language. This enabled a heterogeneous network of computers to be connected in such a way that they could exchange information and resources.[11]

In December 1969 the Advanced Research Projects Agency network (ARPANET)[12] – an interstate network of computers linking four research centres in California and Utah – was born.[13] Two years later it linked 23 computers located on both coasts and in 1973 ARPANET became an international computer network, giving access to its resources to computers located in England and Norway.[14] ARPANET originated as a tool for researchers to enable them to share knowledge for military purposes.[15] Its development was a result of intense research funded by ARPA shortly after Russia's successful launch of Sputnik in 1957.[16] It allowed

---

[11] See, for example, Leiner, B.M., et al., *A Brief History of the Internet*; Zakon H'obbes', R. *Hobbes' Internet Timeline v5.6*.

[12] Roberts, L.G. (October 1967), *Multiple Computer Networks and Intercomputer Communication*.

[13] Ibid. See especially Robert's design of ARPANET.

[14] University College of London in England and Royal Radar Establishment in Norway.

[15] In particular, it enabled execution of programs on remote computers. Abbate, J. (2000), *Inventing the Internet*, p. 2.

[16] See, for example, Gillies, J. and Cailliau, R. (2000), *How the Web was born: the story of the World Wide Web*, pp. 11-18; Rheingold, H. (2000), *The Virtual Community: Homesteading On The Electronic Frontier*, p. 58.

P.P. Polański, Customary Law of the Internet

researchers located in geographically disperse locations to remotely login and transfer files between computers.[17] In 1971 Ray Tomlinson invented e-mail.[18] Two years later, e-mail accounted for 75 per cent of the traffic on ARPANET, and was to play the most important role in the popularisation of the Internet.

However, ARPANET was no more than a private, architecturally closed international computer network. Soon many other similar networks emerged.[19] The problem was connecting these emerging networks, all of which had incompatible protocols, software and hardware. This made the idea of inter-network resource sharing difficult to achieve. The breakthrough came in 1974 when two American engineers, Vinton Cerf and Robert Kahn, proposed

> 'a protocol design and philosophy that supports the sharing of resources that exist in different packet switching networks.'[20]

This protocol, known today as Transmission Control Protocol/Internet Protocol (TCP/IP), became the technological foundation of the Internet. The central idea was based on Kahn's four ground rules:

> 'Each distinct network would have to stand on its own and no internal changes could be required to any such network to connect it to the Internet.
> Communications would be on a best effort basis. If a packet didn't make it to the final destination, it would shortly be retransmitted from the source.
> Black boxes would be used to connect the networks; these would later be called gateways and routers. There would be no information retained by the gateways about the individual flows of packets passing through them, thereby keeping them simple and avoiding complicated adaptation and recovery from various failure modes.
> There would be no global control at the operations level.'[21]

Of particular importance is the fourth rule of Kahn, which proclaims architectural decentralisation of control at the operations level. This design choice has had an enormous impact on Internet regulation, and is the primary reason why there is no central body that can govern the Internet, enacting and enforcing laws.

In the 1980s the idea of a web of pages or domain addresses was unknown. The Internet was used for e-mail communication, file transfer, and later to access

---

[17] Leiner, B.M., et al., *A Brief History of the Internet*; Leiner, B.M., et al. (February 1997), *The Past and Future History of the Internet*, p. 104; Poke (1996), *Internet-history.*

[18] Griffiths, R.T., *History of the Internet, Internet for Historians (and just about everyone else).*

[19] E.g., AlohaNet created at University of Hawaii in 1970, CYCLADES in France in 1972, Telenet in USA in 1974, etc. See, for example, Zakon H'obbes', R. *Hobbes' Internet Timeline v5.6.*

[20] Cerf, V.G. and Kahn, R.E. (May 1974), *A Protocol for Packet Network Intercommunication*, p. 637.

[21] Leiner, B.M., et al., *A Brief History of the Internet*; Leiner, B.M., et al. (February 1997), *The Past and Future History of the Internet*, pp. 103-104.

USENET, which was a network of newsgroups.[22] In 1984 Paul Mockapetris announced the concept of Domain Name System (DNS),[23] laying the foundations for the modern system of Internet addressing. Modern DNS is an automatic system of translating human-readable Internet domain names such as Amazon.com into computer-readable IP addresses like 207.171.181.16.

Arguably, the most important event in Internet history was the invention of the World Wide Web (WWW).[24] The concept of webpages connected to one another via links was developed in 1989 and publicly released to the physics community in 1991 by Tim Berners-Lee,[25] working at CERN, the European Laboratory for Particle Physics in Geneva.[26] Berners-Lee developed three crucial components of the World Wide Web: the Uniform Resource Identifier (URI) to uniquely identify documents on the Internet,[27] the HTML language for creating websites and the HTTP protocol to enable transfer of such websites from one computer to another.[28] It is important to distinguish between the concepts of the *Internet* and the *World Wide Web* since the former is much broader than the latter.

> 'The Web is an abstract (imaginary) space of information. On the Net, you find computers — on the Web, you find document, sounds, videos, ... information. On the Net, the connections are cables between computers; on the Web, connections are hypertext links. The Web exists because of programs which communicate between computers on the Net. The Web could not be without the Net'.[29]

The World Wide Web did not really take off until 1993, when the first graphical, multimedia-enabled, user-friendly web browser Mosaic X was launched,[30,31] followed by the introduction of Netscape 1.0 the following year (Figure 1).

The appearance of freely available, graphically advanced web browsers was the key factor in the popularisation of the WWW and the Internet. In April 1995 the World Wide Web became the most popular service offered by the Internet, surpass-

---

[22] Created by Tom Truscott, Jim Ellis, and Steve Bellovin in 1976. See, for example, Zakon H'obbes', R. *Hobbes' Internet Timeline v5.6.* See also Rheingold, H. (2000), *The Virtual Community: Homesteading On The Electronic Frontier*, pp. 109-148.

[23] Griffiths, R.T., *History of the Internet, Internet for Historians (and just about everyone else)*; Leiner, B.M., et al., *A Brief History of the Internet.*

[24] See, for example, Gillies, J. and Cailliau, R. (2000), *How the Web was born: the story of the World Wide Web.*

[25] Berners-Lee, T., CERN (March 1989), *Information Management: A Proposal*, pp. 35-45.

[26] <http://user.web.cern.ch/user/cern/CERNName.html>, last visited: 06/06/2003.

[27] Berners-Lee, T. and Mark Fischetti (1999), *Weaving the Web: the original design and ultimate destiny of the World Wide Web by its inventor*, p. 2.

[28] Ibid., p. 38.

[29] Berners-Lee, T., *Frequently Asked Questions by the Press.*

[30] See Griffiths, R.T., *History of the Internet, Internet for Historians (and just about everyone else).*

[31] <http://archive.ncsa.uiuc.edu/alliance/press-images/mosaic.1.0.tif>, last visited: 10/06/2003.

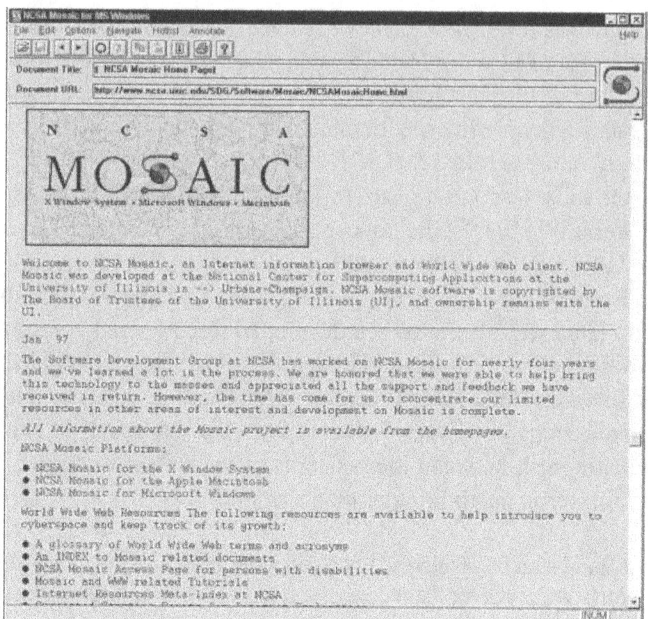

Figure 1 – Mosaic X browser in 1993

ing FTP, e-mail, Usenet and other Internet services.[32] It took the Web less than ten years to revolutionise social life.

The Internet would not be what it is now without the influence of many other important factors, including the invention of time-sharing operating systems, the emergence of cheap personal computers (PCs),[33] the increase of bandwidth on the backbone networks, the commercialisation of the Internet and the active support of governments that have promoted its development. More importantly, however, the Internet would not be where it is now without active engagement of the Internet community through an open and active participation in standardisation forums.[34] In many ways, the author of the Internet is the Internet community.

The Internet is probably the most important social, cultural and economic development of the second half of the twentieth century. The growth of the network of computer networks, originally for American military and research purposes, spread quickly in geographical coverage as well as in purpose of use. Within a few years, nearly the whole world embraced the Internet. In addition, it ceased to be just a research tool built for the military; it started to be used in other ways, including

---

[32] See, for example, Zakon H'obbes', R. *Hobbes' Internet Timeline v5.6.*

[33] See, for example, Rheingold, H. (2000), *The Virtual Community: Homesteading On The Electronic Frontier*, pp. 59-60. On the role of Xerox PARC in this respect see pp. 70-71.

[34] See *below*.

informational, commercial, educational, medical, entertainment and religious purposes.

3. Brief History of Electronic Commerce

One of the most important changes that the Internet brought was the transformation of domestic and international commerce. *Electronic commerce* means many different things that can be put under one heading: commercial activities enabled via digital networking. Although electronic commerce existed long before the Internet, it was limited to inter-business trade, with transactions sent over relatively secure private networks between trading partners who were well-known to each other and with terms of trade set out in detailed written agreements. An example of such computer networking is Electronic Data Interchange (EDI) which can be defined as the electronic transfer from computer to computer of business documents using an agreed standard to structure the information.[35] From the 1960s, some large manufacturing and retail companies[36] adopted EDI and related technologies such as barcode scanners[37] to enable a more efficient supply of goods and services. Another example of proprietary electronic commerce was a collaborative technology enabling joint design, production and product maintenance called Computer Aided Logistics Support (CALS), which was adopted widely in the defence and heavy manufacturing industries.[38] It was from this relatively benign electronic environment that many electronic commerce law attempts began.

The emergence of the World Wide Web brought a crucial change. The Web gave birth to widely accessible Internet commerce,[39] where anyone with access to the Internet could easily set up a commercial website, publish it and start trading online. This had three consequences.

First, by enabling trade with Small-to-Medium Enterprises (SMEs), and with ordinary consumers located anywhere on the globe, the customer base became considerably larger to include entities that could not afford to participate in proprietary e-commerce. Furthermore, the Internet enabled commercial interactions between these groups in all possible manners. This, in turn, led to an intuitive classification

---

[35] UNCITRAL (1996), *General Assembly Resolution 51/162 of 16 December 1996 – UNCITRAL Model Law on Electronic Commerce with Guide to Enactment with additional Art. 5 bis as adopted in 1998*, Art. 2(b). Other authors define EDI as 'the electronic exchange of business documents in a standard, computer-processable, universally accepted format between trading partners.' Bajaj, K.K. and Nag, D. (2000), *E-Commerce: The Cutting Edge of Business*, p. 117.

[36] Bajaj, K.K. and Nag, D. (2000), *E-Commerce: The Cutting Edge of Business*, p. 120.

[37] Clark, R. (December 1998), *Electronic Data Interchange (EDI): An Introduction.*

[38] Also called Computer Assisted Lifecycle Support Timmers, P. (1999), *Electronic commerce: strategies and models for business-to-business trading*, p. 3.

[39] Although Rheingold stated in the context of virtual communities that in the 1996 'e-commerce wasn't even a cloud on the horizon', Rheingold, H. (2000), *The Virtual Community: Homesteading On The Electronic Frontier*, p. 334.

of electronic commerce as Business-to-Business (B2B), Business-to-Consumer (B2C), Consumer-to-Consumer (C2C) and so on. However, it is important to realise that the traditional distinction between commercial and consumer transactions has to some extent lost its significance in the Internet environment.[40] For instance, both consumers and businesses purchase goods from sites such as Amazon.com. The convenient categorisations of electronic commerce as B2B or B2C are no longer distinct but as Rayport and Jaworski put it 'they are linked in a broader network of supply and demand.'[41] This will have an important impact on national laws, as consumers are usually granted much stronger protection compared to professional traders.

Secondly, electronic commerce has become internationalised, which has enabled trading with businesses and consumers located in different jurisdictions. Although some earlier EDI-based electronic networks such as SWIFT[42] enabled international transactions, these were limited only to banks and secured by legal agreements. On the other hand, web-based commerce has enabled purchase of products from sites such as Amazon.com by almost any consumer or business in the world. This has led to uncertainty as to which legal regime would govern such a transaction.

Thirdly, e-business has become anonymous. Unlike earlier forms of electronic commerce, Web commerce facilitates ongoing but also one-off or infrequent transactions between parties who do not know each other. They no longer have a history of previous dealings, which usually provide valuable information about the reliability of another party. Web dealings are not secured by extensive contractual arrangements as was the case with, for example, EDI. Web agreements are less detailed, very rarely read (as they are usually hidden on a separate page) and are very likely to contain provisions which inadequately regulate a given matter. These factors contribute to the creation of an even greater legal uncertainty on the Internet, which is further exacerbated by the lack of globally binding written electronic commerce laws.

Nevertheless, web commerce continues to flourish. The typical web transaction is often based on the shopping cart technology that emulates the traditional way of purchasing goods in supermarkets.[43] Customers first find a product in the electronic catalogue, put it in a shopping basket and then take it to the check-out, where they provide their personal information and financial details, which are customarily secured. The transaction takes place when the buyer clicks the 'order' button and the vendor confirms the purchase. However, the Web has given new impetus to the traditional modes of establishing the price for goods, services or information. In addition to electronic catalogue pricing, other mechanisms are also used, such as traditional auction pricing, reverse-auction pricing, demand-aggregation pricing and

[40] Rayport, J.F. and Jaworski, B.J. (2002), *Introduction to e-Commerce*, p. 5.
[41] Ibid.
[42] See Glossary.
[43] See Glossary.

haggle pricing.[44] Unlike the traditional auction where the buyer with the highest price wins, in a reverse auction the winner is the seller with the lowest price.[45] Demand aggregation sites like MobShop[46] enable multiple buyers to join together in order to negotiate a better price with the supplier. Haggle pricing enables the negotiation of prices over the web although the sales representative is a computer program.[47] Also, the emergence of artificial agents[48] that bid on behalf of a party has changed the way commercial agreements are entered into.

The growth of web commerce was fuelled by rapid advancements in electronic commerce technologies. The area that required special attention was the security of transactions, as the infrastructure of the web transmits information in plain text. With advances in transaction security, especially the development of encryption[49] mechanisms such as Public Key Encryption (PKE)[50] and the Secure Sockets Layer (SSL) protocol,[51] Web trade became more secure. Online traders began to encipher credit card transactions using SSL and perform real-time settlements of accounts. Banks rapidly invested in online banking, and this gave their customers the ability to access accounts, transfer money, pay bills, repay loans or check the history of their transactions. Large manufacturing and retail companies that had large amounts of money tied to the EDI could connect smaller suppliers to their networks via a secure Internet connection.

Other technological innovations such as eXtensible Markup Language (XML) enabled the formal structuring of web documents. This has led to the exchange of business data in a fully portable format, thus making possible complete integration of resources of online companies.[52] Intranets have been built to enable access to electronic resources inside a company, whereas extranets enable employees to connect to electronic resources of a company from outside the office.[53] E-procurement solutions[54] enable business to purchase goods from their suppliers using their online catalogues. The growing popularity of mobile phones and other wireless technologies has led to the emergence of mobile Internet commerce (m-commerce) that enables participation in global trade without a computer.

---

[44] See, for example, Rayport, J.F. and Jaworski, B.J. (2002), *Introduction to e-Commerce*, pp. 229-231.

[45] See also Emiliani, M.L. (2000), *Business-to-business online auctions: key issues for purchasing process improvement*, p. 177; Lucking-Reiley, D. (September 2000), *Auctions on the Internet: What's Being Auctioned, and How?*

[46] See, for example, <http://www.mobshop.com>, last visited: 25/10/2002.

[47] See, for example, <http://www.hagglezone.com>, last visited: 25/10/2002.

[48] See Glossary.

[49] See Glossary.

[50] See Glossary.

[51] See Glossary.

[52] <http://www.w3.org/XML/>, last visited: 06/06/2003. See Glossary.

[53] See Glossary.

[54] See Glossary.

All of this technological innovation has inspired the business world. Merchants have developed innovative business models to fully utilise opportunities created by Internet commerce.[55] Companies such as Dell, Cisco or General Electric have utilised the Web to connect their suppliers in order to streamline their operations. Merchants have started to organise themselves into various forms of electronic marketplaces for more efficient trading of large volume of products, inaccessible to most users of the Internet.[56] Vertical marketplaces, which gather companies from the same industry such as VerticalNet or ChemConnect, have appeared, as have horizontal marketplaces, such as Ariba or Commerce One, which provide products and services across all industries. On the other hand, virtual companies such as Yahoo or Amazon have used the Internet to specialise in online Business-to-Consumer (B2C) trade. Other companies such as eBay provide third party services in Consumer-to-Consumer (C2C) trade. All of these examples show the impact of Internet technology on the way commerce is conducted in the Information Age.

4. Legal Issues Raised by the Internet

The worldwide nature of the Internet has, to a greater or lesser extent, affected every branch of domestic legal systems. Numerous national commissions[57] have been set up to analyse the Internet's impact on national laws. The Internet has been labelled as 'a lawless phenomenon', and the World Wide Web has been compared to the Wild West[58] or recast as The Wild Wild Web.[59] The aim of this section is to provide a brief overview of the most important issues posed by the Internet in order to show how deeply various branches of national legal systems have been affected. Chapter X will provide a more detailed analysis of some of the problems highlighted here.

---

[55] See, for example, Lucking-Reiley, D. and Spulber, D.F. (Winter 2001), *Business-to-Business Electronic Commerce*; Rappa, M. (2002), *Business models on the Web*; Timmers, P. (1999), *Electronic commerce: strategies and models for business-to-business trading*, pp. 35-41.

[56] See, for example, Kaplan, S. and Sawhney, M. (May-June 2000), *E-hubs: The New B2B Marketplaces*, Rayport, J.F. and Jaworski, B.J. (2002), *Introduction to e-Commerce*, p. 373.

[57] See, for example, Australia Electronic Commerce Expert Group (31 March 1998), *Electronic commerce: building the legal framework: Report of the Electronic Commerce Expert Group to the Attorney General*; European Commission (15 April 1997), *A European Initiative in Electronic Commerce (Green Paper), (COM 97) 157*; New Zealand Law Commission (October 1998), *Report 50: Electronic Commerce Part One: A guide for the legal and business community*; New Zealand Law Commission (November 1999), *Report 58: Electronic Commerce Part Two: A basic legal framework*; New Zealand Law Commission (December 2000), *Report 68: Electronic Commerce Part Three: Remaining Issues*; White House (1 July 1997), *A Framework for Global Electronic Commerce: Policy statement issued by President Clinton and Vice-President Al Gore.*

[58] Hamdani, A. (May 2002), *Who's liable for cyberwrongs*, p. 902.

[59] Goodwin, M. (1998), *Wild, Wild Web*; Shipchandler, S. (2000), *The Wild Wild Web: Non-Regulation as the Answer to the Regulatory Question.*

4.1 Intellectual property law

To many researchers the traditional concept of intellectual property (IP)[60] has ceased to exist in the era of the Internet.[61] In particular, copyright protection, which has a territorial scope[62] with significant variations across legal cultures, is entirely ignored by the architecture of the Internet. Web technology is inherently based upon the concept of copying information. Web servers store a website as files containing strings of characters and numbers that may be sent or copied to any requesting web browser. As a result, limiting the copying of information is made impossible by the very construction of the Internet.

The ease, speed, quality and lack of expense of copying and distributing IP worldwide has rendered protection and enforcement of infringed IP moral[63] and economic rights practically impossible. Copyright offenders are practically untraceable if they use anonymisers,[64] which allow their personal details to remain hidden, and if they encipher the transfer of protected materials via encryption.[65] Even technological innovations, such as Digital Rights Management systems[66] and usage rights languages,[67] as well as the existing international IP treaty framework[68] have not managed to change the perception that the Internet is a copyright-free environment,[69] where the free use of works is a rule, rather than an exception.

The decentralised character of the Internet augmented by the use of file-sharing software such as Kazaa, eMule or BitTorrent, in which each participant gives pub-

---

[60] Intellectual Property law provides many forms of protection including copyright, trademark, patents, trade secrets, etc. See, for example, WIPO (May 2000), *Primer On Electronic Commerce And Intellectual Property Issues*.

[61] See, for example, Barlow, J.P. (March 1994), *The Economy of Ideas: Rethinking Patents and Copyrights in the Digital Age*; Weber, R.H. (2001), *Does Intellectual Property Law Become Unimportant in Cyberspace?*

[62] See, for example, Art. 3 of WIPO (1971), *Paris Act of July 24, 1971, as amended on September 28, 1979 of Berne Convention for the Protection of Literary and Artistic Works of September 9, 1886.*

[63] Art. 6 bis in ibid., Art. 5 in WIPO (1996) *Performances and Phonograms Treaty (adopted in Geneva on December 20, 1996).*

[64] See, for example, <http://www.safeweb.com or http://www.anonymizer.com>, last visited: 06/03/2003.

[65] See Glossary.

[66] See, for example, Martens, T. and Garrity, B. (4 November 2005), *Consumers sing copy-protection blues.*

[67] See, for example, Stefik (1997), *Shifting the Possible: How digital property rights challenge us to rethink digital publishing.*

[68] See, for example, WIPO (1996), *Copyright Treaty (adopted in Geneva on December 20, 1996)*; WIPO (1971), *Paris Act of July 24, 1971, as amended on September 28, 1979 of Berne Convention for the Protection of Literary and Artistic Works of September 9, 1886*; WIPO (1996), *Performances and Phonograms Treaty (adopted in Geneva on December 20, 1996)*; WTO (15 April 1994), *Annex 1c: Agreement On Trade-Related Aspects Of Intellectual Property Rights (TRIPS) to Agreement Establishing World Trade Organisation.*

[69] See, for example, ISOC (15 August 2002), *Statement of the Internet Society on Digital Rights Management.*

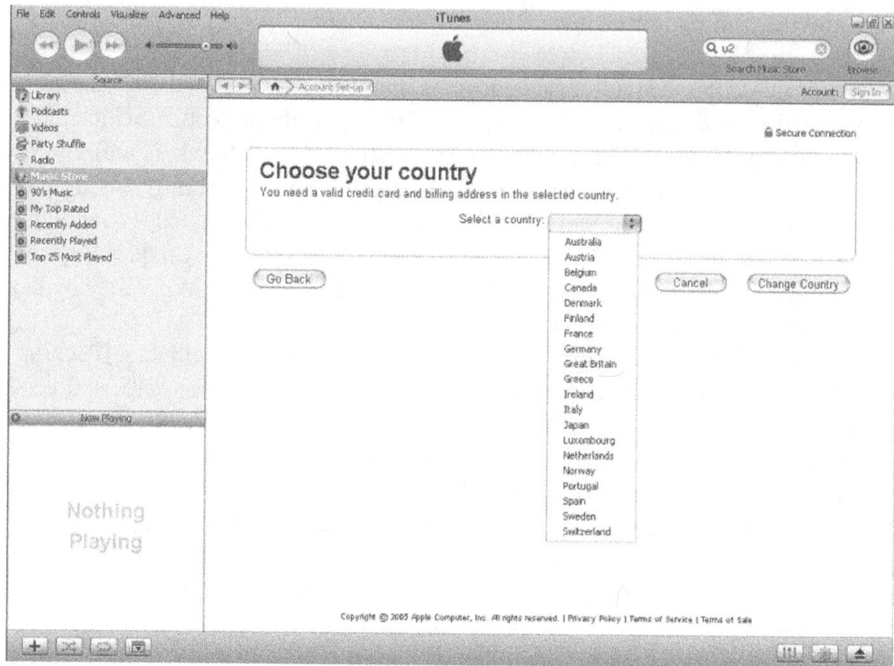

Figure 2 – iTunes, which sells legitimate music files and videos is available only in few industralised countries

lic access to music or video files, renders persecution of copyright violators a practically impossible task. A recent ruling of the US Supreme Court in the already famous *Grokster* case,[70] followed by similar rulings in other jurisdictions[71] might prevent some companies from investing in file-sharing software. In fact, Grokster was forced to shut down its service.[72] It is hard to believe, however, that Internet users will stop using such software. Even if Kazaa implements a filtering technology pursuant to the order of the High Court of Australia,[73] P2P users will have a plethora of other networks to switch to. A recent report from the Electronic Frontiers Foundation confirms this assertion. Despite the fact that as of November 2005 15,000 users of P2P networks have been sued, the usage of file-sharing systems has increased and is more popular than ever.[74]

P2P networks create a huge challenge for the entertainment industry, but copyright issues also arise in the context of other networking technologies such as web browsing. For instance, it is not clear whether it is permissible to link to web re-

---

[70] *Metro-Goldwyn-Mayer Studios, Inc* v. *Grokster Ltd.* [2005] WL 1499402.

[71] See the discussion in Chapter IX.

[72] Boliek, B. (8 November 2005), *Grokster to stop distributing file-sharing service.*

[73] *Universal Music Australia Pty Ltd* v. *Sharman License Holdings Ltd* [2005] FCA 1242 (5 September 2005). See also Goldfarb, J. (24 November 2005), *Kazaa given deadline to alter system.*

[74] Electronic Frontiers Foundation (2005), *RIAA* v. *the People: Two Years Later.*

sources without authorisation or to use thumbnails of third party artwork without consent. Also, technology-driven copying, such as copying to RAM memory or hard disk, is questioned by some commentators. As will be shown in Chapter X, there are already widespread customs in this field that can be utilised to settle these issues.

One of the branches of IP law, the law of trademarks, has also been greatly affected by the Internet, especially in relation to problems posed by a user-friendly address of a website known as a domain name[75] (such as Amazon.com, Rossetta.net, w3c.org, theage.com.au). Domain name registration has customarily been based on 'first-in, first-served' principle and some early Internet users reserved domain names of famous companies in order to later resell these domains for a substantial profit, a practice known as *cybersquatting*.[76] Trademark law, which is territorial in nature, was suddenly confronted with phenomenon that ignores borders and in effect introduces dozens of competing trademark regimes and trademark name holders. Disputes arising out of domain name assignments are difficult, especially given that this area is virtually unregulated on both national and international levels. Online dispute resolution mechanisms have emerged, which tackle the issues of registration of domain names in bad faith.[77] In many countries, such registrations have been regarded as an unfair competition. We will come back to this point in the last chapter.

Patent law has also been affected by the flood of patent claims for almost every invention on the Internet.[78] Some patent claims may have serious consequences for the Internet. Recently, British Telecom lost a case to establish a patent on the hyperlink,[79] which is a fundamental of the World Wide Web. Here again, because of the territorial scope of patent laws, the only way to protect them is to patent them in every country where the Internet is being used, which is exceptionally ineffective, expensive and time-consuming. The situation has been further complicated with the emergence of freely available software code through the Open Source initiative,[80] whose philosophy is in stark contrast to that of software patents. The

---

[75] See Glossary

[76] See, for example, Harris, A. (10 September 2002), *Cybersquatting Law Gets Longer Reach*. See the discussion in Chapter IX.

[77] But see, for example, ICANN (2001), *ICANN Fact Sheet*; ICANN (25 November 1998), *Memorandum Of Understanding Between The U.S. Department Of Commerce And Internet Corporation For Assigned Names And Numbers*; ICANN (1999), *Rules for Uniform Domain Name Dispute Resolution Policy*; ICANN (26 August 1999), *Uniform Domain Name Dispute Resolution Policy.*

[78] Datz, T. (2002), *Who Should Own What? An interview with Lawrence Lessig on Patents and the Internet*. See also Lessig, L. (2001), *The future of ideas. The fate of the commons in a connected world* in which he argues among other things that companies through IP protection will stifle the growth of the Internet.

[79] See Memorandum And Order Granting Summary Judgment (22 August 2002), *British Telecommunications PLC* v. *Prodigy Communications Corp., 00 Civ. 9451 (CM)*. See also, e.g., Delio, M. (23 August 2002), *Judge Tosses BT Hyperlink Case.*

[80] See, for example, <http://www.opensource.org>, last visited: 06/11/2005.

diverging approaches to patentability of software innovation in the United States and the European Union has led the latter to reject a harmonising directive in this respect.

4.2 Contract law

The traditional law of contract has been confronted with difficult issues of online contract formation and acceptability of electronic form and content. In the context of contract formation many questions have been raised as to whether a website of electronic shop constitutes an offer.[81] It has been argued that a basic website (static website) that only advertises products but does not display information about their availability should not be treated as a definitive offer but as an invitation to treat.[82] This is a logical contention because such websites do not enable an immediate or automatic conclusion of a transaction. However, there is a debate concerning the status of the so-called 'interactive website' which contains detailed product catalogues and enables an immediate conclusion of a contract by software without involvement of a human operator. Authors supporting the view that interactive websites should not be treated as offers claim that, in a similar way to displays in shop windows, the seller should not be held bound to an unforeseeable number of acceptances,[83] and that the web vendor may not want to trade with certain jurisdictions[84] or may want to create price differentials for customers from different regions.[85] Unfortunately, arguments like these indicate a large degree of ignorance of electronic commerce capabilities and online mercantile practices, because online merchants already have the relevant technology at their disposal. It is a common practice that trading websites provide real-time access to information about product availability and prices, shipping charges, taxes, packaging and so on. Some web vendors also restrict availability of certain products or use different pricing policies dependant on where a costumer lives. For instance, Amazon.com and its trading partners sell both new and second hand items. However, second hand items are generally available to customers located in the United States only, which is easy to establish as only buyers with a ship-to address in the United States will be accepted by the system. In summary, it is submitted that an interactive website should be presumed to constitute an offer.

[81] See, for example, Hance, O. (1996), *Business and Law on the Internet*, p. 154. Hance supports view that a website constitutes offer. For the opposite view see, for example, Perdue, E.S. (1996), *Creating Contracts Online*, p. 82. Other authors do not give a definitive answer; see, for example, Glatt, C. (Spring 1998), *Comparative issues in the formation of electronic contracts*, p. 51. The question of contract formation via e-mail and other Internet technologies resembles traditional contract formation and is outside the scope of this book.

[82] See, for example, Glatt, C. (Spring 1998), *Comparative issues in the formation of electronic contracts*, p. 50.

[83] Gringras, C. (1997), *The Laws of the Internet*, p. 16.

[84] Smith, G.J.H. (1996), *Internet Law and Regulation*, p. 97.

[85] Gringras, C. (1997), *The Laws of the Internet*, p. 14.

Two recent incidents show the importance of the treatment of a mistake during contract formation. In March 2003, on the basis of a contractual mistake, Amazon.co.uk declined to honour online contracts for handheld Ipaq computers valued at £300 that were sold for £7.32.[86] Soon afterwards, Thai Airlines refused to honour purchases of first class flights from London to Bangkok for a price equal to that of airport taxes.[87] Although resolution of the problem of treatment of mistake is not straightforward, it should be noted that many customers consider the Web to be a bargain place.[88] Given the nature of the commercial Internet, it is much more difficult to distinguish between bargains and mistakes than in the traditional world. Moreover, the payment is usually immediate, and is confirmed by e-mail and website, which proves that a transaction took place. It can then be argued that mistakes should in general be treated with a greater degree of scepticism than in paper-based transactions. Again, time will show in which direction practice will go.

There are many other issues associated with contract formation that will not be analysed at length here. They include: the capacity and intention to form a contract, common law consideration or civil law cause, time and place of contract formation, problems of classification of Internet technologies as instantaneous or non-instantaneous,[89] enabling a communication between present people,[90] various types of online auctions, and so on. This situation is further complicated by the emergence of intelligent agent-mediated contract formation mechanisms[91] that do not merely act as static pre-programmed software devices but can learn from their past experiences and modify their behaviour accordingly, thus having their own autonomy.[92] Finally, there are numerous customs that have emerged in the area of online contracting, which will be analysed throughout this book.

The form of online documents has also created problems of validity and enforceability. All modern national legal systems rely on the importance of handwriting, original documentation and signatures to identify and prove unique features of a given transaction. However, these terms have lost their meaning in an electronic

---

[86] See, for example, Sturgeon, W. (19 March 2003), *Amazon fails to honour Pocket PC bargain*; Sturgeon, W. (20 March 2003), *Amazon.co.uk breaks iPaq news to customers but lawyers still aren't convinced.*

[87] Sturgeon, W. (28 April 2003), *Thai Airways online sales in legal mess.*

[88] Ibid.

[89] See, for example, *Adams* v. *Lindsell* [1818] 1 B&Ald 681; *Brinkibon Ltd* v. *Stahag Stahlwarenhandelsgesellschaft mbH* [1983] 2 AC 34; *Entores* v. *Miles Far East Corporation* [1955] 2 QB 327.

[90] This distinction is known in civil law systems. Telephone conversation although technically is between people that are not present, from a legal perspective is treated as being between present.

[91] See, for example, Allen, T. and Widdison, R. (Winter 1996), *Can Computers Make Contracts?*; Weitzenboeck, E.M. (2001), *Electronic Agents and the Formation of Contracts.*

[92] See, for example, Russell, S.J. and Norvig, P. (1995), *Artificial intelligence: a modern approach*, Wooldridge, M. and Jennings, N.R. (June 1995), *Intelligent Agents: Theory and Practice*. See also, e.g., Allen, T. and Widdison, R. (Winter 1996), *Can Computers Make Contracts?*; Gonzalo, S. (2001), *A Business Outlook regarding Electronic Agents.*

context where there are no tangible documents to which they can be related. In an electronic environment, which document can be considered as the original? Electronic writing does not uniquely distinguish a writer. A word-processor signature cannot uniquely identify a will. Any electronic document can be considered as an original as copies are indistinguishable. To remedy this situation digital signatures have been introduced, which promise to be a better method of guaranteeing the authenticity of a document than its paper-based counterpart.[93] Digital signatures enable not only the verification of a signer of a document, which achieves sender non-repudiation, but can also ensure that a document has not been altered during transmission.[94] Questions relating to electronic signatures and electronic contracts in regard to their legal effect, validity, enforceability and admissibility in court proceedings have been addressed in many countries, mainly as a result of Model Laws developed by UNCITRAL,[95] although, as will be pointed out later, no harmonised solution has so far been developed.[96] However, a major problem with digital signatures is that they are rarely used in practice. Internet users generally use less sophisticated methods of establishing identity, such as usernames and passwords or PGP technology, which seem to work well in practice.

The content of electronic contract has also introduced problems. A difficult matter is the location of parties, which, if a party does not indicate it, may turn out to be impossible to establish. It is unclear whether a domain name creates a presumption in favour of party location or not. Furthermore, the applicability of standard terms and conditions may turn out to be problematic, especially if they contain surprising terms. Another difficulty is the distinction between goods, services and information.[97] Other problems include protection of consumers, as the Internet blurs the distinction between a professional and a consumer. Finally, one of the most important issues is how to evidence electronic contracts or supply the original of a contract.

4.3 Crime and offence law

Like other national legal branches, criminal law and the law of minor offences (or torts) has a territorial scope. However, it has to address supranational issues arising from a negligent or criminal act committed by an intruder in cyberspace that has an adverse effect in a country in question. Of great concern is *malicious hacking*, which is breaking into an information system in order to steal, delete or change important

---

[93] See, for example, Schneier, B. (1997), *Cryptography Primer.*

[94] Koops, B.-J. (1999), *The crypto controversy: a key conflict in the information society*; Schneier, B. (1997), *Cryptography Primer.*

[95] See *below*.

[96] But see 1999 European Electronic Signature Directive. See also draft Convention on Electronic Contracting.

[97] See, for example, Kessedjian, C. (August 2000), *Electronic Commerce and International Jurisdiction. Prel. Doc. No 12. Summary of discussions*, pp. 5-6.

data. Another serious concern is computer viruses or Trojan horses.[98] A virus self-executes and self-replicates to cause harm to a computer by deleting files, formatting hard drives or simply displaying annoying messages. Trojan horses do not replicate themselves and are usually executed by opening an e-mail attachment or downloading a program.[99] Other serious problems are Denial of Service attacks (DoS) and Distributed Denial of Service attacks (DDoS), both of which aim to block access to a given website by overloading Internet servers with requests. These requests are sent from botnets or networks controlled by a perpetrator.[100] One of the most dangerous DoS attacks took place in October 2002. It targeted thirteen Domain Name Servers with the intention of making the Internet malfunction.[101]

An interesting fact is the decreasing age of cyber offenders. A famous DoS attack on the Yahoo portal in February 2000 was instigated by somone called 'Mafia Boy', who turned out to be fifteen years old.[102] It is not surprising that the Internet is considered insecure, especially given the difficulty of tracking down offenders, the free availability of powerful security-breaching programs, as well as new security bugs and a common lack of awareness about potential risks associated with security breaches.[103] The perceived lack of Internet security has given rise to a discussion of self-help or even hacking as a way of fighting online theft.[104] In this respect one should mention the controversial action of the FBI, which hacked into Russian computer systems to obtain the first 'extra-territorial seizure of digital evidence', which involved catching two hackers under the pretext of a job interview in the United States.[105] To counter problems of cybercrime, the Council of Europe has adopted a controversial[106] Convention on Cybercrime,[107] which has only recently come into force.

Recently major problems have been caused by Internet frauds known as *phishing* and *pharming*,[108] in which perpetrators induce innocent users to reveal their usernames and passwords by directing them to bogus websites, which look like

---

98 See Glossary. Also see, for example, Symantec (9 September 2002), *What is the difference between viruses, worms, and Trojans?*

99 Ibid.

100 See, for example, Whitcomb, D. (3 November 2005), *US charges 'Botmaster' in unique computer crime.*

101 ComputerWire (23 October 2002), *Feds investigating 'largest ever' Internet attack*; McGuire, D. and Krebs, B. (22 October 2002), *Attack On Internet Called Largest Ever*; Orlowski, A. (22 October 2002), *Root server DoS attack slows net.*

102 See, for example, Barabási, A.-L. (2002), *Linked: The New Science of Networks*, pp. 1-3.

103 See, for example, Tovey, M. (2001), *Security of eCommerce Systems.*

104 Berman, H., *Peer-to-Peer Piracy Prevention Act Section-by-Section Analysis*; Sinrod, E.J. (13 September 2002), *E-Legal: A Bill to Combat P2P Copyright Infringement.*

105 Reuters (5 October 2002), *Russian hacker gets 3-year sentence.*

106 See American Civil Liberties Union, *Eight Reasons the US Should Reject the International Cybercrime Treaty.*

107 See *below*. Council of Europe (23 November 2001), *Convention on Cybercrime, ETS No. 185, signed at Budapest.*

108 See Glossary.

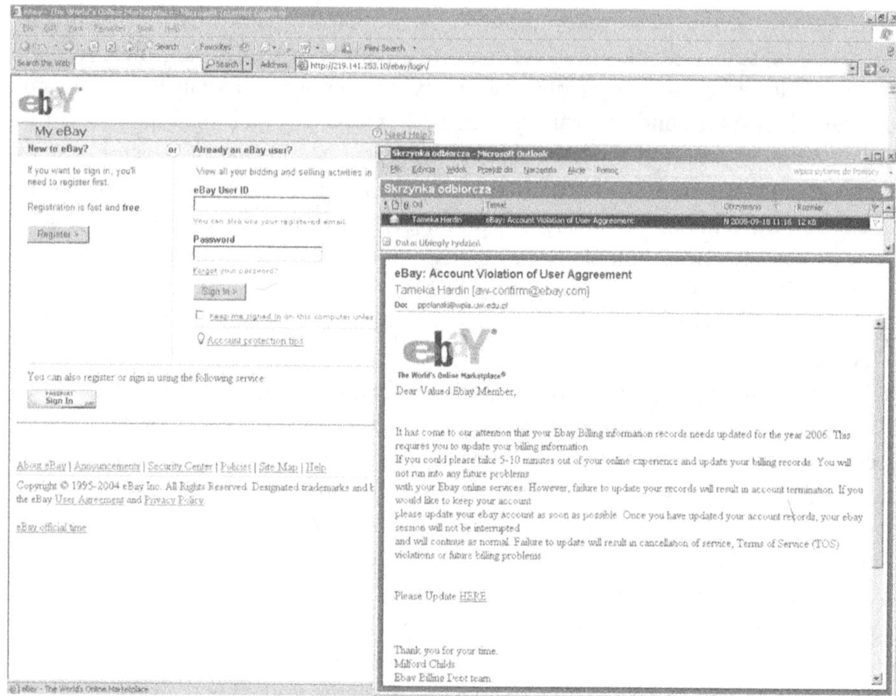

Figure 3 – Example of phishing where a user is induced by e-mail to 'update' his billing records under the pretext of account violation of user agreement. Notice the numeric IP address instead of a domain name

original websites. Usually e-mails are sent in the name of a well-known company asking for a link to be clicked, which then asks for a username and password. In the case shown above, an e-mail has allegedly come from Ebay which asks for the recipient to update their billing information. What should bring suspicion is the lack of a literal domain name, instead, a numeric IP address is used.

Another challenging issue on the Internet is the protection of individuals from defamatory actions or criminal threats referred to as *cyberstalking*.[109] An important problem is the amount of websites displaying content that is usually prohibited by national legal systems, such as child pornography, or websites which give instructions about how to harm others[110] or which solicit the use of force.[111]

---

[109] For a recent trial in America see Costlow, T. (3 September 2002), *As stalkers go online, new state laws try to catch up.*

[110] See, for example, Akdeniz, Y. (2001), *Case Analysis of (the Yahoo case) League Against Racism and Antisemitism (LICRA), French Union of Jewish Students* v. *Yahoo! Inc. (USA), Yahoo France, Tribunal de Grande Instance de Paris (The County Court of Paris), Interim Court Order, 20 November 2000.*

[111] See, for example, EPIC and PI (2002), *Privacy and Human Rights 2002. An International Survey of Privacy Laws and Developments.*

National policymakers have engaged in tough policies aimed at the elimination of this phenomenon, introducing surveillance systems like Echelon and Carnivore.[112] China has blocked access to some search engines, including the very popular Google.[113] On the other hand, the Platform for Internet Content Selection (PICS) has been proposed as a technological solution for classification and filtering of website content. PICS is a specification developed by the World Wide Web Consortium that enables labels (metadata) to be associated with Internet content to help parents and teachers control what children access on the Internet.[114] Another way of approaching the problem of illegal content is the highly controversial attempt to assign liability to Internet Service Providers (ISPs).[115] For instance, the Spanish government forced ISPs to block access to the Batasuna[116] website of separatist Basques.[117] However, ISPs provide community access to the Internet and usually also host websites on their servers, but customarily do not check the content of a site. As a result they have no easy way of finding out what content has been posted on their information system. The side effect of these activities has raised concerns about freedom of speech.[118]

4.4 **Privacy law**

Similarly, privacy laws have been deeply affected by the Internet.[119] One problem is the ease of automatically sending thousands of electronic messages to predetermined addressees without the consent of recipients, which is usually known as *spamming*.[120] This is exacerbated by the fact that the sender's address changes every time messages are sent, making simple blocking of the originator's address an unfeasible solution. Spamming is dangerous as it is sometimes used to bring a server down (DDOS attack), or to hack into a system or to distribute viruses or

---

112 See, for example, Broersma, M. (11 April 2001), *Privacy activists plan assault on Eschelon, Carnivore.*

113 See, for example, BBC News (2 September 2002), *China blocking Google.*

114 <http://www.w3.org/PICS/>, last visited: 06/03/2003.

115 See below Arts. 12-15 of OJ L 178/1 (12.11.2000), *Directive 2000/31/EC of the European Parliament and of the Council of 8 June 2000 on certain legal aspects of information society services, in particular electronic commerce, in the Internal Market (Directive on Electronic Commerce)*; see also, e.g., Hamdani, A. (May 2002), *Who's liable for cyberwrongs*; Shipchandler, S. (2000), *The Wild Wild Web: Non-Regulation as the Answer to the Regulatory Question.*

116 <http://www.batasuna.org>, last visited: 10/10/2002.

117 See, for example, timothy (7 October 2002), *Internet Censorship In Spain.*

118 See, for example, activities of Electronic Frontier Foundation, at <http://www.eff.org>, last visited: 06/03/2003.

119 See, for example, <http://www.epic.org>, last visited: 06/03/2003 or <http://www.privacy international.org>, last visited: 06/03/2003.

120 The term spam is usually used in the context of unsolicited e-mail communication. However, unsolicited bulky messages are also sent to mobile phones, blogs, newsgroups, online forums or games. See Glossary and Chapter IX. See also, for example, Branscomb, A.W. (May 1995), *Anonymity, Autonomy, And Accountability: Challenges To The First Amendment In Cyberspaces*, pp. 1657-1660.

other malicious software. It is also a problem because it shifts the cost from the sender, whose costs are negligible, to the recipient. Some legal systems promote the use of opt-out registers, but rather than providing relief, these often turn out to be used for e-mail validation purposes of the sender.

Moreover, the ease of collection of personal data by means of *cookies* and *web beacons* has raised privacy concerns. A cookie is a file that most major websites store on a user's computer for the purpose of tracking information about browsing preferences, such as the addresses of frequently visited websites, the length of time spent at each of them, and so on.[121] Web beacons are small, transparent image files used to count the number of times a webpage or e-mail is opened.[122] The potential for worldwide dissemination of information gathered in this way, without the knowledge of its owners, has created severe tensions between jurisdictions. Even greater concerns have been caused by widespread use of spyware,[123] which potentially can send any information back to a requesting server without authorisation or knowledge of an end user. The European Union has implemented tough data protection policies whereas the United States has a much more liberal attitude towards the regulation of privacy. In this field some local agreements, such as the United States-European Union. Safe Harbour Agreement became necessary in order to provide a safe legal framework for the conduct of international trade.[124] Also some technological solutions, such as the Platform for Privacy Preferences Project (P3P),[125] have been developed by the Internet community.[126]

Similar controversies have been created by some employers who read their employees' e-mail. There is a growing concern associated with actions of the United States and other governments aimed at an invigilation of electronic records in response to the attacks of September 11.[127] For many, the battle for privacy in this area seems to have already been lost.[128]

4.5 Freedom of expression and jurisdictional problems

All of the above problems are further complicated by the number of national jurisdictions that the Internet spans. Numerous cases could exemplify tensions between different jurisdictions. For instance, in a famous French suit against Yahoo for offering Nazi materials on their website, the American court did not enforce the ruling of the French court ordering the blocking of access to these materials to French

[121] See, for example, <http://www.cookiecentral.com>, last visited: 04/06/2003 and Glossary.

[122] See Glossary.

[123] See Glossary

[124] See <http://www.export.gov/safeharbor/>, last visited: 06/06/2003.

[125] W3C (5 May 1999), *Web Content Accessibility Guidelines 1.0.*

[126] See also Open Profiling System (OPS) developed by Netscape, Firefly and Verisign in 1997.

[127] See, for example, The Associated Press (30 March 2003), *ACLU cyberchief worried about privacy.*

[128] Ibid.

citizens; a decision based on the First Amendment.[129] In a libel case of Gutnick against Dow Jones for publication of defamatory materials, the Australian court allowed Gutnick to sue the American company in the Australian state of Victoria.[130] In another case, the Australian court declared that the American Skybiz.com site was in breach of the pyramid selling prohibition of Australian consumer law.[131] Recently, the Canadian court did not assume jurisdiction in a case brought by Mr. Bangoura against The Washington Post for a defamatory publication, because the plaintiff was not a resident of Canada at the time of publication.[132]

The Internet and electronic commerce have also posed a number of other issues that will not be discussed at length here. For instance, there are serious issues with the collection of consumer rights, data protection, taxes and customs,[133] enforcement of licences required to conduct certain forms of business on virtual organisations[134] or affecting the functioning of traditional financial instruments and institutions.[135]

Jurisprudence has not managed to develop an effective system of solving issues to do with conflict of laws. At the moment this is essentially rooted in national legislature, which prescribes which system of law should be used in case of a dispute. Two difficulties arise here. The first is that there are dozens of such national systems, each prescribing their own rules. The second is that parties or perpetrators on the Internet are difficult to locate. With both these things in mind, it is clear that something new has to be done to enable global adjudication of electronic commerce disputes.

---

[129] See, for example, *Yahoo!* v. *La Ligue Contre le Racisme et l'Antisemitisme* [2001] 169 F.Supp.2d 1181 (N.D.Cal.). See also Akdeniz, Y. (2001), *Case Analysis of (the Yahoo case) League Against Racism and Antisemitism (LICRA), French Union of Jewish Students* v. *Yahoo! Inc. (USA), Yahoo France, Tribunal de Grande Instance de Paris (The County Court of Paris), Interim Court Order, 20 November, 2000.* See also the latest ruling by 9th Circuit US Court of Appeals reported in Auchard, E. (13 January 2006), Court rules against Yahoo in Nazi speech case. *Yahoo!* v. *La Ligue Contre le Racisme et l'Antisemitisme; L'Union des Etudiants Juifs de France* [2006] Appeal from the United States District Court for the Northern District of California, No. 01-17424, D.C. No CV-00-21275-JF.

[130] *Gutnick* v. *Dow Jones & Co Inc* [28 August 2001] VSC 305 and subsequent judgments at Clark, R. (29 June 2002), *Defamation on the Web: Gutnick* v. *Dow Jones*; Vangelowa, L. (19 June 2002), *A Global Audience, a World of Worries? Australian Court's Ruling in Libel Case Could Have a Chilling Effect on Web Publications*.

[131] See, for example, FindLaw Australia (1 October 2002), *U.S. Web-Based Pyramid Selling Scheme Banned.*

[132] *Cheickh Bangoura* v. *The Washington Post* [2005] Court File No. C41379 (16 September 2005) available at <http://www.ontariocourts.on.ca/decisions>.

[133] See, for example, a Model Tax Convention: OECD (29 April 2000), *OECD Model Tax Convention on Income and on Capital*.

[134] See, for example, Reuters (1 October 2002), *House votes to limit online gambling*; The New Zealand Herald (10 September 2002), *Law says no to internet wine sales*; Keller, B.P. (1999), *The Game's the Same: Why Gambling in Cyberspace Violates Federal Law*.

[135] See, for example, Muller, J.D. (November 1998), *Selected Developments In The Law Of Cyberspace Payments*; Winn, J.K. (November 1998), *Regulating The Use Of The Internet In Securities Markets*.

The international community has realised that one way to solve jurisdictional issues is to promote online dispute settlement,[136] in which Internet users could submit complaints, but so far no agreement has been reached.[137] Such methods of resolving conflicts promise to be more flexible in applying legal norms to adjudicate Internet disputes than national courts. Arbitrators can more openly rely on supranational sources of norms, such as the customs of online merchants, for example, and perhaps even accept a set of such norms as a future supranational Internet legal system governing any disputes arising on the Internet.

5. Summary

The Internet was created to provide a decentralised exchange of information without any global control at the operations level. Kahn's four rules have had a decisive impact on the current problems associated with the regulation of the Internet. However, legal issues have become apparent only with the commercialisation of the global network.

Legal issues posed by the Internet are numerous and the above section has briefly summarised the most important of them, together with a number of proposed solutions. National laws are a product of the pre-Internet era, which cannot be easily adapted to the Information Age. All the affected fields of law have a territorial scope, which stems from sovereign rights of states to regulate their internal matters. However, the Internet ignores territoriality. Hence the constant conflicts of laws, which produce serious legal uncertainty.

The territorial approach to regulation of the Internet is further exacerbated by the lack of a 'transnational' approach. Virtually all legal textbooks on Internet law discuss it from the perspective of a given national legal system,[138] although many principles of such systems have a local character and are unknown elsewhere. Such 'nationalisation' of the Internet has adverse effects, as it does not even attempt to build a supranational legal framework that will reflect the global nature of the Internet.[139]

---

[136] See the work of UNCITRAL described *below*. See, for example, UNCITRAL (11-22 October 2004), *A/CN.9/571 – Report of the Working Group on Electronic Commerce on the work of its forty-fourth session.*

[137] See, for example, Kessedjian, C. (August 2000), *Electronic Commerce and International Jurisdiction. Prel. Doc. No. 12. Summary of discussions*, pp. 7-8.

[138] See, for example, Akindemowo, O. (1998), *Information Technology Law in Australia*; Bainbridge, D.I. (2000), *Introduction to Computer Law*; Chissick, M. and Kelman, A. (1999), *Electronic commerce law and practice*; Edwards, L. and Waelde, C. (eds.) (2000), *Law & the Internet;* Forder, J. and Quirk, P. (2001), *Electronic commerce and the Law*; Gringras, C. (1997), *The Laws of the Internet*; Lessig, L. (1999), *Code and other laws of cyberspace*; Lessig, L. (2001), *The future of ideas. The fate of the commons in a connected world*; Lloyd, I. (1997), *Information Technology Law.*

[139] For a more detailed discussion see Polanski, P.P. (2002), *A New Approach to Regulating Internet Commerce: Custom as a Source of Electronic Commerce Law.*

The two most important problems that underlie all the concerns described above are *a lack of central authority* that could govern the Internet, and, as a partial result of this, *a lack of globally binding written Internet laws*. Understanding these two fundamental issues is necessary before a remedy (the concept of *custom* as a source of Internet commerce law) can be presented.

Chapter III
INTERNET GOVERNANCE

1. Introduction

The previous chapter presented the background information about the development of the Internet and electronic commerce from a historical perspective. In particular, Kahn's four rules were introduced to demonstrate its impact upon the regulation of the Internet. Legal issues raised by the development of the global network of networks were also presented from an international point of view.

In this chapter the problem of governing the Internet will be addressed, which is the first major implication of the Internet architecture. The Internet does not possess any central form of government because, as explained earlier, it was built around the concept of architectural decentralisation of control (Kahn's fourth rule). However, there are a number of organisations that are sometimes considered to be some form of Internet government. In fact, all they do is ensure its technological growth and smooth technical functioning.

It is important to understand what role various organisations perform in order to better appreciate the decentralised character of the Internet, and the enormous regulatory problems using traditional top-down measures. The discussion of these organisations is also important in the context of Internet custom to be presented in the next part of the book, as some of these organisations may play an important role in initiating prospective customary practices.

2. Internet Governance

The notion of Internet governance has gained popularity since the first World Summit on Information Society (WSIS), held in Geneva on 10-12 December 2003, and organised under the auspices of the United Nations. The envisaged framework[140] assumed that no single government should have a pre-eminent role in Internet governance and that the organisational form should involve all stakeholders on an equal

[140] See, for example, WSIS (12 December 2003), *Declaration of Principles. Building the Information Society: a global challenge in the new Millennium.* para. 20 and WSIS (12 December 2003), *Plan of Action*, para. A3.

footing.[141] These principles have been reflected in the 'Report of the Working Group on Internet Governance', which has proposed the following definition of the term:

> 'Internet governance is the development and application by Governments, the private sector and civil society, in their respective roles, of shared principles, norms, rules, decision-making procedures, and programmes that shape the evolution and use of the Internet.'[142]

The roles and responsibilities of governments include public policymaking and adoption of laws and standards, the creation of an enabling environment and access to ICT services, oversight functions, development of best practices, promotion of technological research, combating cybercrime as well as dispute resolution and arbitration. The private sector's role is to foster industry self-regulation, develop best practices, policy proposals and organise dispute resolution mechanisms. It is also encouraged to do research and develop technologies, standards and processes, and to contribute to the drafting of national law.[143]

The roles and responsibilities of civil society include such well-defined tasks as awareness-raising and capacity-building (knowledge, training, skills sharing), promoting various public interest objectives, facilitating network-building, mobilizing citizens in democratic processes, bringing perspectives of marginalized groups, including, for example, excluded communities and grass-roots activists, engaging in policy processes, contributing expertise, skills, experience and knowledge in a range of ICT policy areas, and so on.[144] It is to be regretted, however, that The Working Group on Internet Governance (WGIG) did not even mention the potential of customs and trade usages developed by the Internet community as a potential means of supporting the global effort. This book will demonstrate how civil society and the private sector could contribute to the creation of global Internet governance.

> 'Furthermore, the WGIG recognized that the contribution to the Internet of the academic community is very valuable and constitutes one of its main sources of inspiration, innovation and creativity. Similarly, the technical community and its organizations are deeply involved in Internet operation, Internet standard-setting and Internet services development. Both of these groups make a permanent and valuable contribution to the stability, security, functioning and evolution of the Internet. They interact extensively with and within all stakeholder groups.'[145]

---

[141] WSIS (12 December 2003), *Declaration of Principles. Building the Information Society: a global challenge in the new Millennium.* para. 48. WGIG (June 2005), *Report of the Working Group on Internet Governance*, para. 48.

[142] WGIG (June 2005), *Report of the Working Group on Internet Governance*, para. 10.

[143] Ibid.

[144] Ibid., pp. 9-10.

[145] Ibid.

However, the authors are aware that 'there are significant barriers to multi-stakeholder participation in governance mechanisms'.[146] The report enlists the often overlapping roles and tasks each group would have.[147] It is made clear though that Internet governance means more than ICANN's domain name management and includes 'significant public policy issues, such as critical Internet resources, the security and safety of the Internet, and developmental aspects and issues pertaining to the use of the Internet.'[148] WGIG has identified the following four key public policy areas as:

> '(a) Issues relating to infrastructure and the management of critical Internet resources, including administration of the domain name system and Internet protocol addresses (IP addresses), administration of the root server system, technical standards, peering and interconnection, telecommunications infrastructure, including innovative and convergent technologies, as well as multilingualization. These issues are matters of direct relevance to Internet governance and fall within the ambit of existing organizations with responsibility for these matters;
> (b) Issues relating to the use of the Internet, including spam, network security and cybercrime. While these issues are directly related to Internet governance, the nature of global cooperation required is not well defined;
> (c) Issues that are relevant to the Internet but have an impact much wider than the Internet and for which existing organizations are responsible, such as intellectual property rights (IPRs) or international trade. The WGIG started examining the extent to which these matters are being handled consistent with the Declaration of Principles;
> (d) Issues relating to the developmental aspects of Internet governance, in particular capacity-building in developing countries.'[149]

The Report listed several issues within the public policy areas where there is a need to co-ordinate international action.[150] For instance, the problem of the authorisation of changes to the root zone file, which for historical reasons has rested with the US government, has provoked great controversy.[151] To address these issues, the WGIG proposed four organisational models, ranging from the UN-based Global Internet Council to the non-UN-based International Internet Council to the internationalised ICANN and to a hybrid model to be decided during the second World Summit on Information Society.[152]

---

[146] Ibid., para. 19.

[147] Ibid., paras. 11, 29-34. See also WSIS (12 December 2003), *Plan of Action*, para. A3.

[148] WGIG (June 2005), *Report of the Working Group on Internet Governance*, para. 12.

[149] Ibid., para. 13.

[150] Ibid., paras. 15-28.

[151] Ibid., para. 15.

[152] 1. a UN-based Global Internet Council, which would take over the activities of ICANN, conduct arbitration, facilitate treaty-making and set public policy in the relevant areas (Model 1); 2. ICANN-based but enlarged to provide full and equal participation of all stakeholders who could make recommendations and co-ordinate the identified issues (Model 2); 3. not UN-based International Internet Council, which could fulfil the corresponding functions, especially in relation to ICANN/IANA com-

The WSIS summit held in Tunis in November 2005 attracted nearly 20,000 participants from all over the world but did not bring any significant changes. The sole control over the DNS system has therefore been retained by the United States.[153] As will be shown below, however, ICANN cannot be regarded as the government of the Internet because it has no power to issue and enforce laws. Therefore, although this area is politically sensitive it does not seem to be the most important issue for the Internet or for electronic commerce.

The sections below will demonstrate various governmental, business and civil society organisations that influence the functioning of the Internet. First, technical organisations will be presented, as they seem to have the greatest influence on the development of the Internet. Then commercial parties, governmental agencies and non-governmental organisations will be introduced and discussed. This chapter will demonstrate that none of these organisations have enough power to be regarded as a form of Internet government. This is because none of these organisations can issue laws and enforce them.

3. Internet Organisations

There are various bodies concerned with the development of standards on the Internet, including both private and public sector organisations. Within the private sector standards are developed in two communities: non-commercial communities, represented by organisations such as the Internet Engineering Task Force, and commercial organisations such as Microsoft or Netscape. Both types of organisations are important to the development of standards on the Internet and both have an enormous influence on how companies actually behave on the Internet. But none of these organisations can be treated as the Internet government.

For instance, the Internet Society (ISOC) cannot be considered as a government of the Internet. ISOC's mission is to:

> 'assure the open development, evolution and use of the Internet for the benefit of all people throughout the world.'[154]

---

petencies for policy issues involving national interests (Model 3); 4. The hybrid model, which involves different stakeholders taking different roles: 'Public policy development and decision-making on international Internet-related public policy issues led by Governments. Oversight over the body responsible at the global level for the technical and operational functioning of the Internet led by the private sector. Global co-ordination of the development of the Internet through dialogue between Governments, the private sector and civil society on an equal footing.' See ibid., pp. 13-16.

[153] Drake, W.J. (ed.) (2005), *Reforming Internet Governance: Perspectives from the Working Group on Internet Governance (WGIG);* WGIG (2005), *Tunis Agenda for the Information Society. Second Phase of the WSIS (16-18 November 2005, Tunis)*.

[154] See <http://www.isoc.org/isoc/mission/>, last visited: 06/03/2003.

ISOC was founded in 1992 as a non-profit, professional organisation of international character, with more than 100 organisational and 20,000 individual members in over 180 nations worldwide.[155] The primary role of ISOC is to provide institutional home and financial support to the Internet standardisation process, led primarily by the Internet Engineering Task Force (IETF).[156]

IETF is the principal organisation engaged in the formal development of new Internet standard specifications. Areas of interest have ranged from security to data transport to routing to operations and management to standard processes to policy formulation.[157] It is:

> 'a large open international community of network designers, operators, vendors, and researchers concerned with the evolution of the Internet architecture and the smooth operation of the Internet.'[158]

IETF is not a governmental organisation, but an open, virtual community that performs its job in several working groups classified into areas of interest. In its early days, IETF was financed by the US government[159] but over the last ten years it has been financially supported by ISOC.

On the other hand, the Internet Research Task Force (IRTF) is not concerned with the formal development of Internet standards. Instead, its work has a less formalistic character and is more concerned with a futuristic vision of the Internet. IRTF areas of interest include Interplanetary Internet or Internet Digital Rights Management. IETF and IRTF now form the Internet Architecture Board (IAB).[160]

Another important Internet organisation is the Internet Corporation for Assigned Names and Numbers (ICANN), which is:

> 'a non-profit, private-sector corporation formed by a broad coalition of the Internet's business, technical, academic, and user communities.'[161]

Its objective is to:

> 'operate as an open, transparent, and consensus-based body that is broadly representative of the diverse stakeholder communities of the global Internet.'[162]

ICANN has been recognised by the international community as the global consensus entity to co-ordinate the technical management of the Internet's Domain Name

---

[155] <http://www.isoc.org>, last visited: 03/12/2005.
[156] Cerf, V.G. (1995), *IETF and ISOC.*
[157] <http://www.ietf.org>, last visited: 06/03/2003.
[158] <http://www.ietf.org/overview.html>, last visited: 06/03/2003.
[159] Cerf, V.G. (1995), *IETF and ISOC.*
[160] IAB (2002), *A Brief History of the Internet Advisor/Activities/Architecture Board.*
[161] ICANN (2001), *ICANN Fact Sheet.*
[162] See earlier.

System (DNS), the allocation of Internet Protocol (IP)[163] address space, the assignment of protocol parameters, and the management of the root server system. From a legal perspective the most important activity of ICANN is co-ordination of DNS policing. DNS is a global database of domain names.[164] It is maintained at several locations known as Regional Internet Registrars (RIR).

The rising interest of national governments in participating in the management of global and country-level domain names, especially the latter, has led to a debate whether management should be internationalised under the auspices of the United Nations or left in the hands of a privately-owned American company.[165] It is worth noting that ICANN is considered to be controlled by the US Government[166] under a Memorandum of Understanding due to expire in September 2006. The US Government is opposed to the creation of a new international organisation to oversee this process but other countries would clearly like to take part in this process.[167] As mentioned above, the World Summit on the Information Society (WSIS) has retained the *status quo* in this regard.[168]

ICANN has also played a key role in setting up a domain name dispute resolution system. Based on a recommendation[169] from the World Intellectual Property Organisation (WIPO), it has developed a global policy[170] and rules[171] for resolving conflicts in domain name registration which is administered by a number of organisations, including WIPO. 'The Uniform Domain Name Dispute Resolution Policy' and 'the Rules for Uniform Domain Name Dispute Resolution Policy' have been applied and elaborated in numerous panel decisions of WIPO Arbitration and Mediation Centre[172] and other dispute resolution providers. WIPO has also developed its own supplementary rules and remains the most important domain name arbiter, handling a majority of all domain name disputes.[173] Most of the decisions are accessible online and could be regarded as the beginning of a transnational arbiter-made Internet law.

---

[163] See Glossary.

[164] See Glossary.

[165] WGIG (June 2005), *Report of the Working Group on Internet Governance.* For more information see <http://www.wgig.org>, last visited: 02.12./2005.

[166] See Hagen, who argues that the current structure of the DNS is controlled by the US Government. Hagen, G.R. (2003), *Sovereign Domains and Property Claims*, p. 39.

[167] See, for example, BNA Int'l Bus. & Fin. Daily (5 July 2005), *U.S. States Internet Principles: No Change For ICANN, No Support for New Global Body.*

[168] See *below.*

[169] WIPO (30 April 1999), *The Management of Internet Names and Addresses: Intellectual Property Issues.* See also, for example, Valles, C.M. (2003 Supp), *eCommerce in International and Regional Organizations.*

[170] ICANN (26 August 1999), *Uniform Domain Name Dispute Resolution Policy.*

[171] ICANN (1999), *Rules for Uniform Domain Name Dispute Resolution Policy.*

[172] See, for example, WIPO (2005), *WIPO Overview of WIPO Panel Views on Selected UDRP Questions.*

[173] See, for example, WIPO, *Internet Domain Name Disputes: Some Questions and Answers.*

However, one should not overestimate the role of ICANN. It is confined to the management of the domain name system and does not really go beyond it. Although Hagen has argued that 'the norms embedded in the DNS architecture cannot be ignored as merely technical',[174] it is difficult to conclude that ICANN could be considered as a form of Internet government, capable of issuing globally binding laws. There are too many unresolved legal aspects of international e-commerce to allow for such a conclusion.

On the other hand, the World Wide Web Consortium (W3C)[175] is the organisation responsible for developments of the most important Internet technology: the World Wide Web.[176] In October 1994, Tim Berners-Lee founded W3C at the Massachusetts Institute of Technology.[177] The mission of W3C is to:

> 'lead the World Wide Web to its full potential by developing common protocols that promote its evolution and ensure its interoperability.'[178]

W3C concentrates its efforts on vision, design and standardisation of web protocols.[179] W3C's long term goals are:

> '1. Universal Access: To make the Web accessible to all by promoting technologies that take into account the vast differences in culture, languages, education, ability, material resources, and physical limitations of users on all continents;
> 2. Semantic Web: To develop a software environment that permits each user to make the best use of the resources available on the Web;
> 3. Web of Trust: To guide the Web's development with careful consideration for the novel legal, commercial, and social issues raised by this technology.'[180]

W3C activities are generally organised into several types of groups. W3C has developed specifications for, among other things: HTML (used to build websites), XML (a new generation language used to create content on the Web, which is also the technological backbone of the future World Wide Web), Cascading Style Sheets (CCS) to provide rich, content-independent formatting of documents, Scalable Vector Graphics (SVG) to provide efficient vector-based graphics on the Web, Platform for Internet Content Selection (PICS) to help rate the content of websites, Platform for Privacy Preferences (P3P) to better protect private information on the Web, and many others.[181]

---

[174] Hagen, G.R. (2003), *Sovereign Domains and Property Claims*, p. 39.

[175] See W3C (2000), *About the World Wide Web Consortium (W3C)*; W3C (5 May 1999), *Web Content Accessibility Guidelines 1.0.*

[176] See earlier.

[177] W3C (2000), *About the World Wide Web Consortium (W3C).*

[178] Ibid.

[179] W3C (5 May 1999), *Web Content Accessibility Guidelines 1.0.*

[180] W3C (2000), *About the World Wide Web Consortium (W3C).*

[181] See Glossary.

One of the most interesting developments of W3C is the Web Content Accessibility Guidelines.[182] These guidelines help web developers create content which is accessible to everyone, so that 'people with disabilities can perceive, understand, navigate, and interact with the Web, and that they can contribute to the Web.'[183] But web accessibility also benefits people without disabilities. The guidelines are an important tool in establishing what are the best practices for the development of webpages. They have already become the source of inspiration for numerous potential customary practices in this area.

There are other important technological organisations but none of them can be considered as a form of Internet government, capable of issuing and enforcing all-encompassing, globally binding laws. Most of the above organisations deal with the process of standardisation of the Internet protocols. Other organisations, such as ICANN, focus on particular aspects of the Internet technology, sustaining its growth, operation and providing important dispute resolution mechanisms. All of these organisations, however, have a decisive role in shaping architectural constraints in which Internet merchants operate.

4. Private Sector

The Internet is largely dependant upon technological innovations and practices developed by hi-tech giants such as Google, Microsoft, IBM, Sun Microsystems, Cisco, America Online, Macromedia and Adobe, to name just a few. Although these organisations will not be discussed in detail, it is important to realise their role in co-ordinating participants' behaviour on the Internet. Through the provision of software that has such widespread use, they promote certain behaviours and disallow or inhibit others. These companies have developed private standards that have been reigning in cyberspace for a very long time. Despite the movement towards open standardisation,[184] the private sector's influence is undoubtedly still very strong today.

For instance, Microsoft is the provider of the most widely used web browser[185] and the second most widely used web server.[186] It is also highly dominant in the field of operating systems, office software and a host of other software products. With such a strong position in the market, Microsoft enforces its own private standards that provide technological frameworks. The global impact of companies like Microsoft has been noticed by the international community and recently the World

---

[182] W3C (5 May 1999), *Web Content Accessibility Guidelines 1.0*. See also the Draft WCAG version 2.0, which applies to all Web content and is not specific to any one Web technology.

[183] See <http://www.w3.org/WAI/intro/accessibility.php>, last visited: 02/12/2005.

[184] See, for example, Open Source Initiative mentioned earlier.

[185] As of September 2002 the Internet Explorer has won around 95% of the market, See, for example, <http://www.onestat.com/html/aboutus_pressbox7.html>, last visited: 08/06/2003.

[186] Netcraft (2002), *The August 2002 Netcraft Web Server Survey*.

Trade Organisation (WTO) has in fact penalised the American government for supporting the monopolistic position of such software giants.[187]

Similarly, Internet Service Providers (ISPs) may play an important role in regulating the Internet. The biggest intermediaries like America Online (AOL)[188] may actually enforce their own standards of behaviour by disallowing certain forms of activities. AOL, for instance, provides anti-spamming facilities, parental control features and can even limit time children spend online.[189] This situation has led some governments to impose or limit liability on ISPs for illegal traffic that passes through their computers.[190]

The impact of the private sector on the development of the Internet has been so great that it has led Lessig to conclude that the development of standards to fit the goals of the private sector will change the nature of the Internet from a free and open environment to a highly 'regulable' and controlled network.[191] However, the future is difficult to predict. The emergence of freely available and user-friendly software supported by the open source code and open standards initiatives may seriously undermine the future position of today's modern technological giants.

In summary, commercial software and hardware producers, as well as Internet Service Providers, play an important role in supporting the Internet and driving its further development. However, these companies do not govern the Internet or electronic commerce. The disappearance of any of these companies, or even all of them, will not stop the functioning of the Internet.

5. Governmental and Non-Governmental Organisations

There are organisations that have contributed to the discussion or to the development of legal instruments facilitating the Internet and electronic commerce. They have very diverse aims and come from both public and private sectors. Some of these organisations, such as the Electronic Frontier Foundation, TRUSTe, Law and Policy Forum exist primarily on the Internet, whereas others like UNCITRAL, UNIDROIT, ICC, OECD, WIPO and WTO are important international organisations whose primary goals are non-electronic activities such as drafting new laws, international trade or intellectual property. These organisations deal with the Internet only as a sideline, as their scope of activities is much larger than that of specialised Internet regulation forums.

187 WTO allowed EU to seek punitive duties on $4 billion of US exports to Europe – unless the US law is changed. Blustein, P. (15 January 2002), *U.S. Loses Ruling in Trade Fight With Europe. WTO Decision Allows EU to Seek Penalties*.

188 <http://www.aol.com>, last visited: 28/08/2002.

189 <http://www.corp.aol.com/whoweare.html>, last visited: 28/08/2002.

190 See earlier.

191 See, for example, Lessig, L. (1999), *Code and other laws of cyberspace*, p. 30. See also Lessig, L. (2001), *The future of ideas. The fate of the commons in a connected world*, p. 263.

For instance, the United Nations Commission on International Trade Law (UNCITRAL) performs a very important role in drafting global electronic commerce laws. It established Working Group IV to deal with legal aspects of electronic commerce and EDI.[192] As will be discussed later, this working group has produced several ground-breaking documents, including the latest Convention on the Use of Electronic Communications in International Contracting, as well as the Model Law on Electronic Commerce and the Model Law on Electronic Signatures.

In turn, the World Intellectual Property Organization (WIPO)[193] is heavily engaged in dispute resolution processes concerning the improper assignment of Internet domain names. It has developed the Uniform Domain Name Dispute Resolution Policy[194] for resolving such disputes, which was later adopted by ICANN as the global policy binding all its accredited domain name registrars. WIPO is the leading ICANN-accredited domain name dispute resolution service provider, resolving more than half of all domain name disputes.[195] It has also developed very important conventions dealing with intellectual property rights in the digital age and published several interesting documents about electronic commerce law.[196] WIPO is the author of the important 1996 Copyright Treaty and Performances and Phonograms Treaty.[197]

On the other hand, the Electronic Frontier Foundation (EFF) was established in 1990 in San Francisco to defend freedom of speech. It is a donor-supported membership organisation working to protect fundamental rights regardless of technology, to educate the press, policymakers and the general public about civil liberties issues related to technology and to act as a defender of those liberties. EFF opposes misguided legislation, initiates and defends court cases, launches global public campaigns, introduces innovative proposals and papers, hosts frequent education events, engages the press regularly, and publishes a comprehensive archive of digital civil liberties information at its website.[198]

Another important Internet organisation is TRUSTe, established in 1996 to build privacy online and to support self-governance of the Internet.[199] The core of the TRUSTe initiative is the TRUSTe Privacy Seal, a visual symbol that can be displayed by Websites that meet the program's requirements for data gathering and dissemination practices, and which agree to participate in its dispute resolution process. From the legal perspective, the cornerstone of the TRUSTe program is a con-

---

[192] See <http://www.uncitral.org>, last visited: 06/06/2003.

[193] See WIPO (May 2000), *Primer On Electronic Commerce And Intellectual Property Issues*.

[194] ICANN (26 August 1999), *Uniform Domain Name Dispute Resolution Policy*. See also ICANN (1999), *Rules for Uniform Domain Name Dispute Resolution Policy*.

[195] See <http://arbiter.wipo.int/domains>, last visited: 06/03/2003.

[196] See, for example, WIPO (May 2000), *Primer On Electronic Commerce And Intellectual Property Issues*.

[197] See *below*.

[198] <http://www.eff.org/abouteff.html>, last visited: 06/03/2003.

[199] See TRUSTe, *The TRUSTe White Paper: Building Trust Online: TRUSTe, Privacy and Self Governance*.

tract that is signed between TRUSTe and a website. This contract gives TRUSTe the ability to address users' privacy concerns, regardless of their citizenship or the location of the TRUSTe licensee.[200] Websites displaying the TRUSTe logo must inform users what data is being gathered and with whom it is going to be shared. Users must be given an option to disallow dissemination of their data, and they must also be given the opportunity to correct any inaccuracies. Websites must provide reasonable security to protect user data. TRUSTe's alternative dispute resolution system allows any of its users, regardless of their geographical location, to submit complaints to the TRUSTe Watchdog. This might then take various measures ranging from policy change recommendation to informing relevant government bodies of improper business practices.

6. Summary

The Internet does not have a central governing body and it is highly unlikely that it will have a central government in the future. This is simply the consequence of its architecture. As a result, there seems to be no way to effectively impose restrictions in a top-down manner on all participants. No jury-like collective decision-making body has been established.[201] The Internet also does not belong to anyone,[202] although certain parts of the network have owners. Electronic traffic that flows through these networks does not recognise any proprietary rights or legal jurisdictions.

There are many organisations that are actively interested in doing something about the governance on the Internet, but none of them can effectively control it. The majority of the organisations presented above are standards organisations or commercial entities that develop technical specifications, or are organisations of a legal character interested in the development of a coherent regulatory framework for the Internet.

Some of the technical organisations described above, such as ISOC, are sometimes treated like as a quasi-Internet government but in fact they only support its functioning by financing, developing and documenting technical standards on which the Internet is based. ICANN has an important role in administering domain name assignment and supporting a global network of domain name servers, but its role is too limited to consider it an Internet government. On the other hand, international organisations such UNCITRAL only draft international conventions and do not participate in the Internet development or governance at all. Similarly, virtual

---

[200] Ibid.

[201] 'I've described a different ideal, it seems quite alien. I've promised that something different could be done, but not by any institution of government that I know. I've spoken as if there could be hope. But Hope was just a television commercial.' Lessig, L. (1999), *Code and other laws of cyberspace*, p. 233.

[202] See, for example, Loshin, P., et al. (2001), *Electronic Commerce: On-line Ordering and Digital Money*, pp. 55-56.

organisations such as TRUSTe promote privacy and self-governance by adherence to certain self-imposed standards and do not try to control it in top-down manner.

However, these organisations have great influence over how Internet participants behave and trade. Technical organisations and commercial companies promote technological standards that often become implemented in software used by Internet participants. In this sense, software shapes both the Internet and electronic commerce practices. Also, non-technical organisations influence the behaviour of the Internet community by promoting or criticising certain standards of behaviour. All these organisations play an important role in developing practices that might become customary if adopted by the Internet community.

It is important to note, however, that some organisations like ICANN or TRUSTe provide Internet-based alternative dispute resolution (ADR) mechanisms. Both ICANN and TRUSTe have reported hundreds of resolved cases based upon their own rules of procedure and evidence. As will be argued later, electronic adjudication mechanisms might signal the emergence of a supranational legal framework for the Internet and electronic commerce. In summary, the lack of a global authority that can centrally administer the Internet is one of the reasons why it is generally perceived to be a free environment. The following chapter will present another crucial consequence of the architecture of this medium.

Chapter IV
INTERNATIONAL REGULATION OF THE INTERNET

1. Introduction

The second important issue, which to some extent is a consequence of the lack of a centralised Internet government, is the lack of adequate, globally binding written laws. This gap is especially visible in international electronic commerce, where the existing legal framework is inadequate. The consequence of this is the submission of electronic commerce and the Internet to a number of national laws. In turn, these laws may either have no provisions related to the Internet and electronic commerce or, even if they have, they are often not harmonised.

The top-down regulation of the Internet can be classified into three categories: an individual state-based regulation of electronic commerce; harmonised state-based regulation of electronic commerce; and international treaty. State-based regulation of electronic commerce is still important but it brings a great deal of uncertainty when a transaction crosses a border, as there are different legal regimes that might attach different consequences to the same act. This approach has been to some extent superseded by a more harmonised approach as soon as important Model laws were developed by the international community. The harmonisation of Internet law promises equal treatment of Internet participants based on similar principles established upon a commonly accepted framework.

A similar goal lies behind the Internet commerce treaty regulation. International treaty regulation of the Internet can be analysed from the perspective of binding international law, non-binding model laws, and treaties written without electronic commerce in mind but nevertheless potentially applicable. The first category consists of the following international regulations: the 1980 Vienna United Nations Convention on Contracts for the International Sale of Goods (CISG)[203] and the newly adopted Convention on the Use of Electronic Communications in International Contracting[204] (Treaty on electronic contracting). Special treatment will be given to European Union legislation in this field, which is international albeit lim-

---

[203] UNCITRAL (1980), *United Nations Convention on Contracts for the International Sale of Goods*.

[204] United Nations (23 November 2005), *United Nations Convention on the Use of Electronic Communications in International Contracts*. See also UNCITRAL (23 November 2005), *General Assembly adopts new Convention on the Use of Electronic Communications in International Contracting*.

ited to one continent only. In the second category the 1996 UNCITRAL Model Law on Electronic Commerce and 2004 UNIDROIT Principles will be analysed. In the third category there will be brief presentations of the Council of Europe Convention on Cybercrime,[205] the 1996 WIPO Copyright Treaty (Copyright Treaty)[206] and the 1996 WIPO Performances and Phonograms Treaty.[207] Both the treaty approach and the harmonisation approach are important developments in international electronic commerce law and will be examined below in more detail.

2. International e-Commerce Regulation

2.1 1980 Vienna Convention on Contracts for the International Sale of Goods (CISG)

The Vienna Convention on Contracts for the International Sale of Goods (CISG) is probably the most important development in the field of international commercial law. Currently there are 67 states which have ratified the Vienna Convention, including the United States, China, Russia, Australia, Germany, France and Poland.[208] It remains the most popular sales convention so far.

Obviously CISG was not drafted with modern electronic communication in mind. In fact, CISG was actually written before the Internet era. As stated earlier, in 1980 the TCP/IP protocol was not universally used as the basis for inter-network communication and was only implemented as a standard by all networks from 1 January 1983. Therefore, the question of the Convention's suitability to the Internet age remains problematic.

For instance, Article 13 of the Sales Convention states that for the purposes of the Convention the term 'writing' includes also telegram and telex. This article does not mention EDI, which was already in use in 1980. EDI is still in use but telegram and telex have been made obsolete by modern means of distant communication such as e-mail or webpages. As a result, it remains unclear whether Article 13 could be interpreted to cover modern electronic communication technologies.

However, CISG offers several advantages. The major advantage of the Vienna Convention is that it is an autonomous and flexible legal framework for international trade. It is autonomous in the sense that its interpretation should recognise its international character and promote the observance of good faith, which for centuries was called upon to provide equitable solutions to legal disputes. Therefore,

---

[205] Council of Europe (23 November 2001), *Convention on Cybercrime, ETS No. 185, signed at Budapest.*

[206] WIPO (1996), *Copyright Treaty (adopted in Geneva on December 20, 1996).*

[207] WIPO (1996), *Performances and Phonograms Treaty (adopted in Geneva on December 20, 1996).*

[208] See <http://www.uncitral.org/uncitral/en/uncitral_texts/sale_goods/1980CISG_status.html>, last accessed: 06/12/2005.

CISG uses a language that is understandable to business people and which is disconnected from any particular legal culture, in order to create truly universal norms.[209] Furthermore, it provides its own gap-filling mechanism. According to Article 7 of CISG:

> '(1) In the interpretation of this Convention, regard is to be had to its international character and to the need to promote uniformity in its application and the observance of good faith in international trade.
> (2) Questions concerning matters governed by this Convention which are not expressly settled in it are to be settled in conformity with the general principles on which it is based or, in the absence of such principles, in conformity with the law applicable by virtue of the rules of private international law.'

Therefore, if the Convention does not provide any specific guidance, the gaps should be filled with a reference to the general principles on which it is based, and only subsidiarily with a reference to national legal systems. In this sense it is autonomous, as it refers to the municipal legal orders only as a last resort. This feature of the Convention makes it the ideal candidate for one of the pillars of the autonomous Internet law.

CISG is also a very flexible framework. It provides supplementary norms, which are overridden by contrary provisions of the contract or trade usages. Vienna Convention recognises the importance of commercial customs and attaches a special importance to them. As Bernard Audit observed:

> 'The purpose of the Vienna Convention is not only to create new, state-sanctioned law, but also to give recognition to the rules born of commercial practice and to encourage municipal courts to apply them. (…) The provisions of the Convention, however, were not meant to fill a vacuum. International business practice did not have the luxury of waiting until states could come to agreement to establish a suitable legal regime for transactions. The Convention, therefore, acknowledges that other rules exist which it supplements.'[210]

In other words, flexibility of the Convention is achieved thanks to the recognition of the importance of commercial customs, which change with time, unlike conventional norms. Flexibility is one of the tools implemented in CISG to ensure its practical importance over time.

Flexibility of the Convention is also visible in Article 11, which permits the contract to be concluded by any means, which is of fundamental importance in electronic commerce:

---

[209] Audit, B. (1998), *The Vienna Sales Convention and Lex Mercatoria*, pp. 178-180.
[210] Ibid., p. 173.

> 'Article 11. A contract of sale need not be concluded in or evidenced by writing and is not subject to any other requirement as to form. It may be proved by any means, including witnesses.'

It is therefore argued that electronic contracts are recognised by the Vienna Convention. This provision of CISG can be especially helpful with respect to international contracts formed by e-mail or EDI. However, national courts can be reluctant to not to apply the parole evidence rule.[211] These advantages of the Vienna Convention deserve a closer look.

CISG applies to contracts for the international sale of goods where the parties have a place of business in different Member States or where conflict of law rules lead to the application of the Vienna Convention.[212] One of the most apparent drawbacks of CISG is the lack of definition of place of business, which is especially important in web-based commerce.[213] The different places of business must be specified in a contract or disclosed earlier or be known from previous dealings because neither the nationality nor the character of the parties or a contract is to be taken into account.[214] On the Web, such information is usually disclosed on a website, therefore the place indicated there should be taken into account. The situation is usually less clear in case of e-mails, where often such information might be missing. If a party has more than one place of business, then that which has the closest relationship to the contract and its performance shall be selected. On the other hand, if a party does not have a place of business, as the case might be in the online world, the reference shall be made to its habitual place of residence.[215] Obviously, it may turn out to be a rather daunting task to ascertain the location of parties in global electronic commerce.

The Vienna Convention governs the formation of the contract for the sale of goods, obligations of performance by the seller and the buyer, the passing of risk from seller to buyer, and penalties for non-performance on the contract.[216] It does not contain rules on the validity of contracts or usages nor the effect which the contract may have on the property in the goods sold (Art. 4). CISG also does not apply to the liability of the seller for death or personal injury (Art. 5), although it covers the liability for property destruction. The Sales Convention contains also other very important limitations, which will be discussed below.[217]

---

[211] Boersma, M. (1998), International business transactions, the Internet and the Convention on the International Sale of Goods: Preventing unintentional pitfalls, pp. 122-123.

[212] Art. 1.

[213] This problem was addressed in the UN Convention on electronic contracting. See *below*.

[214] Arts. 1(2) and 1(3).

[215] Art. 10.

[216] The Vienna Convention contains 101 articles, divided into four parts: Sphere of application and General Provisions (Part 1), Formation of Contract (Part 2), Sale of Goods (Part 3) and Final Provisions (Part 4).

[217] See, for example, Art. 2.

The Convention aims to uphold international agreements. An offer must fulfil three conditions: be sufficiently precise in its indication of goods, quantity and price;[218] addressed to one or more specific persons, and indicate the intention of the offeror to be bound in case of acceptance.[219] In establishing the intent and a reasonable person standard,[220] the Vienna Convention acknowledges the importance of all relevant circumstances of the case including the negotiations, any practices which the parties have established between themselves, usages and any subsequent conduct of the parties.[221] The offer can be revoked prior to its acceptance, unless it is irrevocable[222] or it was reasonable for the offeree to rely on the offer as being irrevocable and the offeree has acted in reliance on the offer.[223]

The requirements for the offer are usually met by interactive electronic shops, which not only provide detailed information about the product, quantity and price but also force a user to register in the system, thus addressing its proposal to a specific person. Furthermore, the intention to be bound can be inferred from the trade usage of providing an 'Order' button, which enables rapid conclusion of a transaction. Non-interactive shops do not provide such facilities, therefore it can be presumed that such webpages only invite to treat.[224]

The acceptance of an offer can be communicated in a statement or by any other conduct,[225] although inactivity, as a rule of thumb, does not amount to acceptance.[226] Therefore clicking on the 'Order' button communicates acceptance in interactive web-based shopping. The offer must be accepted by the offeree on the terms of the offer, although minor modifications would not constitute a counter-offer. Minor modifications are those that do not pertain to the price, payment, quality and quantity of the goods, place and time of delivery, extent of one party's liability to the other or the settlement of disputes.[227] This provision might be relevant in e-mail-based commerce but is ill-suited to web-based commerce. In electronic shops the buyer is usually allowed to specify the quantity of products and choose from the programmed means of payment, therefore having all other conditions set and unchangeable. According to the above-mentioned provision, specification of quantity on a webpage would constitute a counter-offer. However, one must bear in mind that interactive shops are often linked to their inventory system and specify how many items are available. It is therefore argued that having the indication of the quantity of product left, specification of quantity by the buyer would not constitute a counter-offer. The same applies to the choice of payment method.

218 But see Art. 55.
219 Art. 14.
220 Art. 8(2). Compare with Art. 8(1).
221 Art. 8(3).
222 Then see Art. 15(2).
223 Art. 16.
224 See also the earlier discussion under the heading 'Contract law'.
225 See, for example, Art. 18(3).
226 Art. 18.
227 Art. 19(3).

The acceptance becomes effective when the indication of assent reaches the offeror.[228] A late acceptance is generally valid unless, without delay, the offeror orally informs the offeree that he considers his offer as having lapsed or dispatches a notice to that effect.[229] An acceptance as well as an irrevocable offer can only be withdrawn in very limited circumstances.[230]

CISG contains a general rule that a contract is concluded at the moment when an acceptance of an offer becomes effective, i.e., at the moment the indication of assent reaches the offeror.[231] As stated above, the contract does not need to be in any particular form and can be evidenced by any means.[232] Once concluded, the contract can be modified or terminated by mutual consent in that form.[233]

According to Article 24, for the purposes of formation of contract, an offer, declaration of acceptance or any other indication of intention 'reaches' the addressee if it is made orally or delivered by any other means to him or her personally, to his or her place of business or mailing address or habitual residence. On the other hand, in case of post-contractual communication dealt with in Part III of CISG:

> 'if any notice, request or other communication is given or made by a party in accordance with this Part and by means appropriate in the circumstances, a delay or error in the transmission of the communication or its failure to arrive does not deprive that party of the right to rely on the communication.'[234]

Therefore, CISG adopted the theory of receipt as the main tool with respect to contract formation, and the theory of dispatch, with respect to notifications during the performance of an already existing contract.[235] Means appropriate in Internet-based commerce include e-mail, website or EDI notifications and, rarely, chat or discussion groups.

CSIG imposes detailed obligations on the seller of goods.[236] In general, the seller is obliged to deliver the goods along with any documents of title relating to them and to transfer the property in the goods, as required by the contract and Convention.[237] If the seller has agreed to arrange for carriage of the goods, he must arrange

---

[228] However, an acceptance is not effective if the indication of assent does not reach the offeror within the time he has fixed. In case the time is not fixed, an acceptance is not effective if it does not reach the offeror within a reasonable time, taking into account circumstances of the transaction, including the rapidity of the means of communication employed by the offeror. An oral offer must be accepted immediately unless the circumstances indicate otherwise. See Art. 18(2).

[229] Art. 21(2).

[230] See Arts. 22 and 15(2).

[231] Arts. 23 and 18(2).

[232] See Art. 11.

[233] Art. 29.

[234] Art. 27.

[235] Eiselen, S. (1999), *Electronic Commerce and the UN Convention on Contracts for the International Sale of Goods (CISG) 1980*, pp. 27-34.

[236] See Chapter II of Part III of CISG.

[237] Art. 30.

for carriage appropriate in the circumstances and according to the usual terms for such transportation.[238] The seller is obliged to deliver goods appropriately contained or packaged which are of the quantity, quality and description required by the contract.[239] In particular, the goods should possess the qualities which the seller has held out to the buyer as a sample or model, which may be of special importance in web-based transactions. Furthermore, goods should be free from claims by third parties, including those based on intellectual or industrial property rights.[240]

On the other hand, the buyer must examine the goods as quickly as possible and notify the seller of non-conformance within a reasonable period of time, no less than two years.[241] However, in the case of electronic commerce, the current practice shows that such notifications should be made immediately, within a few hours from receipt. This is especially so in case of digital goods such as software, which should be examined for defects immediately. The most important defect in this context would be the inability to install the full version of the program, as other defects might take more time to discover. The buyer is also obliged to pay the price and take delivery of the goods.[242] As determined by industry practice, the terms of the price are set either in a contract or with a reference to commercial customs.[243]

Breach of contract by any of the parties allows the counterparty to seek two types of remedy: exercise specific rights[244] and claim damages.[245] As a rule of thumb, the injured party is not deprived of any right it may have to claim damages by exercising the right to other remedies.[246] The buyer is entitled to specific performance of the agreement, including the delivery of substitute goods,[247] additional time for performance[248] or he or she may declare the contract voided and terminate the agreement.[249] The contract can be declared voided in case of a serious breach of contract. However, non-delivery would not provide grounds for such drastic remedy unless, for example, the seller did not deliver the goods within the additional period of time fixed by the buyer.[250] If delivery has been made of non-conforming goods, the buyer may reduce the price of the goods.[251] In case of partial performance, the buyer may seek partial remedies for his damages, although in case of

---

238 Art. 32(2).
239 Art. 35.
240 See Arts. 41-44.
241 Arts. 38-40.
242 Arts. 53-60.
243 Art. 55.
244 Arts. 45-52 for the buyer and Arts. 61-65 for the seller.
245 Arts. 74-77.
246 Art. 45(2) and Art. 61(2).
247 Art. 46(2).
248 Art. 47.
249 Art. 49.
250 Art. 49(1)(b).
251 Art. 50.

fundamental breach he may declare the contract voided in its entirety.[252] These provisions may be hard to apply in electronic environment.

If the buyer is in breach of a contract, the seller also has some remedies, albeit weaker.[253] The seller may allow the buyer extra time to perform, as well as retaining the right to require the buyer to pay, take delivery, or perform.[254] The only serious remedy is avoidance of the contract in the case of a fundamental breach of contract by the buyer. However, the contract cannot be voided unless, for example, the buyer would not pay or take the delivery within the additional period of time fixed by the seller.[255] The seller may also set the requirements for the goods if the buyer has not set them.[256]

CISG also includes detailed provisions on the calculation of damages.[257] In general, the injured party can claim not only the actual loss but also lost profits. CISG also includes other important regulations regarding calculation of damages as well as provisions for such things as passage of risk, anticipatory breach, force majeur, and so on, which will not be discussed here.

However, CISG contains very serious limitations, which make it unfit for electronic commerce for the following reasons:

1. CISG is limited to international contracts of sale. As a result it does not apply to contracts of exchange or free exchange, which are not uncommon on the Internet.

2. CISG is limited to contracts for the international sale of goods only. It does not apply to the sale of services or information, which are a fundamental of electronic commerce. This is a very serious limitation of this Convention (Art. 1). Furthermore, the concept of goods is very vague. In particular, it is hard to say whether the sale of software or music over the Internet constitutes sale of goods or merely provision of services.

3. CISG only applies to Business-to-Business or commercial transactions. Article 2 makes it clear that the Convention does not apply to the sale:

> 'of goods bought for personal, family or household use, unless the seller, at any time before or at the conclusion of the contract, neither knew nor ought to have known that the goods were bought for any such use.'

This is another very important limitation of CISG. Although B2B transactions are certainly the most important Internet transactions in terms of their value, consumer

---

[252] Art. 51.
[253] Arts. 61-65.
[254] Arts. 62 and 63.
[255] Art. 64(1)(2).
[256] Art. 65.
[257] Arts. 74-77.

transactions are also very important. Furthermore, as stated earlier, it is very hard to distinguish between consumers and professionals on the Web. Nevertheless, Business-to-Consumer (B2C), Consumer-to-Consumer (C2C), Consumer-to-Business (C2B) and other popular forms of electronic commerce are excluded from the scope of this Convention.

4. CISG does not apply to sales via auctions. This is another huge problem. Auctions are the most important business model on the Internet. In fact, most B2B online transactions are done via auctions. Exclusion of this form of contracting renders the potential applicability of the Convention in a very limited field of B2B sales of goods practically virtual.

5. CISG also does not apply to the sale of financial instruments such as stocks, shares, investment securities, negotiable instruments or money. This is another serious limitation as the Internet has become the most important vehicle for international financial investments through online banking and online investment.

6. CISG does not address the problem of automated interactive ordering systems such as web-based shops, where at least one party is represented by a pre-programmed computer system and where terms and conditions are non-negotiable. The Convention assumes that both parties are human beings that communicate in a less automated manner than the Internet allows.

7. CISG does not define certain terms such as place of business, which is of fundamental importance especially in the virtual world. Without the definition of place of business, one may never be sure whether the Convention is applicable or not. The Vienna Convention also includes a restrictive definition of writing and does not cover such important terms as signature, original, interactive websites, etc.

According to Article 6, the parties may exclude the application of the Vienna Convention or, subject to Article 12, derogate from or vary the effect of any of its provisions. In practice, companies very often derogate from it, and one may wonder if CISG has any serious role to play in the Information Age.

As a result, in its current form, CISG does not offer a solution to global electronic commerce legal issues. Its scope of application, exclusions and old terminology seriously undermine its applicability in the Internet era. Furthermore, the Vienna Convention does not bind all states, as there are less than seventy countries bound by its provision. Nevertheless, CISG might have some role to play if judges and arbitrators properly utilise its autonomous and flexible architecture.

2.2 2005 United Nations Convention on the Use of Electronic Communications in International Contracting[258]

On 23 November 2005 the United Nations General Assembly adopted a new Convention on the Use of Electronic Communications in International Contracting.[259] The Convention on e-contracting is the most important and long awaited development in international electronic commerce law. The Convention was drafted by the UNCITRAL Working Group IV over six sessions since 2002.

The new Convention will be open for signature by all states at the United Nations Headquarters in New York from 16 January 2006 to 16 January 2008.[260] According to communication from the UNCITRAL Secretariat, 'it is expected that a signature event would take place during the UNCITRAL's thirty-ninth session, to be held in New York from 19 June to 7 July 2006, to promote participation in the Convention by states and awareness of its provisions.'[261] The Convention is subject to ratification, acceptance or approval by the signatory states.[262] Arabic, Chinese, English, French, Russian and Spanish texts are equally authentic.[263]

The Convention contains a Preamble and 25 articles. It is organised into four chapters. The first part delineates the sphere of application of the instrument. The second chapter contains general provisions including the definitions of the terms used. Chapter III, which covers the 'use of electronic communications in international contracts' contains provisions on legal recognition of electronic communications, form requirements of a contract or a communication, time and place of electronic communications, invitation to make offers, use of automated systems for contract formation, availability of contract terms and treatment of input error. The last part contains final provisions.

The drafters of the Convention were heavily influenced by the 1980 Vienna Convention and Model Laws on Electronic Commerce and Electronic Signatures. The influence of CISG is clearly visible in the first chapter of the Convention, and to a lesser extent in the remaining parts. On the other hand, the impact of Model laws is noticeable in the third chapter.

The aim of the Convention is to remove legal obstacles to electronic commerce, including those which arose under other instruments, on the basis of the principle

---

[258] This part is largely based on Polanski, P. P. (2006) *Some remarks on the scope of application of the newest Convention on electronic communications*; Polanski, P. P. (5-7 June 2006) *Convention on e-contracting: the rise of international law of electronic commerce?*; Polanski, P. P. (2006) *International Electronic Contracting in the newest UN Convention.*

[259] United Nations (23 November 2005), *United Nations Convention on the Use of Electronic Communications in International Contracts*. See also UNCITRAL (23 November 2005), *General Assembly adopts new Convention on the Use of Electronic Communications in International Contracting*.

[260] Art. 16(1).

[261] UNCITRAL (23 November 2005), *General Assembly adopts new Convention on the Use of Electronic Communications in International Contracting*.

[262] Art. 16(3). So far, only China, Central African Republic, Lebanon, Madagascar, Senegal, Sierra Leone, Singapore and Sri Lanka have signed the Treaty.

[263] Art. 25(2).

of functional equivalence.[264] Furthermore, the Treaty aims to provide a common solution in a manner acceptable to states with different legal, social and economic systems.[265]

As regards the sphere of application, the Convention applies to the use of electronic communications[266] in connection with the formation or performance of a contract between parties whose places of business are in different states.[267] By applying the Convention to electronic communications, the scope of the Convention is broadened significantly. It includes not only contracts but also electronic negotiations and contracts formed partially by digital means. Nationality or character of the parties is irrelevant.[268] Place of business is defined as 'any place where a party maintains a non-transitory establishment to pursue an economic activity other than the temporary provision of goods or services out of a specific location.'[269] A party's place of business is presumed to be the location indicated by that party,[270] and not that where the technological equipment is located or where an information system can be accessed. It may also appear from any previous dealings or from information disclosed by the parties.[271] If a party has not indicated its place of business, or has more than one, then the closest relationship test shall designate one. However, the Convention states that a domain name or electronic mail address connected to a specific country does not create a presumption that a given party has a place of business in that country.[272]

The unique contribution of this Convention can be found in Article 20, which has the goal of removing obstacles to e-commerce found in other international instruments adopted before the Internet era. It reads as follows:

---

264 UNCITRAL (11- 22 October 2004), *A/CN.9/571 – Report of the Working Group on Electronic Commerce on the work of its forty-fourth session*, para. 14.

265 United Nations (23 November 2005), *United Nations Convention on the Use of Electronic Communications in International Contracts*. See Preamble, 6th passage.

266 Art. 4 (b) 'Electronic communication' means any communication that the partie smake by means of data messages;
(c) 'Data message' means information generated, sent, received or stored by electronic, magnetic, optical or similar means, including, but not limited to, electronic data interchange, electronic mail, telegram, telex or telecopy.
The definition of data message has been copied from the Model Law on Electronic Commerce. Although the definition of a data message, is broad enough to encompass new technologies, it does not even mention WWW, although it is the most important Internet technology. For my critique of this approach, see Polanski, P.P. (July 2003), *Custom as a Source of Supranational Internet Commerce Law (PhD Thesis)*, p. 46.

267 Art. 1(1). See also Art. 1(2) which repeats Art. 1(2) of CISG.

268 Art. 1(3).

269 Art. 4(h).

270 Art. 6(1). It should appear from any previous dealings, contract or information disclosed by the parties. See Arts. 1(2) and 1(3).

271 Art. 1(3).

272 Art. 6(5). This provision not only limits the freedom of adjudicator but also ignores the fact that these days ccTLDs give strong indication of parties' location. Although in theory a business can easily register a domain name in another country, modern online entrepreneurs nearly always try to register a domain name in a country where they actually run a business. The current wording seems to have been influenced by early fears in this regard. See, for example Johnson, D.R. and Post, D. (May 1996), *Law and Borders – The Rise of Law in Cyberspace*, section B.

'1. The provisions of this Convention apply to the use of electronic communications in connection with the formation or performance of a contract to which any of the following international conventions, to which a Contracting State to this Convention is or may become a Contracting State, apply:

Convention on the Recognition and Enforcement of Foreign Arbitral Awards (New York, 10 June 1958);
Convention on the Limitation Period in the International Sale of Goods (New York, 14 June 1974) and Protocol thereto (Vienna, 11 April 1980);
United Nations Convention on Contracts for the International Sale of Goods (Vienna, 11 April 1980);
United Nations Convention on the Liability of Operators of Transport Terminals in International Trade (Vienna, 19 April 1991);
United Nations Convention on Independent Guarantees and Stand-by Letters of Credit (New York, 11 December 1995);
United Nations Convention on the Assignment of Receivables in International Trade (New York, 12 December 2001).'[273]

As a result, the Convention applies to the aforementioned conventions to which a Contracting State of this Convention is or may become a party. In consequence, for example, the term 'writing' as used in Article 13 of CISG would be given a new meaning provided that a Contracting State to CISG becomes a Contracting State to the Treaty on e-contracting. Furthermore, the provisions of the Convention also apply to other conventions related to international trade, but a Contracting State may declare that it is not bound by that provision.[274] Such a declaration by Contracting State can be made, changed and withdrawn at any time,[275] unlike reservations, which are not permitted under this Convention.[276]

The Convention, however, differs from CISG in many respects. Firstly, it is not limited to contracts for the sale of goods and it applies to transactions other than sales such as barters. More importantly, the new Convention also applies to transactions regarding services and information. This is a fundamental and long awaited change. Thanks to this provision international e-services have finally been given legal recognition.

The second difference from CISG is that the new Convention applies to contracts between parties located in two different states, even if one or both are not Contracting States. Such wording suggests a universal character of the Treaty. The wording of this provision has been influenced by the 1964 Hague Convention relating to a Uniform Law on the International Sale of Goods,[277] but its interpretation

[273] Art. 20(1).

[274] See Art. 20(2).

[275] Arts. 21(1) and (4).

[276] Art. 22.

[277] UNCITRAL Working Group IV (Electronic Commerce) (2005), *A/60/17 – Report of the United Nations Commission on International Trade Law on the work of its thirty-eighth session, 4-15 July 2005*, para. 19

caused two conflicting interpretations among the drafters.[278] The prevailing view is that the Convention should only apply when the laws of a contracting state applied to the underlying transaction.[279] Therefore the Convention applies, so long as the law of a Contracting State applies to the dealings of the parties. Furthermore, any Contracting State may declare that it will apply this Convention only when the states are Contracting States or when parties have agreed that it applies.[280]

The autonomous character of the Convention is reflected in the provision on interpretation, which is a copy of Article 7 of the Vienna Convention. Therefore, the provisions of the Convention should be interpreted having regard to its international character and the need to promote uniformity and the observance of good faith in international trade. On the other hand, gaps are to be settled in conformity with the general principles on which it is based such as the principles of functional equivalence and technological neutrality, expressly referred to in the Preamble. Only in the absence of such principles, questions not expressly settled in the Convention should be answered by the law applicable by virtue of the rules of private international law.

However, the autonomous character of the Convention is adversely affected by two articles that refer to extra-conventional norms. Both Article 7 on information requirements[281] and Article 13 on the availability of contract terms[282] make reference to some other law that has to be taken into account by online entrepreneurs.[283] In the comment to the draft the authors have offered the following interpretation of the word 'law':

> 'In the context of the draft article, the words "the law" were to be understood as encompassing not only statutory or regulatory law, including international conventions or treaties ratified by a Contracting State, but also judicially created law and other procedural law. However, as used in the draft article, the words "the law" did not include areas of law that had not become part of the law of a state and were sometimes referred to by expressions such as "lex mercatoria" or "law merchant".'[284]

---

[278] Ibid., para. 22.

[279] Ibid., paras. 18-22.

[280] Art. 21(1).

[281] Art. 7. Nothing in this Convention affects the application of any rule of law that may require the parties to disclose their identities, places of business or other information, or relieves a party from the legal consequences of making inaccurate, incomplete or false statements in that regard.

[282] Art. 13. Nothing in this Convention affects the application of any rule of law that may require a party that negotiates some or all of the terms of a contract through the exchange of electronic communications to make available to the other party those electronic communications which contain the contractual terms in a particular manner, or relieves a party from the legal consequences of its failure to do so.

[283] In particular, the European Union Directive on Electronic Commerce, which stipulates numerous informational requirements.

[284] UNCITRAL Working Group IV (Electronic Commerce) (2005), *A/60/17 – Report of the United Nations Commission on International Trade Law on the work of its thirty-eighth session, 4-15 July 2005,* paras. 57-58 and 94. See in particular comment to Arts. 9(2) and 13.

Therefore, on the one hand side, the term 'law' and 'the rule of law' is given a broad scope to include judicially created law and 'other' procedural law. On the other hand, mercantile customary law (*lex mercatoria*) is excluded.[285] In consequence, if there exist commercial customs regarding the disclosure of certain information or making available contract terms, these norms would not become binding on the parties of an electronic contract governed by the new Convention. Such an interpretation obviously does not make much sense and is contrary to commercial standards.

The new Treaty also does not contain the regulation of trade usages akin to the formulation found in Article 9 of the Vienna Convention.[286] Lack of such provision adversely affects the flexibility of the conventional norms. It is impossible to understand why UNCITRAL experts did not recognise the importance of commercial usages in electronic commerce. As the rest of the book will demonstrate, such an approach is deeply flawed as it ignores probably the most powerful source of norms in global electronic commerce.

In general, the sphere of application of the Convention is much broader than that of CISG. However, it does not apply to consumer contracts, electronic financial services and, what is novel, international transferable documents such as bills of exchange.[287] It is to be regretted that this Convention excludes such important areas of electronic commerce, as these are the fields that require international regulation. Furthermore, as in CISG, parties may exclude the application of this Convention or derogate from or vary the effect of any of its provisions.[288]

With respect to the norms regarding electronic communications, a contract or a communication[289] can be made or evidenced in any particular form.[290] The wording of this provision has been influenced by the Vienna Convention and is broad enough to cover electronic contracts. However, the Treaty on e-contracting specifically recognises such contracts as functionally equivalent to paper-based ones:

> 'A communication or a contract shall not be denied validity or enforceability on the sole ground that it is in the form of an electronic communication.'[291]

---

[285] However, the drafters do not define the term *lex mercatoria.*

[286] UNCITRAL Model Law on Electronic Commerce, which also used narrow interpretation of the term 'law' and 'the rule of law'.UNCITRAL (11- 22 October 2004), *A/CN.9/571 – Report of the Working Group on Electronic Commerce on the work of its forty-fourth session*, para. 58.

[287] Art. 2.

[288] Art. 3.

[289] Art. 4(a). 'Communication' means any statement, declaration, demand, notice or request, including an offer and the acceptance of an offer, that the parties are required to make or choose to make in connection with the formation or performance of a contract.

[290] Art. 9(1).

[291] Art. 8(1).

In addition, a contract formed by a computer system and a natural person, or by the interaction of automated message systems,[292] shall not be denied validity or enforceability on the sole ground that no natural person reviewed or intervened in each of the individual actions carried out by the automated message systems or the resulting contract.[293] Parties' agreement to use electronic communications can be inferred from the party's conduct.[294]

Treaty on e-contracting specifies the requirements for electronic writing, signature and originality based on Articles 6-8 of the Model Law on Electronic Commerce. The requirement of writing is met by an electronic communication if the information contained therein is accessible so as to be usable for subsequent reference.[295] On the other hand, the requirement of signature is met if a method is used that identifies the party, indicates its intention and is as reliable as appropriate to its purpose (or proven in fact to have fulfilled the above functions).[296] The requirement of originality is met if the integrity of information is reliably assured from the time when it was first generated in its final form and the information can be displayed to the person requesting it.[297] The integrity of information is assured if it has remained complete and unaltered, apart from any changes that arise in the normal course of electronic data transfer. The standard of reliability shall be assessed in the light of the purpose for which the information was generated and all relevant circumstances.[298]

The Convention contains provisions on time and place of dispatch and receipt of electronic messages, which differ in comparison to the Model Law on Electronic Commerce.[299] As a rule of thumb, the place of business designates the place where the information was dispatched or received, even if supporting information system is located elsewhere.[300] On the other hand, the time of dispatch is the time when a message leaves the computer system of a sender, whereas the time of receipt is the time when it becomes capable of being retrieved by the addressee at a designated electronic address. The message is presumed to be capable of being retrieved when it reaches the addressee's electronic address.[301] The correct electronic address is important, because the time of receipt at another address is when the addressee becomes aware that a message has been sent and that it can be retrieved. The afore-

---

292 Art. 4(g). 'Automated message system' means a computer program or an electronic or other automated means used to initiate an action or respond to data messages or performances in whole or in part, without review or intervention by a natural person each time an action is initiated or a response is generated by the system.

293 Art. 12.

294 Art. 8(2).

295 Art. 9(2).

296 Art. 9(3).

297 Art. 9(4).

298 Art. 9(5).

299 Art. 10. See also art. 24 and art. 27 of CISG and the discussion on p. 54.

300 See Art. 6.

301 Art. 10(2), third sentence.

mentioned provision is well suited to e-mail and EDI-based electronic commerce, but it may not be so easy to establish in case of web-based commerce, because such information would usually be recorded only by one automated system.

The Convention on e-contracting also contains novel principles on invitations to make offers and input error. Article 11 contains the following presumption with regards to the status of interactive ordering systems:

> 'A proposal to conclude a contract made through one or more electronic communications which is not addressed to one or more specific parties, but is generally accessible to parties making use of information systems, including proposals that make use of interactive applications for the placement of orders through such information systems, is to be considered as an invitation to make offers, unless it clearly indicates the intention of the party making the proposal to be bound in case of acceptance.'[302]

This presumption is of particular importance for web-based electronic shops. Therefore, unless the online merchant making the proposal clearly indicates his or her intention on a website, his electronic catalogue will not be treated as a definite offer. However, one should note that this presumption is only valid provided that a proposal is not addressed to one or more specific parties. It is argued that the drafters failed to notice that after a customer logs into such an interactive ordering system, the proposal is always specifically addressed to him or her, which can be easily ascertained if a system has implemented shopping cart technology. In consequence, from that moment in time, such proposals should be treated as offers as they are customarily very specific, addressed to a registered user and allow for immediate placement of an order. Clearly, the provision of Article 11 is not a very fortunate one. It fails to take into account the fact that registration in any online system can be regarded as a communication addressed to a specific person. Furthermore, it does not even define what constitutes an invitation to treat and how it is to be distinguished from an offer.[303] Finally, it uses the confusing term 'interactive applications for the placement of orders' rather than 'automated message system' used elsewhere in the text, which might lead to future unnecessary problems of interpretation.[304]

Furthermore, the Treaty regulates consequences of a contractual mistake. Where a person makes an input error on an interactive website and is not given the opportunity to correct it, he or she has the right to withdraw the portion of the electronic communication if he or she:

---

[302] Art. 11.

[303] See the discussion on this topic under Vienna Convention heading and Contract law section *above*.

[304] See an even more confusing explanation for this choice in UNCITRAL Working Group IV (Electronic Commerce) (2005), *A/60/17 – Report of the United Nations Commission on International Trade Law on the work of its thirty-eighth session, 4-15 July 2005*, para. 87.

'(a) (…) notifies the other party of the error as soon as possible; and
(b) (…) has not used or received any material benefit or value from the goods or services, if any, received from the other party.'[305]

This provision spurred a great deal of controversy. Critics argued that such a provision might conflict with well-established contract law principles, is more appropriate for consumer transactions and that it would create serious difficulties for trial courts, since the only evidence of the error would be the assertion of the interested party that he or she made an error. The proponents argued that the type of error is specific to electronic communication and therefore deserves special treatment, that it provides a much needed uniform rule in view of the differing and possibly conflicting national rules and that it did not in any way aggravate the evidentiary difficulties that already exist in a paper-based environment, because the courts would have to assess all the circumstances anyway.[306] The proponents won, but the purpose of this provision is not entirely clear. It only provides for consequences of input error, but does not oblige online entrepreneurs to introduce systems of error identification and correction, despite the fact that it is a customary practice to do so.[307] The drafters felt that such a prescriptive provision would be incompatible with 'the enabling nature' of the Convention.[308] Furthermore, no time limit was set for the exercise of the right of withdrawal, thereby introducing legal uncertainty.

In summary, although it is definitely too early to draw any serious conclusions, the new Convention is certainly the most important international development in electronic commerce law. Being primarily concerned with the formation of electronic contracts, it recognises the value of electronic communications and modernises the terminology of older conventions to embrace the impact of digital technologies. Another advantage of the Convention is its broader scope of application. Compared to that of CISG it goes beyond sales and covers trade in goods, services and information. It also confirms widely recognised principles such as that of functional equivalency or irrelevancy of the location of information systems.

The Treaty increases the certainty of electronic contracting by expressly recognising this form of transaction. One might argue that it attaches special importance to automated message systems such as online marketplaces, interactive electronic shops or EDI. The Convention also removes the barrier to electronic commerce by specifying the requirements for the recognition of electronic writing, signature and original. Finally it offers a useful definition of parties' place of business, specifies

---

[305] Art. 14(1). See also art. 27 of CISG and the discussion on p. 54.

[306] UNCITRAL (11- 22 October 2004), *A/CN.9/571 – Report of the Working Group on Electronic Commerce on the work of its forty-fourth session*, pp. 185-186. UNCITRAL Working Group IV (Electronic Commerce) (2005), *A/60/17 – Report of the United Nations Commission on International Trade Law on the work of its thirty-eighth session, 4-15 July 2005*, paras. 96-105.

[307] See Chapter IX.

[308] UNCITRAL (11- 22 October 2004), *A/CN.9/571 – Report of the Working Group on Electronic Commerce on the work of its forty-fourth session*, para. 184.

time and place of electronic communication and provides novel regulations on invitation to treat and input error.

However, the new Treaty also has some shortcomings. Having broader scope than CISG, the Convention nevertheless excludes fundamental areas of e-commerce where uniform, international regulation is really necessary. Consumer trade is excluded even though online consumers might not be better protected by their domestic legal systems. Financial transactions are excluded even though they are the fundamental part of global e-commerce. Electronic bills of lading and other transferable documents are excluded although they are a crucial element in international trade. Also its relation to other conventions is not entirely clear.

Flexibility of e-contracting is seriously undermined by lack of recognition of electronic trade usages. In fact, the drafters have expressed their resentment towards *lex mercatoria*. Such an approach ignores the most promising source of norms on the Internet. Taking into account the flexibility that the Convention affords to states making the declarations under Article 21, it is fair to say that its provisions are more flexible to future Contracting States than to online merchants. Recently, Connoly and Ravindra even argued that Article 19, which permits Contracting States to limit the application of the Convention to other Contracting States or when the parties agree that it applies 'has the potential to re-introduce the very legal ambiguities that the Convention is designed to avoid.'[309]

Furthermore, the conventional norms are vague and do not recognize many common practices that have emerged in electronic commerce, such as order confirmation or encryption of transactions. In this sense, it is not a very innovative instrument as it repeats many of the provisions found in the 1980 Sales Convention and the Model Law on Electronic Commerce. The repetitive character is particularly visible in the definition of 'data message', which does not even mention web-based technology. In addition, unnecessarily confusing terminology is sometimes introduced as in the case of 'automated message system' and 'interactive system for placing orders'. At the same time, the Convention is not as comprehensive as CISG or European Union e-commerce directives.

Finally, it is argued that UNCITRAL failed to realise the value of public consultations with the Internet community. Only states and interested international organisations were invited to participate in the preparation of the draft Convention at all the sessions of the Working Group IV with a full opportunity to speak and make proposals.[310] The fact that the Internet community could not participate in the drafting process and express its opinions on UNCITRAL's website is against the spirit of the Internet, which continues to be developed through open sharing of information. Global Internet regulations should at least be consulted with the users.

Despite its shortcomings, the Treaty on e-contracting represents a major step forward in the international regulation of electronic commerce. Many of the critical

---

[309] Connoly, C. and Ravindra, P. (2006), *First UN Convention on eCommerce finalized*, p. 33.
[310] A60/515 p. 7.

comments expressed above might be addressed in the Explanatory Report, which was not yet available at the time of this writing. Therefore, it is advisable for all states to ratify this Convention in order to bring more certainty and predictability to modern international trade. Only time will tell whether the Convention becomes widely adopted, and if international electronic commerce becomes more legally certain.

2.3 European E-commerce Directive

The European Union has created one of the most original and comprehensive frameworks for electronic commerce in the world.[311] Important international develop-

---

[311] See Poullet, Y. (2004), *A European Internet Law?* There are also numerous regulations in the EU that cover Internet commerce and telecommunication sector, for instance:OJ C 376/01 (12.12.1996), *Council Resolution of 21 November 1996 on new policy- priorities regarding the information society*; OJ L 178/1 (12.11.2000), *Directive 2000/31/EC of the European Parliament and of the Council of 8 June 2000 on certain legal aspects of information society services, in particular electronic commerce, in the Internal Market (Directive on Electronic Commerce)*; OJ L 201/37 (31.07.2002), *Directive 2002/58/EC of the European Parliament and of the Council of 12 July 2002 concerning the processing of personal data and the protection of privacy in the electronic communications sector (Directive on privacy and electronic communications)*; OJ L 204/37 (21.07.1998), *Directive 98/34/EC of the European Parliament and of the Council of 22 June 1998 laying down a procedure for the provision of information in the field of technical standards and regulations*; OJ L 271/16 (09.10.2002), *Directive 2002/65/EC of the European Parliament and of the Council of 23 September 2002 concerning the distance marketing of consumer financial services and amending Council Directive 90/619/EEC and Directives 97/7/EC and 98/27/EC*; OJ L 321/41 (06.12.2003), *Council Decision of 17 November 2003 relating to the conclusion on behalf of the European Community of Council of Europe Convention No. 180 on information and legal cooperation on information society services (2003/840/EC)*; OJ L 345/90 (31.12.2003), *Directive 2003/98/EC of the European Parliament and of the Council of 17 November 2003 on the re-use of public sector information*; OJ L 9/3 (15.01.2003), *Directive 2002/92/EC of the European Parliament and of the Council of 9 December 2002 on insurance mediation*; OJ L 12/1 (16.01.2001), *Council Regulation (EC) No. 44/2001 of 22 December 2000 on jurisdiction and the recognition and enforcement of judgments in civil and commercial matters*; OJ L 13/12 (19.01.2000), *Directive 1999/93/EC of the European Parliament and of the Council of 13 December 1999 on a Community framework for electronic signatures*; OJ L 94/37 (13.04.2005), *Statement by the Commission concerning Art. 2 of Directive 2004/48/EC of the European Parliament and of the Council on the enforcement of intellectual property rights (2005/295/EC)*; OJ L 108/7 (24.04.2002), *Directive 2002/19/EC of the European Parliament and of the Council of 7 March 2002 on access to, and interconnection of, electronic communications networks and associated facilities (Access Directive)*; OJ L 108/21 (24.04.2002), *Directive 2002/20/EC of the European Parliament and of the Council of 7 March 2002 on the authorisation of electronic communications networks and services (Authorisation Directive)*; OJ L 108/33 (24.04.2002), *Directive 2002/21/EC of the European Parliament and of the Council of 7 March 2002 on a common regulatory framework for electronic communications networks and services (Framework Directive)*; OJ L 108/51 (24.04.2002), *Directive 2002/22/EC of the European Parliament and of the Council of 7 March 2002 on universal service and users' rights relating to electronic communications networks and services (Universal Service Directive)*; OJ L 134/1 (30.04.2004), *Directive 2004/17/EC of the European Parliament and of the Council of 31 March 2004 coordinating the procurement procedures of entities operating in the water, energy, transport and postal services sectors*; OJ L 134/114 (30.04.2004), *Directive 2004/18/EC of the European Parliament and of the Council of*

ments include two European Union directives: the Electronic Commerce Directive[312] and the Electronic Signature Directive.[313]

The Electronic Commerce Directive (the Directive) is a comprehensive framework for electronic commerce that establishes a set of rules aiming at harmonisation of the laws of European Union members. It includes provisions regarding establishment of service providers, commercial communication, liability of intermediaries, electronic contracts, and out-of-court dispute settlement.[314] The Electronic Commerce Directive promotes freedom of commencing electronic commerce activity without authorisation,[315] although subject to the law of Member State where the service provider is established.[316] Furthermore, the Directive establishes the obligation of e-companies to provide electronic information about its name, geographic and e-mail address, information about any registrars in which it may function or about supervisory authority if present,[317] as well as clear indication of prices including delivery cost and tax information.

In relation to electronic commerce communication, the Directive sets informational requirements for online advertising and unsolicited e-mails, in the latter case establishing a formal requirement of provision of opt-out registrars[318] for participants who do not want to receive such e-mails. It attempts to encourage self-regulation of licensed professions through codes of conduct in order to determine the

---

31 March 2004 on the coordination of procedures for the award of public works contracts, public supply contracts and public service contracts; OJ L 144/19 (04.06.1997), *Directive 97/7/EC of the European Parliament and of the Council of 20 May 1997 on the protection of consumers in respect of distance contracts*; OJ L 159/16 (02.06.2004), *Directive 2004/48/EC of the European Parliament and of the Council of 29 April 2004 on the enforcement of intellectual property rights*; OJ L 167/10 (22.06.2001), *Directive 2001/29/EC of the European Parliament and of the Council of 22 May 2001 on the harmonisation of certain aspects of copyright and related rights in the information society*; OJ L 275/39 (27.10.2000), *Directive 2000/46/EC of the European Parliament and of the Council of 18 September 2000 on the taking up, pursuit of and prudential supervision of the business of electronic money institutions*; OJ L 281/31 (23.11.1995), *Directive 95/46/EC of the European Parliament and of the Council of 24 October 1995 on the protection of individuals with regard to the processing of personal data and on the free movement of such data*.

[312] OJ L 178/1 (12.11.2000), *Directive 2000/31/EC of the European Parliament and of the Council of 8 June 2000 on certain legal aspects of information society services, in particular electronic commerce, in the Internal Market (Directive on Electronic Commerce)*.

[313] OJ L 13/12 (19.01.2000), *Directive 1999/93/EC of the European Parliament and of the Council of 13 December 1999 on a Community framework for electronic signatures*.

[314] See Art. 1.2 of The Electronic Commerce Directive.

[315] See Art. 4 *above*.

[316] The so-called Internal Market clause (Art. 3.1) *above*.

[317] See Art. 5 *above*.

[318] See Arts. 6 and 7 *above*. The article on spam has been modified by Art. 13 of the Directive on privacy in electronic communication, which in general, prohibits sending usolicited e-mails without prior consent of a user. See OJ L201/37 (31.07.2002), *Directive 2002/58/EC of the European Parliament and of the Council of 12 July 2002 concerning the processing of personal data and the protection of privacy in the electronic communications sector (Directive on privacy and electronic communications)*.

types of information that can be given for the purpose of commercial communication.[319]

In regard to liability of intermediaries, the Directive generally exempts them from liability. This is the case with information that passes through their computers (so-called *mere conduit*),[320] 'caching', which is a common practice of automatic and temporary storage of information requested by other users for the purpose of faster onward transmission[321] and 'hosting', which is storage of information at the request of a user, e.g., hosting of a website.[322] Each of these activities is exempted from liability under certain conditions that must be fulfilled by an intermediary.[323] Consequently, the Directive exempts intermediaries from the general obligation to monitor the information they store or transfer and obligation to actively seek illegal activity.[324] However, somewhat contradictorily, it allows Member States to establish obligation of prompt informing of public authorities about alleged illegal activities of recipients of their service and their details.[325]

The Electronic Commerce Directive employs the functional equivalent approach of the Model Law, requiring fifteen EU Member States to implement legislation to remove current requirements, including the requirements of form, which are likely to curb the use of contracts by electronic means.[326] In this respect, the Directive establishes freedom of electronic contracting, specifically listing types of contracts that may be excluded from its scope.[327]

Furthermore, the Directive puts an additional burden on e-businesses to provide certain pre- and post-contractual information on a website but not necessarily in e-mail communication[328] that is compulsory in Business-to-Consumer trade and may be waived by contrary agreement in Business-to-Business commerce. Information that should be provided prior to the conclusion of the contract include the different technical steps that follow to conclude the contract[329] that is customarily provided by trading websites, whether the contract will be filed and accessible[330] for subsequent reference, the ways of identifying and correcting input errors,[331] languages

---

319 See Art. 8.2 *above*.

320 See Art. 14 *above*.

321 See Art. 15 *above* and Glossary.

322 See Art. 16 *above* and Glossary.

323 See Art. 14.1(a-c), Art. 15.1(a-e), Art. 16.1(a-b).

324 See Art. 17.1 *above*.

325 See Art. 17.2 *above*.

326 See recital 34 and Art. 9.1 *above*. See also, for example, Murray, A.D. (2000), *Entering into Contracts Electronically: The Real W.W.W.*, pp. 27-28.

327 EU countries may disallow electronic contracts that create or transfer rights in real estate, contracts requiring by law involvement of public authorities, etc. See Arts. 9.2 and 9.3 *above*.

328 The directive excludes e-mail and equivalent individual communications from the burden of including the information specified *above*.

329 See Art. 10.1(a) *above*.

330 See Art. 10.1(b) *above*.

331 See Art. 10.1(c) *above*.

offered for the conclusion of the contract,[332] codes of conduct to which e-business subscribes and how they can be consulted electronically[333] and links to downloadable general terms and conditions or other ways of enabling the recipient to store and reproduce them.[334] In addition, the Directive requires, prior to the conclusion of the contract, a provision of not only information enabling identification and correction of input errors but also technical ways of doing this.[335] More importantly, however, the Directive requires e-business to acknowledge the receipt of the recipient's order without undue delay and by electronic means,[336] thus, as will be argued later, codifying customary web-commerce practice. The Directive stipulates that such an acknowledgement is deemed to be received when the party to whom it is addressed can access it.[337] Unfortunately, the Directive does not provide any legal consequences for non-provision of such acknowledgement, delegating this task to national legislatures.[338]

The Directive also deals with various issues regarding its implementation.[339] In this respect, the Directive encourages drafting of codes of conduct on all levels of professional activity and their impact 'upon practices, habits or customs relating to electronic commerce'.[340] Moreover, the Directive encourages alternative dispute resolution systems, including electronic ones[341] and dissemination of knowledge about them, their decisions and practices and customs of electronic commerce.[342]

The importance of the Electronic Commerce Directive is that it is the first mandatory, transnational recognition of electronic commerce linking both Civil and Anglo-Saxon legal traditions. It recognises many already practiced e-commerce habits, promotes electronic alternative dispute resolution systems and seems to be aware of the significance of customary Internet practices. Moreover, the regulation not only affects European Union countries but is likely to be adopted by candidate states to the European Union, thus promoting a uniform e-commerce law across all of Europe.

However, the Directive is also somewhat limited, regulating contractual electronic commerce in only three articles, therefore raising many controversies within the EU community itself.[343] Moreover, the Directive does not regulate issues of

---

[332] See Art. 10.1(d) *above.*

[333] See Art. 10.2 *above.*

[334] See Art. 10.3 *above.* Provision of general terms and conditions prior to the conclusion of the contract in such a way that they can be stored and reproduced later is also a requirement in e-mail and equivalent individual communication. See Art. 10.4

[335] See Art. 11.2 *above.*

[336] See Art. 11.1 first indent, *above.*

[337] See Art. 11.1 second indent *above.*

[338] See Art. 20 *above.*

[339] See Chapter 3 of the Directive.

[340] See Art. 16.1(d).

[341] See Art. 17.1.

[342] See Art. 17.3.

[343] See, for example, London Investment Banking Association (17 February 2000), *Proposed directive on certain legal aspects of electronic commerce. A Memorandum on the Common Position by*

jurisdictional issues, taxation, cartel law and other areas excluded from its scope.[344] Furthermore, protests by some web operators clearly indicate a degree of disagreement in relation to the European regulation of electronic commerce.[345]

More importantly, however, the Electronic Commerce Directive is restricted in its application to Europe. Therefore, it does not aim at or guarantee a uniform set of rules for global, intercontinental Internet-based trade.[346] The Directive has been amended and supplemented by other directives, especially the 2002 Directive on Privacy in Electronic Communication[347] and the 2002 Directive on Consumer Financial Services.[348] Similar remarks can be made in relation to the Electronic Signature Directive that establishes the requirements for electronic signature certificates and certification services throughout the EU and includes mechanisms for co-operation with third countries based on mutual recognition of certificates, bilateral and multilateral agreements.

3. Model laws

3.1 1996 Model Law on Electronic Commerce

The first important development in international electronic commerce law was the Model Law on Electronic Commerce adopted by United Nations' General Assembly in December 1996.[349] The Model Law resolution, written in Arabic, Chinese, English, French, Russian and Spanish, is a global framework for electronic commerce, which aims at the facilitation of electronic trade in countries with different legal, social and economic systems.[350]

---

the London Investment Banking Association (LIBA); Poggi, C.T. (2000), *Electronic commerce legislation: an analysis of European and American approaches to contract formation*. See also ICC (27 July 1999), *International business comments on the proposed EU directive on certain legal aspects of electronic commerce*.

344 See Chapter I.

345 The Directive had not been implemented by even a majority of EU Member States by January 17, 2002. See Art. 22 *above*, see also, for example, McGuire, D. and Krebs, B. (22 October 2002), *New e-Commerce regulations*. See also, for example, Avanova (29 October 2002), *Spanish websites go blank to counter web regulation*.

346 However Council of Europe has started work aiming at making certain directives available to non-EU members. See, for example, Council of Europe (2 October 2001), *The Council of Europe provides a harmonised approach to the regulation of on- line services at the Pan-European level*.

347 OJ L 201/37 (31.07.2002), *Directive 2002/58/EC of the European Parliament and of the Council of 12 July 2002 concerning the processing of personal data and the protection of privacy in the electronic communications sector (Directive on privacy and electronic communications)*.

348 OJ L 271/16 (09.10.2002), *Directive 2002/65/EC of the European Parliament and of the Council of 23 September 2002 concerning the distance marketing of consumer financial services and amending Council Directive 90/619/EEC and Directives 97/7/EC and 98/27/EC*.

349 UNCITRAL (1996), *General Assembly Resolution 51/162 of 16 December 1996 – UNCITRAL Model Law on Electronic Commerce with Guide to Enactment with additional Art. 5 bis as adopted in 1998*.

350 See preamble.

The Model Law resolution is based on two principles: functional equivalence,[351] which means that electronic documents are functionally equivalent to paper documents, and technology neutrality,[352] which means that all the provisions of the model law are expressed in technology neutral language in order to remain applicable irrespective of technological progress.

The Model Law is divided into two parts. The first part consists of fifteen articles and contains provisions of general character related to legal recognition of data messages, writing, signature, original, retention and evidence of data messages as well as formation, validity, time and place of contract formation and acknowledgment of receipt. This part also includes provisions related to the sphere of application and interpretation of the Model Law and allows the Model Law to be varied by agreement. The second part is confined to two articles only, which are specific to a contract of carriage of goods and equate transport documents issued in electronic format with paper-based equivalents.

The Model Law is not a statute in the sense that it does not specify all the provisions to govern a specific matter but leaves room for states to specify exceptions to some articles. For instance, states may list exceptions to provisions on electronic writing,[353] signature,[354] original of message,[355] formation and validity of contracts,[356] recognition by parties of data messages,[357] time and place of dispatch and receipt of data messages[358] and transport documents.[359] The Model Law allows states to limit its applicability to international data messages, although the Model Law itself does not contain such a limitation and applies to 'any kind of information in the form of a data message used in the context of commercial activities.'[360]

In summary, the importance of the Model Law is that it offers recognition of electronic writing and signatures and supports admission of computer evidence in court as well as recognises the validity and enforceability of contracts formed through electronic means. The issue of electronic signatures was further discussed by UNCITRAL and led to the adoption of Model Law on Electronic Signatures in 2001.[361]

---

[351] UNCITRAL (1996), *General Assembly Resolution 51/162 of 16 December 1996 – UNCITRAL Model Law on Electronic Commerce with Guide to Enactment with additional Art. 5 bis as adopted in 1998*, para. 15-18.

[352] Ibid., para. 6.

[353] Art. 6(3).

[354] Art. 7(3).

[355] Art. 8(4).

[356] Art. 11(2).

[357] Art. 12(2).

[358] Art. 15(5).

[359] Art. 17(7).

[360] See Art. 1 and comments to it.

[361] UNCITRAL (2001), *General Assembly Resolution 56/80 – Model Law on Electronic Signatures with Guide to Enactment.*

Since its release, the Model Law has been the most important trigger of regulation of electronic commerce. The Model Law and its Guide to Enactment have gained worldwide recognition as a good 'start to defining an international set of uniform commercial principles for electronic commerce'[362] and its provisions have already been voluntarily implemented in a number of states throughout America,[363] Australia,[364] Europe[365] and Asia.[366]

However, the Model Law does not target a development of a global legal framework for electronic commerce. Instead, the Model Law provides the national legislators with a template, a non-binding blueprint that is aimed at helping them enact domestic Internet laws, thus hoping to achieve harmonisation of electronic commerce law. Moreover, the Model Law contains only very general norms and explicitly declares that it is not intended to cover all aspects of electronic commerce. It encourages states to enact detailed technical regulation[367] of such matters, thus promoting a top-down and state-origin regulation of electronic commerce, instead of supporting Internet participants in the development of technical regulatory norms. Furthermore, the Model Law was drafted in the era of Electronic Data Interchange (EDI) and many of its provisions do not reflect the current practice of Internet-based commerce. Although EDI is still important, Internet commerce is primarily based on web transactions. As the hypothetical case study will show, the Model Law is in some respects outdated.

Although all countries enacting laws dealing with Internet commerce have been to a great extent influenced by the Model Law, there is a discrepancy between national Internet law legislations as well as implementations of the Model Law. As a result, no full harmonisation has been achieved. This is a direct consequence of, among other things, the fact that the Model Law allows for various exceptions to its provisions, does not intend to cover all the matters related to electronic commerce and that some of its provisions have not achieved a global consensus.

---

362 See section 3 in White House (1 July 1997), *A Framework for Global Electronic Commerce: Policy statement issued by President Clinton and Vice-President Al Gore*.

363 See, for example, Hultmark, C. (1999), *European and U.S. perspectives on electronic documents and electronic signatures*; Poggi, C.T. (2000), *Electronic commerce legislation: an analysis of European and American approaches to contract formation*.

364 See, for example, Backhouse, B. (2000), *Legal Regimes to Facilitate Electronic Transactions – Their Suitability and Effectiveness – With Particular Reference to the Electronic Transactions Regime Currently Being Adopted in Australia*; Forder, J. and Quirk, P. (2001), *Electronic commerce and the Law*.

365 See, for example, Dickie, J. (1999), *Internet and Electronic Commerce Law in the European Union* Ramberg, C.H. (2001), *The ecommerce directive and formation of contract in a comparative perspective*.

366 See, for example, Ahmad, F. (2001), *Electronic Commerce: An Indian Perspective*; Anil, S. (2001), *Electronic Commerce in Asia: The Legal, Regulatory and Policy Issues*.

367 UNCITRAL (1996), *General Assembly Resolution 51/162 of 16 December 1996 – UNCITRAL Model Law on Electronic Commerce with Guide to Enactment with additional Art. 5 bis as adopted in 1998*, para. 13.

3.2 2004 UNIDROIT Principles of International Commercial Contracts

In contrast to the Model Law on Electronic Commerce, which was addressed at governments, the UNIDROIT Principles of International Commercial Contracts 2004 (second edition)[368] are primarily targeted at the mercantile community. Similarly to the Model Law they are not binding. Therefore, they would usually have to be expressly incorporated into a contract to become operative.

According to the Preamble, the Principles set forth general rules for international commercial contracts. Commercial contracts are given wide interpretation and include contracts for supply or exchange of goods and services, as well as investment contracts and the like. However, consumer contracts are excluded from the scope of the Principles.[369] These shall be applied only when the parties have agreed that their contract be governed by them.[370] Furthermore, they may be applied when the parties have agreed that their contract be governed by general principles of law, such as the *lex mercatoria* or the like. The authors of the Principles also suggest that they may be applied when the parties have not chosen any law to govern their contract. In addition, the Principles may be used to interpret or supplement international uniform law instruments of domestic law and serve as a model for national and international legislators.[371]

According to Bonell, the UNIDROIT Principles of International Commercial Contracts, first published in 1994 and prepared by a group of experts[372] from all major legal systems, have met with extraordinary success in the legal and business community worldwide.[373] The Principles are an international restatement of contract law available in more than twenty languages. In comparison to the 1980 Vienna Convention, they are much more comprehensive, which is partly because they do not have to be negotiated and concluded on a governmental level. For instance, apart from the formation of contracts, rights and obligations of the parties, the Prin-

---

368 UNIDROIT (2004), *UNIDROIT Principles of International Commercial Contracts 2004*.

369 See Official Comment 2 to Art. 1.

370 The Principles suggest the following two versions of the choice of law clauses:
1. 'This contract shall be governed by the UNIDROIT Principles (2004)[except as to the Articles...]'.
2. 'This contract shall be governed by the UNIDROIT Principles (2004)[except as to Articles...], supplemented when necessary by the law of [jurisdiction X]'. See Preamble.

371 See Preamble.

372 Micheal Joachim BONNELL (Chairman, Italy), Luiz Olavo BAPTISTA (Brazil), Paul-André CREPEAU, (Canada), Samuel K. DATE-BAH (Ghana), Adolfo DI MAJO (Italy), Aktham EL KHOLY (Egypt), E. Allan FARNSWORTH (United States of America), Paul FINN (Australia), Marcel FONTAINE (Belgium), Michael P. FURMSTON (United Kingdom), Arthur S. HARTKAMP (The Netherlands), HUANG Danhan (People's Republic of China), Camille JAUFFRET-SPINOSI (France), Alexander S. KOMAROV (Russian Federation), Ole LANDO (Denmark, Chairman of the Commission on European Contract Law), Peter SCHLECHTRIEM (Germany) and Takashi UCHIDA (Japan).

373 Bonnell, M.J. (2004), *UNIDROIT Principles 2004 – The New Edition of the Principles of International Commercial Contracts adopted by the International Institute for the Unification of Private Law*.

ciples cover such areas as agency, limitation periods, set-off and assignment of rights. In addition, the Principles contain extensive and very helpful rules on the interpretation of international contracts, which could be used in the interpretation of Internet contracts.[374] Furthermore, the Principles are an ongoing project, and easy to change in comparison to any conventional law.

What is particularly interesting from the perspective of electronic commerce is that the Principles recognise the importance of electronic communication is international trade. For instance, the definition of *writing* is expressed in functional terms to cover electronic writing.[375] Similarly to the international instruments discussed above, a contract can be formed and evidenced by any means, including witnesses:

> 'The principle, which is to be found in many, although not in all, legal systems, seems particularly appropriate in the context of international trade relationships where, thanks to modern means of communication, many transactions are concluded at great speed and by a mixture of conversations, telefaxes, paper contracts, e-mail and web communications.'[376]

In addition, the Principles provide several useful examples of application of its provisions to electronic commerce. Therefore, knowing that a contract may be concluded either by the acceptance of an offer or by conduct of the parties that is sufficient to show agreement,[377] the drafters give this principle a broad interpretation to cover automated contracting. Then the following illustration of contracting using Electronic Data Interchange is provided:

> 'Automobile manufacturer A and components supplier B set up an electronic data interchange system which, as soon as A's stocks of components fall below a certain level, automatically generates orders for the components and executes such orders. The fact that A and B have agreed on the operation of such a system makes the orders and performances binding on A and B, even though they have been generated without the personal intervention of A and B.'[378]

Another principle provides that where notice is required it may be given by any means appropriate to the circumstances. This reaches the addressee as soon as it is delivered either to the addressee personally or to their electronic mailing address or place of business.[379] The official comment explains that:

---

[374] See Arts. 4.1 to 4.8.

[375] 'Writing means any mode of communication that preserves a record of the information contained therein and is capable of being reproduced in tangible form.' See Art. 1.11 and Official Comment 4.

[376] See Official Comment 1 to Art. 1.2.

[377] See Art. 2.1.

[378] See Official Comment 3 to Art. 2.1.

[379] See Official Comment 4 to Art. 1.10.

> 'For an electronic notice to be "appropriate to the circumstances" the addressee must expressly or impliedly have consented to receive electronic communications in the way in which the notice was sent by the sender, i.e. of that type, in that format and to that address. The addressee's consent may be inferred from the addressee's statements or conduct, from practices established between the parties, or from applicable usages.'

Then the following interesting illustration of the application of this principle is given:

> 'Seller A and buyer B have a longstanding business relationship in the course of which they have regularly communicated by electronic means. On discovering a defect in the goods supplied on one occasion, B immediately sends A notice thereof by e-mail to an e-mail address different from the one normally used. A, who had no reason to expect an e-mail from B at that address, on discovering B's notice three weeks after it had been sent rejects it as being too late. B may not object that it had given prompt notice of the defects since the notice was not given by a means appropriate to the circumstances.'[380]

As a result, by sending e-mail to a different address than customarily used the party has not given notice by appropriate means to the circumstances. Although in general such a conclusion is reasonable, one may only wonder if the drafters would have reached a similar conclusion in a situation in which the regularly used e-mail address was unreachable due to server overload and the other address was available on a website or a business card. There are other examples of electronic contracting provided throughout the Principles that will not be discussed here, but most of them are primarily concerned with e-mail and EDI-based transactions.

The Principles also contain very interesting provisions relating to the use of standard terms and conditions, which are defined as 'provisions which are prepared in advance for general and repeated use by one party and which are actually used without negotiation with the other party.'[381] Such standard contract terms are a common feature of web-based shops, therefore it would be very useful to have some rules in this regard. The Principles expressly recognise that the format of electronic standard terms and conditions is irrelevant. One of the most interesting provisions in this regard is Principle 2.1.20, which deals with surprising terms:

> '(Surprising terms)
> (1) No term contained in standard terms which is of such a character that the other party could not reasonably have expected it, is effective unless it has been expressly accepted by that party.
> (2) In determining whether a term is of such a character regard is to be had to its content, language and presentation.'

---

[380] See Official Comment 2 to Art. 1.10.

[381] See Art. 2.1.19(2).

As a result, a standard term is ineffective if a reasonable person could not have expected it, having regard to its content, language and presentation. Therefore, unless the seller draws the adhering party's attention to such a term and the adhering party expressly accepts it, such a term will not be effective. All of these factors are of importance in web-based shopping and are aimed at the protection of the weaker party.

The Principles also contain other protective provisions. According to Article 7.1.6 an adjudicator or court may disregard exemption clauses, which are very common in international contract practice and which 'tend to give rise to much controversy between the parties':[382]

> 'A contract clause which limits or excludes one party's liability for non-performance or which permits one party to render performance substantially different from what the other party reasonably expected may not be invoked if it would be grossly unfair to do so, having regard to the purpose of the contract.'

The Principles contain an illustration of this principle. Although the example below does not directly speak of electronic commerce, there is no distortion in this illustration if we assume that the tour operator here is very popular:

> 'A tour operator offers at a high price a tour providing for accommodation in specifically designated luxury hotels. A term of the contract provides that the operator may alter the accommodation if the circumstances so require. If the operator puts up its clients in second class hotels, it will be liable to them notwithstanding the contractual term since the clients expected to be accommodated in hotels of a category similar to that which had been promised.'[383]

As a result, a contract clause that permits an online travel agent to render a performance substantially different from what the customer reasonably expects could not be invoked. Provisions such as these extend the protection usually granted to consumers to professional parties and could be regarded as a basis for future uniform electronic commerce principles that apply, irrespective of the character of parties. This is the right approach, because, as stated earlier, in principle the distinction between online consumers and professionals is blurred.[384]

In general, the UNIDROIT Principles offer a very interesting alternative to treaty-based regulation of electronic commerce. They are very popular, have a very broad scope and cover areas such as services that are not regulated in other international conventions. Furthermore, the Principles recognise the importance of electronic contracting and contain interesting examples showing the application of its norms in the digital environment. In addition, although the Principles do not apply to con-

---

[382] See Official Comment 1 to Art. 7.1.6.

[383] See Official Comment 2 to Art. 7.1.6.

[384] See also Chapters I and X.

sumer contracts, they provide interesting protective mechanisms that could in future also extend to online customers. Finally, the Principles are very flexible and recognise the importance of customs and trade usages.

Unfortunately, the 2004 UNIDROIT Principles were drafted primarily for traditional international commerce and not for electronic commerce. The Principles do not expressly recognise many specific features of electronic contracting, such as the need for secure exchange of information or the customary requirements of web-based ordering. Furthermore, the Principles are a private restatement of contract law and are therefore not binding.

4. Other Internet-related Treaties

There are two other important international regulations that pertain to the Internet: Convention on Cybercrime and two WIPO Treaties. These conventions do not directly deal with electronic commerce, as the former regulates criminal activities on the Internet, whereas the latter is devoted to intellectual property law. However, these conventions are of some relevance to electronic commerce and therefore the following sections will briefly present them.

4.1 **2001 Convention on Cybercrime**

The Convention on Cybercrime is an important international development dedicated solely to fighting Internet-related crime. Written under the auspices of the Council of Europe and signed in Budapest on 23 November 2001 it is so far the only international convention dealing with the Internet crimes. The Convention is a very recent development, which entered into force only in July 2004. At this stage only eighteen states have ratified the Convention, including Albania, Armenia, Bosnia Hercegowina, Bulgaria, Croatia, Cyprus, Denmark, Estonia, France, Hungary, Lithuania, Norway, Romania, Slovenia, the former Yugoslav Republic of Macedonia, Ukraine and recently the United States of America and the Netherlands. On the other hand, Additional Protocol to the Convention on cybercrime, concerning the criminalisation of acts of a racist and xenophobic nature committed through computer systems have been ratified by eight states and entered into force in March 2006.

The Convention consists of 48 articles, divided into four Chapters. The first part contains only one article defining four key terms ('computer system', 'computer data', 'service provider' and 'traffic data'). It is quite surprising that there are no provisions outlining the aim and scope of the Convention, exclusions and other typical provisions usually found in modern conventions. There are also no provisions dealing with the interpretations of the Convention, although here the Convention's Preamble is certainly helpful.

The most important part of the Convention is the second part. It is divided into two sections covering substantive criminal law and procedural criminal law. Rather than addressing individuals and companies, the Convention addresses states-signatories and requires them to implement the required provisions. The section devoted to the substantive law, to which the following discussion will be limited, contains definitions of nine computer crimes, grouped into the four categories shown in Figure 4.

The Convention does not contain the definition of a 'cybercrime'. The term 'cyber' implies the Internet or at least a networked environment. That would suggest that the Convention deals only with Internet-related offences. But its scope (intentionally or unintentionally) is broader and as can be seen in the table below it also contains computer-related offences such as computer forgery and fraud.

Furthermore, the Convention may not necessarily create a harmonised system of cybercrime law as in most cases it allows for qualification of the definitions of computer offences. With the exception of system interference[385] and computer-related forgery,[386] in all cases the provisions of the domestic law implementing the Convention can be substantially modified and may either require additional conditions to be satisfied or can be derogated from.

Type of cybercrime	Category
1. Illegal access	Title 1 – Offences against the confidentiality, integrity and availability of computer data and systems
2. Illegal interception	
3. Data interference	
4. System interference	
5. Misuse of devices	
6. Computer-related forgery	Title 2 – Computer-related offences
7. Computer-related fraud	
8. Offences related to child pornography	Title 3 – Content-related offences
9. Offences related to infringement of copyrights and related rights	Title 4 – Offences related to infringements of copyright and related rights
10. Dissemination of racist and xenophobic material through computer systems	Additional Protocol 1 Chapter 2 - Measures to be taken at national level
11. Racist and xenophobic motivated threat	
12. Racist and xenophobic motivated insult	
13. Denial, gross minimisation, approval or justification of genocide or crimes against humanity	

Figure 4 – Classification of cybercrimes

385 Art. 5.
386 Art. 7.

The Convention also penalises intentional attempts as well as aiding or abetting the commission of any of the above listed offences.[387] In the following article it also establishes a liability of legal persons. The Convention does not contain any specific sanctions for the specified crimes and leaves it to the states to ensure that the criminal offences 'are punishable by effective, proportionate and dissuasive sanctions, which include deprivation of liberty.'[388] In general, the drafters understood that insignificant misconducts do not constitute cybercrimes. However, the penalised conduct must be done 'intentionally' and 'without right'. Thus, the domestic law might justify the conduct based on classical legal defences such as self-defence, consent or necessity. Also, other principles or interests might lead to the exclusion of criminal liability such as conduct undertaken pursuant to lawful government authority. One should stress that custom can also serve as a justification for derogation from criminal liability:

> '...legitimate and common activities inherent in the design of networks, or legitimate and common operating or commercial practices should not be criminalised.'
> (Explanatory Report to the Convention on Cybercrime, para. 38)

Apart from substantive provisions the Convention also contains procedural provisions such as those related to expedited preservation and partial disclosure of traffic data[389] or real-time collection of traffic data.[390] Furthermore, each state should empower its competent authorities to search or access a computer system or computer-data storage medium in which computer data may be stored in its territory. Part three of the Convention deals with the international co-operation with respect to fighting online crime.

Although the computer crimes listed in the Convention will not be deeply analysed, some of the most controversial ones from the perspective of electronic commerce will be examined. Certainly, one of such controversial offences is described in Article 6 under the heading of 'misuse of devices'. According to this article, making available of software, hardware or computer access codes with intent that it be used for the purpose of committing illegal access or interception as well as data or system interference constitutes a cybercrime. In consequence, not only producers of programs such as Trojan horses or hacking software can be held liable, but also distributors, importers and other parties. Also, individuals or corporations behind websites that make freely available software keys, key-generators and cracks are cyber offenders under the Convention.

But the Convention goes even further, and outlaws the mere possession of such software, hardware or access codes with the intent to illegally access, intercept data or cause data or system interference. The problem is especially apparent if one

[387] Art. 11.
[388] Art. 13.
[389] Art. 17.
[390] Art. 20.

realises that in today's online underworld the computers of users can easily be infected with dangerous software, which can commit outlawed acts without the user's knowledge or intent. Although the second paragraph of this article allows making available or possessing of such items if not intent to commit the above-mentioned cyber offences is present (for example, the authorised testing or protection of a computer system), this psychological state of mind may not be easy to prove. However, states

> 'may reserve the right not to apply paragraph 1 of this Article, provided that the reservation does not concern the sale, distribution or otherwise making available of the items referred to in paragraph 1(a)(2).'[391]

Other controversial provisions relate to the problem of child pornography. It is a commonly accepted that pornography is one of the most profitable business models on the Internet. Unfortunately, porn websites also sell or sometimes even publicly advertise child pornography. This of course creates an enormous problem of how to fight such practices.

Article 9 of the Convention lists several forms of child pornography. It provides a very wide definition of child pornography, which includes pornographic material that visually depicts a minor (a person under eighteen years of age), engaged in sexually explicit conduct or a person appearing to be a minor engaged in sexually explicit conduct or realistic images representing a minor engaged in sexually explicit conduct. Such a wide definition certainly must have created many problems as, for example, what criteria should be used to ascertain whether a given image depicts a person appearing to be a minor.[392] Furthermore, many legal systems outlaw sexual contact with a person below fifteen years of age, whereas the Convention outlaws the possession of materials with older minors. This obviously might lead to serious complications.

The Convention outlaws the production of child pornography for the purpose of its distribution through a computer system; offering or making available child pornography through a computer system and distributing or transmitting child pornography through a computer system. However, it also outlaws procuring child pornography through a computer system for oneself or for another[393] and even possessing child pornography in a computer system or on a computer data storage medium.[394] These provisions have generated heated debate and probably for this reason the Convention allowed for derogation from penalising purchasing child pornography for oneself or for another, as well as the possession of child pornography.[395]

---

[391] Art. 6(3).
[392] Arts. 9(2) and 9(3).
[393] Art. 9(1(d)).
[394] Art. 9(1(e)).
[395] Art. 9(3).

On the other hand, the Additional Protocol to the Convention on cybercrime outlaws certain type of content on the Internet. Article 6 of the Protocol prohibits distribution or making available materials which deny, grossly minimise, approve or justify acts constituting genocide or crimes against humanity. Furthermore, online distribution of racist and xenophobic material to the public is forbidden (Art. 1 AP). 'Racist and xenophobic material' is defined as:

> 'any written material, any image or any other representation of ideas or theories, which advocates, promotes or incites hatred, discrimination or violence, against any individual or group of individuals, based on race, colour, descent or national or ethnic origin, as well as religion if used as a pretext for any of these factors.'
> (Art. 2(1) of AP)

In addition, insulting publicly, through a computer system, (i) persons for the reason that they belong to a group distinguished by race, colour, descent or national or ethnic origin, as well as religion, if used as a pretext for any of these factors; or (ii) a group of persons which is distinguished by any of these characteristics is also prohibited (Art. 5 AP). Likewise, racist and xenophobic motivated threat is criminalised (Art. 4 AP).

The low popularity of the Convention clearly shows how difficult it is to establish an international framework for Internet-related offences. Many practices that exist on the Internet are undesirable, but should not necessarily be treated as crimes or be penalised.

Furthermore, building a truly international framework has to be co-ordinated by a truly international organisation (and not local in character, such as the Council of Europe). Without widespread participation, especially of large players, even a well-drafted treaty would have problems becoming widely accepted and followed. And in international law this is what is important. Not a letter but a deed.

4.2 1996 WIPO Treaties

The World Intellectual Property Organisation has recently adopted two very important intellectual property related treaties: the Copyright Treaty (WCT) and Performances and the Phonograms Treaty (WPPT). WCT entered into force on 6 March 2002 and WPPT on 20 May 2002. Since both contain similar provisions we will focus on the Copyright Treaty.

The Copyright Treaty is considered to be one of the most important treaties dealing with the impact of modern information technologies. The Preamble of the Copyright recognises:

> 'the need to introduce new international rules and clarify the interpretation of certain existing rules in order to provide adequate solutions to the questions raised by new economic, social, cultural and technological developments.'

These new developments are specified in the next sentence, which stresses

> 'the profound impact of the development and convergence of information and communication technologies on the creation and use of literary and artistic works.'

One must remember, however, that the Convention was drafted in the very early age of the Internet – certainly the most important technological development of recent times. The Copyright Treaty was adopted in Geneva on 20 December 1996. Since then many important technological developments have taken place, such as file-sharing systems, which enable unconstrained swapping of music and video files. Even more important was the rapid growth of Internet-based commerce.

As one can see, even a Treaty less than ten years old may turn out to be too old to deal with constant technological revolution. For these reasons, only the most important technology-related provisions of the Copyright Treaty will be outlined.

The WIPO Copyright Treaty consists of the Preamble and 25 articles to which no reservations are admitted.[396] It extends the Berne Convention for the Protection of Literary and Artistic Works, constituting 'a special agreement' within the meaning of Article 20 of the Berne Convention.[397]

Article 2 of the Treaty confirms the scope of the copyright protection:

> 'Copyright protection extends to expressions and not to ideas, procedures, methods of operation or mathematical concepts as such.'

Technological influence is certainly visible in Articles 4 and 5, which extend copyright protection to computer programs and databases respectively. However, in case of databases the protection does not extend to the data or the material itself. This does not mean, however, that such data or material, if already protected by copyrights, loses its protection.

Articles 6 to 8 enumerate three rights of authors of artistic and literary works including software programs and databases: right of distribution, right of rental and right of communication to the public. Of special importance in the Internet age seems to be the right of communication to the public, which entails the exclusive right of the author of authorising:

> 'any communication to the public of their works, by wire or wireless means, including the making available to the public of their works in such a way that members of the public may access these works from a place and at a time individually chosen by them.'

It is important to realise that according to the Treaty making copyrighted material available to the public is an exclusive prerogative of the author of a webpage. An

---

[396] Art. 22.

[397] Art. 1(1-2).

infringement of this right would be any act of a person other than the author, which would result in making such material available to the public. An infringement would usually be passive (a link to a copyrighted material on a website, a file uploaded to an FTP server or made available on a hard disk for other P2P users).[398] In this sense, Article 8 applies to the potential of making available copyrighted material on the Internet, via a website, newsgroups, file-sharing systems, File Transfer Protocol, and so on. An interesting question arises whether sending such material in an e-mail would be considered as an infringement of Article 8.

Since Internet Service Providers (ISPs) actually enable such communication to the public, an important question is whether such companies can be liable for copyright infringement. Agreed statements concerning Article 8 clearly remove the liability of ISPs:

> 'It is understood that the mere provision of physical facilities for enabling or making a communication does not in itself amount to communication within the meaning of this Treaty or the Berne Convention.'

Therefore the passive provision of electronic services as in the case of ISPs does not infringe the right of communication to the public.

Furthermore, the technological influence is visible in Article 11 which forces Contracting Parties to:

> 'provide adequate legal protection and effective legal remedies against the circumvention of effective technological measures that are used by authors in connection with the exercise of their rights under this Treaty or the Berne Convention and that restrict acts, in respect of their works, which are not authorized by the authors concerned or permitted by law.'

Such circumventions of effective technological measures are greatly facilitated by the use of technological tools, which are mainly software-related. Circumventions are also powered by the ease of distribution through online channels. (The DVD Jon case is the primary example of the ease of circumventing technological measures). This is further elaborated on in the following article that deals with obligations of Contracting States concerning removal or alteration of any electronic rights management information without authority or distribution without authority of works or copies of works knowing that electronic rights management information has been removed or altered without authority.[399] The remaining parts of the Treaty deal primarily with institutional aspects of managing the monitoring and enforcement of the Treaty and for this reason will not be further elaborated.

As stated earlier, the Copyright Treaty cannot be regarded as an Internet-related Convention because, by the time it was drafted, the Internet was not a significant

[398] See Chapter X.

[399] Art. 12.

technological development. For this reason the Treaty concentrated on the extension of copyright protection to computer programs and databases. In consequence, one can at most view this Treaty as international regulation adapted (partially, of course) to the needs of the Information Society.

Despite the large number of signatories, it does not provide any unified legal framework that expressly deals with important Internet-related developments such as the problem of technology-related copying or 'ephemeral copying' as is the case with caching or proxy servers. It also did not address the status of a webpage as a subject of copyright, the use of metatags, the freedom of unconstrained linking to web resources and exceptions to this rule such as the problem of deep linking and framing, inlining, spidering, and so on. Other important aspects of Internet-related IP issues not covered in the Treaty include: the status of file-sharing systems, the relation to Open Source initiatives and the tremendous number of licensing schemes that surround the notion of freely available software, technological security innovations such as watermarking or the problem of admissibility of patenting software and e-commerce novel practices such as Amazon's famous One-click technology.

5. Self-regulation versus Internet Regulation

In his famous 'A Declaration of the Independence of Cyberspace',[400] Barlow, the founder of the Electronic Frontier Foundation, expressed the self-regulatory character of the Internet:

> 'You have no moral right to rule us nor do you possess any methods of enforcement we have true reason to fear. (...)We will create **a** civilization of the Mind in Cyberspace. May it be more humane and fair than the world your governments have made before.'[401]

In this emotional address, Barlow expressed the feelings of perhaps the majority of Internet users, who were afraid that governments might take their Internet freedom away.

Although the idea of self-regulation[402] seems to be self-explanatory, this term has different meanings or at least different scopes of meaning to different authors.[403]

---

400 Barlow, J.P. (8 February 1996), *A Declaration of the Independence of Cyberspace*.

401 Ibid.

402 See, for example, Barlow, J.P. (8 February 1996); Delacourt, J.T. (Winter 1997) p. 208; Hardy, I.T. (Summer 1994) p. 1054; Johnson, D.R. and Post, D. (May 1996) p. 1390; Perritt, H.H., Jr. (1997). For the other side of the argument see, for example, Netanel, N.W. (March 2000). See also Perritt, H.H., Jr. (2001).

403 Hardy, I.T. (Summer 1994), *The Proper Legal Regime For Cyberspace*; Johnson, D.R. and Post, D. (May 1996), *Law and Borders – The Rise of Law in Cyberspace*; Post, D.G. (October 1996), *Anarchy, State, and the Internet: An Essay on Law-Making in Cyberspace (Art. 3)*; Post, D.G. (2000), *What Larry doesn't get: code, law, and liberty in cyberspace*.

Some authors limit its scope to self-regulation by means of a contract, which is supposed to set out all matters among parties in question.[404] Codes of conduct and by-laws of Internet organisations are often included in this category. Other authors extend the meaning of the term to include self-help. There are also authors who, under the heading of self-regulation, seem to include general law-making mechanisms such as custom.[405] The problem with the latter approach is that, contrary to contractual obligation cases, custom may create legal rights and obligations for all subjects and not only for parties to an agreement. Furthermore, these rules may emerge spontaneously and unconsciously, thus escaping the 'rational' way of forming mutual obligations. In this respect, custom belongs to another category of potential sources of Internet and e-commerce law.[406]

However, a majority of authors seem to associate the idea of self-regulation with a conscious act of forming mutual relationships in a form of agreements. Hence self-regulation of the Internet by means of leaving everything for parties to set out in a contract is contrasted with a top-down approach of regulating Internet behaviour by means of harmonised statutes. In this study, the term 'self-regulation' will be understood as consisting of regulating rights and obligations in agreements including codes of conduct and organisation by-laws.

Self-regulation of electronic trade has certainly been facilitated by the emergence of Model Agreements promulgated by the various organisations mentioned above. For instance, in pre-World Wide Web-based commerce, parties often formulated their agreements based on the Model Interchange Agreement for the International Commercial use of Electronic Data Interchange[407] or the European Model EDI Agreement. Drafters of web contracts may draw on the UN/CEFACT Electronic Commerce Agreement[408] or the ICC Model clauses for use in contracts involving transborder data flows.[409] Self-regulation is also fuelled by numerous private initiatives on a national and global level aimed at the development of commonly

[404] See, for example, Boss, A.H. (1992), *The emerging law of international electronic commerce*, p. 304. Perritt, H.H., Jr. (1997), *Cyberspace Self-Government: Town Hall Democracy Or Rediscovered Royalism?*, pp. 433-437.

[405] Hardy, I.T. (Summer 1994), *The Proper Legal Regime For Cyberspace*.

[406] Polanski, P.P. (2002), *A New Approach to Regulating Internet Commerce: Custom as a Source of Electronic Commerce Law*.

[407] UN/CEFACT, *The Model Interchange Agreement for the International Commercial use of Electronic Data Interchange,* reproduced in Bajaj, K.K. and Nag, D. (2000), *E-Commerce: The Cutting Edge of Business*, Appendix 6.

[408] UN/CEFACT (May 2000), *Electronic Commerce Agreement; Recommendation No. 31, first edition, adopted by the United Nations Centre for Trade Facilitation and Electronic Business (UN/CEFACT), Geneva, Source: ECE/TRADE/257.*

[409] ICC (23 September 1998), *Model clauses for use in contracts involving transborder data flows*. See also ICC (July 2002), *Standard Contractual Clauses for the Transfer of Personal Data from the EU to Third Countries, submitted to European Commission*.

accepted rules of conduct on the Internet, such as the Model Privacy Disclosures of TRUSTe[410] or P3P.[411]

The advantage of self-regulation is that it allows for an unconstrained growth of electronic commerce, free from imposed acts that outdate quicker than Internet technology. Moreover, it also offers more legal security, as parties may specify in their agreements not only mutual rights and obligations, but also, in case of a disagreement, which law will govern their dispute or which court or arbitration tribunal will hear their dispute.

However, the disadvantage of this approach is that it does not create binding rights and obligations to non-parties to such agreements and in effect, this approach does not contribute to the development of globally binding Internet and electronic commerce law. Lessig argues that self-regulation fails to respect deeply held local or national values usually embodied in a constitution.[412] Other disadvantages include: the impossibility of removing legal and administrative requirements such as writing and signature requirements, difficulty with forming such agreements among parties not known to each other,[413] almost certainty of non-inclusion of some important terms and conditions into the agreement, problems with potential validity of contract and enforceability of certain terms, and so on.

On the other hand, the idea of top-down regulation is a reflection of states' desire to regulate the Internet in a similar way in which ordinary life is regulated. This approach has obvious advantages as it brings greater certainty as to one's rights and obligations, removes important hurdles like status of electronic documents or signatures, and forces states to devote resources to the enforcement of its regulations, which in turn may boost consumers trust in the electronic commerce, and so on.

There are also serious disadvantages of such an approach. First, it can only work if similar laws are enacted in all Internet connected states, or at least in the most important states in terms of Internet usage. Without fulfilling this requirement, national regulation of the Net will not bring a significant change to the behaviour of the online users. Moreover, harmonised laws would have to be updated regularly and by all participating states. Given the speed of Internet evolution and the current practice of legislatures around the world, this is unrealistic.

There is also a trend that marries both approaches to create a hybrid regulation of the Internet through the combination of general public law frameworks within which private regulatory regimes can work out the details.[414] Some authors argue

---

410 TRUSTe, *TRUSTe Guidance on Model Web Site Disclosures*.

411 See, for example, Electronic Commerce Platform Netherlands (October 2001), *Model Code of Conduct for Electronic Business (Draft 4.0)*. For a very good exposition of these initiatives see ICC (July 2002), *Global Action Plan for Electronic Business, third edition*, pp. 49-83.

412 Lessig, L. (1999), *Code and other laws of cyberspace*.

413 Boss, A.H. (1992), *The emerging law of international electronic commerce*, p. 304.

414 See, for example, Perritt, H.H., Jr. (2001), *Towards A Hybrid Regulatory Scheme For The Internet*.

that self-regulation is insufficient and should be supplemented by a selective legislation[415] or by a more general public law framework.[416] This approach will probably become dominant over time. However, none of these approaches stress the need to research customary practices of Internet users. This is a serious flaw of all these approaches, as neither detailed agreement nor a statute can provide such detailed norms as current common practices can.

In this respect, the widespread adoption of a global Internet convention could potentially help to solve this problem. The new Convention on the Use of Electronic Communications in International Contracting might turn out to be the solution. However, the new Convention would have to be accepted by every country interested in the use of the Internet, which seems unachievable in the near future. It would also have to be revised to reflect changes in technology, which is also a very difficult task. Furthermore, it could provide only a general framework, leaving detailed norms outside its scope, thus providing only a limited legal certainty.

6. Summary

There are already some important developments in international electronic commerce law but so far no globally binding written norms have emerged. The United Nations Convention on the Use of Electronic Communications in International Contracts is certainly the most important development and the best candidate for providing transnational norms for electronic commerce. However, it contains only very general provisions that will not be helpful in solving many Internet disputes. Besides, the Convention on electronic contracting is not as flexible and comprehensive as the Vienna Convention on Contracts for the International Sale of Goods, which provides detailed regulation of parties' rights and obligations. However, the Vienna Convention was drafted in the pre-Internet era, and as a result, its provisions are ill-suited to web-based commerce.

The Model Law, in turn, is a non-binding template that has to be adopted unchanged by all or a majority of states to create a harmonised framework. Furthermore, it was drafted in the pre-web era, which does not make it a good candidate to regulate modern electronic commerce. Similarly, the UNIDROIT Principles are not binding and their application requires express choice in an agreement. Although they recognise the importance of electronic communication, they were not written from the perspective of modern electronic commerce and hence do not expressly recognise many specific features of electronic contracting. On the other hand, the European Directive has a greater thematic scope but pertains only to European

---

[415] See, for example, Netanel, N.W. (March 2000), *Cyberspace Self-Governance: A Skeptical View from Liberal Democratic Theory*.

[416] See, for example, Perritt, H.H., Jr. (2001), *Towards A Hybrid Regulatory Scheme For The Internet*.

countries. This is a very severe limitation of this otherwise important development.

There are interesting international developments in the area of cybercrime and intellectual property law, but these conventions are of only indirect relevance to e-commerce. The Convention on Cybercrime, although comprehensive, did not become widely adopted. On the other hand, WIPO Treaties are concerned with intellectual property issues. Furthermore, similarly to the Model Law on Electronic Commerce, they were drafted in the pre-Web era.

All these developments illustrate the movement towards harmonisation and unification of Internet commerce laws, adversely affected by haphazard national regulation of the Internet. There is also a trend towards self-regulation, which opposes top-down regulation of the Internet law. This approach relies more on contracts and various normative documents issued by Internet commerce participants rather than that of governments or governmental bodies. However, this approach also has many shortcomings. The most important one is that it does not target the development of globally binding Internet laws. Also, if an agreement does not cover all the issues at hand, parties to the dispute will remain uncertain of the outcome.

Finally, there are advocates of combining the self-regulatory scheme with an official public law arrangement. This approach will probably succeed as it combines certainty of the harmonisation movement with self-regulation of more detailed matters in agreements. None of these approaches, however, provide globally binding norms that can be used to solve present Internet disputes: the regulatory approach, because there are no global written laws as yet; and the self-regulation approach, because it is supposed to bind only parties to an agreement.

7. Attempt to Solve Hypothetical Case Studies

Having reviewed the current status of Internet regulation and international electronic commerce law, an attempt will be made to solve the hypothetical case studies introduced at the end of the first chapter. The idea is to apply the relevant provisions of these written laws to assess their usefulness in solving potential Internet commerce disputes.

7.1 **Transaction confirmation case**

In the transaction confirmation case a website designer did not include an order confirmation screen. As a result, one buyer was unsure whether a transaction had taken place and purchased the required items from another website. In this hypothetical case the issue boils down to the question: is a web vendor obliged to immediately confirm an order? And if so: what are the consequences of not confirming the order? The above questions could be restated as: is an order confirmation a necessary step in the successful formation of an electronic contract?

As will be shown in Chapter VII, immediate transaction confirmation is a very widespread practice associated with electronic contract formation on the World Wide Web. Both the Model Law on Electronic Commerce and the European Union Directive on Electronic Commerce have included provisions dealing with some aspects of this practice. However, the United Nations Convention on the Use of Electronic Communications in International Contracts does not contain any specific regulation in this area.

(a) Model Law on Electronic Commerce

Article 14 of the Model Law[417] deals with acknowledgement of receipt of a data message. The Model Law regulates a matter in a dual manner dependent upon an existing agreement (or a request for acknowledgement) or a lack of agreement (or request for acknowledgement.) However, an acknowledgement seems to be given a much wider meaning than order confirmation. Even the TCP/IP protocol[418] provides for acknowledgement of receipt of a data message.[419] In short, ack-

---

[417] Art. 14. Acknowledgement of receipt
(1) Paragraphs (2) to (4) of this article apply where, on or before sending a data message, or by means of that data message, the originator has requested or has agreed with the addressee that receipt of the data message be acknowledged.
(2) Where the originator has not agreed with the addressee that the acknowledgement be given in a particular form or by a particular method, an acknowledgement may be given by
(a) any communication by the addressee, automated or otherwise, or
(b) any conduct of the addressee,
sufficient to indicate to the originator that the data message has been received.
(3) Where the originator has stated that the data message is conditional on receipt of the acknowledgement, the data message is treated as though it has never been sent, until the acknowledgement is received.
(4) Where the originator has not stated that the data message is conditional on receipt of the acknowledgement, and the acknowledgement has not been received by the originator within the time specified or agreed or, if no time has been specified or agreed, within a reasonable time, the originator:
(a) may give notice to the addressee stating that no acknowledgement has been received and specifying a reasonable time by which the acknowledgement must be received; and
(b) if the acknowledgement is not received within the time specified in subparagraph (a), may, upon notice to the addressee, treat the data message as though it had never been sent, or exercise any other rights it may have.
(5) Where the originator receives the addressee's acknowledgement of receipt, it is presumed that the related data message was received by the addressee. That presumption does not imply that the data message corresponds to the message received.
(6) Where the received acknowledgement states that the related data message met technical requirements, either agreed upon or set forth in applicable standards, it is presumed that those requirements have been met.
(7) Except in so far as it relates to the sending or receipt of the data message, this Art. is not intended to deal with the legal consequences that may flow either from that data message or from the acknowledgement of its receipt.

[418] See Glossary.

[419] See, for example, Osterloh, H., (2002) *TCP/IP Primer Plus*.

nowledgement of receipt relates to confirmation of receipt of any data message.[420]

Since in our case there was no prior agreement, or request for acknowledgement, not all provisions of the Model Law related to transaction acknowledgement would find application.[421] In fact, the Model Law creates only two presumptions. The first presumption is that a receipt of acknowledgement by an originator indicates a previous receipt of a message by an addressee. The second presumption is that:

> 'where the received acknowledgement states that the related data message met technical requirements, either agreed upon or set forth in applicable standards, it is presumed that those requirements have been met.'

The second presumption will only find application if a data message states that it meets standard or agreed upon technical requirements. However, the Model Law affirms that it does not deal with legal consequences of acknowledgement of receipt of data message.[422] In short, the Model Law creates two non-significant presumptions of a prior receipt of message being acknowledged and of conformance of acknowledgement with technical standards.

In our case, it could mean that an order confirmation would create a presumption that the order acceptance has been received and that order acknowledgement has met some technical standards. This does not seem to explain much. The Model Law avoids stating whether such practice is obligatory and whether it is necessary to successfully form a contract. Hence it does not help us solve the hypothetical problem. The Model Law provides more extensive regulation of order confirmation only if both a seller and a buyer have previously agreed that such confirmation would be necessary. In short, the purpose and content of the Model Law provisions relating to acknowledgement of receipt of order acceptance is unclear and provides no guidance in solving the hypothetical case problem.

It is important to note that provisions of Article 14 were drafted at the time when Electronic Data Interchange was a primary means of conducting electronic trade, as it was customary in such trade to conclude EDI agreements that would specify such requirements.[423] However, in the World Wide Web environment, which enables one-off transactions between unknown parties, as opposed to closed and predefined EDI communication among trading partners, such contracts are not feasible solutions and are rarely encountered in practice. Parties to a typical web transaction usually do not pre-negotiate contracts. They simply utilise technological means provided by a vendor in the form of a shopping cart, auction mechanism or similar techniques that lead to the conclusion of the contract. As a result the Model Law

---

420 Compare with Art. 3.2 of the Model Interchange Agreement.

421 See Art. 14 (1) in connection with Art. 14(5-7).

422 See Art. 14 (7).

423 EDI agreements usually consisted of two parts: general conditions and technical annex. See, for example, Bajaj, K.K. and Nag, D. (2000), *E-Commerce: The Cutting Edge of Business*, pp. 416-423.

solution does not reflect the current practice of trading on the Internet and does not provide the answer to problems posed in the hypothetical case study.

(b) Electronic Commerce Directive

The European Union Directive on Electronic Commerce contains a specific provision related to order confirmation. Article 11 of the Directive states that:

> 'the service provider has to acknowledge the receipt of recipient's order without undue delay and by electronic means.'

This requirement does not apply to business-to-business transactions in case of contrary agreement and excludes formation of contract by exchange of e-mails or 'equivalent individual communication'.[424] It is of course limited to EU-based electronic commerce participants.

Assuming that the hypothetical professional buyer and supplier were located in the European Union and that they did not sign any agreement excluding application of the Directive, the solution to the case looks deceptively easy. The seller would have to confirm an order without undue delay. But what does 'undue delay' mean? Can it be equated to immediate confirmation? It seems that this is not the case. 'Undue' means 'longer than immediately'. In our case, however, the buyer who has not immediately received order confirmation simply purchased items from another website. It seems that according to the Directive he would have to wait for a reasonable period of time, probably even up to fourteen days to receive the order confirmation. But such a requirement would be against Internet commercial practice, where transactions are confirmed immediately. Moreover, the Directive does not apply to a situation where both buyer and supplier do not reside in the European Union, so it does not guarantee uniform rules for global electronic commerce.

In summary, both the Model Law and the Directive deal with the issue of message acknowledgement so they both confirm the importance of such practice. The Model Law, however, does not specify whether such practice is compulsory, although the European Union Directive does. However, the Directive does not require immediate order confirmation, is mandatory only in relations to consumers as businesses can exclude its application and is limited to members of the European Union. In short, both instruments, although important in the context of the electronic commerce, do not provide rules that adequately reflect current electronic commerce practice and that could be used in truly transnational context required by the Internet to solve the order confirmation problem.

---

[424] See Art. 11.3 *above*.

7.2 Strong encryption case

In this case the problem was associated with lack of provisions in the agreement detailing specific security requirements of the Internet transactions. Because the vendor provided a weakly encrypted channel, important financial information was deciphered, which resulted in financial loss. In this case the question is: does the financial information provider have to encrypt transactions using strong encryption technology?

This hypothetical case is somewhat simplistic in its assumptions about the security of transactions, as there may be many more reasons for breach of security and resulting theft, alteration or deletion of information. Chapter VIII will demonstrate that provision of strong encryption by the financial sector is now a very widespread practice. Most web servers provide 128-bit long keys that enable very secure transmission of data across a wire using the de facto standard Secure Sockets Layer (SSL) protocol.[425]

However, this practice has not found recognition in law. The UN Convention on the Use of Electronic Communications in International Contracts, the Model Law and the Directive on Electronic Commerce are silent on the question of data encryption on the Internet. Even Model Agreements such as the Model Interchange Agreement do not provide any specific guidance in this respect.[426] The issue of security has however been signalled in the European directive on privacy and electronic communication. Article 4 of the Directive obliges the providers of publicly available electronic services to:

> '1. (...) take appropriate technical and organisational measures to safeguard security of its services, if necessary in conjunction with the provider of the public communications network with respect to network security. Having regard to the state of the art and the cost of their implementation, these measures shall ensure a level of security appropriate to the risk presented.
> 2. In case of a particular risk of a breach of the security of the network, the provider of a publicly available electronic communications service must inform the subscribers concerning such risk and, where the risk lies outside the scope of the measures to be taken by the service provider, of any possible remedies, including an indication of the likely costs involved.'[427]

---

[425] See, for example, Freier, A.O., et al. (1996), *The SSL Protocol version 3.0. Internet Draft* and discussion in Part IV.

[426] Art. 2.5. Security Procedures and Services, 'Each party shall implement and maintain security procedures and services, including any specified in the Technical Annex, to protect Messages and their records against untoward events or misuse including improper access, alteration or loss.' The Model Agreement applies to EDI transactions.

[427] See Arts. 4 and 5 and recitals 20 and 21 in OJ L 201/37 (31.07.2002), *Directive 2002/58/EC of the European Parliament and of the Council of 12 July 2002 concerning the processing of personal data and the protection of privacy in the electronic communications sector (Directive on privacy and electronic communications).*

The Directive has therefore created a general obligation to take appropriate security measures, leaving it to a given service provider to decide which ones are suitable, with regard to the cost and risks involved. Since the Directive is silent on such detailed questions as to the appropriate strength of encryption, the answer would require the investigation of industry practice to supplement legislation in this area. This is especially so because in the truly global context there is no law on this point. As a result, one cannot solve this hypothetical case study based on current developments in electronic commerce law.

7.3 **Summary of hypothetical case studies**

Neither of the current developments in international electronic commerce law can provide an adjudicator with legal norms that would enable him or her to settle a dispute in a global Internet context. In the order confirmation case, although both the Model Law and the Directive to some extent recognise the practice of acknowledging receipt of data, only one considers it to be a compulsory practice, albeit with severe limitations. More importantly, however, none of these instruments reflects the actual Internet commerce practice of immediate web-order confirmation and hence cannot serve as a practical solution to the dispute. In the transaction security case the situation is even worse, as there are no transnational provisions relating to the standard of security of web-based systems at all. Taking into account the lack of specific provisions in parties' agreements, the arbitrator would be in a difficult position in attempting to solve these problems. The following chapters will propose the concept of electronic commerce custom as a potential solution to the problems outlined above.

8. Conclusion

The Internet has affected all fields of legal science. Problems created by the global network are difficult to solve because current systems of laws are territorial in nature and are based upon easily identifiable individuals and legal entities: tenets that do not apply to the Internet. Territorial regulation means that different laws might apply to the same situation, which greatly contributes to legal uncertainty.

The Internet does not have any global government. There are organisations that play important roles in its functioning and ensure further growth but they cannot impose rules upon people using it. These organisations cannot promulgate globally binding Internet laws although they can influence the practice of Internet participants.

There are no written internationally binding rules that could be used to solve disputes on the Internet. Existing international electronic commerce instruments cannot be considered to constitute transnational electronic commerce law. UNCITRAL Model laws are not binding, and they are of a very general nature and are largely outdated. European Union directives have only local scope, a general character and also do not reflect the global practice of online trade. The new Convention on e-contracting is not yet binding.

In addition, policymakers and legal advisors tend to ignore the transnational nature of the Internet. Textbook writers present the Internet from a national law perspective, which creates an impression that there is some kind of Internet law. In fact, this is only a national interpretation of parties' rights and obligations should a dispute arise in a given jurisdiction. Such an approach confuses the picture of Internet law.

In response to nationalisation of electronic commerce laws the process of harmonisation of national laws has commenced, based upon principles agreed upon in the Model Laws. On the other hand, the proponents of self-regulation continue to fight the idea of regulating the Internet. Both of these approaches, however, result in very general and vague norm sets that do not have general application and often would not be able to answer many detailed problems encountered on the Internet.

As shown in the hypothetical case studies, the current transnational electronic commerce law does not contain specific norms that could solve non-trivial legal problems. There are either no norms to regulate a given matter, or if there are any, they are incomplete and outdated. To solve these case studies and numerous other problems outlined in the beginning of this chapter, a new approach is necessary. The next part of the study will discuss a potential remedy to this problem.

Part II
CUSTOM

Chapter V
THE ROLE OF CUSTOM

1. Introduction

Custom is probably the oldest form of law-making and is a fundament of every legal system.[428] Customary practices guided the behaviour of humans even before we learnt how to speak. In this sense, this law existed without words and without a lawgiver, who (as Sacco points out) is only 'a recent innovation'.[429] Through the long-lasting process of recognition of certain human behaviours as desirable or mandatory, and the observance of those practices by other members of the society, human communities have managed to develop complex legal systems, now totalling more than 10,000 distinct legal orders.[430]

Customary laws were also a cornerstone of early international trade,[431] long before the emergence of the great religious systems such as Buddhism, Confucianism, Christianity or Islam. Later Arabic domination of trade between East and West provides further evidence for the role of mercantile customary practices[432] that were incorporated by Roman law and rediscovered a millennium later by European traders.[433] Custom is still important in modern international commerce and international law, although its role in national legal systems has been considerably diminished.

Customary law, however, can have an even more important role in supplying norms to ascertain the legal rights and obligations of participants in Internet commerce. A lack of globally binding written laws does not mean that the Internet community has not developed binding rules through widespread, repetitive behaviour. In fact, any community creates binding behavioural norms based on adherence to

---

428 See the discussion in David, R. and Brierley, J.E. (1985), *Major legal systems in the world today*, para. 97. Maine claims that custom is posterior to that of judgment. See Maine, H.S. (1861 reprinted in 1970), *Ancient Law: Its Connection With The Early History Of Society And Its Relation To Modern Ideas*, p. 5.

429 Sacco, R. (Summer 1995), *Mute law*, p. 455.

430 Rouland, N. (1994), *Legal Anthropology*, p. 1.

431 See, for example, Garavaglia, M. (1991), *In Search Of the Proper Law in Transnational Commercial Disputes*, p. 33, citing J. Reddie.

432 Bewes, W.A. (1923), *The Romance of the Law Merchant Being an Introduction to the Study of International and Commercial Law with Some Account of the Commerce and Fairs of the Middle Ages*, p. 77.

433 Ibid., pp. 8-9.

widespread practices. Norms emanating from these practices could form the foundation of global Internet and electronic commerce law. But the mechanism which generates them and the content of these norms first needs to be established.

The aim of this chapter is to discuss various approaches to custom in different epochs and cultures. This part of the book will build a bridge between ancient times and the modern technological age; it will construct a link between primitive societies, Eastern and Western civilisations and international commerce for the purpose of creating a common ground for the understanding of the role of customary practices in human social life in general and legal culture in particular. As will be shown, customary practices govern human life irrespective of technological advancement or the complexity of a society. This multidisciplinary undertaking provides a useful background for both legal and technical audiences in understanding custom as a law-making medium. This is important as contemporary Western societies are largely unaware of the significance of repetitive behaviour of humans in the creation of law.

The following sections explain the historical and contemporary role of custom in various domestic legal cultures and international legal regimes. The distinction between East and West is difficult to make and will be used only to better organise this material. The term *Western legal culture* will refer to the families of laws, European in origin, that embrace the continental legal tradition based upon Roman law, and Anglo-Saxon tradition based upon English common law. In terms of geographical coverage systems rooted in European law cover not only the whole of Europe including Scandinavia and Russia but also Australia, both Americas and some African and Asian countries. The term 'non-Western legal cultures' will refer to legal cultures developed independently from the European legal culture; even if there have been recent influences from it. It will cover the religious systems of Islam and Hinduism as well as Chinese and Japanese legal cultures. In this section the role of custom in indigenous societies located in various parts of the world will also be analysed. The next part will outline the role of custom in modern international legal regimes, focusing on the role of custom in modern transnational commercial law, particularly the New Law Merchant. This part will discuss why international commercial law and commercial custom is not the best candidate to describe and delineate the characteristics of Internet custom. This chapter will end with a discussion of the potential of the notion of custom in the Internet environment. In particular, the role of custom as a source of Internet law, and custom as a source of knowledge about the Internet, will be outlined, followed by a discussion of the emerging Internet Law Merchant.

2. Historical Importance of Custom in Western Culture

2.1 Custom in the Roman Empire

Roman law developed in the philosophical climate of ancient Greece, and is the foundation of continental legal thought that exerted a greater or lesser influence on most modern legal traditions, including the much younger Anglo-Saxon legal tradition. The original law of Rome is generally recognised to be customary.[434] The famous Law of the Twelve Tables, for instance, from the sixth century B.C., is generally recognised as the foundation of ancient Roman law, and is a transcription of ancient customs.[435] According to Rouland, for the next five hundred years private relations were governed mainly by reference to ancestral custom.[436]

However, Roman law was primarily based upon legislation.[437] Custom played an important practical role but did not play a dominant role. Custom was not even always universally recognised as a source of Roman law. For instance, it was recognised by Cicero,[438] but Gaius did not list it in his famous textbook.[439] Nevertheless, it was officially and unequivocally recognised by the emperor Justinian in the sixth century A.D. in the most famous codification of ancient Roman law: the Corpus Iuris Civilis, which became the foundation of the European continental civil law.[440] Justinian confirmed that Roman law is written or unwritten and that the latter:

> 'is that which usage has confirmed, for customs long observed and sanctioned by the consent of those who employ them, resemble law.'[441]

The authority of custom over legislation is well illustrated in the opinion of Paulus:

> 'And indeed, a law of this kind has greater authority, for the reason that it has been approved to such an extent that it is not necessary to commit it now in writing.'[442]

---

[434] Allen, C.K. (1964), *Law in the making*, p. 81. See also Smith, M. (June 1903), *Customary law. I.*, p. 256, who argued that Romans treated custom and legislation as 'equal in potency'.

[435] Rouland, N. (1994), *Legal Anthropology*, p. 39.

[436] Only 26 out of 800 statutory laws enacted in this period dealt with private law. See ibid.

[437] Allen, C.K. (1964), *Law in the making*, p. 81.

[438] Robinson, O.F. (1997), *The Sources of Roman Law. Problems and methods for ancient historians*, pp. 28-29.

[439] Ibid.

[440] See, for example, Jolowicz, H.F. (1957), *Roman Foundations of Modern Law*, p. 21.

[441] See Enactments of Justinian section 3 and 9 in the second volume of Scott, S.P. (1973), *The Civil Law including The Twelve Tables, The Institutes of Gaius, The Rules of Ulpian, The Opinions of Paulus, The Enactments of Justinian, and The Constitutions of Leo*, pp. 6-7.

[442] Paulus, On Sabinus, Book VII in ibid., p. 224 para. 36.

In general, Romans recognised custom as an important source of law but did not construct an explicit theory of custom.[443] Despite the lack of theory, some crucial features of custom were highlighted. As Julianus, the most famous Roman lawyer, explained it, custom can change or abolish legislation:

> 'For as the laws themselves restrain us for no other reason than because they are accepted by the judgment of the people – for it is but proper that what the people have approved without being written should bind all persons – for what difference does it make whether the people have manifested their will by vote, or by acts and deeds? Wherefore the rule has also been most justly adopted that laws shall be abrogated not only the vote of the legislator, but also through disuse by the silent consent of all.'[444]

Julianus also argued that a customary practice consisting of acts and deeds and approved by people, should bind all persons. These are the crucial aspects of custom, which are, as will be shown later, generally accepted in modern international law. On the other hand, Hermogenianus required long practice, resembling a tacit agreement of citizens:

> 'Those rules which have been approved by long established custom and have been observed for many years, by, as it were, a tacit agreement of citizens, are no less to be obeyed than laws which have been committed to writing.'[445]

Allen argued that the reference to consensus should be understood as a requirement of uniform or unanimous practice.[446] As will be shown in the next chapter, the notion of a tacit agreement and the requirement of a long-lasting, uniform practice also have a significant impact on the modern theories of custom.

Although the practical role of custom in transactions between Roman citizens should not be overemphasised, it played a decisive role in the development of a distinct system of rules used to resolve mercantile disputes between Roman citizens and foreign individuals or between foreigners themselves. The so-called *ius gentium* was defined by Gaius as 'the law which all nations employ' and it can be considered as an international Roman law.

> 'All peoples who are ruled by laws and customs partly make use of their own laws and partly have recourse to those which are common to all men.'[447]

---

[443] Allen, C.K. (1964), *Law in the making*, p. 82.

[444] Julianus, Digest, Book XCIV in Scott, S.P. (1973), *The Civil Law including The Twelve Tables, The Institutes of Gaius, The Rules of Ulpian, The Opinions of Paulus, The Enactments of Justinian, and The Constitutions of Leo*, p. 225 para. 32.

[445] Hermogenianus, Eptiomes of Law, Book I in ibid., p. 224 para. 35. Similarly, see Ulpian: 'Mores sunt tacitus consensus populi, longa consuetudine inveteratus'.

[446] Allen, C.K. (1964), *Law in the making*, p. 82.

[447] See section 1 of the First Commentary of Gaius in Scott, S.P. (1973), *The Civil Law including The Twelve Tables, The Institutes of Gaius, The Rules of Ulpian, The Opinions of Paulus, The Enact-*

Ius gentium was especially important as a body of commercial customs in ancient trade as it recognised many not known to Roman law but also highly important commercial transactions, such as informal contracts of sale, agency, bailment or a jointly owned company.[448] *Ius gentium* provides evidence of the spread and importance of commercial customs developed earlier by other trading peoples such as the Phoenicians and the Arabs. For instance, Romans were under the influence of the great customary Sea Law of Rhodes that for hundreds of years was used in the shipment of goods around the Mediterranean.[449] As it was based on commercial customary practices of foreign nations it turned out to be much more flexible than the law of Roman citizens and it greatly influenced further development of that law.[450] *Ius gentium* is a precursor of the medieval customary Law Merchant (*lex mercatoria*), as well as modern transnational commercial law and international public law and, arguably, the transnational customary law of the Internet.

2.2 Custom in the European legal tradition

The evolution of post-Roman European law can be characterised as a fifteen centuries long struggle for the primacy between customary law on one hand and statutory law as well as case law on the other. Figure 5 below below illustrates well the juxtaposition of custom in relation to statute in Europe over the last millennium:

After the fall of the western part of the Roman Empire its legal culture remained forgotten for half a millennium. During the early Middle Ages the Germanic successors of the Roman Empire, as well as Celtic and Slavic tribes, were governed almost exclusively according to their own usually unwritten customs,[451] which also bound their kings.[452] As the Carlyles explained it,

> 'The law was primarily custom, legislative acts were not expressions of will, but records or promulgations of that which was recognised as already binding upon men.'[453]

---

ments of Justinian, and The Constitutions of Leo, p. 81.; also Robinson, O.F. (1997), *The Sources of Roman Law. Problems and methods for ancient historians*, pp. 25-26.

448 See, for example, Goldman, B. (1983), *Lex Mercatoria*, p. 1; Kelly, J.M. (1992), *A short history of western legal theory*, pp. 62-63.

449 Bewes, W.A. (1923), *The Romance of the Law Merchant Being an Introduction to the Study of International and Commercial Law with Some Account of the Commerce and Fairs of the Middle Ages*, p. 9.

450 See, for example, De Ly, F. (1992), *International Business Law and Lex Mercatoria*, pp. 8-15.

451 Gilissen, J. (1982), *La coutume*, p. 42.

452 Kelly, J.M. (1992), *A short history of western legal theory*, p. 101.

453 Carlyle, R.W. and Carlyle, A.J. (1903, 1936), *A History of Medieval Political Theory in the West*, p. 40 Vol. 3.

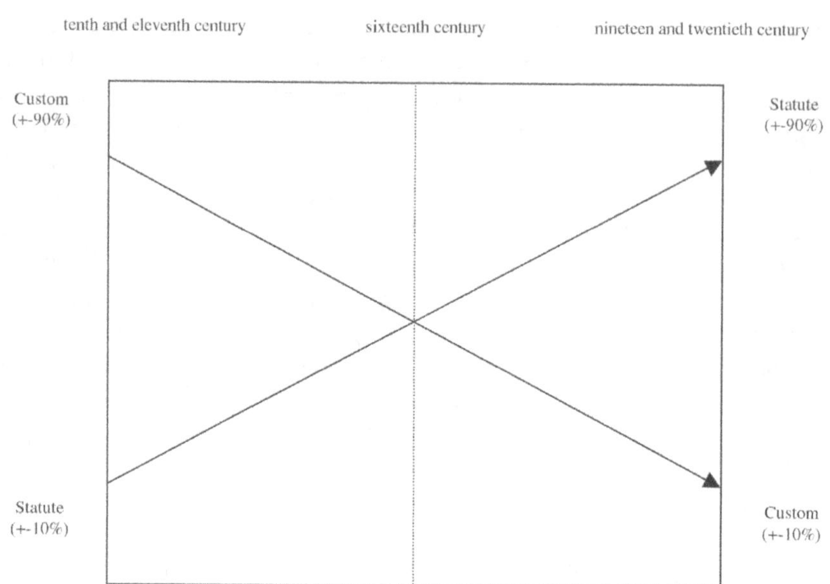

Figure 5 – Custom *v.* Statute. Based on: Gilissen, J. (1982), La coutume, p. 14

In the ninth century, Saint Nicephore equated written law with codified custom.[454] Therefore, legislation, although existing in these times, was primarily confined to what had been established by custom. Even in the newly created kingdom that the Crusaders established in Jerusalem in the eleventh century, laws were established by collecting customs of the various nations represented in their ranks. This vividly illustrates the primacy of custom over legislation in the early Middle Ages.[455]

Medieval Europe had a large number of customary legal systems, of various scope and origin that cannot be equated with modern national laws as the concept of state emerged only in the seventeenth century. Various groups of medieval society, such as noblemen, churchmen, the bourgeoisie and merchants developed their own systems of law, and did so independently of local laws. Custom was very influential in the law of the then very powerful Catholic Church, which was later codified in the Canon law, which required it to be 'reasonable', practiced for forty or a hundred years and confirmed by the superior.[456] The nobles had their feudal law, which was also based upon custom, and the bourgeoisie had their own city law. Medieval merchants developed their own Law Merchant, which was used to settle commercial disputes in fairs and marketplaces. Different customary laws applied to

---

[454] «Quid alium enim est lex nisi scripta consuetudo? Sicuti vicissim consuetudo est lex non scripta. » cited in Gilissen, J. (1982), *La coutume*, p. 16. and the literature there.

[455] See Kelly, J.M. (1992), *A short history of western legal theory*, p. 102.

[456] See Section 3, codes 25-30 in Bouscaren, L.T. and Ellis, A.C. (1957), *Canon Law: A Text and Commentary*, pp. 37-42.

the peasants and artisans.[457] Smith pointed out that these class customs, together with ecclesiastical law, had a European character:[458]

> 'Decisions made in Lombardy were cited in all feudal courts of Europe; judgments rendered at Pisa, at Barcelona and at Oléron enjoyed an equally wide authority in questions of commercial and maritime law.'[459]

From the perspective of territoriality, late medieval Europe was divided between regions of customary law and written law. What is now northern France,[460] Switzerland, Belgium, the Netherlands and Scandinavia were all regions where customary law had special influence. Gillisen points out that Germany,[461] Italy, Spain and England were also governed by customary law but the interest of jurisprudence was lesser there.[462]

In England, where the Anglo-Saxon family of laws was only peripherally influenced by Roman law,[463] custom played a dominant role, especially in the early stages of the development of common law.[464] Even the term *common law* derives from the fact that customary law of England was unified and made common to all the people.[465] Writing in the eighteenth century, Blackstone clearly underlines the importance of custom as the foundation of the Anglo-Saxon legal system,[466] and requires it to be 'good', by which he understands that it is immemorial, continued, peaceable, not unreasonable, certain, compulsory and consistent.[467] With the emergence of centralised judge-made law in the twelfth and thirteenth centuries, and equity in the fifteenth and sixteenth centuries,[468] English jurisprudence focused on these sources of law, leaving custom as a source of unwritten feudal, manorial,

---

457 Smith, M. (June 1903), *Customary law. I.*, p. 258.

458 Ibid., pp. 258-260. Roman law was added to it as a result of its rediscovery, but it had only a subsidiary force.

459 Ibid., p. 258.

460 See, for example, Cohen, E. (1993), *The crossroads of justice: law and culture in late medieval France*.

461 Up until the reception of the Roman law. See, for example, Huebner, R. (1918), *A History of Germanic Private Law*, pp. 5-7.; see also Puchta, G.F. (1928), *Das Gewohnheitsrecht*; von Savigny, F.K. (1840-49), *System des Heutigen Romischen Rechts*; von Savigny, F. K. (1840) *Vom Beruf Unserer Zeit fur Gesetzgebung und Rechtswissgnschaft*.

462 Gilissen, J. (1982), *La coutume*, pp. 17-18.

463 Scotland was exceptional in this regard. See, for example, Zweigert, K. and Kötz, H. (1998), *An Introduction to Comparative Law*, pp. 202-204. On the influence of the Roman law on English custom see, for example, Blackstone, W. (1783 reprinted 1978), *Commentaries on the Laws of England*, p. 78 Vol. 1.

464 See, for example, Kelly, J.M. (1992), *A short history of western legal theory*, p. 139, citing Bracton.

465 Blackstone, W. (1783 reprinted 1978), *Commentaries on the Laws of England*, pp. 66-67 Vol. 1.

466 Ibid., p. 63 Vol. 1.

467 Ibid., pp. 76-78 Vol. 1.

468 See, for example, Zweigert, K. and Kötz, H. (1998), *An Introduction to Comparative Law*, pp. 187-191.

constitutional and mercantile law.[469] Mercantile disputes were settled according to the transnational Law Merchant administered by special courts set up in important places of trade. These courts directly applied the customs of traders, rather than using common law, which was regarded as too inflexibile.[470]

Many transcriptions or codifications of local customs took place both during and after medieval times.[471] Recording of customs created greater legal certainty, but also fixed custom, which eventually led to its loss of importance. Many transcriptions of customary laws took place in France and the Netherlands.[472] One important work is that of Beaumanoir and German Mirror of Saxons (Sachsenspiegel).[473] The Grand Coutumier de la Normandie, also known as the Customs of Normandy, which were transcribed in the thirteenth century, are still legally binding in the English Channel Islands.[474] The sixteenth century Customs of Paris reigned for centuries in Northern France, and extended its influence to other parts of the world.[475] Before the Enlightenment, hundreds of official and private transcriptions of customs were completed, which led to a very complex amalgamate of local customary laws.

A peculiar feature of European medieval customary law was that local customs superseded general laws and customs.[476] As in the Roman Empire, custom was perceived as a source of law that by 'disuse by the silent consent of all'[477] could abolish other customs and also written law (*desuetude*). Sometimes legislators in the Middle Ages confirmed the validity of previously enacted written laws by adding a clause 'as far as these are still in use'.[478] Gratian affirms that legislation is valid only insofar as it is approved by custom:

---

[469] See Gilissen *above*. But see, for example, Kelly, J.M. (1992), *A short history of western legal theory*, p. 185.

[470] See, for example, Mitchell, W. (1904), *An Essay on the Early History of the Law Merchant*, p. 40; Zweigert, K. and Kötz, H. (1998), *An Introduction to Comparative Law*, p. 194.

[471] See, for example, Mitchell, W. (1904), *An Essay on the Early History of the Law Merchant*, p. 29.

[472] See, for example, van Caenegem, R.C. (1992), *An historical introduction to private law*, pp. 35-45.

[473] See, for example, David, R. and Brierley, J.E. (1985), *Major legal systems in the world today*, p. 53.

[474] Zweigert, K. and Kötz, H. (1998), *An Introduction to Comparative Law*, p. 76. At the time when England was conquered by Normans, the Channel Islands belonged to Duchy of Normandy, the fact which leads islanders to joke that England is their oldest colony. See Zweigert, K. and Kötz, H. (1998), *An Introduction to Comparative Law*, pp. 201-202.

[475] Especially Quebec, see Zweigert, K. and Kötz, H. (1998), *An Introduction to Comparative Law*, p. 117.

[476] Smith, M. (June 1903), *Customary law. I.*, pp. 257-258.

[477] See Julianus, Digest, Book XCIV in Scott, S.P. (1973), *The Civil Law including The Twelve Tables, The Institutes of Gaius, The Rules of Ulpian, The Opinions of Paulus, The Enactments of Justinian, and The Constitutions of Leo*, p. 225 para. 32, cited *above*.

[478] Smith, M. (June 1903), *Customary law. I.*, p. 258, citing Leyes de Toro (1505) I.

'laws are instituted when they are promulgated; confirmed when they are approved by the custom of those who observe them.'[479]

The famous thirteenth century philosopher St. Thomas Aquinas clearly summarises the importance of customary law in medieval Europe:

'All law originates from the reason and will of a lawmaker, but men can make known their will by deeds as well as by words, for whatever they do they presumably think good to do. So if expressing what we want and mean in words can alter and expound laws, then laws can also be altered and expounded by repeated behaviour setting up customs which acquire the force of law: for what we do over and over again is surely done deliberately. Custom then has the force of law, can abolish law, and is law's interpreter.'[480]

However, the rediscovery of Roman law in the eleventh century and its reception in university teaching marked the beginning of a very slow and gradual loss of significance of custom as a source of law.[481] In the sixteenth century two radically opposing views on the role of custom versus statute emerged, which were best represented by Jacques Cujas and Jean Bodin. According to Cujas:

'A custom is based on a better reason, together with the common interest, and the passage of a long time in silent and unwritten agreement among the community, together with the authority of judicial decisions, has the effect of abrogating a statute the reason of which has disappeared, or is less substantial, or is of less benefit to the state (...) The disuse of the statute leaves the custom alone in force, and it acquires thus the same force as a statute (...) And no statute binds us, unless it has received the acceptance of custom.'[482]

Bodin, as the most famous supporter of the king's absolutism, gave much greater force to the statute, pointing out that custom cannot establish either punishments or rewards and exist only because of the ruler's willingness to tolerate it.[483] History would favour his doctrine. As Smith pointed out, hostility towards custom was a result of its association with a preservation of class privileges that modern societies wanted to abandon.[484] In effect, custom was subject to legislation and gradually started to lose its importance as an independent source of law. It could no longer

479 Decretum Gratianum, dist. 4, c. 3 cited in ibid.

480 St. Thomas Aquinas (1989), *Summa Theologiae. A concise translation*, p. 293 (Ia 2ae 97.3.).

481 See, for example, David, R. and Brierley, J.E. (1985), *Major legal systems in the world today*, pp. 53-54.

482 Paratitla C. 8. 52 cited in Kelly, J.M. (1992), *A short history of western legal theory*, pp. 185-186.

483 Ibid., p. 186.

484 Smith, M. (June 1903), *Customary law. I.*, p. 264.

abolish written law and existed, as Hobbes' political doctrine maintained, insofar as the absolute monarch tolerated it.[485]

Similarly in the Anglo-Saxon legal tradition, although generally not codified, custom lost its dominant role.[486] It was overtaken by the doctrine of precedent and the statute.[487] In *Pilans* v. *van Mierop*,[488] the customary Law Merchant was nationalised as the common law of the land:

> 'The law of merchants and the law of the land, is the same: a witness cannot be admitted, to prove the law of merchants. We must consider it as a point of law.'[489]

The policy of resentment towards custom has spread among countries that have adopted the doctrine of common law.[490] In modern common law, courts have the power to invalidate a custom if it is unreasonable,[491] and this contention has led some authors to declare the necessity of recognising custom in order for it to be binding.[492]

But it was not until the Enlightenment's move towards rationality, as well as the period of great codifications of law in the nineteenth century, that left custom with only a marginal role to play. New civil codes, following the ground-breaking Code Napoleon, introduced innovative legal rules that often abrogated many older customs. However, it is worth remembering that the Code Napoleon was, with the exception of the law of contract and the law of property, primarily based on the customs of Northern France.[493] A particularly hostile attitude to *ancien régime* customs led French lawyers to abandon the old term 'custom' and replace it with 'usage'. The introduction of this new term to denote essentially the same phenomenon resulted in a linguistic ambiguity[494] and difficulty in distinguishing between the two. This attitude to custom was exported to other parts of the world with the process of colonisation and a systematic replacement of local laws with European developments.

---

485 Chapter 26 of Hobbes, T. (1996), *Leviathan,* cited in Smith, M. (June 1903), *Customary law. I.*, pp. 258-260.

486 But see, for example, Allen, C.K. (1964), *Law in the making*, pp. 76-77.

487 See, for example, de Cruz, P. (1999), *Comparative law in the changing world*, pp. 103-104.

488 *Pilans* v. *van Mierop* 3 Burrr. 1663, 97 Eng. Rep. 1035 (K.B. 1765).

489 Id. at 1670, 97 Eng. Rep. at 1038.

490 See, e.g., Karsten, P. (2002), *Between law and custom: high and low legal cultures in the British diaspora lands- the United States, Canada, Australia, and New Zealand, 1600-1900*; Zweigert, K. and Kötz, H. (1998), *An Introduction to Comparative Law*, pp. 218-237.

491 See, for example, *Johnson* v. *Clark* [1908] I Ch. 303; *Tanistry* case [1608] Dav. 29 See also discussion in Allen, C.K. (1964), *Law in the making*, pp. 144-146.

492 See, for example, Excursus A in Allen, C.K. (1964), *Law in the making*, pp. 152-156.

493 See, for example, Weber, M. (1967), *Max Weber on Law in Economy and Society*, p. 286, citing Ehrlich.

494 Goode, R. (1997), *Usage and its reception in transnational commercial law*, pp. 1-2.

2.3 Medieval Law Merchant

Law Merchant deserves special attention because medieval traders developed an almost universally recognised set of customary norms governing their transactions, which could be an antecedent for global Internet commerce customary law. Medieval merchants had to travel to different trade fairs and cities, which were each governed by different local laws. The opening of trade with the markets of the East and the rise of autonomous cities in Italy created favourable conditions for the development of a customary mercantile law that soon spread to France, Spain, England and the rest of Europe.[495] Law merchant, which is also referred to as *lex mercatoria*,[496] was a set of transnational commercial customs, to a large extent uniform and developed by the mercantile community to avoid application of various local legal systems. It was a self-regulatory system administered and enforced by experienced traders themselves at market fairs, harbours and guilds located in various cities across the Mediterranean basin and northern Europe. However, it is important to note that Law Merchant was not European in origin.[497] It was probably largely developed in the East and brought to Europe by Arabic traders,[498] and only became known to European traders in late medieval times.

Mitchell characterised *lex mercatoria* as customary law of an international character with minor local varieties,[499] having equitable and speedy procedures[500] and administered by merchants rather than by professional judges.[501] Among the norms originated by mercantile custom that were not known to formal Roman law[502] were

---

495 See, for example, Berman, H. and Kaufman, C. (1978), *The law of international commercial transactions (lex mercatoria)*, p. 224; Caemmerer, E. v. (1964), *The influence of the law of international trade on the development and character of the commercial law in the civil law countries (With Particular Reference to the nature of Commercial Law in those Countries as a Separate System of Law)*. p. 88. citing Lopez (1971), The commercial revolution of the Middle Ages, 950-1350 and other literature cited there. See also, e.g., Robinson, O.F., et al. (1985), *An Introduction to European Legal History*, pp. 153-178.

496 Malynes, G. (1686), *Consuetudo, vel, Lex mercatoria, or, The ancient law-merchant: in three parts, according to the essentials of traffic: necessary for statesmen, judges, magistrates, temporal and civil lawyers, mint-men, merchants, mariners, and all others negotiating in any part of the world.*

497 Andersen, C.B. (Fall 1998), *Furthering the Uniform Application of the CISG: Sources of Law on the Internet*.

498 Bewes, W.A. (1923), *The Romance of the Law Merchant Being an Introduction to the Study of International and Commercial Law with Some Account of the Commerce and Fairs of the Middle Ages*, pp. 8-9.

499 Robinson argued that: 'Different customs applied at sea or at land, between the north of Europe and the south, and even between neighbouring cities.' In regard to the international character of the Law Merchant he wrote: 'Its common feature was community of institutions rather than community of rules; there was no central legislation, no central court, through which uniformity of rules might be achieved.' Robinson, O.F., et al. (1985), *An Introduction to European Legal History*, pp. 153-154.

500 Similarly ibid., pp. 154-155

501 Mitchell, W. (1904), *An Essay on the Early History of the Law Merchant*, pp. 1-21.

502 Berman, H. and Kaufman, C. (1978), *The law of international commercial transactions (lex mercatoria)*, p. 226. However, informal agreements were known and applied in the Roman *ius gentium*. Robinson, O.F., et al. (1985), *An Introduction to European Legal History*, p. 155.

developments such as these: informal agreements could be legally binding,[503] that mere possession of a bearer bill of exchange established a right to payment, that the good faith of a purchaser, even of stolen goods, is protected against the original owner when the goods were bought in an open market, that the seller has the right to stop goods in transit on default by the buyer, that partners may sue each other for an accounting, and that the rights and obligations of one partner survive the death of the other.[504]

These mercantile customs dealing with maritime and inland trade were frequently codified by the merchants themselves. The ancient Sea Law of Rhodes, probably dating from about 300 B.C.,[505] was already known to medieval merchants, but soon new compilations were developed. The most famous examples of commercial customs codifications were maritime customs transcribed in the eleventh century Amalphitan Table,[506] the twelfth century Scrolls of Oléron, which were adopted in seaport towns of the Atlantic Ocean and the North Sea, the maritime Law of Wisby, which was compiled around 1350 and used in Baltic Sea towns and the fifteenth century Consolato del mare,[507] which was used in commercial centres of the Mediterranean basin.[508] Other compilations include the judgments of Damme and the laws of Westkapelle.

Rulers aware of the importance of the exchange of goods and services to their own wealth[509] allowed merchants to be governed by their own Law Merchant. The English Carta Mercatoria of 1303 and the Statute of the Staple of 1353 guaranteed that marketplaces could settle disputes according to Law Merchant rather than feudal law or city law.[510] Carta Mercatoria added that if any dispute of a contractual

---

503 See Bewes, W.A. (1923), *The Romance of the Law Merchant Being an Introduction to the Study of International and Commercial Law with Some Account of the Commerce and Fairs of the Middle Ages*, pp. 29-30.

504 Ibid., pp. 28-62, 77-79.

505 See, for example, Berman, H. and Kaufman, C. (1978), *The law of international commercial transactions (lex mercatoria)*, p. 224. It provided that if the cargo was jettisoned in order to save a ship and the ship was saved, the loss had to be shared by all who benefited from it including the owner of the ship, so that the whole loss did not fall on the owners of the cargo. Robinson, O.F., et al. (1985), *An Introduction to European Legal History*, p. 156.

506 See, for example, Berman, H. and Kaufman, C. (1978), *The law of international commercial transactions (lex mercatoria)*, p. 224.

507 For a short description see Goode, R. (1997), *Usage and its reception in transnational commercial law*, pp. 17-18.

508 See, for example, Berman, H. and Kaufman, C. (1978), *The law of international commercial transactions (lex mercatoria)*, p. 225.

509 For economical analysis of this phenomenon see, for example, Greif, A. (June 1993), *Contract Enforceability and Economic Institutions in Early Trade: The Maghribi Traders' Coalition*; Greif, A. (1997), *Contracting, Enforcement, and Efficiency: Economics beyond the law*; Greif, A., et al. (August 1994), *Coordination, Commitment, and Enforcement: The Case of the Merchant Guild*; Milgrom, P.R., et al. (March 1990), *The Role of Institutions in the Revival of Trade: The Law Merchant, Private Judges, and the Champagne Fairs*.

510 See, for example, De Ly, F. (1992), *International Business Law and Lex Mercatoria*, p. 16, and the literature cited there.

nature should arise, the resort should be held to the customs of the fairs and market towns where the contract was made.[511]

Soon, as was the case in the Roman Empire, transnational commercial customs were absorbed into local legal systems to govern disputes between ordinary inhabitants administered by special purpose commercial courts. This process was especially visible in eighteenth century England under Chief Justice Mansfield, who decided that law merchant is a question of law to be decided by the court rather than a matter of custom to be proved by the parties.[512] Absorption of mercantile customs resulted in a loss of internationality, flexibility and adaptability of the mercantile law to the changing needs of the international trade.[513] A similar process of nationalisation of transnational customary law of commerce took place in continental Europe, the United States[514] and other parts of the world with the introduction of civil and commercial codes in the nineteenth and twentieth century that replaced custom as a source of mercantile law.

2.4 Custom in contemporary Western legal tradition

The notion of customary law is weakly entrenched in modern Western legal thinking. Apart from the historical reasons outlined earlier, this is also because of dominant legal theories, which, at least in continental legal systems, permit the operation of custom where this is permitted by written law. As David and Brierly put it:

> 'justification for the recognition of custom is nowadays sought *within* a legislative framework, even if, in doing so, custom must be falsely presented as being in harmony with legislation when really it is either filing in the gaps of a text or is even contrary thereto.'[515]

In other words, although customary law is continuously being created by various communities, this fact seems to require some kind of recognition on the part of judicial or legislative authorities. Another reason for the weak position of custom in modern Western jurisprudence is the lack of proper legal education in this respect. Students are no longer taught the customary law of the land. Usually the notion of custom as a source of law is only mentioned while discussing the theory of law,

---

511 Mitchell, W. (1904), *An Essay on the Early History of the Law Merchant*, p. 6.

512 See *above*. See also, e.g., Bane, C.A. (May / September 1983), *From Holt and Mansfield to Story to Llewellyn and Mentschikoff: The Progressive Development of Commercial Law*; Berman, H. and Kaufman, C. (1978), *The law of international commercial transactions (lex mercatoria)*, p. 226.

513 E.g., Bainbridge, S. (1984), *Trade Usages in International Sales of Goods: An Analysis of the 1964 and 1980 Sales Conventions*, p. 625; Berman, H. and Kaufman, C. (1978), *The law of international commercial transactions (lex mercatoria)*, pp. 227-228.

514 Section 1-103 of the Uniform Commercial Code states: 'Unless displaced by the particular provisions of this Act, the principles of law and equity, including the law merchant (…) shall supplement its provisions.'

515 David, R. and Brierley, J.E. (1985), *Major legal systems in the world today*, pp. 130-131.

international law or commercial law. Therefore, the scant knowledge of customary norms is the greatest enemy of what was once the most important source of law.

Nevertheless, custom continues to play a crucial role, albeit 'unconsciously', especially in the provision of detailed norms to interpret and supplement legislation. Again, as David and Brierly rightly describe it:

> 'Legislation itself, in order to be understood, often has to appeal to custom for the necessary clarification of the idea of the legislators. Without such a reference it cannot be said for example when a person has committed a fault, whether a certain mark constitutes a signature, whether the person committing an infraction may plead attenuating circumstances, whether an object is a family keepsake, whether a person has acted within a "reasonable" delay, or whether there is the moral impossibility of procuring written proof of an obligation. Any effort made to eliminate the role of custom in these respects will result in a conceptualism or in a case-by-case approach contrary to the spirit of the law of Romano-Germanic countries; an attempt to suppress the enormous role which custom, *secundum legem*, has thus acquired seems futile.'[516]

Although it is clear that custom continues to play an enormous role in the interpretation of statutes and contracts (including qualification of some of its provisions), contemporary discussion of the notion of custom is rather modest and full of disparities. One of the most serious difficulties concerns the definition of custom and its recognition as a source of law, the use of different terms (*custom*, *usage*) to describe the same phenomenon, the different consequences attached to these terms and the different position of custom in relation to statutory norms.

Custom is rarely expressly recognised as a source of law in statutes. More often, however, it is left to jurisprudence to agree on its status. For instance, the Swiss civil code provides in Article 1(2) that a judge should apply customary law in the absence of relevant statutory law.[517] Similarly, in Spain, custom is enlisted as a source of legal order.[518] It operates in the absence of written law provided that it is proven and not contrary to morality or public order.[519] In Italy and Germany, statutes introducing civil codes contain provisions recognising custom as a source of law, although it is mainly the teaching of the doctrine that has clarified this issue.[520]

---

[516] Ibid., para. 98.

[517] Art. 1.2 of Swiss Civil Code: '2 A défaut d'une disposition légale applicable, le juge prononce selon le droit coutumier et, à défaut d'une coutume, selon les règles qu'il établirait s'il avait à faire acte de législateur.' See also, e.g., Gutteridge, H.C. (1971), *Comparative Law. An Introduction to the Comparative Method of Legal Study & Research*, pp. 80-81.

[518] See Art. 1.1 of Spanish Civil Code. 'Las fuentes del ordenamiento jurídico español son la ley, la costumbre y los principios generales del derecho.'

[519] See Art. 1.3. 'La costumbre sólo regirá en defecto de ley aplicable, siempre que no sea contraria a la moral o al orden público y que resulte probada.' And further 'Los usos jurídicos que no sean meramente interpretativos de una declaración de voluntad tendrán la consideración de costumbre.'

[520] See Art. 1 of the Introductory Title to Codice Civile and Art. 2 of EGBGB, which defines law as it is used in EGBGB and BGB as including any rule of law, e.g., De Ly, F. (1992), *International Business Law and Lex Mercatoria*, pp. 143, 138.

The Netherlands and Austria used to have provisions to this effect but it seems that custom is still regarded as a source of law in these countries.[521] The Polish Constitution, on the other hand, does not enlist custom as a source of law, but it is widely accepted that customary law can operate alongside written law.[522]

As a result, there are different definitions of custom and its nature in various jurisdictions.[523] They are usually developed by jurisprudence, rarely by courts and almost never expressed in statutes. For instance, in Germany there is no statutory definition of custom. Therefore, the definition is left to jurisprudence. Some authors argue that custom exists if parties follow a certain norm of conduct while feeling bound by it.[524] Therefore, parties need to feel bound by a custom.[525] A similar approach seems to prevail in France, although here the term usage (in French *usage*) is used instead of custom (in French *coutume*). In England, in turn, there is no such requirement. However, the distinguishing features of custom in the United Kingdom are that customs are confined to 'definite, limited locality'[526] and they have to be 'immemorial', i.e., proven to have existed in 1189, when Richard I began his reign. However, the courts recognise customary norms 'if circumstances are proved which raise a presumption that the custom in fact existed at that date'[527] or if they have been established by previous precedents.[528] Apart from this, custom has to be reasonable, certain and consistent; in other words, it must have continued uninterrupted since time immemorial.[529] Thus, only local and long-lasting customs are permitted, which if established can take the place of general common law.[530]

On the other hand, the United States, despite strong common law ties, has a statutory definition of custom, which is actually referred to as a usage. The Uniform Commercial Code appears to distinguish between local and general usages, which are referred to as *courses of dealing* and *usages of trade*. Thus, a course of dealing is defined as:

---

[521] Ibid., pp. 142, 144. But see David, R. and Brierley, J.E. (1985), *Major legal systems in the world today*, pp. 130-131. Austrian Civil Code contains provision that custom can only be taken into consideration where the statute says so: § 10. Auf Gewohnheiten kann nur in den Fällen, in welchen sich ein Gesetz darauf beruft, Rücksicht genommen werden.'

[522] See, for example, Safjan, M. (2005), *Refleksje o roli zwyczaju*; Stelmachowski, A. (2005), *Problemy legislacji*, pp. 109-110.; Radwański, Z. (2004), *Prawo cywilne – część ogólna*, pp. 36-38; Stelmachowski, A. (1998), *Zarys teorii prawa cywilnego*, pp. 308-323.

[523] See, for example, a very good survey of European civil codes and common law approach in De Ly, F. (1992), *International Business Law and Lex Mercatoria*, pp. 134-164.

[524] Ibid., p. 138, citing Hubner, Horn and Böckstiegel.

[525] Ibid., pp. 138-139, citing Sonnenberger and other authors.

[526] Wellwood, J.W. (1975), *Custom and usage*, pp. 2-3.

[527] Ibid., p. 5.

[528] De Ly, F. (1992), *International Business Law and Lex Mercatoria*, p. 138, citing Wortley.

[529] See, for example, Wellwood, J.W. (1975), *Custom and usage*, p. 5. See also, e.g., Chitty, J. (1999), *Chitty on Contracts*.

[530] Wellwood, J.W. (1975), *Custom and usage*, p. 2.

> 'a sequence of previous conduct between the parties to a particular transaction which is fairly to be regarded as establishing a common basis of understanding for interpreting their expressions and other conduct.'[531]

On the other hand, a usage of trade is defined as:

> 'a practice or method of dealing having such regularity of observance in a place, vocation or trade as to justify an expectation that it will be observed.'[532]

Therefore, American jurisprudence rejects the traditional common law requirements of immemoriality, reasonablessness and locality.[533] It also does not subscribe to the psychological element required by continental legal systems such as those in Germany or France.[534] And further:

> 'The existence and scope of such a usage must be proved as facts. If it is established that such a usage is embodied in a trade code or similar record, the interpretation of the record is a question of law.'[535]

In summary, one can see completely different concepts of custom within Western legal thinking. But, as de Ly puts it, custom continues to be accepted as a source of law, however 'requirements are hard to meet and few examples exist'.[536]

Another serious problem is associated with distinguishing between custom and usage. Not all countries distinguish between the two concepts, the most important example being the United States. Such a distinction seems to exist in the United Kingdom,[537] although this is debated.[538] According to Wellwood, custom is 'clearly distinguishable' from trade or local usages, 'although in practice frequently confused with them'.[539] Usages are primarily considered where they were or should be imported as express or implied terms into contracts[540] and they do not have to be immemorial or confined to a definite locality. However,

> 'usages (...) contrary to positive law will not be sanctioned by the courts, while customs may be inconsistent with the general law of the realm.'[541]

---

[531] UCC §1-303 (b).

[532] UCC §1-303 (c). See also Art. 565 of the Italian Commercial Code.

[533] See Comments to UCC. See also De Ly, F. (1992), *International Business Law and Lex Mercatoria*, pp. 138-139.

[534] Berman, H. and Kaufman, C. (1978), *The law of international commercial transactions (lex mercatoria)*, pp. 262-263.

[535] UCC §1-205 (c).

[536] De Ly, F. (1992), *International Business Law and Lex Mercatoria*, p. 138.

[537] Wellwood, J.W. (1975), *Custom and usage*, pp. 4, 28-60.

[538] See De Ly, F. (1992), *International Business Law and Lex Mercatoria*, p. 138.

[539] Wellwood, J.W. (1975), *Custom and usage*, p. 4.

[540] Ibid., citing *Dashwood* v. *Magniac* (1891), 3 Ch 306 at 370, CA per Kay LJ and *Sewell* v. *Corp* (1824) 1 C & P 392 at 393, per Best CJ.

[541] Ibid., footnotes ommited.

On the other hand, in Germany, usages are defined as 'uniform patterns which have been observed for some time leading to a general conviction that they are applicable.'[542] Parties do not need to feel bound by a usage whereas this feeling is necessary in case of a customary rule.[543] Therefore, both in Germany and the United Kingdom usages do not have subjective element, do not have to be long-lasting and seem to be binding irrespective of whether parties are aware of them. On the other hand, usages are binding in France only if agreed to by the parties, which is consistent with the subjective theory of contract interpretation.[544]

Although the majority of Western legal systems seem to distinguish between custom and usage the distinction is very hard to make, as it is tied to the subscribed theory of custom and tradition of interpretation. Many authors who distinguish both concepts seem to apply the same theories of objective and subjective element to both custom and usage.[545] Often both terms are used interchangeably, which can easily create confusion. For instance, one crucial question is whether usage has to be known or agreed to by the parties. Custom binds irrespective of party consent, because it is a source of law but not a usage. However, usage once had to be known or consented to in its application by parties to a contract. This viewpoint still seems to prevail in France, which advocates a subjective method of legal interpretation. However, the majority of Western states seem to require that merchants should know usages, which subscribes to the objective method of interpretation. This is at least the case in the common law countries such as England and in continental legal systems such as those of Germany[546] and Belgium.[547] Therefore, it is impossible to distinguish between both concepts on the ground of party consent. The same can be said with respect to the requirement of time, which has shortened greatly in the modern era. The only differentiator would be the subjective element, which is present in case of a customary norm and absent in case of a usage. However, there seems to be no agreement among a majority of states on this topic, not to mention the practical difficulty of proving someone's convictions. Therefore, Western countries that distinguish between custom and usage create serious obstacles to the application of spontaneous norms in the legal process. Although consequences of custom and usage are different, the distinction between both concepts is very hard to grasp. Taking into account a plethora of domestic theories of custom, it is very hard to tell in practice whether a given norm is a binding custom or is merely a usage.

The role of usages is also presented differently in various jurisdictions. A common feature is that it is always delineated by specific provisions of the civil or

542 German Supreme Court (2 May 1984), WM, 1984, 1000; cited in De Ly, F. (1992), *International Business Law and Lex Mercatoria*, p. 138.

543 Ibid., pp. 138-139, citing Sonnenberger and other authors.

544 See ibid., pp. 148-151.

545 Studnicki, F. (1949), *Działanie zwyczaju handlowego w zakresie zobowiązań z umowy*, p. 36.

546 See, for example, De Ly, F. (1992), *International Business Law and Lex Mercatoria*, pp. 136, 139.

547 Ibid., p. 150, although it is still debatable.

commercial codes.[548] Often supplementary and interpretative functions of a usage are distinguished, although this is not always easy to do. Civil codes usually contain a provision to the effect that an agreement is to be supplemented with relevant statutory provisions, rules of ethics and usages.[549] The famous Article 1135 of Code Napoleon states that 'agreements are binding not only as to what is therein expressed, but also as to all the consequences which equity, usage or statute give to the obligation according to its nature.' Therefore, common practices can qualify the terms of a contract.

More often, however, references to usages are done in the context of contract construction.[550] The German BGB contains a norm, which forces an adjudicator to take into account good faith and usage in contract construction.[551] Furthermore, the German HGB in § 346 states that all the acts and omissions of professional traders should be interpreted according to custom.[552] On the other hand, Code Napoleon states that contract ambiguities are to be interpreted according to the usage prevailing at the place of contract formation[553] and that it should be supplemented with commonly used clauses.[554] Finally, usages are also referred to as a source of norms to guide the performance of a contract.[555] In consequence, a usage in continental legal systems is not treated as an independent source of law, although it plays a fundamental role in contract construction, qualification and performance. From this perspective, the distinction between custom and usage does not seem to have a great importance, because a given customary norm can be referred to by an adjudicator anyway.

In the United States, trade usages (customs) and courses of dealing (local customs) have interpretative as well as supplementary functions.[556] Both can give a particular meaning to the terms of a contract and qualify its terms. Therefore, despite the abandonment of distinction between custom and usage, US jurisprudence

---

[548] See, for example, David, R. and Brierley, J.E. (1985), *Major legal systems in the world today*, pp. 130-131.

[549] See, for instance, Art. 1135 of French Code Napoleon, Art. 56 of Polish Civil Code of 1964, Art. 248, Book 6 of Dutch New Civil Code. German BGB does not contain such provision, though.

[550] See, for instance, Art. 157 of German BGB.

[551] Art. 157 of BGB. 'Verträge sind so auszulegen, wie Treu und Glauben mit Rücksicht auf die Verkehrssitte es erfordern.'

[552] Art. 346 of HGB: 'Unter Kaufleuten ist in Ansehung der Bedeutung und Wirkung von Handlungen und Unterlassungen auf die im Handelsverkehr geltenden Gewohnheiten und Gebräuche Rücksicht zu nehmen.'

[553] See, for instance, Art. 1159 of French Code Napoleon.

[554] See, for instance, Art. 1160 of French Code Napoleon. In this respect see particularly de Ly, who argues that Art. 1160 Cc has no meaning different from Art. 1135Cc. De Ly, F. (1992), *International Business Law and Lex Mercatoria*, pp. 138-139.

[555] In Germany see Art. 242 of BGB. 'Der Schuldner ist verpflichtet, die Leistung so zu bewirken, wie Treu und Glauben mit Rücksicht auf die Verkehrssitte es erfordern.'

[556] Bainbridge, S. (1984), *Trade Usages in International Sales of Goods: An Analysis of the 1964 and 1980 Sales Conventions*, p. 640.

seems to attach similar consequences to common practices as its modern European counterpart associates with the notion of usage.

Finally, there are doubts with respect to the position of custom or usage in relation to statutes or a contract. The Western legal tradition seems to universally accept that parties can derogate from contrary usage or custom. Therefore, contract prevails over contrary custom. Furthermore, the question whether a usage or a customary norm can abolish contrary mandatory provision of statutes seems unthinkable today.[557] Therefore, the operation of a custom *contra legem*, understood as against mandatory provisions, is universally rejected. However, there are some difficulties with respect to potential of custom to modify non-mandatory provisions of statutes. In countries such as Switzerland and Poland, statutory rules, whether mandatory or not, seem to prevail over usage.[558] On the other hand, in countries such as Germany, usage seems to prevail over non-mandatory statutory provisions.[559] In the English legal tradition, custom may only derogate from common law but not from statutory law. The American UCC only settles the hierarchy between contract terms and usage. In case of inconsistency, the contract prevails over both trade usage and course of dealing. In a case of inconsistency between trade usage and course of dealing, the latter prevails.[560]

In summary, the role of custom in civil law and in the Anglo-Saxon legal tradition has been marginalised but not entirely eliminated.[561] Some countries explicitly recognise custom as a source of law to be used in the absence of statutory norms. Contemporary England still does not have a written constitution, and much of its constitutional law is customary in origin.[562] In general, however, custom can be said to have lost its position as a dominant source of domestic law. In relation to a contract, the remnants of custom's authority are visible in continental usages or the Anglo-American doctrine of contractual terms implied by usage. Despite the difficulties of deciphering the differences between both concepts, one can agree with de Ly that the status of usages has, of late, become more important. Usages are one of

---

[557] But see David, R. and Brierley, J.E. (1985), *Major legal systems in the world today*, para. 98.

[558] See for example, De Ly, F. (1992), *International Business Law and Lex Mercatoria*, p. 142; Safjan, M. (2005), *Refleksje o roli zwyczaju*; Studnicki, F. (1949), *Działanie zwyczaju handlowego w zakresie zobowiązań z umowy* .

[559] At least with respect to contract interpretation. See De Ly, F. (1992), *International Business Law and Lex Mercatoria*, p. 140, and the literature cited there.

[560] UCC § 1-303 (e) states that '(e) Except as otherwise provided in subsection (f), the express terms of an agreement and any applicable course of performance, course of dealing, or usage of trade must be construed whenever reasonable as consistent with each other. If such a construction is unreasonable: (1) express terms prevail over course of performance, course of dealing, and usage of trade; (2) course of performance prevails over course of dealing and usage of trade; and (3) course of dealing prevails over usage of trade.'

[561] See, for example, David, R. and Brierley, J.E. (1985), *Major legal systems in the world today*, pp. 130-132.

[562] See, for example, Allen, C.K. (1964), *Law in the making*, pp. 76-77; Smith, M. (June 1903), *Customary law. I.*, pp. 263-264.

the fundaments of contract construction and assessment of parties' performance of the obligation. With the exception of France and Belgium, usages can also supplement contracts without looking at party intent. Nevertheless, the distinction between custom and usage is difficult to justify and therefore, should be abandoned.

2.5 **Summary**

Throughout history, custom has played a very important role in Western legal culture, with the exception of the last two centuries. Although not a dominant force in the Roman Empire, it was a foundation of Roman *ius gentium*, the predecessor of modern international commercial law. In medieval Europe its supreme dominance was clearly visible, although it systematically decreased after the rediscovery of Roman law and especially after the Enlightenment in the eighteenth century. It was during this time that customary Law Merchant has been received and further developed in major European trade centres to assist traders in dispute resolution. However, the modern role of custom in Western legal culture is marginal, mainly as a result of the supreme role of written statutes that tend to establish everything in writing, which petrifies once established practices. Although some traces of the importance of custom can be found in continental modern civil codes or commercial codes, its role seems to be delineated by such codes as if custom did not operate independently. In consequence, the concept of custom as a source of law was and continues to be of no interest to lawyers and legal scholars, who are accustomed to theoretical analysis of existing written laws rather than to examination of empirical sources of law. Even legal historians, although aware of the historical significance of custom, prefer to examine past written laws rather than unwritten ones. These attitudes have led to a serious underdevelopment of this field of knowledge.

History gives the foundation for the discussion of customary practices on the Internet. It shows that custom did bind all persons, thus justifying the claim that it could also be a source of globally binding Internet law. It gives a basis for the contention that Internet customs could abolish or modify obsolete legislation, which will be of great importance in the technological age. Similarly, it allows the conclusion that custom will be the best interpreter of written Internet law. Certain elements of custom identified by Roman lawyers, such as its uniformity and duration, will change their meaning in the concept of e-custom. The historical importance of local customs will also have an effect on the proposed theory of Internet custom. Finally, history shows that merchants transacting internationally have always referred to customs of trade in order to settle their disputes. Custom gave them more flexible and certain norms than particular written laws, which were often not designed to handle mercantile disputes. This allows the conclusion that a similar process will take place on the Internet, and that online merchants, over time, will rely on their own widespread practices in settling electronic commerce disputes.

3. Custom in Other Legal Traditions

Repeated social conduct has played and continues to play an important role in non-Western legal traditions. Western legal thought was based upon Greek cosmology, shaped by Christianity and developed by the rational philosophy of the eighteenth century, and non-Western traditions have developed in isolation from all of this. The great non-Western legal traditions are to an even greater extent based upon religion, sometimes making it difficult for the researcher to distinguish between legal norms and religious precepts. Moreover, in the East, it is a far more frequent occurrence for non-official law practiced by people to modify official law or resist its domination.[563]

These differences, however, create serious problems with analysing aspects such as the role of custom as a source of law. These traditions do not use the same terminology, and often do not identify law as a separate body of norms governing humans' behaviour:

> 'We reject the notion held generally in Western legal thought for over two thousand years that law is something universal. The history of various civilizations, their anthropology and their philosophy, however, tell us that civilizations have developed different concepts as their fundamental principles of social organization. Law is only one such principle, which, in Western civilization, is derived from the Greek concept of nomos. The Chinese civilization has its li. African societies have their own particular patterns. And the Hindu civilization has its dharma, whose meaning is broader than law alone.'[564]

Taking into account the serious difficulties with analysing the role of custom in non-Western normative systems, the following section will limit its discussion to Hindu, Muslim, Chinese and Japanese legal traditions. This will be followed by an analysis of custom in primitive societies from an anthropological perspective. Material presented in this section will, of necessity, be only briefly analysed and should be treated more as a reminder of the importance of custom in the non-Western world rather than as an authoritative discussion of this phenomenon.

3.1 Custom in Islamic tradition

The importance of Arabic traders, long before the emergence of Islam, is difficult to overestimate. Their influence on trade can best be evidenced by modern commercial terminology, which has adopted many Arabic words.[565] Prophet Muhammad

---

[563] Rouland, N. (1994), *Legal Anthropology*, p. 61.

[564] Nanda, V.P. and Sinha, S.P. (eds.) (1996), *Hindu Law and Legal Theory*.

[565] Bewes, W.A. (1923), *The Romance of the Law Merchant Being an Introduction to the Study of International and Commercial Law with Some Account of the Commerce and Fairs of the Middle Ages*, p. 10, citing Lammens.

himself started his career as a caravan merchant, which gave a unique flavour to the importance of trade in Islam.[566] Muslim traders played a very active role in medieval trade[567] as it is probably through them that medieval Europe received customary laws of the trading world. Muslim commercial customs influenced medieval Law Merchant in many ways, laying, for example, the foundation for the modern limited company.[568]

Islamic jurisprudence focuses primarily on the analysis of *Quran*, *Sunnah*, *Ijma* and *Quijas*. Custom (*ᶜurf*) only constitutes an additional basis for legal decisions if it is sound and reasonable.[569] Custom's validity is justified on the rule that

> 'whatever the people consider to be good for themselves is good in the eyes of God.'[570]

Among the four schools of Islamic law, the one that especially favoured the customary practices of the Medina was the Maliki School.[571]

Custom is defined as

> 'recurring practices which are acceptable to people of sound nature.'[572]

Custom must posses certain qualities.[573] It must represent a common and recurrent phenomenon among a large number of people, must be in existence at the time a transaction is concluded and cannot contravene an agreement or the definitive principle of law. Custom can be general or local, verbal or actual. Verbal custom means agreement of the people on the meaning and usage of certain words. Actual custom is based upon recurrent practices other than those associated with the meaning of words. An example of actual custom is the give-and-take sale, which is normally concluded without declarations of offer and acceptance.

Apart from custom, Islamic tradition has another very similar source of law: *Ijma*. *Ijma* seems to be a custom among jurisprudence as opposed to a custom of

---

[566] Mallat, C. (Winter 2000), *Commercial Law In The Middle East: Between Classical Transactions And Modern Business*, p. 92.

[567] See, for example, Greif, A. (June 1993), *Contract Enforceability and Economic Institutions in Early Trade: The Maghribi Traders' Coalition*.

[568] Bewes, W.A. (1923), *The Romance of the Law Merchant Being an Introduction to the Study of International and Commercial Law with Some Account of the Commerce and Fairs of the Middle Ages*, p. 77.

[569] Kamali, M.H. (1991), *Principles of Islamic Jurisprudence*, p. 283.

[570] Ahmad bin Mohamed Ibrahim (1965), *Sources and development of Muslim law*, p. 33.

[571] Same could be said about Hanafi school in regard to statement of Abn Yusuf: 'What matters in all things is the "urf"', cited in Mallat, C. (Winter 2000), *Commercial Law In The Middle East: Between Classical Transactions And Modern Business*, p. 96, citing Sarakhsi, al-Mabsut.

[572] Kamali, M.H. (1991), *Principles of Islamic Jurisprudence*, p. 283.

[573] Ibid., pp. 286-287.

ordinary people.[574] *Ijma* is based upon practice of the learned members of the community and does not depend on the agreement of the layman. *Ijma* requires an absolute agreement of jurisprudence, whereas in case of custom, a minority may act against a rule in question. Custom can evolve, but *Ijma*, once established, cannot be changed. Finally custom requires a certain amount of time to develop whereas *Ijma* may come into existence as soon as learned scholars reach a unanimous agreement. Furthermore, it does not require continuity for its conclusion.[575]

Commercial customs in Islam have still great importance.[576] The validity of this type of custom is illustrated in the maxim:

> 'what is known by custom is equal to what is agreed upon as a clause.'[577]

In regard to the establishment of price, for instance, it is customary practice that authorises how much a merchant can add to the buying price. What practice excludes must be excluded:[578]

> 'In the law of sale custom is decisive.'[579]

British colonial legislators often considered the whole Islamic legal system as customary, despite the fact that custom is a separate source of Islamic law.[580] Nowadays, custom is an important source of law[581] only in some Muslim countries, especially in Morocco.[582] In some countries a special type of Islamic banking law has developed.[583] Custom also plays an essential role in the preservation of the Palestinian customary legal system.[584]

---

574 See, for example, David, R. and Brierley, J.E. (1985), *Major legal systems in the world today*, p. 458.

575 Kamali, M.H. (1991), *Principles of Islamic Jurisprudence*, pp. 288-289.

576 See, for example, Chapter 4 in Gerber, H. (1994), *State, society, and law in Islam: Ottoman law in comparative perspective*.

577 Mallat, C. (Winter 2000), *Commercial Law In The Middle East: Between Classical Transactions And Modern Business*, p. 96, citing Kasani; see also Kamali, M.H. (1991), *Principles of Islamic Jurisprudence*, p. 290.

578 Mallat, C. (Winter 2000), *Commercial Law In The Middle East: Between Classical Transactions And Modern Business*, p. 95, citing Udovitch.

579 Ibid., citing Kasani and Sarakhsi.

580 See, for example, Oba, A. (October 2002), *Islamic Law as Customary Law: The Changing Perspective in Nigeria*.

581 Serjeant, R.B. (1991), *Customary and Shari'ah law in Arabian society*.

582 Ahmad bin Mohamed Ibrahim (1965), *Sources and development of Muslim law*, pp. 33-34; see also Al-Zwaini, L. (1994), *A bibliography of Islamic law, 1980-1993*.

583 See, for example, Mallat, C. (Winter 2000), *Commercial Law In The Middle East: Between Classical Transactions And Modern Business*, p. 90.

584 See, for example, Zilberman, I. (1996), *Palestynian customary law in the Jerusalem area*.

3.2 Custom in Hindu tradition

Originally Hindu law was a rationalised and systematised body of customary law and observances.[585] Central to Hindu law is the concept of *Dharma*, which means 'preserving'. Dharma is not based on a set of specific commands but describes a way of life, such as when an individual should awaken and go to sleep, and how his or her day should he divided. Dharma also provides guidance about relationships with other people, and information about nature and even diet.[586] The oldest source of Hindu law is *sruti* composed from four *Vedas*. Custom known as *sadachara* meaning 'custom of good men'[587] is one of the sources of Hindu law[588] although some English authors question this fact.[589] Legal codes called *Dharmasastras* codified legal principles contained in the *Vedas*, *Dharmasutras*[590] and customary practices of good people. Customary practices of people trained in *Vedas* have had great importance and in case of conflict some authors consider them to be more authoritative than written sources.[591] Custom as a source of law is then limited only to people who are permitted to or who can study the *Vedas*.

Through the process of colonisation, England has significantly changed traditional Hindu law.[592] At first, the British decided that Hindus should be governed by their own laws in several areas, so *Dharmasastras* began to be used in the courts to resolve family law, property, succession and religious usage. The applicable law was subject to modification by custom, which had various local varieties. This approach changed, however.[593] Custom is applied as an exception to statutory law and *Dharmasastras* and its existence is treated as a question of fact and law. Modern Hindu legislation defines custom as follows:

> 'The expression "custom" and "usage" signify any rule which, having been continuously and uniformly observed for a long time, has obtained the force of law among Hindus in any local area, tribe, community, group or family: provided that the rule is

---

[585] See, for example, Derrett, J.D.M. (1963), *Introduction to Modern Hindu Law*, p. 3.

[586] Nanda, V.P. and Sinha, S.P. (eds.) (1996), *Hindu Law and Legal Theory*.

[587] Nagpal, R.C. (1983), *Modern Hindu Law*, p. 27.

[588] See Nanda, V.P. and Sinha, S.P. (eds.) (1996), *Hindu Law and Legal Theory*, p. XIV, referring to Manusmriti II, 6; see also Nagpal, R.C. (1983), *Modern Hindu Law*, p. 28.

[589] E.g., Derrett, J.D.M. (1963), *Introduction to Modern Hindu Law*, p. 12.

[590] Foundation of civil and criminal law, see Nanda, V.P. and Sinha, S.P. (eds.) (1996), *Hindu Law and Legal Theory*, p. XIV.

[591] See Nagpal, R.C. (1983), *Modern Hindu Law*, p. 29 and literature cited there. A similar approach was taken by English jurisprudence, see *Ramnad* case.

[592] See, for example, Chakravarty-Kaul, M. (1996), *Common lands and customary law: institutional change in North India over the past two centuries*.

[593] Soon judges reversed the traditional hierarchy and stated that the wording of the commentary overrules that of the Dharmasastra, and the latter that of the Vedas. Gradually judges abandoned consulting Sanskrit texts by making Hindu law into a regular Anglo-Saxon case law. Nanda, V.P. and Sinha, S.P. (eds.) (1996), *Hindu Law and Legal Theory*, p. XIV.

> certain and not unreasonable or opposed to public policy; and provided further that in the case of a rule applicable only to a family it has not been discontinued by the family.'[594]

Custom can be evidenced by official or unofficial record,[595] or by the observance of a rule. It cannot be evidenced by analogy. Custom must be ancient,[596] continuous, uniform, certain, reasonable, not against public policy and not abolished by a statute.[597] There are four types of customs: local customs applying to residents of certain locality, group customs prevailing in certain groups or castes, family customs and institutional customs.[598]

3.3 Custom in Chinese tradition

Chinese legal tradition[599] is especially difficult to analyse as it has developed very original concepts of social organisation not known in other legal systems. Chinese social organisation is deeply rooted in the thought of Confucius (551-479 BC) which supports a hierarchical order of society where everyone has a place and where the balanced harmony of the world, expressed in unwritten rules of behaviour called *li,* should not be disturbed.[600] The 'ideal man' is conscious of the natural order of things, but represses his subjective interests, remaining willingly obedient and spontaneously and rigorously follows the precepts of *li*.[601] Confucianism considers legal rules (called *Fa*) as a necessary evil, good only for barbarians. It condemns people using litigation, and stresses the virtue of modesty and the importance of peaceful out-of-court dispute settlement.[602] The rules of alternative dispute settlement are based on a conciliator's knowledge of *li* and customary practices of a region.[603]

In consequence, dispute prevention becomes more important than dispute settlement. It is so because no matter how disputes would be resolved, harmony was disturbed whenever people were in dispute.[604] As Confucius put it:

---

594 Sec. 3(a) of HMA, Sec. 3(d) of HAS, Sec. 3(a) of HAMA cited in Nagpal, R.C. (1983), *Modern Hindu Law*, p. 30.

595 E.g., customs transcribed by Rattigan in Punjab under the head 'Riwaj-i-am'. Ibid., p. 31.

596 There is no time limit set for custom like in English law year 1189.

597 Nagpal, R.C. (1983), *Modern Hindu Law*, pp. 32-35.

598 Ibid., p. 36.

599 See Chapter 2 in Poh-Ling Tan (1997), *Asian legal systems: law, society and pluralism in East Asia*.

600 See, for example, Zweigert, K. and Kötz, H. (1998), *An Introduction to Comparative Law*, pp. 288-292, and literature cited there.

601 Ibid., p. 288.

602 Rouland, N. (1994), *Legal Anthropology*, p. 39; Zweigert, K. and Kötz, H. (1998), *An Introduction to Comparative Law*, p. 289.

603 Zweigert, K. and Kötz, H. (1998), *An Introduction to Comparative Law*, p. 291.

604 Wong, B.K.Y. (June 2003), *Dispute Resolution by Officials in Traditional Chinese Legal Culture*, Murdoch University Electronic Journal of Law 10(2), para. 6.

'As to hearing lawsuits, I am no different to an ordinary person; it is best to prevent all disputes.'[605]

Although it is difficult to categorise Chinese sources of law in the way Western countries do, it seems that customary practices of people in their normal life have far greater importance in China[606] than in the West. The unwritten rules of *li* that are followed spontaneously resemble customary practices. Preference is given to them, even in modern China, which has only recently introduced some legislation.

In relation to private commercial transactions, pre-communist China was governed by informal customary rules enforced by families and guild organisations without the need for courts.[607] The recent influence of the Western legal tradition is apparent in the modern approach to custom that is important primarily in regions inhabited by ethnic minorities.[608] With the introduction of the civil code only customs that do not conflict with other regulations have significance as a source of norms of civil law.[609]

3.4 Custom in Japanese tradition

Separated from the Asian mainland, the Japanese legal tradition is very difficult to classify as it was for a long time influenced by Chinese thought and Buddhism. Only recently has it become totally dominated by Western legal culture. Customary rules of behaviour play a very important role in Japan. The unwritten rules of *giri*, that could be equated with custom,[610] direct the lives of the Japanese. In long-lasting merchant-customer relationships the customer who buys products from another merchant breaches *giri*.[611] However, these rules are founded on affection and are not demandable. As a result, they have a much wider meaning than the Western idea of legal custom.

With the reception of codes in the nineteenth century followed by American influence in the twentieth century,[612] Japanese legal thought became dominated by the Western concept of custom where it plays a marginal role. Custom is now considered a source of law within the meaning of Article 2 of the law of 1875, which states that custom that is not contrary to public order or to morality has the value of law, provided that it is not excluded by legislation and that it deals with matters that

[605] Ibid., para. 6 citing Analects: Yan Yuan 《論語．顏淵》55.

[606] Ibid.

[607] Potter, P.B. (1992), *The Economic Contract Law of China. Legitimation and Contract Autonomy in the PRC*, pp. 9-11.

[608] Jones, W.C. (ed.) (1989), *Basic Principles of Civil Law in China*, p. 25.

[609] Ibid.

[610] See Noda, Y. (1976), *Introduction to Japanese Law*, pp. 174-183, citing Lévi-Bruhl, H. (1961), *Sociologie du droit*.

[611] Noda, Y. (1976), *Introduction to Japanese Law*, p. 176.

[612] See, for example, von Mehren, A.T. (ed.) (1963), *Law in Japan. The Legal Order in a Changing Society*.

have not been provided by statute or regulation.[613] On the other hand, Article 92 of the Japanese civil code states that:

> 'If there are customs contrary to the legislation which do not deal with matter of public policy, judgement can be given according to the customs if the parties wish that to be done.'[614]

Both of these rules subject custom to legislation but, as Noda points out, this 'does not express the social reality' as:

> 'judgments often refer to customary rules which are incompatible with imperative rules of law in order to reach an appropriate solution.'[615]

It is interesting to note that Japanese courts seem to be braver than their Western counterparts in safeguarding the validity of certain customs against the contrary provisions of statutes. The examples of customary norms functioning against express provisions of statutory law include: partial recognition of *de facto* marriage, the legal validity of contract in which a debtor gives a pledge without disposition of the property, validity of the transferral of registered shares by way of endorsement[616] and validity of issuing blank bills of exchanges.[617]

3.5 Custom in tribal societies

Tribal societies depend upon the observance of customary norms to an even greater extent than every legal culture mentioned so far. Many anthropologists have studied indigenous[618] systems of social organisations, and the most interesting ones are often produced by researchers who are actually immersed in the community in question. The founder of this approach was Malinowski, who in describing the life of Trobriand islanders pointed out that they have a very efficient set of customary norms, not only in criminal law, but also in economic and non-economic relations. In regard to economic relations, he pointed out the importance of division of work and products and give-and-take customary principles as a fundamental of their social organisation.

---

613 Noda, Y. (1976), *Introduction to Japanese Law*, pp. 218-219; Oda, H. (1999), *Japanese Law*, p. 60.

614 Law No. 10, 1898; On discrepancy of various provisions on custom see Noda, Y. (1976), *Introduction to Japanese Law*, p. 219.

615 Ibid., pp. 219-220.

616 Taniguchi (1964), *La loi et la coutume au Japon*, pp. 575-578, cited by Noda, Y. (1976), *Introduction to Japanese Law*, pp. 220-221.

617 Judgment of the Supreme Tribunal, October 18, 1926 cited in Oda, H. (1999), *Japanese Law*, p. 60.

618 See criteria for indigenousness described in Rouland, N. (2001), *Custom and the Law*, p. 17.

Custom continues to play a fundamental role among native tribes. Recent studies of indigenous people in the Australasian region reveals the rebirth of customs in the post-colonial era.[619] Customary rules of land ownership are a fundamental of the legal system of Australian Aborigines and Torres Straight Islanders that have significantly altered Australian laws.[620] Custom has also played, and continues to play, a fundamental role among indigenous habitants in both Americas.[621] The relations between Eskimos, for instance, are governed primarily by unwritten rules of conduct that could be classified as customary norms. Many African societies, even those which were subjected to Western legal thought for a long period of time, are dependant on customs.[622]

3.6 **Summary**

Non-Western societies seem to value customary practices higher than Western ones. Cultural and ideological differences are certainly the most important cause of this. The Western way of thinking, which favours unrestrained individualism, is at odds with more societal life in non-Western cultures.

Custom played and continues to play an important role in the great religious systems of Islam and Hinduism. Muslim followers developed a very interesting and in-depth concept of binding customary practices which are different among jurists and normal people. Similar distinctions are evident in the Hindu concept of *sadachara*. Chinese people, on the other hand, prefer to follow unwritten rules of *li* rather than written precepts of law. Similar observations can be made about Japan, despite its accession to Western legal culture. Finally, customs are fundamental to the social organisation of tribal societies.

However, the role of custom is also being diminished with the growing acceptance of Western culture, including the reception of civil law and common law legal traditions. Such receptions of foreign laws, however, are very complex phenomena and may remain on paper only for many years, as societies will continue to live according to their own traditions. This will only widen the gap between the law in books and the law in practice.

---

[619] de Deckker, P. and Faberon, J.Y. (eds.) (2001), *Custom and the law*.

[620] See, for example, Bartholomew, G.W. (1996), *Recognition of Aboriginal law and legal pluralism*; Lokan, A. (1999), *From recognition to reconciliation: the functions of Aboriginal rights law*; Office of Indigenous Affairs (1994), *Aboriginal customary laws: report on Commonwealth implementation of the recommendations of the Australian Law Reform Commission*; The Law Reform Commission (1986), *The recognition of aboriginal customary laws. Report No. 31, Vol. 1*.

[621] See, for example, Barroso, R.L. (Summer 1995), *The saga of indigenous peoples in Brazil: constitution, law and policies. Symposium: Tribal Sovereignty: Back to the Future?*; Joh, E.E. (2000-2001), *Custom, tribal court practice, and popular justice*; McNeil, K. (1998), *Aboriginal Rights in Canada: From title to land to territorial sovereignty*.

[622] For a recent very good analysis of various native legal cultures see Scheleff, L. (2000), *The future of tradition: customary law, common law and legal pluralism*. See also, e.g., Berat, L. (1991/1992), *Customary Law in a New South Africa: a Proposal*.

This discussion has provided evidence that custom is a source of law known to different cultures, irrespective of their technological advancement. In turn, this allows the conclusion that custom would be a perfect tool to settle international disputes on the Internet as all cultures either relied on it or continue to rely on it. However, what is required is an explicit theory of custom acceptable to different nations that could be used as a model for Internet commerce custom. The following section will search for such a model in modern international legal orders.

4. Custom in Modern International Legal Orders

Despite the marginal role of custom in modern national legal systems, custom plays a very important role in international legal orders. It is officially recognised as the source of law in international public law, which is considered by the international community as a truly supranational legal order. It also plays a crucial role in international trade law, although the status of *lex mercatoria* as an independent system of law from national legislatures is still the subject of heated debate among scholars.

4.1 Custom in the international commercial law

(a) Rebirth of the Law Merchant

In the twentieth century the idea of independent transnational commercial law similar to that of Roman *ius gentium* or medieval Law Merchant described above was revived. As Berman observed, the commercial world developed universal commercial law because of their history and common problems they confront.

> 'It is the mercantile community that has, in the first instance, generated mercantile law. And it is this same community which continues to develop present day mercantile law (...) through their contract practices and the common understandings on which they are based, and also through regulations of self-governing trade associations and through decisions of arbitration tribunals to which their disputes are submitted. These contract practices, understandings, regulations and decisions constitute a body of customary law which is the foundation on which national and international commercial legislation has been and continues to be built.'[623]

Customary mercantile practices are still very important in modern trade relations. Organisations such as International Chamber of Commerce (ICC) from 1930's codified certain mercantile practices widely used in international trade. The most important examples include several editions of International Commercial Terms

---

[623] Berman, H. and Kaufman, C. (1978), *The law of international commercial transactions (lex mercatoria)*, pp. 222-223.

(INCOTERMS),[624] which describe commonly used commercial terms like Free on Board (FOB) or Cost, Insurance, Freight (CIF) clauses which set rights and obligations of the parties, the moment of passing risk to the buyer, and so on. International banking industry on the other hand developed customary practices regarding financing international trade by means of letters of credit that were also codified by the ICC in several versions of Uniform Customs and Practice for Documentary Credits (U.C.P.).[625] In 2002, the International Chamber of Commerce issued the eUCP, which supplements U.C.P. 'in order to accommodate presentation of electronic records alone or in combination with paper documents.'[626] ICC is currently working eTerms 2004, which could soon become customary principles of the Internet based commerce.[627] The majority of Banker's Associations acceded to various versions of U.C.P. that were also recommended in electronic SWIFT regulations.[628] There are some areas of commerce where custom reigns absolutely and remains largely unwritten as is the case in the insurance market.[629] In other areas like the oil industry, merchants customarily include elaborate and almost uniform in content provisions dealing with various contingencies and especially non-performance terms.[630]

Observing the independence and self-reliance of the international mercantile community, Goldman proposed in the 1960s the idea of autonomous, independent of national legal systems law of international trade that could be used as a law governing the contract.[631] Although the concept was initially met with criticism,[632] after Roman *ius gentium* and medieval Law Merchant it was the third revival of *lex mercatoria* in history.[633] UNIDROIT Principles, Lando Principles together with

---

[624] See, for example, International Chamber of Commerce (1999), *Incoterms 2000: ICC official rules for the interpretation of trade terms: entry into force 1st January 2000 = Regles officielles ICC pour l'interpretation des termes commerciaux: entrée en vigueur 1er janvier 2000.* Some countries, such as the United States, codified their own version of such terms.

[625] See, for example, International Chamber of Commerce (1993), *ICC uniform customs and practice for documentary credits*.

[626] International Chamber of Commerce (2002), *eUCP Version 1.0. Supplement to UCP 500 for Electronic Presentation (in force as of 1 April 2002) (eUCP).*

[627] UNCITRAL (12 August 2004), *ICC eTerms 2004. ICC Guide to electronic contracting. (A/CN.9/WG.IV/WP.113).*

[628] De Ly, F. (1992), *International Business Law and Lex Mercatoria*, pp. 175-182. See also Glossary.

[629] See, for example, Hoffman, W. (1997), *On the use and abuse of custom and usage in reinsurance contracts*.

[630] For the rare example of a case study in the oil industry see Trakman, L.E. (1983), *The Law Merchant: The Evolution of Commercial Law*.

[631] See, for example, Goldman, B. (1983), *Lex Mercatoria*, p. 1.

[632] See especially Chapter 4 in De Ly, F. (1992), *International Business Law and Lex Mercatoria*; Mustill, M. (1987), *The new lex mercatoria: the first twenty-five years, in Liber amicorum for Lord Wilberforce*.

[633] See Goldman, B. (1983), *Lex Mercatoria*, p. 1. For a more recent discussion see, for example, Badinter, R. (December 1995), *Role of the International Lawyer*, p. 506; Bamodu, G. (2001), *Extra-legal principles in the global village: A conceptual examination of transnational law*, p. 6; Bonell, M.J.

the increased interests in independent from national legal systems solutions to international commercial disputes are considered to mark a new stage in the revival of the idea of *lex mercatoria*.[634] The essence of the notion of the modern doctrine of *lex mercatoria* is a resort to well-established, supranational norms of international commerce thus escaping the traditional court-based dispute settlement. Probably the best description of advantages of the modern *lex mercatoria* was provided by Lando in his often cited article:

> 'By choosing the lex mercatoria the parties oust the technicalities of national legal systems and they avoid rules which are unfit for international contract. Thus they escape peculiar formalities, brief cut-off periods, and some of the difficulties created by domestic laws which are unknown in other countries such as the common law rules on consideration and privity of contract. Furthermore, those involved in the proceedings – parties, counsel and arbitrators – plead and argue on equal footing; nobody has the advantage of having the case pleaded and decided by his own law and nobody has the handicap of seeing it governed by a foreign law.'[635]

And further:

> 'the binding force of the lex mercatoria does not depend on the fact that it is made and promulgated by State authorities but that it is recognized as an autonomous norm system by the business community and by State authorities.'[636]

The sources of modern *lex mercatoria* have their basis in codified and uncodified commercial customs, private restatements such as UNIDROIT Principles, commonly used contract terms, as well as in arbitral awards.[637] Based on the analysis of arbitral awards Justice Mustill presented the following rules of *lex mercatoria*:

(2000); *The UNIDROIT Principles and Transnational Law*. A contrary view was presented by De Ly, F. (1992), *International Business Law and Lex Mercatoria*, pp. 8-20; Mustill, M. (1987), *The new lex mercatoria: the first twenty-five years, in Liber amicorum for Lord Wilberforce*.

[634] E.g., De Ly, F. (2001), *Choice of law clauses, Unidroit Principles of International Commercial Contracts and Art. 3 Rome Convention, Lex mercatoria before domestic courts or arbitration privilege?*; De Ly, F. (2000), *Emerging new perspectives regarding lex mercatoria in an era of increasing globalization*; De Ly, F. (2001), *Lex mercatoria (New Law Merchant): Globalization and international self-regulation*; De Ly, F. (1999), *National Report: The Netherlands: An Interim Report regarding the Application of the Unidroit Principles of International Commercial Contracts in The Netherlands*; Goldman, B. (1964), *Frontières du droit et lex mercatoria*; Goldman, B. (1982), *La nouvelle réglementation française de l'arbitrage international*; Goldman, B. (1983), *Lex Mercatoria*; Goode, R. (1997), *Usage and its reception in transnational commercial law*; Lando, O. (1990), *European Contract Law*; Lowenfeld, A.F. (1998), *Lex Mercatoria: An Arbitrator's View*. For critical views see Badinter, R. (December 1995), *Role of the International Lawyer*; De Ly, F. (1992), *International Business Law and Lex Mercatoria*; Lagarde, P. (1983), *Approche critique de la lex mercatoria*; Mustill, M. (2001), *The Historic Evolution of the Lex Mercatoria Doctrine*; Mustill, M. (1987), *The new lex mercatoria: the first twenty-five years, in Liber amicorum for Lord Wilberforce*.

[635] Lando, O. (1985), *The Lex Mercatoria in International Commercial Arbitration*, pp. 747-748.

[636] Ibid., p. 752.

[637] Lando enlists more sources of *lex mercatoria* including international public law. See ibid.

'1. A general principle that contracts should *prima facie* be enforced according to their terms: *pacta sunt servanda*. (...)
2. The first general principle is qualified at least in respect of certain long term contracts, by an exception akin to *rebus sic stantibus*. (...)
3. The first general principle may also be subject to the concept of *abus de droit*, and to a rule that unfair and unconscionable contracts and clauses should not be enforced.
4. There may be a doctrine of *culpa in contrahendo*.
5. A contract should be performed in good faith.
6. A contract obtained by bribes or other dishonest means is void, or at least unenforceable. So too if the contract creates a fictitious transaction designed to achieve an illegal object.
7. A State entity cannot be permitted to evade the enforcement of its obligations by denying its own capacity to make a binding agreement to arbitrate, or by asserting that the agreement is unenforceable for want of procedural formalities to which the entity is subject.
8. The controlling interest of a group of companies is regarded as contracting on behalf of all members of the group, at least so far as concerns an agreement to arbitrate.
9. If unforeseen difficulties intervene in the performance of a contract, the parties should negotiate in good faith to overcome them, even if the contract contains no revision clause.
10. 'Gold clause' agreements are valid and enforceable. Perhaps in some cases either a gold clause or a 'hardship' revision clause may be implied.
11. One party is entitled to treat itself as discharged from its obligations if the other has committed a breach, but only if the breach is substantial.
12. No party can be allowed by its own act to bring about a non-performance on a condition precedent to its own obligation.
13. A tribunal is not bound by the characterisation of the contract ascribed to it by the parties.
14. Damages for breach of contract are limited to the foreseeable consequences of the breach.
15. A party which has suffered a breach of contract must take reasonable steps to mitigate its loss.
16. Damages for non-delivery are calculated by reference to the market price of the goods and the price at which the buyer has purchased equivalent goods in replacement.
17. A party must act promptly to enforce its rights, on pain of losing them by waiver. This may be an instance of a more general rule, that each party must act in a diligent and practical manner to safeguard its own interests.
18. A debtor may in certain circumstances set off his own cross-claims to extinguish or diminish his liability to the creditor.
19. Contracts should be construed according to the principle *ut res magis valeat quam pereat*.
20. Failure by one party to respond to a letter written to it by the other is regarded as evidence of assent to its terms.'[638]

---

[638] Mustill, M. (1987), *The new lex mercatoria: the first twenty-five years, in Liber amicorum for Lord Wilberforce*, pp. 174-177.

The proposed rules of *lex mercatoria* could also be regarded as general principles of law or general principles of contract law. Some of them have a very general character and are known to virtually all legal systems e.g. *pacta sunt servanda.* Most of them are to be found in the 2004 UNIDROIT Principles[639] as well as Lando Principles. The distinguishing feature of these norms is that they are transnational in nature – thus do not belong to national or international legal systems. As Goldman put it:

> 'For it is obvious that the specific problems of transnational commercial custom – is it a rule of law? does it constitute a transnational legal order, distinct from national legal systems as well as from the international legal order sensu stricto? – do not arise with respect to rules of inter-State or State origin. No one contests that the latter are rules of law, nor that they are part of the legal order of the States having adopted them. (…) The criterion for determining the ambit of lex mercatoria (…) does not solely reside in the object of its constituent elements, but also in its origin and its customary, and thus spontaneous, nature.'[640]

It seems however that these days it is not the mercantile community that is leading the development of the New Law Merchant. Instead, it seems that it is actually the legal community that has taken the lead in this respect. As Badinter described it:

> 'globalisation has also led lawyers, in particular those working with international matters, patiently to elaborate, over the years, a veritable *jus communis* of international business, a common business international law of which lawyers are both the practitioners and the authors.'[641]

In this regard, the most important private restatement of modern commercial law is the second edition of UNIDROIT Principles of International Commercial Contracts (UNIDROIT Principles).[642] The Principles are hoped to become a 'world code of international trade law'.[643] It is an open-ended set of principles intended to integrate the most important norms relating to international commercial transactions.[644]

---

[639] UNIDROIT (2004), *UNIDROIT Principles of International Commercial Contracts 2004.*

[640] Goldman, B. (1983), *Lex Mercatoria*, p. 4.

[641] Badinter, R. (December 1995), *Role of the International Lawyer*, p. 506.

[642] UNIDROIT (2004), *UNIDROIT Principles of International Commercial Contracts 2004.* It replaced the 1994 edition. See Chapter IV for more details.

[643] See, for example, Bonell, M.J. (2001), *Do We Need a Global Commercial Code?*, referring to Schmitthoff. See also, e.g., Baron, G., *Do the UNIDROIT Principles of International Commercial Contracts form a new lex mercatoria?*; Bonell, M.J. (1998), *UNIDROIT Principles and the Lex Mercatoria*; Bonell, M.J. (2000), *The UNIDROIT Principles and Transnational Law*; Bonell, M.J. (2000), *The UNIDROIT Principles in practice – the experience of the first two years*; Bonell, M.J., *The UNIDROIT Principles Of International Commercial Contracts: Nature, Purposes And First Experiences In Practice.*

[644] Ibid.

The second edition of Principles recognises the importance of electronic technologies. For instance, the definition of writing is flexible enough to include electronic communication thus explicitly giving recognition the principle of functional equivalence.[645] Furthermore, Article 2.1 which defines the manner of contract formation in terms of the acceptance of the offer or parties conduct sufficient to show the agreement, includes automated contracting.[646] The UNIDROIT Principles are important achievement on the way to codify international commercial law, but their status is yet to be confirmed.[647] One should also mention the Principles of European Commercial Law (PECL)[648] as similar to initiative but limited to the European Union.

(b) Problems with the definition of commercial custom

According to Schmitthoff, international trade law is derived from two sources: international legislation and international custom. Describing international commercial custom, he stated:

> 'International custom consists of commercial practices, usages or standards, which are so widely used that businessmen engaged in international trade expect their contracting parties to conform with them and which are formulated by international agencies, such as International Chamber of Commerce, or United Nations Economic Commission for Europe, or international trade associations.'[649]

There are three striking elements in this definition of international commercial custom. First, as in the previous definition, custom does not need to have a long tradition in order to be binding. Second, commercial practice needs to be widely used and accepted as a binding norm. Finally, formulation of custom by various international trade associations seems to be a necessary condition of a successful formulation of custom.

Goode argues that *lex mercatoria* consists of uncodified customary commercial law, customary rules of evidence and procedure and general principles of commercial law, including international public policy.[650] He defined unwritten trade usage as:

---

645 See, for example, comment 4 to Art. 1.11 in UNIDROIT (2004), *UNIDROIT Principles of International Commercial Contracts 2004*. For more information see section 3.2 in Chapter IV.

646 See comment 3 to Art. 2.1 in ibid.

647 See, for example, Baron, G., *Do the UNIDROIT Principles of International Commercial Contracts form a new lex mercatoria?*

648 Commission on European contract law (1998), *The Principles of European Contract Law – completed and revised version.*

649 Schmitthoff, C.M. (1988), *Clive M. Schmitthoff's Selected Essays on International Trade Law*, pp. 148-149.

650 Goode, R. (1997), *Usage and its reception in transnational commercial law*, p. 1.

> 'a practice or pattern of behaviour among merchants established by repetition which has in some degree acquired normative force.'[651]

This definition accentuates the role of repetitive practice. However, it requires a practice to acquire some degree of normative force – a concept that is not very clear. This definition seems to be a compromise between two theories of unwritten trade usage. One sees trade usage as a particular form of international customary law, which will be analysed in the next chapter. The other, equates it with an implied term into a contract. This approach was adopted in the Vienna Sales Convention,[652] which supplements existing trade usages with a set of directly applicable rules.[653]

Bonell argues that the distinction between custom and usage is irrelevant and defined it as:

> 'any practice or line of conduct regularly observed within a particular trade sector or at a particular market place, irrespective of whether, according to some national law, it would fall within one or the other of the categories mentioned above.'[654]

His definition stresses the necessity of regularly observed conduct without requiring it to be long-standing, confirmed by the court or some legal authorities or accepted as a binding norm. Moreover, this definition does not deal with global customs as it is limited to usages in particular trade sectors or market places. Furthermore, he equated the term usage with custom. In this respect it is important to mention a significant problem created by lawyers who distinguish between custom and usage. Honnold even argued that CISG 'trade usages' are different from 'usage' or 'custom' because the latter one must be long established or even ancient.[655] Some regarded the 'custom' as the source of law and 'usage' as a factual element, which needs to be known to the parties or expressly referred to in the agreement in order to be binding.[656] The problem is to a large degree a consequence of an abandonment of the term 'custom' and replacement of it with 'usage' by the influential French jurisprudence after the French Revolution because of programmatic destruction of anything to do with the pre-revolutionary regime.[657] However no satisfactory dividing line had been drawn between the two allegedly different concepts. As a result, following Bonell's suggestion, the distinction between custom and usage will be abandoned in this study.

---

651 Ibid.

652 Ibid.

653 See, for example, Audit, B. (1998), *The Vienna Sales Convention and Lex Mercatoria*.

654 Bianca, C.M. and Bonell, M.J. (1987), *Commentary on the International Sales Law: The 1980 Vienna Sales Convention*, p. 111.

655 Honnold, J.O. (1982), *Uniform Law for International Sales under the 1980 United Nations Convention*, pp. 146-147.

656 De Ly, F. (1992), *International Business Law and Lex Mercatoria*.

657 See Gilissen, J. (1982), *La coutume*, p. 24.

Unfortunately, no international trade law convention or authoritative private compilation of transnational commercial principles has explicitly defined what usage or custom is. The most important commercial law treaty is 1980 Vienna Convention on Contracts for the International Sale of Goods (CISG)[658] and it does not contain such definition. [659] Neither UNIDROIT Principles nor PECL define usage or deal with the question of proof or validity of a usage. These developments only lay down criteria for the incorporation of trade usages into international contracts.

All the above-mentioned developments include the same provision describing the effects of express reference to customary practices in the agreement and past dealings between the individual parties:

> 'The parties are bound by any usage to which they have agreed and by any practices which they have established between themselves.'[660]

This paragraph deals with two different situations. In the first case, the custom does not have to fulfil any requirements, not even that of being reasonable. Parties may refer to a local, particular or general custom or set of customary principles. In practice, this usually means a reference to trade terms like F.O.B. in ICC's INCOTERMS.[661] As soon as it is agreed to in the contract, it automatically binds the parties. In the second case, they are bound by any practices which they have established between themselves. Here, a course of dealings between parties will bind them – a situation which might be considered as an extreme instance of local custom.

However, when it comes to the description of usage that has not been mentioned in the contract or one which is not related to parties past dealings, the formulations are different. The Vienna Convention which relates to non-domestic international transactions in the offline world stated in Article 9 (2) that:

> '(2) The parties are considered, unless otherwise agreed, to have impliedly made applicable to their contract or its formation a usage of which the parties knew or ought to have known and which in international trade is widely known to, and regularly observed by, parties to contracts of the type involved in the particular trade concerned.'[662]

---

[658] UNCITRAL (1980), *United Nations Convention on Contracts for the International Sale of Goods*.

[659] See, for example, Bianca, C.M. and Bonell, M.J. (1987), *Commentary on the International Sales Law: The 1980 Vienna Sales Convention*, pp. 110-111.

[660] See Art. 9(1) in UNCITRAL (1980), *United Nations Convention on Contracts for the International Sale of Goods*; Art. 1.9 in UNIDROIT (2004), *UNIDROIT Principles of International Commercial Contracts 2004* and Art. 1:105 in Commission on European contract law (1998), *The Principles of European Contract Law – completed and revised version*.

[661] Honnold, J.O. (1982), *Uniform Law for International Sales under the 1980 United Nations Convention*, pp. 145-146.

[662] UNCITRAL (1980), *United Nations Convention on Contracts for the International Sale of Goods*. See also Art. 8 on interpretation of contracts in the light of customary practices.

According to this paragraph, parties will be presumed to have impliedly made applicable to the contract or its formation a usage that must meet three criteria. Firstly, it must be known to the parties or at least it ought to be known to them. Secondly, it must be widely known in the international trade to parties to contracts of the type involved in the particular trade concerned. Thirdly, it must be regularly observed, by parties to contracts of the type involved in the particular trade concerned. The first two conditions require the knowledge of custom among the parties (either express or implied) and the industry in which the parties operate. The second condition related to the actual observance of a given practice in the industry concerned. This formulation seems to limit the scope of commercial customs to industry wide customs. The question of admissibility of local customs is questionable.[663]

This provision generated a considerable debate concerning the scope of usages.[664] To Farnsworth, developed nations liked usages (such as usages in the grain trade in London) because they were creating them, whereas developing and socialist countries felt susceptible to them.[665] The final version was a compromise.[666] Bonell argued that the first requirement was intended to reflect the parties intentions, but it may only be said so if they knew of the usage.[667] If they did not know, 'it is the law itself which confers the binding force on the usage' which makes the doctrine of implied terms a legal fiction.[668] The second requirement is an objective one.[669] Usage must be regularly observed within the particular trade (e.g., wheat trade) and for the contracts of the type involved (e.g., trade with soft wheat and hard wheat).[670] It must also be widely known in international trade. The purpose of this requirement was to avoid domestic usages, to which Convention gave only 'very limited recognition'.[671] Also, the Article is silent on how 'ancient' the usage should be. Honnold argued that usage must be established on an objective basis and it does not have to be 'long standing'.[672]

On the other hand, the 2004 UNIDROIT Principles in Article 1.9(2) stated:

---

663 Honnold, J.O. (1982), *Uniform Law for International Sales under the 1980 United Nations Convention*, p. 148. But see also Berman, H. and Kaufman, C. (1978), *The law of international commercial transactions (lex mercatoria)*. Bonell also speaks of limited recognition of local usages in the Convention. Bianca, C.M. and Bonell, M.J. (1987), *Commentary on the International Sales Law: The 1980 Vienna Sales Convention*, p. 109.

664 Farnsworth, A.E. (1979), *Developing International Trade Law*, pp. 465-466.

665 Ibid. See also Bianca, C.M. and Bonell, M.J. (1987), *Commentary on the International Sales Law: The 1980 Vienna Sales Convention*, p. 105.

666 See, for example, Bianca, C.M. and Bonell, M.J. (1987), *Commentary on the International Sales Law: The 1980 Vienna Sales Convention*, p. 110.

667 Ibid., p. 108.

668 Ibid.

669 Ibid.

670 Ibid., pp. 108-109.

671 Ibid., p. 109.

672 Honnold, J.O. (1982), *Uniform Law for International Sales under the 1980 United Nations Convention*, p. 148.

> 'The parties are bound by a usage that is widely known to and regularly observed in international trade by parties in the particular trade concerned except where the application of such a usage would be unreasonable.'[673]

Commercial custom can bind parties to a contract given that it is widely known and regularly observed by a majority of traders in the particular industry. However, contrary to CISG, it does not have to be known to the parties, nor parties 'ought to have known it'. On the other hand, it may not be applied, if it would be unreasonable in a given circumstances. This is a new requirement that has not been mentioned in CISG formulation. These requirements apply to usages of international, national or local scope if used in international trade. However, as it was the case in CISG formulation, local usages can be applied only exceptionally.[674] Both in case of Vienna Convention and UNIDROIT Principles, the commercial customs prevail over Convention and Principles respectively.[675]

In summary, customary practices play a very important role in international trade. Commercial custom also plays the central role in the revived Law Merchant doctrine. The new *lex mercatoria* has not yet been widely recognised as being independent of national legal systems but such recognition seems to be only a matter of time. However, none of the important written sources of transnational commercial law define it or discuss a methodology of proving it. In consequence, the doctrine of *lex mercatoria* has not developed an explicit theory of commercial custom. The material presented above, suggests only that commercial custom is based on the actual and widespread observance of practice and is confined to particular trade sectors. Furthermore, there seems to be no requirement of acceptance of practice as law. These findings are important for the development of the theory of Internet commerce custom.

4.2 Custom in international public law

Custom has been playing a critical role in international public law, which governs the inter-state relations. Article 38 of the Statute of International Court of Justice lists international custom as a source of international law.[676] Its crucial role in international public law of the sea,[677] law of outer space,[678] law of the treaties,[679] law of

---

673 UNIDROIT (2004), *UNIDROIT Principles of International Commercial Contracts 2004*.

674 See Comment to Art. 1.9 in ibid. and Art. 1.8 in UNIDROIT (1994), *UNIDROIT Principles of International Commercial Contracts*.

675 See Comment to Art. 9 in Bianca, C.M. and Bonell, M.J. (1987), *Commentary on the International Sales Law: The 1980 Vienna Sales Convention*, p. 104. See also Comment 6 to Art. 1.9 in UNIDROIT (2004), *UNIDROIT Principles of International Commercial Contracts 2004*.

676 United Nations Conference on International Organization at San Francisco (26 June 1945), *Statute of the International Court of Justice*.

677 See, for example, Slouka, Z.J. (1969), *International custom and the continental shelf. A study in the dynamics of customary rules of international law*.

678 See, for example, Cheng, B. (1965), *United Nations Resolutions on Outer Space: 'Instant' International Customary law?*

diplomatic and consular relationships,[680] law of human rights[681] or environmental law[682] has been expressed very often in the literature[683] and in judgments of the International Court of Justice.[684]

The concept of international custom has also been very well researched by international jurisprudence that developed very interesting theories of international custom. These analyses of custom in a transnational context are arguably the best available and for that reason the whole of the next chapter will be devoted to the discussion of this concept.

5. The Potential Role of Custom on the Internet

Custom, understood as a source of behavioural norms, has enormous potential in providing knowledge about widespread online practices. This knowledge can then be used to solve problems arising out of the lack of written Internet law. The sections below present the potential role of Internet commerce customary practices from two angles. First, the potential role of custom as a source of Internet law will be discussed. Then, the role of custom in providing knowledge about the Internet environment will be outlined.

5.1 Custom as a source of Internet commerce law

The potentially crucial role of custom as a source of law on an international level would be a result of certain essential features of transnational regimes such as the lack of central governance and, relative to modern legislations, underdevelopment. The Internet, with its bottom-up governance and, at this stage, lack of globally binding written laws is an example of such an environment. In consequence, custom as a source of norms could play a similarly important role on the Internet, but this role has not been realised yet.

Custom may turn out to be the most important source of Internet commerce law because, as history shows, it can bind all persons. Neither an agreement, an interna-

679 See, for example, Kontou, N. (1994), *The Termination and Revision of Treaties in the Light of New Customary International Law*; Villiger, M.E. (1997), *Customary International Law and Treaties. A Manual on the Theory and Practice of the Interrelation of Sources*.

680 See, for example, Briggs, H.W. (October 1951), *The Colombian-Peruvian Asylum* case *and Proof of Customary International Law*.

681 See, for example, Meron, T. (April 1996), *The continuing role of custom in the formation of international humanitarian law*; Simma, B. and Alston, P. (1992), *The Sources of Human Rights Law: Custom, Jus Cogens, and General Principles*.

682 See, for example, Brownlie, I. (1973), *A Survey of International Customary Rules of Environmental Protection*; Palmer, G. (April 1992), *New Ways To Make International Environmental Law*.

683 See, for example, Akehurst, M. (1974-1975), *Custom as a Source of International Law*; D'Amato, A.A. (1969), *The concept of custom in international law*; Danilenko, G.M. (1983), *Law-Making in the International Community*.

684 See Chapter VI.

tional convention nor a statute dealing with the Internet is likely to have such a scope of application. Furthermore, custom petrifies and rises to the level of law, commonly recognised and observed practices. In a fast changing digital world, its ability and flexibility in recognising globally binding e-commerce practices may turn out to be the best if not the only regulatory option available. At the same time, the concept of custom does not contradict other regulatory developments at national and international level, because it can be assumed that a customary norm will be overruled by any contrary treaty, statute, or agreement.

The possible legislative role of a custom appears to be an interesting solution to the lack of written Internet law. Drawing lessons from history, in the next phase of the development of international electronic commerce law, some explicit conventional regulations will codify Internet customs and likely add some new rules. However, customary norms are continuously changing norms and it is crucial to monitor constantly adherence to them. Any codification can only be a snapshot of customary practices within a given timeframe and as a result can be overturned by the proof of subsequent contrary custom.

However, the legal role of a custom is much broader than an interim regulation of some of the aspects of the international electronic commerce. Custom can be viewed as a serious alternative to the idea of harmonisation of Internet law and as a complement to the result of this process. Custom can also widen the scope of applicability of international conventions and national regulations. Further, its capability of modifying existing or future concurrent sources of e-commerce law like conventions, domestic statutes or contracts should be stressed. In particular, custom can abolish written laws that were not adhered to due to, e.g., technological change (*desuetude*).[685] Custom can modify both the way agreements come into being as well as content of contracts. Custom continues to play an important role in interpreting contract clauses. In addition, custom will remain the best filler of gaps left by formal e-commerce-related legislatorial works. Finally, custom can be viewed as a source of already enforced legal norms, which enables effective functioning of such legal system.

In consequence, Internet custom can give national and international judges, and especially national and international arbitrators, a very rich and powerful source of transnational legal norms that could be used in adjudicating cyberspace-related disputes. This source of law may turn out to be of special importance to future online arbitration and online dispute resolution systems as it can help them in creating a global and unified body of Internet case law that, among other things, overcomes traditional problems of conflicts of national laws.

Some authors have already suggested that custom is used on the Internet in the form of the Netiquette,[686] which is a list of norms of behaviour on the Internet.

---

[685] See Glossary.

[686] See Netiquette Guidelines in Hambridge, S. (October 1995), *RFC 1855 Netiquette Guidelines (Also FYI0028) (Status: INFORMATIONAL)* . See also, e.g., Reidenberg, J. R. (Summer 1996), *Gov-*

Status of the Netiquette as a basis for adjudication of disputes has also been confirmed in judicial proceedings *Christophe G.* v. *Société France Télécom Interactive, S.A.*, where a French Tribunal de Grande Instance de Rochefort sur Mer recognised Netiquette as a binding set of Internet customary norms, which prohibit among other things, the practice of spamming.[687] However, one should take these claims with a great degree of caution. First, Netiquette is not a codification of Internet customs, but a list of supposedly good Internet practices. The core rules of Netiquette are very general and resemble more moral or ethical codes, rather than codification of Internet customs. Furthermore, the alleged customary character of the Netiquette has not been confirmed by research studying the level of adherence to its precepts. As of today, one has no basis for treatment of Netiquette as a record of Internet customs.

5.2 **Custom as a source of knowledge about the Internet**

The study of custom can play a fundamental role in the process of learning about the Internet and electronic commerce. Being the empirical source of behavioural norms, it allows the Internet community to learn about past and current common online practices. This knowledge could then inspire the process of drafting written sources of law and thus greatly contribute to their quality. Without a very good knowledge and understanding of current Internet practices, any attempts to regulate the Internet by virtue of abstract statutes or treaties may only produce more harm than good.

Unfortunately, current legislative practices do not recognise the need for analysis and learning about the Internet environment. Rather, legislators in their attachment to the 'rational' creation of law by means of statutes and conventions, search for inspiration almost exclusively in logical deductions. This book calls for a rapid change of attitude in the process leading to the development of norms that are supposed to regulate the Internet.

But knowledge of customary practices can also help IT and online business communities in learning about what is the most common way of online trading these days. This knowledge might turn out to be of special importance to start-up ventures as well as to small-to-medium enterprises that often do not have enough resources to research current widespread practices. Finally, the whole Internet community can benefit from the knowledge of common practices of not only traders but also non-commercial ventures and adopt what is considered by the majority as the most efficient way of organising online distribution of information.

---

erning Networks and Rule-making in Cyberspace. The Randolph W. Thrower Symposium. Legal Issues in Cyberspace: Hazards on the Information Superhighway, p. 920. For opposite view treating Netiquette as rules of online courtesy see Halpern, M. and Mehrotra, A.K. (Fall 2000), *From International Treaties To Internet Norms:The Evolution Of International Trademark Disputes In The Internet Age*, p. 545.

[687] *Christophe G.* v. *Société France Télécom Interactive, S.A.* [28.02.2001] JGT: 64/2001, RG: 00/106.

6. Conclusion

Custom is the foundation of all legal systems on Earth. Humans from prehistoric times built whole societies by following customary practices of their fellow people. The role of custom was very important in the early times of the development of modern civil law and common law traditions in the West. However, with the process of its redaction and subsequent emergence of statute, its role has been diminished in Europe and in such a form exported to other parts of the world through the process of colonisation. Nevertheless, Roman lawyers have identified several important aspects of custom, although no explicit theory has been constructed. These constructs will be discussed in the context of proposed concept of electronic commerce custom.

The role of custom, though minimised in Western legal tradition continues to be important in other parts of the world. Both religion based systems of Islam and Hinduism as well as Far East legal systems value the idea of repetitive practice of other people as it provides a very reliable guideline in human life. With the ongoing penetration of Western legal thought in some of these traditions, the official role of custom may diminish with time. Even indigenous societies will probably be affected by this process, but the role of custom as a tool of regulating behaviour will remain profound for a long time. This in turn, allows concluding that custom as a source of binding norms is known to all cultures and hence, is the best candidate for a source of cross-cultural Internet and electronic commerce law.

However, customary practices play a very important role in international legal regimes. Both international law and international commercial law were built upon customs of states and merchants respectively. The importance of custom in regulating relations between states and merchants is clearly visible in history. Modern international legal regimes have important historical predecessors in the Roman *ius gentium* and the medieval Law Merchant. Custom continues to play a very important role in these regimes by being officially recognised as the source of international law. This is a very important finding and implications of it will be further explored in the context of global electronic commerce. However, the New Law Merchant has not proposed an explicit theory of commercial custom and for this reason a search for a better model in international public law will follow.

This leads to the conclusion that custom could play a fundamental role in settling Internet disputes. It is a source of globally binding norms that emanate from constantly changing practices thus providing the best reflection of the current state of the Internet and electronic commerce. History shows that merchants relied on it in settling their disputes as it always reflected the expectations of the majority of merchants as to their rights and obligations. Internet customary norms could complement norms embodied in contracts or norms contained in international or domestic written laws. They could interpret unclear provisions of written laws and abolish ones that are obsolete.

In summary, this chapter has shown the importance of custom as a source of law in time and space. This knowledge will be useful in fully appreciating the proposed concept of customary practices as a prospective fundament of the global electronic commerce law because almost every society built their legal system upon custom or relied upon it to some extent. Especially, merchants were and continue to be aware of the significance of customs in international commerce. This gives the basis to conclude that history provides the evidence for the potential of custom in regulating electronic commerce and solving Internet commerce disputes.

Chapter VI
INTERNATIONAL CUSTOM AND ITS PROOF

The previous chapter discussed the historical and contemporary role of custom in national and international legal regimes and outlined the potential of custom in regulating the Internet. This chapter will discuss the concept of international custom and its proof in order to provide a starting point for the discussion of Internet custom in the next chapter. Subsequently, the requirements for custom identified in this part of the book will be analysed from the perspective of its practicality in borderless electronic commerce.

1. Introduction

The aim of this chapter is to characterise the concept of custom in the international law context as well as to outline the methodology of evidencing it in order to provide a basis for the analysis of the Internet custom in the subsequent chapters. The approach, to define Internet custom from the perspective of requirements of international custom, is hoped to be more acceptable to various cultures and legal traditions using the Internet for a number of reasons.

Firstly, international law jurisprudence has analysed the concept of custom much more deeply than municipal or particularly, Law Merchant doctrine. As was argued in the last chapter, Law Merchant doctrine is a natural predecessor of transnational electronic commerce law, but the characteristics of mercantile custom has not been the main focus of the doctrine. Goode suggested that *lex mercatoria* doctrine has developed the concept of custom in total isolation from international public law,[688] but it has focused more on the general features of the Law Merchant, rather than on the detailed analysis of the requirements of custom as a source of law. In particular, no definition of custom or commercial usage has been included in any commercial treaties or unofficial restatements. For this reason, the notion of international custom is a better candidate for analysing the phenomenon of custom on the Internet.

Secondly, international public law is the only international legal regime that is unquestionably recognised by the international community as being independent from national legal systems. As a result, international custom is a source of law independent of national legislatures. The modern Law Merchant has so far not gained

[688] Goode, R. (1997), *Usage and its reception in transnational commercial law*, p. 1.

such a widespread recognition,[689] although it is firmly approaching in this direction.[690]

Thirdly, international custom, as the name suggests, has an international character. Its law-making power is accepted by 192 countries[691] that are members of the United Nations. In this sense, international custom as a source of law has a universal scope of application. It is recognised by all countries on the globe despite diverse cultures and legal traditions, although not all of them have had an opportunity to participate in the development of its theory or its norms.

Fourthly, international custom is, next to a treaty, a very important source of international public law. In fact, numerous authors consider it to be the most fundamental source of international public law.[692] Furthermore, international custom has been referred to in a number of cases before the International Court of Justice and generated a very rich literature.

Finally, international customary and treaty law define relations between independent states.[693] Similarly to the Internet, there is no central authority above the states although the international community has developed institutional and judicial infrastructure[694] to streamline international co-operation. In summary, international customary law operates in a framework that is most similar to the supra-national and decentralised character of the Internet.

This chapter has been arranged as a presentation of issues associated with this source of law. The most important one is the necessity of two elements: the element of practice and the subjective element of feeling bound by it. The discussion will centre on these two notions, as they constitute the most fundamental elements of the concept of international custom. This chapter will analyse the views of jurisprudence and the selected International Court of Justice (ICJ) case law on the matter. However, as will be shown, it is mainly the doctrine of international law that has developed the concept of international custom during the last four hundreds years or so. The International Court of Justice did not exist prior to the twentieth century and in consequence, its understanding of custom has been based on earlier doctrinal developments. On the other hand, the ICJ has enriched the theoretical developments and applied them in practice. The importance of the ICJ case law lies especially in the ways the ICJ proved the existence of international custom. It is primarily from this perspective that the judgments of this Court will be examined.

---

[689] See for example, De Ly, F. (1992), *International Business Law and Lex Mercatoria.*

[690] E.g., UNIDROIT (2004) *UNIDROIT Principles of International Commercial Contracts 2004*; Bonell, M.J. (2001), *Do We Need a Global Commercial Code?*

[691] The last country that joined United Nations was Montenegro on 28 June 2006. See http://www.un.org/Overview/growth.htm, last access: 12/12/2006.

[692] See for example, Stern, B. (2001), *Custom at the heart of international law (trans. M. Byers, A. Denise)*, p. 89.

[693] See Art. 2.1 in United Nations Conference on International Organization at San Francisco (26 June 1945), *Charter of the United Nations*.

[694] Ibid., see Art. 7. See Glossary.

The presentation has also some limitations. The issue of custom formation, enforcement as well as the philosophical justification for a binding force of custom will not be the main focus of this chapter. Also, the relation of custom to treaty and other sources of international law will be largely ignored. Finally, the inter-relation between international customary law and national legal systems will be excluded from the scope of this chapter.

The following sections will discuss the most important issues surrounding the concept of international custom in greater detail. First, the role of international custom will be outlined followed by the outline of issues surrounding its definition. Secondly, the constitutive elements of custom will be studied. The characteristics of practice will then be examined, followed by the problems associated with the subjective element of custom. Thirdly, the issue of judicial confirmation of custom will be outlined. Finally, practical problems associated with evidencing international custom will be studied.

2. The Role of Custom in International Law

Custom is a fundamental source[695] of international law.[696] As Westlake put it, in the beginning of the twentieth century,

> 'Custom and reason are the two sources of international law.'[697]

The most profound norms of international law of peace and war such as the freedom of the seas,[698] air[699] and cosmos,[700] principles relating to treaties,[701] status of diplomats and consuls[702] and recently humanitarian norms particularly in non-in-

---

[695] The word source has many potential meanings and some authors suggested abandoning it. See for example, Kelsen, H. (1966), *Principles of International Law*, pp. 437-438. The expression custom as a source of law will nevertheless be used in this study as an equivalent of the expression custom as the law creating fact.

[696] See also, e.g., Bourquin, M. (1931), *Règles Générales du Droit de la Paix*, p. 61; Fauchille, P. (1922), *Traité de Droit International Public*, p. 41; Kunz, J.L. (October 1953), *The nature of customary international law*, p. 663; Oppenheim, L. (1955), *International Law: A Treatise*, pp. 25-26; Stern, B. (2001), *Custom at the heart of international law (trans. M. Byers, A. Denise)*, p. 89; Williams, J.F.S. (1939), *Aspects of Modern International Law: An Essay*, p. 41.

[697] Westlake, J. (1910), *International Law*, p. 14.

[698] See for example, Slouka, Z.J. (1969), *International custom and the continental shelf. A study in the dynamics of customary rules of international law*.

[699] See for example, Kunz, J.L. (October 1953), *The nature of customary international law*, p. 666.

[700] See for example, Cheng, B. (1965), *United Nations Resolutions on Outer Space: 'Instant' International Customary law?*

[701] See for example, Kontou, N. (1994), *The Termination and Revision of Treaties in the Light of New Customary International Law*; Villiger, M.E. (1997), *Customary International Law and Treaties. A Manual on the Theory and Practice of the Interrelation of Sources*.

[702] See for example, Briggs, H.W. (October 1951), *The Colombian-Peruvian Asylum* case *and Proof of Customary International Law*; Nussbaum, A. (1954), *A concise history of the law of nations*.

ternational armed conflicts[703] originated from customary practice of states. Similarly, the principle of *pacta sunt servanda* requiring contractual promises to be upheld or the rule that harm only signatories, can actually give rise to new international customs, therefore binding states that are not parties to a treaty. As the Vienna Convention on the Law of Treaties stipulates in Article 38:

> 'Nothing (...) precludes a rule set forth in a treaty from becoming binding upon a third State as a customary rule of international law, recognized as such.'[704]

Notwithstanding the progressive codification of international customary law, especially in the form of multilateral international treaties, it remains the only source of generally binding international law.

Despite its profound importance in international relations, the characteristic of international custom remains the subject of very hot scholarly and juridical debate. There is a great deal of uncertainty as to what constitutes custom, how it is formed and how to evidence it. Tunkin made the observation:

> 'The whole concept of international law depends upon whether this problem is solved one way or another.'[705]

Unfortunately, the doctrine and ICJ decisions are divided on virtually all the issues concerning this concept. This has led some of the authors to question the very existence, necessity or utility of custom as a source of law.[706] Despite these difficulties, several elements of custom have been identified and they form a useful starting point to the discussion of this phenomenon.

3. The Definition of International Custom

Custom in modern international law is invariably defined with reference to the Statute of the International Court of Justice, itself an integral part of the Charter of the United Nations.[707] Article 38 of the Statute states that:

---

[703] See in particular the unique in history empirical study of international humanitarian customary law in 3 volumes: Henckaerts, J.-M. and Doswald-Beck, L. (2005), *Customary International Humanitarian Law, 2 volumes, Volume I. Rules, Volume II. Practice (2 Parts)*. See also Henckaerts, J.-M. (March 2005), *Study on customary international humanitarian law: A contribution to the understanding and respect for the rule of law in armed conflict*.

[704] International Law Commission (22 May 1969), *Vienna Convention on the Law of Treaties*.

[705] Tunkin, G.I. (1961), *Remarks On the Juridical Nature of Customary Norms of International Law*, p. 419.

[706] See for example, Kelly, P. (Winter 2000), *The twilight of customary international law*; van Hoof, G.J.H. (1983), *Rethinking the sources of international law*, p. 113.

[707] United Nations Conference on International Organization at San Francisco (26 June 1945), *Charter of the United Nations*.

> 'The Court, whose function is to decide in accordance with international law such disputes as are submitted to it, shall apply: (…) international custom as evidence of general practice accepted as law.'[708]

The definition distinguishes two elements of custom: material element of general practice and the subjective element of its acceptance as law and remains the cornerstone of numerous other definitions proposed in the literature.[709]

Many authors have noticed the poor quality of Article 38's definition of international custom and have criticised it on a number of grounds.[710] First, it is illogical to state that custom is evidence of general practice, as in fact, only the opposite can be true, namely that only general practice can serve as the evidence of custom.[711] Second, the Court cannot apply a custom, but only customary law.[712] In addition, the definition requires practice to be general and eliminates the so-called local or particular practices that are of importance in international law.[713] It should be reminded that the customs of local scope were the essential feature of past European law, before the systems of statutory laws emerged.[714] Furthermore, international custom is not required to be old, moral or reasonable, consistent or universally accepted. The issue of objections to the practice and the role of the judiciary in recognising the validity of custom have also not been dealt with.

The International Court of Justice has referred to the international custom in numerous judgments.[715] For instance, in the 1969 *North Sea Continental Shelf* case the Court explained:

---

[708] See Art. 38 para. 1(b) in United Nations Conference on International Organization at San Francisco (26 June 1945), *Statute of the International Court of Justice*. A similar definition was included in the Statute of the Permanent Court of Justice, which was the predecessor of the International Court of Justice in the inter-war period. Both Courts will be referred to as the World Court.

[709] See for example, Brownlie, I. (1990), *Principles of public international law*, pp. 4-11; Hudson, M.O. (3 March 1950), *Article 24 of the Statute of the International Law Commission. Working Paper. Document A/CN.4/16*, p. 26; Judge de Castro (1974), *Separate opinion of Judge de Castro on Fisheries Jurisdiction* case, p. 89.

[710] See for example, Wolfke, K. (1993), *Custom in Present International Law*, pp. 1-8 and the literature cited there. See also, e.g., de Visscher, C. (1925), *La codification du droit international*, p. 352; Sőrensen, M. (1960), *Principes de droit international public: Cours général*, pp. 35-36, citing Kosters, Cheng, B. (1965), *United Nations Resolutions on Outer Space: 'Instant' International Customary law?*, p. 36.

[711] See Kunz, J.L. (October 1953), *The nature of customary international law*, p. 664; Sőrensen, M. (1960), *Principes de droit international public: Cours général*, p. 35. See also *Fisheries* case *(United Kingdom* v. *Norway)* (1951) p. 142; Villiger, M.E. (1997), *Customary International Law and Treaties. A Manual on the Theory and Practice of the Interrelation of Sources*, p. 15.

[712] See for example, Villiger, M.E. (1997), *Customary International Law and Treaties. A Manual on the Theory and Practice of the Interrelation of Sources*, p. 15.

[713] See for example, *Asylum* case *(Columbia/Peru)* (1950); *Case Concerning Right of Passage Over Indian Territory (Portugal* v. *India)* (1960).

[714] See Chapter V.

[715] See especially *Asylum* case *(Columbia/Peru)* (1950); *Case Concerning Delimitation Of The Maritime Boundary In The Gulf Of Maine Area (Canada* v. *United States of America)* (12 October 1984); *Case Concerning Kasikili/Sedudu Island (Botswana/Namibia)* (13 December 1999); *Case Con-*

> 'Not only must the acts concerned amount to a settled practice, but they must also be such, or be carried out in such a way, as to be evidence of a belief that this practice is rendered obligatory by the existence of a rule of law requiring it. The need for such a belief, i.e., the existence of a subjective element, is implicit in the very notion of the opinio juris sive necessitatis. The States concerned must therefore feel that they are conforming to what amounts to a legal obligation. The frequency, or even habitual character of the acts is not in itself enough. There are many international acts, e.g., in the field of ceremonial and protocol, which are performed almost invariably, but which are motivated only by considerations of courtesy, convenience or tradition, and not by any sense of legal duty.'[716]

Here, the acceptance as law is equated with the feeling that a practice is required by law. In the 1985 *Continental Shelf* case the Court confirmed that: 'the material of customary international law is to be looked for primarily in the actual practice and opinio juris of States.'[717] The Court repeated this pronouncement in the *Nuclear Weapons Advisory Opinion* and in the *Nicaragua* case.[718] In the latter case the Court further clarified that:

---

cerning Maritime Delimitation And Territorial Questions Between Qatar And Bahrain (Qatar v. *Bahrain) – Merits* (16 March 2001); *Case Concerning Military and Paramilitary Activities in and Against Nicaragua (Nicaragua* v. *United States of America)* (1986); *Case Concerning Oil Platforms (Islamic Republic Of Iran* v. *United States Of America) – Preliminary Objection* (12 December 1996); *Case Concerning Right of Passage Over Indian Territory (Portugal* v. *India)* (1960); *Case Concerning Rights Of Nationals Of The United States Of America In Morocco (France/United States of America)* (27 August 1952); *Case Concerning The Aerial Incident Of 10 August 1999 (Pakistan* v. *India)* (21 June 2000); *Case Concerning The Arrest Warrant Of 11 April 2000 (Democratic Republic Of The Congo* v. *Belgium)* (14 February 2002); *Case Concerning The Barcelona Traction, Light And Power Company, Limited (New Application: 1962) (Belgium* v. *Spain)* (5 February 1970); *Case concerning the Gabcikovo-Nagymaros project (Hungary/Slovakia)* (1997); *Case Concerning The Land And Maritime Boundary Between Cameroon And Nigeria (Cameroon* v. *Nigeria: Equatorial Guinea Intervening)* (10 October 2002); *Case Concerning the Territorial Dispute (Libyan Arab Jamahiriya/Chad)* (3 February 1994); *Continental Shelf (Libyan Arab Jamahiriya/Malta)* (1985); *The Corfu Channel* case *(Merits)* (1949); *Difference Relating to Immunity from Legal Process of a Special Rapporteur of the Commission on Human Rights (Advisory Opinion)* (29 April 1999); *Fisheries* case *(United Kingdom* v. *Norway)* (1951); *Fisheries Jurisdiction (Federal Republic of Germany* v. *Iceland)* (25 July 1974); *Fisheries Jurisdiction (United Kingdom of Great Britain and Northern Ireland* v. *Iceland)* (25 July 1974); *Interhandel (Switzerland* v. *United States of America)* (1959); *LaGrand* case *(Germany* v. *United States of America)* (27 June 2001); *Legality Of The Threat Or Use Of Nuclear Weapons (Advisory Opinion)* (8 July 1996); *North Sea Continental Shelf (Federal Republic of Germany/Denmark; Federal Republic of Germany/ Netherlands)* cases (1969); *Nottebohm* case *(Liechtenstein* v. *Guatemala)* (1955); *Nuclear Tests (Australia* v. *France)* (20 December 1974); *Reservations To The Convention On The Prevention And Punishment Of The Crime Of Genocide* (28 May 1951); *Western Sahara (Advisory Opinion)* (1975); *The Case of the S.S. 'Lotus'* (1927); *The S.S. 'Wimbledon'* (1923). Recently, see *Difference Relating to Immunity from Legal Process of a Special Rapporteur of the Commission on Human Rights (Advisory Opinion)* (29 April 1999).

[716] *North Sea Continental Shelf (Federal Republic of Germany/Denmark; Federal Republic of Germany/Netherlands)* cases (1969) p. 44, para. 77.

[717] *Continental Shelf (Libyan Arab Jamahiriya/Malta)* (1985) para. 27.

[718] *Case Concerning Military and Paramilitary Activities in and Against Nicaragua (Nicaragua* v. *United States of America)* (1986) p. 97, para. 183; *Legality Of The Threat Or Use Of Nuclear Weapons (Advisory Opinion)* (8 July 1996).

> 'Where two States agree to incorporate a particular rule in a treaty, their agreement suffices to make that rule a legal one, binding upon them; but in the field of customary international law, the shared view of the Parties as to the content of what they regard as the rule is not enough. The Court must satisfy itself that the existence of the rule in the opinio juris of States is confirmed by practice.'[719]

On the other hand, in the *Asylum* case concerning common practice peculiar to Latin American states, the Court examined the concept of regional custom.[720] Referring to contesting Peru and Columbia it stated:

> 'The Party which relies on a custom of this kind must prove that this custom is established in such a manner that it has become binding on the other Party. The Colombian Government must prove that the rule invoked by it is in accordance with a constant and uniform usage practised by the States in question, and that this usage is the expression of a right appertaining to the State granting asylum and a duty incumbent on the territorial State.'[721]

Here the practice does not need to be general as the case discusses the regional custom pertaining to states in Latin America. On the other hand, it has to be constant, meaning that it cannot be interrupted. Moreover, it has to be uniform, meaning that it must be practiced by all states in question.

The discussion of what constitutes international custom continues to be recognised as one of the most difficult problems in international law.[722] In 1936 Basdevant observed that

> 'the ideas of jurists in regard to the character of custom have attained neither the unity nor the clarity.'[723]

The situation has not changed since then. Conversely, one could say that it even became worse, as new interpretations of custom have been proposed that radically changed the traditional association of it with a long lasting and widespread practice of doing something. Legal doctrine favouring the *a priori* analysis of the international customs,[724] greatly contributed to the preservation of endless disputes. More-

---

[719] *Case Concerning Military and Paramilitary Activities in and Against Nicaragua (Nicaragua* v. *United States of America)* (1986) para. 184.

[720] See also, e.g., Briggs, H.W. (October 1951), *The Colombian-Peruvian Asylum* case *and Proof of Customary International Law*; de Visscher, C. (1957), *Theory and Reality in Public International Law*, pp. 148-149.

[721] *Asylum* case *(Columbia/Peru)* (1950) para. 276; see also Guggenheim, P. (1952), *Les Principles de Droit International Public*, p. 70.

[722] See for example, Sőrensen, M. (1960), *Principes de droit international public: Cours général*, p. 47; van Hoof, G.J.H. (1983), *Rethinking the sources of international law*, p. 85.

[723] 'les idées des juristes sur le caractère de la coutume n'ont atteint ni à l'unité ni à la clarté', Basdevant, J. (1936), *Règles Générales du Droit de la Paix*, p. 508.

[724] Ibid.

over, the discussion is obscured by the fact that many authorities use terms such as custom, practice or the psychological element but attach a different meaning to them. Also, many constituent elements of custom are interrelated, which becomes a hurdle to their systematised presentation. Furthermore, some analysts refer to both elements only in the context of describing a customary rule and reject them as an explanation of the process of their formation.[725] The analysis is further complicated by the fact that many authorities remain silent on certain aspects of the problem. In consequence, one can observe a rapid proliferation of works that are very difficult to analyse, not to mention the complexity of their systematisation.

Some patterns, however, can be discerned. In the twentieth century the concept of international custom as consisting of the two elements of practice and its acceptance as law has been widely accepted.[726] However, the dualistic conception quickly turned out to mean different things to different authorities. The jurisprudence is divided as to the meaning of the subjective element. Two different schools of interpretation emerged: one that equates it with a feeling or conviction that the rule embodied in the widespread practice is binding (*opinio iuris*) and the other that interprets it as acquiescence in or acceptance of the practice as law.[727] The latter approach is most often associated with the ancient idea of custom as a tacit treaty (*pactum tacitum*) that will be referred to as a consensual or voluntaristic conception of custom. The former approach, much younger than the voluntaristic conception of custom, will be referred to as the 'belief' approach (or the 'conviction' approach or *opinio iuris* approach). The following sections will discuss these points in greater detail as they constitute 'rules on rules'[728] as far as the ascertainment of the existence of customary norms is concerned.

---

[725] See for example, Ago, R. (1956), *Science Juridique et Droit International*, p. 850. See also, e.g., Stern, B. (2001), *Custom at the heart of international law (trans. M. Byers, A. Denise)*, p. 93.

[726] See for example, Akehurst, M. (1974-1975), *Custom as a Source of International Law*; Akehurst, M. (1987), *A modern introduction to international law*; Bernhardt, R. (1992), *Customary International Law*, vol. 1; Danilenko, G.M. (1983), *Law-Making in the International Community*; Degan, V.D. (1997), *Sources of International Law*; Guggenheim, P. (1967), *Traite de Droit international public: Avec mention de la pratique internationale et suisse*; *Ways and Means of Making the Evidence of Customary International Law More Readily Available, Preparatory Work within the Purview of Article 24 of the Statute of the International Law Commision, Memorandum submitted by the Secretary-General* (1949); Thirlway, H.W.A. (1972), *International Customary Law and Codification*; Tunkin, G.I. (1974), *Theory of International Law*; van Hoof, G.J.H. (1983), *Rethinking the sources of international law*; Villiger, M.E. (1997), *Customary International Law and Treaties. A Manual on the Theory and Practice of the Interrelation of Sources*; Wolfke, K. (1993), *Custom in Present International Law*. See also de Visscher, C. (1957), *Theory and Reality in Public International Law*, pp. 148-156; Ridruejo, J.A.P. (1998), *Le droit international à la veille du vingt et unième siècle: normes, faits et valeurs*, p. 45; Rosenne, S. (2001), *The Perplexities of Modern International Law: General Course on Public International Law*, p. 58; Sőrensen, M. (1960), *Principes de droit international public: Cours général*, p. 36.

[727] See *below.*

[728] Villiger, M.E. (1997), *Customary International Law and Treaties. A Manual on the Theory and Practice of the Interrelation of Sources*, p. 16, citing de Aréchaga.

4. Practice

Practice is the essence of custom but its characteristic is sometimes troublesome. The question is whose practice contributes to the formation of international customary rule. International law has traditionally been concerned with the relations between states.[729] In this sense, states are the primary subjects of international practice. Also, some international organisations like United Nations are recognised as subjects of international law. Recently also private persons and companies started to be considered in a limited sense as subjects of international law.[730]

4.1 The notion of practice

What types of conduct constitute practice is the subject of much argument.[731] The concept of practice is undisputedly taken to refer to actions.[732] The action is traditionally connected with positive activities of organs competent to bind a state internationally (e.g., a head of state, foreign minister, diplomats) although this assumption has been extended to concordant legislation of states and decisions of municipal courts.[733] However, there is a dispute whether statements, negotiating positions or unilateral declarations may constitute the party's practice. Another difficult question is whether abstentions from actions constitute state practice.

One widely represented view, insisted that only positive actions constitute practice.[734] Judge Read in his often-cited dissenting opinion to the *Anglo-Norwegian Fisheries* case said in respect to the practice:

> 'This cannot be established by citing cases where coastal States have made extensive claims, but have not maintained their claims by the actual assertion of sovereignty over trespassing foreign ships. Such claims may be important as starting points, which, if not challenged, may ripen into historic title in the course of time. The only convincing evidence of State practice is to be found in seizures, where the coastal State asserts

---

729 See for example, Thirlway, H.W.A. (1972), *International Customary Law and Codification*, p. 7.

730 See for example, *Nottebohm* case *(Liechtenstein* v. *Guatemala)* (1955); Oppenheim, L. (1955), *International Law: A Treatise*, p. 6. But see also, e.g., Akehurst, M. (1974-1975), *Custom as a Source of International Law*, p. 11.

731 See for example, Barberis, J. (1967), *L'élément matériel de la coutume internationale d'après la Cour de la Haye (1922-1966)*.

732 See for example, Thirlway, H.W.A. (1972), *International Customary Law and Codification*, pp. 57-60; Villiger, M.E. (1997), *Customary International Law and Treaties. A Manual on the Theory and Practice of the Interrelation of Sources*, p. 5; Wolfke, K. (1993), *Custom in Present International Law*, p. 41; van Hoof, G.J.H. (1983), *Rethinking the sources of international law*, p. 107.

733 See for example, Degan, V.D. (1997), *Sources of International Law*, pp. 149-150.

734 See for example, D'Amato, A.A. (1971), *The concept of custom in international law*, p. 88; van Hoof, G.J.H. (1983), *Rethinking the sources of international law*, p. 107; Villiger, M.E. (1997), *Customary International Law and Treaties. A Manual on the Theory and Practice of the Interrelation of Sources*, p. 5; Wolfke, K. (1993), *Custom in Present International Law*, pp. 41-42.

its sovereignty over trespassing foreign ships and by maintaining its position in the course of diplomatic negotiation of international arbitration.'[735]

D'Amato has echoed the above statement:

'a claim is not an act. As a matter of daily practice, international law is largely concerned with conflicting international claims. But the claims themselves, although they may *articulate* a legal norm, cannot constitute the material component of custom.'[736]

According to Wolfke:

'repeated verbal acts are also acts of conduct in their broad meaning and can give rise to international customs, but only to customs of making such declarations, etc., and not to customs of the conduct described in the content of the verbal acts.'[737]

On the other hand, Akehurst argues that this is a minority view.[738] He argues that 'it is artificial to distinguish between what a State does and what it says'[739] because recognition of one State by another 'is no more than a form of words'.[740] Moreover, he argues that physical acts can be no more consistent than words, thus refuting D'Amato's claim that the state can act in only one way at one time.[741] Thirlway on the other hand, argues that claims and other statements can be considered as state practice, but only in the context of some concrete situation.[742] Villiger, in turn, adopted the least restrictive view on qualification of concrete and abstract statements as state practice.[743] The judiciary practice of the ICJ seems to confirm this view. For instance, in the *Nicaragua* case and *Nuclear Weapons Advisory Opinion*, the Court made extensive references to abstract statements as constituting state practice.[744]

In regard to the second problem, there is an ongoing discussion in the literature as to whether abstention or lack of positive acts can be considered as practice and in

---

735 *Fisheries* case *(United Kingdom* v. *Norway)* (1951) para. 191.

736 D'Amato, A.A. (1971), *The concept of custom in international law*, p. 88.

737 Wolfke, K. (1993), *Custom in Present International Law*, p. 42, citing Judge Radhabinod Pal.

738 Akehurst, M. (1974-1975), *Custom as a Source of International Law*, p. 2.

739 Ibid., p. 3.

740 Ibid., citing Parry, C. (1965), *Sources and Evidences of International Law*, p. 65.

741 Akehurst, M. (1974-1975), *Custom as a Source of International Law*, p. 3; D'Amato, A.A. (1971), *The concept of custom in international law*, p. 51.

742 Thirlway, H.W.A. (1972), *International Customary Law and Codification*, p. 58, see also Akehurst, M. (1974-1975), *Custom as a Source of International Law*, pp. 4-8.

743 Villiger, M.E. (1997), *Customary International Law and Treaties. A Manual on the Theory and Practice of the Interrelation of Sources*, p. 19.

744 See for example, *Case Concerning Military and Paramilitary Activities in and Against Nicaragua (Nicaragua* v. *United States of America)* (1986) para. 189; *Legality Of The Threat Or Use Of Nuclear Weapons (Advisory Opinion)* (8 July 1996) para. 70.

consequence, create prohibitory or permissible customary norms.[745] In the *Lotus* case the Permanent Court of International Justice (PCIJ) acknowledged the possibility of practice consisting of abstentions.[746] The case dealt with the abstention from initiating criminal proceedings against foreign citizens. The Turkish representative and some judges argued that such an abstinence from action cannot create custom. On the other hand the French representative Basdevant argued that:

> 'The custom observed by states to refrain from prosecuting foreign citizens charged with causing collisions of vessels in the open sea constitutes a customary norm of international law.'[747]

The Court concluded that:

> 'only if such abstention were based on their being conscious of a duty to abstain would it be possible to speak of an international custom.'

Because such a consciousness was not proved, the Court rejected the claim that such custom had emerged. However, judges Nyholm and Altamira expressly opposed the idea that abstention from action can create customary law.[748] The argument that absence of action cannot create custom has found recognition in the doctrine,[749] but a majority seems to support the opposite view.[750] The role of abstentions turned out to be of crucial importance in the area of international customary humanitarian law, where many rules require abstention from certain conduct, and 'omissions pose a particular problem in the assessment of *opinio juris* because it has to be proved that the abstention is not a coincidence but based on a legitimate expectation.'[751]

In summary, even the relatively simple question of what constitutes 'practice' is problematic in the doctrine of international law. There is no dispute as to whether positive acts constitute practice, but the problem arises in the context of abstentions from acting as well as the treatment of statements about an act. A majority seems to accept the view that abstention can be considered as a practice. Also, a majority

---

[745] See for example, Tunkin, G.I. (1974), *Theory of International Law*, p. 116.

[746] Villiger argues that the position of the Court is not clear. Villiger, M.E. (1997), *Customary International Law and Treaties. A Manual on the Theory and Practice of the Interrelation of Sources*, p. 37.

[747] *The Case of the S.S. 'Lotus'* (1927) para. 25.

[748] *Dissenting Opinion of Judge Altamira on Lotus* case (1927) para. 59, 96; *Dissenting Opinion of Judge Altamira on Lotus* case (1927) para. 112.

[749] See for example, Strupp, K. (1934), *Les Règles Générales du Droit de la Paix*, p. 307. See also Gianni (1931), *La coutume en droit international*, p. 126.

[750] See for example, Kunz, J.L. (October 1953), *The nature of customary international law*, p. 666; Thirlway, H.W.A. (1972), *International Customary Law and Codification*, p. 58. Tunkin, G.I. (1961), *Remarks On the Juridical Nature of Customary Norms of International Law*, pp. 421-422.

[751] Henckaerts, J.-M. (March 2005), *Study on customary international humanitarian law: A contribution to the understanding and respect for the rule of law in armed conflict*, p. 182.

seems to accept the claim that statements whether abstract or general should count as state practice.

4.2 Duration of practice

The second problem relates to the question how old the custom should be. The ordinary meaning of the term 'custom' presupposes the existence of widespread practice for a very long time.[752] Canon law requires forty or a hundred years of practice.[753] Although definition of international custom in Article 38 of the Statute did not mention the importance of time, it was listed by Hudson in his influential characteristic of international custom.[754] Also Kelsen spoke of custom as a long-established practice of states that creates law.[755] Such a requirement could also be inferred from the ICJ requirement of constant and uniform usage in the *Asylum* case and fisheries rights 'attested by very ancient and peaceful usage' formulation in the *Anglo-Norwegian Fisheries* case.[756]

However, the requirement of longevity of practice seems to have been generally relaxed in the contemporary doctrine of international law.[757] Even before the Second World War, authors such as Basdevant argued that international custom could be recognised after a short period of time.[758] Kunz argued that customary norm permitting sovereignty over adjacent airspace developed in a short timeframe before the First World War.[759] But after the war this contention has been almost universally accepted in international law. Tunkin stated that

> 'the element of time does not in itself create presumption in favour of the existence of a customary norm of international law. There is even less ground to think that juridically it is necessary for the customary rule to be "old" or of long standing.'[760]

---

[752] The Oxford English Dictionary provides the following two meanings of the term custom: '1. A habitual or usual practice; common way of acting; usage, fashion, habit (either of an individual or of a community)
2. Law. An established usage which by long continuance has acquired the force of a law or right esp. the established usage of a particular locality, trade, society, or the like.'

[753] Bouscaren, L.T. and Ellis, A.C. (1957), *Canon Law: A Text and Commentary*, pp. 40-41.

[754] Hudson, M.O. (3 March 1950), *Article 24 of the Statute of the International Law Commission. Working Paper. Document A/CN.4/16*, p. 26.

[755] Kelsen, H. (1966), *Principles of International Law*, p. 441; Kelsen, H. (1952), *Principles of International Law*, p. 307.

[756] *Fisheries* case *(United Kingdom* v. *Norway)* (1951) p. 142.

[757] See for example, Baxter, R.R. (1970), *Treaties and Custom*, p. 67; Brownlie, I. (1990), *Principles of public international law*, p. 5; Kunz, J.L. (October 1953), *The nature of customary international law*, p. 666; Lachs, M. (1972), *Some Reflections on Substance and Form in International Law*, pp. 109-110; Ridruejo, J.A.P. (1998), *Le droit international à la veille du vingt et unième siècle: normes, faits et valeurs*, p. 47, para 2.2.4.

[758] Basdevant, J. (1936), *Règles Générales du Droit de la Paix*, p. 513.

[759] Kunz, J.L. (October 1953), *The nature of customary international law*, p. 666.

[760] Tunkin, G.I. (1961), *Remarks On the Juridical Nature of Customary Norms of International Law*, pp. 419-420, references omitted; see also Tunkin, G.I. (1974), *Theory of International Law*, pp. 114-115.

Observing the rapid technological progress in regard to the exploration of cosmos, Cheng formulated his theory of 'instant custom'.[761] Consequently, some authorities claimed that the 'time factor as a separate element in the proof of custom now seems irrelevant.'[762]

Similar views were expressed by the ICJ in the groundbreaking 1969 *North Sea Continental Shelf* cases. Observing the swift technological advances in the exploration of the continental shelf the judges said that

> 'the passage of only a short period of time is not necessarily, or of itself, a bar to the formation of a new rule of customary international law.'[763]

It should be stressed, however, that this requirement was based upon the assumption of the existence of the previous treaty norm and subsequent extensive and virtually uniform practice of states including those whose interests are specially affected together with the recognition of a practice in question as a law.[764] Some authorities outlined the possible timeframe for the development of custom. As Judge Tanaka put it, in his dissenting opinion in this case:

> 'the speedy tempo of present international life promoted by highly developed communication (...) had minimized the importance of the time factor and has made possible the acceleration of the formation of customary international law. What required a hundred years in former days now may require less than ten years.'[765]

However, as far as the proof of time factor is concerned, it is usually omitted, although there are examples of detailed ascertainment of a timeframe of a given practice. For instance, in the *Right of Passage* case dealing with an alleged regional custom of passage over Indian territory to two Portuguese enclaves, the Court stated that:

> '[the] practice having continued over a period extending beyond a century and a quarter unaffected.'[766]

The *North Sea Continental Shelf* cases also had a clearly outlined timeframe, extending from the 1958 as the date of signing the Convention to the date of dis-

---

[761] Cheng, B. (1965), *United Nations Resolutions on Outer Space: 'Instant' International Customary law?*

[762] See for example, Baxter, R.R. (1970) *Treaties and Custom*, p. 67.

[763] See for example, *North Sea Continental Shelf (Federal Republic of Germany/Denmark; Federal Republic of Germany/Netherlands)* cases (1969) para. 74.

[764] Ibid., para. 74.

[765] Judge Tanaka (1969), *Dissenting opinion of Judge Tanaka on Continental Shelf* case, p. 177.

[766] *Case Concerning Right of Passage Over Indian Territory (Portugal* v. *India)* (1960) p. 40.

pute.[767] And the *Nuclear Weapons Advisory Opinion* examined the non-recourse to nuclear weapons over the past fifty years.[768]

In summary, the requirement of a long lasting practice seems to be generally abandoned in the contemporary doctrine of international law. International custom can develop in a short timeframe and it seems that it does not have to be proved separately.

4.3 Generality of practice

Article 38 of the Statute speaks of the general practice accepted as law. The ICJ confirmed in the *Nicaragua* case that

> 'the Court may not disregard the essential role played by general practice'.[769]

In the 1951 *Fisheries* case the Court repeated the requirement of the generality of practice; lack thereof prohibited it from establishing the customary norm of ten-mile rules for bays in this case.[770] In the *North Sea Continental Shelf* cases mentioned above the Court argued that practice must be settled and that custom can be formed quicker given an 'extensive and virtually uniform' practice of states, including states that are 'specially affected'.[771]

Although Article 38 speaks of general practice accepted as law, the ICJ and the doctrine generally recognised the local character of custom.[772] This is in line with the nature of custom, which from a historical perspective was primarily the source of particular or local law.[773] The locality of custom has also been expressly recognised by the PCIJ in the *Asylum* case, the *Rights of US nationals in Morocco* case and the *Right of Passage* case.[774] In the *Right of Passage* case the ICJ conceded that the relation between two states could only result in the establishment of local custom. *The Asylum* case on the other hand, supports the claim that custom can exist only in

---

[767] *North Sea Continental Shelf (Federal Republic of Germany/Denmark; Federal Republic of Germany/Netherlands)* cases (1969), para. 74.

[768] *Legality Of The Threat Or Use Of Nuclear Weapons (Advisory Opinion)* (8 July 1996), para. 67.

[769] *Case Concerning Military and Paramilitary Activities in and Against Nicaragua (Nicaragua* v. *United States of America)* (1986), para. 184.

[770] *Fisheries* case *(United Kingdom* v. *Norway)* (1951), para. 131.

[771] *North Sea Continental Shelf (Federal Republic of Germany/Denmark; Federal Republic of Germany/Netherlands)* cases (1969), para. 74.

[772] See for example, Bourquin, M. (1931), *Règles Générales du Droit de la Paix*, p. 63; Fauchille, P. (1922), *Traité de Droit International Public*, p. 43, para. 47(1); Ridruejo, J.A.P. (1998), *Le droit international à la veille du vingt et unième siècle: normes, faits et valeurs*, p. 49, para. 2.2.6. See especially Barberis, J. (1992), *Les règles spécifiques du droit international en Amérique latine*.

[773] Smith argues that in continental Europe in Middle Ages the word custom was synonymous with local law, Smith, M. (June 1903), *Customary law. I.*, p. 261. See Chapter V.

[774] See for example, *Asylum* case *(Columbia/Peru)* (1950); *Case Concerning Right of Passage Over Indian Territory (Portugal* v. *India)* (1960); *Case Concerning Rights Of Nationals Of The United States Of America In Morocco (France/United States of America)* (27 August 1952).

relation to the particular region of the world. In the *Rights of US nationals in Morocco* case the Court repeated this formulation.[775] In all these cases the Court required a uniform usage.[776] This requirement can be justified by the nature of local custom that the latter case dealt with, as it is impossible to have other than a unanimous practice between two states involved. It can also be accepted in the case of regional custom.

The doctrine remains divided on the question of whether practice should be general or universal in case of non-regional custom. According to Tunkin,

> 'customary norms of international law are premised first of all on universal practice.'[777]

This view is a consequence of a philosophical stance of the voluntarists, who emphasise the importance of a concordant will of states in the creation of custom that in principle, can only bind these states and not others. However, the minority states can be presumed to accept a custom as a result of their silence and lack of protests.[778]

In the view of a majority of the doctrine however, the practice does not have to be universal or unanimous.[779] But the exact formula of what generality means turned out to be a major problem for the jurisprudence. Some authors recognising the relative character of this term leave its ascertainment to the discretion of the judge.[780] Others try to present more precise criteria. For instance, Strupp asserted that if more than a half of states adhered to a given norm, then it could be presumed that it applies to the whole community of states.[781] Other authorities made reference to an overwhelming majority:

> 'The practice must be "general", not universal; but a mere majority of states is not enough. The practice must have been applied by the overwhelming majority of states that hitherto had an opportunity of applying it.'[782]

---

[775] *Case Concerning Rights Of Nationals Of The United States Of America In Morocco (France/United States of America)* (27 August 1952), para. 200.

[776] *Asylum* case *(Columbia/Peru)* (1950), para. 276; *Case Concerning Right of Passage Over Indian Territory (Portugal* v. *India)* (1960), p. 40.

[777] Tunkin, G.I. (1961), *Remarks On the Juridical Nature of Customary Norms of International Law*, p. 422.

[778] Stern, B. (2001), *Custom at the heart of international law (trans. M. Byers, A. Denise)*, p. 98.

[779] See for example, Kunz, J.L. (October 1953), *The nature of customary international law*, p. 666; Villiger, M.E. (1997), *Customary International Law and Treaties. A Manual on the Theory and Practice of the Interrelation of Sources*, p. 29.

[780] See for example, Sőrensen, M. (1960), *Principes de droit international public: Cours général*, pp. 38-39.

[781] Strupp, K. (1934), *Les Règles Générales du Droit de la Paix*, p. 310.

[782] Kunz, J.L. (October 1953), *The nature of customary international law*, p. 666, citing The Paquete Habana (1900), *175 US 677* , see also, e.g., Oppenheim, L. (1955), *International Law: A Treatise*.

Villiger asserted that the term general indicates 'common and widespread practice among many States'.[783] Kelsen maintained that:

> 'A long-established practice of a great number of states, including the states which, with respect to their power, their culture, and so on, are of certain importance, is sufficient.'[784]

Meijers drawing similarities to treaty negotiation claimed that where a small number of countries are involved, the custom must be unanimously approved, 'but if a larger number of states is involved then two-thirds of them is usually enough.'[785]

In this respect one should mention the *North Sea Continental Shelf* cases where the Court argued:

> 'With respect to the other elements usually regarded as necessary before a conventional rule can be considered to have become a general rule of international law, it might be that, even without the passage of any considerable period of time, a very widespread and representative participation in the convention might suffice of itself, provided it included that of States whose interests were specially affected.'[786]

Therefore, a representative participation in a convention, can, in the Court's view, amount to the formation of a general customary norm. In respect to the representative participation, one should mention the opinion of Baxter who argued that 'there must be some weighting of the "votes" cast for and against the rule according to the size of the State, the volume of its international relations and, in general, the contribution that it makes to the development of international law.'[787]

In summary, practice can be of a general, particular or local scope. In the case of particular or local practice the uniformity has to be proved. In the case of practice of a general scope, however, a practice does not have to be uniform but the exact formula of how many states should adhere to a given practice ranges from half of the participants to virtual unanimity of participants.

4.4 Consistency of practice

Another problem is created by the question of how consistent over time the practice should be. The PCIJ in the *Wimbledon* case stated that practice should be con-

---

[783] Villiger, M.E. (1997), *Customary International Law and Treaties. A Manual on the Theory and Practice of the Interrelation of Sources*, p. 29.

[784] Kelsen, H. (1966), *Principles of International Law*, p. 445.

[785] Meijers, H. (1978), *How is international law made? – The stages of growth of international law and the use of its customary rules*, p. 15.

[786] *North Sea Continental Shelf (Federal Republic of Germany/Denmark; Federal Republic of Germany/Netherlands)* cases (1969), p. 42, para. 73. On specially affected states see Sőrensen, M. (1960), *Principes de droit international public: Cours général*, p. 40. Villiger, M.E. (1997), *Customary International Law and Treaties. A Manual on the Theory and Practice of the Interrelation of Sources*, pp. 30-33.

[787] Baxter, R.R. (1970), *Treaties and Custom*, p. 66.

stant.[788] Similar views were expressed in the already cited *Asylum* and *Right of Passage* cases where the Court required a consistent usage.[789] Similarly, the Joint Separate opinion of judges to the 1974 *Fisheries jurisdiction* case stated that:

> 'contradiction in the practice of States or inconsistent conduct, particularly emanating from these very States which are said to be following or establishing the custom, would prevent the emergence of a rule of customary law.'[790]

But the ICJ has sometimes relaxed the requirement of absolute consistency of practice. For instance, in the *Nicaragua* case the Court argued that practice has to be 'in general (…) consistent' but not absolutely perfect:[791]

> 'The Court does not consider that, for a rule to be established as customary, the corresponding practice must be in absolutely rigorous conformity with the rule. In order to deduce the existence of customary rules, the Court deems it sufficient that the conduct of States should, in general, be consistent with such rules, and that instances of State conduct inconsistent with a given rule should generally have been treated as breaches of that rule, not as indications of the recognition of a new rule.'[792]

According to some authorities, the customary norm in question should be evidenced by consistent practices, because diverging practices cannot contribute to the development of customary norm.[793] A majority, however, seems to accept the possibility of interruption of practice. For Tunkin, continuity such as the passage of time does not play a decisive role in the formation of a custom.[794] Brownlie argues that substantial uniformity is required although complete uniformity is not necessary.[795] As Akehurst stated referring to the 1951 *Fisheries* case:[796]

> 'Major inconsistencies in the practice (that is a large amount of practice which goes against the 'rule' in question) prevent the creation of a customary rule. Minor inconsistencies (that is a small amount of practice which goes against the rule in question) do

---

788 *The S.S. 'Wimbledon'* (1923), para. 25.

789 See for example, *Asylum* case *(Columbia/Peru)* (1950); *Case Concerning Right of Passage Over Indian Territory (Portugal* v. *India)* (1960); *Case Concerning Rights Of Nationals Of The United States Of America In Morocco (France/United States of America)* (27 August 1952).

790 Judges Forster, B., Jimenez De Arechaga, Nagendra Singh and Ruda (1974), *Joint Separate Opinion of Judges Forster, Bengzon, Jimenez De Arechaga, Nagendra Singh and Ruda on Fisheries Jurisdiction* case, p. 50 para. 16.

791 *Case Concerning Military and Paramilitary Activities in and Against Nicaragua (Nicaragua* v. *United States of America)* (1986) p. 98, para. 186.

792 Ibid., p. 98, para. 186.

793 See for example, Cavaglieri, A. (1929), *Règles Générales du Droit de la Paix*, pp. 336-337; Kunz, J.L. (October 1953), *The nature of customary international law*, p. 666.

794 See for example, Tunkin, G.I. (1961), *Remarks On the Juridical Nature of Customary Norms of International Law*, pp. 420-421.

795 Brownlie, I. (1990), *Principles of public international law*, p. 5.

796 *Fisheries* case *(United Kingdom* v. *Norway)* (1951), para. 138.

> not prevent the creation of customary rule (...), although in such cases the rule in question probably needs to be supported by a large amount of practice, in order to outweigh the conflicting practice.'[797]

In summary, there are various degrees of consistency suggested by the jurisprudence. However, there seems to be a general agreement that the practice should be consistent although small inconsistencies seem to be accepted.

4.5 **Objections to practice**

Another important issue perplexing international lawyers is the problem of the persistent objector to the customary practice.[798] The concept has appeared in the Anglo-Norwegian *Fisheries* case where the Court argued that the 'ten miles' appertained to the territorial sea 'would appear to be inapplicable against Norway inasmuch as she has always opposed any attempt to apply it to the Norwegian coast.'[799]

Villiger argues that a state is not bound by the eventual customary norm if it opposes a practice from the early stages and does it consistently.[800] The notion of persistent objector is clearly linked with the voluntaristic conception of customary law, which rests on the grounds that a custom binds a given state only if it has consented to it, either expressly or tacitly.[801] However, voluntarists were not always consistent in their argumentation and admitted that the protest of a state is not valid against mandatory norms of international law or *ius cogens*.[802] Even some authors supporting the *opinio iuris* element, thus disfavouring voluntaristic conception of customary law, agree that the will of the state may create an exception in the application of international law.[803] For instance, Kunz argued that protests prevent the emergence of international custom:

---

[797] See for example, Akehurst, M. (1987), *A modern introduction to international law*, p. 28.

[798] See for example, Brownlie, I. (1990), *Principles of public international law*, p. 10; *Fisheries* case *(United Kingdom* v. *Norway)* (1951), para. 131, see also, e.g., Wolfke, K. (1993), *Custom in Present International Law*.

[799] *Fisheries* case *(United Kingdom* v. *Norway)* (1951), p. 131.

[800] See for example, Villiger, M.E. (1997), *Customary International Law and Treaties. A Manual on the Theory and Practice of the Interrelation of Sources*, p. 34.

[801] Ibid., p. 41.

[802] See Art. 53 of the Vienna Convention on the Law of Treaties and Glossary, see also, e.g., *Case Concerning Military and Paramilitary Activities in and Against Nicaragua (Nicaragua* v. *United States of America)* (1986), para. 100-101 and para. 190; Meijers, H. (1978), *How is international law made? – The stages of growth of international law and the use of its customary rules*, p. 22.; Stern, B. (2001), *Custom at the heart of international law (trans. M. Byers, A. Denise)*, p. 99. For the other side of the argument see for example, Wolfke, K. (1993), *Some Persistent Controversies Regarding Customary International Law*, p. 14.

[803] See for example, Brierly, J.L. (1963), *The law of nations*, pp. 59-62; Lauterpacht, H.S. (1958), *The Development of International Law by the International Court*, pp. 379-381; MacGibbon, I.C. (1957), *Customary International Law and Acquiescence*, pp. 125-131; Verdross, A. (1955), *Völkerrecht*, p. 119. See also Wolfke, K. (1993), *Custom in Present International Law*, p. 48.

> 'Protests by other states or declarations that they, even if submitting to this practice, do so only *ex gratia*; protests against the norm on which an international decision is based, even in carrying out this decision, prevent the coming into existence of a new norm of customary general international law.'[804]

In short, however, a majority of writers seem to have accepted this concept, which proves the peculiar character of international relations.[805]

In this context, one should mention the potential consequences of lack of objections on the emergence of international custom. Many voluntarists argue that lack of protests may amount to the acceptance of practice through acquiescence.[806] The creation of such a presumption of a universal acceptance of a given norm is a voluntaristic way of allowing customary norms to bind generally. For instance, Wolfke argues that:

> 'toleration of a practice by other states, considering all relevant circumstances, justifies the presumption of its acceptance as law, which in turn leads to the formation of a new customary rule of international law.'[807]

Tunkin here maintains that when an emerging rule affects a state, its absence of objections after a sufficient time, can be regarded as a tacit recognition of a norm.[808] However, as the ICJ opined in the *Gulf of Maine* case:

> 'while it may be conceded that the United States showed a certain imprudence in maintaining silence after Canada had issued the first permits for exploration on Georges Bank, any attempt to attribute to such silence, a brief silence at that, legal consequences taking the concrete form of an estoppel, seems to be going too far.'[809]

Finally, one should mention the issue of states objecting to an already existing customary practice, also known as the subsequent objectors.[810] Such protest would in fact mean the violation of a customary norm in question. As the ICJ put it in the 1969 Continental Shelf judgment:

> 'customary law rules and obligations which, by their very nature, must have equal force for all members of the international community, (...) cannot therefore be the

---

[804] Kunz, J.L. (October 1953), *The nature of customary international law*, p. 667.

[805] See for example, Degan, V.D. (1997), *Sources of International Law*, p. 164; Villiger, M.E. (1997), *Customary International Law and Treaties. A Manual on the Theory and Practice of the Interrelation of Sources*, p. 33.

[806] See for example, Charney, J.I. (October 1993), *Universal International Law*, pp. 536-537.

[807] Wolfke, K. (1993), *Custom in Present International Law*, p. 48.

[808] Tunkin, G.I. (1974), *Theory of International Law*, p. 129.

[809] *Case Concerning Delimitation Of The Maritime Boundary In The Gulf Of Maine Area (Canada v. United States of America)* (12 October 1984), para. 308.

[810] See for example, Villiger, M.E. (1997), *Customary International Law and Treaties. A Manual on the Theory and Practice of the Interrelation of Sources*, pp. 36-37.

subject of any right of unilateral exclusion exercisable at will by any one of them in its own favour.'[811]

In summary, the issue of the persistent objector seems to be generally accepted by the international jurisprudence despite very difficult theoretical barriers that the explanation of this exception encounters. On the other hand, lack of objections may often be interpreted as acquiescence in the practice of the majority.

4.6 Repetition of practice

The concept of custom presupposes existence of a repeated series of actions. However, there are authors like Strupp for whom the element of repetition in custom is irrelevant.[812] Similarly, Cheng argues that there is no need for repeated practice in the establishment of custom providing that *opinio iuris* can be clearly established.[813] For other authors like Tunkin, custom can be formed after a single repetition of practice, although as he admits, such instances are rare.[814]

On the other hand, a majority of authors argue that practice has to be repeated in order to form a customary norm.[815] The ICJ also seems to require the repetition of practice, which can be inferred from the references to constant, extensive or settled practice.[816] In summary, despite some views to the contrary, the majority of the jurisprudence seems to require the practice to be repetitive.

4.7 Morality and reasonableness of practice

The question of whether the practice that is not morally desirable or reasonable creates customary norms is difficult to answer from the legal point of view. This problem is in essence, the question whether law should be good or at least not bad or unreasonable. On the one hand, it is difficult to imagine having an immoral written statute or bad custom that has to be followed as law. Only extreme positiv-

---

[811] *North Sea Continental Shelf (Federal Republic of Germany/Denmark; Federal Republic of Germany/Netherlands)* cases (1969), para. 63.

[812] Strupp, K. (1934), *Les Règles Générales du Droit de la Paix*, p. 304.

[813] Cheng, B. (1965), *United Nations Resolutions on Outer Space: 'Instant' International Customary law?*, p. 36.

[814] Tunkin, G.I. (1961), *Remarks On the Juridical Nature of Customary Norms of International Law*, p. 419, citing Rousseau; Tunkin, G.I. (1974), *Theory of International Law*, p. 114; see also writing of Klafkowski and Cheng.

[815] See for example, Fauchille, P. (1922), *Traité de Droit International Public*, p. 42, para. 47; Kunz, J.L. (October 1953), *The nature of customary international law*, p. 666; Meijers, H. (1978), *How is international law made? – The stages of growth of international law and the use of its customary rules*, pp. 13-14; Stern, B. (2001), *Custom at the heart of international law (trans. M. Byers, A. Denise)*, p. 90.

[816] See for example, *Asylum* case *(Columbia/Peru)* (1950), para. 276; *North Sea Continental Shelf (Federal Republic of Germany/Denmark; Federal Republic of Germany/Netherlands)* cases (1969) para. 43-44.

ists would consider harmful norms that were created according to the prescribed procedures as legally binding. On the other hand, if law is to be dependant on reason or morality it is not a fully independent body of norms. Since its existence is subjected to the subsequent proof of subjective morality or reason, its content may not be certain.

Blackstone maintained on the grounds of English law that

> 'if it is not a good custom, it ought to be no longer used.'[817]

In his view, custom had to possess certain requisites for it to be good: it had to be immemorial, continued, peaceable, not unreasonable, certain, compulsory and consistent.[818] Reasonableness of custom is also a fundamental requirement of the Canon of law.[819]

Some authorities, however, do not require custom to be good. Kunz for example argues that:

> 'It is doubtful whether (…) the practice must be "just" or "humane" or must not be in violation of existing treaties or of valid international law. For custom may change a valid treaty norm (…) or a valid norm of general international law.'[820]

Such a position is dominant in modern international law that is dominated by legal positivists.

4.8 Summary of practice

Practice is the essential element of custom. However, it can be understood in a number of ways. Although all authors agree that positive acts constitute practice, there is disagreement whether promises of such acts and abstentions can constitute practice. An equally troublesome requirement of custom is the time aspect of practice, which can be long lasting or can be formed instantly. Similarly, the scope of practice can be either general or local, but the troublesome question is what criteria should be used to ascertain generality of practice. Equally diverse answers are given to the question of how consistent the practice should be ranging from uniformity or near uniformity to relative consistency of practice. Even the simple question regarding repeatability of practice has many different answers ranging from lack of repetition through single repetition to unspecified repetition of practice. The picture regarding the understanding of the material element of custom is further cluttered by the doctrine of persistent objector, which provides a way for a state to avoid

---

817 Blackstone, W. (1783 reprinted 1978), *Commentaries on the Laws of England*, p. 76 Vol. 1.

818 Ibid., pp. 76-78 Vol.1.

819 See for example, Bouscaren, L.T. and Ellis, A.C. (1957), *Canon Law: A Text and Commentary*, pp. 37-42.

820 Kunz, J.L. (October 1953), *The nature of customary international law*, p. 666.

application of customary law. Equally difficult are questions of morality and reasonability of practice, which introduce supra-legal sources of norms to the assessment of customary practice.

5. Acceptance of Practice as Law

As was shown above, Article 38 speaks of practice that must be accepted as law. In international law not all uniform practices are considered as amounting to international custom because as the Court explained in the *North Sea Continental Shelf* case, they are not motivated 'by any sense of legal duty.'[821] The question is what this subjective element actually means and how it can be evidenced, as it is difficult to contend that a state can have psychological sensations. An understanding of the source and the nature of this issue is important before embarking upon the task of defining the concept of custom on the Internet in the next chapter.

5.1 The notion of acceptance as law

(a) The 'belief' interpretation

François Geny is regarded as the first jurist who introduced the term *opinio iuris sive necessitates* when referring to the psychological element of custom.[822] This view, having at least a century long tradition,[823] equates the psychological element

---

[821] *North Sea Continental Shelf (Federal Republic of Germany/Denmark; Federal Republic of Germany/Netherlands)* cases (1969), para. 77.

[822] See for example, D'Amato, A.A. (1971), *The concept of custom in international law*, p. 49; Mendelson, M. (1995), *The subjective element in customary international law*, p. 194.

[823] François Gény proposed this idea in 1899 and then in 1919. See Gény, F. (1919 reprinted in 1954), *Méthode d'Interprétation et sources en droit privé positif*. See also D'Amato, A.A. (1969), *The concept of custom in international law*, pp. 64-66; Mendelson, M. (1995), *The subjective element in customary international law*, p. 194. D'Amato, A.A. (1971), *The concept of custom in international law*, pp. 48-49 and Degan, V.D. (1997), *Sources of International Law*, p. 144. Others argue that it was Rivier who first proposed the concept in 1896. Rivier, A. (1896), *Principes du Droit de Gens*, p. 35 Vol. 1. See Mendelson, M. (1995), *The subjective element in customary international law*, p. 194. Walden, R.M. (1977), *The Subjective Element in the Formation of Customary International Law*, p. 358, citing Guggenheim, P. (1958), *Contribution a l'histoire des sources du droit des gens*, p. 52. A number of authors see in this concept the influence of German historical school represented by von Savigny, Puchta and Glück. See Glück (1797), *Ausfürliche Erläuterung der Pandekten*, Vol. 1, p. 461; Puchta, G.F. (1928), *Das Gewohnheitsrecht*; von Savigny, F.K. (1840-49), *System des Heutigen Romischen Rechts*; von Savigny, F.K. (1840), *Vom Beruf Unserer Zeit fur Gesetzgebung und Rechtswissgnschaft*, cited in, e.g.,Guggenheim, P. (1958), *Contribution a l'histoire des sources du droit des gens*, p. 53, para. 11; Kelsen, H. (1952), *Principles of International Law*, pp. 309-310; Wolfke, K. (1993), *Some Persistent Controversies Regarding Customary International Law*, p. 5, citing Puchta, G.F. (1928), *Das Gewohnheitsrecht*, pp. 33-39. Kelsen also points to works of French school of social solidarity and works of Duguit (1901), *L'état, le droit objectif, et la loi positive*, pp. 243-245, 364-365, in Kelsen, H. (1966), *Principles of International Law*, p. 442; Kelsen, H. (1952), *Principles of International Law*,

with the feeling of being bound by a norm embodied in the customary practice in question. This feeling of necessity enables drawing a line between legally binding norms and non-binding social habits.[824] Mendelson argued that the term *opinio iuris* means a belief and not an act of will.[825] He translated the term *opinio iuris sive necessitates* as 'a *belief in (or claim as to) the legally permissible or obligatory nature of the conduct in question, or of its necessity.*'[826] Brierly put it this way:

> 'Custom in its legal sense means something more than mere habit or usage; it is a usage felt by those who follow it to be an obligatory one. There must be present a feeling that, if the usage is departed from, some form of sanction probably, or at any rate ought to, fall on the transgressor.'[827]

Ago points out that *opinio iuris* does not participate in the formation of customary norm which is spontaneous, but is used to describe existing customary rules.[828] On the other hand, MacGibbon suggested that the concept of *opinio iuris* should only be concerned with customary norms expressed as obligations and not rights.[829]

The ICJ has in general endorsed the notion of *opinio iuris* in its judgments. For instance, in the *North Sea Continental Shelf* case it argued that:

> 'The need for such a belief, i.e., the existence of a subjective element, is implicit in the very notion of the opinio juris sive necessitatis. The States concerned must therefore feel that they are conforming to what amounts to a legal obligation.'[830]

Also in the earlier *Lotus* case the Court referred expressly to the belief approach:

> 'for only if such abstention were based on their being conscious of a duty to abstain would it be possible to speak of an international custom.'[831]

---

p. 309. Allen and Parry point to Blackstone, W. (1783 reprinted 1978), *Commentaries on the Laws of England*, p. 78 Vol. 1, in Allen, C.K. (1964), *Law in the making*, p. 137; Parry, C. (1965), *Sources and Evidences of International Law*, p. 61. See also Walden, R.M. (1977), *The Subjective Element in the Formation of Customary International Law*, p. 358.

824 Gény, F. (1919 reprinted in 1954), *Méthode d'Interprétation et sources en droit privé positif*, para. 110.

825 Mendelson, M. (1995), *The subjective element in customary international law*, pp. 184-185.

826 Ibid., p. 195, references omitted.

827 *Asylum* case *(Columbia/Peru)* (1950), para. 276., see also, e.g., Brierly, J.L. (1963), *The law of nations*, p. 59.

828 Ago, R. (1956), *Science Juridique et Droit International*, p. 937. Similarly Stern, B. (2001), *Custom at the heart of international law (trans. M. Byers, A. Denise)*, p. 93.

829 MacGibbon, I.C. (1957), *Customary International Law and Acquiescence*, pp. 127-128. For the other side of the argument see for example, Thirlway, H.W.A. (1972), *International Customary Law and Codification*, pp. 48-49.

830 *North Sea Continental Shelf (Federal Republic of Germany/Denmark; Federal Republic of Germany/Netherlands)* cases (1969), p. 44, para. 77.

831 *The Case of the S.S. 'Lotus'* (1927) para. 26. Repeated in *North Sea Continental Shelf (Federal Republic of Germany/Denmark; Federal Republic of Germany/Netherlands)* cases (1969), p. 44, para.

(b) The 'tacit agreement' interpretation

The wording of Article 38 has led some authors to interpret the second element as a tacit recognition of a binding nature of the norm arising out of a practice.[832] The voluntaristic interpretation of the subjective element has a long pedigree, in the view of some as old as Roman law[833] or at least as far back as the origin of modern international law in the seventeenth century.[834] Tunkin argues that:

> 'Such recognition or acceptance represents a tacit proposal to other states to regard this rule as a norm of international law. If such a tacit proposition is accepted by other states, i.e., if other states demonstrate by their actions that they recognize the given customary rule as juridically binding, it may be taken that a customary norm of international law has appeared.'[835]

Wolfke admits that the distinction between the belief approach and will of the state approach does not remove all the difficulties. Nevertheless, the latter approach is superior because the will of the state is something 'very real in international relations', whereas the legal conviction of the state is 'too vague and objectively unverifiable'.[836] In addition, he claims that:

> 'One might speak of a true opinio juris when custom already exists, but not before.'[837]

---

78. See also, e.g., Stern, B. (2001), *Custom at the heart of international law (trans. M. Byers, A. Denise)*, p. 106.

[832] See for example, Strupp, K. (1934), *Les Règles Générales du Droit de la Paix*, pp. 302-311; Triepel, H. (1923), *Les Rapports entre le Droit Interne et le Droit International*, p. 83. Other supporters include Danilenko, G.M. (1983), *Law-Making in the International Community*, p. 101; Stern, B. (2001), *Custom at the heart of international law (trans. M. Byers, A. Denise)*, p. 108; Suy, E. (1962), *Les actes juridiques unilatéraux en droit international public*, pp. 234-235; Tunkin, G.I. (1961), *Remarks On the Juridical Nature of Customary Norms of International Law*, p. 423; Villiger, M.E. (1997), *Customary International Law and Treaties. A Manual on the Theory and Practice of the Interrelation of Sources*, p. 49; Virally, M. (1968), *The Sources of International Law*, pp. 134-135; Waldock, H. (1962), *General Course of International Law*, pp. 48-49; Wolfke, K. (1993), *Custom in Present International Law*, p. 47.

[833] Walden, R.M. (1977), *The Subjective Element in the Formation of Customary International Law*, p. 344. Also see for example, Allen who argues that the Roman consensus was, in fact, a uniform and consistent usage. Allen, C.K. (1964), *Law in the making*, p. 83, citing Brie. See also Chapter V.

[834] Grotius, H. (1646 reprinted 1925), *De Jure Bellli ac Pacis Libri Tres*, Prolegomena, paras. 1, 11, 17, 40 Book 1. See also Ago, R. (1956), *Science Juridique et Droit International*, p. 936; Guggenheim, P. (1958), *Contribution a l'histoire des sources du droit des gens*, p. 42, para. 7; Mendelson, M. (1995), *The subjective element in customary international law*, pp. 194-202. Lambert pointed to the doctrine of Canon law in Lambert, E. (1903), *La Fonction du droit civil comparé*, pp. 111-112, 125, also cited by Bourquin, M. (1931), *Règles Générales du Droit de la Paix*, p. 62. See also Walden, R.M. (1977), *The Subjective Element in the Formation of Customary International Law*, p. 345.

[835] Tunkin, G.I. (1961), *Remarks On the Juridical Nature of Customary Norms of International Law*, p. 423.

[836] Wolfke, K. (1993), *Custom in Present International Law*, p. 47.

[837] Ibid., p. 48, italics omitted.

Strupp in turn, mixes the consensual and psychological interpretations of the subjective element by arguing that:

> 'the conviction of being internationally bound constitutes (...) a reference to a previous declaration of will, which could be centuries old.'[838]

Similarly, Stern maintains that *opinio iuris* is

> 'the feeling of being bound by a norm to which one consents, giving it existence through this consent.'[839]

The ICJ has also given credit to this interpretation. In the *Nicaragua* case, the Court's 'recognition of validity' of rules 'as customary international law'[840] has been seen by some authors as the acceptance of voluntaristic interpretation of the subjective element.[841] But the Court has also clearly endorsed the 'belief' concept of *opinio iuris* by citing the relevant fragments of the *North Sea Continental Shelf* cases.[842] The Court has referred to a 'belief in a general kind of right'[843] when discussing the customary norm of non-intervention, thus providing a further argument to the contrary. Similarly, in the *North Sea Continental Shelf* cases mentioned above, the contention that state practice should 'show a general recognition that a rule of law is involved' gave the arguments to the proponents of the *pactum tacitum* interpretation.[844] In consequence, both interpretations of the subjective element of custom could be justified in these judgments.

In effect, some authors being aware of the two different interpretations[845] accept either one or the other. Many, however, do not seem to attach importance to this distinction and speak of the requirement of the psychological element as of the

---

838 Strupp, K. (1934), *Les Règles Générales du Droit de la Paix*, p. 302.

839 Stern, B. (2001), *Custom at the heart of international law (trans. M. Byers, A. Denise)*, p. 94.

840 *Case Concerning Military and Paramilitary Activities in and Against Nicaragua (Nicaragua* v. *United States of America)* (1986), p. 98, para 185.

841 See for example, Danilenko, G.M. (1983), *Law-Making in the International Community*, pp. 100-101.

842 *Case Concerning Military and Paramilitary Activities in and Against Nicaragua (Nicaragua* v. *United States of America)* (1986), pp. 108-109, para. 207.

843 Ibid., p. 108 para. 206.

844 *North Sea Continental Shelf (Federal Republic of Germany/Denmark; Federal Republic of Germany/Netherlands)* cases (1969), para. 74.

845 See for example, Basdevant, J. (1936), *Règles Générales du Droit de la Paix*, pp. 504-520; Danilenko, G.M. (1983), *Law-Making in the International Community*, pp. 98-103. Ago, R. (1956), *Science Juridique et Droit International*, p. 936; Cheng, B. (1965), *United Nations Resolutions on Outer Space: 'Instant' International Customary law?*, p. 36; de Visscher, C. (1957), *Theory and Reality in Public International Law*, p. 148; Kunz, J.L. (October 1953), *The nature of customary international law*; Walden, R.M. (1977), *The Subjective Element in the Formation of Customary International Law*; Wolfke, K. (1993), *Custom in Present International Law*, pp. 44-51.

conviction or necessity or feeling being bound by the practice.[846] This approach is also visible in the first empirical study of customary humanitarian law, which referes to 'the legal conviction that a particular practice is carried out "as of right".'[847] Others argue that this distinction was drawn too sharply.[848] On the other hand, most of the textbooks on international law teach young adepts only one approach, mostly the 'belief' or the 'conviction' interpretation of the subjective element.[849] This is certainly one of the causes of the confusion surrounding the dualistic conception of international custom.

5.2 Generality of acceptance

Article 38 speaks of general practice but leaves open the question whether acceptance of the practice as law must be general or universal. The Court took the former stance in the *Lotus* case:

> 'the rules of law binding upon states therefore emanate from their own free will as expressed in conventions or usages generally accepted as expressing principles of law.'[850]

This was confirmed in the *North Sea Continental Shelf* cases where the Court spoke of 'a general recognition' of a rule of law.[851]

Similarly, Villiger argued that:

> 'the basis of the binding character of customary law results from the general consensus of States (...). The essential difference from a contractual obligation derives from the fact that customary law requires general agreement and not unanimity of will.'[852]

---

[846] See for example, Bernhardt, R. (1992), *Customary International Law*, pp. 899-901, Vol. 1, points a, c and e; Ridruejo, J.A.P. (1998), *Le droit international à la veille du vingt et unième siècle: normes, faits et valeurs*, p. 44; Rosenne, S. (2001), *The Perplexities of Modern International Law: General Course on Public International Law*, p. 58. For earlier discussions see for example, de Visscher, C. (1925), *La codification du droit international*, p. 352; Sőrensen, M. (1960), *Principes de droit international public: Cours général*, pp. 47-51.

[847] Henckaerts, J.-M. (March 2005), *Study on customary international humanitarian law: A contribution to the understanding and respect for the rule of law in armed conflict*, p. 181.

[848] See for example, Mendelson, M. (1995), *The subjective element in customary international law*, p. 183.

[849] See for example, Akehurst, M. (1987), *A modern introduction to international law*; Shaw, M.N. (1997), *International Law*, p. 67. See also, e.g., Starke, J.G. (1994), *Starke's international law*, pp. 33-34.

[850] *The Case of the S.S. 'Lotus'* (1927), para. 18.

[851] *North Sea Continental Shelf (Federal Republic of Germany/Denmark; Federal Republic of Germany/Netherlands)* cases (1969), para. 74.

[852] Villiger, M.E. (1997), *Customary International Law and Treaties. A Manual on the Theory and Practice of the Interrelation of Sources*, p. 49.

Stern stressing the importance of the Great Powers maintains that:

> 'states which are in the minority should require a unanimous opinio juris and (...) those which have power, or are in the majority, a general opinio juris.'[853]

This leads her to the conclusion that:

> 'the customary international rule is the one which is considered to be such by the will of those states which are able to impose their point of view.'[854]

However, the recent practice of the Court does not seem to fully support this contention. For instance, in the *Nuclear Weapons Advisory Opinion* the Court has not found the sufficient *opinio iuris* to declare the prohibition of the use of nuclear weapons, despite

> 'the desire of a very large section of the international community to take, by a specific and express prohibition of the use of nuclear weapons, a significant step forward along the road to complete nuclear disarmament.'[855]

If the desire of a very large group of states evidenced in the resolutions adopted each year by a large majority of states was not sufficient to convince the Court as to the existence of necessary *opinio iuris*, then it means that the Court expected a universal *opinio iuris* on this matter.

5.3 Critique of the subjective element

(a) Critique of *opinio iuris*

Tomuschat argued in his recent Hague lectures that the formulation of the element of *opinio iuris* 'leaves no room for criticism'.[856] However, the notion of the psychological element has created two profound theoretical and practical problems:

First, there is a chronological paradox in relation to the custom formation described by Thirlway as 'juridical squaring of the circle':

> 'The simple equation of the opinio iuris with the intention to conform to what is recognized, at the moment of conforming, as an existing rule of law has been exposed to the objection (...) that it necessarily implies a vicious circle in the logical analysis of the creation of custom.'[857]

---

853 Stern, B. (2001), *Custom at the heart of international law (trans. M. Byers, A. Denise)*, p. 104.

854 Ibid., p. 108.

855 *Legality Of The Threat Or Use Of Nuclear Weapons (Advisory Opinion)* (8 July 1996), para. 73.

856 Tomuschat, C. (1999), *International Law: Ensuring the Survival of Mankind on the Eve of a New Century*, p. 324.

857 Thirlway, H.W.A. (1972), *International Customary Law and Codification*, p. 47.

Kunz argued:

> 'On the one hand it is said that usage plus opinio iuris leads to such norm, that, on the other hand, in order to lead to such a norm the states must already practice the first cases with the opinio iuris. Hence, the very coming into existence of such norm would presuppose that the states acted in legal error.'

To Kunz, this problem 'has not yet found a satisfactory solution'.[858] And D'Amato:

> 'But if custom creates law, how can a component of custom require that creative acts be in accordance with some prior right or obligation in international law?'[859]

Also judges are aware of these deficiencies of the theory of custom. Judge Lachs stated in his dissenting opinion to *North Sea Continental Shelf* cases that

> 'to postulate that all States, even those which initiate a given practice, believe themselves to be acting under a legal obligation is to resort to a fiction – and in fact to deny the possibility of developing such rules.'[860]

As a result, the concept of *opinio iuris* created a very serious theoretical problem that is sufficient to render the whole concept unacceptable on the grounds of its internal inconsistency, as it is impossible to accept as a theory a set of statements that cannot logically explain their subject-matter.

Second, there exist practical difficulties with evidencing the psychological element. Customary practice is formed spontaneously and it is difficult to ascertain a precise attitude to it among states. Nevertheless, Briggs in his often cited opinion argued that the psychological element 'has created more difficulty in theory than in practice'.[861] This is so, because as will be discussed below, judges have ignored the direct proof of *opinio iuris* by either inferring it from a party's practice or entirely abandoning its attestation.[862]

Furthermore, as was mentioned above, Geny introduced the notion of *opinio iuris* in order to distil from the set of already existing customs those that have a legal character.[863] However, this is often a difficult task. For instance, the widely

---

[858] Kunz, J.L. (October 1953), *The nature of customary international law*, p. 667.

[859] D'Amato, A.A. (1969), *The concept of custom in international law*, p. 84.

[860] Judge Lachs (1969), *Dissenting opinion of Judge Lachs on Continental Shelf* case, p. 231.

[861] Briggs, H.W. (October 1951), *The Colombian-Peruvian Asylum* case *and Proof of Customary International Law*, p. 730, citing Sorensen, Silving and Guggenheim.

[862] See for example, Brownlie, I. (1990), *Principles of public international law*, p. 8; Jenks, C.W. (1964), *The Prospects of International Adjudication*, pp. 253-254; Kelsen, H. (1952), *Principles of International Law*; Lauterpacht, H.S. (1958), *The Development of International Law by the International Court*, p. 380; Wolfke, K. (1993), *Custom in Present International Law*, p. 123.

[863] Gény, F. (1919 reprinted in 1954), *Méthode d'Interprétation et sources en droit privé positif*, para. 110.

practiced exemption of diplomats' baggage from customs checks was an often-cited example of a non-binding social habit.[864] Tunkin argued, that such norms 'are not norms of international law'.[865] However, somewhat paradoxically, this norm was expressly codified in the 1961 Vienna Convention on Diplomatic Relations.[866] Similarly, the ICJ in the *Lotus* case refused to acknowledge the emergence of a customary norm of non-prosecution of foreign citizens as a result of maritime collision on the high seas based on the alleged lack of *opinio iuris*.[867] Very soon however, this norm was codified in Article 11 of the 1958 Convention on the High Seas.[868] The question is whether these norms were really non-legal norms. For some writers, such a situation is not a problem, as the non-binding usage of the *opinio iuris* was added later on.[869] It could be argued, however, that the above examples are a compelling illustration of the development of customary norms without *opinio iuris*, until their final codification in the international treaties. It also shows how difficult it might be to categorise social norms as legal or non-legal norms.

(b) Critique of *pactum tacitum*

Equally difficult problems are posed by the consensual interpretation of the subjective element of custom.

First, this approach does not correspond to the reality as customary norms are in principium formed in a spontaneous manner and not by an agreement.[870] If one accepts this premise, it is impossible to reconcile the explanation of the subjective element as a conscious acceptance of a legal obligation or right with the impulsive character of this social phenomenon. Spontaneous adherence to a practice precludes a calculated acceptance of it as law. However, one should note that a number of authors agree that states closely observe one another's behaviour and either acknowledge or immediately protest against a practice in question, thus weakening this argument to some extent.[871]

Second, as was the case with *opinio iuris*, the consciousness of an obligation or a right is required as it is impossible to form an agreement – tacit or explicit, with-

---

864 See for example, Guggenheim, P. (1950), *Les deux éléments de la coutume en droit international*, p. 71; Tunkin, G.I. (1974), *Theory of International Law*, p. 115.

865 Tunkin, G.I. (1974), *Theory of International Law*, p. 115.

866 International Law Commission (18 April 1961), *Vienna Convention on Diplomatic Relations*.

867 *The Case of the S.S. 'Lotus'* (1927). See also Starke, J.G. (1994), *Starke's international law*, p. 35.

868 International Law Commission (29 April 1958), *Convention on the High Seas*.

869 See for example, Kunz, J.L. (October 1953), *The nature of customary international law*, p. 667.

870 See Puchta, G.F. (1928), *Das Gewohnheitsrecht*; von Savigny, F.K. (1840-49), *System des Heutigen Romischen Rechts*; von Savigny, F. K. (1840) *Vom Beruf Unserer Zeit fur Gesetzgebung und Rechtswissgnschaft*.

871 See for example, Meijers, H. (1978), *How is international law made? – The stages of growth of international law and the use of its customary rules*; Wolfke, K. (1993), *Some Persistent Controversies Regarding Customary International Law*, p. 8.

out being aware of its terms. Again, one faces evidentiary issues associated with proving this attitude. Some authors try to overcome this problem by suggesting that the consent can be presumed if the state does not protest against a practice in question (acquiescence in).[872] But a party may not protest for a number of reasons,[873] including lack of interest or knowledge, thus confirming the artificiality of this interpretation.

In addition, if every state should individually agree to a customary norm in question, the custom would cease to be a source of generally binding law[874] or at least its role in the creation of generally binding law would be minimal.[875] This consequence is in conformity with the extreme positivist outlook arguing that a majority of independent states cannot legally bind the minority.[876] However, some supporters of the consensual view contradict the underlying concept of state sovereignty, allowing custom to bind the dissenting minority.[877]

Finally, this doctrine also has not convincingly explained why states new to a given practice should be bound by the existing body of customary international law.[878] If custom emanates only from the free will of states, then it should not bind states that had not taken part in its formation. Some authors argue that new states, by seeking admission to the family of states, already give evidence of their recognition of general international law.[879] They more or less willingly recognise already existing customary law; otherwise they would encounter problems regarding their admission to the international community.[880] The artificiality of such an explanation is a product of the voluntaristic doctrine of law that assumes that all the rules of international law are the result of deliberate law-making. The above concept was criticised as a 'pure and simple fiction'[881] or 'a totally fictitious conception'.[882] Kunz put it this way:

---

[872] See for example, Wolfke, K. (1993), *Custom in Present International Law*, p. 48, cited above, Meijers, H. (1978), *How is international law made? – The stages of growth of international law and the use of its customary rules*, p. 18; Wolfke, K. (1993), *Some Persistent Controversies Regarding Customary International Law*, pp. 8-9.

[873] D'Amato, A.A. (1971), *The concept of custom in international law*, pp. 98-102.

[874] Guggenheim, P. (1953), *Traite de Droit international public: Avec mention de la pratique internationale et suisse*, p. 47.

[875] See for example, Basdevant, J. (1936), *Règles Générales du Droit de la Paix*, p. 517; Mendelson, M. (1995), *The subjective element in customary international law*, p. 185.

[876] See for example, Wolfke, K. (1993), *Some Persistent Controversies Regarding Customary International Law*, p. 13.

[877] See for example, Oppenheim, L. (1955), *International Law: A Treatise*, p. 11, see also works of judge Fitzmaurice.

[878] See for example, Basdevant, J. (1936), *Règles Générales du Droit de la Paix*, pp. 507, 515; Kelsen, H. (1966), *Principles of International Law*, pp. 444-445.

[879] See for example, Wolfke, K. (1993), *Some Persistent Controversies Regarding Customary International Law*, p. 13.

[880] Ibid.

[881] Basdevant, J. (1936), *Règles Générales du Droit de la Paix*, p. 515.

[882] de Vischer, C. (1955), *Théories et réalités en droit international public*, p. 188; de Visscher, C. (1957), *Theory and Reality in Public International Law*, p. 188.

> 'The purely fictitious character of this construction, its open contradiction to the practice of states, the untenable consequences to which it leads, its rejection of the overwhelming majority of writers, makes it superfluous to refute this construction once more.'[883]

And further:

> 'As to the problem of how widely the usage must have been practiced, international law demands a "general" practice, not a unanimous one. That shows the untenability of the consent theory, of the *pactum tacitum* construction. For, if it is the case of a customary rule of general international law, created by general practice, such norm is valid for new states and for pre-existing states that hitherto had no opportunity of applying it.'[884]

6. Alternative Approaches

The doctrine has developed alternative interpretations of the twin elements in the theory of custom. These interpretations either reject the element of practice or reject the *opinio iuris* element, or mix all of the approaches in one framework.

6.1 The 'practice only' approach

The 'practice only' approach rejects the necessity of the subjective element and leaves the material element of practice as the only constituent of the notion of custom. In 1937 Kopelmanas, influenced by Hammel,[885] argued that

> 'the formation of custom does not depend on the presence in the minds of the parties of an opinio juris, but on the contrary the content of the customary rule often plays the principal part.'[886]

His motives were dictated by the understanding of the requirements of international trade that often has to function outside the law, the phenomenon that he describes as

> 'a "revolt of the facts against the code" – a revolt realized by the concurrent activity of the subjects of law, an activity determined by the requirements of social life.'[887]

Two years later, Williams rejected *opinio iuris* as an error.

---

883 Kunz, J.L. (October 1953), *The nature of customary international law*, pp. 663-664, and the literature cited there.

884 Ibid., p. 666, citing The Paquete Habana (1900), *175 US 677.*

885 Hammel, J. (1935), *Les formes internationales des credits bancaires*, p. 205.

886 Kopelmanas, L. (1937), *Custom as a Means of the Creation of International Law*, p. 151.

887 Ibid., p. 150, italics omitted.

> 'The Rubicon which divides custom from law is crossed silently, unconsciously, and without proclamation. There is ordinarily no moment at which persons, corporate bodies, or states, which have been following for a long period a particular course of conduct, say to themselves or to each other, "what we are doing is not simply following in the path which our predecessors have followed or cleared, but we are actually making it a legal duty as between ourselves to do what for an indefinite period we and our predecessors for a long time (or 'from time immemorial') have done.'[888]

Kelsen also supported the idea of practice as the sufficient element to form custom because it is too difficult to evidence thoughts of national governments.[889] However, his theory is not very clear. Kelsen clearly required two elements in custom:

> 'the fact that certain actions or abstentions have repeatedly been performed during a certain period of time'

and,

> 'the fact that the individuals must be convinced that they fulfil, by their actions or abstentions, a duty, or that they exercise a right.'[890]

In regard to the second element, however, he stated that parties

> 'must believe that they apply a norm, but they need not believe that it is a legal norm which they apply. They have to regard their conduct as obligatory or right.'[891]

Kelsen emphasises the importance of practice and seems to reject the traditional notion of *opinio iuris* understood as acceptance of practice as law.[892] The problem with his approach is that it requires a belief in the exercise of a subjective right. It will rarely, however, be the case as customary law develops as he noted subsequently, unconsciously and unintentionally.[893] The requirement of exercise of a right or duty and unconsciousness of acts are impossible to reconcile. He also avoids the answer if a proof of such subjective feeling of exercising non-legal right or duty is required or not.

---

[888] Williams, J.F.S. (1939), *Aspects of Modern International Law: An Essay*, p. 44.

[889] Kelsen, H. (1939), *Théorie du droit international coutumier*, p. 264, see also Kelsen, H. (1966), *Principles of International Law*, p. 440; Kelsen, H. (1952), *Principles of International Law*, p. 307.

[890] Kelsen, H. (1966), *Principles of International Law*, p. 440; Kelsen, H. (1952), *Principles of International Law*, p. 307.

[891] Ibid.

[892] D'Amato argues that Kelsen did not reject the psychological component but 'he came close by arguing that the determination of this element is a matter for the absolute arbitrary discretion of an international tribunal.' D'Amato, A.A. (1971), *The concept of custom in international law*, p. 52, citing Kelsen, H. (1939), *Théorie du droit international coutumier*, pp. 264-266.

[893] Kelsen, H. (1966), *Principles of International Law*, p. 441; Kelsen, H. (1952), *Principles of International Law*, p. 308.

Guggenheim argued that the concept of the psychological element makes custom superfluous as an independent source of international law.[894] He was opposing the articulation of Article 38 of the Statute which he considered as an acceptance of the theory of the historical school of Savigny, which in turn did not consider customary practice as a source of law, but only as an evidence of a rule developed by the spirit of the nation.[895] Guggenheim maintained that long lasting and constant repetition of acts is the only one constitutive element of custom and that the subjective element should be eliminated.[896] The main reason for the rejection of the subjective element was difficulties with evidencing it.[897]

Among other important writers who continued to support the traditional reliance upon a practice were Gihl, who recognised difficulties with proving the psychological element without time consuming research,[898] Quadri who associated custom with the tradition that does not require recognition to become the norm of law but creates expectation that will be followed[899] and Lissitzyn, who considered the psychological element to be an artificial construct.[900] On the other hand, Lauterpacht favoured the element of practice, because *opinio iuris* could be presumed on that basis.[901] The ICJ has not explicitly endorsed this approach although, as will be shown later, it has based its decisions on analysis of practice only and disregarded the proof of *opinio iuris*.

In summary, supporters of the importance of practice point to the difficulties with evidencing the subjective element and the artificiality of its theoretical explanatory power. This approach eliminates illogical deficiencies that perplex *opinio iuris* theories. The only objection raised against this way of thinking is that it blurs the line between legally relevant rights and obligations and non-legal norms of comity or morality.[902] The question remains if such a distinction is possible and necessary. As will be shown in the next chapter, the distinction between legal and non-legal norms is rarely clear and what is more important, is a relevance of a given practice in solving legal disputes.

---

894 Guggenheim, P. (1950), *Les deux éléments de la coutume en droit international*, pp. 275-280.

895 Guggenheim, P. (1952), *Les Principles de Droit International Public*, pp. 69-70.

896 Guggenheim, P. (1950), *Les deux éléments de la coutume en droit international*, p. 275; Guggenheim, P. (1953), *Traité de Droit international public: Avec mention de la pratique internationale et suisse*, Vol. 1, pp. 44-45. But see his metamorphosis in Guggenheim, P. (1967), *Traité de Droit international public: Avec mention de la pratique internationale et suisse*, Vol. 1, p. 107.

897 Guggenheim, P. (1950), *Les deux éléments de la coutume en droit international*, p. 275; Guggenheim, P. (1953), *Traité de Droit international public: Avec mention de la pratique internationale et suisse*, Vol. 1, pp. 44-45.

898 Gihl, T. (1957), *The Legal Character and Sources of International Law*, p. 83.

899 Quadri, R. (1963), *Diritto internazionale pubblico*, pp. 95-96, cited by Tunkin

900 Lissitzyn, O. (1965), *International Law Today and Tomorrow*, pp. 34-35.

901 Lauterpacht, H.S. (1958), *The Development of International Law by the International Court*, p. 380, see also writings of Jean Haemmerlé.

902 See for example, Kunz, J.L. (October 1953), *The nature of customary international law*, p. 665; Thirlway, H.W.A. (1972), *International Customary Law and Codification*, p. 48; van Hoof, G.J.H. (1983), *Rethinking the sources of international law*, p. 86.

6.2 The 'instant custom' approach

Cheng's 'instant custom' approach is on the opposite side of the spectrum and equates the custom with consent to a given norm.[903] Witnessing the emergence of the law of cosmos he proposed the theory of 'practice-less' custom developed by a unanimous will of states accepting a resolution:

> 'Not only is it unnecessary that the usage should be prolonged, but there need also be no usage at all in the sense of repeated practice, provided that the opinio juris of the States concerned can be clearly established. Consequently, international customary law has in reality only one constitutive element, the opinio juris.'[904]

Nonetheless, Cheng is aware of the difficulty of speaking about custom without practice.

> 'It is true that in the case of a rule without usage, objection might be taken to the use of the term custom or customary. But whether in such a case one speaks of international customary law or an unwritten rule of international law becomes purely a matter of terminology.'[905]

Interestingly though, Cheng requires general and prolonged practice as the constituent element of custom in municipal legal systems.[906] Recently, Ridruejo argued that the subjective or spiritual element is nowadays much more important than practice. In his view, it is the *opinio iuris* element that allows international law to adapt to changing international conditions and values.[907]

However, rejection of practice stretches the notion of custom to the point where it loses its original sense and for this reason, this concept will not be further investigated.

6.3 Reconciliatory approaches

There are authors who decided to reconcile theories of custom ranging from 'practice only' approaches to dual element theories to 'practice-less' constructs.[908] Kirgis

---

903 See for example, Corbett, P. (1925), *The Consent of States and the Sources of the Law of Nations*; Strupp, K. (1934), *Les Règles Générales du Droit de la Paix*, p. 304; Triepel, H. (1923), *Les Rapports entre le Droit Interne et le Droit International*, pp. 82-83.

904 Cheng, B. (1965), *United Nations Resolutions on Outer Space: 'Instant' International Customary law?*, p. 36.

905 Ibid.

906 Ibid., p. 37.

907 Ridruejo, J.A.P. (1998), *Le droit international à la veille du vingt et unième siècle: normes, faits et valeurs*, p. 45, para. 2.2.3.

908 See for example, Kirgis, F.L.J. (1987), *Custom on a sliding scale*, p. 149, and supporting him Roberts, A.E. (October 2001), *Traditional and modern approaches to customary international law:*

tolerates using both practice without the psychological element and the psychological element without practice or any combination of the above elements dependant upon the activity in question and reasonableness of potential customary norm.[909] Reasonableness and morality are at the core of his idea of custom on a sliding scale because as he asserts

> 'the more destabilising or morally distasteful the activity (...) the more readily the international decision makers will substitute one element for the other.'[910]

One particularly interesting theory was proposed by D'Amato, who replaced the division on material and subjective elements with quantitative and qualitative elements.[911] The quantitative element is 'the act or commitment' which can be equated with the traditional element of practice. The qualitative element is the 'articulation' or pronouncement of legality of the quantitative element by states. This way, D'Amato decided to reconcile traditional issues associated with the proof of subjective element[912] with the insistence on the material element of practice.

On the other hand, many supporters of the twin elements theory of custom allow for custom to be based on a practice only. Mendelson argued that:

> 'it is not an invariable requirement that the subjective element be present (in one or other of its forms) for a practice to constitute or reflect a rule of customary international law.'[913]

Likewise Starke stated that:

> 'the *opinio juris* is not an essential element of custom, but if it is present, it is helpful as distinguishing custom from a course of action followed as a matter of arbitrary choice or for other reasons.'[914]

In the same way, Bernhardt stressing the necessity of the *opinio iuris* argued that

> 'in many cases consistent State practice can be considered as sufficient evidence of customary international law.'[915]

In summary, none of these approaches to date has been explicitly endorsed by the ICJ. Nevertheless, they represent an interesting attempt to explain the

---

A reconciliation, p. 760; Simma, B. and Alston, P. (1992), *The Sources of Human Rights Law: Custom, Jus Cogens, and General Principles*, p. 83.

909 Kirgis, F.L.J. (1987), *Custom on a sliding scale*, pp. 149-151.

910 Ibid., p. 149.

911 D'Amato, A.A. (1971), *The concept of custom in international law*, pp. 73-98.

912 Ibid., p. 2.

913 Mendelson, M. (1995), *The subjective element in customary international law*, pp. 183-184.

914 Starke, J.G. (1994), *Starke's international law*, pp. 33-34, references omitted.

915 Bernhardt, R. (1992), *Customary International Law*, p. 899 Vol. 1.

phenomenon of emergence and existence of international customary law.

7. Judicial Confirmation of Custom

One controversial issue is who should be vested with the ascertainment of the existence of international customs and what should be the value of such a pronouncement. Kunz argues that the ascertainment of custom is a difficult task that must be carried out by the competent international authority and preliminarily by the science of international law.[916] On the other hand, positivists deny the necessity of judicial pronouncement in the formation of custom because they consider the state as the only entity capable of creating law by its own will. As Kopelmanas pointed out:

> 'it is easy to establish by a simple piece of logical reasoning that the judge may be considered as the author par excellence of custom'

but

> 'custom can be developed solely by the action of certain subjects of law without the judge.'[917]

On the other hand, Basdevant seems to consider judicial decisions as constitutive elements of custom.[918] The doctrine seems to remain divided on this question.

8. Evidencing International Custom

8.1 Methods of evidencing custom

The question of how to evidence international custom is one of the most difficult ones. The literature is not particularly abundant in this respect,[919] with the notable exception of latest study on international customary humanitarian law.[920] In the *Lotus* case the Court has sought for the evidence of custom in the teachings of publicists, decisions of municipal and international tribunals, and especially in con-

---

[916] Kunz, J.L. (October 1953), *The nature of customary international law*, p. 667.

[917] Kopelmanas, L. (1937), *Custom as a Means of the Creation of International Law*, pp. 141-142, capital letter and italics omitted.

[918] Basdevant, J. (1936), *Règles Générales du Droit de la Paix*, p. 511.

[919] See for example, Degan, V.D. (1997), *Sources of International Law*, pp. 174-177.

[920] Henckaerts, J.-M. and Doswald-Beck, L. (2005), *Customary International Humanitarian Law, 2 volumes, Volume I. Rules, Volume II. Practice (2 Parts)*. See also Henckaerts, J.-M. (March 2005), *Study on customary international humanitarian law: A contribution to the understanding and respect for the rule of law in armed conflict*.

ventions.[921] Judge Hudson pointed to the following sources of evidence of custom: texts of international instruments, decisions of international courts, decisions of national courts, national legislation, and diplomatic correspondence, opinions of national legal advisors and practice of international organisations.[922] It might be surprising to find in the above lists international conventions and decisions of courts as primary sources of evidence of custom. Conventions create a law but only for the signatories thereof whereas international custom applies *erga omnes* (to all). Furthermore, treaties may codify customary norm, but a practice might change after the codification so the proof of general custom based on a convention is difficult to accept. Similarly, the search for custom in legal decisions is surprising because judgments solve only a given dispute at hand and often refer to old practices that may no longer apply. Equally extraordinary is the search for the proof of custom in the teachings of publicists and legal advisers, which by their very nature will have to be diverse. The analysis of diplomatic correspondence and the examination of practice of international organisations is a potential source of proof of international custom, but their position at the end of the list indicates their relative unimportance in relation to the previous sources of evidence. The most striking element, however, is a complete lack of interest in classic data collection methods such as formal surveys[923] of states' actions or governmental opinions regarding the legality of a given practice. None of the Court judgments or books on the subject presents data of the actual states' actions or states' *opinio iuris* gathered by investigating either all or at least a representative sample of states over a specified period of time.

The following sections will analyse recent customary law-rich judgments of the ICJ in order to establish how the Court establishes international custom in legal proceedings. The three cases analysed below show slightly different approaches that the Court adopted to prove international custom. A knowledge of the jurisprudential techniques of evidencing custom will be used in the next chapter of the book as a starting point for the discussion of the ways and means of evidencing Internet custom.

8.2 Recent evidentiary practice of the ICJ

(a) The 1986 *Nicaragua* case

The 1986 *Case Concerning Military and Paramilitary Activities in and Against Nicaragua* (the *Nicaragua* case)[924] well illustrates this argument. Simplifying the case, the US government was accused by the government of Nicaragua of military

[921] *The Case of the S.S. 'Lotus'* (1927) para. 25-26.

[922] Hudson, M.O. (3 March 1950), *Article 24 of the Statute of the International Law Commission. Working Paper. Document A/CN.4/16*, pp. 26-30.

[923] See Chapter VIII.

[924] *Case Concerning Military and Paramilitary Activities in and Against Nicaragua (Nicaragua* v. *United States of America)* (1986).

and paramilitary intervention and direct and indirect support for the armed opposition (contras).[925] The US government justified its decision on the basis of collective self-defence against an alleged Nicaraguan armed attack on El Salvador, Honduras and Costa Rica[926] and involvement in logistical support for guerrillas in El Salvador.[927] In effect, the Court found the government of United States in breach of several customary norms of international law invoked by Nicaragua: the principle of the prohibition of the use of force,[928] the principle of non-intervention in the internal affairs of state,[929] the principle of respect for territorial sovereignty,[930] the principle of freedom of communications and maritime commerce,[931] the humanitarian principle of giving notice of the mining of ports.[932] The Court also did not uphold the existence of a right of collective self-defence to acts that do not constitute an armed attack and a prohibition of unfriendly acts towards other states as norms of customary law.[933]

The Court stressed the importance of evidencing practice:

> 'The Court must satisfy itself that the existence of the rule in the opinio juris of States is confirmed by practice.'[934]

Therefore, the Court method of proving the custom was first to 'appraise the relevant practice' in the light of the subjective element.[935] However, the aforementioned principles were first declared to have customary character before proceeding to the actual proof of them.[936]

The proof of practice regarding the principle of non-use of force has, in fact, turned out to be an examination of opinions of the US government and the Nicaraguan government contained in the submitted documents.[937] The conclusion was that both governments agreed that this principle is enshrined in Article 2 paragraph 4 of the Charter. One should note here, that the above method could at most be treated as the evidence of *opinio iuris* of the parties and not of a practice. Conversely, the existence of *opinio iuris* was

[925] Ibid., para. 15.
[926] Ibid., para. 229.
[927] Ibid., para. 19.
[928] Ibid., paras. 187-200, 227.
[929] Ibid., paras. 242, 246.
[930] Ibid., paras. 250-252.
[931] Ibid., para. 253.
[932] Ibid., paras. 215, 254.
[933] Ibid., paras. 211, 238, 246-249, 273.
[934] Ibid., para. 184.
[935] Ibid., para. 185.
[936] Ibid., para. 174, citing Judgment of 26 November 1984 (ICJ Reports 1984, para. 73).
[937] Ibid., paras. 187-188.

> 'deduced from, inter alia, the attitude of the Parties and the attitude of States towards certain General Assembly resolutions, particularly the Declaration on Principles of International Law.'[938]

Statements made by state representatives were cited as a further confirmation of the validity of this customary norm.[939] In summary, the custom of non-use of force has been established, based only on the unanimous view of the parties and the doctrine that such a rule exists, without recourse to an analysis of the actual general practice of states over time.

The existence and the content of the right of self-defence were also evidenced by citing the relevant provisions of treaties and resolutions as well as parties' opinions that allegedly testified to their existence.[940] Special emphasis was placed on Article 51 of the Charter of the United Nations that partially codified the right of individual and collective self-defence.[941] Based on the parties' opinions, the right was found to contain the limitations of proportionality and necessity as 'well established in customary international law'.[942] Furthermore, the Court 'defined'[943] additional conditions for the exercise of this customary right: the necessity of an armed attack (by regular forces and by sending armed bands by a third state on behalf of another state), the obligation of the state for whose benefit the right is used to declare itself to be the victim of an armed attack, the requirement of a request by the State which is the victim of an armed attack.[944] These norms were found in the customary law of States but no proof of the actual state practice has been cited. Instead, the Court found them in the treaties allegedly reflecting the state of the international customary law. Conversely, the Court has not found as belonging to the customary norms the requirement of immediate notification to the Security Council of measures taken in the exercise of the self-defence by a state being attacked as required in Article 51 of the Charter. The proof of non-customary nature of this norm was based on a logical reasoning that

> 'a procedure so closely dependent on the content of a treaty commitment and of the institutions established by it'[945]

could not belong to the body of international customary law.

---

[938] Ibid., para. 188.

[939] Ibid., para. 190.

[940] Ibid., paras. 176, 193-201.

[941] United Nations Conference on International Organization at San Francisco (26 June 1945), *Charter of the United Nations.*

[942] *Case Concerning Military and Paramilitary Activities in and Against Nicaragua (Nicaragua* v. *United States of America)* (1986), paras. 176, 194.

[943] Ibid., para. 193.

[944] Ibid., paras. 194-199, 211.

[945] Ibid., para. 200.

It is interesting how the Court approached the evidence of the principle of non-intervention that has not been codified in the Charter.

> 'The principle of non-intervention involves the right of every sovereign State to conduct its affairs without outside interference; though examples of trespass against this principle are not infrequent, the Court considers that it is part and parcel of customary international law.'[946]

And further:

> 'The existence in the opinio juris of States of the principle of non-intervention is backed by established and substantial practice.'

Again, a reference is made to the established and substantial practice but no data is presented. On the other hand, *opinio iuris* is found in the Courts' earlier judgments, resolutions, declarations and treaties.[947] Based on this, the Court declares the existence of this norm as an international custom.

On the other hand, the content of the principle is again defined by the Court:

> 'the principle forbids all States or groups of States to intervene directly or indirectly in internal or external affairs of other States.'[948]

This time, the Court decided to search for the proof of this definition by a reference to a hypothetical contrary custom of the interventions in the internal affairs of states to support the opposition:

> 'There have been in recent years a number of instances of foreign intervention for the benefit of forces opposed to the government of another State. The Court is not here concerned with the process of decolonisation; this question is not in issue in the present case. It has to consider whether there might be indications of a practice illustrative of belief in a kind of general right for States to intervene, directly or indirectly, with or without armed force, in support of an internal opposition in another State, whose cause appeared particularly worthy by reason of the political and moral values with which it was identified. For such a general right to come into existence would involve a fundamental modification of the customary law principle of non-intervention.'[949]

But no detailed examination of the practice followed. Instead the Court declared that:

---

[946] Ibid., para. 202.
[947] Ibid., paras. 202-209.
[948] Ibid., para. 205.
[949] Ibid., para. 206.

> 'the Court finds that States have not justified their conduct by reference to a new right of intervention or a new exception to the principle of its prohibition.'[950]

To support its contention, the Court in very general terms referred to the practice of the United States:

> 'The United States authorities have on some occasions clearly stated their grounds for intervening in the affairs of a foreign State for reasons connected with, for example, the domestic policies of that country, its ideology, the level of its armaments, or the direction of its foreign policy. But these were statements of international policy, and not an assertion of rules of existing international law.'[951]

Since the United States made no claim towards Nicaragua supporting 'the new right of intervention', no such rule was established.[952] In consequence, the restrictive notion of the customary principle of non-intervention was upheld.

It is important to note that the examination of state practice should not be limited to the practice of litigants only, as the practice of all the other states should be taken into account. This flows from the accepted principle of general practice. Furthermore, the examination of state practice should not be reduced to the general observation that certain states adhere to a given practice or not, but should be analysed in more depth, including the statement of how many states have been examined and citing at least the important cases of such an adherence.

The customary principle of respect for state sovereignty is again defined with a reference to specific treaties.[953] No state practice, with the exception of the United States mining of the Nicaraguan ports, is examined. Also no reference to the proof of *opinio iuris* is made, although it can be presumed that the above-mentioned treaties serve this purpose. On this occasion, the Court also mentioned the related customary norm of 'innocent passage in territorial waters for the purposes of entering or leaving internal waters' as codified by the relevant treaty.[954] In this context, the customary principle of giving notice about mining of the ports has been mentioned but no proof of its existence in states practice has been attested to. The Court's strategy in relation to establishing humanitarian customary norms is particularly confusing. First, a reference to such a principle is made in connection with the relevant convention expressing it, but the Court did not declare as a rule of customary international law but as a 'the principle of humanitarian law'. Secondly, a reference to this norm as a norm of customary international law is made only later on in the judgment:

---

[950] Ibid., para. 207.
[951] Ibid.
[952] Ibid., paras. 207-209.
[953] Ibid., paras. 212-214.
[954] Ibid., para. 214.

> 'Mention has already been made (...) of the violations of customary international law by reason of the failure to give notice of the mining of the Nicaraguan ports.'[955]

But in fact, no such mention has been made, and it is unclear whether the Court considered the discussed humanitarian principles as principles of customary law or general principles of law.

Neither has the Court established certain norms as customary ones. For instance, in respect to prohibition of unfriendly acts towards other states bound by the treaty of friendship, the Court stated that:

> 'as a matter of customary international law, it is not clear that the existence of such a far-reaching rule is evidenced in the practice of States.'[956]

However, no such evidence is cited or examined. Also there is no analysis of *opinio iuris* regarding this norm.

In the end of the judgment, the Court has also recalled

> 'the principle that the parties to any dispute, particularly any dispute the continuance of which is likely to endanger the maintenance of international peace and security, should seek a solution by peaceful means.'[957]

Again, its existence was declared with a reference to the relevant treaty provision. On this occasion, however, the Court mentioned the Contadora Process,[958] which could be treated as a proof of state practice. However, to prove the existence of this principle, more evidence of states practice would be necessary.

In general, the ICJ has not provided and analysed sufficient evidence of state practice in relation to any of the alleged customary norms of international law, thus undermining the theory of custom it subscribed to. No data regarding the actual state practice (with the exception of litigants' recent practice) is cited or analysed, leading to the conclusion that in the light of the adopted theory of custom, claims about the existence of a given general state practice and its characteristics are unfounded. This does not mean of course, such principles do not exist as customary norms, but only that they have not been satisfactorily proven. Instead, in some cases, the presented proof could be argued to satisfactorily evidence the existence and content of a general principle of law.

The Court has focused on the proof of *opinio iuris*, often providing an impressive survey of the legal documents enshrining the customary principles. One should note here that the Court made an implicit and risky assumption that a will of a State expressed in a signature to the agreement or a declaration is a conclusive proof of

---

955 Ibid., para. 254.
956 Ibid., para. 273.
957 Ibid., para. 290.
958 Ibid., paras. 290-291.

the feeling that a given norm or set of norms exists and binds it even without such an agreement. However, the proof of *opinio iuris* based on the analysis of treaties, resolutions and case law may not provide the same results as a proper survey of beliefs or convictions among state decision-makers regarding the existence and binding character of a principle in question. In short, it could be argued that the Court has not cited convincing evidence of the existence and the content of the psychological element of custom. Likewise, the proof of content of a given custom was based on a procedure that favoured the analysis of legal texts referring to a given norm, at the expense of the proof of the actual practice of states. In some cases, the Court simply declared the existence or a content of a given norm.

One should note that the methodology of evidencing custom based on the ascertainment of the existence and the content of a given norm in two separate activities also seem to be a result of the *a priori* method of proving custom. If a given customary norm exists, it exists in a given form or has a given content. It cannot exist without a specific content. The establishment of the existence of a customary norm in the practice of states determines its content – it cannot be defined or modified by the Court. Each characteristic of a customary norm should be found in the actual practice of the majority (or unanimity) of participants amounting to its creation and, in the view of the doctrine accepted by the Court, in their *opinio iuris*. Therefore, the Court's method of first establishing the existence of custom in the legal treaties, resolutions and cases and then the "interpretation" of its content in the same sources cannot be regarded as a reasonable and permissible method of evidencing international custom.

(b) The 1996 Nuclear Weapons Advisory Opinion

In the *Advisory Opinion (Nuclear Weapons Opinion)* the Court offered its view on permissibility under international law of the threat or use of nuclear weapons in any circumstances.[959] However, it could not

> 'reach a definitive conclusion as to the legality or illegality of the use of nuclear weapons by a State in an extreme circumstance of self-defence, in which its very survival would be at stake.'[960]

In this opinion, a reference was made to the following customary norms: the right of self-defence,[961] the prohibition of threat or use of force (in the context of nuclear weapons),[962] and the humanitarian principles applicable in the event of a war of the

[959] *Legality Of The Threat Or Use Of Nuclear Weapons (Advisory Opinion)* (8 July 1996), para. 3.
[960] Ibid., paras. 97, 105.
[961] Ibid., para. 41.
[962] Ibid., paras. 64, 52.

protection of civilian population and civilian objects and prohibition of causing unnecessary suffering to combatants[963] as well as the principle of neutrality.[964]

In respect to the right of self-defence, the Court stated:

> 'The submission of the exercise of the right of self-defence to the conditions of necessity and proportionality is a rule of customary international law.'[965]

To prove this assertion however, the Court has referred to the United Nations Charter and to the *Nicaragua* case, where as was shown above, this custom has not been properly established by investigating what the general practice and *opinio iuris* is.

In addition, the Court endeavoured to determine whether a principle of prohibition of threat or use of nuclear weapons flows from the customary international law. The Court took into account the consistent practice of non-utilisation of nuclear weapons since 1945.[966] However, states interpreted this inactivity differently: some argued that it amounted to a formation of custom prohibiting the use such weapons and others that

> 'if nuclear weapons have not been used since 1945, it is not on account of an existing or nascent custom but merely because circumstances that might justify their use have fortunately not arisen.'[967]

In consequence, the Court has not found the satisfying proof of general practice as

> 'a number of States adhered to (...) practice [known as the "policy of deterrence"] during the greater part of the Cold War and continue to adhere to it.'

Likewise, the divergent opinions of states as expressed in resolutions have not satisfactorily proven the existence of general *opinio iuris* on this matter despite, as was argued earlier, 'the desire of a very large section of the international community'.[968] In consequence,

> 'The emergence (...) of a customary rule specifically prohibiting the use of nuclear weapons as such is hampered by the continuing tensions between the nascent opinio juris on the one hand, and the still strong adherence to the practice of deterrence on the other.'[969]

---

963 Ibid., para. 78.

964 Ibid., para. 88. The Court has also referred to the principle of good faith but has not expressly recognised it in this judgment as of customary character. *Legality Of The Threat Or Use Of Nuclear Weapons (Advisory Opinion)* (8 July 1996), paras. 98-103.

965 *Legality Of The Threat Or Use Of Nuclear Weapons (Advisory Opinion)* (8 July 1996), para. 41.

966 Ibid., paras. 64-66, 96.

967 Ibid., para. 66.

968 Ibid., paras. 67-73.

969 Ibid., para. 73.

Noting the relative ease of the proof of passive practice, the Court has made a reference to the policy of deterrents but has not discussed which states actually adhered to it and in consequence, what percentage of states precluded this norm from coming to existence. However, it is important to note that the Court provided the satisfactory proof of inaction and has delineated the timeframe for the investigated customary norm.

The Court also made a reference to the principles of humanitarian law, including: the prohibition of an attack on civilian populations and civilian objects and the resulting prohibition of the 'use of weapons that are incapable of distinguishing between civilian and military targets' and the prohibition of causing unnecessary suffering to the combatants.[970] The Court further stated that:

> 'these fundamental rules are to be observed by all States whether or not they have ratified the conventions that contain them, because they constitute intransgressible principles of international customary law.'[971]

To prove the *opinio iuris* the Court argued:

> 'The extensive codification of humanitarian law and the extent of the accession to the resultant treaties, as well as the fact that the denunciation clauses that existed in the codification instruments have never been used, have provided the international community with a corpus of treaty rules the great majority of which had already become customary and which reflected the most universally recognized humanitarian principles. These rules indicate the normal conduct and behaviour expected of States.'[972]

It is interesting to note in this respect that norms that are considered to flow from a custom indicate behaviour expected of a party – a contention that will be one of the fundaments of the notion of Internet custom. However, no state practice has been examined in relation to humanitarian principles. Again its existence was either declared or inferred from a large body of the relevant conventional norms. In the end, the Court attempted to answer the question whether these customary humanitarian principles in fact prohibit the use of nuclear weapons but found (quite surprisingly) the answer to be negative.

Next, the Court referred to the customary principle of neutrality and contended that it is a customary norm reflected in relevant provisions of the international conventions dealing with this matter.[973] However, no proof of state practice or explicit evidence of *opinio iuris* has been presented.

In summary, this judgment demonstrates that it is far easier to prove a passive conduct than an active practice. The Court has evidenced the abstention from using

[970] Ibid., para. 78.
[971] Ibid., para. 79.
[972] Ibid., para. 82.
[973] Ibid., paras. 88, 93.

nuclear weapons since 1945, but *opinio iuris* was not convincingly presented. It would be far better to state how many states opposed the alleged customary prohibition and how many did not, so as to have a clear picture that the general *opinio iuris* did not exist. Otherwise, as was stated above, the Court could be argued to require a unanimous *opinio iuris*. However, positive practice was not evidenced in the case of the norm of self-defence. On the other hand, principles of humanitarian law and neutrality were declared to have customary character without the proof of the two elements involved. Moreover, principles of humanitarian law were declared as intransgressible, thus disregarding the flexible and unpredictable nature of custom.

(c) The 2002 *Arrest Warrant* case

The case concerned the legality of the issue of the arrest warrant and its international circulation by a Belgian judge against a Minister of Foreign Affairs of the Democratic Republic of Congo accused of war crimes and crimes against humanity. The Court concluded that this act constituted violation of a legal obligation of respect for the immunity from criminal jurisdiction and inviolability of the position of Minister of Foreign Affairs.[974] In judgment the Court made a reference to the customary norm of absolute inviolability and immunity from the criminal process of incumbent foreign ministers[975] and the principle that only a sending state may waive such immunity.[976]

The Court commenced the proof of the general immunity norm with a declaration of the principle that the ambassadors and consuls as well as high-ranking state officials enjoy immunities from criminal and civil jurisdiction, which is 'firmly established' in international law.[977] The Court then discussed conventions embodying this norm and has found that they provide useful guidance but do not deal specifically with the immunities of the Minister of Foreign Affairs.[978] On this occasion, the Court declared the customary character of a norm that only a sending state may waive the immunity as reflected in Article 32 of the Vienna Convention on Consular Relations.[979] No specific proof of the actual practice or *opinio iuris* was presented.

The actual proof of the immunity of foreign ministers was based upon a succinct but useful discussion of the importance of the practice.[980] From the discussion of the functions of a Minister of Foreign Affairs, the Court concluded that: 'through-

[974] *Case Concerning The Arrest Warrant Of 11 April 2000 (Democratic Republic Of The Congo* v. *Belgium)* (14 February 2002), para. 29.
[975] Ibid., paras. 51-52.
[976] Ibid., para. 52.
[977] Ibid., para. 51.
[978] Ibid., para. 52.
[979] Ibid.
[980] Ibid., para. 53.

out the duration of his or her office, he or she when abroad enjoys full immunity from criminal jurisdiction and inviolability.'[981] Again no proof of state practice or *opinio iuris* was discussed.

Then the Court proceeded to the Belgian argument that there is an exception to the rule of immunity when incumbent foreign ministers 'are suspected of having committed war crimes or crimes against humanity.'[982] The Court cited two divergent interpretations by parties to the dispute in respect to two judgments of French and English courts in Qaddafi and Pinochet cases respectively.[983] As a matter of proof of practice, the ICJ

> 'has carefully examined State practice, including national legislation and those few decisions of national higher courts, such as the House of Lords or the French Court of Cassation'

and

> 'the rules concerning the immunity or criminal responsibility of persons having an official capacity contained in the legal instruments creating international criminal tribunals'

including Nuremberg, Tokyo, former Yugoslavia, Rwanda and the International Criminal Tribunal.[984] In conclusion, the Court found that no such exception exists.[985]

The ICJ has not referred to any theory of international custom, in particular the twin elements theory. Two norms declared have customary character based on a specific treaty provision and examination of the role of the subjects of the custom. In contrast to the earlier practice, however, the Court has examined only the state practice in respect to the exception to the principle of jurisdictional immunity of high-ranking state officials when suspected of having committed serious crimes.[986] Although the examination of practice has been limited to only two national judgments submitted by the parties and national and international legislation which in itself may not constitute a strong ground for drawing the conclusion, the judgment indicates a shift in the evidentiary practice of the Court. It marks a departure from the earlier emphasis on the element of *opinio iuris* and stresses the importance of the proof of state practice in the process of evidencing international custom.

---

981 Ibid., para. 54.
982 Ibid., para. 56.
983 Ibid., para2. 56-57.
984 Ibid., para. 58.
985 Ibid., paras. 58-59.
986 Ibid. paras. 51-57.

8.3 Two approaches to evidencing custom by ICJ

Space does not permit analysing all the cases where a particular or general custom was referred to, so only a brief account of the case law will be made. In general, the Court followed a practice of either declaring the existence of custom with a reference to a specific provision of a multilateral treaty or by proving the state practice and inferring from it *opinio iuris* or by simply proving the state practice. The following sections will present a synthesis of the two approaches.

(a) The 'declarative' approach

The 'declarative' approach is most clearly visible in all of the cases discussed above. In this approach, state practice is not evidenced and custom is proved either with a reference to the treaty containing the provision reflecting the norm in question or without any reference at all. A number of recent cases related to the norms governing treaties also prove this assertion. In the *Advisory Opinion on the Construction of a Wall,*[987] the *Avena* case,[988] *LaGrand* case,[989] *Oil Platforms* case,[990] *Kasiki/Sedudu Island* case[991] and the *Territorial Dispute* case,[992] the Court declared the existence of customary norm of good faith in the interpretation of the treaty in accordance with the ordinary meaning to be given to its terms in their context and in the light of the treaty's object and purpose embodied in paragraph 1 of Article 31 of the Vienna Convention on the Law of Treaties.[993] In the *Kasiki/Sedudu Island* case, the Court has specifically declared the customary character of the principle of interpretation of the treaty according to its object and purpose when a comparison of the authentic texts discloses a difference of meaning as reflected in paragraph 4 of Article 33 of the Vienna Convention.[994] In the *Territorial Dispute* case and the *Oil Platforms* case the Court held that all of Article 31 of the Convention reflects customary practices.[995]

---

[987] *Legal Consequences of the Construction of a Wall in the Occupied Palestinian Territory (Advisory Opinion)* (9 July 2004), para. 94.

[988] *Difference Relating to Immunity from Legal Process of a Special Rapporteur of the Commission on Human Rights (Advisory Opinion)* (29 April 1999), para. 83.

[989] *LaGrand* case *(Germany* v. *United States of America)* (27 June 2001), paras. 99, 101.

[990] *Case Concerning Oil Platforms (Islamic Republic Of Iran* v. *United States Of America) – Preliminary Objection* (12 December 1996), para. 23.

[991] *Case Concerning Kasikili/Sedudu Island (Botswana/Namibia)* (13 December 1999), para. 18.

[992] *Case Concerning the Territorial Dispute (Libyan Arab Jamahiriya/Chad)* (3 February 1994), para. 41.

[993] International Law Commission (22 May 1969), *Vienna Convention on the Law of Treaties*.

[994] *Case Concerning Kasikili/Sedudu Island (Botswana/Namibia)* (13 December 1999), para. 48.

[995] *Case Concerning Oil Platforms (Islamic Republic Of Iran* v. *United States Of America) – Preliminary Objection* (12 December 1996), para. 23; *Case Concerning the Territorial Dispute (Libyan Arab Jamahiriya/Chad)* (3 February 1994), para. 41. See also *Legal Consequences of the Construction of a Wall in the Occupied Palestinian Territory (Advisory Opinion)* (9 July 2004), para. 94.

In the *Land and Maritime Boundary* case the Court held that based upon a custom a treaty can enter into force either upon a signature or upon a signature and subsequent ratification.[996] In the *Hungarian Dams* case the Court stated that a number of customary norms relating to the termination and suspension of an operation of a treaty (breach of a treaty, impossibility of performance, and fundamental change of circumstances) are set forth in Articles 60-62 of the Vienna Convention mentioned above.[997] Furthermore, it declared that the state of necessity involves the cumulative coexistence of conditions enlisted in Article 33 of the Draft Articles on the International Responsibility of States and 'is a ground recognized by customary international law for precluding the wrongfulness of an act not in conformity with an international obligation.'[998] In addition, the Court recognised the norm that 'rights and obligations of a territorial character established by a treaty are unaffected by a succession of States' is an international custom reflected in Article 12 of the 1978 Vienna Convention.[999]

The approach avoiding the proof of practice is visible in some of the earlier cases.[1000] For instance, in the *Corfu Channel* case the Court stated:

> 'It is, in the opinion of the Court, generally recognized and in accordance with international custom that States in time of peace have a right to send their warships through straits used for international navigation between two parts of the high seas without the previous authorization of a coastal State, provided that the passage is innocent. Unless otherwise prescribed in an international convention, there is no right for a coastal State to prohibit such passage through straits in time of peace.'[1001]

Similarly in the *Interhandel* case:

> 'The rule that local remedies must be exhausted before international proceedings may be instituted is a well-established rule of customary international law; the rule has been generally observed in cases in which a State has adopted the cause of its national whose rights are claimed to have been disregarded in another State in violation of international law.'[1002]

---

[996] *Case Concerning The Land And Maritime Boundary Between Cameroon And Nigeria (Cameroon* v. *Nigeria: Equatorial Guinea Intervening)* (10 October 2002), paras. 264-265.

[997] *Case concerning the Gabcikovo-Nagymaros project (Hungary/Slovakia)* (1997), paras. 46, 99, 104. See also the cases cited there. The Court has also cited the statements of the parties that Arts. 65-67 if not codify, then generally reflect customary law on procedure regarding termination of a treaty (para. 109).

[998] Ibid., paras. 51-52. See also Art. 25 in International Law Commission (2001), *Draft Arts. on the Responsibility of States for Internationally Wrongful Acts* and similar approach in *Legal Consequences of the Construction of a Wall in the Occupied Palestinian Territory (Advisory Opinion)* (9 July 2004), para. 140.

[999] *Case concerning the Gabcikovo-Nagymaros project (Hungary/Slovakia)* (1997), para. 109.

[1000] See, e.g., Sőrensen, M. (1960), *Principes de droit international public: Cours général*, p. 39.

[1001] *The Corfu Channel* case *(Merits)* (1949), para. 28.

[1002] *Interhandel (Switzerland* v. *United States of America)* (1959), para. 27.

In these two cases there is not even a reference to a treaty allegedly codifying a given custom.

The approach of the Court based on the disregard for the actual practice of state and declaring the existence of custom with or without a reference to written sources of international law is sometimes openly defended by its judges. For instance, judge de Castro in his Separate Opinion to 1974 *Fisheries Jurisdiction* case stated that:

> 'International customary law does not need to be proved; it is of a general nature and is based on a general conviction of its validity (opinio iuris). The Court must apply it ex officio; it is its duty to know it as quaestio iuris: iura novit curia. Only regional customs or practices, as well as special customs, have to be proved.'[1003]

Such an approach assumes that general customs do not change – a contention that is difficult to accept given the enormous changes in international life. Also, with such an attitude new general customary norms could not develop.

The 'declarative' approach might resemble the Islamic concept of *'Ijma'* presented in the last chapter, according to which the unanimity of opinion of lawyers on a question of law creates a fundamental and unchallengeable principle of law.[1004] One could then adopt this concept as an alternative to proving unanimously recognised customary norms and to treat them as a kind of international *Ijma* (or general principles of law). Most of the principles declared as customary in the jurisprudence of the ICJ would probably fall into this category. This approach would relieve a judge from a cumbersome proof of well-known principles of international law thus strengthening the justification of applicable norms in the actual judgment, weakened by a reference to non-proven customary norm. However, this approach seems to be of little use in evidencing practices on the Internet, as most of them are novel and have to be ascertained unquestionably.

(b) The 'inferential' approach

The 'inferential' approach is based on the establishment of a norm in the practice of states and inference from *opinio iuris*, thus disregarding the necessity for a separate proof of the second element. As Akehurst put it,

> 'the modern tendency is not to look for direct evidence of a state's psychological convictions, but to infer opinio iuris indirectly from the actual behaviour of states.'[1005]

This approach is clearly visible in the *Right of Passage* case:

[1003] Judge de Castro (1974), *Separate opinion of Judge de Castro on Fisheries Jurisdiction* case, p. 79. References omitted.

[1004] See Chapter V.

[1005] Akehurst, M. (1987), *A modern introduction to international law*, pp. 29-30. See also, e.g., Virally, M. (1968), *The Sources of International Law*, pp. 133-134.

'The Court, therefore, concludes that, with regard to private persons, civil officials and goods in general there existed during the British and post- British periods a constant and uniform practice allowing free passage between Daman and the enclaves. This practice having continued over a period extending beyond a century and a quarter unaffected by the change of regime in respect of the intervening territory which occurred when India became independent, the Court is, in view of all the circumstances of the case, satisfied that that practice was accepted as law by the Parties and has given rise to a right and a correlative obligation.'[1006]

Similarly, in the *S.S. Wimbledon* case,[1007] the *Nottebohm* case[1008] and the *Fisheries Jurisdiction* case[1009] the psychological element was not proven.

The following passage from the dissenting opinion of Judge Sorensen to *North Sea Continental Shelf* cases is self-explanatory:

'I do not find it necessary to go into the question of the opinio juris. This is a problem of legal doctrine, which may cause great difficulties in international adjudication. In view of the manner in which international relations are conducted, there may be numerous cases in which it is practically impossible for one government to produce conclusive evidence of the motives which have prompted the action and policy of other governments.'[1010]

And further:

'the practice of States (…) may be taken as sufficient evidence of the existence of any necessary opinio juris.'[1011]

Judge Lachs, in his dissenting opinion of the same case, argued that:

'the general practice of States should be recognized as prima facie evidence that it is accepted as law.'[1012]

1006 *Case Concerning Right of Passage Over Indian Territory (Portugal* v. *India)* (1960), p. 40.

1007 *The S.S. 'Wimbledon'* (1923), para. 25, also noted by Kirgis, F.L.J. (1987), *Custom on a sliding scale*, p. 149.

1008 *Nottebohm* case *(Liechtenstein* v. *Guatemala)* (1955), paras. 22-23, also noted by Akehurst, M. (1974-1975), *Custom as a Source of International Law*, p. 32; Kirgis, F.L.J. (1987), *Custom on a sliding scale*, p. 149, citing Jenks, C.W. (1964), *The Prospects of International Adjudication*, pp. 253-258.

1009 *Difference Relating to Immunity from Legal Process of a Special Rapporteur of the Commission on Human Rights (Advisory Opinion)* (29 April 1999), paras. 24-26, also noted by Akehurst, M. (1974-1975), *Custom as a Source of International Law*, p. 32.

1010 Judge Sorensen (1969), *Dissenting opinion of Judge Sorensen on Continental Shelf* case, p. 246.

1011 Ibid., p. 247.

1012 Judge Lachs, ibid., *Dissenting opinion of Judge Lachs on Continental Shelf* case, p. 231.

Such an evidentiary practice is inconsistent with the endorsed twin elements theory of custom and clearly shows its impracticality.

But the problem is not only with the approach to evidencing the psychological element but also the way the practice is proven. In general, the Court has not investigated practices of any significant number of states across a defined period of time. The proof was limited to the statements of litigants about their own practice or contained in judgments of national courts or in national legislation. Some authorities have complained about the lack of materials that could be used to research state practice.[1013] According to Harris, at present only the practice of the United States is available in a comprehensive form, although there are some less extensive digests of British, French, Italian and Swiss and some other states' practice available in the national Yearbooks and international law reviews.[1014] As Mendelson noticed, however, they often fail to distinguish between trivial and important state behaviour,[1015] which only reinforces the claim about the difficulty of distinguishing between legal custom and non-legal usage. However, the problems with accessing state practice can be mitigated by establishing an Internet database of state practice.[1016]

It is submitted that alleged customary norms that are not widely recognised or known ought to be proved with all the diligence required. In particular, the actual practice of states within a specified timeframe should be evidenced. A proof should embrace all or at least a representative sample of states. In the latter case, the sample should contain a reasonable proportion of the population of states (i.e., the activity of twenty states over a specified period of time). The analysis of states' practice based upon a recent practice of litigants does not provide sufficient grounds for a generalisation about the generality of practice. Furthermore, any inconsistencies in practice of chosen states should be analysed and presented in relation to the periods of consistent adherence to it in order to get a picture of relative consistency of practice. Such an analysis would require a great deal of knowledge, especially of a historical and socio-political nature. But there seems to be no alternative to proving the existence of general practice. The Court's approach is an idealistic one, built on premises that whatever is agreed on paper does actually happen in reality. But this may not be the case, and therefore, has to be proven. The existence of a custom in question cannot simply be inferred or deduced from what judges or writers think is the general custom.

[1013] See for example, Goralczyk, W. (1989), *Prawo Miedzynarodowe Publiczne w Zarysie*, p. 103; Harris, D.J. (1998), *Cases and Materials on International Law*, pp. 26-27.

[1014] Harris has also pointed to parliamentary papers, law reports and newspapers as potential sources of knowledge about practice. Harris, D.J. (1998), *Cases and Materials on International Law*, pp. 26-27.

[1015] Mendelson, M. (1995), *The subjective element in customary international law*, p. 186.

[1016] See a reference to such a database in commercial litigation in *MCC Marble Ceramic* v. *Ceramica Nuova D'agostino, S.p.A.,* [29 June 1998] 144 F.3d 1384 (1lth Cir.). See also, Andersen, C.B. (Fall 1998), *Furthering the Uniform Application of the CISG: Sources of Law on the Internet*, pp. 405-406.

8.4 Summary of ICJ's evidencing practice

Judges of the International Court of Justice have fully endorsed the dualistic conception of custom, but have never convincingly applied it in practice. The proof of practice was often sought in the treaties, resolutions or judgments but rarely in the actual state behaviours. The proof of practice, if present, was almost invariably limited to the practice of litigants and did not allow for a generalisation. The situation is especially paradoxical in regard to the subjective element of custom, which has never been independently and satisfactorily proven in practice. Never was any form of survey or similar technique used to collect information about the acceptance of a given practice as law by the international community. As was shown above, the proof of *opinio iuris* was either entirely omitted or its existence was inferred from the practice of states or the agreements or resolutions they accepted. In short, the necessity of evidence of the subjective element has only been visible in the Court's words, but not in the practice.

9. The Study of Contemporary International Customary Humanitarian Law

The notable exception with respect to evidencing international customs[1017] is the latest study of customary humanitarian law, conducted by researchers rather than judges. The Steering Committee of the International Committee of the Red Cross was setup in October 1996 to collect evidence of state practice and *opinio iuris.* It took nearly ten years to complete the undertaking.

The purpose of the study was to overcome problems relating to the application of international humanitarian law arising out of the fact that the relevant treaties do not bind all of the states and that there is a lack of international treaty law dealing with non-international armed conflicts. Since the customary law binds all of the states it was necessary to examine the practice of states in order to determine whether other countries were bound by non-written norms.

> 'The study focused in particular on practice from the last 30 years to ensure that the result would be a restatement of contemporary customary international law, but, where still relevant, older practice was also cited.'[1018]

To achieve a geographical representation researchers were identified in 47 States (9 in Africa, 11 in the Americas, 15 in Asia, 1 in Australasia and 11 in Europe) and asked to produce a report on their respective State's practice. The national legisla-

---

[1017] This study has been published after this book was submitted to press and hence it will be only briefly analysed based on Henckaerts, J.-M. (March 2005), *Study on customary international humanitarian law: A contribution to the understanding and respect for the rule of law in armed conflict.*

[1018] Ibid., pp. 184-185.

tion and other useful documentation such as military manuals of countries not covered by the reports on State practice were also researched and collected. The researchers also conducted extensive studies in international sources and International Committee of the Red Cross archives as well as consulted numerous experts.

The report describes 161 customary norms applicable either only in international armed conflicts, non-international armed conflicts or both. 17 rules are applicable only in international armed conflicts and 5 are specific to non-international armed conflicts, which at this stage are covered by only a handful of norms. The vast majority of customary norms applies ot both types of international conflict.

The norms are grouped into six categories. The first area relates to the principle of distinction, which describes the customary norms relating to the distinction between civilians and combatants, civilian objects and military objectives, indiscriminate attacks, proportionality and precautions in and against attacks (24 customary rules). The second area deals with protection of persons and objects and includes norms relating to the status of medical, religious, humanitarian relief and peacekeeping mission personnel and objects as well as journalists, protected zones, cultural property, the natural environment and installations containing dangerous forces (21 customary rules). The third area deals with specific methods of warfare and contains principles relating to the denial of quarter, destruction and seizure of property, the use of starvation and access to humanitarian forces, deception and the communication with the enemy (24 customary rules). The fourth category of principles covers the use of weapons and contains principles relating to the general use of weapons and prohibitions of the use of poison, biological and chemical weapons, expanding and exploding bullets, weapons primarily injuring by non-detectable fragments, booby-traps, landmines, incendiary weapons and blinding laser weapons (17 customary norms). The fifth category titled Treatment of Civilians and Persons Hors de Combat covers the customary principles establishing the fundamental guarantees for these groups, the status of prisoners, prisoners-of-war, the wounded, sick and shipwrecked, the dead and missing persons, persons deprived of their liberty, displaced persons and others afforded special protection (52 customary norms). The last category on implementation contains customary norms dealing with compliance with and enforcement of international humanitarian law, state responsibility and reparation, individual responsibility and war crimes (23 customary norms).

The breadth of study and the wealth of ascertained humanitarian customary norms is truly astonishing. Of particular importance to any research into customary norms is its emphasis on representativeness of collected evidence. It is the first such kind of study in the history of international law. This remarkable work will certainly serve as the example for the future research into customary norms in other areas of international law.

10. CONCLUSION

International jurisprudence has succeeded in the development of a general twin-elements framework for the concept of custom but has not managed to produce one firmly accepted theory of customary law that would adequately explain this phenomenon. The abundance of material reveals an astonishing division of views and opinions on what international custom is, which results in the lack of one acceptable theory of international custom. The majority of scholars require the element of practice and its acceptance as law. The dispute concerns the degrees of continuity, repeatability and longevity of practice, the value of statements and passivity, permissibility of objections to practice, morality and reasonability of practice as well as judicial confirmation of custom. Deep controversies surround even the interpretation of the subjective element of custom, in particular its interpretation and ways of evidencing it.

The work of the International Court of Justice has clarified certain issues but in general has not contributed much to the resolution of the problems surrounding the notion of customary law. The ICJ has endorsed various interpretations of the twin-elements concept of custom but has never convincingly applied them in practice. The proof of general and positive state practice was either entirely omitted or reduced to a very short and vague discussion. The subjective element was either entirely omitted or inferred from the proof of state practice or deduced from written sources of law. In a majority of cases, the Court has not evidenced custom at all but only declared its existence.

Nevertheless, the doctrine of international custom has produced a very rich literature and case law that provide an excellent basis to draw upon in the analysis of customary practices on the Internet. Several useful concepts identified by international jurisprudence will be utilised in the discussion that follows. Of particular importance is the study of customary humanitarian law. However, the methodology of evidencing custom used by the Court discloses so much informality and inconsistency with the adopted theory of custom that it cannot serve as a good model for evidencing practices on the Internet. For this reason, a new methodology for evidencing customary practices on the Internet will be proposed.

Chapter VII
INTERNET CUSTOM

In previous chapters, the importance of custom in national and international legal systems was outlined. In particular, the significance of this mode of regulation in historical times and in present day legal cultures was presented. Then, the concept of international custom as developed in international public law was studied. However, the theory of international custom cannot be directly applied to electronic commerce. This chapter will explain the reasons for the inapplicability of international custom to the Internet environment. It will also propose a concept of custom tailored to Internet commerce and discuss associated issues. The most significant practical problem is how to evidence customary practices on the Web, which will be discussed in the next part of the book.

1. Introduction

Internet commerce does not function in a regulatory vacuum. Since it is a medium used by people to interact with one another, behavioural patterns similar to those observed in traditional social life emerge. For instance, merchants in both traditional as well as the electronic world aim at finding, negotiating and executing a financial deal. To achieve this goal all merchants would try to find the best supplier and customer. In this sense, as was introduced in Chapter II, electronic commerce has not changed the basic paradigm of trade. What has changed is that transactions can now be executed and monitored more efficiently, on a global scale and 24 hours a day.

In their interactions, online trade participants adhere to certain standards of conduct on the Web thus consciously or unwittingly supporting certain behaviours and deterring others. In other words, Internet participants apply norms of behaviour that have spontaneously arisen between them at some point in time. These online interactions can be subjected to research that promises to understand and predict human behaviour better.

As was outlined in Chapter VI, norms embodying certain widespread Internet practices could be used to solve many legal disputes on the Web in the absence of written law. In fact, it will be argued that Internet participants have already created a set of electronic commerce customary practices that are specific to this medium and do not find an equivalent in the offline world. For instance, the first-in first-served rule of domain name registration has been customarily applied by the Internet community. Similarly, freedom of linking to any site via hyperlink without the permission of a site being linked to has also been a widely followed customary practice peculiar to the web. In the same way, many security practices as well as transaction-related routines are customarily followed by the Internet community.[1019]

The key idea offered in this book is that custom is a source of unwritten legal norms that could be used by judges to solve Internet-related problems, especially those in the field of Internet commerce. The aim of this part of the book is to discuss the requirements of Internet commerce custom from a practical perspective. International custom discussed in the last chapter, provides an excellent starting point for understanding customary practices on the Internet. It has been used for a long time in international law and has generated rich and thoughtful literature as well as a number of judgments of international courts that based their decisions upon it. Moreover, contrary to the status of customary Law Merchant, international law enjoys the status of the only universally accepted system of supra-national law in which custom plays the key role.

The concept of international custom, however, cannot be used directly in electronic commerce because international law governs inter-state relations that possess certain peculiarities that do not exist on the Internet. On the other hand, electronic commerce possesses certain features not encountered in inter-state relations. Moreover, the concept of international custom has several deficiencies already described, which should be resolved in order to create a practical tool for Internet adjudicators. For the above reasons a separate notion of electronic commerce custom will be developed.

In order to achieve this goal, the concept of electronic commerce custom will be studied based upon the previously described concept of international custom. First, the justification for the development of a new concept of international e-commerce custom, instead of reusing the existing theory of international custom to Internet commerce, will be outlined. Then a definition of electronic commerce custom will be proposed, followed by an in-depth discussion of its elements. Finally, the role of a judge in establishing custom will be outlined followed by an illustration of how to solve hypothetical cases.

2. Problems with Applicability of International Custom to Internet Commerce

There are at least nine reasons why the concept of international custom cannot be directly applied to Internet commerce:

First, as was reiterated a number of times, international custom applies to states and some international organisations, whereas on the Internet common routines are

---

[1019] See Chapter IX.

entered into by individuals and companies. Moreover, on the Internet interactions might take place only between pre-programmed computers, which do not happen in the world of classical international relations. In other words, there is a fundamental difference in regard to who generates customary practices in traditional international relations and on the Internet.

Second, international custom can be particular or local, meaning that it is confined to a larger or smaller geographical area. In this sense, the scope of custom is determined by the geographical adherence to a given practice. The Internet, however, does not recognise geo-political borders. The geographical ties of Internet websites can only be established by reference to its domain name and other factors such as language used.[1020] However, this is not a perfect indication because there are many sites that use global top-level domain names like .com or .net. Moreover, even country-level domain names like .au or .pl are not perfect indicators of the origin or location of a given site because they can be purchased by anyone from anywhere. In this sense, the Internet custom has none or at most very weak ties with geographical location. Any reference in this book to geography in the context of the Internet custom should be understood as a reference to the domain name convention.

Third, the population of states (191) and international organisations is small, slightly exceeding 200. On the other hand, the population of electronic commerce participants is much larger, to be expressed in millions rather than hundreds. Despite the fact that a large number of participants might use the same information system to manage access to their websites,[1021] the concept of international custom applies to a much smaller population of subjects than is the case of the Internet.

Fourth, states are bound by a large number of bilateral and multilateral treaties, resolutions of international organisations and customary practices recognised by international courts. On the other hand, Internet participants are rarely bound by any formal relationships with one another unless a transaction takes place. Even then, the level of convolution of relationships between Internet participants is much lower than that of states. In other words, the level of complexity of relations between states and between Internet commerce participants is different.

Fifth, states are very complex structures with many organs being responsible for actions that are of significance on the international arena, whereas Internet participants usually represent themselves. Even large online organisations that structurally present a complex entity would usually act only in one way in a given time on the Internet. However, in the case of a state, one organ may say different things on TV, radio and the Internet, or the statement of one organ may be contradicted by a statement or an action of another organ. In other words, the structural complexity of international law subjects is far greater than one of the Internet participants.

[1020] See Chapter II and IV.

[1021] See Netcraft reports on the popularity of hosting providers. Available at <http://www.netcraft.com>, last visited: 07/05/2003.

Sixth, states in international law developed a peculiar attitude to practices of other states, quickly protesting or affirming their actions. The reasons behind this behaviour of states is to make sure that the practice in question will not develop into a customary norm based on the absence of protest on the side of other states (acquiescence).[1022] Such a peculiarity of international law does not exist on the Internet. Internet users are not aware at this stage of the existence of customary Internet law and its potential consequences. In other words, international custom is applied more consciously these days by the international community of states, which is not the case with the Internet.

Seventh, international custom deals with complex entities that are nevertheless directed by groups of humans. On the Internet, however, a lot of behaviour is being programmed once and left to the software components to execute it infinitely. Moreover, some software components can even learn through experience about the environment in which they function, adjusting their behaviour accordingly, thus making predictions about their future behaviour even less certain. In other words, international law custom relates to humans' behaviour, whereas the Internet participants also have to deal with pre-programmed behaviour of software components that may turn out to be very unpredictable.

Eighth, customary practices in the international arena are reflected in the actions of state officials, which are often recorded in legal documents and writings, international agreements, resolutions and case law. In this sense, they are visible, although, e.g. it may not be that easy to get access to diplomatic correspondence between states in question. On the other hand, practices on the Internet are not being officially recorded yet. They can be learnt by examination of website content or the behaviour of the web browser. They can also be learnt by studying the non-visible behaviour of Internet infrastructure. In other words, there are differing modes of manifestation of customary practices in the international arena and on the Internet.

Ninth, customary practices in international law relate to physical processes in the tangible world. On the other hand, customary practices on the Internet exist only in electronic format. The former are cognisable only insofar as social structures and relationships between them can be deciphered and interpreted. On the Internet, learning about processes can be automated and left to intelligent agents to be discovered and reinterpreted. Internet practices can be easily recorded on a daily basis in relation to a far greater number of subjects than is practical in the traditional world. In this sense, the Internet has potential for use of automated intelligence in the discovery of routine behaviours of a large number of participants. Figure 6 below summarises all the key differences.

The differences between the traditional world and the digital one necessitate the development of a new concept of custom that would take into account specific

---

[1022] See for example, Charney, J.I. (October 1993), *Universal International Law*, pp. 536-537; Goralczyk, W. (1989), *Prawo Miedzynarodowe Publiczne w Zarysie*, pp. 100-101; Wolfke, K. (1993), *Custom in Present International Law*, p. 48. See Chapter VI.

	International law	Internet
Who creates custom?	States, organisations	Individuals, companies, computers
The role of geography	High	Low-to-none
Population size	Small, around 200	Large, couple of millions
Complexity of relations	High	Low
Complexity of subjects	High	Low-medium
Community awareness of custom	Very high	Low
Presence of artificial agents	No	Yes
Manifestation of custom	Actions of state officials	Website content, behaviour and source code, infrastructure setup
Visibility of customs	Physical world	Electronic world
Potential for automation	Low	Mid-High

Figure 6 – The differences between international custom and the Internet custom

features of the Internet and electronic commerce. But they are not the only reasons. As was discussed in the previous chapter, the notion of international custom involves presence of both the material element of practice and the subjective attitude to it, which is even more difficult to prove in the largely anonymous and automated world of the Internet. On the other hand, if this subjective element will be equated with an express or tacit recognition of a practice as law then the scope of the application of Internet custom and hence its effectiveness as a source of global Internet law would be limited to the highest degree. In other words, long-lasting theoretical controversies regarding the characteristics of international custom as well as practical problems associated with evidencing it, provide another argument for searching for a better explanation of this phenomenon.

3. Objectives of the New Concept of Custom

The proposed model of electronic commerce custom will have to achieve three objectives:

1. To facilitate practical application of custom in solving Internet-related disputes.
2. To develop the concept of custom independent of national legal systems and tailored to the needs of the Internet.
3. To provide a consistent theoretical explanation of custom as a potential source of Internet law, taking into account the peculiar features of the Internet.

The first objective stresses the practical importance of the new theory of custom. As was shown in the case of international law, the theory accepted there is not practical, because it is difficult to apply. As was shown, the International Court of Justice has never successfully applied it in practice. Practical viability is a very important feature of the proposed concept of Internet commerce custom.

The second objective stresses the importance of adopting a global perspective on the Internet. The proposed concept of Internet custom is constructed taking into account the unique features of the Internet, in particular its global scope and lack of control. It disregards particular national values that could be embedded in domestic theories of custom.

The third objective is to provide a consistent explanation of the phenomenon of legal custom on the Internet. As was shown in Chapter VI, the concept of international custom relies on the presence of a psychological element, which cannot satisfactorily explain the phenomenon. The proposed model will reject any elements that might cause illogical consequences on an abstract level. Furthermore, to make the proposed concept tailored to the needs of the Internet it will take into account the unique features of the Internet.

The proposed concept of electronic commerce custom will rest on the following principles:

1. Computers and humans are equally important actors in online transactions
2. Only actions of actors or their results are identifiable and not their psychological attitudes
3. Widespread Internet practice creates global rights and obligations for everyone involved

The first principle stresses the importance of automation of online commerce. Software plays a preponderant role on the Internet, as it is a medium through which humans execute their deeds. However, software components do not have 'psychology', although intelligent software agents have a limited decision-making autonomy and can adapt their behaviour based on experience. As a consequence, according to the second principle, the concept of custom should not be analysed using human characteristics. In consequence, the psychological element of custom will be rejected. Instead, customary practices should be assessed only from the perspective of their widespread adoption. The third principle assumes a globally binding nature of custom. Without this assumption the power of custom as a source of law would be severely limited. However, this principle is, as was shown, generally accepted in domestic and international legal systems.

4. Proposed Definition of Electronic Commerce Custom

There is no single accepted understanding of what international custom is. Taking this into account as well as the differences between the traditional world and the Internet, the new notion of Internet commerce custom will be proposed. In order to structure better discussion of Internet commerce custom, its definition will be proposed first. Then each of the elements of the definition will be further analysed.

An international electronic commerce custom (e-custom) can be defined as a legally relevant practice of trading on the Internet, which is sufficiently widespread within a given timeframe as to justify the expectation that it should be observed.[1023]

This concise definition hides some important issues that should now be expanded upon. Mercantile practice *per se* must be of legal importance. For example, an Internet practice of using a certain type of font can be presumed to be legally unimportant and hence non-binding. Unless of course there is a dispute involving the usage of certain fonts, e.g., in the context of readability of web documents where such practices may turn out to be legally relevant. Further, the practice must be repetitive – a single instance of a practice is insufficient to form a custom. In addition, this definition does not require e-custom to be a long lasting practice, meaning practice extending over a considerable time. As will be argued below, custom can develop nowadays within a couple of days or even hours because of the intensity of transactions in so dynamic an environment as electronic commerce and the ability to trace them.

What is important is that a practice must be widespread, meaning that it must be followed by the majority of web companies in one or more industry or geographical region or the whole world and intensive in terms of number of transactions within a given time period. Intensiveness of practice is a result of multiple repetition of a given practice within a defined timeframe. In other words, the term widespread is used here to mean the practice is extensive geographically (or industrially) as well intensive in time. Only sufficiently widespread practice may generate the expectation that it should be followed. The concept of expectation as to the observance of the practice means that other Internet traders in the same set of circumstances have a legal prospect of being treated in the same manner. Expectation means that parties willing to deviate from it must have a very good reason to do so. Finally, the notion of expectation implies that the practice is not followed from the feeling of legal necessity or because the practice was tacitly accepted as law.

The next two sections are devoted to justifying all aspects of this definition in the context of the theory of international custom. Particular emphasis will be put on analysis of the material element of practice and the subjective element of the concept of custom in the context of Internet commerce.

5. Practice

Practice is the essence of the concept of custom in general. This gives rise to the question of whose practice contributes to the development of practice. Since we are dealing with international e-commerce transactions, the major players in the devel-

---

1023 See Chapter I. See also Polanski, P.P. and Johnston, R.B. (7-10 January 2002), *International Custom as a Source of Law in Global Electronic Commerce*, p. 4.

opment of customary rules are companies and physical persons, but possibly also international organisations and states acting as a party in e-trade environment. However, one should mention here that the acts of persons might often be replaced by the acts of computers. Nevertheless, such actions will nearly always be attributable to a human being. In consequence, humans rather than computers establish customs.

5.1 The notion of practice

What should be understood as practice in the context of the Internet? Is an electronic statement an action? If so, what if a website promises one thing but does not implement their assertions in practice? The following sections will discuss the concept of practice from the perspective of positive actions, promises to act and conscious abstentions.

(a) Actions

The concept of practice is generally taken to refer to positive actions.[1024] However, what is an action on the Internet? For instance, provision of encryption by a web server could be regarded as an action. Similarly, inclusion of a link to other websites without the consent of the web designer is a physical action. Registration of a domain name is an action of a person. In short, the term action will be used here as a synonym for a positive activity directed towards achieving some goal.

There are two types of positive actions on the Internet. Some actions are not predetermined, can be changed and are carried out in an *ad hoc* manner by human beings. For instance, linking to a website without seeking permission of this website to include a link is a positive action. However, a programmer might in some circumstances change this practice and ask for permission or delete a link if he is afraid of unknown legal consequences. Similarly, copying information from the Web is a physical action. In principle, it will be carried out by a human on an as-needed basis. These types of actions are not pre-determined although they have potential for automation. They may also not provide uniform results under the same circumstances. These types of actions will be referred to as simple actions or actions for short.

However, the unique element in the majority of Internet actions is the fact that they are often pre-programmed and respond in a uniform manner to the event triggering them. For instance, strong encryption has to be enabled first, before any transaction will be secured in this manner. Similarly, registration of a domain based on first-in first-out principle, requires coding of this functionality in the first place. In the same vein, provision of order summary or order confirmation requires pre-programming of this functionality in a web system. These types of actions will

[1024] See Chapter VI.

provide the same behaviour in the same set of circumstances. For this reason, the discovery of the actual functionality is more important than learning about how many times a given functionality was used. This finding will find its application in the context of evidencing Internet customs outlined in the next chapter. These types of actions will be referred to as pre-programmed or predetermined actions.

In summary, there is no doubt that positive actions constitute a practice. In consequence, the same action performed by a majority of web systems over some time may lead to the formation of custom. To be more precise, it may lead to the formation of an expectation that such actions will be performed in similar circumstances by other websites.

(b) Promises to act

However, it is far more difficult to say whether a general or concrete statement or a promise to act can be considered as a practice capable of creating Internet custom. For instance, if all e-shops assure their visitors that they provide a secure environment does it mean that there is a customary practice of providing a secure Internet environment? Or, if a majority of web systems assure their clients that their private data will not be transferred to third parties, does it mean that there is a custom of not transferring such information?

From the logical perspective, the answer is negative. A promise to act or claim about actions that e-businesses make, no matter how solemn or official, cannot be equated with the action itself. Consequently, a promise to act in a given way announced by a majority of websites cannot, in itself, constitute evidence of a customary character of action described in such statements. For example, if most commercial websites claim that they provide secure 128-bit encryption, this information should not be used as the only evidence of existence of custom of providing such a level of encryption. In order to test the validity of such a claim, one would have to check if these businesses actually implement this level of encryption in practice.

However, statements about actions are not without significance. Promises to act may lead to the emergence of a common practice of providing such a promise. In other words, written assurance of encrypted communication can lead to the emergence of a customary norm requiring provision of such information to all website visitors. This can be important when it comes to the provision of highly technical or detailed legal information regarding, e.g., security and privacy of information or common legal clauses. For example, since most commercial websites contain assurance as to the treatment of private data, one can legitimately expect provision of such information from all commercial sites. Furthermore, statements about actions that are concordant with a practice they promise to implement provide additional confirmation of an adherence to a practice in question.

However, a distinction between actions and statements about them is often more difficult to make. This is a result of the fact that the Internet is centred on the provision of information. Is the display of a transaction-confirmation webpage a positive action or simply an electronic statement? In this case, it is important both that the purchase order will be confirmed and that order confirmation will contain specific information. In this scenario, the physical act and the statement are inseparable.

It is submitted then that the term practice refers primarily to positive actions and not to general or concrete statements about them. However, statements about acts can also be viewed as actions, but only as actions that may lead to the formation of custom of making such statements.

(c) Abstention from action

One of the most challenging questions regarding the concept of electronic commerce custom deals with the treatment of lack of action. Can lack of positive actions be considered as a practice? If so, can a common inaction amount to a custom prohibiting contrary positive action or give a right to act?

To exemplify the above questions the phenomenon of spamming[1025] will be analysed. It may be assumed that the majority of Internet participants do not send spam or unsolicited e-mails. In addition, the latest research clearly shows that the vast majority of the Internet population does not like spamming.[1026] Some authorities realising the potentially disruptive nature of this type of communication have decided to regulate it.[1027] Taking into account the above remarks, would it be rational to argue that spamming is prohibited by Internet custom because most of the Internet population does not send spam and expresses a negative attitude to spamming?

The answer is not simple. Rather, it prompts further questions opening a challenging research area. It could be argued that the majority of Internet users may not send spam because they do not know what spamming is or are not interested in it. Can such unconscious abstention from action be considered as a practice? If it is not a practice then what is it? Can such inaction amount to the formation of customary law prohibiting given behaviour in the future?

There are several important issues here. The problem of legal value of common inaction cannot be separated from the motives driving it. However, it is going to be very difficult if not impossible to realise what are the motives behind widespread social abstention from action on the Internet. The problem is whether the inaction is a conscious activity on the side of Internet participants aiming at avoiding or minimising certain negative consequences of contrary positive action. Or, whether inaction is a result of unconscious activity being itself a result of lack of awareness regarding existence of such activity or for a similar reason. In contrast to custom

---

[1025] See Glossary and the discussion in Chapter IX on spam and spandexing.

[1026] See, for example <http://en.wikipedia.org/wiki/Spam (electronic)>, last visited: 30/12/2005.

[1027] See, for example, 2003 CAN SPAM Act, Article 13 of EU Directive on privacy in electronic communications. See also Article 7 of the Directive on electronic commerce.

based on widespread positive actions where motives behind following a given norm are not important because actions are 'visible' and as a result, quantifiable, here one has to ascertain if there are any motives at all because there is no ascertainable activity in the physical space. The whole process takes place only in the psychological sphere of the Internet participants. In order to ascertain whether inaction is a conscious act or just unconscious inactivity, one should delve into the psychological sphere of the subjects taking part in it.

However, there are serious evidentiary problems. The nature of custom implies a sequence of positive acts, because only those are objectively identifiable and quantifiable. In the case of absence from action, it would be necessary to prove the consciousness of non-participation in a given set of circumstances in a representative sample of those not involved. One would also need to address the tricky issue of the repetitiveness of such a practice. Finally, the questions of legal relevance or morality of inaction should be addressed. In this scenario, the evidentiary requirements addressed above could possibly bring us back to the traditional dual requirements of the concept of custom and the problems associated with them. Moreover, allowing creation of law based on lack of practice is very risky, since lack of certain activities may imply prohibition to act in this way in the future. Such an argument would be very difficult to accept, since in the future no positive custom could develop without first breaking the existing customary norm.

On the other hand, a prohibitory norm emanating from widespread abstention from action could be inferred, in certain situations, from the proof of a positive practice that is an exception to the alleged customary norm in question. For instance, the principle of non-use of force could be deduced from the proof of positive actions of self-defence in the event of the use of force. This proposition is very controversial and might be difficult to apply in practice, due to potential difficulties with agreeing which positive practice is a legitimate exception to the alleged prohibitory custom inferred from a common inaction. This very matter will be further researched.

In summary, the consideration of practice as consisting of both positive action as well as abstention from positive action introduces new complexities. Without ruling out the possibility of treating abstention from action as a material for Internet custom,[1028] this study will use the term practice in the context of positive actions and in a limited sense, promises to act. This matter requires further research.

5.2 The notion of legally relevant practice

Not all common Internet practices could amount to legal norms, because some of them in the most typical transactions have no legal relevance.[1029] The legal rel-

---

[1028] See the application of this concept in further discussion on spam and spamdexing in Chapter IX.

[1029] Polanski, P.P. (2002), *A New Approach to Regulating Internet Commerce: Custom as a Source of Electronic Commerce Law.*

evance of practice means that a norm emanating from a practice in question could be helpful in adjudicating a dispute, or in short, is important to law. Being important to law means that it can solve a dispute at hand, for which there are no written norms, written norms are in conflict or there are some other problems.[1030] Hence, there is a need for a judgment of a reasonable person – a judge, arbitrator, researcher or the international community – whether a given practice is legally important or not.

The view taken here is that not all practices even if generally followed will automatically create legally binding norms. As an example, the practice of sending e-mails written using Times New Roman font will never create a customary norm stating: 'All e-mails should be written using Times New Roman font'. It is common sense that will allow judges or arbitrators to ascertain whether a particular practice is legally relevant or not. A common practice of displaying advertising banners in the form of a long rectangle is not legally important but a common routine of providing encryption of transactions is. Judgment is unavoidable but it eliminates the need for the establishment of a subjective attitude to a practice among parties following it.

Some widespread practices may not have an apparent legal character. For instance, it is a common practice to write agreements on white paper or in case of the Internet using Times New Roman font in e-mail communication. However, these apparently non-legal customs may attain, in rare cases, a legal status. For instance, one can imagine a case where the Internet website contained certain obligations written in a font very difficult to read and very rarely used. Would such a written statement create binding legal obligations? The answer could be negative, because it is customary to provide legal information on the website in a more readable format. Therefore, although some popular practices may not have apparent legal relevance, in some cases they may turn out to be useful.

In summary, the concept of electronic commerce custom deals with positive actions as well as statements about acts that must have legal significance. Nevertheless, in some rare cases, a practice considered hitherto as legally irrelevant might turn out to be helpful in solving a legal problem and for this reason acquires the status of legal relevance. To distinguish between legally relevant and irrelevant practices, the judgment of a reasonable person is necessary.

5.3 **The notion of sufficiently widespread practice**

The definition of electronic commerce custom proposed above, defines it as a sufficiently widespread practice. The term widespread embraces three distinct issues:

[1030] As the ICJ put it referring to international law, the questions 'framed in terms of law and rais[ing] problems of international law (…) are by their very nature susceptible of a reply based on law (…) [and] appear (…) to be questions of a legal character.' Western cited in the *above* format in *Legality Of The Threat Or Use Of Nuclear Weapons (Advisory Opinion)* (8 July 1996) para. 13.

1. The question of what is the scope of adherence to a given practice (practice widespread in space).
2. The question of what constitutes a majority of e-commerce participants engaged in a given practice for the purpose of establishing e-custom (the notion of majority).
3. The question of how many occurrences of a given practice should be recorded (practice widespread in time).

The concept of widespread practice is the most important element of the definition of electronic commerce custom and for this reason, it will be analysed below.

(a) Practice widespread in space

Custom may be general, particular or local.[1031] In consequence, even a practice of two e-companies would be sufficient to form a local custom that would bind them. In such a scenario, the customary norm would not extend its force onto other companies. Of course, if other companies then follow the electronic practice of these two companies, this could lead to enlargement of the scope of application of a local customary rule, or maybe even to the formation of a general customary rule. In the latter scenario, the customary norm would be binding upon all companies engaged in electronic commerce in a given industry or across all industries.

Electronic commerce practice can have global or general scope meaning that it is observed by companies of all sizes across all or a majority of industries and across the world. A given practice has particular scope if it is peculiar to a number of companies exhibiting some commonality, e.g., are confined to one or several industries or to one or several geographical regions as indicated by the country-level domain names. A practice has local scope if it occurs between two or only a few trading participants.

To be more precise, however, one should look at practices from the perspective of geographical and industrial coverage. As was stated earlier, the Internet has weak connections with geography and for this reason one can speak about geography only to the extent a domain name and language allows such an inference. One could replace geographical scope with cultural scope or use of similar software. In short, the Internet world can be segmented by any relevant variable. For instance, a practice that is widespread in a geographical sense can be confined to only one or several industries. An example of such a practice is provision of strong encryption of transactions. Such a practice is geographically global as it pertains to all the countries whose banks provide online banking facilities. At the same time, such a practice is limited to industries dependant upon a safe completion of transactions such as the banking industry. On the other hand, a practice can be both geographically global and found in all or a large number of industries. For instance, Internet trans-

1031 See Chapter V i VI.

actions are traditionally instantly confirmed. This is visible in all geographical areas engaged in electronic commerce and applies to a number of industries including e-shops, e-marketplaces, online banking, etc.[1032] One can also imagine a practice of all major industries of a given region but not known in other parts of the world due to differences in language or cultural common heritage.

A practice can be considered widespread for the purpose of custom even if it applies only to one geographical region or industry. In such a case, serious problems might arise when parties in dispute rely on two conflicting customary practices having local or regional scope. Such cases would probably be very rare. Nevertheless, there is no easy way to solve this problem, and it would have to be addressed on a case-by-case basis.

	Geographically global	Geographically particular	Geographically local
All or majority of industries	Global custom	Particular custom	Local custom
Minority of industries	Particular custom	Particular custom	Local custom
One industry	Local custom	Particular custom	Local custom

Figure 7 – The table illustrating potential combinations of geographical and industrial coverage of a given practice and their scope of application

In summary, a practice can be considered widespread in a physical sense looking from different angles. The table above illustrates possible combinations of geographical and industrial comprehensiveness of adherence to a given practice. Both geography and industrial criteria can be replaced with other determinants. For instance, a practice can be analysed from the perspective cultural unanimity of traders, common software use among traders in a given industry, etc. As can be seen, a practice can be considered widespread even if it is adhered to in one industry located in one region of the world. In such a case, however, a potential customary norm arising out of such practice would not have a globally binding effect. This book, however, will focus on practices that are adhered to in geographically dispersed locations and are recognised by many industries.

(b) The notion of majority

How many e-companies must adhere to a given practice in order to consider it widespread? Is an ordinary majority of participants a sufficient indicator of widespread character of practice? Should bigger companies be given greater power than Small-to-Medium Enterprises (SMEs)? The questions are debatable.

A given practice can be adhered to by all, a majority or a minority of Internet traders. In the simplest case scenario, a practice will have 100 per cent adherence to

[1032] Classification of industries might turn out to be a problem in some instances, but this aspect of the proposed classification will be omitted from the scope of the book.

it. The case of unanimity provides the strongest evidence of customary character of a given practice. However, in most of the cases, the answer will not be that straightforward.

If adherence to a given practice is not unanimous, then there must exist one or more competing practice. One could argue that if 51 per cent of Internet trade participants follow a given practice, it is a sufficient argument in favour of the widespread character of this practice. However, a simple majority is not sufficient if a competing practice or competing practices are popular. For instance, if an alleged customary practice has 60 per cent of adherence and a competing practice has 40 per cent adherence then one should not be able to argue that an alleged customary practice is sufficiently widespread because the competing practice is too popular. Instead, such a practice could be regarded as a custom in formation. The graph below illustrates this problem.

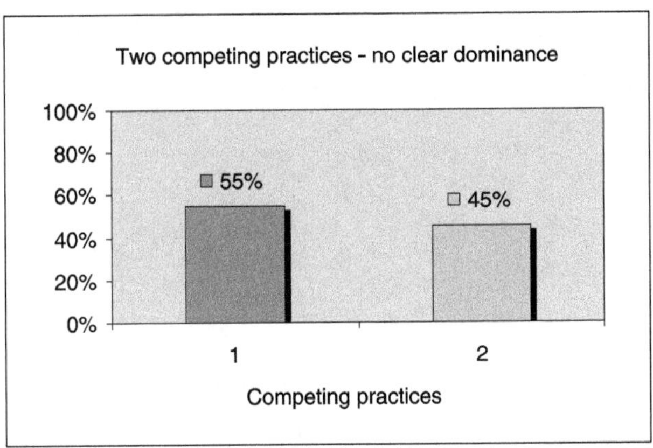

Figure 8 – Two competing practices with no clear dominance

This leads to the question of how prevalent a non-unanimous practice must be in relation to competing practices in order to consider it sufficiently widespread. Any answer will have a degree of arbitrariness. However, this arbitrariness can be minimised by clearly stating the principles on which the answer is based. The notion of majority will be based on the following principles:

1. The practice must have a clear dominance over competing practices.
2. A reasonable person ascertains whether a given practice is clearly dominant.

Clear dominance can be established quantitatively or qualitatively. To establish the dominance quantitatively statistical analysis must be performed. Ability to generalise to the population is ensured by standard techniques from sampling theory. To establish dominance qualitatively, an analytical or inductive generalisation must be performed. As Chapter VIII will show, the quantitative answer can be given by probability sampling, whereas a qualitative generalisation may employ certain types of non-probability sampling.

a. *Quantitative majority*

As far as quantitative dominance is concerned, it is proposed that a practice is clearly dominant if the difference between adherence to such a practice and adherence to the second most widespread practice is greater than 50 per cent. The principle of clear dominance can be summarised in the following equation:

$$\mathbf{D >= C + 50\%}$$

where D = adherence to dominant practice and C = adherence to the second most important competing practice. In case there is only one competing practice, this quantitative principle means that a competing practice should not have more than 25 per cent adherence. The graph below illustrates this scenario:

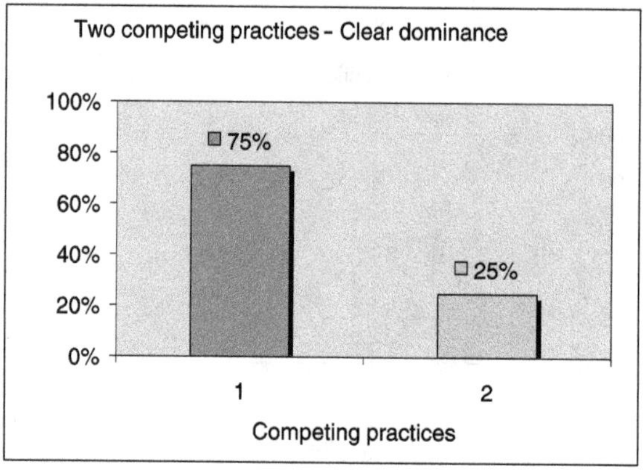

Figure 9 – A clearly dominant practice over one competing practice

When there is more than one competing practice, this formula ensures that the dominant practice must represent no less than 50 per cent of all practice. Thus this approach appears to capture all the essential elements of the notion of a clear majority. The same principle applies in case there is more than one competing practice (Figure 10).

Figure 11 below illustrates this problem well. By March 2002, around 150,000 web servers out of the total number of 160,000 researched by Netcraft offered strong encryption. In other words, the data suggests that in March 2002, 93 per cent of web servers offered strong encryption of transactions and only 7 per cent of servers offered exclusively old ciphers. Since the difference between the practice in question and a competing practice is greater than 50 per cent, the practice of offering strong encryption of transactions is a dominant practice. This seems to be very strong evidence of the customary character of a norm requiring web servers to provide the capability to transact using strong encryption. One should also note, however, that such a practice started to become distinctly popular only from the

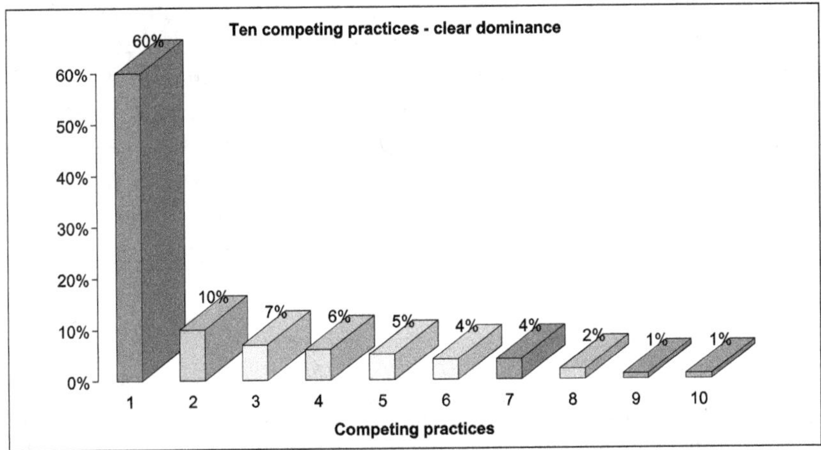

Figure 10 – A clearly dominant practice over nine competing practices

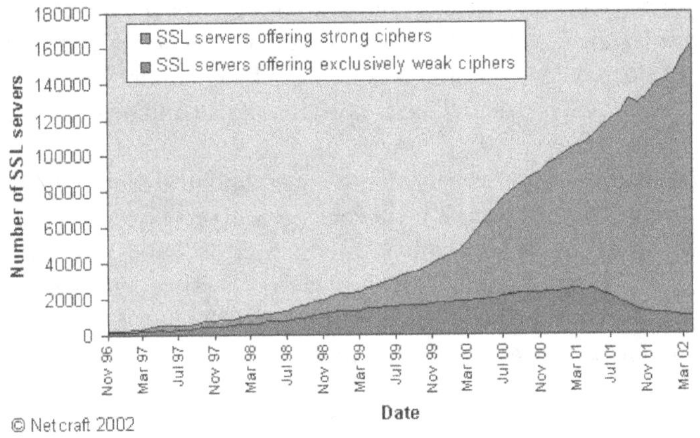

Figure 11 – The notion of majority. Source: Netcraft April 2002 Web Survey

period of March to July 2000. It is only from the end of this period that one could start considering a given norm as having customary character.

The principle of clear dominance is to serve more as a guide rather than a formula that should be strictly adhered to. This is in line with the principle of ascertainment of clear dominance by a reasonable person. The second principle implies that borderline cases should be interpreted in favour of existence of customary practice. For instance, in a case where there is only one competing practice, the quantitative principle of clear dominance means that a competing practice should not exceed 25 per cent of adherence. If, however, a practice in question has 74 per cent adherence and a competing practice has 26 per cent adherence a reasonable person could decide that a given practice is sufficiently widespread.

Practices that could be presumed to be customary would have around 75-100 per cent adherence to it. A practice that is 75-100 per cent popular will be referred to as a common practice. Uniformity of practice suggests that action in conformity with a norm arising out of such practice is expected by all-size participants in electronic commerce. Only a high level of adherence to a given practice provides a strong presumption in favour of customary character of a given routine. The reason is that such practice can much more easily create the presumption of longevity (or time intensiveness), repeatability and consistency thus greatly simplifying the proof of e-custom.

b. *Qualitative majority*

It may not always be possible to establish in numerical terms what the dominant practice is. In such a case the dominance of a given practice must be inferred from other indicators such as the practice of influential companies or other factors that that can indirectly indicate the nature of majority practice. It is important to note here that smaller companies usually follow what big enterprises do, but until this actually happens, one cannot speak of a widespread practice or e-custom. A practice can be considered dominant if it is adhered to by important Internet companies such as, e.g., Amazon.com or Dell.com as well as small and medium e-commerce companies.

Qualitative analysis requires very strong methodological tools that would allow such generalisations. As Chapter VIII will demonstrate, very powerful generalisations can be drawn from analysis of software tools used to build Internet commerce websites because of the constraints they place on possible variation of practice. This matter will be taken up more fully in Chapter VIII where a definite methodology for combining statistical and analytical evidence for the dominance of a practice will be presented.

(c) Practice widespread in time

Internet practice can be widespread not only in a physical sense but also in time. The section below will discuss the element of time in detail.

5.4 Duration of Internet practice

The concept of custom has traditionally been associated with a long lasting practice of doing something.[1033] Since the digital economy relies on fast dissemination of information, practices of companies in the era of the Internet are formed much faster than in the past. The sections below will present the traditional horizontal

[1033] See previous chapters and the definition of custom in Chapter I.

perception of time and the arguably more important vertical element of time in the context of the development of electronic commerce custom.

(a) Horizontal element of time

The ordinary meaning of the term custom presupposes the existence of a widespread practice for a very long time. This notion of the term has changed in international law where it has been accepted that international custom can be recognised after a short time period, since developments in society, particularly in commercial or technology law, take place at a quicker pace.[1034]

These findings are of paramount importance to the concept of electronic commerce custom. Certain e-mercantile practices can become binding within a very short time frame. If thirty years ago, it could take less than ten years[1035] in international public law to develop binding practices it can also take less than ten years to develop binding e-commerce practices nowadays. In fact, given the enormous tempo of the digital revolution, one could argue that binding e-commerce practices could develop in a much shorter time frame, arguably within one year or sometimes even less.

A good illustration of this point is provided by the practice of automatic update of software over the Internet, which has become more and more popular. Thanks to this very powerful capability of the Net, which allows unconscious downloading of patches and updates for any kind of software, millions of computers may be upgraded simultaneously with new features often rapidly changing established patterns of software execution. In consequence, new Internet customs could develop instantly with the widespread adoption of this practice. This calls for a new interpretation of the concept of longevity of customary practices. In less clear-cut cases, however, one should investigate a practice of recent years – 'the more the better'.

(b) Vertical element of time – Volume of transactions

The traditional understanding of the concept of custom implies longevity of practice as the necessary condition of its existence. This one-dimensional, 'horizontal' approach does not take into account other potential measures for assessing the practical importance of a given routine like the intensity of certain practices within a given period ('vertical' measure). Using a simple analogy, two hundred years ago there could be 100 instances of adherence to one commercial practice within one year. Nowadays there can be 100 instances of adherence to one commercial prac-

1034 See Polanski, P.P. (2002), *A New Approach to Regulating Internet Commerce: Custom as a Source of Electronic Commerce Law*; Polanski, P.P. and Johnston, R.B. (7-10 January 2002), *International Custom as a Source of Law in Global Electronic Commerce*; Polanski, P.P. and Johnston, R.B. (2002), *Potential of Custom in Overcoming Legal Uncertainty in Global Electronic Commerce*.

1035 See Judge Tanaka (1969), *Dissenting opinion of Judge Tanaka on Continental Shelf* case, p. 177, discussed in Chapter VI.

tice within one day. In other words, one day nowadays can be as important as one year in the past as far as formation of a custom is concerned.

This study challenges the traditional understanding of the concept of custom as it is argued that, in the case of electronic commerce custom, it is also the volume of the transactions that can contribute to the faster formation of international Internet customary norms. Traditional custom used duration as a measure of significance because intensity was not easily measurable. The electronic commerce environment provides a unique opportunity to measure the number and type of transactions that took place in a given timeframe, thus providing an excellent proof of mercantile adherence to certain practices. For instance, transaction logs or intelligent software agents might gather information about the intensity of certain types of transactions that might contribute to the faster formation of e-custom. This in turn leads to the conclusion that the number of transactions within a given unit of time, rather than some fixed number of time units, is more important when assessing the longevity of Internet customs.

The difficult question is how many adherences to a given practice within a given unit of time would justify considering it as having customary character. Rather than providing some arbitrary figure, more important is the realisation of how popular a given practice is over some period, taking into account its growth trend. Instant practice could be considered customary if it is very widespread and has an indication of the growth in the early stages of its adoption. Proof of custom then, could completely disregard the time factor, although information about when the practice started to occur and when it started to become popular could become very useful.

(c) New meaning of time factor

Electronic commerce custom does not need to have long continuance if adherence to the practice in question provided it could be evidenced using electronic means that it was very intensive within a given timeframe. As it was suggested earlier, it is not unrealistic to assume that sometimes new e-customs could be developed instantly and without the consciousness of the user, provided that most Internet users would have broadband Internet connection and turned on automatic software updates. It is possible to imagine a sudden shift in some security practices because of one update that is instantly disseminated to millions of computers around the world in just a couple of minutes. It is not difficult to imagine that within just a couple of hours, the majority of the commercial web servers and browsers might start to use, e.g., 168-bit encryption of e-commerce transactions. The sites that did not respond quickly to this new standard of transacting would in effect create a less secure environment. If there is a breach of security, the adjudicator could base his or her decision on the customary practice of using higher encryption that was formed within just couple of hours. This new customary practice would follow from another practice that could already be considered as customary and requiring all software to be updated as soon as possible and when there is a direct connection to the Internet – automatically.

The time factor then is still important as far as the nature of custom is concerned but it has changed its meaning. The passage of time is no longer of sole decisive importance, as today most web practices cannot be older than ten years anyway, because web browsers were introduced less than a decade ago. Nevertheless, they could be considered customary based on their very intensive application. As a result, a proof of passage of time would not be necessary, given an indication of popularity of practice.

What is interesting to note is the fact that custom could become a faster mode of development of both domestic and international Internet and electronic commerce law than statutory laws or case law. Since, as it is argued, a customary practice could be developed very rapidly, the new unwritten laws could be established in a much shorter time-frame than traditional laws. This introduces new interesting challenges that will need to be further investigated.

5.5 Consistency of practice

Consistency of Internet practice should be understood as a steady adherence to a given practice over the timeframe in question. From the practical perspective, this boils down to the question of the characteristic of a trend that a given practice exhibits. Steady growth patterns of adoption of a given practice would certainly fuel the argument that such practice is of customary character. Conversely, inconsistent tendencies could provide arguments against the customary character of a given Internet practice.

The trend analysis should be performed especially when the practice in question cannot be regarded as a common practice. If a given practice has 75-100 per cent of adherence, the question of consistency of this practice seems to be unnecessary, as in a given time it fulfils the most important requirement for establishing electronic commerce custom, which is its widespread character. In case of practices that are popular but are not common, a trend analysis seems to be necessary. This type of analysis may turn out to be very important in judicial hearings that always deal with a situation that occurred some time ago. Without being able to see the propensity of a practice within a given timeframe, it may be impossible to argue for the existence of a customary norm in a given moment in the past.

An analysis of consistency of practice from the perspective of the passage of time could reveal major or minor inconsistencies in the tendency of given practice. Major inconsistencies should always lead to the conclusion that a practice in question has not reached a maturity expected from the customary norm. Minor inconsistencies could be tolerated, although in case of electronic commerce, one should expect more linear trends of adoption of a given practice.

However, to establish the trend of a practice may prove to be difficult in real life. If a question regarding the existence of Internet customary norm refers to one or more years back, one may have to gather information about a given practice over this period. One way of approaching this problem is to analyse the current popularity and growth trend of the practice in question taking the last couple of months and then attempt to draw a line back in time. Such a method of establishing consistency of practice is far from ideal and may provide false information for practices that are a couple of years old. For this reason, it is also important to gather information about the time the practice was born and how quickly it was adopted in the industry. In the case of non-common practices, the trend analysis may prove to be difficult to conduct and for this reason should be discouraged.

5.6 Objections to practice

The question of consistency of practice is related to another important issue – that of treatment of conscious objectors to the practice in question. Uniformity of practice suggests that action in conformity with the norm arising out of such practice is expected by other participants in electronic commerce. Practice of an electronic commerce participant, which does not conform to what the majority does, but achieves the same goal as the practice of the majority should not be viewed as an inconsistent practice, but rather should be treated as practice contributing to the uniformity of practice. For if a company does not use strong SSL encryption, but achieves the goal of equally secure data transmission using other methods, then such a practice should be considered as consistent with the practice of the majority.

Transplanting this concept from international law would lead to the result that an e-commerce participant who objects to a given practice from the beginning will not be subjected to the norm arising out of the practice of majority.[1036] There are two issues here. First, as was discussed in the beginning of this chapter, international law has only around two hundred participants, whereas in global electronic commerce there are hundreds of thousands of entities. As a result, in international law, objection to a prevailing practice is made public and is easily noticeable and other states usually react very quickly to such behaviour, either approving it or not. In the case of electronic commerce, there are many more participants who are not aware of the role of custom as a potential source of law and do not make their objections public.

Moreover, in international law, the goal of a state objecting to a given practice is to disturb eventual formation of a custom. The objecting state has to react if it does not want to be considered as acquiescing in the practice of the majority, by virtue of silence, interpreted as an unvoiced compliance. Contrary to international law, many conducts that do not conform to the practice of the majority are unconscious. Frequent reasons for non-conformance would possibly be an ignorance or lack of funds or willingness to implement a given technology. If allowed, such behaviours, could actually lead to a justification of non-conformance with any Internet customary practice thus yielding customary law irrelevant. In short, allowing simple non-con-

---

[1036] See for example, Villiger, M.E. (1997), *Customary International Law and Treaties. A Manual on the Theory and Practice of the Interrelation of Sources*, pp. 33-37.

formance with a practice of the majority, for whatever reason, could undermine the sensibleness of custom as a source of Internet law.

However, does this mean that any practice consciously and openly objecting to a practice of a majority should be denied legal validity in the case of a dispute? The answer is no. As was noted above, the practice of the minority which is different yet achieves the same goal as the practice of the majority, should be considered as a valid exception. Obviously, if the objector follows a practice that is better than an industry standard the same rule should apply. Again, a judgment of a reasonable person (or an expert) will be necessary to assess whether a given practice serves the same purpose as the practice of the majority.

If a competing practice does not achieve the same goal as the practice of the majority, it should be treated as a breach of the norm arising out of the practice of the majority. One should note here, that such a practice should also be assessed from the perspective of its reasonableness or morality of its goal. Similar remarks could be made in the context of the doctrine of a subsequent objector, which could be an e-company that objects to e-custom after it has been established. Again, such an objection would be permissible but only if the practice that it follows is better than the industry standard or at least achieves the same goal as the practice of the majority. In general, however, such behaviours should be interpreted with a great degree of caution.

5.7 Repetition of practice

Repetition of practice over time can result in the formation of custom, which has the force of law.[1037] This apparently obvious statement has been undermined by some international lawyers who argued that international custom could be formed after a single instance of practice.[1038] Although this matter is of little practical importance, it is argued that Internet custom can be formed only through the repetition of acts over some time, even if it is a very short period. Without such a repetition, the notion of custom would be stretched too far from its original meaning. Repetition can be presumed in the case of predetermined actions and non-predetermined actions, given that the practice in question is widespread.

5.8 Morality and reasonableness of practice

The question of whether a practice that is not morally desirable or reasonable creates customary norms is difficult to answer for many lawyers.[1039] As was argued in the previous chapter, allowing such tests introduces uncertainty to the body of legal

---

[1037] See important definitions in Chapter I.

[1038] See Chapter VI.

[1039] Although morality and reasonability are different concepts, they will be discussed as equivalent terms *below*.

norms. On the other hand, written law is certain – even if it is bad, it will usually bind until changed. In contrast, custom is in many legal traditions subjected to the test of reasonableness or morality, which can deny its legal value.[1040] Should Internet practice be subjected to the test of morality and reasonability as a precondition for the establishment of e-custom?

It is argued that an undesirable practice even if widely followed (for example, spam constitutes 42 per cent of e-mail traffic in the United Kingdom[1041]) should not create legally binding rules. This argument introduces an uneasy degree of subjectivity in ascertaining e-custom. Nevertheless, customary law should not be harmful in order to create desired effects in the society. One cannot imagine incorporation into a body of laws, norms that are morally undesirable, illogical or unreasonable. If one assumes that even a harmful or unreasonable common practice can amount to a legally binding norm then the integrity of a system of law is endangered. This could lead to the justification of, e.g., child porn on the Internet on the ground that it is a widespread practice in the Internet porn industry to give access to such materials to people above the age of 18. Or, one would have to accept an unauthorised installation and use of spyware, given a widespread proliferation of such software on the Internet.

One should note, however, that in most cases this verification would not stop the development of customary norms on the Internet. One can safely assume that most of the practices are morally indifferent and not harmful to the Information Society as are the norms in traditional commercial settings. As a result, it is argued that it can be presumed that all norms arising in international Internet commerce are morally desirable and reasonable. If one wants to rebut this presumption, then it would have to be proved to the adjudicator that a given practice violates some widely accepted morals or global standards. This matter then requires further research.

5.9 Summary of the notion of practice

Practice is the cornerstone of the concept of custom. Internet practice consists of positive practice and statements about these practices, although in the latter case, e-custom can amount only to the norm requiring making such statements. An Internet practice is one that is adhered to by Internet companies, individuals as well as international organisations and governments in the course of electronic trading. Such a practice should posses certain qualities in order to consider it as a material for electronic commerce custom. It should be widespread, meaning that it is practiced by the dominant majority of all-size e-commerce participants either globally or locally, across all or some industries and is intensive in terms of number of transac-

[1040] See Part II of the book.

[1041] See for example, Cieslak, D. (31 March 2003), *Brytyjczycy walcza ze spamem.* However, the amount of spam does not create a presumption that the majority of users sends spam. In fact, the opposite is true. See the discussion on spam and spamdexing in Chapter IX.

tions. The last requirement leads to the conclusion that the traditional element of longevity of practice can be replaced by the vertical element of time. Not every Internet practice could amount to custom but only one that is helpful in solving legal problems. Moreover, a practice should be repetitive, as a single instance of practice cannot lead to the formation of e-custom. Furthermore, it should be consistent over time, although minor inconsistencies should not affect the development of custom. Finally, it should not be harmful or unreasonable in order to create the desired effects in the global society.

6. The Subjective Element

According to the majority of international law scholars, practice alone is not a sufficient element to form a legal rule. What is also required is a special psychological attitude towards the practice that could be described as a feeling of being bound by the norm that could be inferred from this practice or that it is accepted by the international community. As a logical consequence, a person violating the custom should be aware of the fact that he/she is breaking the rule of law that is binding him/her.

As was shown in the previous chapter, this approach has been severely criticised in the literature. It was pointed out that it is very difficult to evidence this element in practice as it relates to capturing the intangible state of mind of all the participants. In addition, the formation of new norms or change of existing ones is impossible to explain by psychological theory. Similarly, the reasons for mandatory adoption of all customary norms by new participants could not be successfully explained by acceptance theory.

6.1 **Rejection of subjective element in e-custom**

The idea of a psychological attitude of feeling bound by some practice as a constituent of the definition of custom is extremely problematic, especially when the parties are not people as may indeed be the case in electronic commerce. In the electronic commerce environment, where all transactions may be automated, very fast, and deeply hidden from an end-user, it would be even more difficult to prove the existence of psychological attitude towards some norm especially in the case where machines rather than humans respond to predetermined events.

Consequently, this study challenges the need for the subjective element in the definition of electronic commerce custom. Extreme practical problems with evidencing a psychological attitude toward some norm combined with an unacceptable theoretical explanation of the concept of *opinio iuris* has led to the rejection of the classical 'two elements' theories of custom. Instead, it is argued that the notion of the expectation that a given practice will be observed better explains the formation of customary norms in general and Internet customs, in particular.

On the other hand, some theories of custom presented in the last chapter argue that only the element of practice is necessary for the formation of international custom. Such an approach eliminated deficiencies of *opinio iuris* element in the theory of custom. The main objection against this approach was the argument that the lack of *opinio iuris* eliminates the distinction between custom as a source of law and norms of international comity and morality. The proposed concept of Internet custom eliminates this deficiency by introducing the concept of legally relevant practice, introduced above. Only practice that can help solve legal problems can be considered as having legal applicability. Such practice must also be sufficiently widespread to justify the expectation that it should be observed. Now any practice of trading on the Net that fulfils these requirements shall be considered as a customary right or obligation of Internet commerce. The section below will further elaborate on the meaning of expectation that a given practice should be observed.

6.2 Expectation of practice observance

It is argued that rather than searching for the subjective conviction that a given norm is a law or that it has been tacitly accepted by the community, it is sufficient to prove that a given practice is sufficiently widespread. The reason is that if a given routine were really well-known and practiced, then such a habit would create a natural expectation that it should be followed by other members of the community. Internet trade participants will simply expect such behaviour from the rest of the trading partners. This is the reason why non-conforming parties should adhere to it.

The concept of expectation as to the observance of the practice assumes that Internet traders in the same set of circumstances have a legal prospect of being treated in the same manner in the same set of circumstances. If a party does not live up to the expectation, then it does not necessarily mean that it has breached customary law of the Internet. However, the party must have a very good reason to do so. Such a reason could be a better routine practiced by this participant. However, if a party expecting an adherence to a widespread practice suffered a loss, or his or her right was in any way adversely affected by non-conformation with the widespread practice, then it is highly likely that an adjudicator will conclude that customary practice has been breached.

The expectation then, is a consequence of a widespread adherence to a given practice. This is the expectation of a reasonable person rather than the actual practitioner in any instance of the practice and, in principle, it does not have to be proved. But if it has to be, it can. If a practice is followed by a majority of web trade participants then the expectation that it should be followed could be presumed. For if 80 per cent or 90 per cent of web participants trade in a particular way, it is obvious that such a behaviour will be expected. However, in less clear-cut cases the proof of expectation might be required. The concept of expectation is of a psychological nature but if the need arises, it is certainly easier to prove than the feeling of being bound by the norm in question. The reason here is that it should be less cumbersome to gather evidence in favour of the existence of an expectation that a given practice should be followed as opposed to proving feeling bound by the practice in question. Humans have a tendency of rejecting new norms limiting their freedom, thus making the proof of psychological feeling doomed to failure. In this case, however, it should be much easier to gather information about expectation to act in a given manner because it is the expectation of an outsider rather than that of every single practitioner.

In summary, the concept of e-custom stresses the dominant role of widespread practice that can solve legal problems. The two-elements theory of international custom should not be applied to electronic commerce because of practical and theoretical problems with making use of this idea. Instead, the subjective element should be replaced with the concept of expectation that a given practice will be followed because of a routine that is sufficiently widespread to create such anticipation in a reasonable person.

7. Summary of the Concept of E-custom

In summary, the concept of electronic commerce custom is based on the idea of a legally relevant practice of trading on the Internet that is so widespread that it can justify the expectation that it will be followed. The research has challenged the need for the traditional subjective element of custom, claiming that practice is the only constituent element of e-custom. It does not need to be supported by a feeling of being bound by the practice, due to the impossibility of evidencing this feeling as well as the theoretical chronological paradox created by the 'two elements' theory of custom. Similarly, the consensual interpretation of the subjective element is rejected, on the basis that new participants in Internet commerce could argue that since they have not participated in the creation of customary norms then they are not bound by them.

In order to overcome practical and theoretical problems associated with subjective element of custom, it was replaced with the idea of an expectation of following a norm created by a widespread adherence to a given practice. The expectation can be presumed only given a very widespread adherence to a given practice. In order to distinguish between customary law and some conventional habit of doing something, the concept of legally relevant practice has been introduced. The judge will have to use common sense to make a distinction between legally relevant and legally irrelevant practices of trading on the Internet.

The practice must possess certain qualities. It must be repetitive and widespread in terms of space and time. The practice must also be widespread, meaning that it must be followed by a clear majority of subjects across one Internet industry, some industries or all industries globally or regionally. Local custom, however, can also exist, although it binds only the parties in question. The practice does not need to be long-lasting meaning that it can be established within a short period, arguably even in a couple of hours if there is a high frequency of adherence to a given practice within a specified period of time. Practice changes with time, meaning that it may not be consistent. Nevertheless, consistency of practice automatically creates a presumption that the observation of it is expected. Repetitive practice means repetitive positive behaviour, consisting of both positive physical acts as well as declarations to do something, although in the latter case the scope of custom is limited. Repetition must take place a number of times in order to create an impression that it is a widely followed practice – a single occurrence of a practice cannot give birth to electronic commerce custom. If a practice is followed by 75 per cent or more participants, the presumption can be made that it created an expectation that it should be followed.

Summing up, an electronic commerce custom can be objectively established by researching the adherence in space and in time of Internet companies to the routine in question. This is the primary task of researchers. However, a judge may reject a given practice as being legally irrelevant, 'bad' or unreasonable.

8. The Role of an Adjudicator

Before explaining the role of an adjudicator in establishing customary norms, it is important to realise how various customary law is compared to statutory law. Only then, the role of a judge in adjudicating disputes involving Internet commerce custom can be tackled.

It is submitted that customary norms in general and e-customary norms in particular, are formed unconsciously. In other words, customary rights or obligations come into being whenever there is a community of interacting people or programmed devices, whose majority adheres to certain legally relevant norms irrespective of those norms being known to everyone or established by some official body. Standards organisations or important software companies have a very influential role in shaping dominant practices, but their standards in order to become customary have to be actually adopted by a community, which cannot be presumed. The reason is that companies or individuals usually follow what their competitors or people close to them do, which may be far from what the standard requires. As a result, the extensive adherence to certain practices may create express or unconscious expectations on the part of the majority engaged in the practice in question – that others would either follow it or an equally good or better way of trading.

Consequently, custom as a source of regulatory norms continues to exist without any convention, constitution, or statute enlisting it as a source of law or confirming its binding normative character. Similarly, customary norms continue to exist without official recognition of their existence and their legal character by lawyers, parliaments, or international organisations. In particular, customary norms do not require any judicial confirmation in order to become binding or valid. They simply exist and continue to be adhered to by the members of a given community. In this sense, custom is an autonomous source of norms, as it continues to produce them and influence participant's behaviour 'on its own'.

If custom does not require any official confirmation, then what is the role of the judicial apparatus in establishing and applying it? First, it should be noted that it is the task of Internet researchers to try to find and monitor potential global and particular Internet customary practices. It is difficult to imagine judges being versed with such a complicated and time-consuming challenge. In other words, researchers first of all should deal with questions such as which Internet practices are widespread within a given timeframe, are they consistent over time, are there objections to them, etc. Judges would then have a much easier task of stating whether a given practice is moral or reasonable and whether it could be used to solve a given problem at hand.

Having said that, it is clear that judicial declaration as to the existence of a given norm as customary is important. The importance of confirmation lies in the fact that it may lead to widespread acceptance of a given customary norm by the legal community. This seems to be the best way to promote the potential of custom in other communities. This remark applies especially to IT and the business community that is in general unaware of the potential role of custom as a source of rights and obligations. However, such confirmation of the customary character of a given norm would only have a declaratory power in respect to the customary practice in question. It has to be stressed that a judicial confirmation would only be valid temporarily – in respect to a given practice within a given timeframe. Practices change and new research could prove that existing custom is no longer adhered to by the Internet participants. Such a research should be continued in the Information Systems discipline as well as the legal community in order to find current ways of dealing in the online world.

In summary, the view taken here is that custom exists independently of any other sources of law and it does not require judicial confirmation in order to become binding. The effect of such confirmation may only be declaratory as to the existence of such custom. However, a judge should be able to deny legal effect to a customary practice that is evidently bad or legally irrelevant in given circumstances. A judge or arbitrator should gain knowledge about custom from researching what companies actually do on the Internet by using various forms of measuring electronic practices such as intelligent agents, software logs, etc.

9. Hypothetical Examples

The two examples below will demonstrate how custom can affect both the norms governing formation as well as content of a contract. The first example will show how the web customary practice of immediate transaction confirmation has potentially modified the formation of an electronic contract. The second example will show how common practice among financial institutions to support high encryption of transactions might affect the content of a contract.

9.1 Transaction confirmation practice

A transaction can take place on the Internet in several ways. The most common method is through a website with a shopping cart facility or an auction mechanism. There is of course a possibility of forming a contract via an exchange of e-mails or using proprietary systems such as EDI or electronic marketplaces, but the discussion below will be restricted to publicly available websites.

Web-based transactions usually require several steps to conclude a contract. In the case of purchasing goods, it usually starts with placing a selected item in a shopping cart, which is followed by a screen that requires personal details, then information regarding quantity of the purchased items and packaging, then shipping address details and payment details. After clicking an order button, the order is often not considered to be placed yet, but a purchaser is shown another screen, an order review screen (often misleadingly called an order confirmation or payment confirmation screen), which summarises all the personal, shipping and financial purchaser data. It is at this point that a purchaser may or may not click an order button that will trigger the performance of a transaction. After clicking the order button now, the parties enter into a contract, the transaction will be recorded, and the purchaser will be presented with an order confirmation screen as well as an e-mail being sent confirming the transaction.

It is important to distinguish two distinct customary practices in relation to the conclusion of the web transaction: transaction summary and transaction confirmation. The first practice aims to provide an order summary prior to the final placement of the order. The second practice aims to provide an immediate order confirmation after placement of the order, as proof of the formation of the contract.

Order summary practice either takes the form of a separate order summary screen or is a part of the payment details step. In either case, the transaction is summarised, meaning that all important transaction details are provided on one screen to allow a purchaser to review the transaction prior to the final placement of an order. There are very good reasons for such a practice. Since a purchaser has to provide his information on several screens, he or she may want to see it in one piece to review it before a final commitment. Also, a purchaser is given a last chance to recheck the purchase and to correct input errors or withdraw from the transaction, should they change their mind.

The non-provision of such a screen (Figure 12) could justify avoidance of a contract by a purchaser based on a contractual mistake, although this matter requires further research. In consequence, it is argued that a customary norm has emerged that states: 'All web-based transactions should be summarised by the Internet merchant prior to the acceptance of an order.' A proof of the widespread character of this practice will be presented elsewhere.

On the other hand, an analysis of a number of commercial websites shows that an order confirmation practice usually takes the form of a screen that immediately follows an order placement screen. It usually provides all the details of the transac-

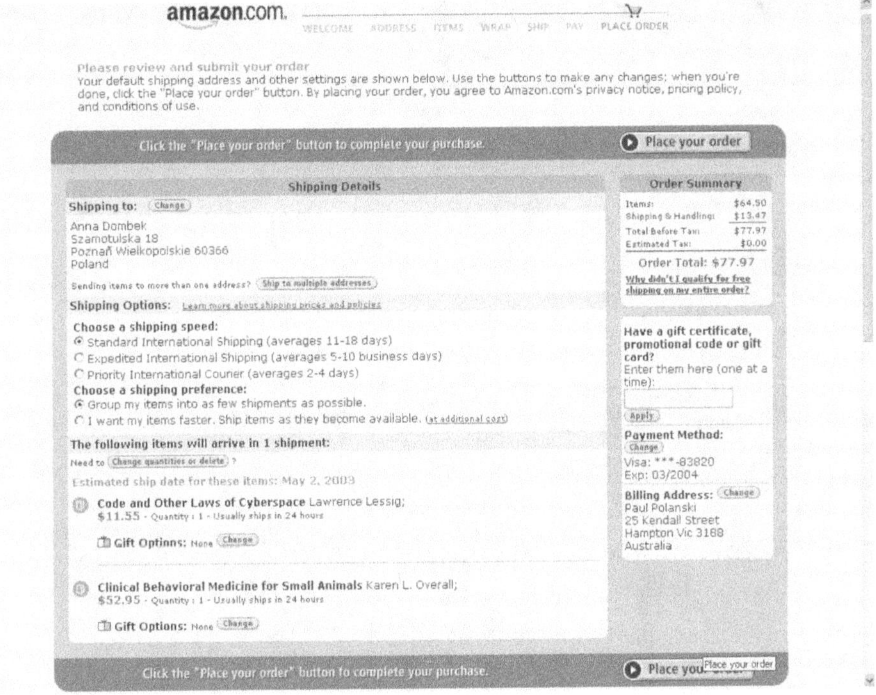

Figure 12 – Amazon.com transaction summarisation practice

tion and a transaction reference number, so the customer can actually track the progress of their order. Immediate transaction confirmation is usually also followed by e-mail confirmation that has the advantage of allowing the customer to easily access the purchase information after the transaction. The necessity of transaction confirmation is recognised by both software product specialists[1042] as well as web design experts.[1043]

The two screen shots (Figures 13 and 14) show that the transaction confirmation practice might take different forms. In the first case scenario, Amazon.com confirms transaction on the Web, informing a purchaser that a confirmation has been sent in the e-mail. Interestingly, Amazon.com did not provide an order tracking number on the Web, but sent it in the e-mail.[1044] However, the sole use of an e-mail as a confirmation medium may not be sufficient, since it is relatively easy to mistype one's e-mail address, which would mean an order would not be confirmed. On the

[1042] See for example, Libertone, D. and Scoppa, A. (2000), *Microsoft Site Server 3.0 Commerce Edition: An E-Commerce Solution*, p. 3.

[1043] See for example, Nielsen, J. (2000), *Designing Web Usability: The Practice of Simplicity*, p. 188.

[1044] The practice has been slightly modified in 2005 and now the order number can be accessed from the order confirmation screen. See also Nielsen, J. (25 July 2005), *Amazon: No Longer the Role Model for E-Commerce Design*.

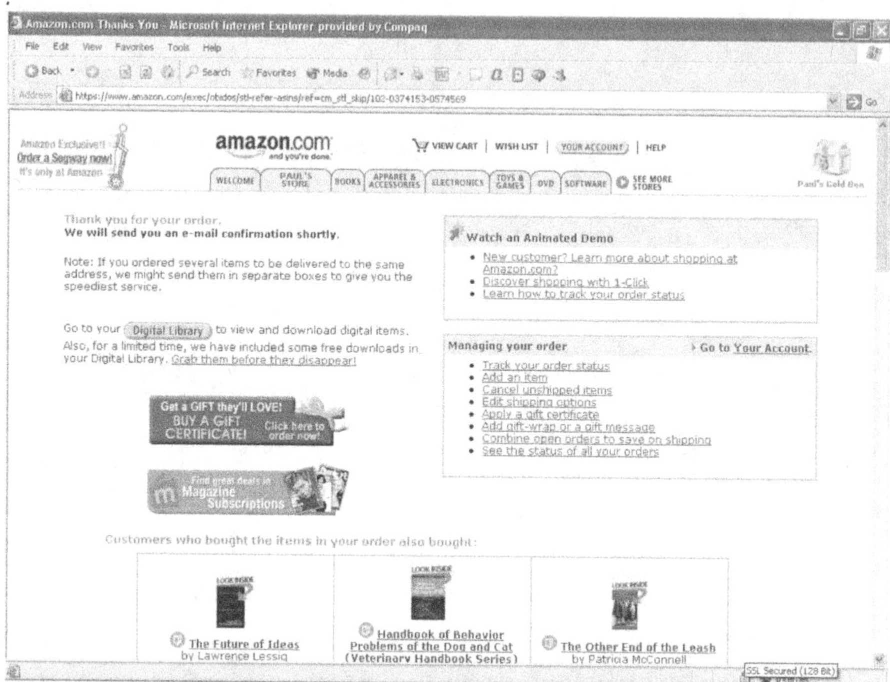

Figure 13 – Amazon.com confirmation page without order tracking number which is sent in the e-mail

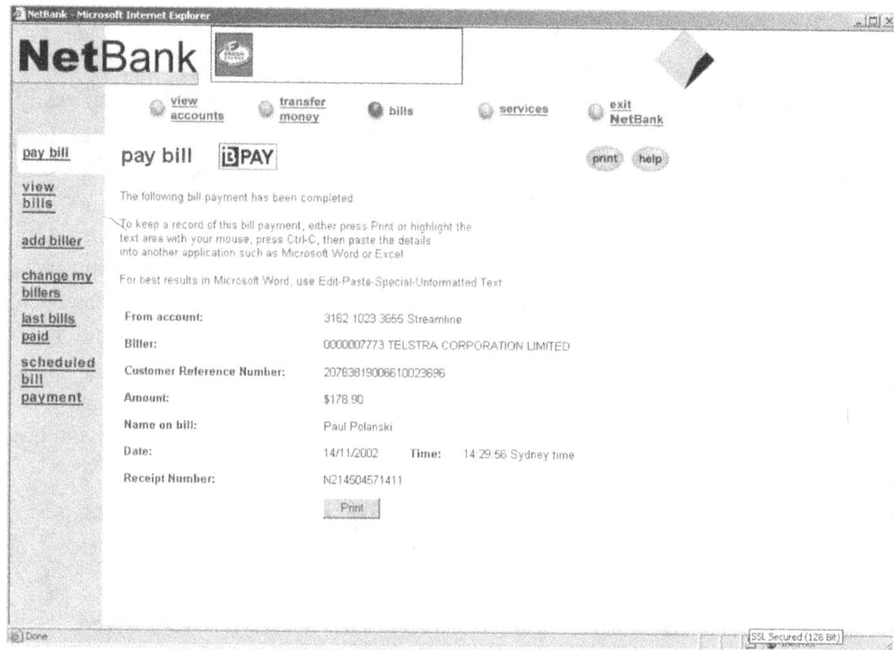

Figure 14 – Web-based transaction confirmation by Commonwealth Bank of Australia without e-mail confirmation

other hand, CBA's banking software did provide immediate online confirmation that included the transaction reference number together with the summarisation of the transaction, but did not confirm it in the e-mail. E-mail confirmation of banking transaction rarely takes place, however. Usually both a detailed web-based transaction confirmation as well as e-mail confirmation takes place. This, it can be seen, is certainly the best practice.

An Internet mercantile community has developed an order confirmation practice that has gained universal recognition. It seems to be a global custom, a common practice across all industries and countries, irrespective of the fact that it is business-to-business, business-to-consumer, business-to-administration, or any other possible form of transaction. Even some web development products have incorporated an order summary screen as a mandatory functionality, thus forcing web developers to include it in their final product.

There are very good reasons for such a practice. First, it is the best way to provide evidence of the conclusion of the contract. The transaction confirmation screen and confirmation e-mail repeat the essential terms of the contract and provide a transaction reference number that would otherwise be unavailable. Second, the order acceptance notification provides an immediate proof of the transaction. Sending the confirmation by post causes delay and provides an unacceptable uncertainty as to whether the order has been accepted or not. Immediate knowledge of that fact would allow a customer to wait calmly for the delivery instead of looking for other options. Third, it enables the tracking of the status of the order.

The practice of providing transaction confirmation is now so common that it justifies the expectation that any Internet merchant will adhere to it. As a result, it is claimed that an international electronic commerce custom has emerged. It states that: 'All web-based transactions should be electronically confirmed immediately after the placement of an order.'

Transaction confirmation practice is a custom concerning the formation of the contract, not a custom as to the content of an agreement. It is argued that it is an essential step in the formation of a web contract, akin to exchange of contracts. An Internet merchant who does not immediately provide an order confirmation could be in breach of an e-commerce custom. In such a case, it could be argued that a business customer has the right to refrain from a contract, although he may not want to exercise it.

Furthermore, it is argued that this global custom has been partially 'codified' in Article 11 of the European Union Directive on Electronic Commerce, which require electronic acknowledgement of recipient's order without 'undue delay'. Problems may arise in connection with the term 'undue delay' employed to set the timeframe for order confirmation. Nevertheless, the directive does not provide for sanctions in case of non-compliance with a required rule. Also, as was mentioned earlier, the directive does not have global scope, so only European Union companies and customers will benefit. However, because of the customary nature of a transaction confirmation norm, the rule requiring merchants to confirm immediately orders that were placed via the web binds all Internet merchants across the whole globe. It could also be argued that the European 'unconscious' codification of this global practice is an important evidence (although an indirect one) of the existence of an international electronic commerce custom.

In order to illustrate better the concept of custom in the formation of the agreement, consider the hypothetical case below. The hypothetical case will be limited to transaction confirmation customary practice.

9.2 Hypothetical transaction confirmation case

In this case a website manager did not include an order confirmation screen in his Web system and in consequence, an international client refused to pay for the delivery, arguing that it is customary nowadays to immediately confirm the ordering of goods. As was demonstrated in Chapter IV, existing international regulations of electronic commerce do not provide adequate means to solve the problem in question. There is a legal vacuum as far as written international electronic law is concerned. However, in order to solve this case we can make use of the idea of custom. The first thing to do is to evidence the existence of an alleged order confirmation practice. This can be done by visiting a specified sample of business websites and checking if all of them provide an order confirmation screen. The other possibility could be automation of this procedure by the use of a software component that would do this for us. Outcomes of surveys and e-business opinions of experts could further strengthen the claim that there is a global Internet customary practice of providing an order confirmation immediately following the submission of an order. Finally, additional evidence could be found in the written laws, which codify, often 'unconsciously' an already existing customary norm. In the next chapter, more detailed ways of evidencing this custom will be presented.

Assuming convincing proof of the widespread character of transaction confirmation practice, one can conclude that it could be expected by a web client. Furthermore, as was explained above, this practice is reasonable and moral as it introduces greater reliability and legal certainty as to the existence of an agreement. In consequence, such a practice is of legal relevance, as it can be used in adjudicating disputes involving formation of e-commerce contracts.

As a result, successfully evidencing the alleged customary norm would relieve a customer from paying for the delivery due to non-observance by a first supplier of a global Internet custom, which requires an immediate provision of an order confirmation screen. Consequently, a contract has not been formed and the client's claim would be considered justified.

9.3 Transaction encryption practice

It is now common practice that nearly all banking transactions on the Internet are secured, mainly using cryptography. The permanent presence of computer hackers who browse the Internet in order to intercept valuable financial data have made e-commerce a highly risky and vulnerable environment. The recent 'Global Security Survey 2003' by Deloitte Touche Tohmatsu reported that 39 per cent of financial institutions

> 'acknowledged that their systems had been compromised in some way within the last year.'

Sixteen per cent of the reported attacks came from external sources, 10 per cent from internal sources and 13 per cent from both sources.[1045]

On the other hand, there is no international regulation that forces IT developers to use cryptography or other security techniques in order to protect the flow of information over the Internet channel. Although this study does not attempt to provide a detailed analysis of online banking, it simply observes that a new banking custom has emerged that states: 'All Internet banks should support strong encryption of transactions.' This translates to observing current practice of at least using the Secure Sockets Layer (SSL) version 3.0 protocol (or higher)[1046] with 128-bit encryption. The discussion of the SSL protocol will be greatly simplified in order to make it easier for a non-technical audience to comprehend it.

The Secure Sockets Layer protocol (SSL) developed by Netscape Communications[1047] is by far the most popular way of encrypting transactions on the Web.[1048] Encryption is the process of scrambling or ciphering information by applying a mathematical function in such a way that it is extremely difficult for anyone other that an intended recipient to obtain the original information.[1049] Central to this process is the mathematical value or a key, which is used by the mathematical function to cipher the message. The longer the key the more secure the transaction is.[1050]

> 'The SSL protocol uses a combination of public-key and symmetric key encryption. Symmetric key encryption is much faster than public-key encryption, but public-key encryption provides better authentication techniques.'[1051]

In symmetric key encryption, which SSL uses as the primary encryption technique, the same key (called the session key) is used for encryption of transaction by the

---

[1045] Deloitte Touche Tohmatsu (2003), *Global Security Survey 2003*, pp. 10, 16.

[1046] The term Secure Sockets Layer will be used to refer to TLS protocol. For an introduction to SSL and TSL see, for example, Rescorla, E. (2000), *SSL and TLS: Designing and Building Secure Systems*.

[1047] See for example, Freier, A.O., et al. (1996), *The SSL Protocol version 3.0. Internet Draft*; Netscape Communications Corporation (1998), *Introduction to SSL*; RSA Security *SSL Basics for Internet Users*.

[1048] See for example, Burnett, S. and Paine, S. (2001), *RSA Security's Official Guide to Cryptography*, p. 242, Rescorla, E. (2000), *SSL and TLS: Designing and Building Secure Systems*.

[1049] See Microsoft *About Encryption*.

[1050] Ibid.

[1051] Netscape Communications Corporation (1998), *Introduction to SSL*.

sender and decryption by the receiver so the challenge is to secure the transmission of the key between the two parties. In order to secure a transmission of the session key, SSL uses public key encryption (also known as asymmetric key encryption), which requires two keys mathematically related and independent of each other: the public key (which can be known to everyone) and private key (which should be kept secret). The public key is embedded in a digital certificate, which is required for all web servers attempting to use the SSL protocol. The server's digital certificate is a digital identification containing information about the web server and the organisation sponsoring the server's web content[1052] and has to be separately acquired from the certificate authorities like Verisign,[1053] Geotrust,[1054] Comodo,[1055] Entrust[1056] or Globalsign.[1057] In SSL, only the web server has to authenticate itself to the client's web browser,[1058] so the client's browser does not need the digital certificate.

After exchanging the session key using asymmetric key encryption, this key is used to encrypt and decrypt information by the server and the client for the rest of the Internet session. It is therefore crucial that the session key be long enough to encrypt the messages adequately. Typically, the key comes in two lengths: 40-bit (which is the default) and 128-bit. The 40-bit key has a little over one trillion possible combinations and is commonly considered insecure.[1059] An RSA-sponsored competition in January 1999 demonstrated that the 40-bit key could be broken in less than eight hours and a 56-bit key in 22 hours and 15 minutes.[1060] On the other hand, the use of 128-bit keys requires 309,485,009,821,345,068,724,781,056 times more computations, which given the same resources as in the previous test, would take two trillion years to complete.[1061]

According to a March 2002 Netcraft study, 18 per cent of SSL servers worldwide use vulnerable key lengths, with more than 40 per cent of them located in France.[1062] The report argues that the uneven result of adoption of strong encryp-

---

[1052] See Microsoft *About Certificates.*

[1053] <http://www.verisign.com>, last visited: 29/04/2003.

[1054] <http://www.geotrust.com/index_flash.htm>, last visited: 03/11/2002.

[1055] <http://www.comodogroup.com>, last visited: 03/11/2002.

[1056] <http://www.entrust.com/index.cfm>, last visited: 03/11/2002.

[1057] <http://www.globalsign.com>, last visited: 03/11/2002.

[1058] Netscape Communications Corporation (1998), *Introduction to SSL.*

[1059] Ibid.; RSA Security (14 February 1997), *Swiss-based Ph.D. Student Solves 48-bit Key in RSA Data Security's Secret-Key Challenge*; Verisign (18 May 1998), *Lotus Joins With Verisign To Provide Secure Global Communications And Commerce With Strongest Encryption Approved By The U.S. Government.*

[1060] See RSA Security (19 January 1999), *RSA Code-Breaking Contest Again Won by Distributed.Net and Electronic Frontier Foundation (EFF).*

[1061] See RSA Security, *SSL Basics for Internet Users*; Verisign (18 May 1998), *Lotus Joins With Verisign To Provide Secure Global Communications And Commerce With Strongest Encryption Approved By The U.S. Government*, see also, e.g., <http://www.fortisbank.com.pl>, last accessed: 01/05/2003.

[1062] Netcraft (2002), *The March 2002 Netcraft Web Server Survey*. See also Chapter II.

tion is due to the American export ban on strong cryptography products.[1063] In its later report, Netcraft claims that:

> 'the percentage of servers internet-wide offering exclusively weak ciphers has fallen from around 40% in December 1997, to below 6% in April 2002.'[1064]

It should be noted, however, that the spread of 128-bit encryption was initially severely limited due to the American ban on the export of strong encryption software that seems to be the main reason behind the non-uniform adoption of it in a number of countries.[1065] However, the Internet community has developed several ways to walk around American restrictions. The famous SSLeay[1066] implementation of the SSL protocol developed by Australian Eric Young enabling 128-bit encryption in Apache web servers was used subsequently in the Stronghold server sold outside America.[1067] After the lifting of export restrictions by the US government on 14 January 2000 regarding the selling overseas of 128-bit encryption, the IDs can be acquired by commercial entities around the world with the exception of Afghanistan (Taliban-controlled areas), Cuba, Iran, Iraq, Libya, North Korea, Sudan and Syria.[1068] Also some e-companies offer products that enable strong encryption over weakly secured links by means of special 'enhancements' to SSL protocol.[1069]

Therefore, a professional party acting on the Internet should support strongly encrypted messages. This is especially so in the case of financial or medical institutions who keep and transfer highly sensitive information about their customers. Consequently, a party to the Internet transaction should have the right to expect that its corresponding partner, for instance, an international bank, will provide strong cryptography (or a similarly secure technology) in order to safeguard their transactions. As a result, if a professional party were to break this rule, the other could expect compensation. According to the case being made here, this e-custom would become the implied term that could be incorporated in any e-commerce software license agreement. Therefore, even if a contract would be silent in respect to the

---

1063 See *above*.

1064 Netcraft (2002), *The April 2002 Netcraft Web Server Survey*.

1065 See for example, Koops, B.-J. (1999), *The crypto controversy: a key conflict in the information society*, pp. 98-99. See also Netcraft (2002), *The March 2002 Netcraft Web Server Survey*; Netscape Communications Corporation (1998), *Introduction to SSL*.

1066 See for example, Hudson, T.J. and Young, E.A. (24 September 1998), *SSLeay and SSLapps FAQ*, SSLeay is now known as OpenSSL, see for example, Netcraft *Glossary*.

1067 See Netcraft *Glossary*.

1068 See for example, <http://support.microsoft.com/support>, last visited: 28/04/2003, Verisign *128-bit SSL Global Server IDs: Frequently Asked Questions,* see also US Export Administration Regulations (EAR), 15 C.F.R. Parts 730-774.

1069 See for example, <http://www.globalsign.net/digital_certificate/hypersign/index.cfm>, last visited: 03/11/2002 and HyperSign certificate. Also Microsoft Server-Gated Cryptography, offered financial institutions the solution for worldwide secure financial transactions using 128-bit encryption during the US strong encryption export ban, but these days what is necessary is a 128-bit digital certificate.

obligatory nature of this practice, it would be appended to this agreement by virtue of the customary norm requiring it.

9.4 Hypothetical banking case

In this case, a software developer produced a web-based system for a bank that did not provide strong encryption and as a result a loss occurred to an international client. The issue of strength of encryption was not explicitly addressed in a contract. As was shown in the previous chapters, there exists legal uncertainty as far as security of transactions is concerned. There are no international instruments that require it, not to mention legal treaties detailing cryptographic requirements or other forms of securing a transaction channel. Here the legal vacuum is the most evident. Again, in order to solve this problem we can again make use of the idea of custom. What is required is evidence that there exists a customary rule stating: 'All Internet banks should support strong encryption of transactions'. In order to do this one should evidence the general and worldwide practice of using state-of-the-art Internet security precautions by online banks. Visiting banking web pages could be one way to gather the necessary information. There is usually information available online regarding security features that their software provides. If a product uses encryption, it can then be verified by running the software and checking in the browser's status bar as to what level of encryption it provides. Outcomes of electronic surveys and opinions of banking security experts could also strengthen the evidence of widespread current practice that nowadays, online banks provide 128-bit encrypted sessions (Figure 15). In the next chapter, a more detailed proof of this practice will be presented.

Given proof of widespread adherence to a given practice, one can conclude that a web client could expect that his transactions will be secured appropriately. Furthermore, this practice is not immoral or unreasonable as it allows the Internet community to secure exchange of valuable information. It is also legally relevant as it can be very helpful in establishing the legal responsibility of online banks, their clients and possibly e-commerce systems developers.

As a result, successfully evidencing the alleged customary rule would in consequence imply a term in the online banking software license agreement stating that the transaction session should be secured using state-of-the art technological precautions. Consequently, the claim of the international client would be considered justified.

10. Consequences for the IT Industry

As can be seen from these examples, Internet commerce customs could play a very significant role in Internet development. Since this role is based on adding legal value to certain practices, it can force IT companies to design their products and

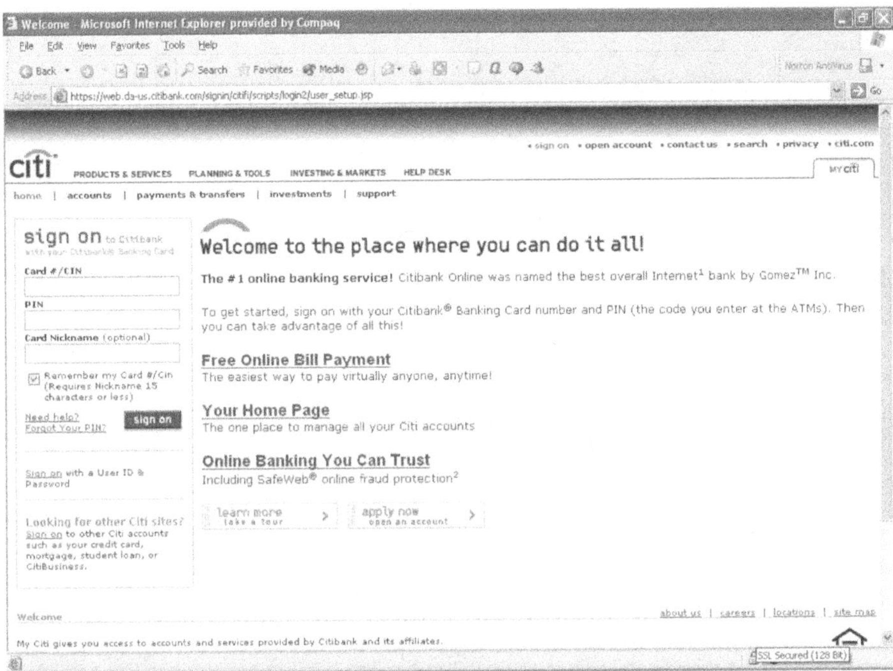

Figure 15 – Citibank's encryption. Note the tool tip over the padlock in the lower right hand corner of the browser indicating 128-bit encrypted session between the user's web browser and Citibank's web server

processes carefully, use state-of-the-art technology, and constantly upgrade their knowledge. It puts a greater burden on the users of technology. The basic premise is: if you do not know how to use it, do not use it for commercial purposes. In a sense, this is not different to traditional commerce.

Best practices have the greatest influence on custom formation, and it is arguably mainly larger companies engaged in the Internet that create these practices. The influence of technology providers such as IBM, Microsoft or Google, or best practice originators like E-bay or Dell is clearly visible on the Net. These practices are being developed quickly but at the same time, are also followed by the vast majority of e-commerce companies.

The consequence is that IT companies may, through adherence to certain practices and standards, directly influence the development of international and national law in this area. This is a very important privilege. But it also means a greater responsibility for IT companies as far as the development of the Internet is concerned.

Part III
EVIDENCING CUSTOM

Chapter VIII
EVIDENCING CUSTOM ON THE WEB

1. Introduction

The Internet itself, although apparently chaotic and irregular in its growth and functioning, is actually governed by regularities. Individuals and enterprises engage in similar activities on the Internet thus creating a truly social phenomenon. Some of these habits are similar to those in the offline world, but some are peculiar to the Internet. Discovery of these behavioural patterns could give us a set of norms, some of which could be used as the adjudicatory basis in Internet-related disputes. But a key issue is how to learn about these Internet customs.

The aim of this part of the book is to propose a methodology that could be used to learn about customary behaviours of Internet participants. The proposed methodology should be consistent with the theory of custom proposed in the previous chapter. In this respect, it will focus on evidencing the actual practice of Internet participants rather than on opinions about them in the literature. This chapter will be limited to potential ways and means of evidencing custom in the electronic environment. The focus will be placed on unobtrusive methods of gathering information. In other words, methods of gathering data in ways that do not require the user's participation will be the preferred method of investigation (unobtrusive research). This approach promises to introduce less bias than traditional data gathering methods. In this respect, the study will not investigate potential ethical issues involved in the conduct of such study. However, the potential for recognition of this methodology in legal proceedings will be accordingly signalled.

2. Problems with Traditional Methodology

Conscious knowledge of the existence of behavioural patterns of Net participants could provide a surrogate written Internet law that could be used to resolve many legal problems on the Internet. The problem is that the law making power of customary norms is not widely known. Its legal relevance is absent in the minds of Internet entrepreneurs and other Net users who consider it to be a lawless sphere. Unfortunately, it is also not widely known in the legal profession.

Judges who are supposed to know the law and apply it in legal proceedings do not know customary law because they are educated only in the written law. In order to professionally apply the unwritten law they have to be educated in the nature and content of customary law. Moreover, judges also have to be educated as to how to find customary law. For instance, in the Anglo-Saxon tradition the existence of custom is considered to be a question of fact and not a question of law. Consequently, custom has to be proved to judges. One could add that it is a rather paradoxical situation that a judge is at the same time a student of customary law and a decision-maker as to its existence.

However, there is no methodology for evidencing traditional custom. Legal doctrine has totally failed in this respect and the case of international law custom is the best evidence for this claim.[1070] As was shown in Chapter VI, evidence of a custom is not sought in the practice of states but in legal opinions. In this sense, the methodology applied by the legal community is inconsistent with the prevailing theory to which it is supposed to apply. The situation is better in the science of anthropology where a lot of research has been carried out in the field of indigenous customary law.[1071] However, even in this field no stringent methodology for conducting research of custom seems to have been developed,[1072] Paradoxically, the most 'scientific' method of proving custom known as the group inquest or *enquête par turbe* can be found in the history of medieval Western Europe where the custom was established by the unanimous claim of ten virtuous men from a given territory.[1073] This institution, originated in the early Middle Ages, later evolved into the jury in the Anglo-Saxon system.[1074] Here we find a simple example of the use of a representative sample of the population, which provides the highest possible assurance of the existence of the customary norm in question.

The lack of methodology for evidencing customary practices must have had an enormous impact on the usefulness of custom as a source of legal norms that could be used to solve disputes at hand. If one does not know how to prove rights or obligations following from common practice, the obvious approach is to avoid it. Professor Berman observed in regard to commercial custom 'hostility toward proof of mercantile custom', which impedes the adaptation of law to new economic circumstances.[1075] In consequence, all the potential advantages of custom, such as its

---

[1070] With the exception of the latest study of international humanitarian law by Henckaerts, J.-M. and Doswald-Beck, L. (2005), *Customary International Humanitarian Law, 2 volumes, Volume I. Rules, Volume II. Practice (2 Parts)*.

[1071] See Chapter V.

[1072] On the proof of native customs see for example, Scheleff, L. (2000), *The future of tradition: customary law, common law and legal pluralism*, pp. 377-409. On the proof of Aboriginal customs see especially The Law Reform Commission (1986), *The recognition of aboriginal customary laws. Report No. 31, Vol. 1*, pp. 453-478.

[1073] See especially Dawson, J.P. (1968), *The Oracles of the Law*, p. 269. and Gilissen, J. (1982), *La coutume*, pp. 65-68, and the literature cited there.

[1074] Gilissen, J. (1982), *La coutume*, p. 66; Robinson, O.F., et al. (1985), *An Introduction to European Legal History*, p. 195.

[1075] Berman, H. and Kaufman, C. (1978), *The law of international commercial transactions (lex mercatoria)*, p. 228.

flexibility, adaptability and reflectivity of what the majority of people do, are lost.

In short, evidencing customary practices is the most difficult part of making use of the idea of custom. It requires a long lasting and cumbersome research into how a society behaves. Taking into account lack of methodology for the conduct of such research, lawyer's lack of empirical background and also lack of agreement as to what constitutes custom and what its role is in a modern legal system, the impracticality of such a source of law must be rather obvious. It is probably the most important reason for its non-use in modern legal proceedings. However, the Internet offers new exciting possibilities for learning about widespread practices of e-commerce participants. The next section will outline the proposed solution.

3. Overview of the Proposed Methodology

In order to remedy these problems, this part of the research is going to propose new methodology for evidencing customary practices that will be consistent with the proposed conception of custom and tailored to the needs of the electronic environment. As the following sections will demonstrate, the Internet has created entirely new possibilities for evidencing custom. The traditional role of the human expert researching patterns of behaviour can be greatly enriched by the use of software agents that could automatically and on a daily basis gather information. Tasks that cannot be fully automated may be facilitated by the use of software components to perform part of the job in an automated fashion. Moreover, time-consuming data collection processes based on sampling a representative number of websites may not even take place, as knowledge of the environment used to create websites may turn out to be a sufficient tool, to answer the question of the existence of a given Internet custom.

The proposed framework will draw upon social science methodology. However, the main resemblance will be the fact that sampling a large population is still the easiest method of getting an insight into its characteristics. However, many aspects of traditional issues associated with sampling large populations will obtain a new dimension. For instance, the Internet enables very large samples, in fact, measuring whole populations. On the other hand, drawing conclusions about the customary norm in question from the analysis of software used to implement web systems promises to introduce data free of bias. In short, the potential intelligence of the Internet forces us to consider it as an entirely new environment that demands a separate methodology.

The proposed methodology will be only a starting point in the discussion of what should be done to prove customary norms on the Internet and how to go about it. It is hoped that this work will be further refined by other researchers leading to a more stringent framework. The idea is that this methodology will remain open so that anyone can test its usefulness and further improve it. Only a methodology that allows verification of results by other researchers may offer a solution to the lack of clear and unambiguous ways of evidencing custom in judicial proceedings.

The proposed methodology will be presented in three sections. The first section will analyse the issues associated with sampling large populations on the Internet that is of special importance to the proposed methodology. The second section will present some Internet-specific methods that could be employed in the search for Internet customary norms. This part will also discuss the role of humans and software in establishing widespread practices. The third section will be devoted to analysis of a concrete three-test methodological framework for evidencing Internet customary norms. The last section of the chapter, will apply this framework to prove the existence of customary norms in the hypothetical case studies given.

4. Sampling the Internet

This discussion of sampling forms the first part of the proposed methodological framework for evidencing Internet customary norms. Because of its importance in the whole framework, it will be examined in detail before the final framework in section 6.

The cornerstone of proving a web custom is to establish that a given practice is widely followed. In order to achieve certainty one should analyse the whole e-commerce population in order to see if a given routine is adhered to by a majority of web participants. But examination of the whole population would be very time-and-money-consuming, unless automated methods of data collection could be used.

As a matter of fact, in some cases, the Internet offers the possibility of investigating a whole or nearly whole population. For instance, it should be relatively easy to research a population of software tools used to build websites, as there are a finite number of them, probably fewer than 100. It is also not impossible to try to build a list of all web servers used in a given industry, although such an endeavour would certainly ruin the budget of an average researcher. For instance, Netcraft (an Internet research company) polls hundreds of thousands of web servers on a daily basis, which might constitute a large proportion of the web servers on the Internet.[1076] A study embracing the whole or nearly whole population would undoubtedly provide the most reliable answers as to the nature of an Internet practice in question.

But in most cases, it is unfeasible to conduct research on a very large population. This is especially so when its size is not known or difficult to estimate. To overcome this problem, researchers from many disciplines analyse samples of a population in order to generalise from them the characteristics of the whole population. Generalisation can be statistical or analytical. Statistical generalisation is based on numerical data gathered during the data collection process such as the Netcraft surveys. For instance, if data shows that in March 2002 93 per cent out of 160,000 web servers supported strong encryption that allows generalising that such practice was a customary practice on the Internet at that time. However, it is not always

[1076] <http://www.netcraft.com>, last accessed: 11/04/2003.

possible to gather numerical data. In such a case one may examine non-quantitative factors, such as a software environment or opinions to be able to generalise about the existence of a given Internet custom. Knowledge of sound non-statistical factors that shape e-commerce practices may allow strong analytical generalisations. For instance, as will be shown below, knowledge of software tools that automatically generate websites provides a very strong ground for analytical generalisations about the dominant practices encoded in products of such tools. On the other hand, opinions of writers about dominant practices, unless supported by numerical data, provide a weak basis for analytical generalisations. In general, however, the use of sampling does not provide 100 per cent accurate answers but if used properly can provide a close approximation of the actual numerical usage of a practice. The important point is to apply a reliable procedure to produce a sample that accurately represents the population.

There are several methods of sampling a population that fall into two broad categories: probability or random sampling and non-probability or purposive sampling.[1077] Both approaches are extensively used in the social sciences and they could be utilised in researching Internet customary practices. In general, probability sampling aims to generate a representative sample by randomly selecting elements from the population (or more precisely from an appropriate listing also known as a sample frame).[1078] On the other hand, non-probability sampling does not randomly select elements but obtains a sample by choosing elements using various research criteria in order to, e.g., maximise variance. The two techniques have their advantages and disadvantages and the choice depends on the scientific goals of the researcher. The problems associated with sampling are not specific to the Internet environment but are universal problems encountered by researchers in the social sciences who cannot afford to study the whole population.

Often researchers mix both approaches in order to answer a research question.[1079] As was recently argued:

> 'Nearly any complex research question requires more than one sampling technique and often involves both probability (i.e., representative) and purposive sampling techniques.'[1080]

The proposed methodology for evidencing customary practices also combines both approaches. As a matter of principle, the researcher should choose probability sampling to provide a statistical answer to the question of dominant character of a given

---

1077 See for example, Kemper, E.A., et al. (2003), *Mixed Methods Sampling Strategies in Social Science Research*, p. 277; Neuman, W.L. (2000), *Social Research Methods*, pp. 195-196.

1078 See Glossary.

1079 See for example, Kemper, E.A., et al. (2003), *Mixed Methods Sampling Strategies in Social Science Research*; Neuman, W.L. (2000), *Social Research Methods*, pp. 214-216.

1080 Kemper, E.A., et al. (2003), *Mixed Methods Sampling Strategies in Social Science Research*, p. 273.

practice. On the other hand, non-probability sampling should be chosen if access to statistical data is not possible but equally convincing generalisations could be drawn from non-numerical data.

The section below is going to provide only a very limited discussion of both techniques in the context of establishing Internet commerce customs. In order to broaden this topic, one would have to consult a number of books on social sciences research methods.[1081]

4.1 Random sampling

It is commonly asserted that random sampling provides greater assurance that a sample will be representative.[1082] For many social science researchers it is the proper way of investigation into the characteristics of a population,[1083] because it is based on statistical analysis and thus allows rigorous statistical generalisation. There are at least three important questions that the Internet researcher would need to answer using random sampling. First, what is the target population and how to obtain a list of all the elements in it? Second, which random selection method to use? And third, what is the desired sample size. This section will attempt to outline the issues involved in answering the first two questions.

In order to be able to sample a population one has to have access to a listing of all the elements in the population. In most cases it is practically impossible to have such a list, especially when one takes into account movements in a population. In

---

[1081] See for example, Abranovic, W.A. (1997), *Statistical Thinking and Data Analysis for Managers*; Alreck, P.L. and Settle, R.B. (1995), *The survey research handbook*; American Association for Public Opinion Research (1997), *Best Practices for Survey and Public Opinion Research*; Bock, T. and Sergeant, J. (Second Quarter 2002), *Small sample market research*; Bouma, G.D. (1993), *The Research Process*; Bryman, A. (2001), *Social Research Methods*; Crano, W.D. and Brewer, M.B. (2002), *Principles and Methods of Social Research*; Frankfort-Nachmias, C. and Nachmias, D. (1996), *Research Methods in the Social Sciences*; Freedman, D., et al. (1978), *Statistics*; Gay, L.R. and Diehl, P.L. (1992), *Research methods for business and management*; Harrison, S.R. and Tamaschke, R.H.U. (1993), *Statistics for Business, Economics and Management*; Henry, G.T. (1997), *Practical Sampling*; Hill, R. (1998), *What sample size is 'enough' in Internet survey research?*; Ilieva, J., et al. (Third Quarter 2002), *Online surveys in marketing research: Pros and cons*; Judd, C., et al. (1991), *Research Methods in Social Relations*; Kellehear, A. (1993), *The Unobtrusive Researcher: A guide to methods*; Kemper, E.A., et al. (2003), *Mixed Methods Sampling Strategies in Social Science Research*; Kish, L. (1995 (1965)), *Survey Sampling*; Kumar, R. (1996), *Research Methodology: A step-by-step guide for beginners*; McLaughlin, M., et al. (1999), *Measuring Internet Audiences: Patrons of an On-Line Art Museum*; Moser, C.A. and Kalton, G. (1971 (reprinted 1985)), *Survey Methods in Social Investigation*; Nachmias, D. and Nachmias, C. (1976), *Research Methods in the Social Sciences*; Neuman, W.L. (2000), *Social Research Methods*; Roscoe, J.T. (1975), *Fundamental Research Statistics for the Behavioural Sciences*; Rosnow, R.L. and Rosenthal, R. (1996), *Beginning Behavioural Research: A Conceptual Primer.*

[1082] See for example, Bock, T. and Sergeant, J. (Second Quarter 2002), *Small sample market research*; Neuman, W.L. (2000), *Social Research Methods*, p. 203; Rosnow, R.L. and Rosenthal, R. (1996), *Beginning Behavioural Research: A Conceptual Primer*, p. 189.

[1083] Nachmias, D. and Nachmias, C. (1976), *Research Methods in the Social Sciences*, p. 254.

order to overcome this problem, researchers usually establish what is called a sampling frame in probability sampling jargon. A sampling frame is a close approximation of all the elements in the population.[1084]

> 'It includes physical lists and also procedures that can account for all the sampling units without the physical effort of actually listing them.'[1085]

Examples of sampling frame include telephone directories, city directories, membership lists of organisations,[1086] tax records, driver's license records, etc.[1087] or maps[1088] although often a researcher has to compile his own substitute list.[1089] The correspondence between the actual population and sample frame is the most crucial factor in providing assurance that the selected sample will be representative.[1090] Without a proper sample frame, the greatest advantage of random sampling would be lost.

Having a sampling frame, the researcher could then randomly select participants from it. In order to do this he or she could simply employ random selection process by using, e.g., a table of random digits or simply throwing a dice. Alternatively, a researcher could choose every first, second, third or nth element of the sample frame (systematic random sampling) although he or she should be certain that the elements are not ordered in some way. However, in the case of customary practices it would be very important to make sure that participants are chosen based on various criteria including their popularity on the web, size, main specialisation or location. For this purpose, proportional or non-proportional stratified sampling methods[1091] could be used. In stratified sampling, the web businesses would first be divided into several groups or strata based upon, e.g., industry criteria before being randomly sampled. The proportions between groups could be proportional or disproportional in relation to the population dependant upon the goal of the researcher. These two methods could be useful in establishing global Internet customary norms. There are more complicated variants of these techniques but more detailed coverage is outside the scope of this book.[1092]

1084 See for example, Kumar, R. (1996), *Research Methodology: A step-by-step guide for beginners*, p. 149; Neuman, W.L. (2000), *Social Research Methods*, p. 201.

1085 Kish, L. (1995 (1965)), *Survey Sampling*, p. 53.

1086 Frankfort-Nachmias, C. and Nachmias, D. (1996), *Research Methods in the Social Sciences*, p. 181.

1087 Neuman, W.L. (2000), *Social Research Methods*, p. 201.

1088 Kish, L. (1995 (1965)), *Survey Sampling*, p. 53.

1089 Frankfort-Nachmias, C. and Nachmias, D. (1996), *Research Methods in the Social Sciences*, p. 181.

1090 See for example, Kish, L. (1995 (1965)), *Survey Sampling*, pp. 53-59.

1091 See for example, Kemper, E.A., et al. (2003), *Mixed Methods Sampling Strategies in Social Science Research*, pp. 277-279; Rosnow, R.L. and Rosenthal, R. (1996), *Beginning Behavioural Research: A Conceptual Primer*, pp. 192-201.

1092 Cluster sampling – a variant of stratified sampling, is designed for situation where there is a geographical listing of the population and for this reason may not be appropriate in the context of the

The greatest benefit of random sampling techniques is that they provide greater assurance than non-random sampling techniques that a sample will be representative and hence, enable a researcher to generalise on the basis of that sample.[1093] However, there are some problems as well. The problem for electronic commerce is that there is no readily available listing of all or at least major participants engaged in online trade. This is going to be one of the most challenging tasks, namely, to actually develop publicly available large sampling frames that would be helpful in analysing the Internet. In many cases, however, it may not be that hard to create a relatively small listing of elements of a target population and select a sample from it using either probability or non-probability sampling methods. Many such lists are compiled by various organisations, e.g., The Fortune 2002 Global 500 largest companies by the revenue[1094] or Quazell, which claims to list the largest number of banks having a website.[1095]

One should also note that the Internet commerce population consists of companies, international organisations, governments and individuals engaged in digital commerce. Dependant upon the customary norm sought, the population will comprise of all participants engaged in a trade, or will be a subset of it, e.g., when an alleged customary norm pertains to one or few industries. One should note, however, that in the case of the Internet, often the object of the research would not be a company or an individual, but an information system that it uses to manage website content delivery. This introduces another level of complexity as, e.g., many small and medium size companies do not have their own web servers but rent a space on such a computer from firms specialising in providing hosting services. On the other hand, many large companies have a number of web servers in order to streamline access to their websites. In summary then, whenever a reference is made to a company or individual participating in electronic commerce, it will often mean that the discussion refers to their information system.

4.2 Non-random sampling

Non-random sampling techniques do not establish a rigorous scheme for drawing a sample. There is no need to establish a sampling frame, because selection of sampling units will not be random. Non-probability sampling embraces several popular sample selection methods[1096] of which the following could be of interest to the

---

Internet. Multistage sampling is a more complex variant of this technique. For more information see the literature listed in the footnote *above.*

[1093] Kemper, E.A., et al. (2003), *Mixed Methods Sampling Strategies in Social Science Research*, p. 277.

[1094] <http://www.fortune.com/fortune/global500/industry/0,15130,,00.html>, last accessed: 22/04/2003.

[1095] <http://www.quazell.com/bank/default.html>, last accessed: 03/05/2003, see also, e.g., Online Banking (2002), *100 Largest Banks (USA).*

[1096] See for example, Neuman, W.L. (2000), *Social Research Methods*, pp. 196-203.

Internet researcher: convenience sampling, quota sampling, judgmental sampling and sequential sampling. Convenience sampling involves drawing elements which are easily accessible to researchers and for this reason is often dismissed as producing non-representative results.[1097] In quota sampling, the researcher first identifies relevant groups and assigns a number of sampling units to each group before selecting as many units as possible to each group.[1098] In judgmental sampling, the researcher chooses samples with a specific purpose in mind in order to: select unique, especially informative cases or to sample a difficult-to-reach population or where cases are to be deeply investigated.[1099] In sequential sampling, new cases are gathered 'until the diversity of information or cases is filled'.[1100]

Non-random sampling allows analytical rather than statistical generalisation. It is usually chosen where the relevance of cases to the topic is more important than simply their representativeness. There are many other non-random sampling methods but what all of them have in common is that units are not randomly selected using a sample frame but instead are selected on some other theoretically-driven basis, e.g., to maximise variance. The advantage of non-random sampling is that it is usually faster as no sampling frame has to be built and frequently smaller sample sizes suffice. Non-random selection methods are often criticised because they do not guarantee the representativeness of the sample.[1101]

In summary, both types of sampling have a role in evidencing Internet customary norms. Probability sampling is the preferred technique for establishing the dominance of a practice quantitatively. To do this it must be possible to access a sampling frame. In cases where access to such information may be difficult or economically unfeasible, non-random sampling can be used to establish dominance on qualitative criteria provided an analytical generalisation from the sample to the population can be made. The three-step framework that will be described in section 6 below will make use of both methodologies.

4.3 Sample size

In regard to the issue of sample size, it should be noted that it has been a subject of debate among social scientists,[1102] although some experienced researchers tend to minimise the importance of this topic, considering it to be over-rated.[1103] There are

1097 See for example, Kemper, E.A., et al. (2003), *Mixed Methods Sampling Strategies in Social Science Research*, p. 280.

1098 See for example, Neuman, W.L. (2000), *Social Research Methods*, p. 197.

1099 Ibid., p. 198.

1100 Ibid., p. 200.

1101 Ibid., p. 196, citing Flick.

1102 Some authors associate researchers using smaller samples as qualitative researchers as opposed to quantitative, which are supposed to use larger samples. See for example, Bock, T. and Sergeant, J. (Second Quarter 2002), *Small sample market research*; Kemper, E.A., et al. (2003), *Mixed Methods Sampling Strategies in Social Science Research*, p. 277.

1103 See for example, Moser, C.A. and Kalton, G. (1971 (reprinted 1985)), *Survey Methods in Social Investigation*, p. 146.

two methods of determining sample size used in practice: one based on the application of a rule of thumb and the other based on the application of a statistical formula. The first method produces the sample size that is relative to the size of the population. The second one produces the absolute size of the sample, irrespective of the population size.[1104]

Neuman argues that the more frequently used method of calculating sample sizes is the application of rules of thumb, which:

> 'are not arbitrary but are based on past experience with samples that have met the requirements of the statistical method.'[1105]

One such rule is that larger populations permit smaller sampling ratios. He proposes 30 per cent for populations under 1,000, 10 per cent for 10,000, 1 per cent for over 150,000 down to 0.025 per cent for populations over ten million.[1106] Alreck and Settle suggest examination of 10 per cent of the population as a rule of thumb and place a sample size of 1,000 as the upper limit.[1107] This technique, however, is useful only when the population size is known, which will often not be the case with the Internet. On the other hand, Roscoe argues that in behavioural sciences there is seldom justification for sample sizes below 30 and above 500.[1108] However, whenever sub-samples or some form of stratification is used, the above rule of thumb should apply to all the sub-samples.[1109] Similar guidelines are offered by other researchers.[1110] Finally, some authors recommend a sample size should be 'large enough'[1111] despite the obvious uncertainty of this proposal.

On the other hand, other authors tend to prefer the use of absolute sample sizes based on sampling theory.[1112] Nachmias for instance, claims that percentage-based or fixed number-based rules of thumb are not adequate.[1113] Similarly, the rule stating that any increase in the sample size will increase the precision of the sample results is rejected.

[1104] Crano, W.D. and Brewer, M.B. (2002), *Principles and Methods of Social Research*, p. 189.

[1105] Neuman, W.L. (2000), *Social Research Methods*, p. 217.

[1106] Ibid.

[1107] Alreck, P.L. and Settle, R.B. (1995), *The survey research handbook.*

[1108] Roscoe, J.T. (1975), *Fundamental Research Statistics for the Behavioural Sciences*, p. 168.

[1109] Ibid.

[1110] Bouma, G.D. (1993), *The Research Process*, p. 128; Hill, R. (1998), *What sample size is 'enough' in Internet survey research?*

[1111] See for example, Bouma, G.D. (1993), *The Research Process*, p. 128; Gay, L.R. and Diehl, P.L. (1992), *Research methods for business and management.*

[1112] See for example, Crano, W.D. and Brewer, M.B. (2002), *Principles and Methods of Social Research*, p. 189; Nachmias, D. and Nachmias, C. (1976), *Research Methods in the Social Sciences*, p. 254; Rosnow, R.L. and Rosenthal, R. (1996), *Beginning Behavioural Research: A Conceptual Primer*, p. 189.

[1113] Nachmias, D. and Nachmias, C. (1976), *Research Methods in the Social Sciences*, p. 254.

> 'The size of the sample is properly estimated by deciding what level of accuracy is required and, hence, how large a standard error is acceptable.'[1114]

The following equation[1115] is used for calculating the sample size in the simple random sampling:

$$\textbf{Sample size} = p * (1-p) / (S.E.)^2$$

where: p = estimated proportion of the population following a given practice and S.E. = the standard error of the sample proportion that a researcher can tolerate (also known as sampling error). Disregarding the effect of smaller populations,[1116] as soon as a researcher estimates the proportion of the population adhering to a given Internet practice and chooses the tolerable error, the following sample sizes can be calculated:

Standard	Estimated adherence level to the Internet practice in question (p)					
	50%	**60%**	**70%**	**80%**	**90%**	**99%**
5%	100	96	84	64	36	4
2%	625	600	525	400	225	25
1%	2500	2400	2100	1600	900	99

Figure 16 – The absolute sample sizes given various degrees of estimated adherence to a given practice (p) and the accepted sampling error (S.E)

The statistical method to be used in simple random sampling recommends sample sizes that range from 4 to 2500. A 5 per cent error margin is usually considered sufficient in social science unless the issue is either controversial or related to life and death issues. Given the fact that most customary practices are expected to present a very high level of homogeneity, the application of the formula would probably lead to the choice of sample sizes between 36 and 100 sampling units. However, as soon as the proportionate stratification of the sample is chosen, the proportions for each stratum must be assessed first and the weighted average of the proportions calculated before they can be used in the formula.[1117] A similar operation must be performed for disproportionate stratified sampling,[1118] although detailed coverage of these techniques is outside the scope of this chapter.

[1114] Ibid.

[1115] Crano, W.D. and Brewer, M.B. (2002), *Principles and Methods of Social Research*, p. 189; Moser, C.A. and Kalton, G. (1971 (reprinted 1985)), *Survey Methods in Social Investigation*, p. 147. See also Kish, L. (1995 (1965)), *Survey Sampling*, p. 50.

[1116] For simplicity reasons, this equation does not take into account the so-called finite population correction or FPC, which would generally lead to a decrease of the sample size. See for example, Kish, L. (1995 (1965)), *Survey Sampling*, p. 50.

[1117] See for example, Moser, C.A. and Kalton, G. (1971 (reprinted 1985)), *Survey Methods in Social Investigation*, p. 88.

[1118] See for example, ibid., pp. 93-99.

The choice of either relative or absolute sample size calculation methods should be left to the researcher. The first method is quite arbitrary and sometimes requires knowledge of the population size. On the other hand, the absolute sample size method relies upon the previous knowledge of the characteristics of the Internet population, which in many cases might not be available. Then, proportions in a population would have to be guessed, based on proportions in a sample, which may be simply incorrect.[1119] In this case scenario 'a reasonable guess will be adequate', because moderate errors in estimating proportion will have a small effect on the calculation of the sample size.[1120] However, such a guess can be strengthened by a pilot study.

Finally, it is certainly true that the larger the sample size the more compelling the evidence will be for the adjudicator. It may turn out, however, that larger sample sizes may not always be necessary in the case of proving Internet customary practices. There are at least three reasons for this. First, as was already mentioned several times, customary practices should display a very high degree of uniformity or homogeneity. In situations where the sample results are homogenous or 'all (or none)',[1121] the generally accepted practice of drawing conclusions from smaller samples[1122] could be accepted. Another argument could be that large sample sizes may not be necessary because what is important is to establish what is done by the top companies in terms of number of participants in the online commerce. Companies like Amazon.com or eBay.com are such important Internet brands that the majority of other websites to a large degree try to emulate their practices.[1123] Finally, a 'large sample size (...) is not sufficient to guarantee the accuracy of the results' but can only give a greater precision of the sample results.[1124] Nevertheless, if a researcher can afford it, he or she should use as large a sample size as possible.

4.4 Representativity of the sample

The pure number of queried respondents is not going to provide the correct results, if the sample is not representative. Hill points out that apart from problems with identifying population size on the Internet, it is difficult to establish a representative sample size when one conducts research only 'with computers', and the choice of the timeframe for the research creates difficulty.[1125] The famous story of American

---

[1119] Henry, G.T. (1997), *Practical Sampling*, p. 123.

[1120] Moser, C.A. and Kalton, G. (1971 (reprinted 1985)), *Survey Methods in Social Investigation*, p. 149.

[1121] Bock, T. and Sergeant, J. (Second Quarter 2002), *Small sample market research.*

[1122] See, for example, Bouma, G.D. (1993), *The Research Process*, p. 127; Rosnow, R.L. and Rosenthal, R. (1996), *Beginning Behavioural Research: A Conceptual Primer*, p. 191. See also Kish, L. (1995 (1965)), *Survey Sampling.*

[1123] One should note however, that recently Amazon's design has been criticised by Nielsen as being 'so different from other e-commerce sites that what's good for Amazon is not good for normal sites'. Nielsen, J. (25 July 2005), *Amazon: No Longer the Role Model for E-Commerce Design.*

[1124] Moser, C.A. and Kalton, G. (1971 (reprinted 1985)), *Survey Methods in Social Investigation*, p. 146.

[1125] Hill, R. (1998), *What sample size is 'enough' in Internet survey research?*

presidential elections in the 1930's illustrates this well.[1126] Simplifying the story, a large sample of 2.4 million respondents was chosen based upon randomly selected names from sources such as a phonebook. But the election results turned out to be drastically different to the ones suggested by the polls and only then was it realised that the sample data was unrepresentative. Because at that time most poor Americans did not have a telephone and hence only wealthy respondents were chosen, thus skewing the true trend in the population. As a result of the choice of an improper sampling frame, the sample turned out to be not representative. In short, a large sample size does not guarantee accurate results if both well-known and less-known subjects are not properly represented.

Researchers of Internet practices using both random and non-random sampling must make sure that their samples are representative of the whole target population in question. In the case of random sampling, it is of paramount importance to assure that the sampling frame is representative. Similarly, in the case of non-probability sampling, it is important that a sample will be categorised and will include both large and smaller ventures, companies using different country-level domain names or coming from different industries in the proportions that reflect that of the population. For this reason, it is advisable to use some form of stratification in order to create as representative a sample of Internet traders as possible.

Stratification may, in some cases, turn out to be a difficult task. For instance, if one decides to create a sample that would consists of all the industries on the Internet the question is how many industries there are and whether all of them are necessary. The problem may be with simple classification of industries especially when some of them do not benefit from the Internet, and some others only partially benefit from it, relying on it more as an advertising channel rather than the core activities medium. The Fortune 500 lists 51 different industries based upon the list of the 500 largest companies in the world,[1127] but this listing applies to brick-and-mortar companies not necessarily heavily dependent upon Internet commerce. It could be argued that a sample of general customary practices is representative when it takes into account all industries where the Internet plays an important role. Such industries include: advertising, printing, manufacturing, banking, insurance, government, etc. If one wants to test for the existence of a certain practice in the market segment that sells goods, it should look at all major representatives of sale markets on the Net. This matter, however, requires further research.

1126 Story described in, e.g., Crano, W.D. and Brewer, M.B. (2002), *Principles and Methods of Social Research*, p. 191; Frankfort-Nachmias, C. and Nachmias, D. (1996), *Research Methods in the Social Sciences*, pp. 182-183; Freedman, D., et al. (1978), *Statistics*, pp. 302-307; Moser, C.A. and Kalton, G. (1971 (reprinted 1985)), *Survey Methods in Social Investigation*, pp. 79-80; Rosnow, R.L. and Rosenthal, R. (1996), *Beginning Behavioural Research: A Conceptual Primer.*

1127 <http://www.fortune.com/fortune/global500/industry/0,15130,,00.html>, last visited: 22/04/2003.

4.5 Summary

The above section analysed the issue of designing samples in the context of the Internet. Although the Internet potentially enables the examination of the whole Internet population (e.g., all web servers) it is unlikely that such research will be often carried out due to time and money constraints. Instead, a sample of the population will have to be researched. This framework proposes to adapt the social sciences sampling techniques to measure customary practices on the Internet. There are various sampling methods available, each having advantages and disadvantages. Of particular importance is the question of sample size and its representativeness, which have to be carefully considered by a researcher. A researcher should use probability-sampling techniques to formulate statistical generalisations about dominant practices. On the other hand, a researcher should choose the non-random sampling technique to formulate analytical generalisations about Internet customs.

5. Overview of Means of Evidencing Internet Custom

The Internet presents a unique opportunity to measure behaviour of its participants in an automated fashion. Its digital nature enables construction of software agents that could gather necessary information without human intervention. This is such a significant feature of this environment that it actually demands an entirely new level of analysis. Moreover, custom can not only be established in an automated manner but also observed and recorded on an everyday basis – something that is not possible in the traditional world.

In law, even if custom is established in the court's proceedings, it states what custom is on a given date or actually on the day the incident in question had occurred. Despite the reliance of probably all lawyers on the establishment of custom in a previous court decision, it should be kept in mind that custom can change and as a result, the court's earlier judgment should never be treated as a proof of subsequent custom. New research needs to be carried out, which is rarely if ever done because it is so difficult, time-consuming and expensive in the traditional environment.

On the Internet this can be easily done. Consequently, one can expect floating adherence to a given practice over time and as such, the floating nature of the Internet law. For instance, one can imagine software gathering information about daily adherence to some security practices based on the analysis of the inclusion of certain software components in the web servers hosting a given website. Such activities are already carried out on the Net. For instance, Netcraft gathers information and publishes it regularly about the usage of web servers of different brands as well as tests for certain security features of the web servers.[1128] Others already automatically

[1128] See for example, Netcraft (2002), *The August 2002 Netcraft Web Server Survey.*

gather information about the usage of the most popular web browsers or, like DoubleClick[1129] collect data about website use in order to create a profile of a customer. Gartner and Forrester Research also provide extensive research in the area of technology. Rather than doing research, an alternative is to purchase evidence from companies like those mentioned above.

The following methods could be used to evidence customary practices on the Net:

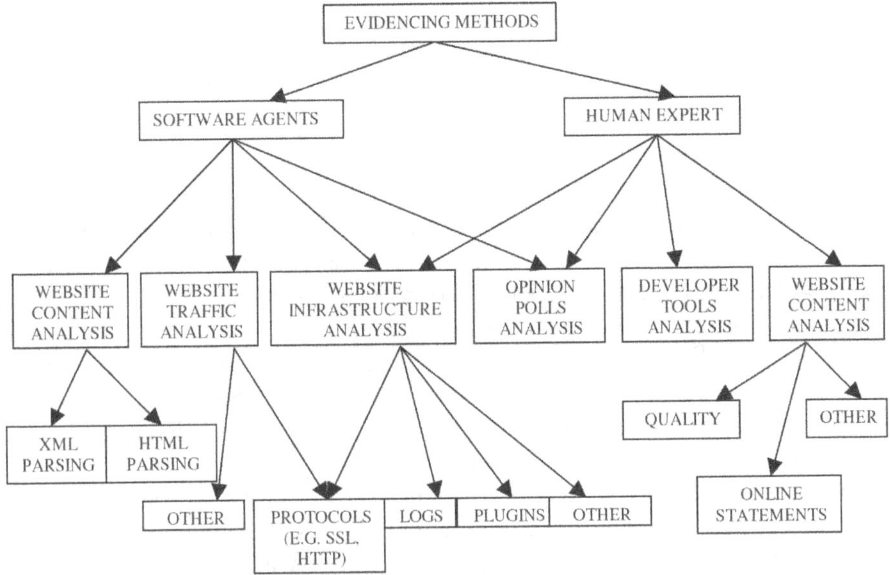

Figure 17 – Summary of potential evidencing methods of customary web practices

5.1 Human versus automation

In the online world, data collection can be performed either by a human expert or by a software component. The potential of automation and intelligence offered by the Internet does not mean that the human role is marginal. Both 'tools' are important, and each is better for certain types of activities over the other. Apart from the obvious fact that someone has to program software components and then analyse data gathered by them, the human being is still superior in many respects to digital technology.

Some tasks such as analysis of the quality of the website or even a task such as a search for particular content on the website will for a long time yet have to be done by human experts. It is difficult at this stage to design software that can interpret the content of a website with the same degree of flawlessness that a human being can.

1129 See <http://www.doubleclick.com>, last visited: 09/10/2002.

Also, a human expert is irreplaceable when it comes to the appraisal of the functionality of a software package used to create websites. Moreover, even relatively simple tasks such as finding certain information on the website will have to be done by humans as the current search engines mechanisms cannot meaningfully locate textual data. This is due to the unstructured nature of the HTML language, which until replaced by semantically structured languages like XML,[1130] will hinder the development of reliable tools enabling automatic analysis of website content. In other words, all the qualitative, interpretative or evaluative work has to be done by humans.

On the other hand, many quantitative, repeatable and invisible tasks can be allocated to computers. For instance, analysis of protocols for certain kind of information can be best performed by a software component. Also software can much better test for support of certain plug-ins by the web browser or web server or for tracking user behaviour in the form of cookies.

The greatest promise of automation for establishing customary norms is that the whole process can be repeated infinitely. This in turn can provide very valuable historical data depicting the rise and fall of a given customary norm in question. Moreover, automation of data gathering can be especially helpful when combined with the analysis of invisible information exchange on the protocol level or as far as configuration of web software is concerned. In addition, automation can lead to automatic detection of new web entities, thus enlarging the population under investigation. This in turn can lead to outcomes scientifically close to error free.

Finally, there are tasks, which can be completed by using both human expert and software. For instance, analysis of browser or web server capabilities can be performed by a human expert and confirmed by the software agent. Similarly, surveys can be done automatically by web software or done in the traditional way. From the perspective of evidencing Internet custom, the tasks to be performed by the human expert and software agent can be divided into five categories: analysis of website content, website traffic, web server/browser configuration, analysis of tools used to create websites and web participant opinion poll. Not all of these areas of investigation will be necessary to examine in the context of the Internet custom in question. Figure 18 below shows in which of these tasks software is better than a human, and vice versa.

Website Content Analysis refers to the establishment of habits of providing certain kinds of visible information on the site. *Website Traffic Analysis* refers to the establishment of habits of providing invisible information by the web system. *Web Server/Browser Analysis* (or *Web Infrastructure Analysis*) aims at the establishment of common configuration and operation patterns of the Internet communication channel. *Developer Tools Analysis* aims at establishing common functionalities inside the design software that will 'force' a designer to accommodate given function on a website. Finally, *Web Participants Opinion Poll* aims to gather information

[1130] See Glossary.

	Human Expert (=Manual)	Software Component (=Automatic or Semi-automatic)
Website Content Analysis	Yes	Soon
Website Traffic Analysis	No	Yes
Web Server/Browser Analysis	Yes	Yes
Developer Tools Analysis	Yes	No
Web Participants Opinion Poll	Yes	Yes

Figure 18 – Usefulness of human expert *v.* software in gathering data about web customs

about human perception of certain aspects of the customary practice in question. The following section will discuss each of these tasks in greater detail.

5.2 Website Content Analysis

The aim of Website Content Analysis is to collect evidence of common provision of certain kinds of information visible to the user. For instance, it may be required to confirm that it is customary to provide order summary or confirmation screen. It may be necessary to confirm that it is a common practice to provide certain precautions to the Internet participants or include certain clauses in a web contract. It may even be necessary to establish the common look and feel of certain websites, e.g., display of steps to follow to conclude a contract.

This aspect of establishing customary practice shows the superiority of human beings. There are enormous problems with automating search for common content on websites because web software has trouble dealing with context. For instance, for a search engine the word 'order confirmation' will have the same value if used on a mercantile site or when used in a novel published on the website. This is due to the design of the HTML language,[1131] which is not structured in the sense that it mixes content and display of data. As a result, although HTML documents can be easily parsed (analysed), the outcome will contain a lot of accidental and unwanted data. If one adds to it synonyms that are used on the websites, the task of reliably establishing common content in an automated fashion seems unreachable.

However, there is a chance that in the near future at least part of this difficult task will be automatically examinable. The new generation Internet languages especially the XML-family languages that are now being deployed on the Net, will allow for a separation of content and its display characteristics. Once coupled with libraries of business terms such as ebXML, it will be possible to search for common content of commercial websites. Nevertheless, as was indicated above, certain aspects of content analysis, e.g., assessment of the quality of the website or content of company policies, statements seem to remain the domain of humans.

[1131] See Chapter II.

5.3 Website Traffic Analysis

The aim of Website Traffic Analysis is to establish the common content of invisible information exchanged during the web session. For instance, one may want to establish that the majority of websites use the SSL protocol with 128-bit long keys to secure sessions. It may also turn out to be necessary to establish common content of the non-displayable part of HTML documents called metatags.[1132] In addition, one may want to analyse references to other sites, e.g., references to Certification Authorities or subscription to peculiar service providers like TRUSTe or PICS.

In this respect, the potential of software agents should be clearly visible. For a human being, establishment of these things would be difficult. For instance, the existence and level of encryption can be ascertained by looking at the padlock icon on the status bar of a browser, but information displayed in a tool-tip may not necessarily be correct.[1133] Moreover, analysis of this aspect of web behaviour would force a researcher to repeat the same operation every day.

Software components could provide a solution in this respect. First, the number of web servers to be analysed needs to be established. Then, the software can repeatedly poll them in order to initiate a 'conversation'. Then, the software could simply record the exchange of protocol messages, until it reaches the desired one. Knowledge of Internet protocols like HTTP, SSL or TCP/IP is the essential requirement for this type of analysis. This simplified procedure could be used on a daily basis in order to record historical adherence to the practice in question.

5.4 Web Infrastructure Analysis

Web Infrastructure Analysis focuses on gathering data regarding common configuration and operation of web servers, and, if necessary, web browsers, routers, etc. This information can be accessed via direct 'conversation' with a given tool in an automated fashion, manual analysis of configuration and operation of it, or manual analysis of outputs from it. The first task will often overlap with website traffic analysis. The second and the third will usually require access to the computers examined. It may involve analysis of options chosen by the administrator, installation of certain plug-ins, analysis of cookies, etc.

On the other hand, analysis of web server logs can provide important data regarding the use of a given website. Logs can keep track of who has visited the site based on unique IP addresses, when the visitors came, what they requested, how much time they spent on each page, where they were before they came to this site, what country they were from, what browser they were using and other elements.[1134]

[1132] See Chapter II and Glossary.

[1133] See *below*.

[1134] See for example, McLaughlin, M., et al. (1999), *Measuring Internet Audiences: Patrons of an On-Line Art Museum*, p. 167.

Analysis of the so-called referrer logs can provide information whether users arrived at a given page from a search engine or a net guide, what keywords they used to find a given website, etc.[1135] This information can be analysed by a human expert or by specialised data extraction software, e.g., Webtrends.[1136] It is important to be aware of problems connected with the validity of information about the number of unique visitors to the site. The results are most likely only a rough estimate of the actual site usage because of dynamic IP allocation used by many ISPs as well as caching of web pages both by visitor's web browser and ISP's proxy servers.[1137] Dynamic IP allocation means that the same user visiting a given site during different times will appear to a log as if there were many unique visitors to the site thus leading to gross overestimation of the real number of unique visitors. On the other hand, visits to web pages cached by a proxy server or a web browser will not be recorded by the web server log, leading to the underestimation of the number of actual visits to a website. However, because server logs are not accessible from the outside their usefulness in establishing customary practices is limited. For this reason this aspect will not be further referred to in this study.

5.5 Developer Tools Analysis

This analysis aims to establish common functionality provided by the software used to construct websites. It can be performed only by humans. However, it offers unusual benefits to the problems of establishing customary norms and for this reason will be analysed in-depth below under the heading: E-commerce development tools capability test.

5.6 Web Participants Opinion Poll

This analysis aims to survey opinions of e-commerce participants in regard to a given customary practice. For instance, a survey could establish whether Internet participants feel free to provide a link to any site they want. It could ascertain whether they consider the first-in first-out principle of domain name registration as the customary norm on the Web, etc.

A survey can be performed manually and semi-automatically. The most important difference between semi-automatic examination and a fully automated one is the fact that in the latter, data gathering depends on the user's input. It is impossible to gather this type of information without asking a user some specific questions. Semi-automatic methods may include provision of forms to be filled by the users. However, the most important form of gathering data both online and offline is a survey of opinions.

[1135] Ibid., pp. 169-170.

[1136] See <http://www.webtrends.com>, last visited: 01/11/2002.

[1137] See Glossary.

The Internet has given a new impetus to well-known data gathering methods such as survey. Online surveys are used extensively by companies and are heavily recommended by marketing specialists. They can overcome traditional problems associated with paper-based surveys by mail such as the poor and slow response rate, the non-response issue and the necessity to manually copy data from questionnaire to a statistical program which may result in additional data entry errors.[1138] Moreover, the low cost of online surveys enables designation of a much greater sample size than is practical or economically feasible in the traditional world. For instance, McKinsey has recently announced an online survey in Germany, which was addressed to 170,000 respondents and supplemented by an offline survey of 2,700 respondents to filter out biases. It has been declared the largest in-depth online survey ever done in Europe.[1139] One of the most important issues is to make sure that the analysed sample is representative of the whole population.[1140]

5.7 **Summary**

The above section presented an overview of possible methods that could be used to evidence the existence of Internet customary norms. It was argued that the Internet offers potential for automation of the data gathering process, but the involvement of human experts is often a necessity. Various activities could be performed to establish Internet customary practices that range from website content analysis to survey of opinions.

6. Proposed Three-step Methodology

The following section will propose a three-step methodology for evidencing Internet customary norms as a series of steps that should be performed in order to prove the existence of a web custom. These steps include: the e-commerce development tools capability test, practice examination test and literature review test. The two first steps allow both analytical and statistical generalisations about the dominant character of a given practice. The e-commerce development tools capability test allows primarily analytical conclusions but it can be strengthened statistically by studies of the most widely used software tools. The literature review test allows only analytical generalisations. These tests will draw on the methods for evidencing customary practices outlined above.

[1138] See for example, Ilieva, J., et al. (Third Quarter 2002), *Online surveys in marketing research: Pros and cons*.

[1139] Fassbender, H., et al. (2002), *What Germans Really Think*.

[1140] See for example, Ilieva, J., et al. (Third Quarter 2002), *Online surveys in marketing research: Pros and cons*.

6.1 E-commerce development tools capability test

This test is concerned with measuring the software tools that are used to create Internet commerce solutions rather than examining their products. The basic idea is that if one manages to establish that a searched functionality is automatically generated by the most popular software tools used to build commercial websites, then there is no need to perform a traditional study of actual adherence to a given practice. Internet commerce software development tools not only crystallise acceptable practices but also enforce them mechanically. As a result, electronic commerce websites contain similar functionality and in consequence, are more standardised than non-commercial websites. In other words, if the most popular website development tools add certain functionality to each web system they produce, then one can generalise analytically that a majority of websites created with these tools contain such functionality. This argument provides further evidence that Internet customary practices are formed without any psychological element.

It is envisaged that software development tools will be limited to the so-called rapid development tools and web server software. E-commerce rapid development software suits provide a lot of wizard[1141] based functionality that generates core aspects of the e-business on the fly, which is very important from the time-to-market perspective. In addition, this approach ensures that thoroughly tested components will be included in the web application. However, a website designer may choose to implement a site using either a popular e-commerce software package or a basic or advanced HTML editor. A basic HTML editor can be any text editor like Windows Notepad. Important advanced HTML editors include Macromedia Dreamweaver and Homesite, Adobe GoLive!, NetObjects Fusion or Microsoft FrontPage.[1142] Advanced HTML editors are often used to customise or enhance the raw sites generated by e-commerce rapid development tools. But experience suggests that many e-commerce projects, especially large and medium ones, are done using rapid development tools.[1143] From the perspective of evidencing customary practices, only wizard-tools[1144] are worth consideration, as it is impossible to discern any functionality patterns in using plain text editors. Apart from e-commerce development packages, one may also have to examine the functionality provided by web software particularly web servers. This might be necessary as some functionality, such as SSL encryption of transaction, can only be enabled on the server side.

There are several steps that need to be performed in this test. First, a category of required software tools should be established. The search may include general e-

---

1141 See Glossary.

1142 For a list of other HTML code editors see, for example, <http://builder.cnet.com/webbuilding/0-3881-6-7255.html?tag=more>, last visited: 04/11/2002.

1143 Remark made by Milutinovic at the Hawaian Conference in January 2002. See Milutinovic, V. (2002), *Tutorial*.

1144 See Glossary.

commerce development tools or may be more specific. In the former category there may be software tools that are used to enable B2B or B2C communication over the Net or ones that are suited only to content management, etc. Second, a representative sample of rapid e-commerce tools should be selected. The sample will be representative if it includes the most widely used software to build large websites. But it should also contain small-to-medium size category software products. It may be advisable to conduct a small pilot study in order to establish which software development tools are most popular among companies developing e-commerce tools. Such a pilot study can also add the power of statistical generalisation. Since the population of development tools is not large, dependant upon the budget, it should be possible to research all or a large proportion of them. Third, the required software should be acquired and installed. Since the Internet is independent of an operating system run on computers connected to it, usually one operating system version of the software should be sufficient. Fourth, the sample should be thoroughly examined from the perspective of the practice in question. One would have to check whether a given functionality is always included in a given system or whether it can be opted-out during the design phase. Production of sample websites may turn out to be necessary. In order to do this, software wizards should be thoroughly explored. Likewise, sample websites delivered with the software should be explored. Similarly, software manuals should be thoroughly investigated. Also, official websites of such software tools often offer free demonstration and multimedia information that should be thoroughly investigated for the sought after functionality. Fifth, a conclusion should be formulated. It should include information about whether the practice in question is compulsorily included in the production process or whether the designer can turn it off or exclude it.

The software development tools test has many important advantages. First, the test has great potential for saving time. It is highly likely that it will take less time to investigate the most widely used software tools from the perspective of a given functionality rather than to probe all the websites produced by them. There are obviously fewer e-commerce site building tools than websites created by them. Second, the scope of applicability of results is potentially much greater than in the case of traditional practice adherence examination. From a smaller sample of tools used to build websites one can be more certain about the spread of a given practice. Third, the test can be performed at the computer desk, without the need for engaging in a potentially biased interaction with respondents. The only exception may be the survey of the most popular e-commerce solutions among website development firms and in-house computer departments of larger brick-and-mortar companies. Fourth, a great number of e-commerce development tools are freely available on the Net. More expensive software is available for a trial period, which should be sufficient to perform the test.

However it also has some disadvantages. First, it is a test that in principle has to be performed by a human expert and not by a computer. It is impossible to automate checking the capabilities of the most popular e-commerce solutions. The exception is a check of the type of web server that a given site is running, which can be automated and from which it can be inferred what capabilities a given server possesses. The process that has potential for automation is checking which software was used to create a given website in order to build a picture of relative popularity of various development tools. Second, the test requires possession of software that sometimes can be very expensive. This problem is alleviated by the fact, that most expensive software is available in trial versions. But the expensive part of the research may be to set up the software, taking into account various platform and operating system requirements. Third, one may have to learn the functionality provided by the software. Fourth, a website designer may still alter the code generated by the development tools.

In short, this test offers a number of very important advantages. If the results of this test show a uniformity of practice there is no need for further investigation as to the existence of the customary practice in question. For these reasons it should be performed before the actual practice examination test. If, however, this test fails or it is not be possible to use it, then the researcher should turn to the practice examination test described below.

6.2 **Practice examination test**

The second type of test is the application of the classic technique for establishing patterns in a given population using examination of a representative sample of commercial websites, software or users. The aim of this test is to establish how common the practice is. If possible, this research should establish some timeframe for a given practice. Examination of this could show if a practice was continuous or not. The questions of reasonability or morality of practice should not be examined at this stage.

There are many conditions that need to be met before the research can be conducted. Most of these conditions will be similar to those encountered in the social sciences. The most important one is establishing the sample frame and sample size. Others may include searching for software capable of automatic discovery of patterns on the Web or design and implementation of customised software. Finally, the researcher will have to spend some time on researching the characteristics of the technology in question.

(a) **Automatic analysis of practice**

As was argued above, web traffic, web infrastructure and to some extent opinion polls can be examined automatically. The most interesting aspect of automatic analysis of practice is the examination of web traffic and web infrastructure. This usually means the examination of underlying Internet protocols such as HyperText Transfer Protocol (HTTP) or Secure Sockets Layer (SSL).[1145] The construction of such

[1145] See Glossary.

software should not be very difficult as the Internet protocols are widely known and standardised. Such software can operate on the basis of polling a sample of web servers on which the websites sought reside in order to examine exchange of messages establishing client-server communication.

As was argued earlier, it is much more difficult at this stage to design software to analyse content of websites automatically. This is due to the unstructured character of HTML language, which mixes content and display. This problem is easily illustrated by problems Internet users face when searching information on the Web using any of the popular search engines. These websites, despite their high level of sophistication, list results that are often taken out of context and hence of no use. The same problems will face any automatic HTML document analyser (parser). For this reason, the human expert will still play a very important role in the establishment of e-customary practices.

The power of an automated survey of web practice lies in the fact that it can be performed on a daily basis and hence can provide historical data crucial to the analysis of the formation of customary practices.[1146] Trends can be analysed using days, weeks, months or years as time units. This is a very important advantage of automation of data collection as it can provide historical context to the data, which in legal proceedings is very rarely known and usually either guessed or not proved. However, as was stated in the previous chapters, the time factor is no longer important in the proof of custom but can be helpful is solving a particular case.

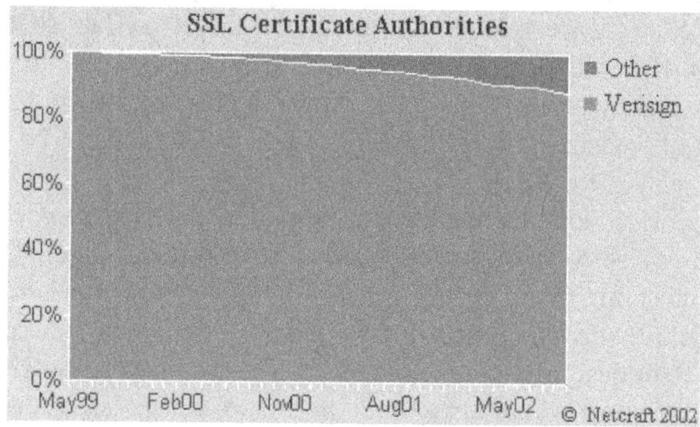

Figure 19 – SSL Certificate Authorities. The graph illustrates the gradual win of share from Verisign by other SSL Certificate Authorities. Source: Netcraft October 2002 Report

Another important advantage of automatic analysis of web practice is the ability to survey a large number of participants, which is impossible using traditional survey techniques. Netcraft surveys for instance, examine between 35,000,000 to nearly 75,000,000 web servers every month (see Figure 20). This aspect of automation of data collection means that issues associated with sampling are no longer relevant.

[1146] See Netcraft surveys described *below*.

Such a method is certainly preferable although it involves establishment of a special purpose data collection organisation. In addition, one can envisage proliferation of various software components or web services capable of tracking user's behaviour on the Net. Re-use of these web services may speed up the establishment of customary practices to the degree not possible before.

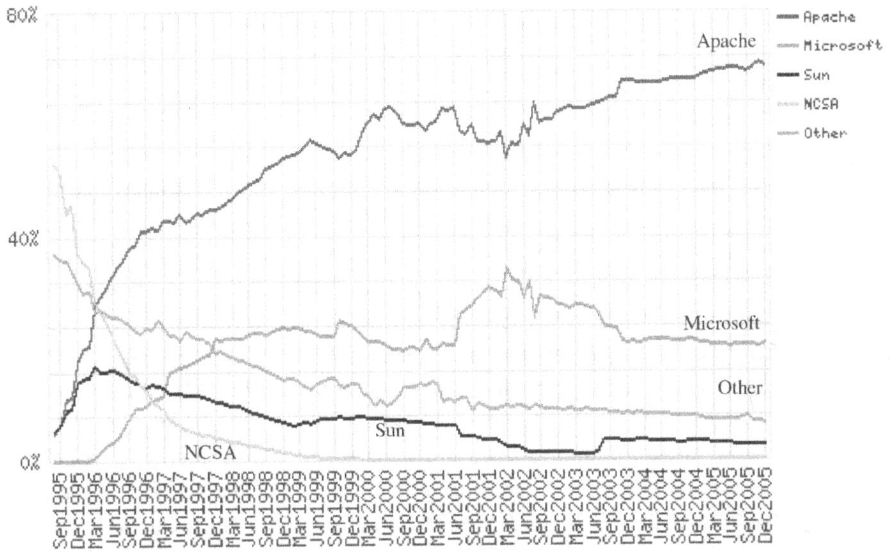

Figure 20 – Market Share for Top Servers Across All Domains August 1995 – December 2005. Response was received from 74,353,258 sites. Source: Netcraft December 2005 Report

There are also some disadvantages of automatic analysis of practice. First, it may be time-consuming to develop software to collect required information automatically. It is necessary to possess very good programming skills as well as a very deep knowledge of the Internet functionality. This may turn out to be a very expensive skill to acquire. Second, it is difficult to forecast if every single practice in question will be examinable in automatic fashion. Apart from content-related customs, there may be problems with the establishment of some traffic or infrastructure-related information.

(b) Manual analysis of practice

Manual analysis of practice is especially relevant in the context of website content analysis, web infrastructure analysis and survey of the Internet participants' opinions. Manual analysis of websites is in reality the only option when it comes to examining their content. As was indicated earlier, software components cannot easily interpret the required text information on the website. A human expert is also necessary when it comes to the analysis of provision of common information e.g. common practice of providing security-related information, or common content of legal agreements on commercial websites. Similarly, a human expert can much more effectively analyse any promises, demonstrations and instructions provided by e-commerce businesses.

Manual analysis of practice may also include examination of web infrastructure. Here the actual configuration of web browsers, web servers, routers, interpreters and the like could be tested. The problem with this type of analysis is that access to a given software or hardware is required, thus making this task very difficult to resolve. Remote examination is possible, but it would require permission from the company being subjected to such an analysis. Once such permission is granted, the practice analyst could investigate content of log files, supported third party components, etc.

In addition, manual analysis will be commonly used in online and offline surveys of opinions. A human expert has to prepare a survey first and other humans have to respond to it. There may be important problems with the preparation of questions and trustworthiness of responses received from the participants. Issues surrounding surveys are commonly known and will not be reiterated in this work.[1147]

The simplified process of analysis could be as follows. First, dependant upon sampling strategy, the sampling frame should be defined. Then, a sample of websites, participants or elements of web infrastructure should be selected. Websites have to be thoroughly investigated for the required functionality. This may include recording of browser behaviour (e.g., appearance of various icons on status bar in the web browser, check of website properties) or website content (e.g., searching for required information). Internal search engines and site maps can be used to speed up the search. This analysis should lead to a detailed list of researched subjects and their sought after behaviour. From this data one should be able to conclude whether or not a majority of sites, software or participants adhered to a given practice.

This test has advantages and disadvantages similar to any social science research project. For this reason, more detailed analysis of the above will be excluded from the scope of this chapter. However, one should mention one particular advantage of this test in the Internet context. A human expert there can make use of third-party software that will analyse one site at a time, thus providing a semi-automatic examination of a web system. A major disadvantage of manual analysis, apart from time and money aspects, is that historical analysis of adherence to a given practice is much more difficult to carry on. As a result, it may turn out to be impossible to ascertain whether at a given point in time, the practice in question was observed by a majority of Internet users or not. But as was argued in Chapter VII, the question of time will rarely be important given the widespread adherence to a practice in space.

[1147] See for example, Moser, C.A. and Kalton, G. (1971 (reprinted 1985)), *Survey Methods in Social Investigation*.

In summary, the manual or automatic examination of web infrastructure, traffic and opinion polls may provide invaluable opportunities for establishing the customary norms in question. If results of the practice examination test show unanimous adherence to a given practice, the custom can be considered to be established. If not all sites adhere to a given practice, but a number of sites adhering to it exceed 75 per cent, the custom can also be considered established. On the other hand, if access to a sampling frame is not be possible but the data suggests that all major websites adhere to a given practice, it can be compelling evidence of its high frequency of observance. In such a case, one might be able to analytically generalise that a given practice is customary, although there may be a need for the examination of the timeframe of such practice.

6.3 Literature review test

A reference to the literature could be very helpful in evidencing Internet custom. The outcome of this test may reinforce findings from the previous tests. If done properly, it may also provide valuable confirmation of the legitimacy of certain practices. In principle, however, it does not have to be done, if the results of previous tests clearly indicate the existence or non-existence of a customary norm in question.

If used, a literature review test should never be treated as an independent way of proving custom, however. It cannot be used as the only method of proving custom because customary practices change over time and for this reason what is written on paper may not reflect reality. In this sense, one cannot strongly generalise about the customary character of a given Internet practice based on the literature review test. It is essential that new evidence of custom be produced whenever a litigant refers to it. It is only when certain customary practices become so widespread and widely known that almost everyone will be aware of it and that subsequently, the empirical proof of custom may not be required.

A literature review test is based upon searching for evidence of custom in legal and technical writings. Legal writing includes treaties, statutes, judgments, books and other publications dealing with Internet practices. Technical writing includes apart from books and articles, standards, formal recommendations, etc. From the legal perspective especially important are treaties or agreements referring to the customary norm in question, statutory law codifying the custom, judgments of the courts establishing the custom, books, articles and other publications discussing it, etc.[1148] Books or articles, could be written both by lawyers or by technical authors. Technical writers may suggest for instance certain uses of technology, web design or various aspects of Internet activities. Technical standards and recommendations are of importance, especially if they come from trusted sources such as Internet

[1148] See for example, Hudson, M.O. (3 March 1950), *Article 24 of the Statute of the International Law Commission. Working Paper. Document A/CN.4/16.*

Engineering Task Force or the World Wide Web Consortium. A great number of very important sources of information about web design and practices are available on the Web itself.

During legal disputes, the analysis of legal literature will usually be performed by practising lawyers, especially judges. Conversely, technical writing will be the domain of an expert who will usually be called by the Court. Since this type of activity is familiar to lawyers and does not introduce anything novel to the technical audience, more detailed analysis of this form of searching a proof of custom will be omitted.

One should mention here, that this test might resemble evidence of *opinio iuris* proposed by D'Amato, who equated the subjective element with statements about the legality of a practice in question.[1149] However, the concept of e-custom proposed here disregards the *opinio iuris* element. In consequence, even having such a tolerant interpretation of the subjective element would be of little help in evidencing custom, if the actual practice did not conform to what has been agreed to in the literature. Furthermore, the subjective element equated with legal writings, either in the form of treaties or resolutions, or non-binding but authoritative case law and literature is useful to the extent that such material exists about the Internet practice in question. However, at this stage, such materials are very scarce, thus making it impossible to prove custom solely on this basis.

In summary, this test is based upon searching the proof of custom in legal and technical writing. Because of the flexible nature of custom as a source of law this test should always be used in conjunction with empirical tests outlined above. It should never be used as the only method of proving custom and it may be disregarded entirely, if previous tests succeeded or failed or an adjudicator wishes so or if there are no technical publications or laws dealing with a matter in question.

7. Hypothetical Case Studies

Throughout this study reference has been made to the two hypothetical case studies introduced at the end of Chapter I. In Chapter IV it was demonstrated that it is impossible or very difficult to solve those cases using current developments from international electronic commerce law. In Chapter VII the concept of electronic commerce custom was introduced to show how it can resolve the cases in question, using references to the notion of common Internet practices. This solution assumed that the customary practices were properly evidenced.

In this section, it will be shown how these practices could be evidenced using the methodology proposed above. However, because of the limitations of this study,

---

[1149] See for example, D'Amato, A.A. (1971), *The concept of custom in international law*, pp. 2, 89-90; Roberts, A.E. (October 2001), *Traditional and modern approaches to customary international law: A reconciliation*, pp. 757-758. See also Chapter VI.

the empirical work will not be presented below in a comprehensive manner. In consequence, the cases below will be evidenced using small samples relying primarily on non-random sampling techniques. The aim of the examples presented below is not to prove definitively the existence of web customs in question but to exemplify how the evidence supporting the existence of these custom could be gathered using the proposed methodology.

7.1 Transaction confirmation case

In this case the website operator did not include an order confirmation screen. The buyer, unsure about the successfulness of his transaction, decided to purchase items another website. He argued that it is customary nowadays to provide an order confirmation screen and he expected it. How can we prove the customary character of the order confirmation practice?

As was proposed above, one has to make sure that the majority of websites actually employs the order confirmation screen. Because there are a vast number of commercial websites on the Net and their number is growing, the proposed solution to the problem was based on establishing such a practice by looking either at the functionality of a representative sample of the most popular web building software or the observance of functionality provided by a representative sample of websites.

(a) E-commerce development tools capability test

The idea is to employ the E-commerce development tools capability test first because if one manages to establish that the most popular software used to construct commercial websites includes an order confirmation screen automatically, then it will be obvious that the majority of websites will contain such functionality. Of course, it is possible to build a commercial website using just an HTML editor, but experience shows that commercial websites are constructed using packages that deliver certain functionality not available in HTML editors.[1150] Top e-commerce solutions provide among other things user profiling, content personalisation, catalogue management, order processing, languages and currencies and advanced online business analytics.

So the first step is to look at how many web development tools there are on the market and select a representative sample of them. Here a small pilot study would be the best way to ascertain which software tools are used and which ones are most popular. In the absence of this, one has to study available sources on the Web and in bookshops in order to learn what is currently being used on the market.

In order to ensure representative design of the sample, website software could be split into two categories: large-website software and small-to-medium e-business software. In the first category one should mention Microsoft Site Server 3.0

[1150] See Milutinovic, V. (2002), *Tutorial* mentioned earlier. This matter, however, requires a separate study.

Commerce Edition,[1151] replaced by Commerce Server 2002.[1152] Together with Microsoft Biz Talk Server used for B2B electronic commerce integration, both products make up the Microsoft Solution for Internet Business.[1153] According to some technical experts at this stage it seems to be the only all-in-one solution for large e-commerce sites.[1154] Other big players have also developed e-commerce solutions although the functionality in respect to e-commerce site building could not be easily asserted. IBM developed several products in the WebSphere package including IBM WebSphere Commerce editions and IBM WebSphere Studio HomePage Builder for Windows.[1155] Allaire developed ColdFusion, which was recently purchased by Macromedia.[1156] But the rapid development of e-commerce sites is not easily ascertainable in relation to these packages.

In the second category, there are a number of products available. A good way to obtain a sampling frame of small e-commerce development tools is to visit payment gateway providers like WorldPay,[1157] CardService[1158] or Authorize.Net.[1159] For instance, WorldPay integrates its secure payment gateway with the following software solutions:[1160]

WorldPay.com Catalogue and Shopping Cart partners				
1ShoppingCart	Accounts Online	AceFlex 4.0	Actinic	ActivShopping
AliGrafix	Apoogee	Ardeo	B-Com	Beans Cappuccino
Cactushop	Click and Build	ClickCart Pro	ComAdvance	Cows
CybershopUK	Dansie Cart	ecBuilder	EMerchantPro	EROL
Evolve 2000 Store	Expocentric	Extropia	EzStore	Get Trolleyed
IBM WebSphere	iDomainCart/iHostingCart	IGrapeVine	iHTML/Inline	INEX
InstanteStore.com, Internet Treasure Chest	Internolix	Intershop	Intershop ePages	JShop Professional
Mamut	M Cart	Mercantec	Miva Merchant	Netc./Net-Store
PDG Software	PERL Shop	Pulse 2000	QDCat	Qhost
RealCart	Sage	shop@home.pro	Shop@ssistant	ShopCreator
ShopFactory	ShopFitter	ShopMaster	Shopping Cart	Shopping Cart 2000
StoreSense	TKPoint	Transaction 2000	VIPCart.com	VirtualShop
VP-ASP	WebContactPro	WebGenie	WebLogic	Web Widgets
WS4D	(Integra Europe)			

Figure 21 – WorldPay.com Catalogue and Shopping Cart partners

[1151] See for example, Libertone, D. and Scoppa, A. (2000), *Microsoft Site Server 3.0 Commerce Edition: An E-Commerce Solution.*

[1152] See Commerce Server 2002 FAQ.

[1153] See Rosoff, M. (18 February 2002), *Commerce Server 2002 Showcases .NET.*

[1154] See Kaufman, S.J. (14 May 2002), *Easy e-commerce with Microsoft Commerce Server 2002.*

[1155] <http://www.ibm.com>, last accessed: 04/11/2002.

[1156] <http://www.macromedia.com>, last accessed: 04/11/2002.

[1157] <http://www.worldpay.com>, last accessed: 22/04/2003.

[1158] <http://www.cardservice.com>, last accessed: 22/04/2003.

[1159] <http://www.authorize.net>, last accessed: 22/04/2003.

[1160] <http://www.worldpay.com/aus/index.html>, last accessed: 04/11/2002.

On the other hand, Card Service International provides the following list of software integrated with its LinkPoint Secure Payment Gateway:[1161]

Card Service International Catalogue and Shopping Cart software producers				
Merchant Helper	Shop Factory	EZShopper	AbleCommerce	Americart
Bcentral	Beacon	Beanbasket	Bigstep.com	Breakthrough
Commerce.cgi	Cart32	Cartit	Cart Manager	Catalogue Builder Cart
Ccedwards.com	CheckItOut	CoolCart	Dansie Shopping Cart	DesignCart
DreamCommerce	EasyCart	ECSI	CartComplete	Express Shopper
iHTML Merchant	Marketplace Manager	iLM	iTool	LinkPointCart
Make-a-Store	MaxEngine.com	Customised Shopping Cart	Mercantec SoftCart	Miva Merchant
moonSlice	Hazel	PDG Shopping Cart	Platinum Cart	EZ Cart
Quick Cart	Quick Store	@Retail	SecureNetShop	Shop Factory
Shop Site	Store Front	StoresOnline.com	uShop	uStoreKeeper
VirtualCart	VisualTrends OnlineStoreBuilder	Web.site.express		

Figure 22 – Card Service International catalogue and shopping cart software producers

One should also mention NetObjects Matrix Builder,[1162] Yahoo! Store,[1163] Main Street Store (FedEx Store),[1164] ShopFactory[1165] or ecBuilder.[1166]

The distinction between small-to-medium and large e-commerce web solutions is sometimes not easy to make because large software products usually come in several editions providing varying degrees of functionality. For instance Microsoft Commerce Server 2002 comes in Evaluation Edition, Developer Edition, Standard Edition, and Enterprise Edition. And so:

> 'Standard Edition is ideal for medium-sized businesses that have a need for basic e-commerce functions and basic reporting.'

whereas the

1161 <http://www.cardservice.com/partnerships/p_catalog_a_thru_f.aspx>, and linked sites, last accessed: 22/04/2003.

1162 <http://matrix.netobjects.com/destinations/netobjects/login.html>, last accessed: 04/11/2002.

1163 <http://store.yahoo.com/>, last accessed: 26/10/2002.

1164 <http://mybiz.mainstreet-stores.com/apps/smb/clients/FedEx/>, last accessed: 26/10/2002.

1165 <http://www.shopfactory.com/>, last accessed: 27/10/2002.

1166 <http://www.ecbuilder.com>, last accessed: 27/10/2002. See the presentation of Milutinovic, V. on a very similar topic presented as a tutorial at the 35th International Conference on Systems Sciences in Hawaii in January 2002. See Milutinovic, V. (2002), *Tutorial.*

> 'Enterprise Edition has been designed for high-traffic, global sites that need advanced functionality and advanced analysis options.'[1167]

Examination of the widely used Microsoft Site Server 3.0 Commerce Edition shows that it automatically generates an order confirmation. The order confirmation is included in the file titled confirmation.asp that includes an order tracking number.[1168] The order confirmation is included in illustrative websites contained in the system.[1169] More importantly, it is also automatically generated by the Site Builder Wizard, which in fourteen steps can create a site tailored to e-business needs.[1170] The designer can modify these automatically generated files as they are nothing more than a set of text files. Libertone and Scoppa for instance, show how to display shorter order tracking numbers on the order confirmation as well as how to send an order confirmation by e-mail.[1171] The same functionality is embedded in the file Receipt.aspx in Microsoft Commerce Server 2002[1172] and in ColdFusion 4.0 and later versions.[1173] As June 2002 Netcraft report argues:

> 'There are around 36,000 sites using Commerce Server [or Site Server, its predecessor] including a significant number of e-commerce sites and banks.'[1174]

Easier to check are e-commerce sites generation software packages freely available on the Internet. Their common feature is that they use shopping cart technology to handle online purchases that is supposed to imitate purchases in offline supermarkets.[1175] However, the main limitation of this software is that it cannot handle a large amount of data. As a result of its very limited functionality it is probably used only for the development of small websites, although it also has potential to be used by medium sites. The point is that although this type of software is probably rarely used in practice, it provides evidence of what functionality small-to-medium sized e-commerce sites must provide.

[1167] There are also differences as to the number of processors, web servers and applications supported. See Commerce Server 2002 FAQ.

[1168] See for example, Libertone, D. and Scoppa, A. (2000), *Microsoft Site Server 3.0 Commerce Edition: An E-Commerce Solution*, pp. 46-47. See also receipt_view.asp file on pp. 47-52. On commerce interchange pipeline facility that 'ensures the secure data exchange of business data objects such as purchase orders and order confirmations' see p. 112.

[1169] See for example, Volcano Coffee Company default web page.

[1170] See especially step 13 titled Order History. See also p. 70.

[1171] Libertone, D. and Scoppa, A. (2000), *Microsoft Site Server 3.0 Commerce Edition: An E-Commerce Solution*, pp. 101-103.

[1172] See Help file for Microsoft Commerce 2002 Enterprise Edition. See, for example, Commerce Server Tutorials/Commerce Server Developer Tutorials/Exploring the International Retail Site/Shopping the Adventure Works Catalogue.

[1173] See for example, Hoffer, J.A., et al. (2002), *Modern Database Management*, pp. 373-383.

[1174] Netcraft (2002), *The June 2002 Netcraft Web Server Survey*.

[1175] See Chapter II and Glossary.

Examination of software tools in the second category clearly shows that order confirmation is a built-in capability that cannot be opted-out by a site designer during the production stage. For instance, Yahoo!Store or ecBuilder and other products are, similarly to Microsoft Site Server, based upon wizards, which automatically generate order confirmation functionality.

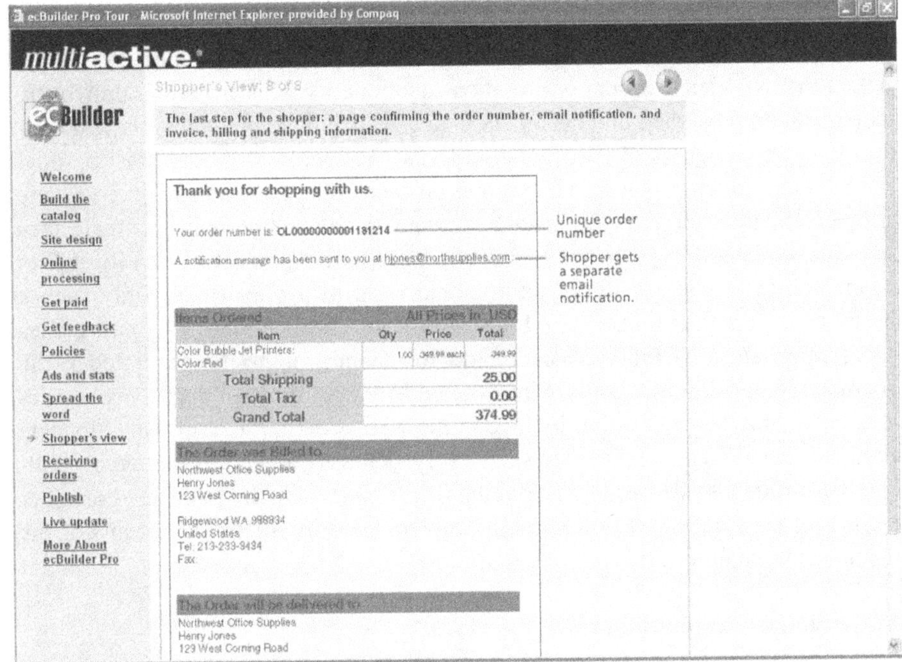

Figure 23 – An order confirmation screen automatically generated by ecBuilder

One should also mention that payment gateways such as Authorize.Net are pre-configured to send e-mail confirmations to e-commerce sites and can also be configured to e-mail automatic transaction confirmation directly to the customers.[1176] In this case, the confirmation of a transaction would not come from the merchant, but from the middleman between the e-merchant and a bank. It is interesting to note that for some payment gateways, e-mails 'are a courtesy function and should be treated as a "useful but not vital" facility.'[1177]

In summary, both large and small-to-medium e-commerce software development tools provide automatic generation of order confirmation screens. This functionality is considered to be standard. From this one could infer that since the majority

[1176] See for example, Authorize.Net (2003), *Advanced Integration Method Implementation Guide Card-Not-Present Transactions Versions 1.0*, p. 32; Authorize.Net (2003), *Shopping Cart Certification Advanced Integration Method (AIM) Implementation Guide Card-Not-Present Transactions*, p. 33.

[1177] See SECPay, *FAQ's technical.*

of rapid e-commerce development tools provide such functionality, then the majority of commercial websites must posses such functionality. This in turn proves existence of a customary norm that requires provision of such functionality to the end-user. Since rapid development tools are globally accessible, this means that a given functionality must be provided by international merchants across a range of industries.

This conclusion has two important limitations, however. First, this approach assumes that sites created by rapid development tools will not be altered in such a manner that will delete order confirmation functionality. This is a minor drawback, since it can be presumed that designers who use such development tools will conform to what designers of their creation tools considered to be the most optimal approach to a given problem. The second problem is more serious. Some website designers do not use rapid e-commerce software development tools but create sites using just code editors. It is not possible to state how many commercial websites are created in this way without doing some form of a pilot study. Only such a survey could confirm that code editors are rarely used to build e-shopping sites from scratch and serve more as a handy tool to enhance rough sites generated by the e-commerce development tools. Since the code editors do not impose any restrictions on what a designer might include in the web system, it is impossible to state whether e-business sites created in such a way, possess order confirmation capability. This introduces a degree of uncertainty, which might actually force the researcher to check if the alleged custom is really implemented in practice by means of the practice examination test.

(b) Practice examination test

The practice examination test should be used only if the e-commerce development tools capability test cannot be performed or if its results are inconclusive. To many adjudicators the arguments presented above about the widespread inclusion of order confirmation generation mechanisms would be sufficient to establish the customary norm in question. However, for those who would not regard this evidence as conclusive, one would have to examine actual practice.

(i) *Automatic analysis*

This is the only test that can be performed automatically. However in respect of order confirmation one faces a serious problem. As was discussed earlier, it is impractical to design a software component that would track the presence and the content of the order confirmation screen because of the unstructured character of HTML language. The problem is best illustrated with the reference to search engines that return any website that contains a searched keyword irrespective of the context in which a given keyword was used (see Figure 24).

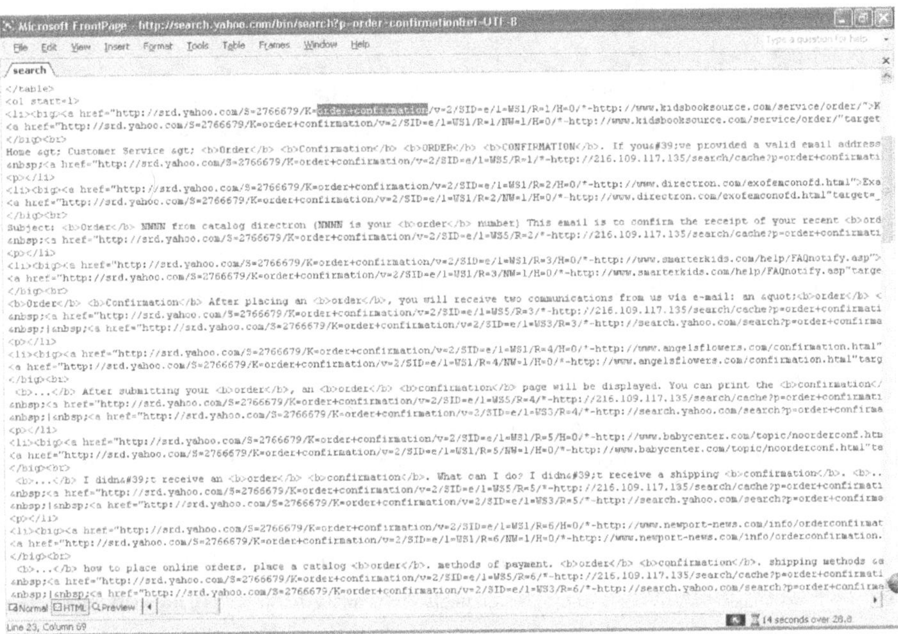

Figure 24 – The results of search of 'order confirmation' keyword using Yahoo search engine and displayed in HTML format using Microsoft FrontPage editor

Moreover, without common terms used to describe a particular moment of a transaction, it is difficult to establish in a given context, the meaning of words such as 'order confirmation' or 'transaction confirmation' or 'purchase confirmation' or any combination thereof. This problem may be overcome when one separates content and display of data and builds a common library of unique keywords that could be searched on all websites. This is already happening with respect to XML language that is going to be the successor of HTML. Common libraries of keywords are already being developed similarly to the electronic business terms used by Electronic Data Interchange EDIFACT and ANSI X.12 libraries. Examples of e-business keyword libraries include ebXML, RosettaNet and others. Until these developments become widespread and change the way commercial websites are designed, a search for content specific information in an automated fashion for the purpose of establishing an e-custom will not be possible.

(ii) *Manual analysis*

Thus one is forced to visit a representative number of websites manually and test if they provide an order confirmation. In order to do this one should choose a random or non-random sampling technique. Irrespective of the method chosen, it is very important when establishing a sample to include well-known and often-visited commercial websites such as Amazon.com. Sites such as Amazon.com account for a large percentage of commercial traffic on the Web and also serve as the benchmark for other commercial sites.

There are some problems with manual analysis of transaction confirmation practices. First, it may be very time consuming to define a sampling frame and for this reason the convenience sampling method will be used as an example. Since it may turn out to be an expensive enterprise to actually purchase products to see if an order confirmation is included, it may be necessary to actually make fake orders, with the permission of a website administrator if possible. Another problem that can be encountered is that some websites will not allow the tester to purchase products from it unless the person testing it has a business or belongs to a business association. In such a case, such a website can either be replaced by one that is publicly available or a special request may be sent to website operator with a kind request to test the website for a given functionality.

One should also note that a transaction confirmation is often linked with the shopping cart facility of which it is the last step. It is therefore advisable to take notice of whether or not a given site provides this functionality and displays the number of steps that it takes to complete a given transaction. When it does, one could also infer from it that a given site includes instant order confirmation capability.

Figure 25 – The example of Amazon.com shopping cart facility indicating various stages of a transaction

Nevertheless, a review of a convenient sample of several more and less popular commercial sites clearly shows that instant order confirmation is a widespread customary practice of global scope. It is used by electronic shops, online banks and financial institutions, and government agencies. One can encounter this practice across all industries that rely on the Internet while selling goods or services. For instance, the domain name registrars like GoDaddy.com, online bookshops like Dymocks, travel agencies like Greyhound Pioneer, online lotteries like Tattslotto or banking institutions like Westpac, all provide instant order confirmation containing a receipt number. The following 5 screen shots (Figures 26–30) show various ways of implementing this functionality.

It is also very common to confirm simultaneously the order in an e-mail. E-mail confirmation is important because it is almost as fast as a Web-based confirmation but is more persistent proof of a transaction. However, e-mail transaction confirmation, although very common and very useful, should not be used as the only means of confirming transactions, as serious problems might arise if a purchaser misspelled his or her e-mail address. The e-mail confirmation usually contains not only a receipt number together with all the transaction details but also a link to the pur-

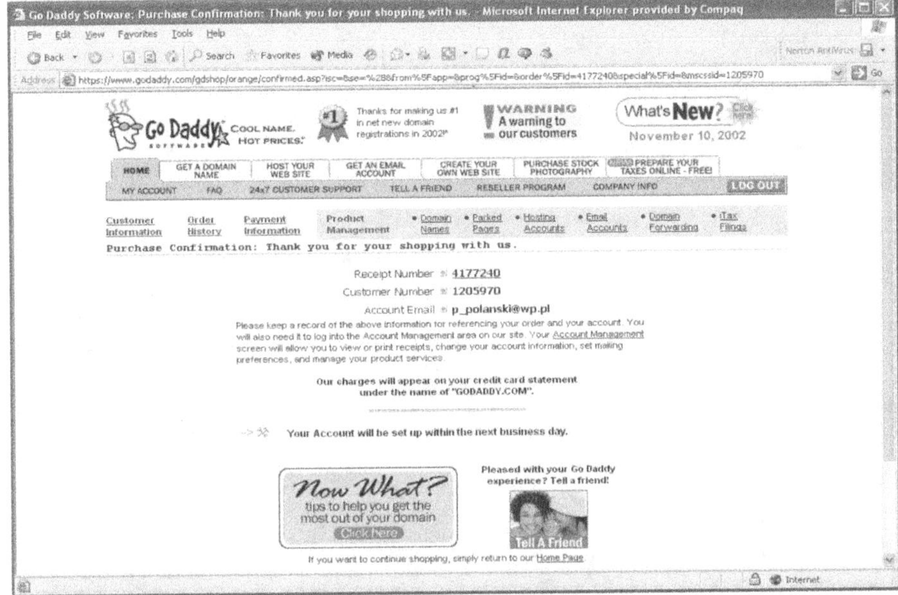

Figure 26 – GoDaddy.com registrar purchase confirmation of the domain name with the receipt number

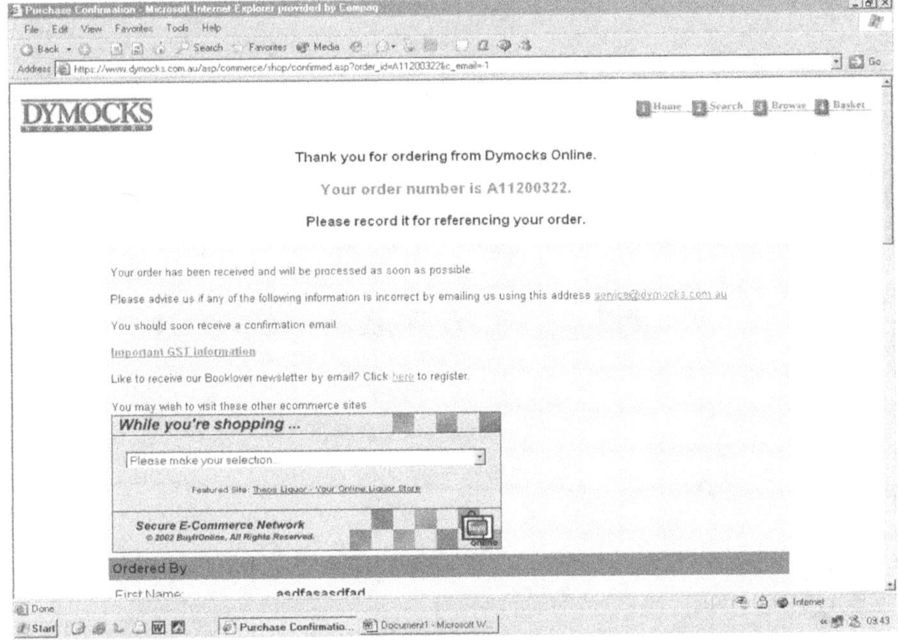

Figure 27 – Dymocks Online purchase confirmation screen containing transaction number

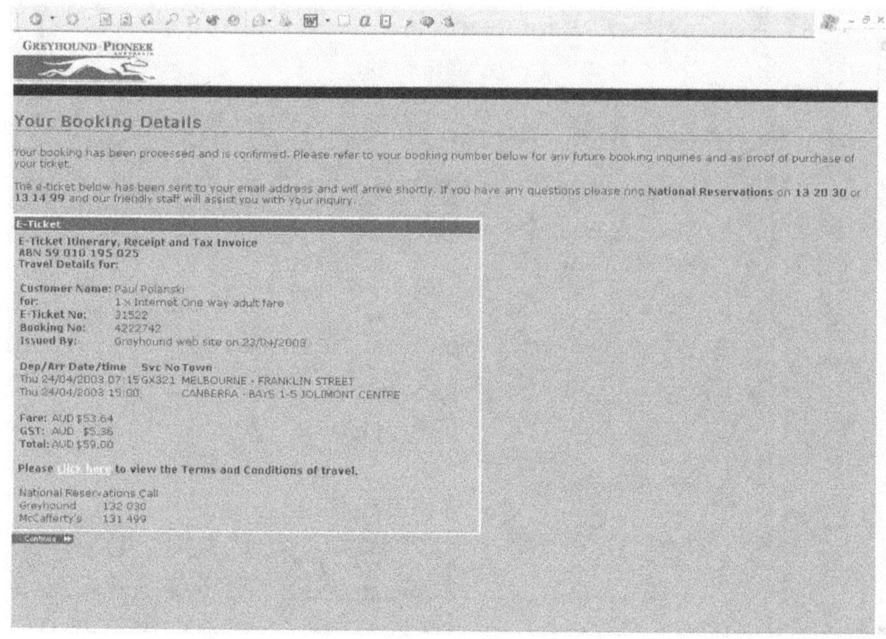

Figure 28 – Greyhound Pioneer coach service confirmation screen with the e-ticket and booking number

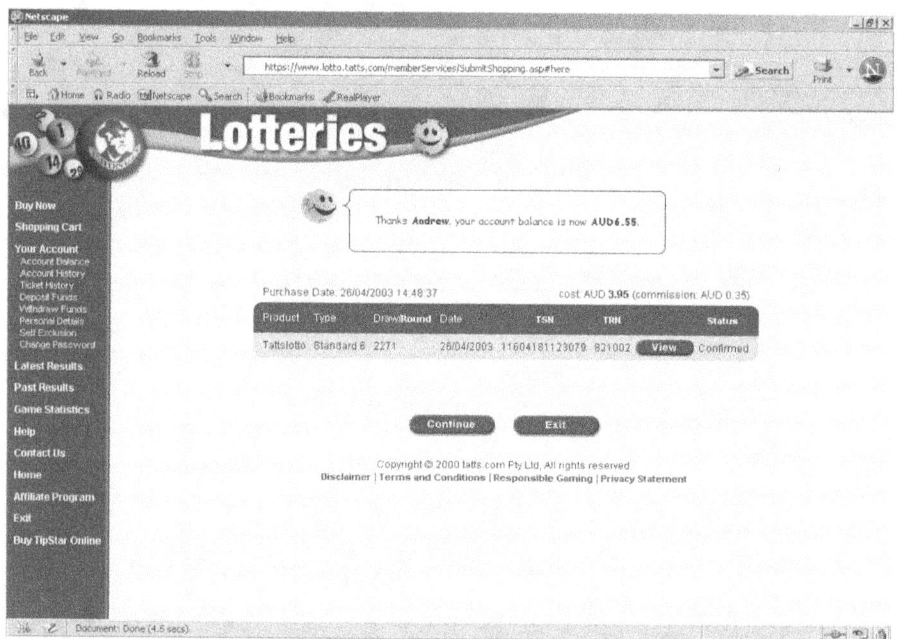

Figure 29 – Tatslotto lottery transaction confirmation screen on Netscape 7.0 web browser

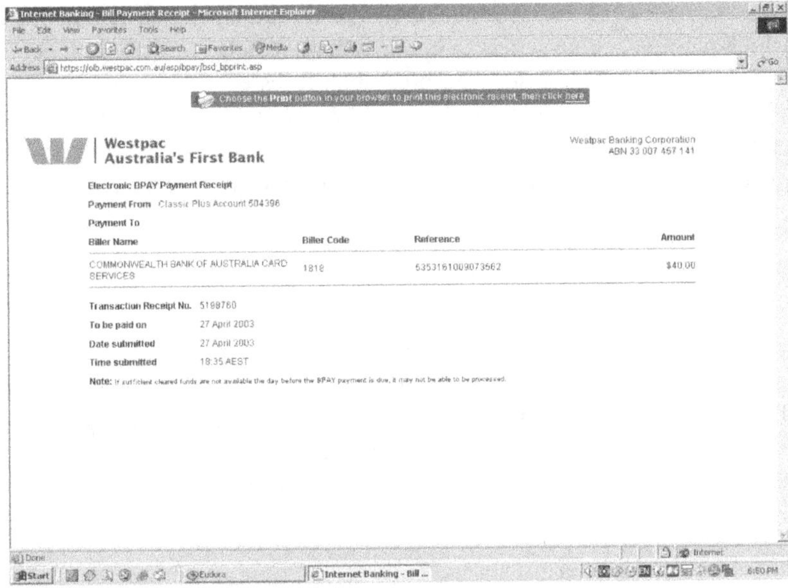

Figure 30 – Transaction confirmation page of Westpac bank with a reference number

chased products so that buyer can track progress of his order, or as in the case of digital product, e.g., edit its features. A combination of both Web-based and e-mail transaction confirmation is the most common and the best way of communicating the deal (Figure 31).

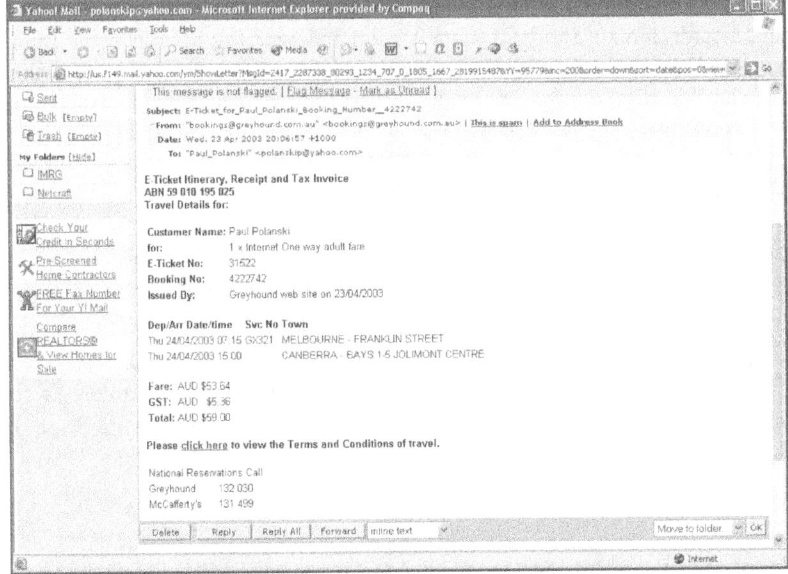

Figure 31 – E-mail confirmation sent by Greyhound pioneer coach service website

The above survey clearly indicates that there is a common practice across all industries, which requires online sellers to confirm immediately purchase orders placed via the Web. This practice is so widespread that it justifies the expectation that it should be provided by all of e-commerce vendors as a natural step in the formation of electronic contract. This expectation is compounded as so far, no sites have been found that do not provide this functionality, although with more resources and space, a more stringent survey could be done.

(c) Literature review test

The emergence of the new practice of immediate transaction confirmation is visible both in technical as well as in legal writings. As far as technical books are concerned, the importance of order confirmation can be deduced from the references to related concepts like shopping cart or tracking order or tracking order number. One finds such references in the writing of the web usability expert, Jakob Nielsen, in the context of the shopping cart:

> 'Shopping carts are now so common on e-commerce sites that they have morphed from metaphor to interface standard. When users encounter a web shopping cart these days, they don't think of a physical supermarket as the reference system. Instead, they think of all the other websites where they have seen shopping carts. Once something becomes sufficiently widely used, it becomes an interface convention and people simply know what to expect.'

And further:

> 'The standardisation of shopping carts is good and bad. The benefits come from consistency, which is even stronger than metaphor as a learning tool. In fact, the user doesn't have to learn *anything* as long as an interface element behaves exactly like the user is accustomed to. At the same time, shopping carts are an inappropriate interface for many applications, and yet designs are forced to use a shopping cart because that is what users expect.'[1178]

It is remarkable that Nielsen speaks about designers who are forced to provide certain functionality because users expect it. Although his remarks are directed towards creation of a Web that is easier to use, they provide an interesting confirmation of the role of customary practices in the electronic commerce.

Similarly, authors writing guides about software solutions to e-commerce websites confirm the necessity of an order confirmation practice. Liberton suggested that

---

[1178] Nielsen, J. (2000), *Designing Web Usability: The Practice of Simplicity*, p. 188.

> 'to make it easy for a customer to track an order, the E-commerce system should generate a tracking number that can be displayed and, possibly, e-mailed to the customer.'[1179]

The order confirmation customarily contains an order tracking number. So from this suggestion, one can deduce that an order should be confirmed instantly by a display of a separate website and confirmed optionally in an e-mail, thus reinforcing earlier findings.

On the other hand, web design expert Jeffrey Veen, while discussing the most frequent customer complaints, cites the March 2000 report of BizTalk.com, which showed that 25 per cent of customer complaints were due to their inability to track orders.[1180] Orders can be tracked only thanks to an order number that must have been supplied either immediately after the transaction took place or in e-mail confirmation. This clearly shows that there is still a large percentage of commercial websites that does not conform to the Internet standards, thus creating a major source of problems to online customers, be it consumers or businesses.

In contrast to technical writing, legal writing is generally silent on the matter of the necessity of an instant order confirmation in e-commerce transactions. Practical matters like Internet practices are of no interest to the legal community. This is in line with the attitude of the legal community to the notion of custom as a source of law, which is considered as irrelevant by modern legal culture, focusing on the interpretation of existing statutes or cases. In consequence, modern literature on electronic commerce law deals only with the interpretation of local and international statutes and case law pertaining to this phenomenon.[1181]

However, it is mandatory to recall that the European Union Directive on Electronic Commerce obliges online businesses to acknowledge the receipt of recipient's order without undue delay and by electronic means.[1182] In consequence, as was argued earlier, Article 11 of the Directive 'unconsciously' codified the customary practice, because there is no single reference to the existence of such practice in the text. It is important to remember, however, that such an order did not have to be confirmed immediately and that businesses-to-business transactions could exclude its application by a contrary agreement.[1183] Nevertheless, it is a very important confirmation of the legal relevance of the order confirmation practice.

In summary, the technical literature review test clearly shows that the practice of confirming orders is expected from e-commerce systems. Although the authors do not explicitly mention that the order must be confirmed immediately, this can be

---

1179 Libertone, D. and Scoppa, A. (2000), *Microsoft Site Server 3.0 Commerce Edition: An E-Commerce Solution*, p. 3.

1180 Veen, J. (2001), *The Art & Science of Web Design*, p. 172.

1181 For more on this matter see Polanski, P.P. (2002), *A New Approach to Regulating Internet Commerce: Custom as a Source of Electronic Commerce Law.*

1182 See Art. 11.1 first indent. See also discussion in Chapter IV and VI.

1183 See Chapter IV and VI.

inferred from the fact that they refer to the shopping cart facility or to website confirmation, which can only provide such feedback in an instantaneous manner. On the other hand, legal writing is generally silent on this matter, although as this practice was 'unconsciously' and partially codified in the European Union Directive on Electronic Commerce.

(d) Case summary

Transaction confirmation practice is global and pertains to web commerce, although it has its predecessor in Electronic Data Interchange. Both empirical tests as well as literature tests provided strong evidence for the existence of the common practice of immediate order confirmation in electronic commerce. The e-commerce development tools test has clearly shown that a convenient sample of big and small-to-medium software packages automatically generate order confirmation capability. These findings were confirmed in the test of actual adherence to such a practice, which has shown that in a convenience sample of large and small online vendors, all of them immediately confirmed purchase orders with a page containing an order reference number and by e-mail. The literature review test has provided further evidence that such practice is known, recommended and legally relevant, thus reinforcing the expectation that it should be observed. The only limitation of this proof were restrictions that had to be put on the number of visited sites and its discussion, which were due to the scope of this book. In a real life case scenario, more formal application of the outlined methodology could be made.

The results of all of the above tests indicate that there is a widespread practice of instantly confirming online orders and that it is widespread enough to create a justified expectation that it should be provided by every Internet merchant. The above proof of the Internet custom should convince an adjudicator as to the existence of a global customary norm that states: 'All web-based transactions should be electronically confirmed immediately after the placement of an order.' This norm could then be used to solve the dispute outlined in the hypothetical case study in favour of the buyer.

7.2 The banking case

In this case the designer of a banking site did not provide 128-bit encryption of the web-based banking system because the agreement did not require it. One of the bank's business clients suffered a financial loss while using the system, despite the fact that his browser could support strong encryption. As was argued in Chapter VII, the client sued the bank on the basis of breach of a customary norm arguing that it should be implied in the contract. This customary norm required the bank to provide state-of-the-art technological security, which is the provision of a 128-bit encryption channel nowadays.

The proof of the case is not going to assess all the potential security practices that are necessary for the safe electronic commerce.[1184] Instead, it will focus on one particular aspect of this very complex subject-matter – the analysis of the Secure Sockets Layer (SSL).[1185] As was shown in the previous chapter, SSL is the most important security standard on the Web. Analysis of the SSL protocol, being a combination of fast symmetric key and the more secure asymmetric key encryption,[1186] will be restricted to the symmetric key encryption, which typically uses the session keys of 40-bit or 128-bit length these days.[1187]

(a) E-commerce development tools capability test

This test deals with the examination of the tools used to build websites. In this case, one would need to examine e-commerce development software capability of providing ciphering mechanisms. However, e-commerce production tools are not designed to handle the set-up of client-server transaction encryption. Although some more advanced products like Microsoft Commerce 2002 Enterprise Edition provide some basic security features, they are related mainly to integrating web system login with Windows authentication.[1188] Similarly, low-to-medium end e-commerce software does not posses capabilities that would enable an inference as to the automatic inclusion of the SSL protocol. In short, existing e-commerce rapid development tools do not cater for automatic inclusion of the SSL based data transmission in the client-server environment.

Instead, encryption is provided by the Web infrastructure. The most important elements of a secure web infrastructure are: the web server, the web browser and the possession of permission to use 128-bit technology by means of a server digital

---

[1184] See for example, Tovey, M. (2001), *Security of eCommerce Systems*.

[1185] See for example, Burnett, S. and Paine, S. (2001), *RSA Security's Official Guide to Cryptography*; Diffie, W. and Hellman, M.E. (November 1976), *New Directions in Cryptography*; Freier, A.O., et al. (1996), *The SSL Protocol version 3.0. Internet Draft*; Hudson, T.J. and Young, E.A. (24 September 1998), *SSLeay and SSLapps FAQ*; Joshi, B.D.J., et al. (2001), *Security models for web-based applications. Using traditional and emerging access control approaches to develop secure applications for the Web*; Koops, B.-J. (1999), *The crypto controversy: a key conflict in the information society*; Netscape Communications Corporation (1998), *Introduction to SSL*; Schneier, B. (1996), *Applied cryptography: protocols, algorithms, and source code in C*; Schneier, B. (1997), *Cryptography Primer*; Tovey, M. (2001), *Security of eCommerce Systems*; Verisign *128-bit SSL Global Server IDs: Frequently Asked Questions*; Verisign (2002), *Securing Your Website for Business: A step by step guide for secure online commerce*; Wells Fargo (2002), *Browser Frequently Asked Questions*; Wells Fargo (2002), *Online Security Guarantee*; Wells Fargo (2002), *Online Security Guarantee: Frequently Asked Questions*.

[1186] See for example, Netscape Communications Corporation (1998), *Introduction to SSL* and Glossary.

[1187] It is possible to use other key lengths, e.g., 56-bit or 168-bit, see, for example, Schneier, B. (1996), *Applied cryptography: protocols, algorithms, and source code in C*; Schneier, B. (1997), *Cryptography Primer*.

[1188] See Help file for Microsoft Commerce 2002 Enterprise Edition. See especially section: Securing Your Site.

certificate or Global Server ID.[1189] Both the web browser and the web server have to possess 128-bit encryption capabilities in order to create a strong encryption environment.

The browser that completely dominates the market nowadays is Microsoft Internet Explorer in several versions.[1190] Microsoft Internet Explorer and other browsers have built-in support for SSL protocol in various versions.

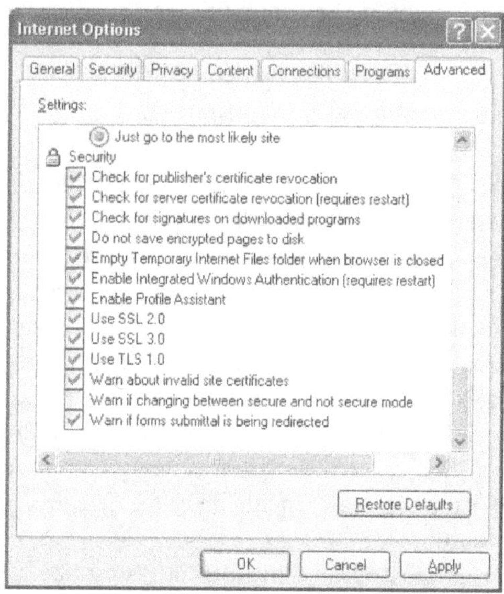

Figure 32 – Microsoft Internet Explorer 6.0 supports SSL 2.0, SSL 3.0 and TLS 1.0

However, not all browsers enable strong encryption automatically. The recent version 6.0 includes automatic support for 128-bit encryption, but previous versions (still popular today) have not supported it, unless a High Encryption Pack was separately downloaded and installed.[1191] This is an important finding, because it is likely that in such a case, it might be the client who will be held responsible for weak encryption of the transaction and in consequence, a legal challenge.

On the other hand, as Figure 20 above shows, the two most important web servers are Apache and Microsoft Internet Information Server (IIS), also in several versions.[1192] These web servers have the ability to encrypt transactions using SSL.

[1189] Netscape Communications Corporation (1998), *Introduction to SSL*. See Glossary.

[1190] See various Netcraft reports, e.g., Netcraft (2002), *The April 2002 Netcraft Web Server Survey*; Netcraft (2002), *The August 2002 Netcraft Web Server Survey*; Netcraft (2002), *The June 2002 Netcraft Web Server Survey*; Netcraft (2002), *The March 2002 Netcraft Web Server Survey*; Netcraft (2002), *The October 2002 Netcraft Web Server Survey*.

[1191] See <http://support.microsoft.com>, last accessed: 28/04/2003, <http://www.microsoft.com/windows/ie/downloads/recommended/128bit/default.asp>, last accessed: 28/04/2003.

[1192] See Figure 20 *above* and Netcraft reports, e.g., Netcraft (2002), *The April 2002 Netcraft Web Server Survey*; Netcraft (2002), *The August 2002 Netcraft Web Server Survey*; Netcraft (2002), *The*

However, as Figure 33 shows, SSL has to be activated by the special purpose digital certificate.

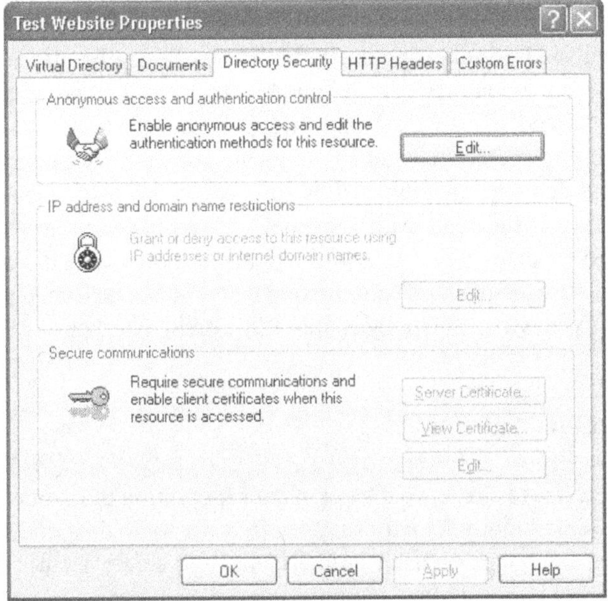

Figure 33 – IIS Web Server Directory Security dialog box. Note the secure communications section, which requires server certificate to enable SSL communication

The most popular one is Verisign's 128-bit Global Server ID, which, the company claims, is used by the 'top 40 e-commerce sites, all of the 500 Fortune companies with a Web presence, and thousands of other leading sites.'[1193] Other players that only recently[1194] emerged on the digital certificate market to compete with Verisign include: Geotrust,[1195] Comodo,[1196] Entrust[1197] and Globalsign.[1198] Some banks, however, have assured their customers that they provide strong encryption even when client's browser supports only 40-bit or 56-bit encryption, but this seems to be related to banking inter-server communication only.[1199] In this respect, one should mention that a link between a merchant and a bank is usually secured using third-

June 2002 Netcraft Web Server Survey; Netcraft (2002), *The March 2002 Netcraft Web Server Survey*; Netcraft (2002), *The October 2002 Netcraft Web Server Survey*.

1193 Verisign (2002), *Securing Your Website for Business: A step by step guide for secure online commerce*, p. 1.

1194 Netcraft (2002), *The October 2002 Netcraft Web Server Survey*.

1195 <http://www.geotrust.com/index_flash.htm>, last visited: 03/11/2002.

1196 <http://www.comodogroup.com>, last visited: 03/11/2002.

1197 <http://www.entrust.com/index.cfm>, last visited: 03/11/2002.

1198 <http://www.globalsign.com>, last visited: 03/11/2002.

1199 Wells Fargo (2002), *Online Security Guarantee: Frequently Asked Questions*, see also Wells Fargo (2002), *Browser Frequently Asked Questions*.

party payment gateways that act as a middleman between an e-commerce site and a bank that processes credit card transactions. [1200] In principle, however, strong encryption on the web server side can be enabled only by having the 128-bit digital certificate that has to be acquired separately. For this reason, the level of encryption cannot be established by analysing the web server software functionality.

In summary, the e-commerce development tools test has not established that developers are 'forced' to provide strong encryption of Web transactions as rapid e-commerce development tools cannot automatically embed strong encryption. However, this test has demonstrated that SSL is the most widely used secure protocol on the Web as it is embedded in the most popular web browsers and web servers. Nevertheless, SSL can use keys of various lengths thus providing different levels of security. As a result, the practice examination test will be performed next to establish whether banking servers actually enable 128-bit SSL encryption of online transactions.

(b) Practice examination test

The aim of this test is to check what level of data encryption of Internet transactions online financial institutions actually support. In order to do this, one should establish a conceptual population of all online banks and select a random sample of online banking websites (random sampling) or create a sample based on non-random selection process (non-random sampling). Then, automatic or manual investigation of each site included in the sample should be performed. In this case, the random sampling methodology will be applied.

(i) *Automatic analysis*

In order to perform the practice examination test in an automated fashion one has to build software that will enable this operation. Since it is outside the scope of this book, only a general overview of such a software design will be presented. The feasibility of such an endeavour can be illustrated by the Netcraft web software, [1201] which performs similar tasks.

The main object of investigation for the practice of provision of strong encryption should be the web server. It is this software that enables an online bank to provide its services over a secure or insecure channel. In other words, if one manages to establish that the majority of web servers run by online banks support 128-bit encryption then a claim that it is a customary obligation of the bank to provide strong encryption would be justified. It is important to stress, however, that the above statement does not mean that the majority of transactions will be performed

[1200] See, for example, Authorize.Net (2003), *Advanced Integration Method Implementation Guide Card-Not-Present Transactions Versions 1.0*, p. 4.

[1201] See <http://www.netcraft.com/sslwhats>, last accessed 22/04/2003 discussed later.

using strong encryption because, as was discussed earlier, it is also dependant upon the client web browser's ability to support strong encryption.

The software to be useful should poll a number of selected banking web servers in the sample and examine underlying SSL protocol on port 443 for supported ciphers (port 443 is a default port for SSL). It should be relatively easy to make the software scalable in order to poll automatically new websites.

The aim of the software is to record encryption algorithms supported by the web server also known as the cipher suite. The exchange of basic information about supported security algorithms takes place in the so-called handshake phase of the communication.[1202] The software should establish communication with a web server and extract the information about algorithms supported by the web server. The information at this stage is unencrypted, as parties have to agree on the cipher algorithms to be used before they can use them. SSL supports 31 various cipher suits, not all of them providing security in today's world.[1203] In the classical working of the SSL protocol, the client sends a hello message to the server together with among other things, a list of supported ciphers in the order of importance.[1204] Below is the typical list of supported ciphers:

- RC4 with MD5
- RC4 with MD5 (export version restricted to 40-bit key)
- RC2 with MD5
- RC2 with MD5 (export version restricted to 40-bit key)
- IDEA with MD5
- DES with MD5
- Triple DES with MD5

The server responds with the 'Hello' message and among other parameters chooses the cipher suite to be used in the communication. This is the value of interest to our software. The most widely used are RC4 and RC2 symmetric key algorithms[1205] that come in two versions: 40-bit (marked as export version) and the plain one indicating support for 128-bit transactions. IDEA also uses 128-bit long keys.[1206] On the other hand, DES is an old standard supporting 56-bit communication, which is also too weak taking into account state-of-the-art technology because 56-bit keys are vulnerable to exhaustive search.[1207] Triple DES in turn, provides strong encryp-

---

1202 See for example, Freier, A.O., et al. (1996), *The SSL Protocol version 3.0. Internet Draft*; Netscape Communications Corporation (1998), *Introduction to SSL.* See also TLS specification (also known as SSL 3.1) which replaced current version of SSL 3.0 in Burnett, S. and Paine, S. (2001), *RSA Security's Official Guide to Cryptography*, pp. 233-242; Dierks, T. and Allen, C. (January 1999), *RFC 2246 The TLS Protocol Version 1.0 (STATUS: Standard) (STD 1).*

1203 Burnett, S. and Paine, S. (2001), *RSA Security's Official Guide to Cryptography*, pp. 240-241.

1204 Ibid., p. 236.

1205 Ibid. See Glossary.

1206 See Glossary and Netcraft *Glossary.*

1207 See for example <http://www.rsasecurity.com/rsalabs/faq/3-2-2.html>, last visited: 08/07/2003.

tion and for this reason will be treated as an equivalent of 128-bit ciphers. If a company lists only 40-bit or 56-bit ciphers it means that it cannot provide a strongly encrypted communication channel and is vulnerable to brute force attack.[1208] If it lists 128-bit ciphers together with weaker ones, it means that it can, in principle, provide strong encryption, unless a client cannot support it – in which case it will use a weaker one.

In summary, construction of such software should not create major difficulties but the benefits of it would be enormous to the case. It could not only ascertain the customary practice of providing strong encryption but also provide historical data as far as changes in the supported ciphers are concerned. If the development of automatic scanning of web servers proved to be too difficult, the same analysis could be performed using a manual approach.

(ii) *Manual analysis*

The aim of this test is to investigate manually a selected number of online banking websites in order to ascertain whether or not they support 128-bit encryption. The first important task is to define the sampling frame of online banks from which a sample should be drawn. In this case, the sampling frame was built by joining two groups of online banking sites: one containing the largest banks with e-banking capabilities and one of the others containing smaller ones. The first category was represented by the listing of the largest banks in the list of 500 largest companies by revenue in Fortune 500 magazine. The 2002 edition lists the 62 largest banks in the world 2002.[1209] To fill in a second category, Quazell[1210] and Qualisteam[1211] websites were visited. Both sites contain links to a large number of banking websites throughout the world, categorised by continent, country or some other criteria. Qualisteam contains links to 2819 banking websites, whereas Quazell claims that it has the largest collection of banking sites online. Websites from each major category were chosen on a random basis from each continent as well as major and minor countries. Five online banks were added, based on references to these banks on other websites.

Having established the sampling frame, the next issue was determination of the sample size. In this example a probability sampling technique was used. Taking into account that common practice should have 75 per cent or more of adherence to it, 80 per cent was chosen as an estimate of adherence to encryption practice in question among online banks (p). As far as accepted error (S.E.) is concerned, 5 per cent error was selected. Applying it to the formula presented earlier, 64 sampling

[1208] See Burnett, S. and Paine, S. (2001), *RSA Security's Official Guide to Cryptography*, p. 236.

[1209] <http://www.fortune.com/fortune/global500/industrysnapshot/0,15133,10,00.html>, last accessed: 22/04/2003.

[1210] <http://www.quazell.com/bank/default.html>, last accessed: 22/04/2003.

[1211] <http://www.qualisteam.com/Banks/index.html>, last visited: 05/05/2003.

units would be necessary. Taking into account large banks – smaller banks stratification, 128 banks should be visited. In order to balance the potential problem arising from the fact that not all banks with the online presence will have online banking capabilities, the sample size was increased to 146 units.

66 selected banks based on Fortune 500 global banks listing				
Deutsche Bank	Credit Suisse	BNP Paribas	Bank of America Corp.	J.P. Morgan Chase
UBS	HSBC Holding PLC	Mizuho Holdings	Fortis	ABN AMRO Holding
HypoVereinsbank	Crédit Agricole	Royal Bank of Scotland	Santander Central Hispano Group	Sumitomo Mitsui Banking
HBOS	Barclays	Wells Fargo	Mitsubishi Tokyo Financial Group	DZ Bank
UFJ Holdings	Bank One Corp.	Société Générale	Banco Bilbao Vizcaya Argentaria	Commerzbank
Westdeutsche Landesbank	Lloyds TSB Group	Wachovia Corp.	Rabobank	IntesaBci
Industrial & Commercial Bank of China	FleetBoston	Dexia Group	Crédit Lyonnais	Almanij
Bank Of China	Abbey National	Washington Mutual	Landesbank Baden-Wurttemberg	Groupe Caisse d'Épargne
Royal Bank of Canada	National Australia Bank	U.S. Bancorp	Bayerische Landesbank	UniCredito Italiano
Banco Bradesco	Canadian Imperial Bank of Commerce	Bank of Nova Scotia	Toronto-Dominion Bank	China Construction Bank
Norinchukin Bank	Nordea	Banco Do Brasil	Bank of Montreal	Danske Bank Group
Fokus bank	Östgöta Enskilda Bank	Daiwa Bank Holdings	Agricultural Bank of China	Bankgesellschaft Berlin
Berliner Bank	Berliner Sparkasse	Norddeutsche Landesb.	Kreditanstalt für Wiederaufbau	Itaæsa-Investimentos Itaæ
MBNA				

Figure 34 – The 66 selected banks based on Fortune 500 global banks listing

The first category comprised 66 banks, the second 80 banks (Figures 34–35). The smaller number of banks in the second category was due to the fact that the Fortune list included only 62 banks, all of which were investigated. However, online banking facility could not be found or accessed on some of them because they were either brick-and-mortar banks without online banking facilities, or represented a holding, or required a digital certificate to be installed or for other reasons like language barriers or temporary inaccessibility of a web server. In the case of some banking holdings, sometimes banks belonging to this holding were identified and examined. In consequence, 4 additional banking sites were added to the Fortune

80 selected banks based on Qualisteam and Quazell listings				
WBK	Kredyt Bank	ING BankOnline Polska	Mbank	Inteligo
Yemen Commerial Bank	National Bank of Abu Dhabi	ABN Amro	Canara Bank	Allahabadbank
Dena Bank	UTI Bank	ING Vysya Bank	Corporation Bank	Baroda Bank
IBA	Bank of East Asia	Bank BNI	Bank Mandiri	Lippo Bank
OCBC Bank	United Overseas Bank	Union National Bank	Arab Bank	Groupe Saradar
Banque Audi	Fransa Bank	Korea First Bank	KorAm Bank	Cairo Amman Bank
Investec Bank	Hapoalim Bank	First Bank	Republic Bank	Banco de la Nacion Argentina
Banco Patagonia	Diamond Bank	First Bank of Nigeria	Continental Trust Bank Limited	Union Bank of Nigeria
Indo-Nigerian Merchant Bank	Magnum Bank	National Bank of Nigeria	NBM Bank	Egyptian American Bank
National Societe General Bank	MISR Exterior Bank	National Bank of Egypt	Banque Al Baraka d'Algérie	Banque Nationale d'Algerie
Banque extérieure d'Algérie	Union Bank	Banque Belgolaise	The Trust Bank	Biao
Akiba Bank	Kenya Commercial Bank Group	Standard Bank of South Africa	Griffon Bank	Banco Santos
Banco Real ABN Amro	Banco Itau	Interbank	Bank Leumi Le Israel	Bank Otsar Ha Hayal
First International Bank of Israel	Israel Discount Bank	Mercantile Discount Bank	Mizrahi Bank	The Maritime Bank of Israel
Union Bank of Israel	Emirates Bank Group	Middle East Bank	Bank of Ikeda	Chugoku Bank
Secure Trust Bank	Salem Five direct banking	Fleet	Hapo's Internet Teller	Virtual Bank

Figure 35 – The 80 selected banks based on Qualisteam and Quazell listings

500 global banks list. In the category of major banks, out of 66 visited, 15 could not be used in the study. In the second category, which embraced the whole globe, 31 out of visited 80 banks had to be dropped for similar reasons as in the first category. In effect, out of 146 visited websites 100 of them possessed online banking capabilities that were further investigated.

To reflect geographical, technological and cultural diversity of the globe the sample included banks from Western and Eastern Europe, Northern and Southern America, Asia, Middle East and Australia. The first group included online banks from the following fifteen countries: Australia, Belgium, Brazil, Canada, China, England, France, Germany, Italy, the Netherlands, Norway, Spain, Sweden, Switzerland and the United States. The second group included online banks from the following eighteen countries: Abu Dabi, Argentina, Belgium, Brazil, China/Hong

The final sample of online banking sites selected from Fortune 500 magazine				
Deutsche Bank	Credit Suisse	BNP Paribas	Bank of America Corp.	J.P. Morgan Chase
UBS	HSBC Holding PLC	ABN AMRO Holding	HypoVereinsbank	Royal Bank of Scotland
Santander Central Hispano Group	HBOS	Barclays	Wells Fargo	Bank One Corp.
Société Générale	Banco Bilbao Vizcaya Argentaria	Commerzbank	Westdeutsche Landesbank	Lloyds TSB Group
Wachovia Corp.	Rabobank	IntesaBci	Industrial & Commercial Bank of China	FleetBoston
Dexia Group	Crédit Lyonnais	Bank Of China	Abbey National	Washington Mutual
Landesbank Baden-Wurttemberg	Groupe Caisse d'Épargne	Royal Bank of Canada	National Australia Bank	U.S. Bancorp
Bayerische Landesbank	UniCredito Italiano	Banco Bradesco	Canadian Imperial Bank of Commerce	Bank of Nova Scotia
Toronto-Dominion Bank	China Construction Bank	Nordea	Banco Do Brasil	Bank of Montreal
Fokus bank	Östgöta Enskilda Bank	Berliner Bank	Berliner Sparkasse	Norddeutsche Landesb.
MBNA				

Figure 36 – The final sample of 51 online banking sites selected from Fortune 500 magazine

The final sample of online banking sites banks selected from Qualisteam and Quazell listings				
WBK	Kredyt Bank	ING BankOnline Polska	Mbank	Inteligo
National Bank of Abu Dhabi	Allahabadbank	UTI Bank	ING Vysya Bank	Corporation Bank
IBA	Bank of East Asia	Bank Mandiri	Lippo Bank	OCBC Bank
United Overseas Bank	Union National Bank	Arab Bank	Groupe Saradar	Banque Audi
Investec Bank	Hapoalim Bank	Banco de la Nacion Argentina	Banco Patagonia	First Bank of Nigeria
Banque Belgolaise	Standard Bank of South Africa	Griffon Bank	Banco Santos	Banco Real ABN Amro
Banco Itau	Interbank	Bank Leumi Le Israel	Bank Otsar Ha Hayal	First International Bank of Israel
Israel Discount Bank	Mercantile Discount Bank	Mizrahi Bank	The Maritime Bank of Israel	Union Bank of Israel
Emirates Bank Group	Middle East Bank	Bank of Ikeda	Chugoku Bank	Secure Trust Bank
SalemFive direct banking	Fleet	Hapo's Internet Teller	Virtual Bank	

Figure 37 – The final sample of 49 online banking sites banks based on Qualisteam and Quazell listings

Kong, Dominica, India, Indonesia, Israel, Japan, Jordan, Lebanon, Nigeria, Peru, Poland, Singapore, South Africa and United Arab Emirates. In this category seven cyber banks were included. To reflect diversity in the financial power of the banks, the 51 banks selected from the Fortune magazine list could be regarded as representing the most powerful online banks on the globe. The less powerful banks were randomly selected from the references in the websites cited above.

From a technical perspective, the analysis was performed using Internet Explorer v.6.0 or earlier versions with enabled 128-bit client-side encryption on Windows XP Home Edition, Windows 2000 Professional Edition and Windows 98 operating systems. The support for strong encryption was also tested using Netcraft Query SSL engine.[1212] Online banking was tested using both business and home banking websites because it was assumed that the bank will apply the same security policy towards business and non-business transactions.

As far as the investigation method is concerned, the websites were investigated by manually accessing online home or business banking links in order to invoke secure login screens. In this type of unobtrusive, manual analysis, the strength of the session key was established based on information contained in the tool-tip above the padlock icon in the web browser. In order to invoke it, one should find a website where a user can enter login and password details. Usually then web system designers activate transaction encryption. If such an icon does not appear by that time, the investigator will have to enter a fake login and password in order to trigger encryption of the transaction.

Figure 38 – The padlock icon in Internet Explorer, which symbolises encryption of the communication

The following five screen shots show the diversity of online banking login screens all secured using 128-bit encryption (Figures 39–43).

The approach of relying on the information contained in the tool-tip, however, had one disadvantage. Information gathered in this manner was not always reliable when, e.g., a secured website was divided using invisible frames, each with different levels of security. In such a case, the tool-tip did not appear, as only a portion of the document was secure and the padlock appears only when the whole visible screen is secure.[1213] In order to mitigate this problem the properties of the web document containing login boxes were invoked in order to test for supported protocol (Figure 44).

1212 See <http://www.netcraft.com/sslwhats>, last accessed: 05/05/2003.

1213 See SECPay, *FAQ's technical.*

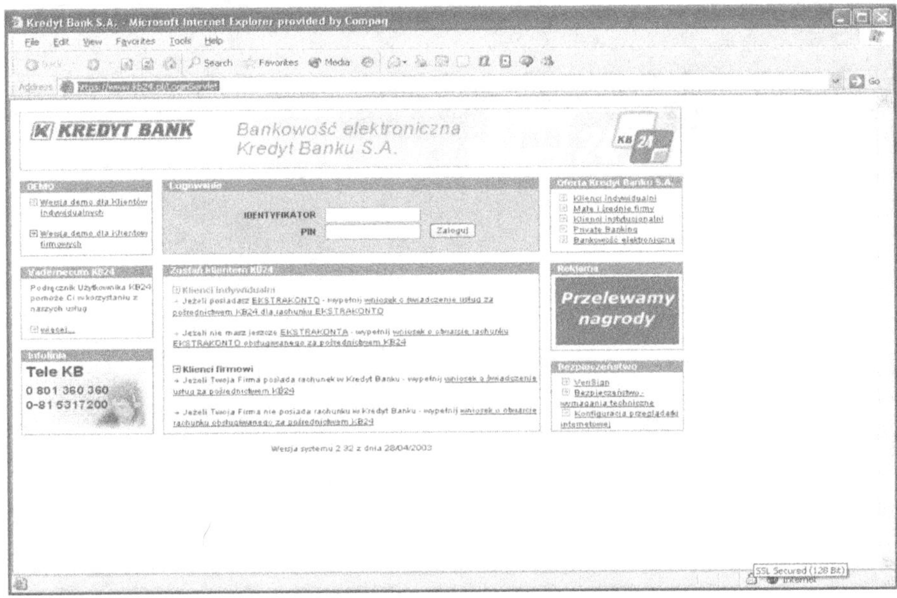

Figure 39 – Kredyt Bank. 128-bit encrypted SSL session

Figure 40 – 128-bit encryption supported by Indian Allahabadbank

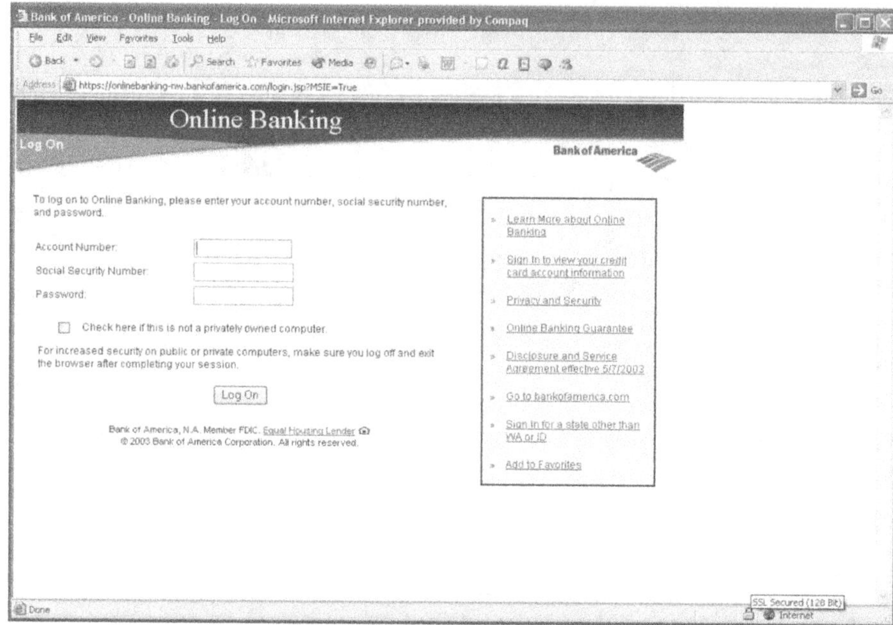

Figure 41 – Bank of America 128-bit transaction security padlock

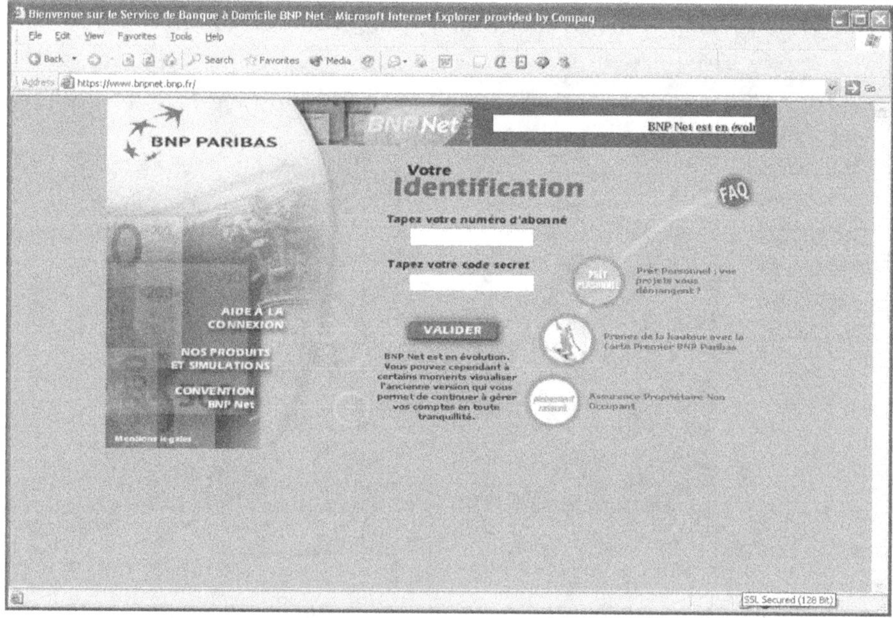

Figure 42 – French BNP Paribas also uses 128-bit encryption

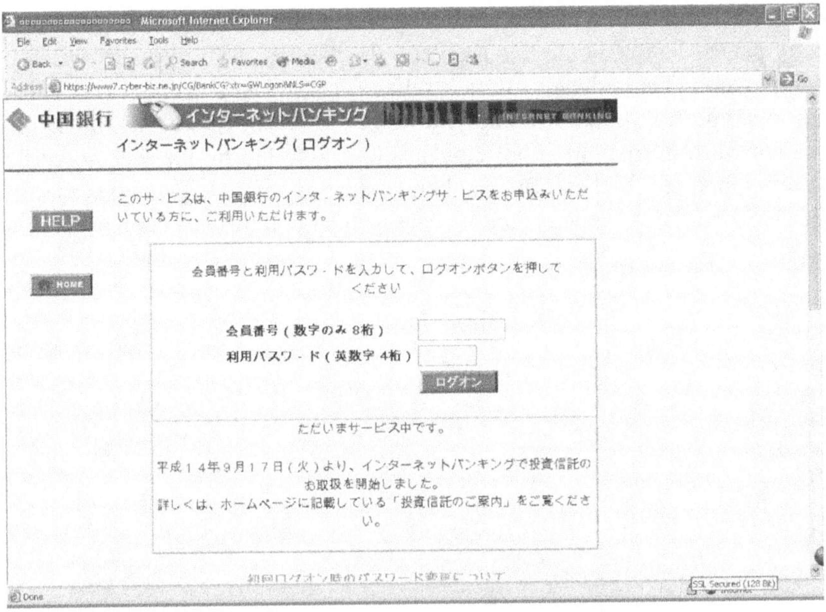

Figure 43 – Japanese Chugoku bank supports strong 128-bit encryption

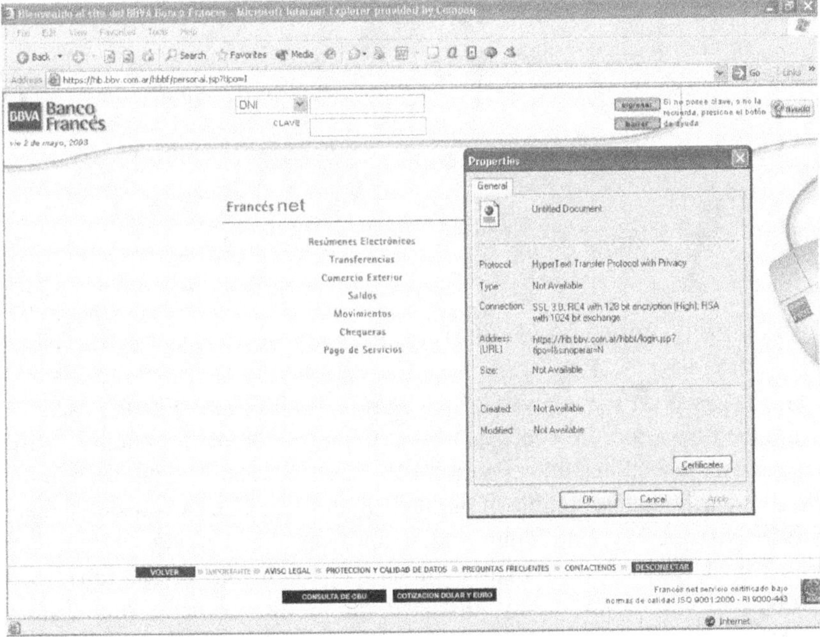

Figure 44 – Banco Bilbao Vizcaya Argentaria (Argentina Branch) site supported 128-bit encryption although the tooltip over padlock is not visible. However, as the site property page indicates in the Connection part, this site is secured using SSL 3.0 RC4 algorithm with 128-bit encryption

However, in some online banking systems, web administrators disabled access to property pages. To overcome this problem, the Netcraft SSL web server analyser was employed. This software offers a reliable test of web server capabilities in regard to supported strength of encryption. In particular, the results of the query engine contain information about cipher suits supported by the web server. If a given site supported RC4 and RC2 ciphers in the non-restricted versions as well as Triple DES and IDEA ciphers, then it was assumed that this site supported 128-bit encryption.

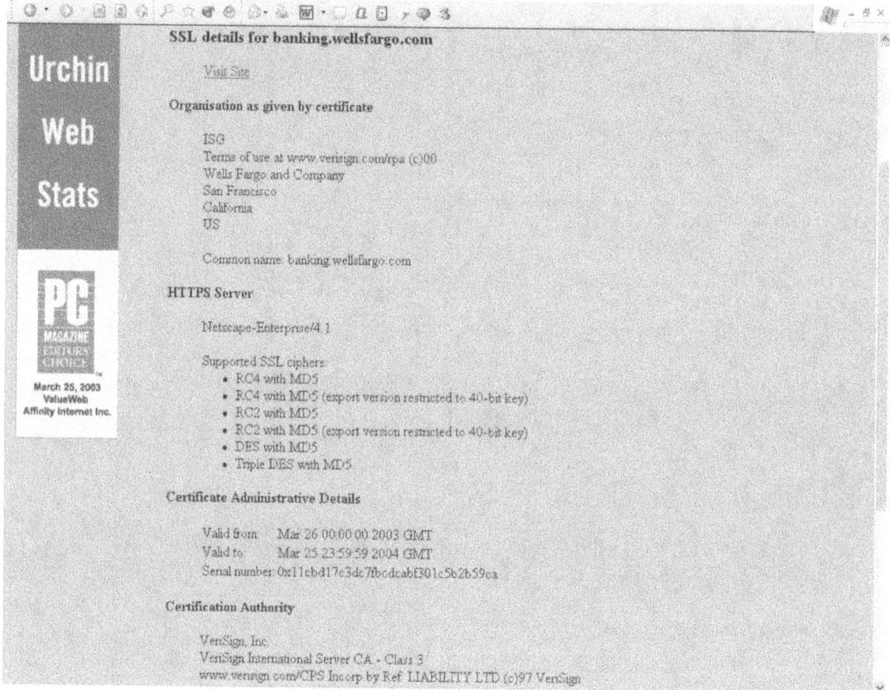

Figure 45 – The result of query of Wells Fargo Bank web server using Netcraft software

As a result, based on the analysis of the sample of 100 online banks using both manual unobtrusive tool-tip check as well as the semi-automatic Netcraft software test, it was established that all supported 128-bit encryption. Having such uniform results in a representative sample of online banking sites one can conclude that the support for strong encryption is universal in the electronic banking community and could legitimately be expected of all the Internet participants. In consequence, one can firmly state that the customary norm stating: ‘All Internet banks should support strong encryption of transactions’ has emerged.

(c) Literature review test

It is natural to search for support for widespread adoption of strong cryptography in technical rather than legal literature.[1214] Technical literature clearly indicates the widespread adoption of SSL protocol developed in 1994 by Netscape. As Burnett and Paine noted:

> 'SSL is by far the most widely distributed security protocol when it comes to e-commerce. One reason for SSL's widespread use is that it is incorporated in every copy of Netscape and Internet Explorer available today. SSL is also found within the operating system of various platforms.'[1215]

However, these comments remain silent about the strength of SSL encryption keys in use nowadays.

Schneier suggested in 1996 that the choice of a key length is dependant upon the situation. He suggested answering three questions:

> 'How much is your data worth? How long does it need to be secure? What are your adversaries' resources?'[1216]

Taking into account that banking and financial services are in possession of data worth billions of dollars that need to remain secure for a long time and adversaries' resources remain unknown, it is not surprising that it is expected that these institutions will provide the highest security possible. This principle has been reiterated by the Basel Committee on Banking Supervision, which argued:

> 'All confidential bank data are maintained in a secure manner and protected from unauthorised viewing or modification during transmission over public, private or international networks.'[1217]

However, the Basel Committee report does not mention the current state of the art with respect to key lengths. Schneier suggested relative usage of key lengths; the longest symmetric key discussed was the 128-bit long key.[1218]

1214 The legal work that came close to this topic was work by Koops that surveyed various cryptography related laws. See especially Chapter 5 of his book. Koops, B.-J. (1999), *The crypto controversy: a key conflict in the information society*. For updated information see Koops, B.-J. (October 2002), *Crypto Law Survey*; van der Hoff, S. (5 July 2002), *Digital Signature Law Survey*.

1215 Burnett, S. and Paine, S. (2001), *RSA Security's Official Guide to Cryptography*, p. 242.

1216 Schneier, B. (1996), *Applied cryptography: protocols, algorithms, and source code in C*, pp. 165-167.

1217 See Principle 10 in

1218 Schneier, B. (1996), *Applied cryptography: protocols, algorithms, and source code in C*, pp. 165-167.

On the other hand, surveys conducted by Netcraft provide very useful information about current trends in the utilisation of strong encryption in general. In the March 2002 Survey already cited Netcraft found that:

> 'Internet-wide, around 18% of SSL Servers use potentially vulnerable key lengths. However, these tend to be concentrated in geographical areas outside the United States and its close trading partners. In the U.S., where over 60% of SSL sites are situated, and Canada only around 15% of sites are using short keys. In most European countries over 25% are still using short keys, and in France, which had laws restricting the use of cryptography until relatively recently, over 40% of sites are using short keys.'[1219]

This survey clearly shows that from the global perspective in March 2002, 82 per cent of web servers worldwide were supporting 128-bit encryption or higher.

In the April 2002 survey Netcraft stated:

> 'Looking at data collected since the SSL survey first started in 1996 serves to illustrate the progress being made in eliminating servers that do not support strong encryption. Not only has the percentage of servers internet-wide offering exclusively weak ciphers fallen from around 40% in December 1997, to below 6% in the April 2002 survey, but also in absolute numbers from 25,000 a year ago, to 9,595 now.'[1220]

The figure below also provides very clear indication of the development of a customary norm in question over time. Similar graphs could be of enormous value to adjudicators resolving Internet-related disputes.

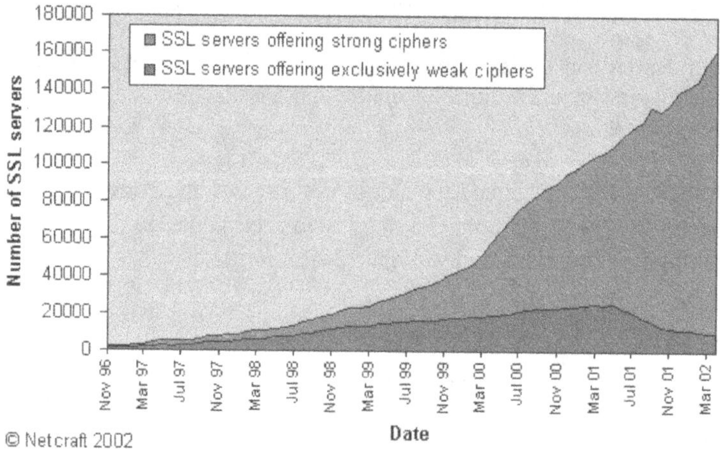

Figure 46 – SSL Servers over time. Source: Netcraft April 2002 Web Survey available at <http://www.netcraft.com.>

[1219] Netcraft (2002), *The March 2002 Netcraft Web Server Survey.*

[1220] Netcraft (2002), *The April 2002 Netcraft Web Server Survey.*

From this graph one can infer that probably the same or higher percentage of web servers used a high level of encryption in the banking environment as it is logical to expect a higher level of awareness in the financial industry. It is important to realise, however, that these figures may vary locally and one can expect higher percentage of non-use of strong encryption in, e.g., France or Taiwan.[1221]

Nevertheless, the data provided by Netcraft clearly proves a very widespread adherence to strong encryption practice both in space and time. The space aspect is clearly indicated by the fact that around 150,000 web servers offer strong ciphers. The time aspect is clearly indicated by the fact that in April 2002 94 per cent level of web servers provided support for strong encryption. Furthermore, the curve clearly indicates a consistent adherence to a given practice over the last 5 years. A strong growth tendency exhibited by the curve further reinforces the argument about very widespread character of this practice.

In summary, although the literature does not speak about the encryption strength of online banking transactions, it is clear that strong encryption is potentially enabled by the majority of web servers on the Net. Taking into account the specific nature of the financial industry, one can expect an adherence to a given practice by all the online banks, thus reinforcing earlier findings.

(d) Case summary

The first empirical test, based on the analysis of the sample of the web design products turned out to be of little help in the context of establishing encryption of online banking transactions because such capabilities are usually not provided by such software. However, this test has confirmed that SSL is the most widely used Web encryption technology as it is implemented by all major web servers and web browsers. SSL though, can use encryption keys of various lengths and for this reason, a practice examination test had to be carried out. The second empirical test established that the practice of securing transaction using 128-bit keys is customary in the online banking industry based on the analysis of 100 online banks randomly selected from around the world. Also, a very promising automatic method of polling web servers and analysis of the underlying Secure Sockets Layer handshake protocol using software similar to that of Netcraft was described. Finally, the literature test also confirmed that the practice of providing secure connection using 128-bit encryption is common nowadays in the security industry. In summary, it can be concluded that the existence of the following customary norm has been proven: 'All Internet banks should support strong encryption of transactions.' This norm could then be used to solve the dispute outlined in the hypothetical case study in favour of the purchaser.

In future, it would be interesting to see how the practice of supporting 128-bit encryption by online banks will change over time, given the new developments in

[1221] Ibid. See also Chapter VI.

the IT industry. Having more resources available, larger sample sizes could be used as the Internet offers the potential for tracking encryption practice of all the online banks. Moreover, similar studies could be performed in other industries including the whole financial industry, insurance industry, medical industry as it is expected that such practices are also very common there. It would be especially interesting to see if such customary practices apply to the retail and wholesale Internet industries. Such studies would also give better insight into which countries still lag behind in the adoption of the Internet. This research has shown that e-banking is not widely available yet as Africa and Asia in general lag behind Internet developments and online banking is slowly being implemented there, thus reinforcing the argument about existence of the digital divide.

The same approach could be taken to analyse the customary practice of securing transmission of the session key using the asymmetric key encryption (both public and private keys are typically of 1024-bits long).[1222] Furthermore, similar analysis could prove that not only banking transactions but also all web-based transactions are secured using 128-bit encryption. In addition, it would be interesting to learn if the custom of actually enforcing the use of 128-bit encryption by banks or online businesses has emerged, leading to the denial of service if the client's web browser did not support a strong encryption. This practice is especially important, given the popularity of 'weak' web browsers. In a similar vein, it would be interesting to see if there is a custom of requiring client-side certificates in order to transact online.

8. Conclusion

The concept of customary practices is not currently used in solving legal disputes in either the offline or online world. The main reason for this is that it is very difficult to establish custom. This part of the book discussed potential methods that could be employed in ascertaining customary practices on the Internet. These methods could be used to examine web content, traffic, and infrastructure. They could also be used to survey human participants and examine software tools.

This chapter proposed a methodology for evidencing such practices taking into account unique features of the Internet, especially its potential for automation of data gathering. A three-step methodology was proposed. The first, to research software that is used to build websites as very often certain capabilities of websites are automatically included by such software. Establishment of this capability among a representative sample of web design software could prove that such functionality is a common practice in Internet commerce. Secondly, to investigate manually or automatically a representative sample of websites to test the capability of a given site.

[1222] Schneier suggested for 128-bit private key, equivalent of 2304-bits for the public key. The criterion for this suggestion was similar resistance to brute force attacks. See Schneier, B. (1996), *Applied cryptography: protocols, algorithms, and source code in C*, pp. 165-166.

Automatic test is especially useful when it comes to the examination of the underlying protocol messages. This, however, does not apply to the analysis of HTML language because of its unstructured nature. In all other cases, manual analysis of website content will be necessary. Very valuable information can be found in server logs, but outside access to it is not possible. The final step of the methodology is related to the analysis of legal and technical literature dealing with a given practice. Legal literature may already contain some commentaries on interpretation of a given practice in statutory or case law. Technical literature may provide better insights as far as industry adoption of a given practice or technical functioning of a given piece of software is concerned. However, the literature test should only be used to confirm the results of the empirical tests, and should never be used as the only means of proving the existence of the customary norm in question.

In order to prove alleged e-customs the above methodology was applied using both probability and non-probability sampling techniques. Non-probability sampling was used to evidence transaction confirmation practice. Convenience sampling was applied both to e-commerce development tools test as well as the practice examination test. The choice of a very small sample size was dictated by the fact that first test has already established a wide range of potential e-commerce sites that would use order confirmation. For this reason, only a very small, conveniently selected sample of actual sites employing this practice was deployed. On the other hand, the transaction confirmation development tools test could not be used to establish the existence of such practice. For this reason, the probability sampling technique was used to select a larger sample of online banking sites. In both cases, the samples were stratified to reflect diversity of the population as much as possible.

The results of the tests clearly indicated the existence of two customary norms in global electronic commerce. The first one states that: 'All web-based transactions should be electronically confirmed immediately after the placement of an order'. The second one states that: 'All Internet banks should support strong encryption of transactions'. In the course of the analysis, other potential customary norms were identified, including the norm requiring the online seller to summarise the transaction prior to the acceptance of an order and the norm requiring the use of 1024-bits public and private keys in the exchange of the session key in the SSL protocol. More elaborate proof of the above norms, as well as others not mentioned in this work, will be presented elsewhere.

It is important to stress that various new methods for proving customary practices need to be developed. The application of the above framework will be dependant upon the practice in question. In time, unobtrusive research of practices may prove to be insufficient to establish custom. It may be necessary to actually visit companies that create websites in order to obtain more valuable information. Similarly, traditional surveys may have to be used to obtain data about the feelings of users and developers in regard to the practice in question. This, however, needs to be further researched and remains outside the scope of this study.

Part IV
TOWARDS SUPRANATIONAL INTERNET LAW

Chapter IX
POTENTIAL INTERNET CUSTOMS

As has been demonstrated in the preceding chapters, there exist trade usages, especially in the field of online contracting and online security, which could be utilised to fill in gaps in national and international regulation of electronic commerce. Obviously, there are numerous practices that have emerged in the online world, which could be regarded as Internet customs.[1223]

The aim of this chapter is to present several potential customs developed by the Internet community. This part of the book does not intend to be an exhaustive or formal treatment of customary norms of the Net. Firstly, there are certainly more customary practices than will be covered here. Secondly, although it is relatively easy to identify the most important principles of the Internet law, it is not so easy to delineate their scope.

It is also important to stress that the norms presented below should not be treated as proven customary principles and therefore one should not yet attach to these norms a legally binding force. Instead, the following list should be rather treated as a proposal that has to be verified by future research. In other words, the aim of this part of the book is to signal the emergence of potential customary norms in global Internet-based commerce.

1. Introduction

The process of 'uncovery' of Internet customs remains one of the essential tasks in the search for a global Internet law. As Trotter Hardy rightly predicted in 1994:

> 'Customs are developing in cyberspace as they might in any community, and rapid growth in computer communications suggests that there may be a great many such customs before long.'[1224]

The objective of this chapter is to identify some of the most important Internet common practices and therefore to show how many potential Internet customs have

[1223] This chapter is based on two of my articles: Polanski, P.P. (6-8 June 2005), *Common practices in the electronic commerce and their legal significance*; Polanski, P.P. (2005), *Information Society and the Internet Law Merchant*.

[1224] Hardy, I.T. (Summer 1994), *The Proper Legal Regime For Cyberspace*, p. 1010.

developed.[1225] No such list of potential customs – akin to Justice Mustill's list presented earlier[1226] – has been offered yet. Although some customary practices have been identified in the previous chapter,[1227] most Internet practices have not yet been described.

Internet customs can be categorised based on whether they exist in the offline world (universal legal customs) or not (Internet-specific customs). In the former category one could mention principles such as *pacta sunt servanda,* which is the basis of both traditional and online commerce. Both of these general principles apply to the Internet and electronic commerce. However, universal legal customs, because of their generic nature, will not be discussed below.

There are, however, numerous Internet-specific customs or that are particularly important in electronic commerce. This chapter will focus on the following Internet-specific customs:

1. Freedom of linking without authorisation.
2. Right to copy certain online materials without permission.
3. Freedom of registration of a domain name based on the first-in first-served principle.
4. Right to explore user's behaviour.
5. Obligation of an online business to support non-trivial username and password authentication.
6. Obligation of an online business to support strong encryption of all web-based transactions.
7. Obligation of an online business to deny a service if client's web browser does not support strong encryption.
8. Obligation of an online business to automatically sign the user out if a web browser is not used for some time (timeout).
9. Obligation of an online bank to use valid digital certificates issued by trusted authorities.
10. Obligation of an online business to display steps that follow to conclude an electronic contract.
11. Obligation of an online business to provide a means of identifying and correcting input errors.

[1225] See Perritt, H.H., Jr. (1999-2000), *The Internet is changing the public international legal system*, pp. 898-899, who argues that 'one of the difficulties with customary international law always has been the difficulty in determining its content.'

[1226] See Chapter V.

[1227] Polanski, P.P. (July 2003), *Custom as a Source of Supranational Internet Commerce Law (PhD Thesis)*; Polanski, P.P. (2002), *A New Approach to Regulating Internet Commerce: Custom as a Source of Electronic Commerce Law*; Polanski, P.P. and Johnston, R.B. (7-10 January 2002), *International Custom as a Source of Law in Global Electronic Commerce*; Polanski, P.P. and Johnston, R.B. (2002), *Potential of Custom in Overcoming Legal Uncertainty in Global Electronic Commerce*.

12. Obligation of an online business to summarise the transaction before accepting payment.
13. Obligation of an online business to confirm an online order instantly and by electronic means.
14. Obligation of an online business to refrain from sending spam.
15. Right of search engines to block spamdexed websites.
16. Obligation of an online business to enable closure of interactive advertising.
17. Right to information.

These practices will be grouped into four categories: online property, online security and online contracting and online advertising. Right to information will be outlined separately. The following subsections will briefly describe these potential customs of the Internet.

2. Online Property

The field of intellectual property has been affected by the Internet to a greater extent than other areas. As has been outlined in Chapter II, this is because the Internet has enabled easy and fast copying of information. This in turn, has led to the proliferation of disputes in this respect.

In this part, four Internet rights and freedoms will be discussed.[1228] These freedoms have a general character, and adherence acceptance of these principles is visible both in the commercial and the non-commercial Internet. Because of their general character, one could actually speak of them as of general principles of Internet law. It is interesting to note that all of these emerging customary rights are connected to the field of intellectual property.

2.1 Freedom of linking without authorisation

One of the major uncertainties surrounding the use of Web resources is whether it is permissible to link to any website without authorisation from the author or website administrator. At this point, one should clearly differentiate between various practices that have been established in this area. Firstly, one should discuss the concept of simple linking or linking to a home page of another Internet user. Secondly, one should investigate the issue of deep linking or linking to web pages other than the home page. Thirdly, it is important to discuss the problem of frames and displaying the deep content of third party website within someone else's frame.

With respect to the problem of simple linking, observation shows that there is a widespread practice of Internet website designers to provide links to any website

---

1228 Three of these norms have been discussed in Polanski, P.P. (2006), *Fundamental Rights in Cyberspace and Internet Customary Law.*

they want, without any agreement or consent of the author of the resource. This seems to be a common practice. This is especially so with respect to search engines, whose job is to index all the resources on the Web and display links to them. However, this may not always be as simple as it sounds. Recently Perfect 10 brought a suit against Google, alleging copyright infringement for the display of photos of their works through Google's images feature, which presents graphical links to other websites.[1229] Nevertheless, considering the history of the development of the Internet and the way search engines have been functioning so far, it is strange to even consider the possibility of requiring permission to link to electronic resources.

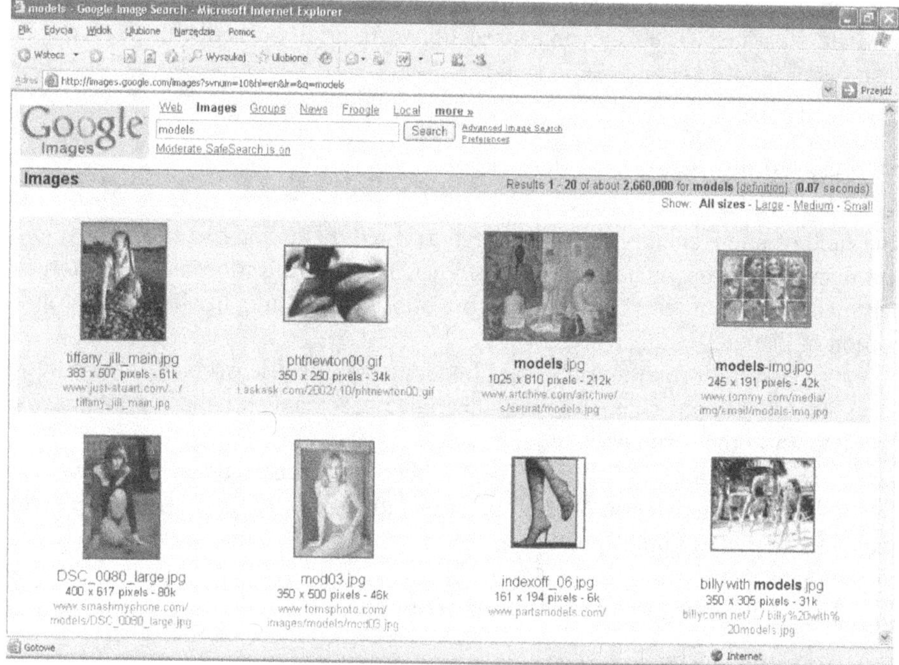

Figure 47 – Google search engine and its image search functionality. Online businesses such as Google would have to cease to operate if there was no freedom of linking to any resource without authorisation

However, there are some companies that demand formal permission to link to their websites, as the story of Chris Raettig demonstrates.[1230] Raettig provided a link to the KPMG website without asking permission, and KPMG sent a letter to Raettig with the following announcement:

[1229] But see Kawamoto, D. (26 August 2005), *Adult-site publisher takes action against Google*. See also AP (23 November 2004), *Adult entertainment site sues Google*; timothy (23 November 2004), *Porn Site Sues Google Over Linked Images*. See also the discussion of a right to copy *below*.

[1230] Manjoo, F. (6 December 2001), *Big Stink Over a Simple Link*.

> 'please be aware such links require that a formal Agreement exist between our two parties, as mandated by our organization's Web Link Policy.'

Raettig replied to this letter:

> 'my own organization's Web link policy requires no such formal agreement. (…) If every hyperlink used on the Web required parties at both sides of the link to enter into a formal agreement, I sincerely doubt that the Web would be in existence today.'[1231]

To further illustrate the deeply embedded feeling of freedom of linking on the Web it is mandatory to point to David Sorkin's 'Don't Link to Us!' website which 'links to sites that attempt to impose substantial restrictions on other sites that link to them.'[1232] The aim of the website is to ridicule the 'stupid linking policies' of many websites including that of law.com, Sonic Foundry, Nikon Precision Inc., The International Trademark Association and numerous others in order to 'encourage some of these sites to move forward into the twentieth century.'[1233]

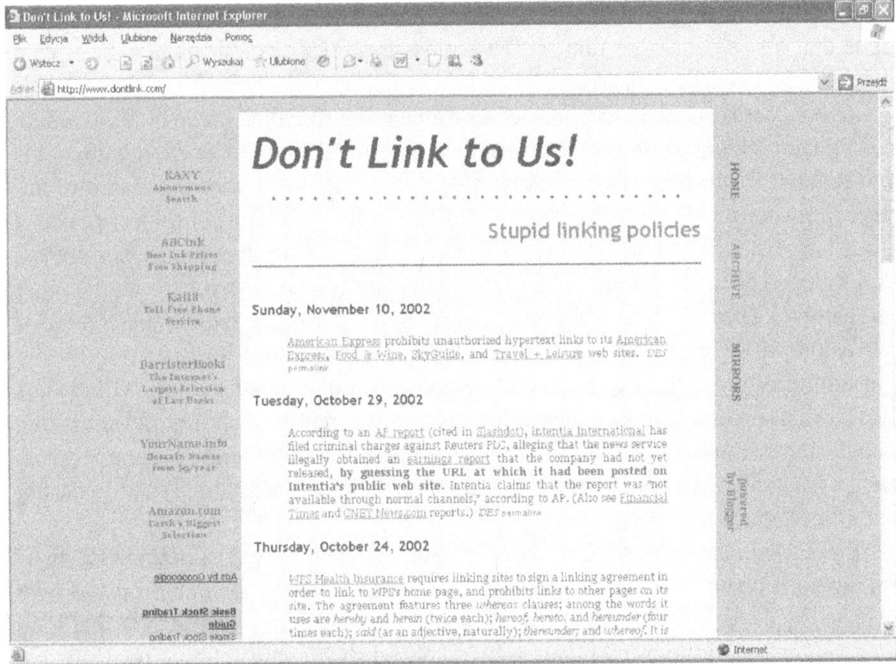

Figure 48 – David Sorkin's website which discusses linking policies

---

[1231] Ibid.

[1232] Sorkin, D.E. (2002), *Don't link to us: Stupid linking policies*.

[1233] Ibid.

It is clear therefore that Internet users feel they have a right to link to any resource they want. And observations seem to confirm that the majority of designers link to resources on the WWW without asking for permission. One can state that this practice is certainly in line with the nature of the medium.

At the same time, however, sites such as those listed on Sorkin's website show that there is opposition against freedom of linking. The debate is especially hot in regards to the second area of our interest – the so-called 'deep linking', or linking to a page other than the front page. Some courts have started to recognise, although prematurely, claims in this regard. For instance, the Danish court prevented Newsbooster from deep linking to the Danish Newspaper Publishers Association's sites.[1234]

However, this practice is in line with the spirit of WWW, which is to allow for a wide dissemination of knowledge through linking. Linking is the essence of the Web, and the essence of the HTML language. One could argue that if someone does not want his or her resource to be linked to, then he or she should consider either securing access to its content or removing it from the Internet. Furthermore, there are technical measures, which automatically take the reader to the home page if he or she visits the deeper content bypassing the home page. Therefore, one could argue that if someone does not use these measures then he or she cannot complain about linking to deep resources.

For many authors, the most problematic area is the so-called 'deep linking' where a webpage of company X may be displayed within a frame or a portion company's Y webpage.[1235] In this case, a linked resource is displayed within a frame of another website, which, in turn, might lead to confusion about who has created a given site. One should stress here, however, that these arguments are not always well founded because the linked resource will usually look different, with the other company's logos, colours, and fonts, which should seriously reduce the chance of confusion. More importantly, it is possible to program a website in such a manner that frames of the calling website will be ignored and a linked website will always display in a separate window. Therefore, it is only a matter of choice and skills of a web designer. Finally, the use of frames is no longer recommended as a good web design practice, and therefore the problem of deep linking is gradually disappearing from the Web.

Another interesting variation of this problem is the question of permissibility of linking to a document for which there is no link publicly available on the host website, by deducing the URL from the sequence of previous URLs. Not that long ago, Reuters linked to a financial report of Swedish Intentia International[1236] that

---

1234 Bowman, L.M. (8 July 2002), *Court: Hands off that hyperlink*.

1235 See for example, the discussion on framing and linking in the context of spamdexing in Nathenson, I.S. (Fall 1998), *Internet Infoglut and Invisible Ink: Spamdexing Search Engines with Meta Tags*, Part II c).

1236 <http://www.intentia.com/w2000.nsf/index>, last accessed: 31/10/2002.

was not 'officially' available on the SII website. Is URL guessing permissible or is it a privacy invasion? Since such incidents happen very rarely, it is difficult to establish what the common practice is. One can however say that if a given resource is published on a publicly accessible webserver, it does not seem unfair to link to any unprotected file.

Finally, one should make it clear that although linking is customarily permitted, it should not be confused with potential liability for content, which is an entirely separate issue. Every author of a website should remain liable for the content he or she disseminates. Therefore, if a link points to a resource which turns out to infringe third party rights or is in contravention of the laws of a given country, only the author of that resource should be held liable. A website operator that includes a link to such a resource shall, as a rule of thumb, be exempted from liability, because they cannot guarantee the content of a resource being linked to. Similar remarks can be made with respect to spamdexing.[1237]

In summary, the practice of linking to a publicly available resource without permission seems to be adhered to by a vast majority of users and hence it seems to be a well established right on the Internet. And there are very strong reasons for defending this basic freedom. However, there are companies that try to enforce their own policies in this respect and demand permission to do this. In order to ascertain whether such a custom exists one has to measure how widespread the practice actually is. Only then will one be able to definitely state, in the absence of any higher written law governing a given case, what a majority of Internet users actually do, and hence, what the prevailing norm on the Internet is.

2.2 Right to copy certain online materials without permission

Unrestricted copying of information enabled by the Internet continues to be one of the most controversial issues in the Information Age. Can one state that it is customary to freely copy information on the Internet? And if yes, does this give the right to freely copy information on the Internet, based on Internet custom? The answers to these fundamental questions involve an in-depth assessment of copying, which can occur both automatically and by human effort. Furthermore, one would have to distinguish between various levels on which electronic copying occurs, i.e., the Internet infrastructure level and the application level. The following discussion will only set the scene for a detailed analysis of this potential customary freedom.

At this stage, one can only make the following remarks. With respect to information exchanges at the Internet infrastructure level, one can clearly state that the very architecture of the Internet is based on the concept of copying information. It is done automatically by computers – not by humans. For instance, in case of the WWW it is the copy of the website that is sent to the requesting browser – not the original. Before it is received by the requesting browser it may also be filed or

---

[1237] See *below.*

cached by a proxy server, in order to speed up future retrieval of the information. As one can see the concept of copying is embedded in the very architecture of the Web and hence one cannot speak of any violations of national copyright laws. To do that would be to question the legality of the Internet itself. Therefore, there exists a right to copy information at the infrastructural level, provided that it is done for the purpose of enabling or making more efficient the transfer of data.

One cannot say the same, however, with respect to the right to copy the electronic content. As opposed to copying at the infrastructural level, which is done by computers rather done human beings, the copying of content is usually done by humans. Furthermore, it usually does not aim at enabling functioning or faster performance of the Internet. As a result, the issues raised by the practices of copying of content, be it text or multimedia files, have different intensities at various Internet application levels. Therefore, the scope of the potential customary freedom of copying content would have to be clearly delineated. The following discussion will be limited to e-mail, www and peer-to-peer networks.

(a) E-mail copying

E-mail is one of the oldest and the most widely used Internet applications. Since conveying electronic messages over the Internet has created a new potential for unauthorised copying, the common practice of doing so has raised legal controversies. As early as 1994, Trotter Hardy described the customary norm of forwarding e-mails without the consent of the original author:

> 'we can look at the well recognized cyberspace custom of copying e-mail messages and forwarding them to others. In real space, this might be a clear copyright violation, but if everyone in cyberspace "does it all the time", and knows that others do it all the time, might not some sort of estoppel or implied waiver of copyright rights arise?'[1238]

The observation shows that e-mail forwarding without authorisation is still a common practice among Internet users and no one considers himself or herself in breach of copyright laws. This practice enables better communication as the addressee knows better what point the sender tries to make. Despite the fact that such practice might be considered illegal in some countries with respect to traditional letters, it is legal in cyberspace. Again, one can see how Internet customary norm changes the traditional legal paradigms.

(b) WWW copying

As opposed to e-mail, website copying without authorisation would in most instances infringe author's copyrights. It has been considered illegal to copy someone's

---

[1238] Hardy, I.T. (Summer 1994), *The Proper Legal Regime For Cyberspace*, p. 1010.

content and present it as one's own (plagiarism), unless the use is partial and done in the context of, say, critical analysis or news reporting. On the other hand, news syndication technologies such as RSS feeds are examples of copying information with the consent of authors, because providers themselves agree to display their information on any webpage capable of handling RSS feeds.

However, there are instances where website content copying without authorial consent has been widely practiced. The most important exception to the general prohibition of content copying without authorisation is the activity of search engines. It goes without saying that web crawlers continue to copy some or all of a website in order to index and classify it. The content of an indexed website would not be fully revealed – only an excerpt of it will be presented to a person searching for information. Most search engines only reveal the content of the so-called 'metatags', which are invisible to a person viewing a website. The metatag 'description' will usually be displayed, together with a link to a resource. But this is not always the case, because some search engines (such as Google) seem to present a different description of content to that found in metatags.

Nevertheless, it seems to be a customary practice to copy a website in order to analyse it as well as to present only a small portion of it to a user without authorisation. To claim otherwise would be to hinder the evolution of the World Wide Web and to ignore widely accepted practice.

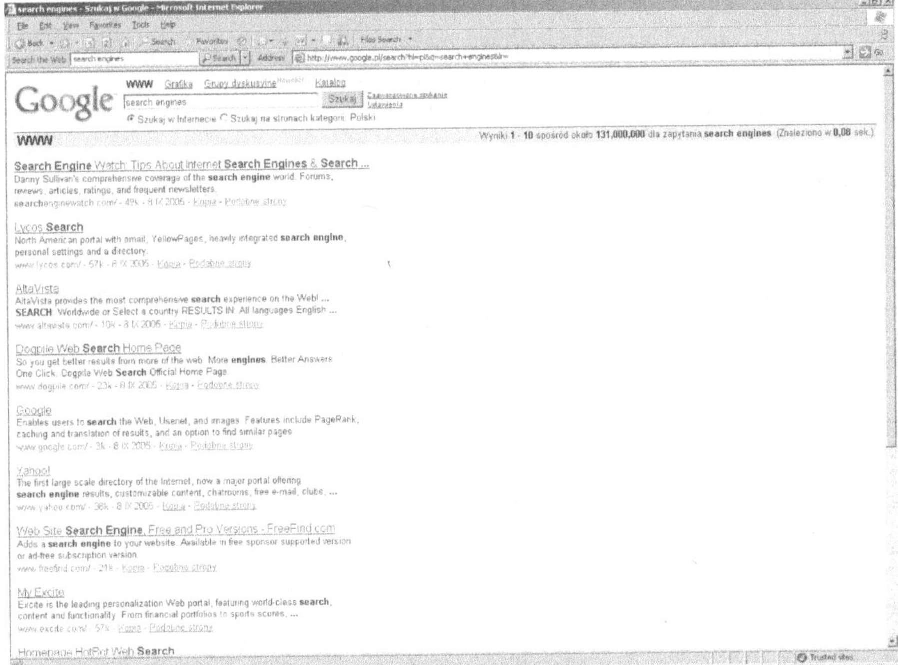

Figure 49 – The Google search engine customarily displays only a small portion of website content

Furthermore, this contention extends to multimedia search engines. Nearly all major search engines, such as Google, AltaVista, Yahoo AskJeeves or DogPile, have provided options to search not only textual information but also pictures, videos, music and so on. It has become a widely accepted practice to display thumbnail images of third party artwork without authorisation, in order to provide visual linking capabilities. Thumbnails are small versions of original images, compressed to the extent that their commercial or even private use is very limited. The aim is to use thumbnails as visual links to the author's original images located on the website of the copyright holder. Search engines usually provide not only explicit links to original resources but also a description of the picture. Therefore, this practice seems to be morally justified, or at least indifferent, provided that images are cut down versions of original artwork used as a link to original resources. As a result, given more extensive proof, it could be argued that there exists a customary right to display thumbnails of third party artwork without authorisation.

However, image search capabilities have created legal challenges as some copyright holders have argued that display of their images has infringed their copyrights. In *Kelly* v. *Arriba Soft Corp*[1239] Arriba used thumbnails in their search engine but displayed a complete picture within the Arriba website and not as a link to the original resource. The American District Court and the appeal court have confirmed that thumbnails were legal on the basis of the doctrine of fair use.[1240] However, the use of thumbnails has been challenged in the recent case brought by Perfect 10 against Google.[1241]

In summary, one can argue that there exists a customary right to copy some or all of a website in order to index it and provide better search capabilities. This does not mean that one can legally copy and paste the whole content of a website. It only means that search engines are customarily entitled to copy content in order to provide better search capabilities. Furthermore, search engines are customarily entitled to copy and display a small portion of an indexed website in order to give informational clues about the website. This seems to extend not only to content of metatags but also to the content of a visible part of a website. Finally, there seems to exist a customary right to display thumbnails in order to provide links to original images. All these exceptions to a general prohibition of copying without consent might be regarded as a fair use.

[1239] *Leslie A. Kelly* v. *Arriba Soft Corp.* [1999] Case No. SA CV 99-560 GLT[JW].

[1240] See the discussion in Quirk, P. and Forder, J. (2003), *Electronic commerce and the law*, pp. 201-202.

[1241] *Perfect 10* v. *Google, Inc.* [2006] Court File No.CV 04-9484 AHM (SHx). See also press releases: Kawamoto, D. (26 August 2005), *Adult-site publisher takes action against Google*. See also AP (23 November 2004), *Adult entertainment site sues Google*; timothy (23 November 2004), *Porn Site Sues Google Over Linked Images*.

(c) P2P copying

However, the most controversial legal issue surrounding copying is associated with the emergence of peer-to-peer networks such as FastTrack, BitTorrent, eDonkey or Gnutella that enable file-sharing between all the users connected to a given network, by means of programs such as Kazaa, Azureus, eMule or LimeWire.[1242] These networks are often regarded as 'the largest international networks of illegality in human history'.[1243] Such networks are accessed *ad hoc*, therefore the number of users varies from time to time. However, the most popular networks can have as many as 3 million users connected at the same time.

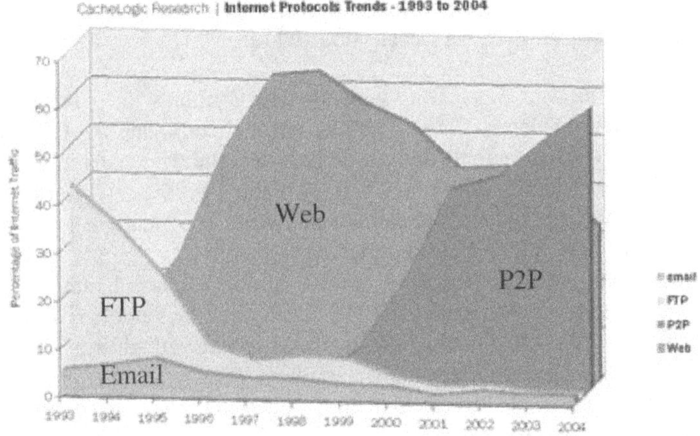

Figure 50 – P2P still represented 60% of Internet Traffic at the end of 2004. Source: Parker Andrew (2006) P2P in 2005[1244]

The peculiar feature of file-sharing systems is that they are used to exchange files directly between users. In consequence, such networks rely on 'computing power and bandwidth of the participants in the network rather than concentrating it in a relatively low number of servers.'[1245] The most popular P2P networks such as BitTorrent or eDonkey still use multiple servers in order to ease the circulation of information about the location of files. The servers however, do not store files, only information where to find them. Furthermore, file sharing networks such as Freenet or Gnutella do not have servers at all and location information as well as files are exchanged directly between users. Nevertheless, in all modern P2P networks, files reside on users' computers, so the exchange takes place between peers.

1242 See Glossary.

1243 Strahilevitz, L.J. (May 2003), *Charismatic Code, Social Norms, and the Emergence of Cooperation on the File-Swapping Networks*, p. 507.

1244 Parker Andrew (2006), *P2P in 2005*, CacheLogic, available at <http://www.cachelogic.com/research/2005_slide07.php>, last visited: 25/02/2005.

1245 Wikipedia (2006), *Peer-to-peer.*

The observation shows that P2P community has developed two customary norms that govern their behaviour with respect to file-sharing: 'the right' to download any file regardless of the potential intellectual property infringement and 'the obligation' to make the content available to other file sharers.[1246] These norms have certainly customary origin but the problem is that they exist in direct conflict with international and national intellectual property law (*consuetude contra legem*). In consequence, to regard these norms as the Internet customary law one would have to analyse how widespread they are in space and time and to address other important issues, in particular, the reasonableness of these practices.

One of the issues that would have to be addressed is how much material that resides in P2P networks violates copyrights. This is important as not all shared materials violate copyright laws, as some are private documents or works no longer protected by local copyrights. As Lessig pointed out:

> 'A. There are some who use sharing networks as substitutes for purchasing content. Thus, when a new Madonna CD is released, rather than buying the CD, these users simply take it. We might quibble about whether everyone who takes it would actually have bought it if sharing didn't make it available for free. Most probably they wouldn't have, but clearly there are some who would. The latter are the target of category A users who download instead of purchasing.
> B. There are some who use sharing networks to sample music before purchasing it. Thus, a friend sends another friend an MP3 of an artist he's not heard of. The other friend then buys CDs by that artist. This is a kind of targeted advertising, quite likely to succeed. If the friend recommending the album gains nothing from a bad recommendation, then one could expect that the recommendations will actually be quite good. The net effect of this sharing could increase the quantity of music purchased.
> C. There are many who use sharing networks to get access to copyrighted content that is no longer sold or that they would not have purchased because the transaction costs off the Net are too high. This use of sharing networks is among the most rewarding for many. Songs that were part of your childhood but have long vanished from the marketplace magically appear again on the network. (One friend told me that when she discovered Napster, she spent a solid weekend "recalling" old songs. She was astonished at the range and mix of content that was available.) For content not sold, this is still technically a violation of copyright, though because the copyright owner is not selling the content anymore, the economic harm is zero – the same harm that occurs when I sell my collection of 1960s 45-rpm records to a local collector.
> D. Finally, there are many who use sharing networks to get access to content that is not copyrighted or that the copyright owner wants to give away.'[1247]

However, the observation shows that such networks are primarily used to exchange copyrighted materials without the authorisation of the owner. In consequence, peer-

[1246] Strahilevitz refers to these norms as mere social norms. See Strahilevitz, L.J. (May 2003), *Charismatic Code, Social Norms, and the Emergence of Cooperation on the File-Swapping Networks*, p. 507.

[1247] Lessig, L. (2004), *Free culture*, pp. 68-69.

to-peer networks are fought on the grounds that they enable piracy and discourage innovation and creation of art. The business of some larger corporations 'has been, not destroyed, but substantially affected – even say afflicted – the ability of people to pirate music, essentially through what is called file sharing between computers.'[1248] In consequence, the battle has moved to courts.

In the already famous judgment *Metro-Goldwyn-Mayer Studios, Inc* v. *Grokster Ltd*[1249] the US Supreme Court found Grokster and StreamCast Networks liable on the grounds that:

> 'one who distributes a device with the object of promoting its use to infringe a copyright, as shown by clear expression or other affirmative steps taken to foster infringement is liable for the resulting acts of infringement by third parties.'

The judgment can be interpreted as reversing the principles of the 1984 Sony Betamax case that legalised the use of video recorders despite protests from the movie industry that it would destroy Hollywood.[1250] One might also argue though, that the development of peer-to-peer software is still legal under US law, provided that it is not distributed with a clear intention to be used to infringe copyrights. Similar rulings have been made in other parts of the world.[1251]

Soon afterwards, however, in *Universal Music Australia* v. *Sharman Licence Holding* the High Court of Australia went even further and forced Kazaa to modify its software in such a way that finding infringing materials would not be possible. The Court ordered that continuation of Kazaa is possible provided:

> '(i): that:
> (a) the software program received by all new users of the Kazaa file-sharing system contains non-optional key word filter technology that excludes from the displayed blue file search results all works identified (by titles, composers' or performers' names or otherwise) in such lists of their copyright works as may be provided, and periodically updated, by any of the applicants; and
> (d) all future versions of the Kazaa file-sharing system contain the said non-optional key word filter technology; and
> (e) maximum pressure is placed on existing users, by the use of dialogue boxes on the Kazaa website, to upgrade their existing Kazaa software program to a new version of the program containing the said non-optional key word filter technology; or

---

[1248] Parsons, R.D. (2005-2006), *An Evening with Richard D. Parsons*, p. 4.

[1249] *Metro-Goldwyn-Mayer Studios, Inc* v. *Grokster Ltd.* [2005] WL 1499402.

[1250] Cooper, M.N. (March 2005), *Time For The Recording Industry To Face The Music: The Political, Social And Economic Benefits Of Peer-To-Peer Communications Networks*, p. 2.

[1251] See the ruling in Kuro.com.tw case in Taiwan, where the management of P2P software Kuro was sentenced to imprisonment and fines for encouraging their subscribers to swap copyrighted music. Also one of the community members was sentenced to imprisonment and a fine. As the author noted: 'The verdict came as a surprise to some observers as Kuro's smaller rival, Ezpeer, was found not guilty of copyright infringement by the Shilin District Court in July.' See Ho, J. (10 September 2005), *Kuro bosses guilty of IPR violations*.

(ii) that the TopSearch component of the Kazaa system will provide, in answer to a request for a work identified in any such list, search results that are limited to licensed works and warnings against copyright infringement and that will exclude provision of a copy of any such identified work.'[1252]

It seems that conformance with the High Court's decision might be very difficult or even impossible. In the first case scenario, the music industry would have to provide a list of materials that are copyrighted and therefore non-viewable. Such a list would have to be modified regularly and take into account various naming conventions used by P2P community. Furthermore, existing users would have to somehow be forced to upgrade their existing versions to the new version. However, there are already 'light' versions of Kazaa freely available that would not conform to this ruling. Furthermore, Internet users still have a plethora of other applications that could be used to download copyrighted materials. Nevertheless, courts around the world began to send a clear message to file-sharing companies to the effect that, from 2005, production and dissemination of P2P software might be a dangerous business.

On the other hand, there is a growing understanding of political, social and economic benefits of peer-to-peer networks.[1253] Given the fact that peer-to-peer networks are not different to video players, CD recorders or photocopiers, have even led some judges to defend the emerging culture. A French judge illustrates this point well:

'We are in the process of creating a cultural rupture between a younger generation that uses the technologies that companies and societies have made available, such as the iPod, file download software, peer-to-peer networks, etc., (...) It's like condemning people for driving too fast after selling them cars that go 250 kmh.'[1254]

The argument about 'creating a cultural rupture between generations' finds some justification in an American survey conducted in January 2001, which found that:

'72 percent [of Internet users] believed that using Internet file-sharing sites, such as Napster, Gnutella and Scour, was either not a copyright violation, or they weren't sure of the legality of the practice.'

A recent report from the Electronic Frontier Foundation titled 'RIAA v. the People: Two years later' shows that despite a campaign of large lawsuits, the recording industry failed to change the behaviour of Internet users:

[1252] *Universal Music Australia Pty Ltd* v. *Sharman License Holdings Ltd* [2005] FCA 1242 (5 September 2005).

[1253] See, for example, Cooper, M.N. (March 2005), *Time For The Recording Industry To Face The Music: The Political, Social And Economic Benefits Of Peer-To-Peer Communications Networks*; Cortell, J. (20 May 2005), *Lecturer censored in Spanish University (UPV) for defending P2P networks*.

[1254] Gain, B. (23 May 2005), *Volez ce MP3!*

> 'The lawsuits, however, are not working. Today downloading from P2P networks is more popular than ever, despite the widespread public awareness of the lawsuits. After two years, one thing has become clear: suing music fans is no answer to the P2P dilemma.'[1255]

It should also be taken into account that some commercial P2P networks such as 'the new' Napster that started to sell legitimate copies of works are not available in most countries.[1256] As a result, buying cheap music or video files over the Internet in developing countries is impossible.

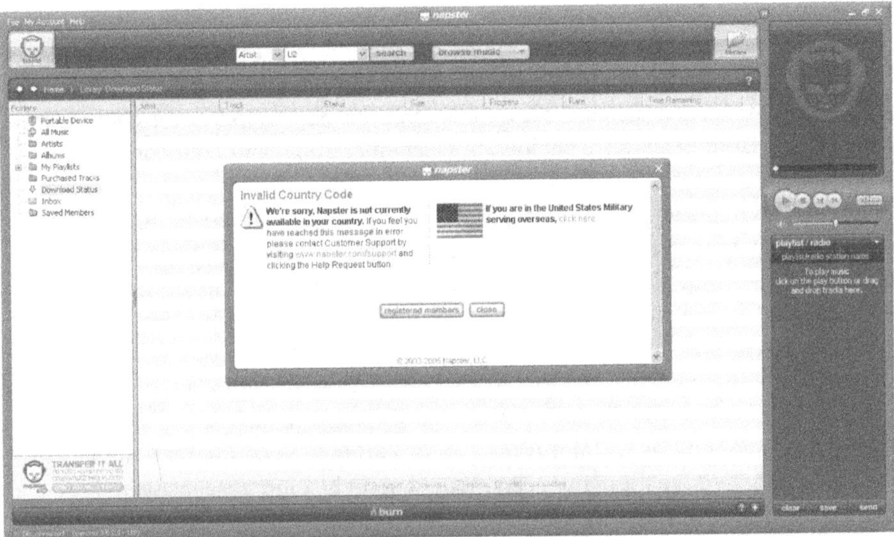

Figure 51 – Napster started a new business model, which permits buying copies of music online. However, the service seems to be directed primarily to American citizens

One of the most interesting questions is therefore whether file-sharing could be defended on the basis that there exists a customary right to download files for private use. Before giving a definite answer, one would have to investigate a number of issues highlighted earlier, which is outside the aim and scope of this book. It should be pointed however, that in December 2005 the lower house of the French Parliament voted to legalise free sharing of files for private use. Under the amendment that is still during the legislative process:

> '(...) authors cannot forbid the reproduction of works that are made on any format from an online communications service when they are intended to be used privately.'[1257]

1255 Electronic Frontiers Foundation (2005), *RIAA* v. *the People: Two Years Later*, p. 2.

1256 Similarly, iTunes is available only in few industralised countries. See Chapter II.

1257 Cited in Viscusi, G. (22 December 2005), *French Parliament Votes to Allow Web File Sharing (Update1)*, Bloomberg.com, available at <http://www.bloomberg.com/apps/news?pid=10000085&sid=avOoTq8aXkU8#>, last visited: 02.01.2006.

In *Société Civile de Producteurs Phonographiques (S.C.P.P.)* v. *Anthony G.*,[1258] Tribunal de Grande Instance de Paris did not find the defendant guilty of file-sharing 1875 files on the grounds that P2P networks enable access to both protected and unprotected works and programs such as Kazaa do not permit to distinguish between them. This case can be contrasted with *BMG Music* v. *Cecilia Gonzalez*[1259] where the US Court of Appeals for the Seventh Circuit rejected defendant's arguments that 1370 songs downloaded using Kazaa was just for sampling music to determine what she liked and therefore constituted a fair use. [1260] Therefore, the Court rejected the argument that file-sharing might actually be considered as a 'kind of advertising', although it did not investigate how many users who downloaded copyrighted materials would have bought it, had they had not access to the free materials on P2P networks. Since the defendant admitted that she never owned 30 of all the downloaded songs the Court ordered her to pay $750 for each downloaded song. Both cases were decided in December 2005, and both courts reached the completely opposite verdicts.

Regardless of the legal standpoint, observation shows that file-sharing is so widespread, and so intensive in terms of number of transactions and in terms of time that it has become common. The controversial question is whether the norm permitting downloading for private use without authorisation and the obligation to make it available to other file-sharers could be regarded as a part of a customary law of the Internet or not. In many jurisdictions a positive answer may sound revolutionary, as it is highly debatable whether custom can abolish existing law (*consuetude contra legem*). But one thing is certain: if the law prohibits file-sharing then the law has been totally ineffective for many years. Would not it be more reasonable to accept a long and widespread practice, which has some merits as a legal right?

Summarising the right to copy, it is argued that the scope of the right of reproduction without authorisation on the Internet is much broader than in the offline world. It is undisputed that there is a widespread practice of copying information on the Internet. This is clearly visible at the infrastructural level as well as at the application level. This allows the formulation of a generalised statement that it is very likely that there exists a customary right to copy information without authorisation at the infrastructural level, as well as, in some instances, on the application level, such as e-mail forwarding or the display of image thumbnails. However, the question of legality of file-sharing for private use is very difficult and requires further research.

[1258] *Société Civile de Producteurs Phonographiques (S.C.P.P.)* v. *Anthony G.* [8 December 2005] Case No. 0504090091.

[1259] *BMG Music* v. *Cecilia Gonzalez* [2005] Court File No. 05-1314 (9 December 2005).

[1260] Ibid., pp. 3-4.

2.3 Freedom of registration of a domain name

Registration of the domain names is not governed by any international convention. It is regulated by the Internet community in various domain name policies and by international domain name arbitrage.[1261] However, the US Government has enacted AntiCybersquatting Consumer Protection Act 1999 (US)[1262] to provide a parallel means of court-based dispute resolution in this area.

It is argued that one of the most fundamental principles of the domain name registration is a customary norm according to which a given domain name is registered to an applicant on a first-come first-served principle for a fee and for a limited period of time. Registration practice is that it is usually free from any formal checks as to the potential conflict of the domain name with, for example, locally registered trademarks. This makes the registration very quick and informal. As of 2003 the informal procedure was used in many countries, including the United States, the United Kingdom, Switzerland, Denmark, Austria, Belgium[1263] and Poland.

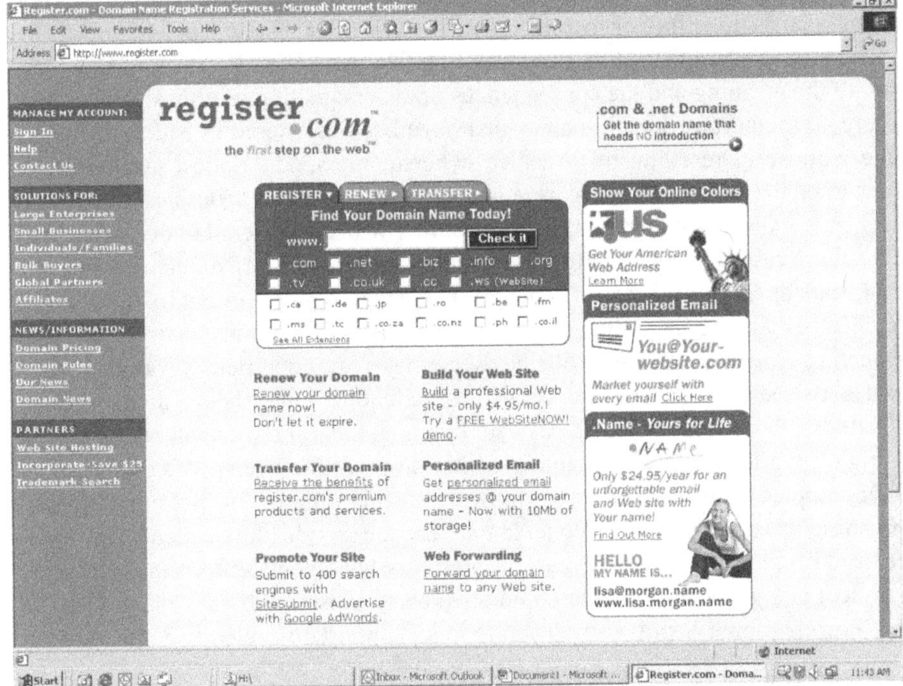

Figure 52 – Register.com, like any other domain name seller, registers domain names on a first-in first-served principle

1261 But see the discussion on the role of ICANN and WIPO in Chapter IV.
1262 See especially section 1125(d) in Chapter 22. Trademarks of 15 USC.
1263 See, for example, Quirk, P. and Forder, J. (2003), *Electronic commerce and the law*, p. 226.

However, there is also a more restricted registration approach, particularly on ccTLD level, although it does not seem to alter the nature of the first-in first-served principle. It can take many forms. In countries such as Bolivia a private person cannot register a domain name, whereas in Brazil, the owner of the domain is required to be a citizen or resident of the country.[1264] Many countries require a local business presence or a local trade mark. Such restrictions exist in Australia, Sweden, Finland, the Netherlands, Germany, France, Portugal, Greece, Italy, Spain and Luxembourg.[1265] However, many countries such as Australia have since relaxed their registration procedures,[1266] therefore it remains to be established which countries follow which model. On the other hand, the new European domain .eu was launched in two phases: the Sunrise period, during which only the holders of certain 'prior rights' were allowed to register their names; and the Land Rush period, where registrations would be open to everyone on a first-in, first-served basis.[1267] Furthermore, with generic top-level domains such as .edu one can expect more stringent requirements to be fulfilled by an applicant. Finally, one would also have to investigate policies and practices that have emerged in the new generic top-level domains such as .biz, .info or .name.

Another aspect of freedom of registration that has to be researched is the question of the meaning and the consequences of cybersquatting or offensive domains. There are numerous domain names that have been registered in bad faith for the sole purpose of reselling by so-called cybersquatters. The hottest disputes have concerned the validity of registering names of famous people, businesses or products, especially when there was a clear conflict with a registered trademark. However, these cases are not as simple as they may sound because a domain name and a trademark are entirely different concepts. In the majority of Western legal traditions intellectual property rights have to be expressly provided for in a national law (the *numerous clausus* principle). With the exception of few countries such as the United States, no such rights have been created for defending interests in a domain name. Therefore, there seems to be no basis for claiming the right to something that is not 'a right' in a legal sense. It is thus essential to present evidence of countries that have adopted some regulatory framework in this regard. Furthermore, 'cybersquatting' is unclear, as is its scope. In one recent example, the Scotland Law Society paid £10,000 to an alleged cybersquatter for the lawscot.co.uk domain.[1268] Clearly Lawscot is a generic name that could have been registered by anyone wishing to run a service about Scottish law. Therefore, it is important to clearly delineate what

---

[1264] See, for example, BNA Int'l Bus. & Fin. Daily (5 July 2005), *U.S. States Internet Principles: No Change For ICANN, No Support for New Global Body.*

[1265] Quirk, P. and Forder, J. (2003), *Electronic commerce and the law*, p. 226.

[1266] Ibid., p. 227.

[1267] The Land Rush period will start on 7 April 2006. See EURid website at <http://www.eurid.edu/en/registrant/>, last visited: 07/12/2005.

[1268] McCarthy, K. (13 June 2003), *Law Society of Scotland pays £10K to 'cybersquatter' for domain.*

constitutes cybersquatting by research of the relevant decisions of domain name arbitrage and the relevant case law. Finally, there are many examples of registering offensive domain names that contain vulgar or controversial words, often in conjunction with a globally recognised brand. Domain names such as airfrancesucks.com may clearly affect the perception of well-known brands.[1269] At this stage, it is unclear whether such practices have been widely recognised by domain name arbitration as exceptions to the general freedom of registration.[1270]

In summary, freedom of registration of domain name can be argued to constitute a customary principle of the Internet, having a global scope. However, there are different aspects to this freedom, such as informal and formal registration procedures and policies for gTLDs, as well as exceptions to this freedom caused by activities such as cybersquatting or the use of offensive names. Therefore, more research is required in order to ascertain the scope of this freedom.

2.4 **Right to explore user's behaviour**

It is also a global practice of website operators to employ cookies or web beacons for the purpose of tracking user behaviour or storing important personal data to personalise a website. The whole online advertising industry relies on the legal permissibility of this practice. Cookies are small text files that are sent by the web server to the requesting web browser and are stored there, unless a user turns the cookie acceptance option off. Web beacons are transparent image files, used to collect information about visits to a website. Cookies and web beacons give a website operator the ability to record certain information about a user, and continue to do this over time.

This practice has raised various privacy concerns. It may be considered a trespass of the user's electronic domain. But again, the practice seems to be in line with the spirit of the medium. The Internet is so powerful because it enables customisation of websites according to the preferences of the user.[1271] Cookies are also used to store some sensitive information, such as the name of the user. This information is used for various purposes, such as enabling faster login to a given website. Some companies use cookies to track user buying habits, observe how much time is spent on a given website, which other sites are visited, and so on. This enables such companies to create a profile of the user, which in turn enables them to better target advertisements.

Cookies are accepted by all browsers currently available on the market. The user has the ability to turn cookies off, which will not affect their use of this technology, and which means that their behaviour will not be tracked. But it also means that

---

[1269] WIPO Arbitration and Mediation Centre (24 May 2005), *Societe Air France* v. *Virtual Dates, Inc. Case No. D2005-0168.*

[1270] WIPO (2005), *WIPO Overview of WIPO Panel Views on Selected UDRP Questions*.

[1271] See, for example, Rayport, J.F. and Jaworski, B.J. (2002), *Introduction to e-Commerce*, p. 212.

some potential benefits, such as website customisation, will be lost. This aspect is an important counterpart of the freedom of using cookies. Internet users have the right to expect that all the browser manufacturers will continue to provide them in the future the capability to turn off the use of cookies. Finally, one should mention new technologies that are emerging to replace cookies.[1272]

Cookies, web beacons and other means of observation of customers' behaviour are closely associated with Internet security, as discussed below.

3. Online Security

The security of transactions is one of the most important areas of concern for both businesses and customers alike. However, because of the highly technical nature of the field there are virtually no national or international laws that deal with this matter. Even laws on electronic signatures tend to be highly general, partly because of the widely accepted principle of technological neutrality, which precludes the technological lock-in by law.

One observes a proliferation of numerous interesting security practices in this area. Many of these practices have been developed in the banking industry, which was one of the earliest adopters of electronic technologies. For instance, it is customary these days to expect username and password forms in order to authenticate access to a system. As Figure 53 below indicates, there are some banks which even require client-side certificates to authenticate a user. Although such practice allows for unique identification and reduces the risk of transaction repudiation,[1273] it is not widely followed because it forces a bank to demand certificates from every single client, which is burdensome, considering that client authentication is optional in SSL-based transactions.

Some of these practices are widely followed, others continue to gain popularity. In case of a dispute, the reliance on commonly accepted standards may turn out to be decisive. The field of online security is clearly governed by established technical practices and standards, which ought to be known and followed by all Internet merchants. Some of these practices will, sooner or later, probably become the provisions of relevant statutes.

It is important though to remember that there are numerous e-banking practices that cannot be established by web research. This is so because many of these practices are internal and range from appropriate board and management oversight, through implementation of appropriate security controls to legal and reputational

---

[1272] See, for example, Microsoft technology embedded in 2002 Commerce Server that relies on the appending information about user to the URL in order to create 'cookieless' state management, see Rosoff, M. (18 February 2002), *Commerce Server 2002 Showcases .NET*.

[1273] Basel Committee on Banking Supervision (July 2003), *Risk Management Principles for Electronic Banking*, p. 15.

Figure 53 – Some banks require client-side authentication for e-banking

risk management.[1274] Some of these internal practices are so important that one might argue the whole security of modern banking rests on them. For instance, one cannot overemphasise the importance of proper backup procedures, without which a bank might lose evidence of invaluable data. It is precisely the lack of backup procedures, as well as reliance on physical transport of magnetic tapes, rather than online transfer of data, that led Citibank's Singapore branch to a loss of data of more than 120,000 customers in March 2004.[1275] It is astounding to learn to what extent major banks might be ignoring trade usages of e-banking in the twenty-first century.

It is important therefore to show which security practices, framed as obligations, have already become or have the potential to become a supranational Internet customary law:

3.1 Obligation of an online business to support non-trivial username and password authentication

It is trivial to speak about username and password-based authentication methods on the Web. One finds them virtually everywhere. Login forms stop intrusion of our

---

1274 For more on this see the two reports by Basel Committee on Banking Supervision: Basel Committee on Banking Supervision (July 2003), *Management and Supervision of Cross-Border Electronic Banking Activities*; Basel Committee on Banking Supervision (July 2003), *Risk Management Principles for Electronic Banking*.

1275 BNA Int'l Bus. & Fin. Daily (22 March 2004), *Citibank Japan Tape Holding Account Data On 230,000 Customers Is Lost in Singapore*.

access to e-banking facilities, web-based e-mails, VoIP accounts, game accounts, online shopping client information and so on. It is a customary obligation of an online business to provide such forms and make sure that they are properly safeguarded.

Online businesses implement this simple principle differently. There are businesses that accept username and passwords of any length and complexity. However, there are many online businesses which require passwords to be not shorter than a certain length (usually six symbols) in order to better secure access to resources. Other practices involve the rejection of passwords that are identical to personal data (e.g., contain a username). It is often required to use a combination of letters and numbers in order to make the password harder to crack. Furthermore, it is also common for online merchants to request periodical changes of passwords, which is easily implemented in modern computer networks. In addition, there are online businesses, particular in the online financial sector that requires additional safeguards such as codewords or one-off numbers in order to log in to a system. Finally, some financial institutions require a company number and password as well as username and password.[1276] It remains to be researched which of these practices are dominant.

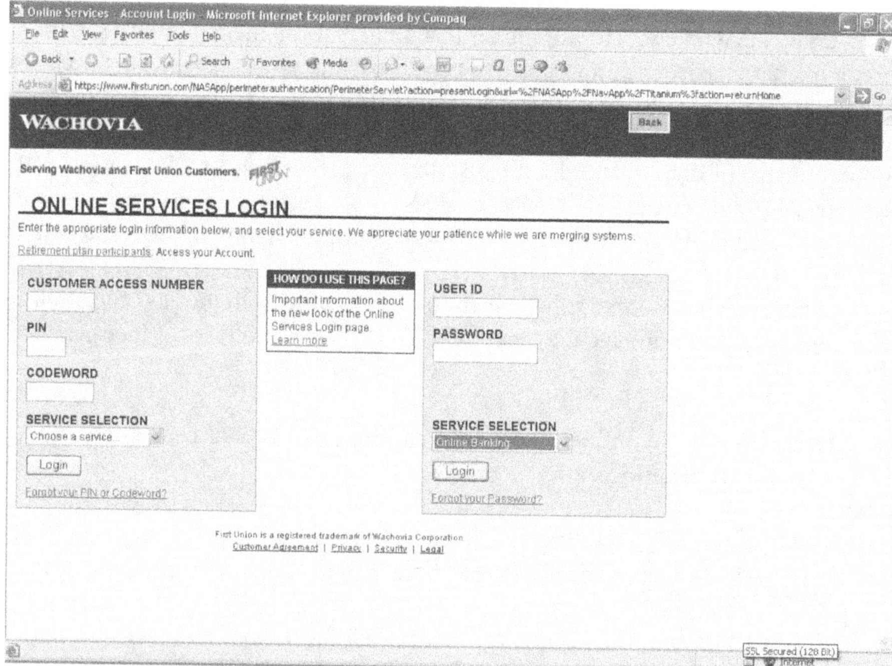

Figure 54 – Wachovia bank requires username and password for online banking but for other financial services one has to provide a codeword as well. Last accessed: 23/04/2003

[1276] See, for example, <http://powerpay100.ceridian.com/default.asp?banner=chase>, last accessed: 23/04/2003.

In addition, obligation of secure authentication implies that an online account should be suspended if a user fails to log in after a certain number of attempts (customarily three times.) Another aspect of obligation of non-trivial authentication is the customary obligation to provide a means for password recovery. This is usually done by means of asking a secret question together with a valid e-mail address.

Therefore it is customary these days not only to have access to one's resources secured by means of username and password but to also have it appropriately safeguarded by the enforcement of passwords of a certain length, which use a combination of letters and numbers and non-trivial words as well as by suspension and password recovery policy. This customary norm is a very detailed and multiform one, which supplements existing legislation and contracts. Failure to adhere to this norm may thus entitle a customer to damages. Finally, one should stress that this customary norm overlaps with customary obligation to provide strong encryption of all exchanges of sensitive data, as discussed below.

3.2 Obligation of an online business to support strong encryption of all exchanges of sensitive information

As explained earlier, the architecture of applications running on the top of the Internet infrastructure such as the World Wide Web or e-mail is based on the exchange of plain-text information. Since confidentiality is essential for online payments or for the sending of other sensitive information, special encryption techniques were developed to disguise the content of messages. One such technique is the universally used Secure Sockets Layer (SSL) protocol, which comes with different key lengths.[1277] As RSA Security experts put it:

> 'Most or all web-based online purchases and monetary transactions are now secured by SSL. When you submit your credit card to purchase a compact disk from CDNOW, for example, the order form information is sent through this secure tunnel so that only the folks at CDNOW can view it.'[1278]

As was shown in the case study of online banks, it is a universal custom in the banking industry to provide strong 128-bit encryption of transactions. This is in line with the common expectation that banks should provide a high security of transactions.

However, the question is whether this practice extends to typical online businesses such as electronic shops or portals. This is important because these businesses also accept credit card payments, process personal information or provide access to free e-mail. Observation shows that this is the case. It is clear from observation of Web commerce, as well as the above quotation, that transactions involving the use of online payments are secured using strong SSL encryption.

1277 See discussion in the hypothetical case studies.

1278 See, for example, RSA Security, *SSL Basics for Internet Users*.

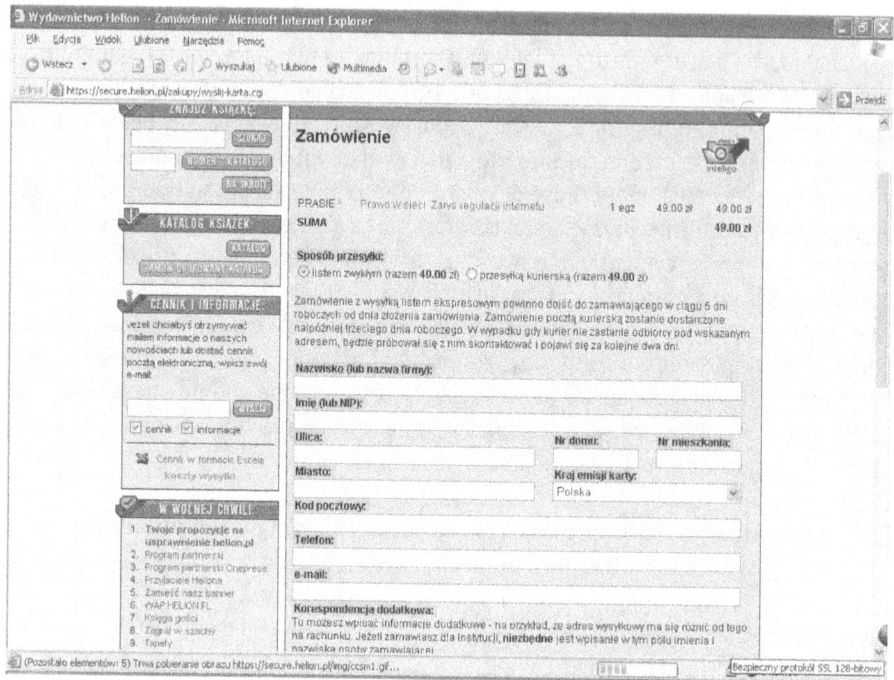

Figure 55 – SSL-based encryption of a transaction in the Polish Helion online bookstore

The term 'transaction' in this context is treated broadly and extends not only to payment transactions but also to any exchanges involving the flow of sensitive information. The encryption practice extends not only to actual purchases but also to other activities where privacy is at risk, such as the exchange of sensitive information while registering online. Submission of such information for server processing is commonly done with the help of strong encryption.

Furthermore, one should also clearly state that strong encryption in SSL also involves the transfer of private keys during the shake-in phase, which is encrypted with a 1024-bit key. However, there are still banks and online entrepreneurs that use shorter keys for the initial exchange of a symmetric key.

Another important aspect of this principle is the duration of encryption. Experience shows that majority of online banks provide encrypted sessions for the whole duration of transaction. This is also in line with 'Risk Management Principles for Electronic Banking' issued by the Basel Committee on Banking Supervision, which provides the following advice:

> 'Authenticated e-banking sessions remain secure throughout the full duration of the session or in the event of a security lapse the session should require re-authentication.'[1279]

[1279] Basel Committee on Banking Supervision (July 2003), *Risk Management Principles for Electronic Banking*, p. 14.

If research shows that this practice is so common as to justify that it will be observed, one can conclude that it is no longer a matter of choice for an online entrepreneur to provide strong encryption of sensitive information or not. In such a case it will be an obligation to support the strong encryption of any exchange of sensitive information between a client and a server. Failure to do so would constitute a breach of Internet custom, which could result in serious financial consequences for an online vendor in case of a loss suffered by a customer. In such a case scenario, the customary norm of supporting strong encryption would supplement existing laws or agreements on the matter.

3.3 Obligation of an online business to deny a service if client's web browser does not support strong encryption

The previous customary norm requires the service provider only to support the strong encryption of transactions. However, if a given web browser is an old one and does not support 128-bit encryption, then the SSL server will select the strongest of the remaining ciphers supported by the web browser in question. This will lead to the channel being encrypted using a shorter key, which may result in a security compromise.

To guard against this, only a denial of service by the website's operator SSL server could actually enforce the usage of strong encryption on the Internet. The practice of denial amounts to the configuration of a web server in such a manner that it supports exclusively strong ciphers. A number of leading online banks including Credit Swiss and UBS bank, ABN Amro, Barclays, Banco Bilbao, Vizcaya Argentaria bank, Commerzbank, Westdeutsche Landesbank, Banco Patagonia and most Israeli online banks have already implemented this practice (Figure 56).[1280]

However, the majority of online banks still do not follow this practice. In consequence, the practice of denial has not yet reached the stage where it could be considered as a customary norm. At most, it could be regarded as a custom in formation or custom *in statuu nascendii*. This, in turn, has an important consequence, because a customer who suffers a loss due to a weakly encrypted channel could not claim that this was a breach of an already existing Internet custom.

Strong encryption is certainly 'the best practice', and it should be quickly adopted by other online entrepreneurs. This example also shows an important difference between common practices and best practices, as both terms overlap. Usually common practices are best practices, because the majority of people act in a reasonable way and choose the best means to achieve a desired goal. However, there are marginal cases, where a better practice has appeared, but it has not yet been adopted widely. Time will tell whether this practice turns into the established customary principle or not.

[1280] As of July 2003.

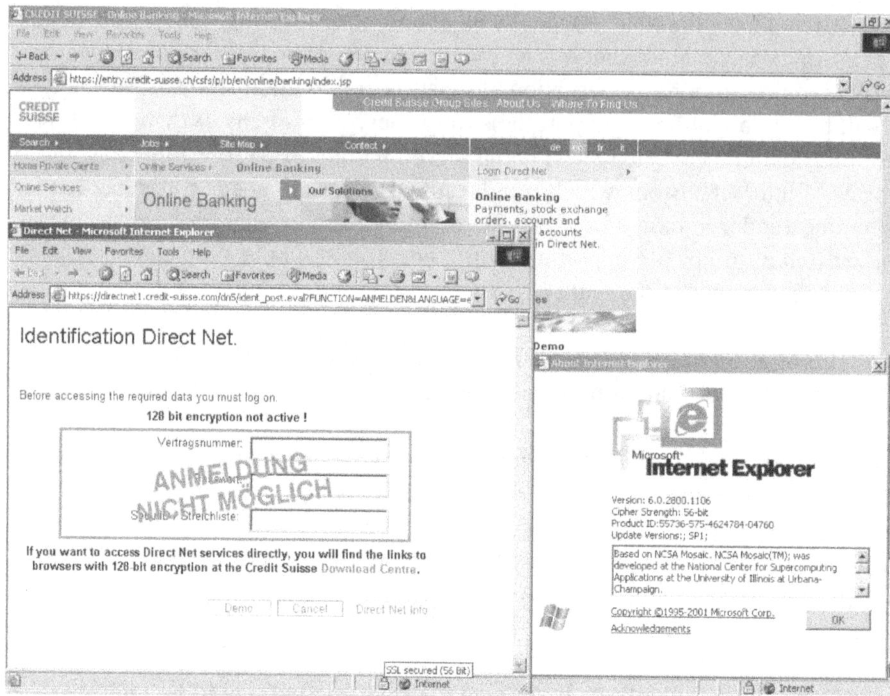

Figure 56 – Credit Suisse e-banking server is configured so that it will not let a browser with less than 128-bit encryption to login to the system

The norm embodied in this practice has not yet been codified in positive law. Neither international law nor municipal laws deal with norms on encrypting transactions to such a level of detail. However, unless parties agree to such practice in an agreement, parties will not be able to rely on it as customary law, because it is not widely followed. Given widespread adoption, the customary norm will clearly supplement existing laws or agreements.

3.4 Obligation of an online business to automatically sign a user out if a web browser is not used for some time (timeout)

The online banking industry has developed several very important practices in order to provide secure electronic banking. Online banks automatically sign a user off the online account after a set period of web inactivity. Once a window has been opened for more than five to fifteen minutes and the system does not receive any input from a user, a session should be cancelled. If the user wants to continue online banking he or she would have to re-login (Figure 57).

The purpose of this practice is to provide better security in Internet banking. The timeout practice ensures that the user will not forget to log out of the system. Fail-

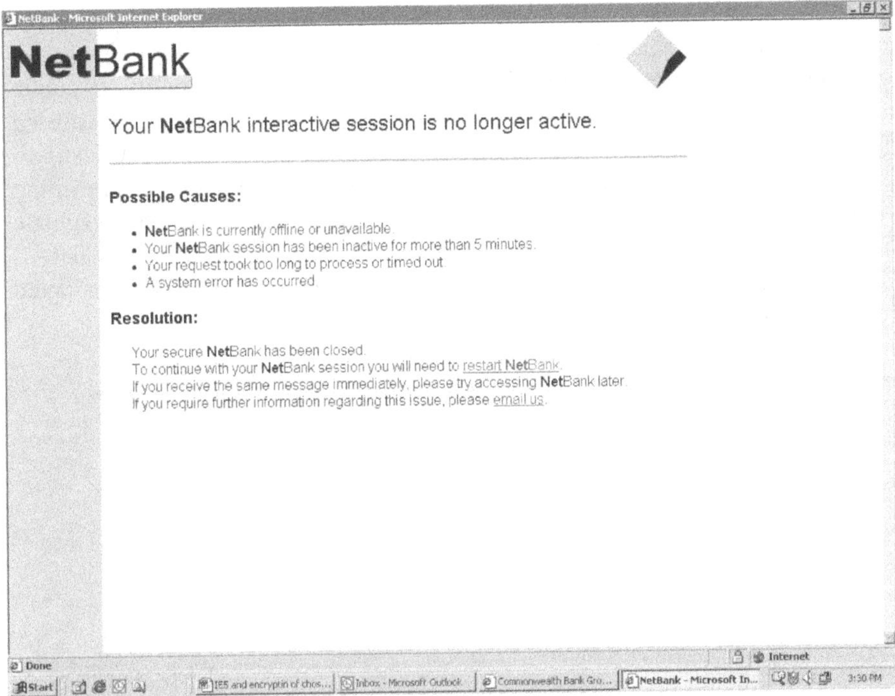

Figure 57 – Timeout practice as implemented by the Commonwealth Bank of Australia

ing to log out means that someone else can gain access to all financial information of the user, as well as transfer funds, change the password, and so on.

Some banks explicitly force a user to sign-off manually. For instance, Wells Fargo Online 'cannot be responsible for customer errors or negligent use of the service and will not cover losses due to: (…) Leaving a computer unattended during an Online session – click "Sign Off" to end your session.' Nevertheless, Wells Fargo promises to sign the user off automatically after ten minutes of inactivity.

This style of transaction has a global scope in the banking industry. However, as in the case of encryption practices, it also exists in other industries. Sometimes even freely available e-mail websites specify a timeout period. So it is possible that this practice has a global scope or is evolving in this direction. Failure to observe this custom may result in financial loss to a customer, and consequently, in the legal proceedings, against an online entrepreneur. The customary norm supplements existing legislative and contractual arrangements.

3.5 Obligation of an online bank to use valid digital certificates issued by trusted authorities

This topic is related to the customary practice of supporting encryption of the Internet channel because SSL protocol requires server-side digital certificates to identify servers. Without a valid digital certificate, the provision of strong SSL-based encryption would not be possible.

Observation of electronic trade shows that the significant majority of public institutions, banks and insurance companies use digital certificates issued by trusted authorities. For instance, it is now a customary practice in the banking industry to use digital certificates issued by trusted authorities such as Verisign. The prevailing format of digital certificate is X.509v3. However, despite early attempts to regulate digital certificates by means of harmonised legislation based on the UNCITRAL Model Law on Electronic Signatures, not all web-based institutions have adopted them, and not all that have adopted them use them properly.

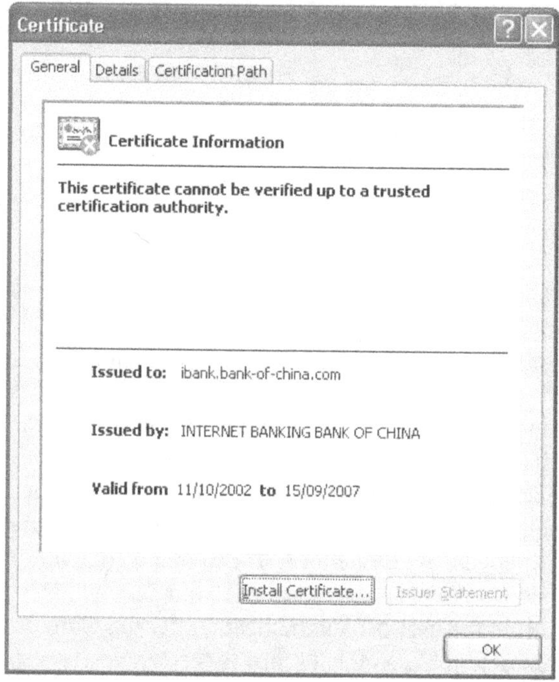

Figure 58 – Certificate verified by a non-trusted authority

An important aspect of using digital certificates by website operators is the assurance that trusted authorities generate or authenticate their certificates. This is important because modern operating systems, such as Windows 2003 Server, enable auto-generation of digital certificates without the need for third-party authorisation. Such certificates do not provide assurance as to the authenticity of the website operator in question and are meant mainly for the internal secure transfer of data.

Internet users can also expect that all online entrepreneurs will have valid digital certificates issued by widely recognised certificate authorities. A certificate that is no longer valid because it has expired or been revoked should be replaced in timely

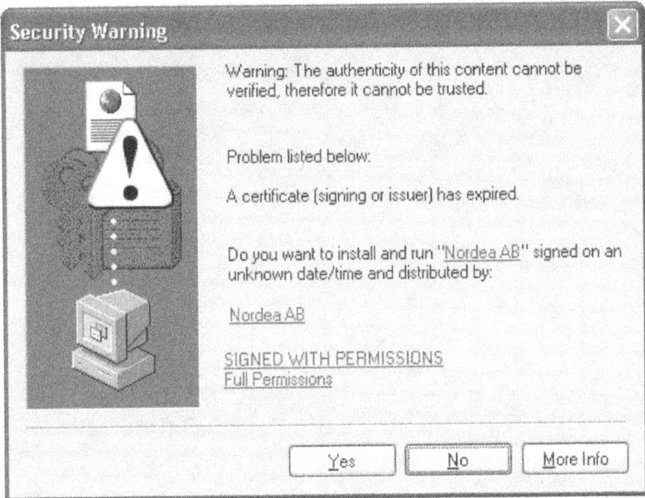

Figure 59 – An expired certificate

fashion by a website operator. Failure to do so may result in a compromise of web security and hence result in a financial loss to a customer.

4. Online Contracting

Online contracting is another interesting area where numerous practices have been developed. These have been created by the Internet community itself in order to allow Internet users to more easily conclude transactions. By following these practices, sellers provide assurance to buyers that a transaction will take place without serious problems. Therefore, the customs described below provide important mechanisms for ensuring the proper conclusion of web-based contracts. These practices will be described in the order akin to the sequence of a typical transaction.

4.1 Obligation of an online business to display steps that follow to conclude an electronic contract

Most electronic businesses that earn their revenue from selling products or information over the Internet provide a clear indication to the user of all the steps that follow to conclude an online contract. Often a picture with a number of steps on it that highlight the stage of the transaction is displayed. Other sellers provide textual clues as to the stage of the transaction. Thanks to this information, users can better assess what stage of the transaction they are at.

This practice is common to all businesses dealing with the sale of goods or information, and graphical clues became widespread with the introduction of shopping cart technology. Auction sites also usually provide textual indicators.

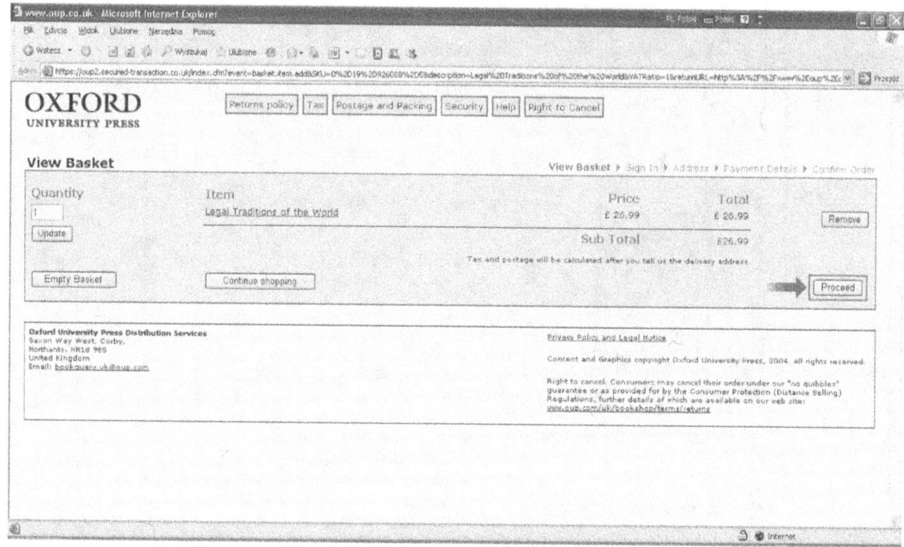

Figure 60 – Arrows and bold text indicates the stage of a transaction at Oxford University Press

The practice has a purely informative character. However, it is difficult to say what happens if an online business does not provide such an indicator. According to the European Union Directive on Electronic Commerce, every website operator should include such a facility, but the regulation is silent on potential sanctions for non-conformance. It is likely that a user will be entitled to claim that he or she made a mistake, and hence that a contract was not validly concluded. The customary practice has been codified in the European Union, but could supplement existing laws of non-EU countries.

For instance, in a case of *Wei Zhu* v. *Merill Lynch*, which dealt with an e-commerce trading platform that was:

> 'incapable of giving to a customer a simple instruction that he should not continue with a request for a trade or cancellation until he or she is advised specifically that the request has been successfully and completely dealt with, or that his transaction is pending until he is advised to the contrary.'[1281]

This case could well be settled based on a breach of customary principle of requiring provision of clear steps to conclude a contract, as well as another customary norm requiring the provision of means of identification and the correction of input errors, which could be implicit in an agreement.

[1281] *Wei Zhu* v. *Merrill Lynch* [2002] HSBC, BCPC 0535 discussed in Prins, J.E.J. (June 2003), *Consumers, Liability, and the Online World*, p. 152.

4.2 Obligation of an online business to provide means of identifying and correcting input errors

The peculiar characteristic of Internet transactions is that they take place very rapidly and in the absence of parties to the transaction. Therefore, it is of paramount importance to allow buyers to easily spot and correct input errors. The current state of technology enables implementation of such mechanisms.

This principle has a very broad scope and can be implemented in numerous ways. In fact, it consists of two obligations: to identify input errors and to enable error correction. The mechanisms for identifying input errors include the double check of passwords, the automatic check of e-mail addresses for presence of the @ symbol, the double check of e-mail addresses, the verification of postal codes or credit card numbers. Furthermore, as the figure below indicates, missing information is customarily signalled with coloured textual information next to the required field or an appropriate message box.

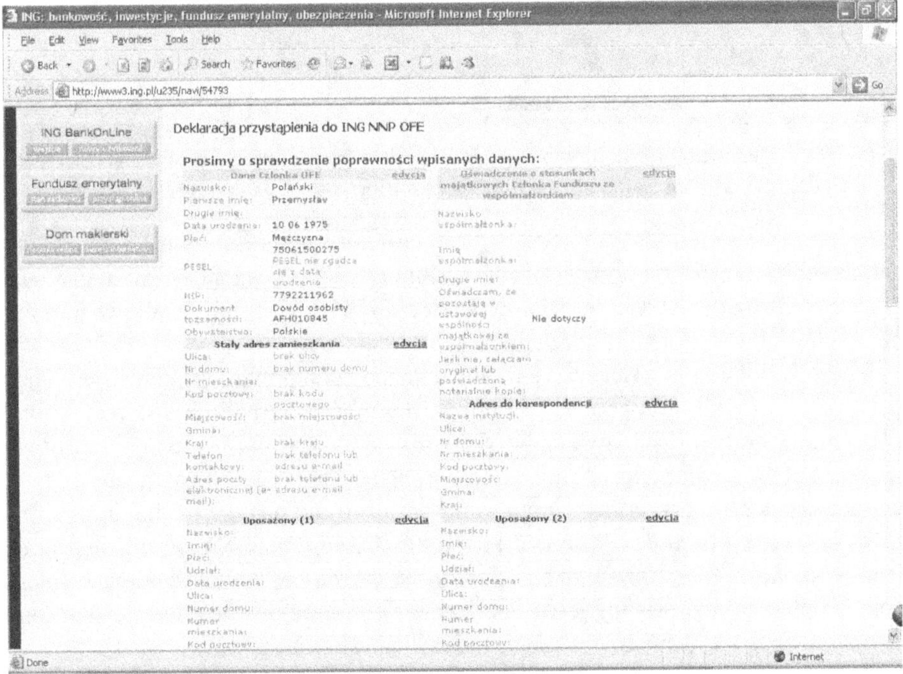

Figure 61 – Bold text in different colour (red) indicates missing information to be supplied on the ING Poland website

On the other hand, mechanisms that allow for correction of input error, as the figure below indicates, usually take the form of an 'Edit' or 'Change' button displayed next to all the important sections of the webpage. This allows a buyer to change the

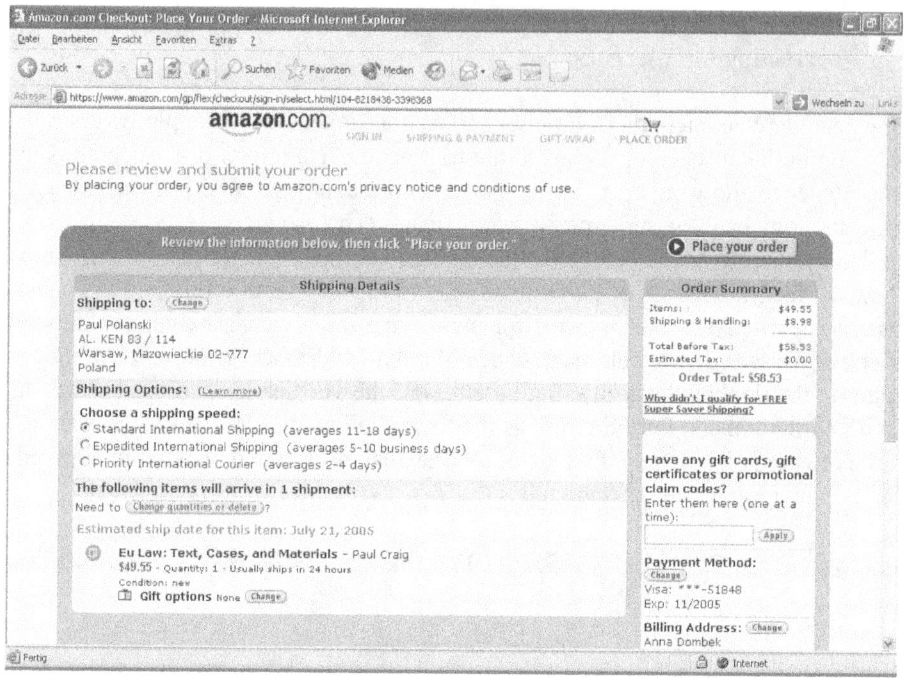

Figure 62 – Change buttons on Amazon website allow for modification of items selected for purchase, as well as the payment method, billing address, shipping address, etc.

details of the transaction prior to its conclusion. Finally, a customer is often given a double confirmation screen, especially in electronic banking, which allows him or her to check the transaction once again.

These validation practices have a global scope and apply to all industries. The practice is generally not codified, although the aforementioned EU Directive on Electronic Commerce has mandated website operators to make 'available to the recipient of the service appropriate, effective and accessible technical means allowing him to identify and correct input errors, prior to the placing of the order.'[1282] However, as has been demonstrated above, this requirement can be fulfilled in a number of ways. Therefore, one can clearly see the way in which customary practices supplement the existing legal framework with more detailed norms. One can also appreciate the value of custom as the law's best interpreter.

The sanction for failure to adhere to this principle could be a loss of a contract or, in some circumstances, financial liability. The United Nations Convention on the Use of Electronic Communications in International Contracting provides the right of withdrawal if a website operator did not provide the person with an oppor-

---

[1282] See Art. 11 para. 2 of .

tunity to correct the input error.[1283] This is a custom as to the formation of a contract.

4.3 Obligation of an online business to summarise the transaction before accepting payment

This customary obligation has been extensively discussed in the previous chapters. The practice of summarising electronic transactions is especially popular in electronic shops. It allows a customer to read once again the details of the transaction and to correct errors prior to placing of the order. It is a custom as to the formation of a contract as opposed to a custom as to the content of a contract. Failure to include this functionality may result in an annulment of a contract or a right to withdrawal from a portion of the electronic communication.

4.4 Obligation of an online business to confirm an online order instantly and by electronic means

This customary obligation has been extensively discussed in the previous chapters. The instant confirmation of online orders is one of the most fundamental principles of online contracting. Without it a buyer would not be certain whether or not a transaction took place. The confirmation usually takes the form of web confirmation and/or e-mail confirmation. The confirmation customarily includes an order tracking number together with other details of the transaction. Often, the confirmation allows customers to track the status of the order.

This is a custom as to the formation of a contract. Therefore, it is a necessary step in order to validly conclude an agreement. The lack of order confirmation provides strong justification for rescinding the online contract. This customary practice has been codified in the European law, although very imprecisely. The aforementioned directive on electronic commerce is silent as to the content of such confirmation, which should be established with a reference to the customary practices of online merchants. Other countries and international organisations should include this principle as one of the fundamentals of the online contract laws. This custom has been established in the previous chapter using a three-test methodology and for this reason the discussion will not be repeated here.

5. Online Advertising

Advertising on the Internet is one of the oldest fields where customary practices have developed. This area is particularly interesting because revenue that is gener-

1283 See the discussion in Chapter IV on Art. 14 of the Convention. United Nations (23 November 2005), *United Nations Convention on the Use of Electronic Communications in International Contracts*.

ated by online marketing is the cornerstone of the majority of business models encountered on the Net. For instance, information portals or search engines rely mostly on advertising revenues to support their operations. It is therefore particularly important to observe certain customary practices that have emerged in this area.

5.1 Obligation of an online business to refrain from sending spam

In the early days of the Internet, sending commercial e-mails was unthinkable. When in 1994 a Phoenix law firm Canter & Siegel posted an immigration law advertisement on bulletin boards, the community of users reacted furiously and effectively blocked their e-mail account by sending thousands of e-mail messages. The law firm's account was soon revoked on the grounds that the company abused its privileges. As the system administrator of a company providing Internet access to Canter & Siegel explained: 'They took 15 or 20 years of Internet tradition and said the hell with it.'[1284]

The early customary norm prohibiting commercial use of the Internet proved transitory. Commercial advertising was finally accepted by the Internet community. As Bodansky observed:

> 'Although violators suffered sanctions, these sanctions ultimately proved insufficient to serve as an effective deterrent. Instead, over time, the non-compliant behavior established a new custom permitting advertising on the Internet, and by now this behavior no longer entails any penalties.'[1285]

However, certain advertising practices are still not tolerated. It is particularly so with respect to spam or unsolicited, bulky email advertising that is difficult to block.[1286] In general, the rules of Netiquette justify this prohibition in the following words:

> 'The cost of delivering an e-mail message is, on the average, paid about equally by the sender and the recipient (or their organizations). This is unlike other media such as physical mail, telephone, TV, or radio. Sending someone mail may also cost them in other specific ways like network bandwidth, disk space or CPU usage. This is a fundamental economic reason why unsolicited e-mail advertising is unwelcome (and is forbidden in many contexts).'[1287]

[1284] Cited in Bodansky, D.M. (Fall 2004), *Customary International Law: Diplomatic Immunities (electronic classes)*, University of Georgia, available at <http://www.law.uga.edu/~bodansky/courses/International_Law/class12.html>, last visited: 28/08/2006.

[1285] Ibid.

[1286] This is a rather narrow definition of spam. Usually, all unsolicited forms of electronic communication are considered spam, including Usenet newsgroups. See, for example, Edwards, L. (2000), *Canning the Spam: Is There a Case for Legal Control of Junk Electronic Mail?*, p. 309.

[1287] Hambridge, S. (October 1995), *RFC 1855 Netiquette Guidelines* (Also FYI0028) (Status: INFORMATIONAL) p. 4. See also, Hambridge, S. and Lunde, A. (June 1999), *RFC 2635 Don't spew.*

It is worth repeating here that status of the Netiquette as a basis for adjudication of disputes has been confirmed in *Christophe G.* v. *Société France Télécom Interactive, S.A.*, where a French court recognised the prohibition of spamming as a binding custom.[1288]

One of the most evident examples of unwelcome (and forbidden) spam is bulky email advertising that contains arbitrary sender addresses. It is difficult to fight this kind of spam, because a sender address keeps changing every time in order to avoid simple text filtering. Such examples of spam have never been tolerated by Internet users and this attitude is common worldwide. It has also been recognized in Article 13 of the European directive on privacy and electronic communications, which outlaws this kind of spam in the following manner:

> '4. In any event, the practice of sending electronic mail for purposes of direct marketing, disguising or concealing the identity of the sender on whose behalf the communication is made, or without a valid address to which the recipient may send a request that such communications cease, shall be prohibited.'[1289]

Similarly, section 5 of the American 2003 CAN-SPAM Act prohibits false or misleading transmission information:

> 'It is unlawful for any person to initiate the transmission, to a protected computer, of a commercial electronic mail message, or a transactional or relationship message, that contains, or is accompanied by, header information that is materially false or materially misleading.'[1290]

This Act also prohibits deceptive subject headings, e-mails that do not contain a functioning return electronic mail address and commercial advertising after objections.

However, there are spam messages that are even more difficult to fight, for instance, e-mails that contain advertisements in graphical format (see Figure 63 below). The reason for embedding advertisement in a graphical image is to circumvent the operation of e-mail filters that can only operate on text. As a result, it is virtually impossible to stop companies that utilize this technique to advertise their products. Unless advanced techniques (maybe OCR) are applied in the area of information filtering, Internet users will have to bear graphical spam.

A Set of Guidelines for Mass Unsolicited Mailings and Postings (spam) (Status: INFORMATIONAL).* See also section 5.2.

1288 See section 5.1 in Chapter V.

1289 See, for example, OJ L 201/37 (31.07.2002), *Directive 2002/58/EC of the European Parliament and of the Council of 12 July 2002 concerning the processing of personal data and the protection of privacy in the electronic communications sector (Directive on privacy and electronic communications).*

1290 15 USC 7704.

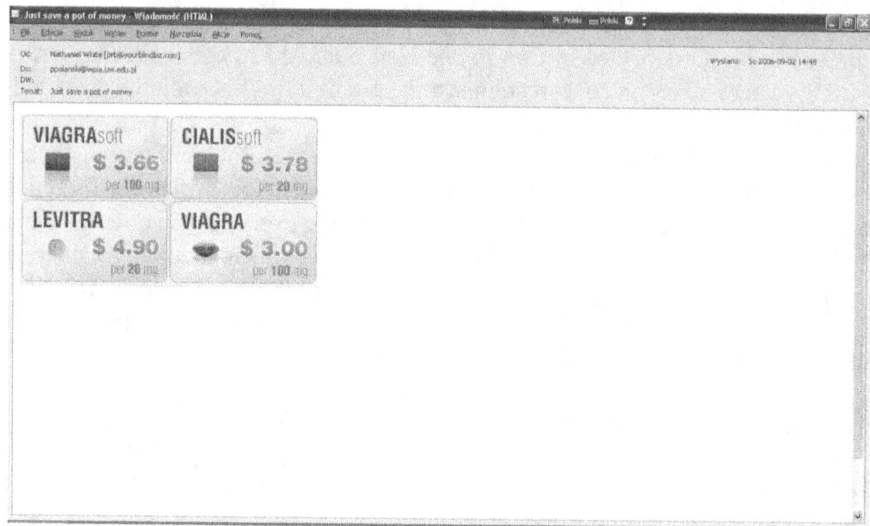

Figure 63 – Recent example of commercial spam that is difficult to block because of its graphical character

Another type of e-mail advertising that is particularly unwelcome and very hard to fight is spamming in order to undermine the network security, e.g., to spread viruses. Fortunately, nearly all email server administrators use anti-virus software that deletes dangerous attachments before they reach client computers (see Figure 64 below). One can therefore argue that it is a customary obligation of email service providers to use anti-virus software on their servers in order to reduce the amount of spam and to fight the spread of viruses and other forms of malicious software.

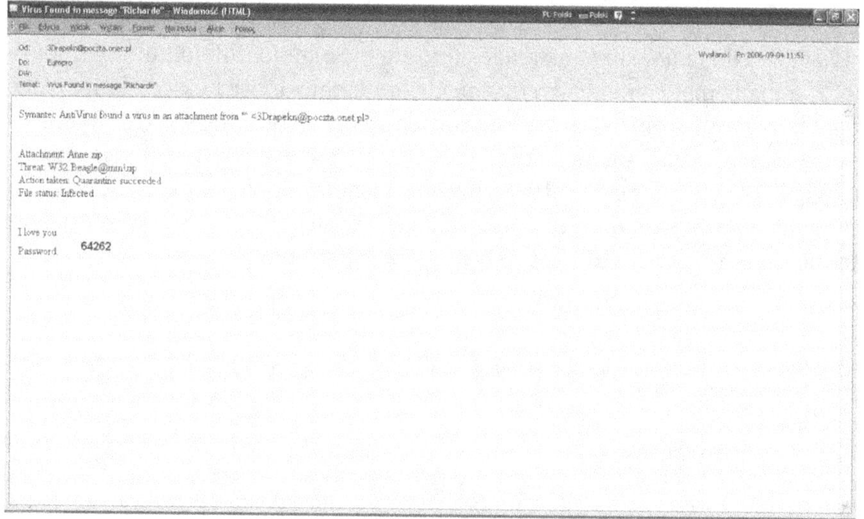

Figure 64 – Example of e-mail message with automatically deleted dangerous attachment

However, spam is also often used in order to forge Distributed Denial of Service (DDoS) attacks,[1291] which result in temporary unavailability of Internet services such as a website or an email server. Spam is also used by hackers in order to hack into computer systems. This use of spam is probably the most dangerous but is much harder to stop.

The negative attitude towards spam is further visible in the works of international organisations that try to fight it. As an example, the Internet Research Task Force (IRTF) has established the Anti-Spam Research Group in order to investigate tools and techniques to mitigate the sending and effects of spam. In particular, the research group focuses on anti-spam tools and techniques that 'include those to prevent spam from being sent, to prevent spam from being received, to distinguish spam from legitimate mail, to facilitate management responses to spam activity, and to ensure that legitimate mail is delivered in the presence of other anti-spam measures.'[1292]

Furthermore, the continuous development of technologies targeted at fighting spam is another proof of the common intention to get rid of it. The vast majority of Internet users and probably all e-mail server administrators use spam filters in order to block the flood of unwanted electronic communications. This argument can serve as another proof of the customary nature of prohibition in respect to commercial spam.

In summary, there are plenty of legal, technical and organisational efforts to remove spam. These undertakings clearly signify the intention of the majority of users to block spam advertising that is generated by a very small fraction of the Internet community. One can therefore argue that it is customary for online business to refrain from sending spam.

5.2 Right of search engines to block spamdexed websites

Successful advertising on the WWW involves an appropriate modification of a webpage so that search engines would list it highly. A typical Web user would not read beyond the first ten to twenty search results. In consequence, a high ranking within the results of a search engine is critical for the success of an online business.

Spamdexing (or web spam) refers to spamming the index of a search engine. In other words, web spam refers to 'actions intended to mislead search engines into ranking some pages higher than they deserve.'[1293] Although the term spamdexing is similar to spam, these two practices should not be confused. According to Wikipedia 'spamdexing refers exclusively to practices that are dishonest and mislead search and indexing programs to give a page a ranking it does not deserve.'[1294]

1291 Hambridge, S. and Lunde, A. (June 1999), *RFC 2635 Don't spew. A Set of Guidelines for Mass Unsolicited Mailings and Postings (spam*) (Status: INFORMATIONAL)*, p. 3.

1292 <http://www.irtf.org/charter?gtype=rg&group=asrg>, last visited: 28/08/2006.

1293 Gyöngyi, Z. and Garcia-Molina, H. (2005), *Web Spam Taxonomy*, p. 1.

1294 <http://en.wikipedia.org/wiki/Spamdexing>, last visited: 28/08/2006.

Unfortunately, because of the financial gain in achieving a high search engine rank, the amount of spamdexing has increased dramatically, leading to a degradation of search results.[1295]

In the early days of WWW, search engines relied on matching queried keywords in available electronic documents. Such simple text searches were especially vulnerable to manipulation by repetition of targeted keywords on a page. Consequently, search engines abandoned this philosophy and the next generation of search engines used more sophisticated techniques. Lycos was first to develop the concept of 'implicit voting', which treated a link to a page as a 'vote' for it.[1296] As a result, a webpage with many links pointing to it would be more 'important' than pages with few links. Google's PageRank algorithm has improved this concept with the notion of the 'importance' of a page. In consequence, pages that are referenced from often cited pages such as Yahoo would be given higher ranking than pages that might have more links but from more obscure places.[1297] Therefore, 'for a page to get a high PageRank, it must convince an important page, or a lot of non-important pages to link to it.'[1298] However, despite its apparent immunity to manipulation, this concept has not turned out to be entirely bullet-proof. For instance, Google bombing,[1299] which involves creating pages that directly affect the rank of other sites is used particularly in non-commercial settings, e.g., to ridicule political leaders.[1300]

Spamdexing can take multiple forms. Common spamdexing techniques are classified into two broad classes: content spam and link spam.[1301] With respect to content spam, keywords can be placed in various so-called 'text fields': a body of a page, its title, meta tags, URL or anchor text. Depending upon the aim of a web spammer, a specific term can be repeated numerous times in these text fields or a great variety of words can be placed there. The content spam category includes techniques that place keywords as a hidden text (e.g., font colour is the same or similar to background colour). If such keywords are repeated in the body of a webpage one speaks of keyword stuffing. On the other hand, repeating keywords in meta tags is referred to as a meta tag stuffing. Other techniques include doorway pages, which contain very little content but are 'stuffed' with keywords and redirecting sites that redirect a user to a different website, without showing him the spammed website.

Link spam embraces even more techniques. A web spammer will be primarily interested in using his own pages and other accessible pages to link to. It is fairly

---

[1295] Gyöngyi, Z. and Garcia-Molina, H. (2005), *Web Spam Taxonomy*, p. 1.

[1296] Jones, T. (2005), *Both Sides of the Digital Battle for a High Rank from a Search Engine*.

[1297] Page, L., Brin, S., Motwani, R. and Winograd, T. (29 January 1998), *The PageRank Citation Ranking:Bringing Order to the Web*, p. 3.

[1298] Ibid., p.12

[1299] <http://en.wikipedia.org/wiki/Google_bomb>, last visited: 28/08/2006.

[1300] BBC News (7 December 2003), *'Miserable failure' links to Bush*.

[1301] See also <http://en.wikipedia.org/wiki/Spamdexing>, last visited: 28/08/2006. Or hiding techniques and boosting techniques – see Gyöngyi, Z. and Garcia-Molina, H. (2005), *Web Spam Taxonomy*, pp. 3-4.

easy to use a spammer's own sites to link to a target website to boost its ranking. However, web spammers will also try to link from pages maintained by others, e.g., to link from a blog to a target website. As a result, spamdexing is closely associated with blog spam. The most common linking technique is link farm (or spam farm), which involves any group of web pages that all hyperlink to every other page in the group.[1302] By creating large spam farms with all the pages pointing to the target, a spammer can boost Google's PageRank.[1303] Web spammers may also use invisible links in order to increase the importance of a page. Sometimes spamdexers purchase expired domains in order to replace the pages with links to their pages. There are also other techniques such as cloaking, which refers to presenting a different page to a web crawler than will be seen by human users.[1304]

Gyöngyi and Garcia-Molina estimate that 10-15 per cent of the content on the Web is spam.[1305] Spamdexing decreases the quality of search results and inflates search engines with useless pages therefore increasing the cost of processing queries.[1306] Furthermore, it forces some honest webmasters to spamdex in order to be found. However, there is still a lack of technical measures for combating this. For instance, 'Search engine SPAM detector' tries only the three most common spamdexing methods: keyword stuffing, doorway farms and hidden text.[1307] In addition, most companies providing search engine optimization (SE) services engage in spamdexing.[1308]

One of the major problems associated with spamdexing is that these techniques can be used for both legitimate and illegitimate purposes. There are numerous techniques that have been accepted in the industry as procedures for making a website indexable by search engines, without misleading the indexing process (known as search engine optimization). On the other hand, the most dangerous forms of spamdexing involve repeated use of certain keywords such as registered trademarks, brand names or famous names in one's webpage to take advantage of their goodwill.[1309] Such practices have been tested in courts worldwide and a consensus has emerged that they violate either competition laws (in Europe) or trademark laws (in the USA).[1310] In other cases, however, there is no law that explicitly prohibits spamdexing.

In consequence, search engines have established and enforced their own web spam policies. Webmasters are usually provided with detailed guidelines that ex-

---

1302 <http://en.wikipedia.org/wiki/Link_farm>, last visited: 28/08/2006.

1303 Gyöngyi, Z. and Garcia-Molina, H. (2005), *Web Spam Taxonomy*, p. 5.

1304 See Glossary. See also Jones, T. (2005), *Both Sides of the Digital Battle for a High Rank from a Search Engine*.

1305 Gyöngyi, Z. and Garcia-Molina, H. (2005), *Web Spam Taxonomy*, p. 8.

1306 Ibid., p. 1.

1307 <http://tool.motoricerca.info/spam-detector/>, last visited: 28/08/2006.

1308 Gyöngyi, Z. and Garcia-Molina, H. (2005), *Web Spam Taxonomy*, p. 2.

1309 See, for example, Nathenson, I.S. (Fall 1998), *Internet Infoglut and Invisible Ink: Spamdexing Search Engines with Meta Tags*, footnote 15.

1310 For a list and the discussion of early cases, see ibid., Part II and footnotes 21-23.

plain how to structure a webpage. For instance, Google specifies quality guidelines and warns that if a site does not meet them, it may be blocked from the index.[1311] Similarly, Yahoo has designed Content Quality Guidelines 'to ensure that poor-quality pages do not degrade the user experience in any way.'[1312] The company has reserved 'the right, at its sole discretion, to take any and all action it deems appropriate to insure the quality of its index.'[1313]

In consequence, based on the evidence of positive actions taken by Internet users to fight spamdexing, one can argue that a new customary right has emerged permitting search engines to block web spam. It is too early, however, to speak about a customary obligation to refrain from spamdexing, because techniques such as cloaking or hidden text can be used for both legitimate and illegitimate purposes. However, this area is evolving rapidly and such customary obligation might emerge soon. Clearly, more research is required.

5.3 Obligation of an online business to allow for closure of interactive advertising

With the advent of web-based advertising, new marketing practices have emerged. This is particularly so thanks to the rapid and widespread adoption of Macromedia Flash software that is being used to create animated website introduction, ad banners and full screen, transparent animations. The latter form of multimedia advertising is particularly intrusive when the full screen animation quite often is very loud, occupies the whole screen and it is hard to find a way to get rid of it.

Figure 65 – Example of Flash advertising on AOL website with close button

1311 <http://www.google.com/support/webmasters/bin/answer.py?answer=35769>, last visited: 28/08/2006.

1312 <http://help.yahoo.com/help/us/ysearch/indexing/indexing-14.html>, last visited: 28/08/2006.

1313 Ibid.

However, the majority of such advertisements usually contain a 'close' button or similar means that allow to close the animation. It is therefore possible that a customary norm requiring provision of such functionality has emerged.

6. Right to Information

Many of the customary norms presented above are derivatives of the basic freedom of speech, which seems to be one of the core values of the Information Society. However, certain types of information simply must be made accessible, particularly in Internet commerce.[1314] Online merchants are expected to provide certain information in a legible and accurate manner, such as the description of goods, prices, delivery conditions and privacy policy. These are not only legitimate expectations of an online customer but also a legal requirement in many jurisdictions, particularly in the European Union. A number of directives set out informational requirements that online businesses have to provide to their customers including information about the company itself, codes of conducts to which it subscribes, contractual information minimum, and so on.[1315] However, the kind of information customarily provided by online merchants will require a more in-depth study.

Interesting customs have also emerged in the area of online auctions. The concept of the reserve price on English auctions, although not new, has been widely used in electronic auctions. What is new, however, is the kind of information that is customarily supplied on various electronic auctions globally: start and end time of the auction, current price, reserve price if set, item location, the seller profile, and so on. Probably the most important of these is the custom of providing detailed information about the seller, including the comments of other buyers and the 'objective' overall rating based on his or her past dealings. A lot of work is necessary to learn about different practices that have emerged in the area of online auctions, especially these related to banning a seller from further sales because they have fraudulently manipulated their score. There are many types of online auctions and each of them requires a special treatment.

Furthermore, another fundamental principle that seems to be taken for granted in electronic commerce is an expectation that an online e-commerce service will be constantly available. This customary principle is especially important in electronic

---

1314 Or in electronic government. However, e-government is outside the scope of this book.

1315 See, for example, OJ L 178/1 (12.11.2000), *Directive 2000/31/EC of the European Parliament and of the Council of 8 June 2000 on certain legal aspects of information society services, in particular electronic commerce, in the Internal Market (Directive on Electronic Commerce)*. See also OJ L 108/51 (24.04.2002), *Directive 2002/22/EC of the European Parliament and of the Council of 7 March 2002 on universal service and users' rights relating to electronic communications networks and services (Universal Service Directive)*; OJ L 144/19 (04.06.1997), *Directive 97/7/EC of the European Parliament and of the Council of 20 May 1997 on the protection of consumers in respect of distance contracts*.

commerce as it guarantees access to services contracted for. However, it covers not only the actual availability of a website or other service but also the assurance of a satisfactory or reasonable level of performance. This implies that online merchants have to ensure that their system will be available 24 hours a day and 365 days a year with a reasonable level of performance. This in turn means that online merchants will have to consider investment in additional servers and technologies such as load balancing. Furthermore, assurance of availability also means that customer data is protected and properly backed-up. In the case of a system failure, other servers should not only allow for continuation of service but should also restore any potentially lost or corrupted data.

One can also envisage the proliferation of customary practices in the area of Web accessibility. Although web developers have detailed guidelines prepared by W3C in this regard,[1316] many practices emerge spontaneously, often to meet the needs of people with disabilities. This area is particularly important for governments and major Internet players, because content that is inaccessible to people with limited vision, say, can not only harm their reputation, but also lead to lawsuits.

7. Conclusion

This chapter has discussed emerging customary practices in the areas of online security, online contracting, online advertising and intellectual property. The principles were only outlined and need to be properly evidenced according to the methodology presented in the previous chapter. It is useful, however, to have a list of at least some potential customary norms, so as to see the potential power of custom as a source of legal rights and obligations.

Some of the norms presented here are so important and so widely used that they could be regarded as general principles of Internet law. This is the case with right to information, freedom of registration of a domain name on first-in first-served basis or freedom of linking to any resource without permission. Other norms are more specific but concern fundamental issues of online security and online contracting.

Clearly, the customary principles presented in this chapter represent only a fraction of the norms that the Internet community has already developed. More research is needed to identify other norms, and to better delineate exceptions to norms that are already well established. However, the aforementioned potential Internet commerce customs might in the future become the basis of the autonomous Internet law.

[1316] See, for example, W3C (5 May 1999), *Web Content Accessibility Guidelines 1.0.*

Chapter X
TOWARDS A SUPRANATIONAL INTERNET LAW

1. The need for a supranational solution

As soon as the commercialisation of the Internet started, it became apparent that there is a need for uniform international law as the reliance on the traditional systems of conflict of norms or private international law brings an intolerable amount of uncertainty.[1317] The first problem is that the rules that decide which law applies usually depend upon the location of the party,[1318] which may not always be possible to indicate. For instance, very often the law of the seller's place of business will be designated as a proper system for ascertaining parties' rights and obligations arising out of a contract. In case a virtual business did not indicate his geographical address, such rules might be impossible to apply.

The second problem is that each domestic legal system has its own legal rules on international disputes, which decide whether a legal system of a plaintiff or a defender will apply. Therefore, a judge in one country may be forced to apply a law of another country, of which he or she has no actual knowledge. Furthermore, such legal system may have no proper rules for the Internet. In such case scenario, it would be difficult for any attorney to convince his client that he can be certain of the outcome of a dispute where another legal system than that where the court sits, was found applicable.

Finally, since each country has its own conflict rules, a different legal system might be designated only as a result of the selection of a court. Therefore, one dispute being submitted to two courts established in two different countries, might lead to opposite verdicts. And even if one party would have won in his country, it might not be able to enforce a favourable judgment in another country. If one adds to this that each legal system considers some of its laws as having mandatory character, which means that they have to be applied by a judge even if another law was selected as applicable by virtue of conflict rules, this clearly shows that the existing system is inadequate for the Internet Age.

[1317] This chapter has been reproduced in the conference paper, subsequently published in the JICLT. See Polanski, P.P. (2006), *Towards a supranational Internet law*.

[1318] See, for example, section I. Breaking Down Territorial Borders in Burnstein, M.R. (1996), *Conflicts on the Net: Choice of Law in Transnational Cyberspace*, p. 81; Johnson, D.R. and Post, D. (May 1996), *Law and Borders – The Rise of Law in Cyberspace*.

As a result, some authors suggested that the Internet needs a supranational or an autonomous legal system.[1319] The proposed concepts were inspiring but rather vague. For instance, some authors already in the 1990-ies have already noted the similarity of electronic commerce practices and the medieval Law Merchant.[1320] Trotter Hardy, who was probably the first to notice the similarity, argued that the parallels of medieval trade with online commerce are strong because:

> 'Many people interact frequently over networks, but not always with the same people each time so that advance contractual relations are not always practical. Commercial transactions will more and more take place in cyberspace, and more and more those transactions will cross national boundaries and implicate different bodies of law. Speedy resolution of disputes will be as desirable as it was in the Middle Ages! The means of an informal court system are in place in the form of on-line discussion groups and electronic mail. A "Law Cyberspace" co-existing with existing laws would be an eminently practical and efficient way of handling commerce in the networked world.'[1321]

The comparison of medieval commercial customs and modern Internet customs is justified to the extent that it recognises the peculiarities of the electronic medium. Trotter Hardy published his excellent article in 1994, and this is the primary reason why he refers only to online discussion groups and electronic mail. These days he would have included the World Wide Web as the primary technology for establishing an informal court system. Furthermore, another interesting feature of his idea of autonomous Internet law is its supplementary character in relation to existing laws. However, his comparison to medieval Law Merchant should go even further. In the reverse order of importance: firstly, because customary mercantile practices were the cornerstone of the Roman *ius gentium*.[1322] Secondly, because Internet customary practices usually apply both to professional as well as consumer trade. Thirdly, because many online customs apply to commercial as well as to non-commercial

---

[1319] Hardy, I.T. (Summer 1994), *The Proper Legal Regime For Cyberspace*; Johnson, D.R. and Post, D. (May 1996), *Law and Borders – The Rise of Law in Cyberspace*.

[1320] Hardy, I.T. (Summer 1994), *The Proper Legal Regime For Cyberspace*, pp. 1019-1021; Johnson, D.R. and Post, D. (May 1996), *Law and Borders – The Rise of Law in Cyberspace*, pp. 1389-1390; Perritt, H.H., Jr. (1997), *Cyberspace Self-Government: Town Hall Democracy Or Rediscovered Royalism?*, pp. 461-463; Post, D.G. (October 1996), *Anarchy, State, and the Internet: An Essay on Law-Making in Cyberspace (Art. 3)*, footnote 15. See also Branscomb, A.W. (May 1995), *Anonymity, Autonomy, And Accountability: Challenges To The First Amendment In Cyberspaces*, p. 1667. Burnstein, M.R. (1996), *Conflicts on the Net: Choice of Law in Transnational Cyberspace*; Burnstein, M.R. (1998-2000), *A Global Network in a Compartmentalised Legal Environment*; Reidenberg, J.R. (February 1998), *Lex Informatica: The Formulation of Information Technology Rules Through Information Technology*, p. 553. Recently, see Michaels, R. (2005), *The Re-State-ment of Non-State Law: The State, Choice of Law, and the Challenge from Global Legal Pluralism*; Trakman, L.E. (Summer 2003), *From the Medieval Law Merchant to E-Merchant Law*.

[1321] Hardy, I.T. (Summer 1994), *The Proper Legal Regime For Cyberspace*, p. 1021.

[1322] Goldman, B. (1983), *Lex Mercatoria*, p. 1.

activities. Although the purpose of this book, was to focus on e-commerce customs many of them in fact, can be found non-commercial sphere.

It is therefore submitted that the emergence of customary practices on the Internet could be considered as the beginning of the formation of the body of rules independent from national legal systems to be used on the Internet in general, and in international electronic commerce, in particular. The proliferation of online dispute resolution mechanisms[1323] provides another argument in support of the similarity of traditional Law Merchant and its online counterpart.[1324] Online adjudicators have not yet resorted to Internet customs as a basis for settling e-commerce disputes and that is why it is crucial to promote this idea among them. Similar remarks can be made about domestic courts, although they will be less flexible in applying written and unwritten laws other than their own. Taking lessons from history one might anticipate that a body of e-commerce customs, once developed, will be incorporated into national and international legal systems.

Internet commerce could be regarded as another example of an environment where in the absence of an agreement or written law, rights and obligations could be inferred from the common practices or customs of e-merchants.[1325] And these customs could be regarded as the foundation of another reincarnation of the idea of the Law Merchant – the modern *Internet lex mercatoria.* This is so, because, in principle, there is no difference between the early trade, modern international commerce and electronic commerce.[1326]

As Badinter put it:

> 'In the Middle Ages, the big trade fairs in the Piémont, in Champagne, in Flanders, on the banks of the Rhine or the Thames were attended by merchants from all corners of Europe. Practices, custom, and arbitrators, even then, elaborated a merchants' law from them, which was acknowledged by all. In the same way, our era has seen the *jus communis* assert itself in all the large financial, industrial and business centres. Law firms are its laboratory, negotiations are its testing ground and arbitration is the combat area of *jus communis*. Even better, thanks to the development of computer science and communication techniques, the regional and temporary trade fair of the olden days has become global and permanent. And, travelling on all the information highways, tomorrow the *jus communis internationalis* will enfold all international transactions in the tight mesh of this law of which we are the tireless Penelopes.'[1327]

Despite the fact that there are no fundamental differences between Internet-based commerce and traditional commerce, some differences nevertheless remain. For

[1323] But see, for example, IntelliCourt that has been closed at <http://www.arbitrationsolutions.com/>, last visited: 06/03/2003. See also Chapter II.

[1324] Karavas, V. i Teubner, G. (2003), <http://www.CompanyNameSucks.com>*: The Horizontal Effect of Fundamental Rights on 'Private Parties' within Autonomous Internet Law*, pp. 1351-1355.

[1325] Polanski, P.P. (July 2003), *Custom as a Source of Supranational Internet Commerce Law (PhD Thesis).*

[1326] Ibid.

[1327] Badinter, R. (December 1995), *Role of the International Lawyer.*

instance, traditional international commerce is accessible primarily to larger business players, is built around strategic business relationships and is rather slow. On the other hand, Internet commerce is fast, enables both spot-buying and strategic relationships and is accessible to small and medium sized enterprises. Consequently, Internet Law Merchant will slightly differ in comparison to the offline *lex mercatoria*. For instance, one of the major differences is that one can observe and measure customs of the online traders in an automated fashion, which is not possible in offline commerce.

Furthermore, arbitral awards are just starting to play a greater role in electronic commerce thanks to, for example, the ICANN dispute resolution policy or the European consumer-focused FIN-NET. In a matter of fact, some authors argue that ICANN-based autonomous Internet law exhibits better quality than traditional *lex mercatoria*:

> 'The practices of still adolescent ICANN Panels, the precedent system and the nature of the norms applied, taken together with their stronger degree of political legitimation and, above all, the mode in which their decisions are effectively enforced, furnish the *lex digitalis* witha far stronger degree of legal quality than that provided by the practices of a by now old and treasured *lex mercatoria*, whose recognition as an autonomous legalorder by national courts and international legal doctrine, although not complete, is,at the very least, far more developed.'[1328]

In offline trade, as the compilation of Justice Mustill clearly shows, arbitral awards are the fundamental source of legal rules and knowledge about customary *lex mercatoria*. Also, standard contract forms commonly used in the traditional international commerce have been replaced on the Internet with web-forms, standard electronic contracts and online contracting mechanisms.

However, a body of norms cannot be regarded as a system, unless there exists a theory of sources of norms as well as a way to sort out conflicts between norms and a gap-filling mechanism. It is very difficult to propose such system and it is certainly outside the scope of this book to provide a detailed discussion of it. Nevertheless, one can make the following initial remarks about the possible theory of sources.

2. Potential Sources of Supranational Internet Law

The norms of supranational Internet law have various sources of origin: practices established between people (custom in narrow sense), judicial decisions, normative provisions established by specialised interest groups. The last category, which is

---

[1328] Karavas, V. i Teubner, G. (2003), <http://www.CompanyNameSucks.com>*: The Horizontal Effect of Fundamental Rights on 'Private Parties' within Autonomous Internet Law*, pp. 1354-1355.

the broadest one, includes deliberately created provisions such as model laws and conventions.

It should be emphasised however, that with the exception of conventions, all other sources are subordinate to custom, because unless the norms originating from them become customarily adhered to or used, they will not attain the status of binding rights or obligations. Therefore, the term 'source' will be used to denote a distinct source of origin or a source of inspiration for a customary practice. And the term 'custom' will be used to denote both an existing body of usages or a formation mechanism that can be triggered by spontaneous acts of Internet users or be the outcome of a deliberate rule-making process.

The primary sources of norms in the proposed concept of supranational Internet law would consist of spontaneously developed customs, consistent arbitral awards and judgments of national courts, general principles of Internet law and norms developed by specialised organisations that include technical standards, models laws, model agreements and commonly used contract terms as well as some conventions. This is not a closed list as there might be other sources that might inspire the creation of customary norms.

However, these norms irrespective of their source of origin, have to be widely applied in practice in order to become binding. In other words, they have to be confirmed or 'sealed' by custom. Only widespread acceptance of these norms in practice can rise them to the level of global Internet law. The various sources of supranational Internet law are thus subjected to customary acceptance, without which they would not attain supranational binding force.

2.1 **Custom**

Custom offers the richest body of globally followed norms on the Internet. Provided that a given customary practice is widely followed by a dominant majority of Internet users it creates an expectation that such behaviour is permissible or obligatory. This is so, even if it was formed in a relatively short period of time, for instance a year or even less than a year.[1329] The previous chapters have provided numerous examples of widely accepted rights and obligations in the area of access to information, online advertising, online contracting, online property and online security. Numerous others exist or are in the process of being formed particularly in the area of online auctions, web accessibility, data protection, online payment systems, and e-government and so on.

However, custom understood as a process of creating norms also validates the norms originating from other sources such as arbitral awards, Model laws or contract clauses. Therefore, unless such awards or some provisions of Model laws express norms that are actually widely followed in practice, they cannot be regarded as binding norms based on which an arbitrator or a judge could settle a

[1329] See the discussion in Chapter VII.

dispute. The mere fact that a given norm is promulgated by an international organisation or a judicial body is not in itself sufficient to attach to it a binding character. Such norm must be followed by adjudicators in other cases or by the Internet community itself in order to be considered binding. In this sense, these other sources are subordinate to custom.

So far the focus of the book was on the essence of custom as a source of law. However, the idea of supranational Internet law requires the examination of relation of custom to other sources of norms, particularly to international conventions. Custom can supplement existing international or domestic legislation when it is specifically referred to (*consuetudo secundum legem*), fill in gaps where there is no actual provision in the existing body of law (*consuetudo praeter legem*) or be conflict with existing body of law (*consuetudo contra legem*).

(a) *Consuetudo secundum legem*

Internet customs can supplement international legislation when, for instance, written norms expressly refer to customs or usages to resolve ambiguities or fill in gaps (*consuetudo secundum legem*). In such case scenario, custom plays subordinate role to that of legislation. This is the case with Article 8(3) of the Vienna Convention on Contracts for the International Sale of Goods, which states that in determining the intent of a party or the understanding a reasonable person due consideration is to be given to all relevant circumstances of the case including usages.

Furthermore, quite often international instruments or domestic statutes do not contain an explicit reference to custom or usages, but other terms are used that in fact mean the same thing. For instance, the aforementioned Vienna Convention stipulates in Article 55 that where a contract does not expressly or implicitly determines the price, the parties are considered:

> 'to have impliedly made reference to the price generally charged at the time of the conclusion of the contract for such goods sold under comparable circumstances in the trade concerned.'[1330]

Therefore, to establish what price was generally charged at the time of the formation of the contract, an adjudicator would have to establish what the particular price usage was at that time.

As we can see, an adjudicator should refer to custom, whenever a conventional or domestic regulation contains a specific reference to custom or a similar term to that effect. Such customs supplement existing laws with more detailed provisions.

[1330] See Art. 55 of CISG discussed in Chapter IV.

(b) *Consuetudo praeter legem*

Internet customs can also supplement written law when there is no law on the point even though a treaty or a statute does not contain an explicit reference to a custom. In this sense, custom is independent source of law that fills in gaps (*consuetudo praeter legem*). For instance, neither the new United Nations Convention on the Use of Electronic Communications in Electronic Contracting or the Vienna Sales Convention contains any provisions relating to the security of online contracting. It is clear that customary practices that have emerged in this field could fill in gaps left by these instruments.

Furthermore, customary norms can also supplement provisions that are too vague. For instance, the aforementioned UN Convention on Electronic Contracting contains a provision dealing with input error, which gives a user a right to withdraw from a portion of the communication if 'the automated message system does not provide the person with an opportunity to correct the error.'[1331] However, the provision is silent on how such opportunity to correct the error should look like. This provision does not contain a reference to customary norms or usages to fill in these gaps. But as it was discussed in the previous chapters, there are numerous techniques that are customarily employed in this regard and which could be utilised by an adjudicator.

Customs can also help with the interpretation of vague provisions. For instance, as it was repeated throughout the book, the European Directive on Electronic Commerce 'unconsciously' put in writing a custom of immediate order confirmation by requiring electronic acknowledgement of recipient's order without undue delay. This provision seems to be specific but the terms *undue delay* and *electronic acknowledgment* are certainly unclear. A resort to customary practice that requires an immediate order confirmation would sort out the dispute. On the other hand, the electronic acknowledgement should be provided on a website and via e-mail. In addition, it should contain at least an order reference number together with the summary of the most important terms of the agreement and/or a hyperlink to the terms of the agreement.[1332]

In all these cases, customary norms exist 'next' to the body of written law that contains gaps or ambiguities, although it appears to be complete as it does not contain any references to usages. But existing customs are more specific and hence can either fill in a gap or help with the interpretation of a vague provision. Sometimes, supplementary and interpretative functions of custom are distinguished, but as the aforementioned examples demonstrate, in practice such distinctions are very difficult to make.

[1331] See Art. 14 of the Convention and the discussion in Chapter IV.

[1332] See, for example, the Transaction Confirmation case in Chapter VII.

(c) *Consuetudo contra legem*

It is therefore clear that custom can supplement existing developments on international and domestic level irrespective of whether a specific reference to usage is made or not. However, a custom can also function in direct opposition to existing written instruments (*consuetudo contra legem*). This is certainly the most controversial function of a custom. However, if a legal norm is vague, unreasonable or unenforceable people might actually engage in a widespread practice that at the first glance, seems to be 'against the law'. But one should not forget that a conventional or statutory obligation that has not been followed in practice and that has been replaced by a contrary one could be regarded as extinguished or fallen into disuse (*desuetude*).

For instance, as it was argued in the previous chapter, intellectual property law is an area where such tensions are clearly visible. According to Article 9(1) of the Berne Convention the authors of literary and artistic 'shall have the exclusive right of authorizing the reproduction of these works, in any manner or form.'[1333] WIPO Treaties explain that the reproduction right fully applies in the digital environment and that the storage of a copyrighted work, performance or phonogram in digital form in an electronic medium constitutes a reproduction.[1334] As a result, a reproduction of a website in the client's computer memory, or in the server's memory without authorisation of the author or the producer would infringe upon these rights. However, it became customary to reproduce digital works without authorisation as it would be clearly unreasonable to ask for such authorisation each time such technological process takes place. Therefore, a custom *contra legem* emerged that abrogated the prohibition in this regard. Similar examples were cited in the previous chapter with respect to forwarding e-mails without authorisation, using thumbnails or textual hyperlinks and so on. In all these cases, it could be argued that a specific customary practice is in conflict with a general provision set out in the convention or a statute.

Similarly, uploading the copyrighted artwork on peer-to-peer networks such as Kazaa clearly violates the international conventions such as the 1996 WIPO Internet Treaties and numerous domestic legal systems. As was discussed in Chapter IV, the 1996 WIPO Treaties give the author the exclusive right of authorising any communication to the public of their works, by wired or wireless means. Giving access to a protected work on someone's hard drive without the consent of the right holder violates the said provision. However, a widespread practice has emerged in this area that is undoubtedly *contra legem*. Nevertheless, so far it turned out to be virtu-

---

[1333] Similar provision is included in Art. 10 of the 1961 Rome Convention for the Protection of Performers, Producers of Phonograms and Broadcasting Organizations, which states: 'Producers of phonograms shall enjoy the right to authorize or prohibit the direct or indirect reproduction of their phonograms.' See also Art. 7c.

[1334] Agreed statements concerning Art. 1(4) of WCT and Arts. 7, 11 and 16 of WPPT. See Chapter IV.

ally impossible to enforce the conventional right. It is so despite rulings of courts in various jurisdictions. It is too early to state whether uploading files on peer-to-peer network could be permitted by virtue of the operation of the customary norm to that effect. Certainly, at this stage, the legal community is not ready for such change.

2.2 Consistent arbitral awards and domestic court judgments

Arbitral awards or judgments provide a unique and very important source of norms that could be used to settle disputes on the Internet. They are important also because they might confirm or apply a customary norm that has emerged in practice. However, a norm expressed in an arbitral award or a judgment would not achieve the status of a binding norm, unless it is repeatedly and consistently upheld in similar cases. It must achieve a status of a 'judicial custom' to be considered binding.

A recent informal overview of panel positions on key procedural and substantial issues produced by WIPO under the Uniform Domain Name Dispute Resolution Policy and Rules (UDRP) provides an excellent example of judicial norms that could have attained a customary character.[1335] On most of the issues, consensus or clear majority views have developed. As an example, the consensus view has emerged with respect to the question whether the content of a website is relevant in determining confusing similarity:

> 'Consensus view: The content of a website (whether it is similar or different to the business of a trademark owner) is irrelevant in the finding of confusing similarity. This is because trademark holders often suffer from "initial interest confusion", where a potential visitor does not immediately reach their site after typing in a confusingly similar domain name, and is then exposed to offensive or commercial content. The test for confusing similarity should be a comparison between the trademark and the domain name to determine the likelihood of confusion.'[1336]

On the other hand, the majority view emerged with respect to the question whether a domain name consisting of a trademark and a negative term is confusingly similar to the complainant's trademark ('sucks cases'):

> 'Majority view: A domain name consisting of a trademark and a negative term is confusingly similar to the complainant's mark. Confusing similarity has been found because the domain name contains a trademark and a dictionary word; or because the disputed domain name is highly similar to the trademark; or because the domain name

---

1335 WIPO (2005), *WIPO Overview of WIPO Panel Views on Selected UDRP Questions*.

1336 Question 1.2. Ibid., citing the following relevant decisions: 'Relevant decisions:
Arthur Guinness Son & Co. (Dublin) Limited v. Dejan Macesic D2000-1698 <guiness.com>, Transfer
Ansell Healthcare Products Inc. v. Australian Therapeutics Supplies Pty, Ltd. D2001-0110 <ansellcondoms.com>, Transfer
Dixons Group Plc v. Mr. Abu Abdullaah D2001-0843 <dixons-online.net>, Transfer
AT&T Corp. v. Amjad Kausar D2003-0327 <attinternet.com>, <attuniversal.com>, Transfer.'

> may not be recognized as negative; or because the domain name may be viewed by non-fluent English language speakers, who may not recognize the negative connotations of the word that is attached to the trademark.'[1337]

Since that view has not achieved the overwhelming majority, the position of the opposing minority is also cited:

> 'Minority view: A domain name consisting of a trademark and a negative term is not confusingly similar because Internet users are not likely to associate the trademark holder with a domain name consisting of the trademark and a negative term.'[1338]

Only consensus views could be regarded as establishing norms of customary character. The majority views should in principle be regarded as representing custom in formation. On the other hand, consistent rulings of various domestic courts should also be taken into account as this may lead to the formation of international Internet custom. This matter requires however, more in-depth analysis.

2.3 Conventions

International conventions such as the new 2005 Convention on the use of electronic communication in international contracts were always regarded as a separate source of law, independent from international custom. However, the downside of international conventions is that very often they have very few participants and hence do not provide globally binding legal framework.

Although conventions bind because of the will of the parties, they could become binding upon third parties by virtue of the operation of custom. One should repeat again that according to Article 38 of the Vienna Convention on the Law of Treaties nothing

> 'precludes a rule set forth in a treaty from becoming binding upon a third State as a customary rule of international law, recognized as such.'

[1337] Ibid. Question 1.3 citing 'Wal-Mart Stores, Inc. v. Richard MacLeod d/b/a For Sale D2000-0662 <walmartsucks.com>, Transfer
A & F Trademark, Inc. and Abercrombie & Fitch Stores, Inc. v. Justin Jorgensen D2001-0900 <aber crombieandfilth.com>, Transfer
Berlitz Investment Corp. v. Stefan Tinculescu D2003-0465 <berlitzsucks.com>, Transfer
Wachovia Corporation v. Alton Flanders D2003-0596 <wachovia-sucks.com> among others, Transfer.'

[1338] Ibid., citing 'Lockheed Martin Corporation v. Dan Parisi D2000-1015 <lockheedmartinsucks.com>, Denied
McLane Company, Inc. v. Fred Craig D2000-1455 <mclanenortheastsucks.com>, Denied
America Online, Inc. v. Johuathan Investments, Inc., and Aollnews.com D2001-0918 <aollnews.com>, <fucknetscape.com> Transfer, Denied in Part.'

In this sense, international conventions could be utilised by arbitrators or judges even if a given state is not a signatory of it, provided that the provisions enshrined in it became customarily adhered to. Chapter IV provided detailed examination of conventions applicable to Internet so it will not be repeated here.

2.4 General principles of Internet law

General principles of Internet law could be regarded as a special category of customs that have general character, broad scope and enjoy wide recognition. The previous chapter has mentioned the principle of *pacta sunt servanda* as an example of a universal custom that also applies in the online world. On the other hand, the Model Law on Electronic Commerce proposed two principles of functional equivalency and technology neutrality that could possibly also be regarded as general principles of Internet law. These principles have been confirmed in legislations of numerous states. However, one should be mindful of the fact that the mere adoption of a law may not be sufficient, unless these principles are actually applied in practice. As a result, more research is necessary in this regard.

2.5 Model laws

State-oriented model laws such the UNCITRAL Model Law on Electronic commerce or private parties oriented model laws as 2004 UNDIROIT Principles or should be included within the framework of supranational Internet law, as they represent important developments in this area. Although the UNCITRAL Model laws normally are only guidelines for legislator, they can attain a global importance if principles enshrined in them become customarily adhered to.

2.6 Model agreements and commonly used contract terms

As in traditional *lex mercatoria* model agreements and contract clauses could attain a legal value, provided that they are widely used in practice. As a result, if parties did not include certain provision in a contract or in electronic standard terms and conditions, such clause could be implied provided that it was commonly used in online trade practice.[1339] Likewise, if electronic standard terms contain surprising provisions that are uncommon in electronic commerce such regulations should not be given legal effect by an adjudicator.[1340]

1339 See also Art. 1160 of the Code Napoleon and the discussion in Chapter IV.

1340 See also Art. 2.1.20 of the 2004 UNIDROIT Principles discussed in Chapter IV.

2.7 **Technical standards**

Technical standards created by organisations as IETF, W3C or ISO have a tremendous impact on the Internet.[1341] These standards create architectural confines, within which the Internet operates. Obligation to adhere to such standards might become apparent especially in the context of provision technology-neutral Internet solutions. For instance, the newly adopted Regulation of the Council of Ministers of Poland specifies the minimum technical standards that e-governmental bodies should support. The list of required standards range from network protocols developed by IETF, to Web standards created by W3C, to document standards created by various commercial players such as Microsoft, Adobe or OASSISS.[1342] Again, such standards are important only when they become widely followed in practice.

3. Potential Benefits

The concept of supranational Internet law has the following advantages:

Firstly, it can serve as a basis for solving Internet disputes in cases where contract parties either failed to choose a national legal system governing the interpretation of their contract or explicitly chose *lex mercatoria* as a law governing it. In such a case scenario, national courts hearing a dispute or more likely arbiters could solve the dispute with a reference to transnational commercial customs and other common trade principles that ought to be known to all merchants.

Secondly, supranational Internet law can coexist and supplement recognised international and domestic legal regimes. For instance, where a particular legal system selected as the law applicable in a given case would not contain relevant norms, a judge or an arbitrator could fill in gaps with a reference to customary norms of Internet *lex mercatoria*. The idea of peaceful coexistence of such systems rather than that of mutual exclusion is of particular importance.

Thirdly, detailed knowledge of actual business practices is essential for drafting sound national, regional and international legislation in this field. Customary Internet law could thus serve as a source of inspiration for future international and domestic regulation of electronic commerce. Furthermore, it could help harmonise existing national regulations of the Internet. In other words, common practices in a rapidly changing technological world are invaluable sources of inspiration for legislators dealing with not only B2B e-commerce but also consumer- and government- centric online trade. The last point is worth continuous emphasising as in principle the differences between consumers and businesses in the online world have been blurred.

[1341] See Chapter III.

[1342] Dz.U. nr 212 poz. 1766 (11.10.2005), *Rozporządzenie RM w sprawie minimalnych wymagań dla systemów teleinformatycznych*.

Fourthly, norms embodied in common commercial practices could be used in the interpretation of both contractual gaps and national or supranational regulation. For instance, several provisions of the EU directives related to electronic commerce would have to be supplemented with a reference to the customs of the Internet in order to fully reflect the needs of European electronic commerce.

4. Issues to Consider

Although there are potential sources of norms that could be utilised in providing justice in cyberspace, much work is required to build effective online dispute resolution mechanisms applying them. We have a precursor of such a system in the ICANN arbitration panels, but they are limited to domain name disputes only. Without new online dispute resolution systems and their wide usage, no precedents will be established that will help to interpret existing body of norms and inspire the creation of new ones.

The solution could be to broaden the prerogatives of existing panels settling domain name disputes to embrace other areas, in particular e-commerce contracts and delicts. For instance, an online seller that sells defective products could be punished by blocking access to his domain name thus preventing him from continuation of his dishonest practices. In consequence, such system could help prevent many anomalies that have appeared on the Net. The enforcement of the decision could be strengthened by co-operation of arbitral panels with for example, search engines that could inform people looking for a given company that it had been blacklisted.

In addition, such framework would have to be available not only in professionals but also to consumers. As it was already recognised in the business literature,[1343] online consumers are often better equipped with the technological knowledge than many professionals. The demarcation line should no longer be drawn between consumers and professionals but between computer literate and illiterate. In consequence, one should create unified framework for both computer savvy professionals and consumers.

Such unified framework would certainly boost the confidence in international electronic commerce as in fact, existing national consumer protection laws create serious obstacles to global online trade. They give only fictious protection to consumers who will very rarely if ever try to enforce their rights in other jurisdictions. They also put unduly heavy burdens on online professionals, who must be prepared to comply with numerous consumer protection regimes. For instance, online traders in the European Union must be prepared to accept consumer's withdrawal from a deal within 7 days or more for any reason.

[1343] See Chapter I.

The proposed vision of existing arbitrage panels settling disputes in other than domain name cases and broadened to include consumers might be difficult to accept by national judges, who may oppose the enforcement of such arbitral awards. It is obvious that more time would be necessary for national legal systems to get familiar and accept the just sketched alternative vision of dispute resolution in cyberspace. Soon, maybe other, better ideas appear. But what is necessary is to start creating such systems and testing them in practice. The time will tell whether such solutions inspire domestic legal systems or not.

5. Conclusion

As it was stated at the beginning of this chapter, the proposal of the detailed framework required for Internet law requires a separate analysis.[1344] Such a framework would involve a comprehensive analysis of the interrelation between custom and other potential general and particular sources of Internet supranational law, especially national legislation, treaties, contracts and case law. It would also need to analyse the practice of online arbitration and domestic courts. This book outlined only some of these interrelations and focused instead on the analysis of custom as the most important potential source of the supranational Internet law.

Furthermore, much still needs to be done in order for such a system to be accepted by the legal and mercantile community. Of particular importance to the success of the notion of Internet customary law is the identification, exploration and publication of new cyberspace customs. These should be sought out on a global level as well as in local settings.

Similarly to what transcribers of local customs in the Middle Ages did in relation to their local laws, so should the researcher of Internet practices do in relation to the online world. New customs should be identified and evidenced, and knowledge about them should be disseminated to the legal community as well as the Internet community. The system of electronic commerce law certainly needs more well evidenced examples of customary norms before their impact can become more visible. Similarly, the Internet community must be given more examples of potential impacts of conformance and ignorance of common practices before the knowledge of them becomes obligatory. Finally, judges and arbitres must be educated about the culture of the Internet society in order to better understand its needs and provide better justice.

1344 More on this topic in Polanski, P.P. (2005), *Information Society and the Internet Law Merchant*; Polanski, P.P. (12 May 2005), *W poszukiwaniu autonomicznego prawa Internetu*.

CONCLUSION

Modern understanding of law is often equated with a top-down, 'rational' regulation of social life in written acts prescribing rights and obligations to its addressees. This approach ignores the existence of the oldest source of law – the foundation of any legal system on earth – the concept of custom as a basis of regulatory norms between humans. Before any centralised system of legislation emerged, humans relied on their past conduct in relation to one another. This knowledge gave them a basis for settling disputes.

Nowadays, in modern domestic legal systems, this empirical basis has been almost completely eradicated by the written law. In consequence, modern legislators search for regulation of the Internet utilising a tool that is best known to them: a domestic statute. The resort to national regulation of the Internet is a natural choice as law making on a national level is much easier than in an international forum.

But the Internet is a truly global phenomenon, which does not recognise geopolitical borders and which can deliver information to the other side of the earth in less than a second. Regulating the Internet via domestic means ignores the architecture of the medium that was created to enable a rapid, decentralised and global exchange of information. This national approach to regulating the Internet may end up creating islands of regulation, where Internet users will not know their rights and obligations, thus increasing uncertainty rather than eliminating it. Domestic regulation may help to solve some Internet-related legal disputes but only if it reflects the real expectations of Internet users. Nevertheless, its influence will necessarily be limited by the concept of sovereignty.

Hence the international legal community has turned to the idea of harmonisation of domestic Internet laws through the process of adoption and implementation of Model laws developed under the auspices of the United Nations. But even this idea has not produced a global legal framework for the Internet. The majority of states have not enacted any laws dealing with the Internet. The states that have adopted Model laws have changed them slightly, thus creating the potential for different interpretations and ultimately disputes in this regard. Besides, the content of Model laws and the implementing legislation are too general to provide real assurance of one's rights and obligations in cyberspace.

On the other hand, existing international treaties have not been designed for the Information Age. For instance, the Vienna Convention on Contracts for the International Sale of Goods (CISG) was drafted before the emergence of the modern Internet.

P.P. Polański, Customary Law of the Internet

It applies only to the sale of goods and does not cover trading in services and information. Furthermore, it does not apply to sales via such fundamental Internet mechanisms as auctions and does not cover trade in shares and other areas where the Internet has drastically changed current practice.[1345] In addition, CISG applies only to Business-to-Business transactions, thus excluding Business-to-Consumer or Consumer-to-Consumer transactions.

The solution could be to develop an international agreement governing the rights and obligations in electronic commerce. In fact, the United Nations has just adopted Convention on the Use of Electronic Communications in International Contracts, largely based on the Vienna Convention and UNCITRAL Model laws.[1346] However, it is too early to discuss the impact of this Convention, as it has not been open for signature yet.

In consequence, the Internet community functions to a large extent in a legal vacuum. This is despite the fact that some states have begun to regulate e-commerce and other states could potentially apply existing rules to settle certain types of Internet disputes. But in many new cases the old rules are unsuitable to electronic commerce or are not universally recognised by other legal systems. Such a situation hinders the development of global Internet commerce.

Therefore, unless Internet users agree on their rights and obligations in contracts, their legal standing will be uncertain. The problem becomes clear in the context of Internet commerce. Since there are no top-down written laws that govern electronic commerce, a party to the transaction has to rely on its own intuition when dealing with an electronic supplier of goods and services. Even a party that has signed a contract cannot feel safe, because a contract may and probably will contain many gaps. Moreover, the questions of law governing a contract or law of forum may turn out to be difficult to answer.

However, custom could provide a viable solution to the lack of globally binding norms on the Internet. Internet customary practices are formed without regard for geopolitical borders or sovereign authorities. Lack of central authority on the Net inhibits the promulgation of globally binding laws, which at this stage can be formed only in a bottom-up manner.

The main focus of this study has been the concept of custom or a widespread and legally relevant practice of trading on the Internet analysed from a global, rather than domestic, perspective. It was argued that Internet commerce participants have developed and widely follow certain practices, and that some of these practices might have considerable legal importance. In other words, there is already a law on the Internet. But it is an unwritten, constantly changing law, one that needs to be

[1345] UNCITRAL (1980), *United Nations Convention on Contracts for the International Sale of Goods*.

[1346] UNCITRAL Working Group IV (Electronic Commerce) (2005), *A/60/17 – Report of the United Nations Commission on International Trade Law on the work of its thirty-eighth session, 4-15 July 2005*.

discovered rather than enacted. It is the law of Internet commerce participants, created by them through conscious or unconscious following of certain online practices. These practices are largely unwritten, but they are there. One of the aims of this study was to articulate them and make the Internet community aware of them.

To enhance the theoretical understanding of custom, a new theory of Internet commerce custom was proposed. In summary, custom should be understood as a widespread practice of how something is done. It was argued that any custom can become a legal one, if it can help solve a dispute at hand. Theoretical deficiencies of international custom were eliminated by rejecting the need for a psychological element in its definition. It was also argued that custom no longer needs to be ancient or immemorial.

To overcome the practical limitations of the notion of custom as a source of law, so clearly visible in international law, a new methodology for evidencing has been offered. The proposed framework is a major achievement as lawyers have not been interested in the development of a coherent empirical framework for evidencing customary practices. As the case law of the International Court of Justice clearly shows, they would rather declare or infer the existence of a given customary norm from an amount of practice that does not permit any generalisation.

This new methodology takes into account the peculiar features of the Internet, in particular, its digital character, where the role of a human is equal to that of machine, its global nature and its decentralised, uncontrollable character. Having a practical application in mind, the methodology provides new ways of establishing customs using software components and human experts. A three-test framework has been proposed, based on examination of the production tools used to build the digital environment, the products of these tools and opinions of legal and technical experts on the practice in question.

As was shown in the hypothetical case studies, this new methodology can be used to successfully prove the existence of different Internet customary practices. In particular, the analysis of software packages used to build websites, together with the analysis of a sample of commercial websites, has clearly shown the existence of widespread practice of immediate order confirmation via the Web and e-mail. Similarly, the analysis of one hundred randomly chosen online banking websites has clearly established the custom of strong encryption being supported on banking web servers. The norms arising out of these facts were used to solve the hypothetical case studies, which could not be adjudicated on the basis of generally binding international law or a contract agreement between the parties. Thus, custom was used to provide norms in the absence of globally binding law.

Having both the theory as well as a methodology with which to apply it in practice, this study makes a call to undertake a broader research into the customary practices on the Internet. It is to be hoped that this exploration will open a new area of research. Its thorough investigation is vital for the development of a solid legal framework for global Internet commerce and for the further development of the Internet.

GLOSSARY OF LEGAL AND TECHNICAL TERMS

Alternative Dispute Resolution (ADR) – a way of settling disputes outside the court system. The most important form of ADR is Arbitration.

Arbitration – an informal way of resolving legal disputes. A party to a dispute usually chooses one arbitrator and both of them choose a third arbitrator. Arbitrators are not bound by specific rules of a particular legal system, unless an agreement states to the contrary. Arbitrators can also devise their own procedure of settling a dispute, which usually is less formal than one applied by national courts. National courts usually uphold arbitration awards.

Arbitrator – a person that adjudicates disputes. Arbitrators are chosen by the parties and do not (necessarily have) a legal background.

ARPANET (Advanced Research Project Agency Network) – a computer network developed by Advanced Research Project Agency (ARPA) in the United States. A precursor of modern Internet based on packet switching technology.

Artificial agent – or intelligent agent – a software program that possesses a degree of autonomy and can communicate with other agents. Artificial agents can have goals, which they can realise without explicit control of a user. Unlike normal software programs that perform a set of operations in given circumstances (reactive behaviour), some artificial agents can learn and modify their behaviour accordingly (proactive behaviour).

Asymmetric Encryption – in asymmetric encryption two different but related keys are used for encryption and decryption. See Public Key Encryption, Public key, Private key, SSL.

ATM (Automatic Teller Machine) – is a mechanical cash dispenser used primarily by a bank's customers to make cash withdrawals at any time without human intervention. Many ATMs also allow people to select different languages, deposit cash and transfer money between their bank accounts. The technology was developed in the 1960s and became very widespread in modern times.

B2B (Business-to-Business) – refers to electronic commerce between professionals, for instance between warehouses and electronic outlets or between a factory and electronic outlets. See B2C, C2C.

B2C (Business-to-Consumer) – refers to electronic commerce between a professional and a consumer. This classification is particularly important for consumer protection laws. However, it is increasingly difficult to distinguish between B2C and B2B web pages because many online sellers offer their products to both categories of buyers without any distinction. See B2B, C2C.

Blog – an electronic diary on a website, where people write about their daily life and thoughts. Anyone can read it. It is usually created using freely available software tools that require only a very basic computer knowledge.

Botnet – a network controlled by a software robots or bots. Such networks are attacked by hackers, which install software robots that act autonomously. Botnets are often used for DDoS attacks. See DoS attack.

Brute force attack – a way of breaking a secret code by trying all the possible combinations.

Caching – a technology that allows storing a copy of a website in a browser's memory or other computer's memory to speed up the process of retrieving a website. Once a website is cached, a browser will not need to request a website from a web server, but will fetch it directly from the cache memory, thus reducing network traffic and improving performance of a system.

Cascading Style Sheets (CSS) – a language of the Web that is concerned with presentation of a web page, which enriches HTML. It allows setting different fonts, colours, borders, etc.

Certificate – a digital ID, equivalent to offline identification documents such as a passport or a driver licence. It is granted by the Certification Authority after presenting the required number of documents. It contains the Certificate Authority's name, the Subject's name, the Public Key of the subject and some time stamps. The certificate is signed with the Certificate's Authority private key. The certificate is valid for a certain period of time and has to be renewed. Certificates can be issued to different subjects including persons, businesses or servers. See also Certificate Authority, Public key, Private key, Public Key Encryption, SSL.

Certificate Authority – an organisation, usually a respected public institution such as a bank or post office that issues digital certificates. Certificate Authorities are linked in a hierarchy, in which Certificate Authorities below are certified by authorities above in the chain. Such a structure allows recognition of certificates issued by other Certificate Authorities. See Certificate, SSL.

CIF (Cost, Insurance, Freight) – one of the most widely used commercial terms in international sales contracts when sea transport is used. When a price is quoted CIF, it means that the selling price includes the cost of the goods, the cost of marine insurance and transport (freight) costs. CIF has been defined in International Commercial Terms (INCOTERMS). See FOB, INCOTERMS, custom.

Cipher – an encryption algorithm, e.g., RC2, RC4, IDEA, DES, Triple DES. See Symmetric Encryption, Asymmetric Encryption, Public Key Encryption, SSL, RC2, RC4, IDEA, DES, Triple DES.

CISG (Convention on Contracts for the International Sale of Goods) – the most important convention that deals with international sale of goods. It covers contract formation and rights and obligations of buyers and sellers. As of August 2006 there are 67 parties to this treaty.

Client-Server technology – a technology based on an exchange of messages between two computers in which one plays the role of a client requesting the services from a server, which provides them. Servers usually provide services to many clients. On the Web, the server software is called a Web server and the client software is called a Web browser. A web browser requests a web page from a web server that stores it.

Cloaking – the practice of serving one version of a page to search engine spiders and another version to human visitors. See Metatags.

Computer Aided Logistics Support (CALS) – an early form of collaborative electronic commerce adopted by the heavy manufacturing and defence industries. CALS enabled joint design, production and product maintenance. The WWW enabled a new level of collaborative e-commerce sometimes referred to as collaborative commerce (c-commerce).

C2B (Consumer-to-Business) – refers to electronic commerce between consumers and a business, for instance individuals offer products (e.g., photos) and services (e.g., his or her work) to companies and the companies pay them. C2B electronic commerce is a complete reversal of traditional business model where companies offer goods and services to consumers. Online comparison services have often been regarded as a form of Consumer-to-Business e-commerce (e.g., Priceline.com). For more, see <http://c2b.typepad.com/>. See also B2B, B2C, C2C.

C2C (Consumer-to-Consumer) – refers to electronic commerce between consumers that is facilitated by a professional party that acts as a middle-man. Most often used in the context of electronic auctions offered by, for instance eBay. There are also other types of electronic commerce. See B2B, B2C, C2B.

Consuetudo – in Latin means custom. See Custom.

Consuetudo contra legem – in Latin, custom against the law. The expression is used to describe a situation where customary norm is contrary to written provision of a statute or a convention. Modern Western legal systems usually do not recognise customs that are contrary to written law.

Consuetudo praeter legem – in Latin, custom 'next to' law. The expression used to describe a situation when custom fills in gaps even when the written law does not expressly refers to custom. Western legal systems not unusually recognise customs operating next to written law.

Consuetudo secundum legem – in Latin, custom supplementing law. Usually used to describe a situation when a provision of a convention or a statute expressly refers to custom to fill in details. Western legal systems often contain written laws that refer to customs or usages to fill in gaps. See Consuetudo praeter legem, Consuetudo contra legem.

Cookie – a small text file that keeps information about user's activity between HTTP sessions. Since HTTP is a stateless protocol, meaning that it does not keep any information between sessions, cookies were developed to store some necessary temporary information, e.g., login information, financial data, user's profile, etc., without the need to enter them every time. A user can turn the cookies off in his or her web browser. Such action will also block web beacons. See Web beacon.

Cryptography – the study of secret (or coded) communication. See Encryption.

Custom – a common practice of doing something.

The Oxford English Dictionary provides the following two meanings of the term custom:

'1. A habitual or usual practice; common way of acting; usage, fashion, habit (either of an individual or of a community);

2. Law. An established usage which by long continuance has acquired the force of a law or right esp. the established usage of a particular locality, trade, society, or the like.'[1347]

Custom has different definitions in international law and in electronic commerce. See International custom, Electronic commerce custom (e-custom), Usage, Implied terms.

Cybersquatting – reserving well-known domain names (e.g., juliaroberts.com) in order to resell them.

Cyberstalking – threatening victims using Internet technology.

Denial of Service (DoS) attack – an attack based on overloading the web server with requests for web pages. The attack is more dangerous in its mutated form called Distrib-

1347 Simpson, J.A. and Weiner, E.S.C. (eds.) (1989), *The Oxford English Dictionary*.

uted Denial of Service (DDoS) attack, where the requests come from a number of different computers on the Web. This type of attack will usually block access to a given website but is often used to enable hacking into the overloaded system. See Web Server, WWW, Botnet.

DES – an acronym for the Data Encryption Standard. DES is a symmetric cipher developed by IBM and adopted as a federal standard in 1975 in the United States. It uses 56-bit key to encrypt blocks of data, which is considered insecure. See Cipher, Symmetric Encryption, Encryption, SSL.

Desuetude – literally means disuse. It is a mechanism of abolishing certain provisions of statutes and other sources of written law through a long disuse.

Digital Signature – see Electronic Signature.

DNS (Domain Name System) – a global database of domain names maintained by domain name servers located throughout the Internet. This database is maintained at several locations called Regional Internet Registrars (RIR). ICANN co-ordinates the Domain Name System policing. DNS is important because a web browser before requesting a given web document has to find a numeric address of a computer on which this document is stored and for this reason, it first contacts domain name servers. Existing top level domains such as .com are managed by a number of private companies. Country level domains were managed so far by volunteers but at this point they are managed by accredited registrars. See ICANN, Domain name, HTTP, Web browser, Web server, WWW, URL.

Domain name – a reader-friendly address of an electronic document. A domain name has a unique numeric equivalent, which is stored in the Domain Name System database. There are two types of top-level domains, global and country code top level domains, plus a special top-level domain (.arpa) for the Internet infrastructure. The root of system is unnamed. Top level domain names (TLDs) consist of global TLDs (gTLDs) (EDU, COM, NET, ORG, GOV, MIL, and INT), and two letter country codes (ccTLDs) based on the ISO-3166 standard. Global top level domains (gTLDs) were created for use by the Internet public, while country code domains (ccTLDs) were created to be used by individual countries as they deemed necessary. An example of a gTLD domain name is Amazon.com and ccTLD domain name is theage.com.au. See Domain Name System, ICANN, URL.

Dynamic IP address allocation – a service performed by a network server which allocates IP addresses for each session or dynamically. IP addresses can also be allocated statically and then each computer on a network will have only one possible IP address.

EDI (Electronic Data Interchange) – the electronic transfer from computer to computer of business documents using an agreed standard to structure the information. EDI was an early (pre-Internet) form of electronic commerce between businesses.

Electronic commerce – doing business over the Internet. There are numerous other definitions of e-commerce of various scope, e.g., '…technology-mediated exchanges between parties (individuals or organization) as well as the electronically-based intra- or interorganizational activities that facilitate such exchanges.'[1348]

Electronic commerce custom (e-custom) – the legally relevant practice of trading on the Internet, which is sufficiently widespread as to justify the expectation that it will be observed. Synonyms: Internet commerce custom, e-custom, Internet custom, Internet

[1348] Rayport, J.F. and Jaworski, B.J. (2002), *Introduction to e-Commerce*, p. 4.

common practice, Internet widespread practice, online custom, digital usage, etc. See Custom, International custom.

Electronic Frontiers Foundation (EFF) – is a non-profit group working to protect digital rights of Internet users. The Electronic Frontier Foundation is based in USA and was founded in July 1990 by Mitch Kapor, John Gilmore and John Perry Barlow.

Electronic Signature – a secure way of signing documents that utilises Public Key Encryption. A sender signs a hash of the document with a public key. See Public Key Encryption, Public Key, Private key, Hash.

E-mail – an electronic mail.

Encryption – a process of scrambling or ciphering data in order to make it unreadable.

E-procurement – a complex of sourcing, ordering, category management, design and logistics collaboration with suppliers enabled by the Internet.

EU (European Union) – is an intergovernmental and supranational union of 25 (soon 27) democratic Member States in Europe.

E-tailer – an online vendor.

Extranet – a corporate inter-organisational network using the Internet which is inaccessible to general Internet users.

FTP (File Transfer Protocol) – one of the most important services enabled by the Internet which allows transferring files between computers connected to the Internet.

File sharing systems – Internet-based computer networks that enable sharing files, especially music and video files. In such systems, each user gives access to part of his or her hard drive, where files to be shared are stored, to the public. In such systems there is no central control over exchanges of files, e.g., Kazaa, Audio Galaxy, etc. However, central servers are often used for indexing purposes.

FOB (Free on Board) – One of the most commonly used commercial terms in international contracts requiring the seller to deliver goods on board a vessel designated by the buyer. The seller fulfills its obligations to deliver when the goods have passed over the ship's rail. See INCOTERMS, CIF, custom.

Form – a type of a website where a user can type in information, e.g., financial information are entered on a payment form that is usually composed of several text boxes.

Global Server ID – a server digital certificate that enables 128-bit or 40-bit SSL encryption of transactions. See also Certificate.

Hacker – originally this term meant a very good computer programmer or specialist. These days it is usually associated with person who breaks into a computer over the Internet or any network.

Handshake protocol – a first phase of the SSL protocol that aims to establish a secure communication channel between an SSL-enabled web browser and an SSL-enabled web server. See SSL.

Hash – a number derived from the characters contained in a document. Any change in a document would change the hash number and for this reason, hashing is used as a document integrity check. See also Electronic Signature.

Historical School – in law, a doctrine developed by F. Savigny. According to this school, legal norms including customary norms are only the evidence of the spirit of the nation.

Hosting – a service offered by Internet Service Providers (ISPs) that enables storage of a website on a web server for a fee. This service takes the burden of a web author associated with purchasing a computer and dedicated connection to the Internet as well as installation and configuration of web server.

HTML (HyperText Markup Language) – an unstructured language used to create websites.

HTTP (HyperText Transfer Protocol) – a language used by web browsers and web servers to communicate between each other.

HTTPS – A version of the HTTP protocol secured by Secure Sockets Layer (SSL) protocol. See SSL.

IAB (Internet Architecture Board) – IAB was established in 1984 to replace the Internet Configuration Control Board (ICCB) created in 1981 by Vint Cerf to advise him on technical issues of the Internet. Initially it consisted of several technical workforces but in 1989 IAB was reorganised, leaving only two workforces: IETF and IRTF. In June 1992 it associated its activities with a newly formed Internet Society and was renamed to Internet Architecture Board. IAB consists of 13 members: chair of IETF and 12 sitting members. Nowadays IAB serves a technical advisory board to the Internet Society and an appeal board in Internet standardisation process. See IETF, IRTF, ISOC.

IANA (Internet Assigned Numbers Authority) – has been established in 1988 by Jon Postel, one of the most prominent figures in the history of the Internet. Contrary to common misconceptions, its role as American government sponsored organisation has never been limited to the assignment of domain names and management of the Domain Name System (DNS), including the delegation of top-level domains and oversight of the root name server system. Instead it has also acted as a registrar of the IETF activities. In particular it registered detailed, low level specifications of protocols used on the Internet including registrar of numbers (types of numbers range from unique port assignments to the registration of character sets), keywords, and other parameters that must be uniquely assigned for the Internet to function properly.[1349] With the privatisation of DNS assignment functions its functions have been overtaken by ICANN. Under ICANN, the IANA continues to distribute addresses to the Regional Internet Registries, coordinates with the IETF and other organisations assignment of protocol parameters, and oversees the operation of the DNS.[1350] See DNS, RIR, ICANN, IETF.

ICANN (Internet Corporation for Assigned Names and Numbers) – is an internationally organized, non-profit corporation that has responsibility for Internet Protocol (IP) address space allocation, protocol identifier assignment, generic (gTLD) and country code (ccTLD) Top-Level Domain name system management, and root server system management functions.[1351] It has been established to take over some of the activities performed by IANA as a result of US government privatisation of Domain Name System management in 1998.[1352] Its objective is to operate as an open, transparent, and consensus-based body that is broadly representative of the diverse stakeholder communities of the global Internet. The technical work of ICANN is referred to as the IANA function. ICANN takes also an active role in policing DNS management. It has developed a global *Uniform Domain Name Dispute Resolution Policy* and *Rules for Uniform Domain Name Dispute Resolution Policy* for resolving conflicts in the domain name registration that is administered by a number of organisations including World Intellectual Property Organisation (WIPO).

[1349] Hovey, R. and Bradner, S. (1996), *RFC 2028 The Organizations Involved in the IETF Standards Process*, p. 4.

[1350] <http://www.icann.org/general/glossary.htm>, last visited: 28/08/2006.

[1351] Ibid.

[1352] ICANN (25 November 1998), *Memorandum Of Understanding Between The U.S. Department Of Commerce And Internet Corporation For Assigned Names And Numbers.*

ICANN is managed by Board of Directors and 3 supporting organisations: Domain Name Supporting Organisation, Address Supporting Organisation and Protocol Supporting Organisation. Board of Directors are elected in global elections from the community at large. The 2005 World Summit on the Information Society agreed not to get involved in the technical operations of ICANN although it established international Internet Governance Forum, with a consultative role on the future governance of the Internet.[1353] ICANN's Government Advisory Committee (GAC), is currently set up to provide advice to ICANN regarding public policy issues and has participation by many of the world's governments. See IANA, WIPO, DNS, Domain name, WGIG, WSIS, RIR.

IDEA – Symmetric cipher developed in 1991 that uses 128-bit keys to encrypt blocks of data. See Encryption, Symmetric Encryption, SSL, RC2, RC4.

IETF (Internet Engineering Task Force) – IETF is the principal organisation engaged in the development of new Internet standard specifications. Areas of interest have ranged from security to transport to routing to operations and management to standard processes to policy formulation. Work is carried on protocols seen by user programs such as email or WWW, different ways of moving IP packets and DNS information, network monitoring, configuration and operation, improving routing of packets, improving security, authentication and privacy, special services for special packets and internal to IETF procedures. IETF proposes standards in Requests for Comments (RFC) some of which became Internet standards.

IETF has officially emerged from IAB in 1986. In the early days, IETF was financed by US government but with the establishment of Internet Society and its association with IAB, IETF became the most important Internet standard organisation financially supported by ISOC. IETF 'is a large open international community of network designers, operators, vendors, and researchers concerned with the evolution of the Internet architecture and the smooth operation of the Internet.' [1354] It is a virtual organisation in a sense that it is not an incorporated organisation, has no board of directors or members.

IIS (Internet Information Services) – the world's second most popular web server developed by Microsoft (after Apache web server). IIS currently includes FTP, SMTP, NNTP and HTTP/HTTPS. See Web server, WWW, FTP, HTTP, SSL.

Implied terms – in Anglo-American legal systems contractual terms (or express terms) can be supplemented or modified by other terms or 'implied terms'. Such terms can be implied from statute, usage (custom) or from common law. See custom, usage.

Implied terms (by usage) – A contract may incorporate any usage of the market, locality or trade unless it is inconsistent with the express terms of the contract or its nature. Such usage will be binding on both parties if it is notorious, certain, reasonable and not contrary to law. It must be widely known in the particular trade or place so that an outsider making inquiry could not fail to discover it.The parties do not have to be aware of the existence of custom.[1355] See Implied terms, custom, usage.

INCOTERMS (International Commercial Terms) – are standard trade definitions most commonly used in international sales contracts. Devised and published by the International Chamber of Commerce (ICC), they are customarily used by international merchants worldwide. ICC introduced the first version of Incoterms in 1936 and updated

---

1353 <http://en.wikipedia.org/wiki/ICANN>, last visited: 28/08/2006.

1354 <http://www.ietf.org/overview.html>, last visited: 26/08/2006.

1355 Chitty, J. (1999), *Chitty on Contracts, sec.13-018.*

them six times since. Among the best known Incoterms are EXW (Ex works), FOB (Free on Board), CIF (Cost, Insurance and Freight). See CIF, FOB, UNCITRAL, ICC, custom.

Intellectual Property (IP) law – a branch of a national law that provides protection of products of intellect. In general, IP law protects an expression of an idea rather than an idea itself. IP law protection includes copyright, trademark, patents and trade secrets.

International Chamber of Commerce (ICC) – was founded in 1919 in Paris. It promotes an open international trade and investment system and the market economy. ICC conducts its activities through publications of important documents relating to international trade as well as through dispute settlement via ICC International Court of Arbitration, generally considered to be the leading arbitral tribunal in the world. ICC is best known for a number of codifications of customary mercantile practices especially those relating to common commercial terms used in international agreements as well as those relating to international letters of credits. In regards to electronic commerce ICC has released a number of very important reports and proposals dealing with the issues posed by the new medium. In particular, ICC proposed for instance Model clauses for use in contracts involving transborder data flows and prepared important guidelines and reports about legal aspects of electronic commerce. It has also been actively participating in the development of the Convention on the Use of Electronic Communications in International Contracts and developed ICC eTerms 2004 to supplement to conventional norms.[1356] See custom, UNCITRAL, INCOTERMS, UCP.

International Court of Justice (ICJ) – an international court set up in 1945 to settle disputes between states. ICJ sits in The Hague, the Netherlands.

International custom – Article 38 of the Statute of International Court of Justice defines international custom as '(…) evidence of general practice accepted as law'.[1357] See Custom, Electronic commerce custom, International Court of Justice.

Internet – a global network of computer networks based on TCP/IP protocol. The Federal Networking Council (FNC) proposed the following definition of the Internet in its resolution passed unanimously on 24 October 1995: '"Internet" refers to the global information system that — (i) is logically linked together by a globally unique address space based on the Internet Protocol (IP) or its subsequent extensions/follow-ons; (ii) is able to support communications using the Transmission Control Protocol/Internet Protocol (TCP/IP) suite or its subsequent extensions/follow-ons, and/or other IP-compatible protocols; and (iii) provides, uses or makes accessible, either publicly or privately, high level services layered on the communications and related infrastructure described herein.'[1358]

Internet Society (ISOC) – Internet Society is sometimes considered to be a form of Internet governance. Internet Society is a non-profit, professional, and incorporated in USA organisation of international character, with more than 100 organisational and 20,000 individual members in over 180 nations worldwide.[1359] ISOC mission is to 'assure the open development, evolution and use of the Internet for the benefit of all people throughout the world.' In particular, the Internet Society:

[1356] <http://www.iccwbo.org/policy/law/id3668/index.html>, last visited: 28/08/2006.

[1357] United Nations Conference on International Organization at San Francisco (26 June 1945), *Statute of the International Court of Justice*.

[1358] Resolution passed by FNC on 24/10/1995, see also Leiner, B.M., et al., *A Brief History of the Internet*.

[1359] <http://www.isoc.org/isoc>, last visited: 28/08/2006.

1. Facilitates open development of standards, protocols, administration and the technical infrastructure of the Internet;
2. Supports education in developing countries specifically, and wherever the need exists;
3. Promotes professional development and opportunities for association to Internet leadership;
4. Provides reliable information about the Internet;
5. Provides forums for discussion of issues that affect Internet evolution, development and use — technical, commercial, societal, etc.;
6. Fosters an environment for international cooperation, community, and a culture that enables self-governance to work;
7. Serves as a focal point for cooperative efforts to promote the Internet as a positive tool to benefit all people throughout the world;
8. Provides management and coordination for on-strategy initiatives and outreach efforts — humanitarian, educational, societal, etc.[1360]

ISOC was founded in 1992 in order to provide institutional home and financial support to the Internet standardisation process led primarily by IETF. It raises funds through variety of activities including conferences, workshops and donations from industry and governments on an international level. It also manages .ORG top level domain through the Public Interest Registry (PIR). ISOC is managed by ISOC Trustees. See IETF, IRTF, IAB, IANA, ICANN.

Intranet – a private network of computers that uses Internet protocols to enable sharing information within a company.

IP (Internet Protocol) – See TCP/IP.

IP address – a unique 32-bit address of any computer on the Internet.

IRTF (Internet Research Task Force) – IRTF similarly to IETF was established in 1986 as the second arm of IAB. IRTF is not concerned with the development of Internet standards. Instead, it is concerned with more futuristic vision of the Internet comparing to areas of interest in IETF. 'It investigates topics considered to be too uncertain, too advanced, or insufficiently well-understood to be the subject of Internet standardization.'[1361] Similarly to IETF, it is comprised of several small Working Groups but its methods of operations are less formal than that of IETF. As of August 2006 IRTF has 13 active working groups including AntiSpam and Peer-to-Peer research working groups. The IRTF is managed by the IRTF Chair appointed by IAB. See IETF, ISOC, IAB.

ISP (Internet Service Provider) – a company that allows public to connect to the Internet.

Ius cogens – in Latin means mandatory law. According to Article 53 of Vienna Convention on the Law of Treaties 'a peremptory norm of general international law is a norm accepted and recognized by the international community of States as a whole as a norm from which no derogation is permitted and which can be modified only by a subsequent norm of general international law having the same character.'

Log – a file that contain information about a given activity of a computer – e.g., information about access to a given computer over time.

1360 <http://www.isoc.org/isoc/mission/>, last visited: 28/08/2006.

1361 Hovey, R. and Bradner, S. (1996), *RFC 2028 The Organizations Involved in the IETF Standards Process*, p. 4.

Metatags – non-visible parts of a website that contain information such as site description or expiration time. Meta keywords were used in various ways to improve site ranking. Currently, all major search engines including Google do not use meta elements to index web sites.

Methodology – the structured set of directives designed to solve a particular problem.

Newsgroups – a popular service on the Internet that allows users to publish information to users in a given group. USENET is a collection of newsgroups.

Organisation of Economic Co-operation and Development (OECD) – The forerunner of the OECD was the Organisation for European Economic Co-operation (OEEC) established in 1948, which was formed to administer American and Canadian aid under the Marshall Plan for reconstruction of Europe after World War II. In 1961 OECD replaced OEEC in order to build stronger economies in its member countries. It consists of 30 member states and has active links with 70 other states and organisations. OECD is best known for its economical publications and statistics. In regards to electronic commerce its distinct influence can be noticed in the area of taxation of digital trade where it proposed model convention on taxation as well as in the area of anti-spam analysis where it set up a task force on spam.[1362] It has also published a number of surveys, case studies, guidelines, projections and policy briefs on various aspects of electronic commerce including ways to measure the new economy, trade related aspects of the new economy, information and communication policy, knowledge economy, etc.

Opinio iuris – *opinio juris* or *opinio juris sive necessitatis* – a belief in the legally permissible or obligatory nature of the conduct in question, or of its necessity. The term was introduced by F. Gény in 1899 in French law and subsequently adopted by international law theorists.

OPS (Open Profiling Standard) – is a proposed standard for exchanging profile information between individuals and service-providing parties, with built-in safeguards for individual privacy developed by W3C. OPS gives individuals the ability to enter the information once, and to give specific rules about how and when that information can be exchanged with services. See W3C, PICS, P3P.

Open Source Initiative – an initiative of the Internet community that stresses the importance of freely available source code of software in order to enable open discussion and improvement of it. The most prominent examples of open source programs are the Apache web server, the Perl language, and recently the Netscape web browser.

Operating system – software that enables functioning of any computer. Without an operating system a computer would not be able to perform its most basic functions such as running programs or copying information. Windows XP or Linux are examples of operating systems.

Packet – a small sub part of the electronic message the user wants to send. See Packet-switching network.

Packet-switching network – a network of computers whose task is to disassemble a message at one end into a number of equal size packets each including the addresses of an addressor and an addressee; send these packets across potentially different routes if some of these routes were busy or destroyed, resending missing packets as necessary; and then assemble the packets back into the original message at the destination node. See Packet.

Pacta sunt servanda – In law, a Latin phrase meaning that agreements should be honoured.

[1362] <http://www.oecd-antispam.org/>, last visited: 28/08/2006.

Pactum tacitum – In law, a Latin phrase meaning a silent agreement.

PageRank – an underyling philosophy implemented in Google search engine. 'a page has high rank if the sum of the ranks of its backlinks is high. This covers both the case when a page has many backlinks and when a page has a few highly ranked backlinks.'[1363] See Search engine, Spamdexing.

Parol evidence rule – parties cannot adduce extrinsic evidence to add to, vary or contradict the written document. This rule is subject to many exceptions in Anglo-American legal systems.

Peer-to-peer (P2P) network – a network used primarily for the exchange of music and video files in a compressed format. P2P network relies on the users' computers and their Internet links rather than on servers. In such networks, servers do play a role, although usually only limited to facilitating files finding (BitTorrent, eDonkey, FastTrack, DirectConnect). The exchange of files takes place between peers. In 'pure' P2P networks, all tasks are performed by users' computers (Freenet, Gnutella). P2P networks should be distinguished from P2P programs. Every major network has one or more programms that can be used to access it, e.g., Kazaa (Fast Track), eMule (eDonkey) or Azureus (BitTorrent).

Permanent Court of International Justice (PCIJ) – a middle-war predecessor of the International Court of Justice.

Persistent objector – a doctrine peculiar to international law, which asserts that if a state has persistently objected a given customary practice, it would not be bound by it.

Pharming – a fraud, similar to phishing, based on inducing a user through redirection to a bogus website in order to obtain data such as username and password. See Phishing.

Phishing – a fraud based on inducing a user via e-mail to click on a link that opens a bogus website resembling user's, e.g., e-banking website. By filling in username and password a user actually provides this data to the middle-man, which may later use it to get access to user's account. See Pharming.

Platform for Privacy Preferences Project (P3P) – a standard developed by the World Wide Web Consortium that helps setting the privacy levels on the browser. See W3C, PICS, OPS, SVG.

Platform for Internet Content Selection (PICS) – a standard developed by the World Wide Web Consortium (W3C) that helps rating the content of web pages. See W3C, P3P, OPS, SVG.

Plug-in – a software program that performs a special job such as playing video files or music that is attached to a web browser, e.g., Flash plug-in, Shockwave plug-in, etc.

Population – all the elements in a group that are the subjects of research.

Positivism – in law, a very influential doctrine that equates law with norms promulgated by a sovereign. Legal positivists are in opposition to the theory that law should be moral to be binding.

Principles of European Contract Law (PECL) – Commission on European Contract Law led by prof. Ole Lando drafted the non-binding Principles of European Contract Law in order to re-state the European contract law. Part 1 of the Principles dealing with perfor-

---

1363 Page, L., Brin, S., Motwani, R. and Winograd, T. (29 January 1998), *The PageRank Citation Ranking:Bringing Order to the Web*, Stanford University, available at <http://dbpubs.stanford.edu:8090/pub/showDoc.Fulltext?lang=en&doc=1999-66&format=pdf&compression=&name=1999-66.pdf>, last visited: 28/08/2006.

mance, non-performance and remedies was published in 1995. PECL Parts I and II was published in 1999 and Part III in 2003.

Private key – a key that is mathematically related to a public key. It should be kept secret. A message encrypted with a private key can only be decrypted with a corresponding public key. This ensures authentication and non-repudiation of a document as only the possessor of a private key could sign it.

Proxy server – a computer that 'represents' a computer network to the outside world. It checks whether a given person will be allowed to enter the private network.

Public key – a publicly available key that is mathematically linked to the private key in Public Key Encryption (PKE). Knowledge of a public key does not allow inferring a private key. Only the possessor of the related private key can read a message encrypted with a public key, thus ensuring confidentiality.

Public Key Encryption (PKE) – also known as Asymmetric Key Encryption (AKE), is an encryption technique that uses a pair of asymmetric keys for encryption and decryption. Each pair of keys consists of a public key and a private key. Data encrypted with a public key can only be decrypted with a corresponding private key and vice versa. In other words, different or asymmetrical keys are used to encrypt and decrypt information. See Public key, Private key, Encryption, SSL.

Rapid development tools – software packages used to quickly develop software applications, e.g., certain types of websites, financial software, etc.

RC4 – a widely used symmetric cipher that encrypts a stream of data using 128-bit key. RC2 was developed by RSA Data Security. See Cipher, IDEA, Symmetric Encryption, Encryption, SSL.

RC2 – a widely used symmetric cipher that encrypts blocks of data using 128-bit key. RC2 was developed by RSA Data Security. See Cipher, IDEA, Symmetric Encryption, Encryption, SSL.

Regional Internet Registrar (RIR) – is an organisation overseeing the allocation and registration of Internet number resources within a particular region of the world. There are five RIRs in operation today: the American Registry for Internet Numbers (ARIN), the Asia Pacific Network Information Centre (APNIC), the RIPE Network Coordination Centre (RIPE NCC), Latin American and Caribbean Internet Address Registry (LACNIC) and African Network Information Centre (AfriNIC). Each of these organisations operates as an open industry self-regulatory body, structured as a not-for-profit membership association. RIRs are not responsible for domain name management (see ICANN) but are responsible for 'reverse' DNS management. IANA delegates Internet resources to the RIRs, and in turn, the RIRs follow their regional policies for further sub-delegation of resources to their customers, which include Internet service providers and end-user organisations.[1364] See DNS, IANA, ICANN.

RSS (Really Simple Syndication) – is a widely used technology for news syndication, which enables sharing content between websites. RSS is based on XML. It was designed for sharing headlines and other WWW content. The technology was created by UserLand in 1997 and subsequently used by Netscape to fill channels for Netcenter. Currently, two major standards are used for RSS feeds.[1365]

1364 See, for example, <http://en.wikipedia.org/wiki/Regional_Internet_Registry>, last visited: 28/08/2006.

1365 See, for example, <http://www.webreference.com/authoring/languages/xml/rss/intro/>, last visited: 01/11/2005.

Sample – the subgroup of a population to which a survey is administered.

Sampling frame – a listing or a method of obtaining a close approximation of all the elements in the population, e.g., a telephone directory.

Search engine – a software that permits finding information on the Web. Search engines provide results that are relevant and important to the query. Relevance is established by matching a text in a query and in a page. Importance is usually inferred from the link structure. A combined score is usually computed and resulting webpages are presented to the user. See PageRank, Spamdexing.

Session key – a key used by a web browser and a web server to encrypt data in SSL protocol. Typically, it comes in two lengths: 40 bit key and 128-bit key. Data encrypted using a 40-bit key is relatively easy to break by a brute force attack, whereas data encrypted using a 128-bit key guarantees immunity against a brute force attack. A session key is used only within one session between a web browser and a web server. It is discarded after the session ends. Since the same key is used by both a web browser and a web server the crucial thing is to securely agree on a given key. The session key is transmitted between a web browser and a web server in a Handshake phase of SSL protocol using Public Key Encryption.

Shopping carts – a widely used technology in web-based commerce to facilitate purchasing of goods over the Internet. It is the software equivalent of the shopping process in offline supermarkets where the goods first have to be put in a basket, then taken to a cash register, paid for and confirmed by a receipt. Different stages in an online purchase are indicated on a shopping cart graphic display.

SMEs (Small-to-Medium Enterprises) – in the Europan Union, companies with fewer than 50 employees are small, and those with fewer than 250 are medium enterprises.

Spamming – sending unsolicited, bulky e-mails. See Spamdexing.

Spamdexing or web spam – the practice of deliberately creating web pages which will be indexed by search engines in order to get a good ranking in search engines. Usually referred to practices that are dishonest and mislead search engines. See Spamming, Search engine, PageRank.

Spyware – software that is usually installed without user's consent and knowledge and which reports back to server information on user's activity as well as other important data.

SSL (Secure Sockets Layer) – a protocol developed by Netscape to provide security over the Internet. SSL is an open, non-proprietary protocol that provides data encryption, server authentication, message integrity, and optional client authentication. It is primarily used to secure web-based financial and credit card transactions between a web browser and a web server in conjunction with the HTTP protocol (HTTP/S), although it can be used with other protocols such as Telnet or FTP. When SSL is used the URL begins with https:// and a padlock on the status bar of the web browser indicates the strength of the encryption. Its latest version is SSL 3.0, which became the basis for the proposed TLS (Transport Layer Security) standard. SSL requires both a SSL enabled web browser and SSL enabled web server to establish a secure channel. A web server must have a valid digital certificate. A web browser does not have to have a digital certificate. SSL uses PKE to secure transmission of a session key that is used throughout a given web session to encrypt transactions. After the session ends, the session key is discarded.

Symmetric Encryption – in symmetric encryption the same key is used for encryption and decryption of transactions. See Session key, Encryption, SSL.

Scalable Vector Graphics (SVG) – a standard developed by the World Wide Web Consortium (W3C) that helps to display two-dimensional vector graphics. See W3C, P3P, OPS.

SWIFT – an international proprietary network of computers used to settle international banking transactions.

TCP/IP – Transmission Control Protocol/Internet Protocol – a language of the Internet that allows different computer networks to be interconnected. Internet Protocol (IP) allows computers located in different networks to communicate with each other based on a 32-bit IP address. Transmission Control Protocol (TCP) ensures that data transmitted between these computers will not be altered and will arrive in sequence.

TLS (Transport Layer Security) – a security transaction protocol based on SSL 3.0 proposed by IETF (Internet Engineering Task Force). See SSL.

Triple DES – a block cipher that encrypts data three times using DES cipher and at least two different keys. In SSL, three separate keys are used, and the middle step is a decryption. It is considered much safer than DES. See DES, Encryption, Cipher, SSL.

Trojan horse – software program that installs itself on a client machine and then sends any important information over the network to the hacker's computer.

UCP (Uniform Customs and Practice for Documentary Credits) – an international standard for drawing up letters of credit. Similarly to INCOTERMS, there are several versions of UCP. The latest version of UCP – UCP 500 has been developed by ICC in 1993 and is widely practiced in international banking. ICC also developed e-UCP to allow for electronic presentations of commercial letters of credit. See ICC, INCOTERMS, Custom.

UDRP (Uniform Domain Name Dispute Resolution Policy) – a policy that has been developed by ICANN and adopted by ICANN-accredited registrars in all gTLDs (.aero, .biz, .cat, .com, .coop, .info, .jobs, .mobi, .museum, .name, .net, .org, .pro, .tel and .travel). The UDRP is a policy between a registrar and its customer and is included in registration agreements for all ICANN-accredited registrars. According to UDRP, dispute proceedings arising from alleged abusive registrations of domain names may be initiated by a holder of trademark rights and heard by ICANN panels. See ICANN, cybersquatting, DNS, Domain Name, RIR.

UNCITRAL (United Nations Commission on International Trade Law) – established by the United Nations General Assembly in 1966 with the mandate to further progressive harmonisation and unification of the law of international trade. UNCITRAL performs its work in 6 Working Groups that work on the following legal matters: privately-financed infrastructure projects, international arbitration and conciliation, transport law, electronic commerce, insolvency law and security interests.

UN (United Nations) – The most important international organisation established in 1945 on an international conference at San Francisco. The UN replaced the between-wars predecessor the League of Nations. As of July 2003 there are 191 countries that are part of the United Nations. The principal organs of the United Nations are: a General Assembly, a Security Council, an Economic and Social Council, a Trusteeship Council, an International Court of Justice, and a Secretariat.

UNIDROIT (The International Institute for the Unification of Private Law) – is an independent intergovernmental organisation whose purpose is to study needs and methods for modernising, harmonising, and co-ordinating private law and in particular commercial law between states. UNIDROIT has drawned up several conventions and published UNIDROIT Principles of International Commercial Contracts 2004. See PECL, ICC.

URI (Uniform Resource Identifier) – is a compact string of characters used to identify or name a resource. See URL.

URL (Uniform Resource Locater) – the most widely used form of URI (Uniform Resource Identifier) to address websites. It can be loosly defned as a web address. An example of a URL is <http://www.amazon.com>. See Domain name, DNS.

Usage – used particularly in international trade literature as a synonym of custom of the trade. In Anglo-American legal systems contractual terms can be implied by usage i.e. customary practices can supplement or modify the terms of the agreement. Similar role can be found in continental legal systems, e.g., in French or Polish civil codes. See custom, Implied terms, implied terms (by usage).

WCT (WIPO Copyright Treaty) – one of the most important treaties dealing with copyright protection in the digital age and drafted by WIPO. See WIPO, WPPT.

Web beacon – a small transparent image file (.gif format), which is used often by advertisers to count the number of visits. Often used in combination with cookies in order to help understanding behaviour of viewers. When a user's browser requests information from a website the following additional information can also be gathered: the IP address, time of viewing, the type of browser and the existence of cookies previously set by that server.[1366] See Cookie.

Web browser – a program that is used to browse web pages. A web browser requests a web page from a web server. A request is sent whenever a user clicks a hyperlink or enters a URL. Modern web browsers also give access to e-mails, newsgroups, files using FTP, streaming audio and video and instant messaging. The most popular web browsers are Microsoft Internet Explorer, Mozzila Firefox, Apple Safari, Netscape and Opera in different versions.

Web server – a computer program running on a computer on the Internet that stores a website identified by a URL. A given web server may host only one or hundreds of websites, all identified by different URLs. A web server sends a copy of a web page in response to a request from a web browser. A web page can be sent as a plain text or as an encrypted page. Popular web servers include the Apache web server and the Microsoft Internet Information Services (IIS) in different versions. See IIS.

WGIG (Working Group on Internet Governance) – was a UN working group set up after the 2003 World Summit on the Information Society first phase Summit in Geneva to agree on the future of Internet governance. See WSIS, UN, ICANN.

WIPO (World Intellectual Property Organisation) – is an organisation based in Geneva and created formally by the Convention Establishing the World Intellectual Property Organisation in 1967. WIPO which currently has 183 member states, was established in order to promote the protection, dissemination and use of intellectual property throughout the world for economic, cultural and social development. The organisation is heavily engaged in dispute resolution process concerning the improper assignment of Internet domain names. It has developed the UDRP for resolving such disputes that was later adopted by ICANN as the global policy binding all its accredited domain name registrars. WIPO is the leading ICANN-accredited domain name dispute resolution service provider, resolving more that 50% of all domain name disputes. It has also developed very important conventions dealing with intellectual property rights in the digital age

1366 See, for example, <http://www.allaboutcookies.org/web-beacons/index.html>, last visited: 06/11/2005.

and published several interesting documents about electronic commerce law. See UDRP, ICANN.

Wizard – in software, a quick way of obtaining results by following a number of steps. Wizards are used in popular software such as Windows to, e.g., connect a user to the Internet. They are also used in development software such as Visual Basic 6.0 to, e.g., connect to a database without actually programming this functionality. The advantage of using wizards is time-saving.

WPPT (WIPO Performances and Phonograms Treaty) – is an international treaty signed by the member states of the World Intellectual Property Organisation in 1996. It largely mirrors the provisions of WCT with respect to the rights of performers and producers of phongrams. See WCT, WIPO.

WSIS (World Summit on the Information Society) – it refers to two conferences organised by UN that took place in 2003 and 2005 to discuss Internet governance. See WGIG, ICANN.

WTO (World Trade Organisation) – established in 1995 by Marrakech Agreement concluding Uruguay Round negotiations (1986-94) and located in Geneva, WTO is one of the largest international inter-governmental organisations having as of August 2006 149 member countries. WTO functions as a result of a set of intergovernmental trading agreements that provide rules for governments to facilitate international trade with the goal to help exporters, importers and manufacturers of goods and services to conduct their business. With respect to electronic commerce, WTO has established various councils and committees to examine all trade-related issues relating to international electronic commerce. In particular, it promotes the policy of not imposing custom duties on electronic commerce. The WTO has organised a number of seminars and has published a number of works related to various aspects of global electronic commerce. Agreement establishing WTO apart from covering trade in goods and services contains also important agreement (TRIPS) dealing with intellectual property rights. See WIPO.

World Wide Web (WWW) – a web of pages connected by hyperlinks, written in the HTML language, identified by URLs and accessed using HTTP or HTTP/S protocol. It is the most important service over the Internet, which accounts for 75% of Internet traffic. It is also the fundament of Internet commerce. The design principles of the WWW are based upon 4 tenets: interoperability achieved by industry consensus and open forum discussion, evolvability into a better web, decentralisation and richer multimedia.

World Wide Web Consortium (W3C) – is the most important organisation responsible for the development of World Wide Web standards. The mission of W3C is to 'lead the World Wide Web to its full potential by developing common protocols that promote its evolution and ensure its interoperability.'[1367] W3C concentrates its efforts on vision, design and standardisation of web protocols. From its inception, W3C has published over 90 standards called W3C Recommendations. Prior to its creation, incompatible versions of HTML were offered by different vendors, increasing the potential for inconsistency between web pages.

W3C was created in October 1994 by Tim Berners-Lee who left the European Organization for Nuclear Research (CERN) and founded W3C at the Massachusetts Institute of Technology. In 1995, the Institut National de Recherche en Informatique et Automatique

---

[1367] <http://www.w3.org/Consortium/>, last visited: 28/08/2006.

(INRIA) became the first European W3C Office, followed by Keio University of Japan in 1996. See HTML, HTTP, WWW, CSS, SVG, PICS, P3P.

Virus – a small program that self-replicates causing damage ranging from displaying annoying messages to the deletion of all information on a computer.

Voluntarists – or consensualists, the doctrine of international law that assumes that all law originates from states' will the will of states. In consequence, a state might be bound by a legal rule only if it has agreed to it, either expressly or implicitly. See positivism.

XML (eXtensible Markup Language) – a new generation language for the Web that allows structuring of the content of documents. It enables separation of content from presentation and deals only with the structuring the content of a website. A very important standard used by many online businesses to exchange data in standardised form among themselves. See W3C.

BIBLIOGRAPHY

Abbate, J. (2000), *Inventing the Internet*, Cambridge, Mass.: MIT Press.

Abranovic, W.A. (1997), *Statistical Thinking and Data Analysis for Managers*, Reading: MA: Addison-Wesley.

Adams v. *Lindsell* [1818] 1 B&Ald 681.

Ago, R. (1956), *Science Juridique et Droit International*, Recueil des Cours de l'Académie de Droit International 90(2): 851-958.

Ahmad bin Mohamed Ibrahim (1965), *Sources and development of Muslim law*, Singapore: Malayan Law Journal Ltd.

Ahmad, F. (2001), *Electronic Commerce: An Indian Perspective*, International Journal of Law and Information Technology 9(2): 133-170.

Akdeniz, Y. (2001), *Case Analysis of (the Yahoo case) League Against Racism and Antisemitism (LICRA), French Union of Jewish Students* v. *Yahoo! Inc. (USA), Yahoo France, Tribunal de Grande Instance de Paris (The County Court of Paris), Interim Court Order, 20 November 2000*, Electronic Business Law Reports 1(3): 110-120.

Akehurst, M. (1974-1975), *Custom as a Source of International Law*, British Yearbook of International Law 47: 1-53.

Akehurst, M. (1987), *A modern introduction to international law*, 6th edn., Boston: London Unwin Hyman.

Akindemowo, O. (1998), *Information Technology Law in Australia*, 1st edn., Sydney: LBC.

Allen, C.K. (1964), *Law in the making*, 7th edn., Oxford: Oxford University Press.

Allen, T. and Widdison, R. (Winter 1996), *Can Computers Make Contracts?*, Harvard Journal of Law & Technology 9: 25-52.

Alreck, P.L. and Settle, R.B. (1995), *The survey research handbook*, Chicago: Irwin.

Al-Zwaini, L. (1994), *A bibliography of Islamic law, 1980-1993*, Leiden, New York: E.J. Brill.

American Association for Public Opinion Research (1997), *Best Practices for Survey and Public Opinion Research*, available at <http://www.aapor.org/ethics/best.html>, last visited: 08/10/2002.

American Civil Liberties Union, *Eight Reasons the US Should Reject the International Cybercrime Treaty*, available at <http://www.aclu.org/issues/privacy/Cybercrime_Feature.html>, last visited: 10/09/2002.

Andersen, C.B. (Fall 1998), *Furthering the Uniform Application of the CISG: Sources of Law on the Internet*, Pace International Law Review 10: 403-410.

Anil, S. (2001), *Electronic Commerce in Asia: The Legal, Regulatory and Policy Issues*, International Journal of Law and Information Technology 9(2): 93-114.

AP (23 November 2004), *Adult entertainment site sues Google*, Fairfax Digital, available at <http://www.smh.com.au/news/World/Adult-entertainment-site-sues-Google/2004/11/23/1100972358406.html#>, last visited: 26/08/2005.

Audit, B. (1998), *The Vienna Sales Convention and Lex Mercatoria*, in T.E. Carbonneau (ed.), Lex Mercatoria and Arbitration: A Discussion of the New Law Merchant, Dobbs Ferry, N.Y.: Juris Publishing 173-195.

Australia Electronic Commerce Expert Group (31 March 1998), *Electronic commerce: building the legal framework: Report of the Electronic Commerce Expert Group to the Attorney Gen-*

eral, Attorney-General's Department, available at <http://www.law.gov.au/aghome/advisory/eceg/single.htm>, last visited: 23/08/2002.

Authorize.Net (2003), *Advanced Integration Method Implementation Guide Card-Not-Present Transactions Versions 1.0*, available at <http://www.authorizenet.com/support/AIM_guide.pdf>, last visited: 22/04/2003.

Authorize.Net (2003), *Shopping Cart Certification Advanced Integration Method (AIM) Implementation Guide Card-Not-Present Transactions*, available at <http://www.authorizenet.com/support/AIM_guide_SCC.pdf>, last visited: 22/04/2003.

Avanova (29 October 2002), *Spanish websites go blank to counter web regulation*, available at <http://www.ananova.com/news/story/sm_699101.html?menu=news.technology>, last visited: 31/10/2002.

Backhouse, B. (2000), *Legal Regimes to Facilitate Electronic Transactions - Their Suitability and Effectiveness - With Particular Reference to the Electronic Transactions Regime Currently Being Adopted in Australia*, available at <http://www.lawnow.com/Products/LegalRegArticles/LegalRegArticles.htm>, last visited: 03/02/2001.

Badinter, R. (December 1995), *Role of the International Lawyer*, International Business Lawyer: 505-506.

Bainbridge, D.I. (2000), *Introduction to Computer Law*, 4th edn., Harlow: Longman.

Bainbridge, S. (1984), *Trade Usages in International Sales of Goods: An Analysis of the 1964 and 1980 Sales Conventions*, Virginia Journal of International Law 24: 619-665.

Bajaj, K.K. and Nag, D. (2000), *E-Commerce: The Cutting Edge of Business*, New Delhi: Tata McGraw-Hill Publishing Company Limited.

Bamodu, G. (2001), *Extra-legal principles in the global village: A conceptual examination of transnational law*, International Arbitration Law Review 4(1): 6-16.

Bane, C.A. (May/September 1983), *From Holt and Mansfield to Story to Llewellyn and Mentschikoff: The Progressive Development of Commercial Law*, University of Miami Law Review 37: 351-377.

Barabási, A.-L. (2002), *Linked: The New Science of Networks*, Cambridge, Massachusetts: Perseus Publishing.

Barberis, J. (1967), *L'élément matériel de la coutume internationale d'après la Cour de la Haye (1922-1966)*, Nederlands Tijdschrift XIV: 367-381.

Barberis, J. (1992), *Les règles spécifiques du droit international en Amérique latine*, Recueil des Cours de l'Académie de Droit International 235: 81.

Barlow, J.P. (8 February 1996), *A Declaration of the Independence of Cyberspace*, Electronic Frontier Foundation, available at <http://www.eff.org/~barlow/Declaration-Final.html>, last visited: 10/09/2002.

Barlow, J.P. (March 1994), *The Economy of Ideas: Rethinking Patents and Copyrights in the Digital Age*, available at <http://www.wired.com/wired/archive/2.03/economy.ideas_pr.html>, last visited: 10/09/2002.

Baron, G., *Do the UNIDROIT Principles of International Commercial Contracts form a new lex mercatoria?*, Pace Law, available at <http://www.cisg.law.pace.edu/cisg/biblio/baron.html>, last visited: 02/06/2003.

Barroso, R.L. (Summer 1995), *The saga of indigenous peoples in Brazil: constitution, law and policies. Symposium: Tribal Sovereignty: Back to the Future?*, St. Thomas Law Review 7: 645-669.

Bartholomew, G.W. (1996), *Recognition of Aboriginal law and legal pluralism*, Darwin: Centre for Southeast Asian Law, NTU.

Basdevant, J. (1936), *Règles Générales du Droit de la Paix*, Recueil des Cours de l'Académie de Droit International 58(IV): 470-690.

Basel Committee on Banking Supervision (July 2003), *Management and Supervision of Cross-Border Electronic Banking Activities*, Bank for International Settlements.

Basel Committee on Banking Supervision (July 2003), *Risk Management Principles for Electronic Banking*, Bank for International Settlements.

Baxter, R.R. (1970), *Treaties and Custom*, Recueil des Cours de l'Académie de Droit International 129(I): 25-105.

BBC News (02 September 2002), *China blocking Google*, available at <http://news.bbc.co.uk/2/hi/technology/2231101.stm>, last visited: 12/09/2002.

Berat, L. (1991/1992), *Customary Law in a New South Africa: a Proposal*, Fordham International Law Journal: Second Annual Philip D. Reed Memorial Issue: 92-128.

Berman, H., *Peer-to-Peer Piracy Prevention Act Section-by-Section Analysis*, available at <http://www.house.gov/berman/p2psection.html>, last visited: 10/09/2002.

Berman, H. and Kaufman, C. (1978), *The law of international commercial transactions (lex mercatoria)*, Harvard International Law Journal 19: 221-277.

Berners-Lee, T., *Frequently Asked Questions by the Press*, available at <http://www.w3.org/People/Berners-Lee/FAQ.html>, last visited: 23/07/2002.

Berners-Lee, T., CERN (March 1989), *Information Management: A Proposal*, available at <http://www.w3.org/History/1989/proposal.html>, last visited: 23/07/2002.

Berners-Lee, T. and Mark Fischetti (1999), *Weaving the Web: the original design and ultimate destiny of the World Wide Web by its inventor*, HarperSanFransisco.

Bernhardt, R. (1992), *Customary International Law*, in R. Bernhardt (ed.), Encyclopedia of Public International Law: published under the auspices of the Max Planck Institute for Comparative Public Law and International Law under the direction of Rudolf Bernhardt, Amsterdam, London, New York, Tokyo: North-Holland 898-905.

Bewes, W.A. (1923), *The Romance of the Law Merchant Being an Introduction to the Study of International and Commercial Law with Some Account of the Commerce and Fairs of the Middle Ages*, London: Sweet & Maxwell, Limited.

Bianca, C.M. and Bonell, M.J. (1987), *Commentary on the International Sales Law: The 1980 Vienna Sales Convention*, Giuffrè, Millan.

Blackstone, W. (1783 reprinted 1978), *Commentaries on the Laws of England*, D.S. Berkowitz and S.E. Thorne (eds.), New York & London: Garland Publishing, Inc.

Blustein, P. (15 January 2002), *U.S. Loses Ruling in Trade Fight With Europe. WTO Decision Allows EU to Seek Penalties*, Washington Post, p. E01.

BMG Music v. *Cecilia Gonzalez* [2005] Court File No. 05-1314 (9 December 2005).

BNA Int'l Bus. & Fin. Daily (22 March 2004), *Citibank Japan Tape Holding Account Data On 230,000 Customers Is Lost in Singapore*, available at <http://pubs.bna.com/ip/BNA/ibd.nsf/is/A0A8G0X9K0>, last visited: 01.04.2004.

BNA Int'l Bus. & Fin. Daily (5 July 2005), *U.S. States Internet Principles: No Change For ICANN, No Support for New Global Body.*, BNA Int'l Bus. & Fin. Daily, available at <http://pubs.bna.com/lp/BNA/ibd.nsf/ls/A0b1A7K7W8>, last visited: 25/07/2005.

Bock, T. and Sergeant, J. (Second Quarter 2002), *Small sample market research*, International Journal of Market Research 44(2): 235-244.

Boersma, M. (1998), *International business transactions, the Internet and the Convention on the International Sale of Goods: Preventing unintentional pitfalls*, Journal of International Law and Practice 7: 107.

Boliek, B. (8 November 2005), *Grokster to stop distributing file-sharing service*, Reuters, available at <http://today.reuters.com/news/newsarticle.aspx?type=internetNews&storyid=2005-11-08T103010Z_01_RID834949_RTRUKOC_0_US-GROKSTER.xml>, last visited: 08.11.2005.

Bonell, M.J. (1998), *UNIDROIT Principles and the Lex Mercatoria*, in T.E. Carbonneau (ed.), Lex Mercatoria and Arbitration: A Discussion of the New Law Merchant, Juris Publishing: 249-257.

Bonell, M.J. (2000), *The UNIDROIT Principles and Transnational Law*, available at <http://www.unidroit.org/english/publications/review/articles/2000-2.htm>, last visited: 24/08/2002.

Bonell, M.J. (2000), *The UNIDROIT Principles in practice - the experience of the first two years*, International Institute for the Unification of Private Law, available at <http://www.cisg.law.pace.edu/cisg/biblio/pr-exper.html>, last visited: 03/06/2003.

Bonell, M.J., (2001), *Do We Need a Global Commercial Code?*, Dickinson Law Review 106: 87-100.

Bonell, M.J., *The UNIDROIT Principles Of International Commercial Contracts: Nature, Purposes And First Experiences In Practice*, available at <http://www.unidroit.org/english/principles/pr-exper.htm>, last visited: 24/08/2002.

Bonnell, M.J. (2004), *UNIDROIT Principles 2004 – The New Edition of the Principles of International Commercial Contracts adopted by the International Institute for the Unification of Private Law*, Uniform Law Review: 5-40.

Boss, A.H. (1992), *The emerging law of international electronic commerce*, Temple International and Comparative Law Journal: 294-309.

Bouma, G.D. (1993), *The Research Process*, rev. edn., Melbourne: Oxford University Press.

Bourquin, M. (1931), *Règles Générales du Droit de la Paix*, Recueil des Cours de l'Académie de Droit International 35(I): 1-232.

Bouscaren, L.T. and Ellis, A.C. (1957), *Canon Law: A Text and Commentary*, 3rd edn., Milwaukee: The Bruce Publishing Company.

Bowman, L.M. (8 July 2002), *Court: Hands off that hyperlink*, CNet News.com, available at <http://news.com.com/2100-1023-942187.html>, last visited: 22/08/20002.

Branscomb, A.W. (May 1995), *Anonymity, Autonomy, And Accountability: Challenges To The First Amendment In Cyberspaces*, Yale Law Journal 104: 1639-1679.

Brierly, J.L. (1963), *The law of nations*, S.H. Waldock (ed.) 6th edn., Oxford: Clarendon Press.

Briggs, H.W. (October 1951), *The Colombian-Peruvian Asylum Case and Proof of Customary International Law*, The American Journal of International Law 45(4): 728-731.

Brinkibon Ltd v. *Stahag Stahlwarenhandelsgesellschaft mbH* [1983] 2 AC 34.

Broersma, M. (11 April 2001), *Privacy activists plan assault on Eschelon, Carnivore*, ZDNet.com (UK), available at <http://zdnet.com.com/2102-11-529264.html>, last visited: 10/09/2002.

Brownlie, I. (1973), *A Survey of International Customary Rules of Environmental Protection*, Natural Resources Journal 13(2): 179-189.

Brownlie, I. (1990), *Principles of public international law*, 4th edn., Oxford: Clarendon Press.

Bryman, A. (2001), *Social Research Methods*, Oxford: Oxford University Press.

Burnett, S. and Paine, S. (2001), *RSA Security's Official Guide to Cryptography*, New York: Osborne/McGraw-Hill.

Burnstein, M.R. (1996), *Conflicts on the Net: Choice of Law in Transnational Cyberspace*, Vanderbilt Journal of Transnational Law 29: 75.

Burnstein, M.R. (1998-2000), *A Global Network in a Compartmentalised Legal Environment*, in K. Boele-Woelki and C. Kessedijan (eds.), Internet. Which Court Decides? Which Law Applies?, The Hague, London, Boston: Kluwer Law International.

Caemmerer, E. v. (1964), *The influence of the law of international trade on the development and character of the commercial law in the civil law countries (With Particular Reference to the nature of Commercial Law in those Countries as a Separate System of Law),* in C.M. Schmitthoff (ed.), The sources of the law of international trade with special reference to East-West Trade, London: Stevens & Sons 88-100.

Carlyle, R.W. and Carlyle, A.J. (1903, 1936), *A History of Medieval Political Theory in the West*, Edinburgh: Blackwood.

Cavaglieri, A. (1929), *Règles Générales du Droit de la Paix*, Recueil des Cours de l'Académie de Droit International 26(I): 315-585.

Cerf, V.G. (1995), *IETF and ISOC*, available at <http://www.isoc.org/isoc/related/ietf/>, last visited: 15/08/2002.

Cerf, V.G. and Kahn, R.E. (May 1974), *A Protocol for Packet Network Intercommunication*, IEEE Transactions on Communications 22(5): 637-648.

Chakravarty-Kaul, M. (1996), *Common lands and customary law: institutional change in North India over the past two centuries*, Delhi: Oxford University Press.

Charney, J.I. (October 1993), *Universal International Law*, American Journal of International Law 87(4): 529-551.

Cheickh Bangoura v. *The Washington Post* [2005] Court File No. C41379 (16 September 2005).

Cheng, B. (1965), *United Nations Resolutions on Outer Space: 'Instant' International Customary law?*, Indian Journal of International Law 5: 23-48.

Chissick, M. and Kelman, A. (1999), *Electronic commerce law and practice*, London: Sweet and Maxwell.

Chitty, J. (1999), *Chitty on Contracts*, H.G. Beale (ed.), 28th edn., London: Sweet & Maxwell.

Christophe G. v. *Société France Télécom Interactive, S.A.* [28.02.2001] JGT: 64/2001, RG: 00/106.

Cieslak, D. (31 March 2003), *Brytyjczycy walcza ze spamem*, IDG.pl, available at <http://www.idg.pl/news/news.asp?id=54044>, last visited: 01/04/2003.

Clark, R. (December 1998), *Electronic Data Interchange (EDI): An Introduction*, available at <http://www.anu.edu.au/people/Roger.Clarke/EC/EDIIntro.html>, last visited: 01/08/2001.

Clark, R. (29 June 2002), *Defamation on the Web: Gutnick* v. *Dow Jones*, available at <http://www.anu.edu.au/people/Roger.Clarke/II/Gutnick.html>, last visited: 10/09/2002.

Cohen, E. (1993), *The crossroads of justice: law and culture in late medieval France*, Leiden, New York: E.J. Brill.

Commission on European contract law (1998), *The Principles of European Contract Law - completed and revised version*, available at <http://www.storme.be/PECL2en.html>, last visited: 03/06/2003.

ComputerWire (23/10/2002), *Feds investigating 'largest ever' Internet attack*, The Register, available at <http://www.theregister.co.uk/content/55/27738.html>, last visited: 24/10/2002.

Cooper, M.N. (March 2005), *Time For The Recording Industry To Face The Music: The Political, Social And Economic Benefits Of Peer-To-Peer Communications Networks*, Stanford Law School Center For Internet And Society.

Corbett, P. (1925), *The Consent of States and the Sources of the Law of Nations*, British Yearbook of International Law 6: 20-30.

Cortell, J. (20 May 2005), *Lecturer censored in Spanish University (UPV), for defending P2P networks*, available at <http://jorge.cortell.net/>, last visited: 25/05/2005.

Costlow, T. (03 September 2002), *As stalkers go online, new state laws try to catch up*, csmonitor.com, available at <http://www.csmonitor.com/2002/0903/p02s01-usju.htm>, last visited: 10/09/2002.

Council of Europe (2 October 2001), *The Council of Europe provides a harmonised approach to the regulation of on- line services at the Pan-European level*, 695a(2001),10/09/2002.

Council of Europe (23 November 2001), *Convention on Cybercrime, ETS No. 185, signed at Budapest*, available at <http://conventions.coe.int/Treaty/en/Treaties/Html/185.htm>, last visited: 23/08/2002.

Crano, W.D. and Brewer, M.B. (2002), *Principles and Methods of Social Research*, 2nd edn., Hahwah, New Jersey: Lawrence Erlbaum Associates, Publishers.

D'Amato, A.A. (1969), *The concept of custom in international law*, Michigan: UMI Information Dissertation Service.

D'Amato, A.A. (1971), *The concept of custom in international law*, Ithaca and London: Cornell University Press.

Danilenko, G.M. (1983), *Law-Making in the International Community*, Dordrecht, Boston, London: Martinus Nijhoff Publishers.

Datz, T. (2002), *Who Should Own What? An interview with Lawrence Lessig on Patents and the Internet*, Darwin Magazine, available at <http://www.darwinmag.com/read/080102/lessig_content.html>, last visited: 06/09/2002.

David, R. and Brierley, J.E. (1985), *Major legal systems in the world today*, 3rd edn., London: Stevens & Sons.

Dawson, J.P. (1968), *The Oracles of the Law*, Ann Arbor: The University of Michigan Law School.

de Cruz, P. (1999), *Comparative law in the changing world*, 2nd edn., London, Sydney: Cavendish Publishing Limited.

de Deckker, P. and Faberon, J.Y. (eds.), (2001), *Custom and the law*. Canberra, ACT, Asia Pacific Press at the Australian National University.

De Ly, F. (1992), *International Business Law and Lex Mercatoria*, Amsterdam, London, New York, Tokyo: T.M.C. Asser Instituut - The Hague.

De Ly, F. (1999), *National Report: The Netherlands: An Interim Report regarding the Application of the Unidroit Principles of International Commercial Contracts in The Netherlands*, in M.J. Bonell (ed.), A new Approach to International Commercial Contracts: the Unidroit Principles of International Commercial Contracts, The Hague: Kluwer Law International 203-235.

De Ly, F. (2000), *Emerging new perspectives regarding lex mercatoria in an era of increasing globalization*, in Festschrift für Otto Sandrock, Heidelberg: Verlag Recht und Wirtschaft 179-204.

De Ly, F. (2001), *Choice of law clauses, Unidroit Principles of International Commercial Contracts and Article 3 Rome Convention, Lex mercatoria before domestic courts or arbitration privilege?*, in Mélanges Mercadal, Paris: 12 pp.

De Ly, F. (2001), *Lex mercatoria (New Law Merchant): Globalization and international self-regulation*, in V. Gessner (ed.), Legal culture and globalization, Oxford: Hart 28 pp.

de Visscher, C. (1925), *La codification du droit international*, Recueil des Cours de l'Académie de Droit International 6(1): 325-455.

de Vischer, C. (1955), *Théories et réalités en droit international public*, 2nd edn.

de Visscher, C. (1957), *Theory and Reality in Public International Law*, P.E. Corbett (trans.), Princeton, New Jersey: Princeton University Press.

Degan, V.D. (1997), *Sources of International Law*, The Hague, Boston, London: Martinus Nijhoff Publishers.

Delio, M. (23 August 2002), *Judge Tosses BT Hyperlink Case*, Wired, available at <http://www.wired.com/news/politics/0,1283,54721,00.html>, last visited: 03/09/2002.

Deloitte Touche Tohmatsu (2003), *Global Security Survey 2003*, available at <http://www.deloitte.com/dtt/cda/doc/content/GFSI-Security-Survey-2003-final(1)pdf>, last visited: 16/05/2003.

Derrett, J.D.M. (1963), *Introduction to Modern Hindu Law*, Bombay: Oxford University Press.

Dickie, J. (1999), *Internet and Electronic Commerce Law in the European Union*, Oxford: Hart Publishing.

Dierks, T. and Allen, C. (January 1999), *RFC 2246 The TLS Protocol Version 1.0 (STATUS: Standard), (STD 1)*, available at <http://www.ietf.org/rfc/rfc2246.txt?number=2246>, last visited: 16/08/2002.

Diffie, W. and Hellman, M.E. (November 1976), *New Directions in Cryptography*, IEEE Transactions on Information Theory IT-22(6): 644-654.

Drake, W.J. (ed.) (2005), *Reforming Internet Governance: Perspectives from the Working Group on Internet Governance (WGIG).* New York, The United Nations Information and Communication Technology Task Force.

Duguit (1901), *L'état, le droit objectif, et la loi positive.*

Dz.U. nr 212 poz. 1766 (11.10.2005), *Rozporządzenie RM w sprawie minimalnych wymagań dla systemów teleinformatycznych.*

Edwards, L. and Waelde, C. (eds.) (2000), *Law & the Internet,* Oxford: Hart Publishing.

Eiselen, S. (1999), *Electronic Commerce and the UN Convention on Contracts for the International Sale of Goods (CISG), 1980*, The EDI Law Review 6(1): 21-46.

Electronic Commerce Platform Netherlands (October 2001), *Model Code of Conduct for Electronic Business (Draft 4.0),* available at <http://www.ecp.nl/ENGLISH/publication/cocdraft4.0ENG.pdf>, last visited: 10/09/2002.

Electronic Frontiers Foundation (2005), *RIAA* v. *the People: Two Years Later*, available at <http://www.eff.org/IP/P2P/RIAAatTWO_FINAL.pdf>, last visited: 06.11.2005.

Emiliani, M.L. (2000), *Business-to-business online auctions: key issues for purchasing process improvement*, Supply Chain Management: An International Journal 5(4): 176-186.

Entores v. *Miles Far East Corporation* [1955] 2 QB 327.

EPIC and PI (2002), *Privacy and Human Rights 2002. An International Survey of Privacy Laws and Developments*, Electronic Privacy Information Center and Privacy International, available at <http://www.privacyinternational.org/survey/phr2002/>, last visited: 10/09/2002.

European Commission (15 April 1997), *A European Initiative in Electronic Commerce (Green Paper), (COM 97), 157*, available at <ftp://ftp.cordis.lu/pub/esprit/docs/ecomcom.pdf>, last visited: 23/08/2002.

Farnsworth, A.E. (1979), *Developing International Trade Law*, California Western International Law Journal 9: 461-471.

Fassbender, H., Kliger, M. and Kluge, J. (2002), *What Germans Really Think*, The McKinsey Quarterly, Number 3, available at <http://www.mckinseyquarterly.com/article_print.asp?ar=1220&L2=19&L3=67&srid=27&gp=0>, last visited: 09/10/2002.

Fauchille, P. (1922), *Traité de Droit International Public*, H.M. Bonfils (ed.), 8th edn., Paris: Librairie Arthur Rousseau.

FindLaw Australia (1 October 2002), *U.S. Web-Based Pyramid Selling Scheme Banned*, available at <http://www.findlaw.com.au/news/default.asp?task=read&id=11293&newstype=L&site=NE>, last visited: 10/10/2002.

Forder, J. and Quirk, P. (2001), *Electronic commerce and the Law*, John Wiley & Sons Australia.

Frankfort-Nachmias, C. and Nachmias, D. (1996), *Research Methods in the Social Sciences*, 5th edn., New York: St. Martin's Press.

Freedman, D., Pisani, R. and Purves, R. (1978), *Statistics*, New York: Norton.

Freier, A.O., Karlton, P. and Kocher, P.C. (1996), *The SSL Protocol version 3.0. Internet Draft*, available at <http://home.netscape.com/eng/ssl3/ssl-toc.html>, last visited: 17/10/2001.

Gain, B. (23 May 2005), *Volez ce MP3!*, Wired.com, available at <http://www.wired.com/news/print/0,1294,67594,00.html>, last visited: 30/05/2005.

Garavaglia, M. (1991), *In Search Of the Proper Law in Transnational Commercial Disputes*, New York Law School Journal of International and Comparative Law 12: 29-106.

Gay, L.R. and Diehl, P.L. (1992), *Research methods for business and management*, New York: Maxwell Macmillan International.

Gény, F. (1919 reprinted in 1954), *Méthode d'Interprétation et sources en droit privé positif*, 2nd reviewed edn., Paris: Librairie Generale de Droit & de Jurisprudence.

Gerber, H. (1994), *State, society, and law in Islam: Ottoman law in comparative perspective*, Albany: State University of New York Press.

Gianni (1931), *La coutume en droit international.*

Gihl, T. (1957), *The Legal Character and Sources of International Law*, Scandinavian Studies in Law 1: 53.

Gilissen, J. (1982), *La coutume*, Turnhout-Belgium: Brepols.

Gillies, J. and Cailliau, R. (2000), *How the Web was born: the story of the World Wide Web*, Oxford: Oxford University Press.

Glatt, C. (Spring 1998), *Comparative issues in the formation of electronic contracts*, International Journal of Law and Information Technology 6(1): 34-68.

Glück (1797), *Ausfürliche Erläuterung der Pandekten.*

Goldfarb, J. (24 November 2005), *Kazaa given deadline to alter system*, Reuters, available at <http://today.reuters.com/news/newsarticle.aspx?type=internetNews&storyid=2005-11-24T155118Z_01_KNE452508_RTRUKOC_0_US-MEDIA-KAZAA-COURT.xml>, last visited: 27.11.2005.

Goldman, B. (1964), *Frontières du droit et lex mercatoria*, Archives de philosophie du droit IX: 177-192.

Goldman, B. (1982), *La nouvelle réglementation française de l'arbitrage international*, The Art of Arbitration, Essays on International Arbitration, Liber Amicorum Pieter Sanders: p. 153.

Goldman, B. (1983), *Lex Mercatoria*, Forum internationale No. 3: 24.

Gonzalo, S. (2001), *A Business Outlook regarding Electronic Agents*, International Journal of Law and Information Technology 9(3): 189-203.

Goode, R. (1997), *Usage and its reception in transnational commercial law*, International and Comparative Law Quarterly 46: 1-36.

Goodwin, M. (1998), *Wild, Wild Web*, in R.M. et al. Baird (ed.), Cyberethics: Social and Moral Issues in the Computer Age, New York: Promotheus Books 215-221.

Goralczyk, W. (1989), *Prawo Miedzynarodowe Publiczne w Zarysie*, 4th edn., Warszawa: Panstwowe Wydawnictwo Naukowe.

Greif, A. (June 1993), *Contract Enforceability and Economic Institutions in Early Trade: The Maghribi Traders' Coalition*, The American Economic Review 83(3): 525-548.

Greif, A. (1997), *Contracting, Enforcement, and Efficiency: Economics beyond the law*, Annual World Bank Conference on Development Economics 1996: 239-265.

Greif, A., Milgrom, P.R. and Weingast, B.R. (August 1994), *Coordination, Commitment, and Enforcement: The Case of the Merchant Guild*, Journal of Political Economy 102(4): 745-776.

Griffiths, R.T., *History of the Internet, Internet for Historians (and just about everyone else)*, available at <http://www.let.leidenuniv.nl/history/ivh/frame_theorie.html>, last visited: 23/07/2002.

Gringras, C. (1997), *The Laws of the Internet*, N. Nathanson (ed.), London: Butterworths.

Grotius, H. (1646 reprinted 1925), *De Jure Bellli ac Pacis Libri Tres*, J.B. Scott (ed.), F.W. Kelsey (trans.), Oxford: Clarendon Press.

Guggenheim, P. (1950), *Les deux éléments de la coutume en droit international*, in La Technique et les Principes du Droit Public: Etudes en l'Honneur de Georges Scelle, Paris: Librairie générale de droit et de jurisprudence.

Guggenheim, P. (1952), *Les Principles de Droit International Public*, Recueil des Cours de l'Académie de Droit International 80(1): 1-189.

Guggenheim, P. (1953), *Traite de Droit international public: Avec mention de la pratique internationale et suisse*, Genève: Librairie de L'Université, Georg & Cie S.A.

Guggenheim, P. (1958), *Contribution a l'histoire des sources du droit des gens*, Recueil des Cours de l'Académie de Droit International 94(2): 1-84.

Guggenheim, P. (1967), *Traite de Droit international public: Avec mention de la pratique internationale et suisse*, 2nd rev. edn., Genève: Librairie de L'Université, Georg & Cie S.A.

Gutnick v. *Dow Jones & Co Inc* [28 August 2001] VSC 305.

Gutteridge, H.C. (1971), *Comparative Law. An Introduction to the Comparative Method of Legal Study & Research*, Cambridge: Cambridge University Press.

Hagen, G.R. (2003), *Sovereign Domains and Property Claims*, International Journal of Law and Information Technology 11(1): 5-39.

Halpern, M. and Mehrotra, A.K. (Fall 2000), *From International Treaties To Internet Norms: The Evolution Of International Trademark Disputes In The Internet Age*, University of Pennsylvania Journal of International Economic Law 21: 523-561.

Hambridge, S. (October 1995), *RFC 1855 Netiquette Guidelines (Also FYI0028), (Status: INFORMATIONAL),* available at <http://www.ietf.org/rfc/rfc1855.txt?number=1855>, last visited: 16/08/2002.

Hamdani, A. (May 2002), *Who's liable for cyberwrongs*, Cornell Law Review 87: 901-957.

Hammel, J. (1935), *Les formes internationales des credits bancaires*, Recueil des Cours de l'Académie de Droit International LI(I): 203-285.

Hance, O. (1996), *Business and Law on the Internet*, Best of Editions ed., McGraw Hill.

Hardy, I.T. (Summer 1994), *The Proper Legal Regime For Cyberspace*, University of Pittsburgh Law Review 55: 993-1054.

Harris, A. (10 September 2002), *Cybersquatting Law Gets Longer Reach*, Law.com, available at <http://www.law.com/jsp/printerfriendly.jsp?c=LawArticle&t=PrinterFriendlyArticle&cid=1030821185175>, last visited: 10/09/2002.

Harris, D.J. (1998), *Cases and Materials on International Law*, 5th edn., London: Sweet & Maxwell.

Harrison, S.R. and Tamaschke, R.H.U. (1993), *Statistics for Business, Economics and Management*, New York: Prentice Hall.

Henckaerts, J.-M. (March 2005), *Study on customary international humanitarian law: A contribution to the understanding and respect for the rule of law in armed conflict*, International Review of the Red Cross 87(857): 175-212.

Henckaerts, J.-M. and Doswald-Beck, L. (2005), *Customary International Humanitarian Law, 2 volumes, Volume I. Rules, Volume II. Practice (2 Parts),* Cambridge University Press.

Henry, G.T. (1997), *Practical Sampling*, in L. Bickman and D.J. Rog (eds.), Handbook of Applied Social Research Methods, Thousand Oaks: Sage Publications 101-126.

Hill, R. (1998), *What sample size is 'enough' in Internet survey research?*, Interpersonal Computing and Technology: An Electronic Journal for the 21st Century 6(3-4): 10.

Ho, J. (10 September 2005), *Kuro bosses guilty of IPR violations*, Taipei Times, available at <http://www.taipeitimes.com/News/front/archives/2005/09/10/2003271076>, last visited: 11/09/2005.

Hobbes, T. (1996), *Leviathan*, J.C.A. Gaskin (ed.), Oxford, New York: Oxford University Press.

Hoffer, J.A., Prescott, M.B. and McFadden, F.R. (2002), *Modern Database Management*, 6th edn., International Edition: Prentice Hall, Pearson Education International.

Hoffman, W. (1997), *On the use and abuse of custom and usage in reinsurance contracts*, Tort and Insurance Law Journal 33(1).

Honnold, J.O. (1982), *Uniform Law for International Sales under the 1980 United Nations Convention*, Deventer/the Netherlands: Kluwer Law and Taxation Publishers.

Hudson, M.O. (3 March 1950), *Article 24 of the Statute of the International Law Commission. Working Paper. Document A/CN.4/16*, Yearbook of the International Law Commission 2: 24-32.

Hudson, T.J. and Young, E.A. (24 September 1998), *SSLeay and SSLapps FAQ*, available at <http://www2.psy.uq.edu.au/~ftp/Crypto/>, last visited: 31/10/2002.

Huebner, R. (1918), *A History of Germanic Private Law*, F.S. Philbrick (trans.), London: John Murray.

Hultmark, C. (1999), *European and U.S. perspectives on electronic documents and electronic signatures*, Tulane European and Civil Law Forum 14(123): 124-153, available at westlaw.com.

IAB (2002), *A Brief History of the Internet Advisory/Activities/Architecture Board*, available at <http://www.iab.org/iab-history.html>, last visited: 15/08/2002.

ICANN (25 November 1998), *Memorandum Of Understanding Between The U.S. Department Of Commerce And Internet Corporation For Assigned Names And Numbers*, available at <http://www.icann.org/general/icann-mou-25nov98.htm>, last visited: 20/08/2002.

ICANN (1999), *Rules for Uniform Domain Name Dispute Resolution Policy*, available at <http://www.icann.org/dndr/udrp/uniform-rules.htm>, last visited: 19/08/2002.

ICANN (26 August 1999), *Uniform Domain Name Dispute Resolution Policy*, available at <http://www.icann.org/dndr/udrp/policy.htm>, last visited: 19/08/2002.

ICANN (2001), *ICANN Fact Sheet*, available at <http://www.icann.org/general/fact-sheet.htm>, last visited: 19/08/2002.

ICC (23 September 1998), *Model clauses for use in contracts involving transborder data flows*, available at <http://www.iccwbo.org/home/statements_rules/rules/1998/model_clauses.asp>, last visited: 10/09/2002.

ICC (27 July 1999), *International business comments on the proposed EU directive on certain legal aspects of electronic commerce*, available at <http://www.iccwbo.org/home/statements_rules/statements/1999/proposed_eu_directive.asp>, last visited: 10/09/2002.

ICC (July 2002), *Global Action Plan for Electronic Business, third edition*, available at <http://www.iccwbo.org/home/electronic_commerce/word_documents/3rd%20Edition%20Global%20Action%20Plan.pdf>, last visited: 10/09/2002.

ICC (July 2002), *Standard Contractual Clauses for the Transfer of Personal Data from the EU to Third Countries, submitted to European Commission*, available at <http://www.iccwbo.org/home/electronic_commerce/word_documents/Final%20version%20July%202002%20Model%20contract%20clauses.pdf>, last visited: 10/09/2002.

ICJ Reports (1949), *The Corfu Channel* case *(Merits).*

ICJ Reports (1950), *Asylum* case *(Columbia/Peru).*

ICJ Reports (1951), *Fisheries* case *(United Kingdom* v. *Norway).*

ICJ Reports (28 May 1951), *Reservations To The Convention On The Prevention And Punishment Of The Crime Of Genocide.*

ICJ Reports (27 August 1952), *Case Concerning Rights Of Nationals Of The United States Of America In Morocco (France/United States of America).*

ICJ Reports (1955), *Nottebohm* case *(Liechtenstein* v. *Guatemala).*

ICJ Reports (1959), *Interhandel (Switzerland* v. *United States of America).*

ICJ Reports (1960), *Case Concerning Right of Passage Over Indian Territory (Portugal* v. *India).*

ICJ Reports (1969), *North Sea Continental Shelf (Federal Republic of Germany/Denmark; Federal Republic of Germany/Netherlands)* cases.

ICJ Reports (5 February 1970), *Case Concerning The Barcelona Traction, Light And Power Company, Limited (New Application: 1962) (Belgium* v. *Spain).*

ICJ Reports (25 July 1974), *Fisheries Jurisdiction (Federal Republic of Germany* v. *Iceland).*

ICJ Reports (25 July 1974), *Fisheries Jurisdiction (United Kingdom of Great Britain and Northern Ireland* v. *Iceland).*

ICJ Reports (20 December 1974), *Nuclear Tests (Australia* v. *France).*

ICJ Reports (1975), *Western Sahara (Advisory Opinion).*

ICJ Reports (12 October 1984), *Case Concerning Delimitation Of The Maritime Boundary In The Gulf Of Maine Area (Canada* v. *United States of America).*

ICJ Reports (1985), *Continental Shelf (Libyan Arab Jamahiriya/Malta).*

ICJ Reports (1986), *Case Concerning Military and Paramilitary Activities in and Against Nicaragua (Nicaragua* v. *United States of America).*

ICJ Reports (3 February 1994), *Case Concerning the Territorial Dispute (Libyan Arab Jamahiriya/ Chad).*

ICJ Reports (8 July 1996), *Legality Of The Threat Or Use Of Nuclear Weapons (Advisory Opinion).*

ICJ Reports (12 December 1996), *Case Concerning Oil Platforms (Islamic Republic Of Iran* v. *United States Of America) - Preliminary Objection*, available at <http://www.icj-cij.org/icjwww/idocket/iop/iopframe.htm>, last visited: 16/05/2003.

ICJ Reports (1997), *Case concerning the Gabcikovo-Nagymaros project (Hungary/Slovakia).*

ICJ Reports (29 April 1999), *Difference Relating to Immunity from Legal Process of a Special Rapporteur of the Commission on Human Rights (Advisory Opinion).*

ICJ Reports (13 December 1999), *Case Concerning Kasikili/Sedudu Island (Botswana/Namibia),* available at <http://www.icj-cij.org/icjwww/idocket/ibona/ibonaframe.htm>, last visited: 16/05/2003.

ICJ Reports (21 June 2000), *Case Concerning The Aerial Incident Of 10 August 1999 (Pakistan* v. *India),* available at <http://www.icj-cij.org/icjwww/idocket/ipi/ipiframe.htm>, last visited: 16/05/2003.

ICJ Reports (16 March 2001), *Case Concerning Maritime Delimitation And Territorial Questions Between Qatar And Bahrain (Qatar* v. *Bahrain) - Merits*, available at <http://www.icj-cij.org/icjwww/idocket/iqb/iqbframe.htm>, last visited: 16/05/2003.

ICJ Reports (27 June 2001), *LaGrand* case *(Germany* v. *United States of America),* available at <http://www.icj-cij.org/icjwww/idocket/igus/igusframe.htm>, last visited: 16/05/2003.

ICJ Reports (14 February 2002), *Case Concerning The Arrest Warrant Of 11 April 2000 (Democratic Republic Of The Congo* v. *Belgium),* available at <http://www.icj-cij.org/icjwww/idocket/iCOBE/icobejudgment/icobe_ijudgment_20020214.PDF>, last visited: 16/05/2003.

ICJ Reports (10 October 2002), *Case Concerning The Land And Maritime Boundary Between Cameroon And Nigeria (Cameroon* v. *Nigeria: Equatorial Guinea Intervening),* available at <http://www.icj-cij.org/icjwww/idocket/icn/icnjudgment/icn_ijudgment_20021010.PDF>, last visited: 16/05/2003.

ICJ Reports (9 July 2004), *Legal Consequences of the Construction of a Wall in the Occupied Palestinian Territory (Advisory Opinion).*

Ilieva, J., Baron, S. and Healey, N.M. (Third Quarter 2002), *Online surveys in marketing research: Pros and cons*, International Journal of Market Research 44(3): 361-376.

International Chamber of Commerce (1993), *ICC uniform customs and practice for documentary credits*, Paris: ICC.

International Chamber of Commerce (1999), *Incoterms 2000: ICC official rules for the interpretation of trade terms: entry into force 1st January 2000 = Regles officielles ICC pour l'interpretation des termes commerciaux: entrée en vigueur 1er janvier 2000.*, Paris.

International Chamber of Commerce (2002), *eUCP Version 1.0. Supplement to UCP 500 for Electronic Presentation (in force as of 1 April 2002), (eUCP),* Paris: ICC.

International Law Commission (1949), *Ways and Means of Making the Evidence of Customary International Law More Readily Available, Preparatory Work within the Purview of Article 24 of the Statute of the International Law Commission, Memorandum submitted by the Secretary-General*, United Nations, United Nations Publications Sales No. 1949. V.6.

International Law Commission (29 April 1958), *Convention on the High Seas*, available at <http://www.un.org/law/ilc/texts/hseas.htm>, last visited: 19/05/2003.

International Law Commission (18 April 1961), *Vienna Convention on Diplomatic Relations*, United Nations Conference on Diplomatic Intercourse and Immunities, available at <http://www.un.org/law/ilc/texts/dipfra.htm>, last visited: 19/05/2003.

International Law Commission (22 May 1969), *Vienna Convention on the Law of Treaties*, United Nations Conference on the Law of Treaties, available at <http://www.un.org/law/ilc/texts/treaties.htm>, last visited: 19/05/2003.

International Law Commission (2001), *Draft articles on the Responsibility of States for Internationally Wrongful Acts*, available at <http://www.un.org/law/ilc/texts/State_responsibility/responsibilityfra.htm>, last visited: 19/05/2003.

ISOC (15 August 2002), *Statement of the Internet Society on Digital Rights Management*, available at <http://www.isoc.org/isoc/media/releases/020815pr.shtml>, last visited: 10/09/2002.

Jenks, C.W. (1964), *The Prospects of International Adjudication*, London.

Joh, E.E. (2000-2001), *Custom, tribal court practice, and popular justice*, American Indian Law Review 25: 117-132.

Johnson, D.R. and Post, D. (May 1996), *Law and Borders - The Rise of Law in Cyberspace*, Stanford Law Review 48: 1367-1402.

Johnson v. *Clark* [1908] I Ch. 303.

Jolowicz, H.F. (1957), *Roman Foundations of Modern Law*, Oxford: Clarendon Press.

Jones, W.C. (ed.) (1989), *Basic Principles of Civil Law in China*. Chinese Studies on China. New York, M.E.Sharpe, Inc.

Joshi, B.D.J., Walid, A., Ghafoor, A. and Spafford, E. (2001), *Security models for web-based applications. Using traditional and emerging access control approaches to develop secure applications for the Web*, Communications of the ACM 44(3): 38-44.

Judd, C., Smith, M., Eliot, R. and Kidder, L., H. (1991), *Research Methods in Social Relations*, Fort Worth: Harcourt Brace Jovanovich College Publishers.

Judge Altamira (1927), *Dissenting Opinion of Judge Altamira on Lotus* Case.

Judge de Castro (1974), *Separate opinion of Judge de Castro on Fisheries Jurisdiction* case, in ICJ Reports 1974, 72-125.

Judge Lachs (1969), *Dissenting opinion of Judge Lachs on Continental Shelf* case, in ICJ Reports 1969, 216-240.

Judge Nyholm (1927), *Dissenting Opinion of Judge Altamira on Lotus* Case.

Judge Sorensen (1969), *Dissenting opinion of Judge Sorensen on Continental Shelf* case, in ICJ Reports 1969, 240-257.

Judge Tanaka (1969), *Dissenting opinion of Judge Tanaka on Continental Shelf* case, in ICJ Reports 1969, 171-178.

Judges Forster, B., Jimenez De Arechaga, Nagendra Singh and Ruda (1974), *Joint Separate Opinion of Judges Forster, Bengzon, Jimenez De Arechaga, Nagendra Singh and Ruda on Fisheries Jurisdiction* case, in ICJ Reports 1974, 45-52.

Kamali, M.H. (1991), *Principles of Islamic Jurisprudence*, rev. edn., Cambridge: Islamic Texts Society.

Kaplan, S. and Sawhney, M. (May-June 2000), *E-hubs: The New B2B Marketplaces*, Harvard Business Review: 97-103.

Karavas, V. i Teubner, G. (2003), <http://www.CompanyNameSucks.com>*: The Horizontal Effect of Fundamental Rights on 'Private Parties' within Autonomous Internet Law*, German Law Journal 4(12): 1335-1358.

Karsten, P. (2002), *Between law and custom: high and low legal cultures in the British diaspora lands- the United States, Canada, Australia, and New Zealand, 1600-1900*, New York; Cambridge: Cambridge University Press.

Kaufman, S.J. (14 May 2002), *Easy e-commerce with Microsoft Commerce Server 2002*, Builder.com, available at <http://builder.com.com/article.jhtml?id=u00320020514SKJ01.htm>, last visited: 04/11/2002.

Kawamoto, D. (26 August 2005), *Adult-site publisher takes action against Google*, available at <http://www.zdnet.com.au/news/software/soa/Adult_site_publisher_takes_action_against_Google/0,2000061733,39208888,00.htm>, last visited: 26.08.2005.

Kellehear, A. (1993), *The Unobtrusive Researcher: A guide to methods*, St. Leonards, NSW: Allen & Unwin.

Keller, B.P. (1999), *The Game's the Same: Why Gambling in Cyberspace Violates Federal Law*, Yale Law Journal 108: 1569-1609.

Kelly, J.M. (1992), *A short history of western legal theory*, Oxford: Clarendon Press.

Kelly, P. (Winter 2000), *The twilight of customary international law*, Virginia Journal of International Law: 450-535.

Kelsen, H. (1939), *Théorie du droit international coutumier*, Revue internationale de la théorie du droit 13: 253-274.

Kelsen, H. (1952), *Principles of International Law*, New York: Holt, Rinehart and Winston.

Kelsen, H. (1966), *Principles of International Law*, R. W. Tucker (ed.), 2nd edn., New York: Holt, Rinehart and Winston.

Kemper, E.A., Stringfield, S. and Teddlie, C. (2003), *Mixed Methods Sampling Strategies in Social Science Research*, in A. Tashakkori and C. Teddlie (eds.), Handbook of Mixed Methods in Social & Behavioral Research, Thousand Oaks: Sage Publications 273-296.

Kessedjian, C. (August 2000), *Electronic Commerce and International Jurisdiction. Prel. Doc. No. 12. Summary of discussions*, Hague Conference on Private International Law, Ottawa, 28 February to 1 March 2000, available at <ftp://hcch.net/doc/jdgmpd12.doc>, last visited: 09/09/2002.

Kirgis, F.L.J. (1987), *Custom on a sliding scale*, The American Journal of International Law 81: 146-151.

Kish, L. (1995 (1965)), *Survey Sampling*, New York: John Wiley & Sons, Inc.

Kontou, N. (1994), *The Termination and Revision of Treaties in the Light of New Customary International Law*, I. Brownlie (ed.), New York: Oxford University Press Inc.

Koops, B.-J. (1999), *The crypto controversy: a key conflict in the information society*, The Hague: Kluwer Law International.

Koops, B.-J. (October 2002), *Crypto Law Survey*, Version 21.0, available at <http://rechten.uvt.nl/koops/cryptolaw/index.htm>, last visited: 14/11/2002.

Kopelmanas, L. (1937), *Custom as a Means of the Creation of International Law*, British Yearbook of International Law 18: 127-151.

Kumar, R. (1996), *Research Methodology: A step-by-step guide for beginners*, Melbourne: Longman.

Kunz, J.L. (October 1953), *The nature of customary international law*, The American Journal of International Law 47(4): 662-669.

Lachs, M. (1972), *Some Reflections on Substance and Form in International Law*, in W. Friedmann, L. Henkin and O. Lissitzyn (eds.), Transnational Law in a Changing Society. Essays in honor of Philip C. Jessup, New York and London: Columbia University Press.

Lagarde, P. (1983), *Approche critique de la lex mercatoria*, Le droit des relations économiques internationales. Etudes offertes a Berthold Goldman (LITEC).

Lambert, E. (1903), *La Fonction du droit civil comparé*, Paris: Giard & Brière.

Lando, O. (1985), *The Lex Mercatoria in International Commercial Arbitration*, International and Comparative Law Quarterly 34.

Lando, O. (1990), *European Contract Law*, in P. Sarcevic (ed.), International Contracts and Conflicts of Laws. A collection of essays., London: Graham & Trotman/Martinus Nijhoff 1-13.

Lauterpacht, H.S. (1958), *The Development of International Law by the International Court*, rev. edn., New York: Praeger.

Leiner, B.M., Cerf, V.G., Clark, D.D., Kahn, R.E., Kleinrock, L., Lynch, D.C., Postel, J., Roberts, L.G. and Wolff, S., *A Brief History of the Internet*, available at <http://www.isoc.org/internet/history/brief.shtml>, last visited: 23/07/2002.

Leiner, B.M., Cerf, V.G., Clark, D.D., Kahn, R.E., Kleinrock, L., Lynch, D.C., Postel, J., Roberts, L.G. and Wolff, S. (February 1997), *The Past and Future History of the Internet*, Communications of the ACM 40(2): 102-108.

Leslie A. Kelly v. *Arriba Soft Corp.* [1999] Case No. SA CV 99-560 GLT[JW].

Lessig, L. (1999), *Code and other laws of cyberspace*, New York: Basic Books.

Lessig, L. (2001), *The future of ideas. The fate of the commons in a connected world*, New York: Random House.

Lessig, L. (2004), *Free culture*, New York: The Penguin Press.

Lévi-Bruhl, H. (1961), *Sociologie du droit*, Paris: Presses Universitaires de France.

Libertone, D. and Scoppa, A. (2000), *Microsoft Site Server 3.0 Commerce Edition: An E-Commerce Solution*, Upper Saddle River, New Jersey: Prentice Hall PTR.

Lissitzyn, O. (1965), *International Law Today and Tomorrow*, New York: Oceana Publications.

Lloyd, I. (1997), *Information Technology Law*, London: Butterworths.

Lokan, A. (1999), *From recognition to reconciliation: the functions of Aboriginal rights law*, Melbourne University Law Review 23: 65-120.

London Investment Banking Association (17 February 2000), *Proposed directive on certain legal aspects of electronic commerce. A Memorandum on the Common Position by the London Investment Banking Association (LIBA),* London Investment Banking Association, available at <http://www.parliament.the-stationery-office.co.uk/pa/ld199900/ldselect/ldeucom/95/95we40.htm>, last visited: 23/08/2002.

Loshin, P., Vacca, J. and Murphy, P. (2001), *Electronic Commerce: On-line Ordering and Digital Money*, 3rd edn., Hingham, Massachusetts: Charles River Media, Inc.

Lowenfeld, A.F. (1998), *Lex Mercatoria: An Arbitrator's View*, in T.E. Carbonneau (ed.), Lex Mercatoria and Arbitration: A Discussion of the New Law Merchant, Juris Publishing 71-93.

Lucking-Reiley, D. (September 2000), *Auctions on the Internet: What's Being Auctioned, and How?*, Journal of Industrial Economics 48(3): 227-252.

Lucking-Reiley, D. and Spulber, D.F. (Winter 2001), *Business-to-Business Electronic Commerce*, Journal of Economic Perspectives 15(1): 55-68.

MacGibbon, I.C. (1957), *Customary International Law and Acquiescence*, The British Year Book of International Law: 115-145.

Maine, H.S. (1861 reprinted in 1970), *Ancient Law: Its Connection With The Early History Of Society And Its Relation To Modern Ideas.*, Gloucester: Peter Smith.

Mallat, C. (Winter 2000), *Commercial Law In The Middle East: Between Classical Transactions And Modern Business*, American Journal of Comparative Law 48: 81-141.

Malynes, G. (1686), *Consuetudo, vel, Lex mercatoria, or, The ancient law-merchant: in three parts, according to the essentials of traffic: necessary for statesmen, judges, magistrates, temporal and civil lawyers, mint-men, merchants, mariners, and all others negotiating in any part of the world,* The third edition, wherein are inserted the three tracts following, never before printed in any former impression. I. The jurisdiction of the admiralty of England asserted, by Richard Zouch ... II. The ancient sea laws of Oleron, Wisby, and the Hanse-towns, still in force: rendered into English for the use of navigators, by G. Miege ... III. The sovereignty of the British seas, proved by records, history, and the municipal laws of this kingdom, by Sir John Burroughs ... ed., London: Printed for T. Basset ... [and 3 others].

Manjoo, F. (6 December 2001), *Big Stink Over a Simple Link*, Wired.com, available at <http://www.wired.com/news/print/0,1294,48874,00.html>, last visited: 29/09/2002.

Martens, T. and Garrity, B. (4 November 2005), *Consumers sing copy-protection blues*, Reuters, available at <http://today.reuters.com/news/newsarticle.aspx?type=internetNews&storyid=2005-11-05T043623Z_01_FOR516536_RTRUKOC_0_US-SOFTWARE.xml>, last visited: 06/11/2005.

MCC Marble Ceramic v. *Ceramica Nuova D'agostino, S.p.A.,* [29 June 1998] 144 F.3d 1384 (1lth Cir.).

McCarthy, K. (13 June 2003), *Law Society of Scotland pays £10K to 'cybersquatter' for domain*, The Register, available at <http://www.theregister.co.uk/content/6/31184.html>, last visited: 16/06/2003.

McGuire, D. and Krebs, B. (22 October2002), *Attack On Internet Called Largest Ever*, WashingtonPost.com, available at <http://www.washingtonpost.com/wp-dyn/articles/A828-2002Oct22.html>, last visited: 24/10/2002.

McGuire, D. and Krebs, B. (22 October 2002), *New e-Commerce regulations*, ZDNet.com, available at <http://techupdate.zdnet.co.uk/cgi-bin/uk/printerfriendly.cgi?id=2124154&tid=481&b=tu>, last visited: 24/10/2002.

McLaughlin, M., Goldberg, S.B., Ellison, N. and Lucas, J. (1999), *Measuring Internet Audiences: Patrons of an On-Line Art Museum*, in S. Jones (ed.), Doing Internet Research: Critical Issues and Methods for Examining the Net, Thousand Oaks, London, New Delhi: Sage Publications 163-178.

McNeil, K. (1998), *Aboriginal Rights in Canada: From title to land to territorial sovereignty*, Tulsa Journal of Comparative and International Law 5: 253-298.

Meijers, H. (1978), *How is international law made? - The stages of growth of international law and the use of its customary rules*, Netherlands Yearbook of International Law IX: 3-26.

Memorandum And Order Granting Summary Judgment (22 August 2002), *British Telecommunications PLC* v. *Prodigy Communications Corp., 00 Civ. 9451 (CM),* United States District Court Southern District Of New York, available at <http://www.nysd.uscourts.gov/courtweb/pdf/D02NYSC/02-07733.PDF>, last visited: 03/08/2002.

Mendelson, M. (1995), *The subjective element in customary international law*, British Yearbook of International Law: 177-208.

Meron, T. (April 1996), *The continuing role of custom in the formation of international humanitarian law*, American Journal of International Law 90: 238-249.

Metro-Goldwyn-Mayer Studios, Inc v. *Grokster Ltd.* [2005] WL 1499402.

Michaels, R. (2005), *The Re-State-ment of Non-State Law: The State, Choice of Law, and the Challenge from Global Legal Pluralism*, Duke Law School Working Paper Series (Paper 21), available at <http://lsr.nellco.org/cgi/viewcontent.cgi?article=1020&context=duke/fs>, last visited: 02.12.2005.

Microsoft, *About Certificates*, Documentation for IIS 5.0, available at <http://localhost/iishelp/iis/htm/core/iiabcsc.htm>, last visited: 23/04/2003.

Microsoft, *About Encryption*, Documentation for IIS 5.0, available at <http://localhost/iishelp/iis/htm/core/iicrysc.htm>, last visited: 23/04/2003.

Milgrom, P.R., North, D.C. and Weingast, B.R. (March 1990), *The Role of Institutions in the Revival of Trade: The Law Merchant, Private Judges, and the Champagne Fairs*, Economics and Politics 2(1): 1-23.

Milutinovic, V. (2002), *Tutorial*, available at <http://galeb.etf.bg.ac.yu/~vm>, last visited: 26/10/2002.

Mitchell, W. (1904), *An Essay on the Early History of the Law Merchant*, New York: Burt Franklin.

Moser, C.A. and Kalton, G. (1971 (reprinted 1985)), *Survey Methods in Social Investigation*, 2nd edn., Aldershot: Gower.

Muller, J.D. (November 1998), *Selected Developments In The Law Of Cyberspace Payments*, Business Lawyer 54: 403-441.

Murray, A.D. (2000), *Entering into Contracts Electronically: The Real W.W.W.*, in C.W. Lillian Edwards (ed.), Law and The Internet. A Framework for Electronic Commerce, Oxford: Hart Publishing.

Mustill, M. (1987), *The new lex mercatoria: the first twenty-five years, in Liber amicorum for Lord Wilberforce*, in M. Bos, Brownlie, I. (eds.), Oxford: Clarendon Press 149-182.

Mustill, M. (2001), *The Historic Evolution of the Lex Mercatoria Doctrine*. Presentation at One Day Conference: Transnational Business in the Age of Globalisation, Muenster, Central: Center for Transnational Law.

Nachmias, D. and Nachmias, C. (1976), *Research Methods in the Social Sciences*, New York: St. Martin's Press.

Nagpal, R.C. (1983), *Modern Hindu Law*, Lucknow: Eastern Book Company.

Nanda, V.P. and Sinha, S.P. (eds.), (1996), *Hindu Law and Legal Theory*. The International Library of Essays in Law and Legal Theory: Legal Cultures 12. Aldershot, Dartmouth.

Nathenson, I.S. (Fall 1998), *Internet Infoglut and Invisible Ink: Spamdexing Search Engines with Meta Tags*, Part II c.

Netanel, N.W. (March 2000), *Cyberspace Self-Governance: A Skeptical View from Liberal Democratic Theory*, California Law Review 88: 395-498.

Netcraft (2002), *The March 2002 Netcraft Web Server Survey*, available at <http://www.netcraft.com/Survey/index-200203.html>, last visited: 18/08/2002.

Netcraft (2002), *The April 2002 Netcraft Web Server Survey*, available at <http://www.netcraft.com/Survey/index-200204.html>, last visited: 18/08/2002.

Netcraft (2002), *The June 2002 Netcraft Web Server Survey*, available at <http://www.netcraft.com/Survey/index-200206.html>, last visited: 18/08/2002.

Netcraft (2002), *The August 2002 Netcraft Web Server Survey*, available at <http://www.netcraft.com/Survey/index-200208.html>, last visited: 29/08/2002.

Netcraft (2002), *The October 2002 Netcraft Web Server Survey*, available at <http://www.netcraft.com/Survey/index-200210.html>, last visited: 03/11//2002.

Netcraft, *Glossary*, available at <http://www.netcraft.com/https/glossary.html>, last visited: 31/10/2002.

Netscape Communications Corporation (1998), *Introduction to SSL*, available at <http://developer.netscape.com/docs/manuals/security/sslin/index.htm>, last visited: 17/10/2001.

Neuman, W.L. (2000), *Social Research Methods*, 4th edn., Boston: Allyn and Bacon.

New Zealand Law Commission (October 1998), *Report 50: Electronic Commerce Part One: A guide for the legal and business community*, New Zealand, prepared by Law Commission, available at <http://www.lawcom.govt.nz/documents/publications/R50.pdf>, last visited: 23/08/2002.

New Zealand Law Commission (November 1999), *Report 58: Electronic Commerce Part Two: A basic legal framework*, New Zealand, prepared by Law Commission, available at <http://www.lawcom.govt.nz/documents/publications/R58.pdf>, last visited: 23/08/2002.

New Zealand Law Commission (December 2000), *Report 68: Electronic Commerce Part Three: Remaining Issues*, New Zealand, prepared by Law Commission, available at <http://www.lawcom.govt.nz/documents/publications/r68.PDF>, last visited: 23/08/2002.

Nielsen, J. (2000), *Designing Web Usability: The Practice of Simplicity*, Indianapolis, Indiana: New Riders Publishing.

Nielsen, J. (25 July 2005), *Amazon: No Longer the Role Model for E-Commerce Design*, Jakob Nielsen's Alertbox, available at <http://www.useit.com/alertbox/20050725.html>, last visited: 01/08/2005.

Noda, Y. (1976), *Introduction to Japanese Law*, A.H. Angelo (trans.), University of Tokyo Press.

Nussbaum, A. (1954), *A concise history of the law of nations*, rev. edn., New York: The Macmillan Company.

Oba, A. (October 2002), *Islamic Law as Customary Law: The Changing Perspective in Nigeria*, International and Comparative Law Quarterly 51(4): 817-850.

Oda, H. (1999), *Japanese Law*, 2nd edn., Oxford: Oxford University Press.

OECD (29 April 2000), *OECD Model Tax Convention on Income and on Capital*, available at <http://www.oecd.org/pdf/M00005000/M00005346.pdf>, last visited: 22/08/2002.

Office of Indigenous Affairs (1994), *Aboriginal customary laws: report on Commonwealth implementation of the recommendations of the Australian Law Reform Commission*, Canberra: Australian Government Publication Service.

OJ C 376/01 (12.12.1996), *Council Resolution of 21 November 1996 on new policy- priorities regarding the information society*.

OJ L 178/1 (12.11.2000), *Directive 2000/31/EC of the European Parliament and of the Council of 8 June 2000 on certain legal aspects of information society services, in particular electronic commerce, in the Internal Market (Directive on Electronic Commerce).*

OJ L 201/37 (31.07.2002), *Directive 2002/58/EC of the European Parliament and of the Council of 12 July 2002 concerning the processing of personal data and the protection of privacy in the electronic communications sector (Directive on privacy and electronic communications).*

OJ L 204/37 (21.07.1998), *Directive 98/34/EC of the European Parliament and of the Council of 22 June 1998 laying down a procedure for the provision of information in the field of technical standards and regulations.*

OJ L 271/16 (09.10.2002), *Directive 2002/65/EC of the European Parliament and of the Council of 23 September 2002 concerning the distance marketing of consumer financial services and amending Council Directive 90/619/EEC and Directives 97/7/EC and 98/27/EC.*

OJ L 321/41 (06.12.2003), *Council Decision of 17 November 2003 relating to the conclusion on behalf of the European Community of Council of Europe Convention No. 180 on information and legal cooperation on information society services (2003/840/EC).*

OJ L 345/90 (31.12.2003), *Directive 2003/98/EC of the European Parliament and of the Council of 17 November 2003 on the re-use of public sector information.*

OJ L 9/3 (15.01.2003), *Directive 2002/92/EC of the European Parliament and of the Council of 9 December 2002 on insurance mediation.*

OJ L 12/1 (16.01.2001), *Council Regulation (EC), No. 44/2001 of 22 December 2000 on jurisdiction and the recognition and enforcement of judgments in civil and commercial matters.*

OJ L 13/12 (19.01.2000), *Directive 1999/93/EC of the European Parliament and of the Council of 13 December 1999 on a Community framework for electronic signatures.*

OJ L 94/37 (13.04.2005), *Statement by the Commission concerning Article 2 of Directive 2004/48/EC of the European Parliament and of the Council on the enforcement of intellectual property rights (2005/295/EC).*

OJ L 108/7 (24.04.2002), *Directive 2002/19/EC of the European Parliament and of the Council of 7 March 2002 on access to, and interconnection of, electronic communications networks and associated facilities (Access Directive).*

OJ L 108/21 (24.04.2002), *Directive 2002/20/EC of the European Parliament and of the Council of 7 March 2002 on the authorisation of electronic communications networks and services (Authorisation Directive).*

OJ L 108/33 (24.04.2002), *Directive 2002/21/EC of the European Parliament and of the Council of 7 March 2002 on a common regulatory framework for electronic communications networks and services (Framework Directive).*

OJ L 108/51 (24.04.2002), *Directive 2002/22/EC of the European Parliament and of the Council of 7 March 2002 on universal service and users' rights relating to electronic communications networks and services (Universal Service Directive).*

OJ L 134/1 (30.04.2004), *Directive 2004/17/EC of the European Parliament and of the Council of 31 March 2004 coordinating the procurement procedures of entities operating in the water, energy, transport and postal services sectors.*

OJ L 134/114 (30.04.2004), *Directive 2004/18/EC of the European Parliament and of the Council of 31 March 2004 on the coordination of procedures for the award of public works contracts, public supply contracts and public service contracts.*

OJ L 144/19 (04.06.1997), *Directive 97/7/EC of the European Parliament and of the Council of 20 May 1997 on the protection of consumers in respect of distance contracts.*

OJ L 159/16 (02.06.2004), *Directive 2004/48/EC of the European Parliament and of the Council of 29 April 2004 on the enforcement of intellectual property rights.*

OJ L 167/10 (22.06.2001), *Directive 2001/29/EC of the European Parliament and of the Council of 22 May 2001 on the harmonisation of certain aspects of copyright and related rights in the information society.*

OJ L 275/39 (27.10.2000), *Directive 2000/46/EC of the European Parliament and of the Council of 18 September 2000 on the taking up, pursuit of and prudential supervision of the business of electronic money institutions*.

OJ L 281/31 (23.11.1995), *Directive 95/46/EC of the European Parliament and of the Council of 24 October 1995 on the protection of individuals with regard to the processing of personal data and on the free movement of such data*.

Online Banking (2002), *100 Largest Banks (USA),* Online Banking Report: Strategies for the Internet, available at <http://www.onlinebankingreport.com/resources/100.html>, last visited: 01/11/2002.

Oppenheim, L. (1955), *International Law: A Treatise*, 8th edn., London: Longmans.

Orlowski, A. (22/10/2002), *Root server DoS attack slows net*, The Register, available at <http://www.theregister.co.uk/content/6/27731.html>, last visited: 24/10/2002.

Osterloh, H. (2002), *TCP/IP Primer Plus*, Indianapolis, Indiana: Sams Publishing.

PCIJ (1923), *The S.S. 'Wimbledon'*, ser. A, No. 1.

PCIJ (1927), *The Case of the S.S. 'Lotus'*, ser. A, No. 10.

Palmer, G. (April 1992), *New Ways To Make International Environmental Law*, American Journal of International Law 86: 259-283.

Parry, C. (1965), *Sources and Evidences of International Law*, Manchester: Manchester University Press.

Parsons, R.D. (2005-2006), *An Evening with Richard D. Parsons*, Media Law & Policy 15(1): 1-6.

Perdue, E.S. (1996), *Creating Contracts Online*, in T.J. Smedinghoff (ed.), Online Law, the SPA's legal guide to doing business on the Internet, Redding, Mass.: Addison-Wesley.

Perfect 10 v. *Google, Inc.* [2006] Court File No. CV 04-9484 AHM (SHx).

Perritt, H.H., Jr. (1997), *Cyberspace Self-Government: Town Hall Democracy Or Rediscovered Royalism?*, Berkeley Technology Law Journal 12: 413-482.

Perritt, H.H., Jr. (1999-2000), *The Internet is changing the public international legal system*, Kentucky Law Journal 88: 885-955.

Perritt, H.H., Jr. (2001), *Towards A Hybrid Regulatory Scheme For The Internet*, University of Chicago Legal Forum 2001: 215-322.

Pilans v. *van Mierop* 3 Burrr. 1663, 97 Eng. Rep. 1035 (K.B. 1765).

Poggi, C.T. (2000), *Electronic commerce legislation: an analysis of European and American approaches to contract formation*, Virginia Journal of International Law 41(224): 225-277.

Poh-Ling Tan (1997), *Asian legal systems: law, society and pluralism in East Asia*, Sydney: Butterworths.

Poke (1996), *Internet-history*, available at <http://community.silverlink.net/poke/IIP/history.html>, last visited: 08/08/2002.

Polanski, P.P. (2002), *A New Approach to Regulating Internet Commerce: Custom as a Source of Electronic Commerce Law*, Electronic Communications Law Review 9(6): 165-205.

Polanski, P.P. (July 2003), *Custom as a Source of Supranational Internet Commerce Law (PhD Thesis),* The University of Melbourne, available at <http://eprints.unimelb.edu.au/>, last visited: 01/06/2005.

Polanski, P.P. (12 May 2005), *W poszukiwaniu autonomicznego prawa Internetu*. Proceedings of the Conference "Prawo E-Biznesu" organised by Fundacja Wspierania Edukacji Informatycznej PROIDEA, Kraków, Poland available at <http://www.proidea.org.pl/pii/>.

Polanski, P.P. (6-8 June 2005), *Common practices in the electronic commerce and their legal significance*, Proceedings of the 18th Bled eCommerce Conference "eIntegration in Action", Bled, Slovenia.

Polanski, P.P. (2005), *Information Society and the Internet Law Merchant*, in A. Łazowski, R. Ostrihansky (eds.), Współczesne wyzwania europejskiej przestrzeni prawnej, Warszawa: Zakamycze.

Polanski, P.P. (2006), *Some remarks on the scope of application of the newest Convention on electronic communications*, in: E. Schweighofer, D. Liebvald, M. Drachsler, A. Geist (eds.) e-Staat und e-Wirtschaft aus rechtlicher Sicht. Tagungsband des 9. Internationalen Rechtsinformatik Symposiums IRIS 2006, Stuttgart: Boorberg, 426-433.

Polanski, P.P. (2006), *Fundamental Rights in Cyberspace and Internet Customary Law*. Proceedings of the First International Conference on Legal, Security and Privacy Issues in IT (LSPI), (30 April - 2 May 2006), Hamburg, Germany, CompLex (Computer Lex).

Polanski, P.P. (2006), *Towards a supranational Internet law*. Proceedings of the First International Conference on Legal, Security and Privacy Issues in IT (LSPI), (30 April - 2 May 2006), Hamburg, Germany, CompLex (Computer Lex), reproduced in Journal of International Commercial Law and Technology 1(1): 1-9.

Polanski, P. P. (2006) *International Electronic Contracting in the newest UN Convention*, Proceedings of the International Conference on Business, Law and Technology Issues, Copenhagen, Denmark.

Polanski, P. P. (5-7 June 2006) *Convention on e-contracting: the rise of international law of electronic commerce?* Proceedings of the 19th Bled eCommerce Conference 'eValues', Bled, Slovenia

Polanski, P.P. and Johnston, R.B. (7-10 January 2002), *International Custom as a Source of Law in Global Electronic Commerce*, Proceedings of the 35th Hawaii International Conference on System Sciences, Big Island, Hawaii.

Polanski, P.P. and Johnston, R.B. (2002), *Potential of Custom in Overcoming Legal Uncertainty in Global Electronic Commerce*, Journal of Information Technology Theory and Application 4(2): 1- 16.

Post, D.G. (October 1996), *Anarchy, State, and the Internet: An Essay on Law-Making in Cyberspace (article 3),* Journal of Online Law, available at <http://www.wm.edu/law/publications/jol/articles/post.shtml>, last visited: 30/08/2002.

Post, D.G. (2000), *What Larry doesn't get: code, law, and liberty in cyberspace*, Stanford Law Review 52: 1439-1459.

Potter, P.B. (1992), *The Economic Contract Law of China. Legitimation and Contract Autonomy in the PRC*, Seattle and London: University of Washington Press.

Poullet, Y. (2004), *A European Internet Law?*, in Jurgen Taeger and A. Wiebe (eds.), Informatik-Wirtschaft-Recht. Regulierung in der Wissensgesellschaft. Festschrift fur Wolfgang Kilian zum 65. Geburstag, Baden Baden: Nomos Verlagsgesellschaft 533-559.

Prins, J.E.J. (June 2003), *Consumers, Liability, and the Online World*, Information & Communication Technology Law 12(2): 143-164.

Puchta, G. F. (1928), *Das Gewohnheitsrecht*.

Quadri, R. (1963), *Diritto internazionale pubblico*, IV edn., Palermo: G. Priulla Editore.

Quirk, P. and Forder, J. (2003), *Electronic commerce and the law*, 2nd edn., Singapore: John Wiley & Sons Australia, Ltd.

Radwański, Z. (2004), *Prawo cywilne - część ogólna*, 7th edn., Warszawa: C.H. Beck.

Ramberg, C.H. (2001), *The ecommerce directive and formation of contract in a comparative perspective*, European Law Review 26(5): 429-450.

Rappa, M. (2002), *Business models on the Web*, available at <http://digitalenterprise.org/models/models.html>, last visited: 02/08/2002.

Rayport, J.F. and Jaworski, B.J. (2002), *Introduction to e-Commerce*, International Edition: McGraw-Hill/Irwin marketspaceU.

Reidenberg, J.R. (Summer 1996), *Governing Networks and Rule-making in Cyberspace. The Randolph W. Thrower Symposium. Legal Issues in Cyberspace: Hazards on the Information Superhighway*, Emory Law Journal 45: 911-930.

Reidenberg, J.R. (February 1998), *Lex Informatica: The Formulation of Information Technology Rules Through Information Technology*, Texas Law Review 76(3): 553.

Rescorla, E. (2000), *SSL and TLS: Designing and Building Secure Systems*, New York: Addison-Wesley.

Reuters (1 October 2002), *House votes to limit online gambling*, News.com, available at <http://news.com.com/2102-1023-960377.html>, last visited: 10/10/2002.

Reuters (5 October 2002), *Russian hacker gets 3-year sentence*, News.com, available at <http://news.com.com/2102-1001-960933.html>, last visited: 07/10/2002.

Rheingold, H. (2000), *The Virtual Community: Homesteading On The Electronic Frontier*, rev. edn., Cambridge, Mass: The MIT Press.

Ridruejo, J.A.P. (1998), *Le droit international à la veille du vingt et unième siècle: normes, faits et valeurs*, Recueil des Cours de l'Académie de Droit International 274: 9-308.

Rivier, A. (1896), *Principes du Droit de Gens*.

Roberts, A.E. (October 2001), *Traditional and modern approaches to customary international law: A reconciliation*, The American Journal of International Law 95(4): 757-791.

Roberts, L.G. (October 1967), *Multiple Computer Networks and Intercomputer Communication*, Proceedings of the ACM symposium on Operating System Principles, Gatlinburg, Tennessee: 3.1-3.6.

Robinson, O.F. (1997), *The Sources of Roman Law. Problems and methods for ancient historians*, London, New York: Routledge.

Robinson, O.F., Fergus, T.D. and Gordon, W.M. (1985), *An Introduction to European Legal History*, Abingdon, Oxon.: Professional Books Limited.

Roscoe, J.T. (1975), *Fundamental Research Statistics for the Behavioural Sciences*, 2nd edn., New York: Holt Rinehart & Winston.

Rosenne, S. (2001), *The Perplexities of Modern International Law: General Course on Public International Law*, Recueil des Cours de l'Académie de Droit International 291: 1-471.

Rosnow, R.L. and Rosenthal, R. (1996), *Beginning Behavioural Research: A Conceptual Primer*, 2nd edn., Englewood Cliffs, New Jersey: Prentice Hall.

Rosoff, M. (18 February 2002), *Commerce Server 2002 Showcases .NET*, Directions on Microsoft, available at <http://www.directionsonmicrosoft.com/sample/DOMIS/update/2002/03mar/0302cs2sn.htm>, last visited: 4/11/2002.

Rouland, N. (1994), *Legal Anthropology*, P.G. Planel (trans.), London: The Athlone Press.

Rouland, N. (2001), *Custom and the Law*, in P. de Deckker and J.Y. Faberon (eds.), Custom and the Law, Canberra, ACT: Asia Pacific Press at Australian National University.

RSA Security (19 January 1999), *RSA Code-Breaking Contest Again Won by Distributed.Net and Electronic Frontier Foundation (EFF)*, available at <http://www.rsasecurity.com/company/news/releases/pr.asp?doc_id=462>, last visited: 01/05/2003.

RSA Security *SSL Basics for Internet Users*, available at <http://www.rsasecurity.com/standards/ssl/basics.html>, last visited: 01/05/2003.

RSA Security (14 February 1997), *Swiss-based Ph.D. Student Solves 48-bit Key in RSA Data Security's Secret-Key Challenge*, available at <http://www.rsasecurity.com/company/news/releases/pr.asp?doc_id=638>, last visited: 01/05/2003.

Russell, S.J. and Norvig, P. (1995), *Artificial intelligence: a modern approach*, Englewood Cliffs, N.J.: Prentice Hall.

Sacco, R. (Summer 1995), *Mute law*, American Journal of Comparative Law 43: 455-467.

Safjan, M. (2005), *Refleksje o roli zwyczaju*, in A. Nowicka (ed.), Prawo prywatne czasu przemian, Poznań: Wydawnictwo Naukowe PWN 79-104.

Scheleff, L. (2000), *The future of tradition: customary law, common law and legal pluralism*, London, Portland: Frank Cass.

Schmitthoff, C.M. (1988), *Clive M. Schmitthoff's Selected Essays on International Trade Law*, London: Stevens & Sons.

Schneier, B. (1996), *Applied cryptography: protocols, algorithms, and source code in C*, 2nd edn., New York: Wiley.

Schneier, B. (1997), *Cryptography Primer*, in B. Schneier and D. Banisar (eds.), The Electronic Privacy Papers, New York: John Wiley & Sons, Inc. 258-263.

Scott, S.P. (1973), *The Civil Law including The Twelve Tables, The Institutes of Gaius, The Rules of Ulpian, The Opinions of Paulus, The Enactments of Justinian, and The Constitutions of Leo*, New York: AMS Press.

SECPay *FAQ's technical*, available at <http://www.secpay.com/tech.html>, last visited: 22/04/2003.

Serjeant, R.B. (1991), *Customary and Shari'ah law in Arabian society*, Hampshire: Gower Pub. Co.

Shaw, M.N. (1997), *International Law*, 4th edn., Cambridge, New York, Melbourne: Cambridge University Press.

Shipchandler, S. (2000), *The Wild Wild Web: Non-Regulation as the Answer to the Regulatory Question*, Cornell International Law Journal 33: 435.

Simma, B. and Alston, P. (1992), *The Sources of Human Rights Law: Custom, Jus Cogens, and General Principles*, Australian Yearbook of International Law 12: 82-108.

Simpson, J.A. and Weiner, E.S.C. (eds.) (1989), *The Oxford English Dictionary*. Oxford, Clarendon Press.

Sinrod, E.J. (13 September 2002), *E-Legal: A Bill to Combat P2P Copyright Infringement*, Law.com, available at <http://www.law.com/jsp/printerfriendly.jsp?c=LawArticle&t=PrinterFriendlyArticle&cid=1029171603269>, last visited: 22/08/2002.

Slouka, Z. J. (1969), *International custom and the continental shelf. A study in the dynamics of customary rules of international law*, The Hague: Martinus Nijhoff Publishers.

Smith, G.J.H. (1996), *Internet Law and Regulation*, London: FT Law and Tax.

Smith, M. (June 1903), *Customary law. I.*, Political Science Quarterly 18(2): 256-281.

Societe Civile de Producteurs Phonographiques (S.C.P.P.) v. *Anthony G.* [8 December 2005] Case No. 0504090091

Sorkin, D.E. (2002), *Don't link to us: Stupid linking policies*, available at <http://www.dontlink.com/>, last visited: 22/08/2002.

Sőrensen, M. (1960), *Principes de droit international public: Cours général*, Recueil des Cours de l'Académie de Droit International 101(III): 1-254.

St. Thomas Aquinas (1989), *Summa Theologiae. A concise translation*, T. McDermott (ed.), London: Eyre and Spottiswoode.

Starke, J.G. (1994), *Starke's international law*, I.A. Shearer (ed.), 11th edn., London: Butterworths.

Stefik (1997), *Shifting the Possible: How digital property rights challenge us to rethink digital publishing*, Berkeley Technology Law Journal 12(1): 137-159.

Stelmachowski, A. (1998), *Zarys teorii prawa cywilnego*, Warszawa: Wydawnictwa Prawnicze PWN.

Stelmachowski, A. (2005), *Problemy legislacji*, in A. Nowicka (ed.), Prawo prywatne czasu przemian, Poznań: Wydawnictwo Naukowe PWN 105-111.

Stern, B. (2001), *Custom at the heart of international law* (trans. M. Byers, A. Denise), Duke Journal of International & Comparative Law 11: 89-108.

Strahilevitz, L.J. (May 2003), *Charismatic Code, Social Norms, and the Emergence of Cooperation on the File-Swapping Networks*, Virginia Law Review 89(3): 505.

Strupp, K. (1934), *Les Règles Générales du Droit de la Paix*, Recueil des Cours de l'Académie de Droit International de La Haye 47(1): 263-595.

Studnicki, F. (1949), *Działanie zwyczaju handlowego w zakresie zobowiązań z umowy*, Kraków: Polska Akademia Umiejętności.

Sturgeon, W. (19 March 2003), *Amazon fails to honour Pocket PC bargain*, silicon.com26/03.2003.

Sturgeon, W. (20 March 2003), *Amazon.co.uk breaks iPaq news to customers but lawyers still aren't convinced*, silicon.com, available at <http://www.silicon.com/news/500022/1/3396.html>, last visited: 26/03/2003.

Sturgeon, W. (28 April 2003), *Thai Airways online sales in legal mess*, ZDNet, available at <http://news.zdnet.co.uk/cgi-bin/uk/printerfriendly.cgi?id=2133949&tid=269>, last visited: 12/05/2003.

Suy, E. (1962), *Les actes juridiques unilatéraux en droit international public*, Paris: Librairie générale de droit et de jurisprudence.

Symantec (9 September 2002), *What is the difference between viruses, worms, and Trojans?*, available at <http://service4.symantec.com/SUPPORT/nav.nsf/docid/1999041209131106>, last visited: 16/09/2002.

Taniguchi (1964), *La loi et la coutume au Japon*, in Etudes juridiques offertes à Julliot de La Morandière, Paris: Librairie Dalloz.

Tanistry case [1608] Dav. 29.

The Associated Press (30 March 2003), *ACLU cyberchief worried about privacy*, CNN.com, available at <http://www.cnn.com/2003/TECH/ptech/03/30/profile.steinhardt.ap/index.html>, last visited: 01/04/2003.

The Law Reform Commission (1986), *The recognition of aboriginal customary laws. Report No. 31, Vol. 1*, Canberra: Australian Government Publishing Service.

The New Zealand Herald (10 September 2002), *Law says no to internet wine sales*, The New Zealand Herald Online, available at <http://www.nzherald.co.nz/storyprint.cfm?storyID=2351227>, last visited: 10/09/2002.

The Paquete Habana (1900), *175 US 677*

Thirlway, H.W.A. (1972), *International Customary Law and Codification*, Leiden: A.W. Sijthoff.

Timmers, P. (1999), *Electronic commerce: strategies and models for business-to-business trading*, Chichester: John Wiley & Sons, Ltd.

timothy (7 October 2002), *Internet Censorship In Spain*, Slashdot.org, available at <http://yro.slashdot.org/yro/02/10/07/2235243.shtml?tid=153>, last visited: 10/10/2002.

timothy (23 November 2004), *Porn Site Sues Google Over Linked Images*, Slashdot, available at <http://yro.slashdot.org/yro/04/11/23/0356223.shtml?tid=123&tid=217&tid=95&tid=1>, last visited: 27/08/2005.

Tomuschat, C. (1999), *International Law: Ensuring the Survival of Mankind on the Eve of a New Century*, Recueil des Cours de l'Académie de Droit International 281: 324-334.

Tovey, M. (2001), *Security of eCommerce Systems*, A Netcraft White Paper, available at <http://www.netcraft.com/security/whitepaper.html>, last visited: 10/12/2001.

Trakman, L.E. (1983), *The Law Merchant: The Evolution of Commercial Law*, Littleton: Fred B, Rothman & Co.

Trakman, L.E. (Summer 2003), *From the Medieval Law Merchant to E-Merchant Law*, University of Toronto Law Review LIII(3),

Triepel, H. (1923), *Les Rapports entre le Droit Interne et le Droit International*, Recueil des Cours de l'Académie de Droit International 1: 77-121.

TRUSTe, *TRUSTe Guidance on Model Web Site Disclosures*, Truste.com, available at <http://www.truste.org/docs/Model_Privacy_Policy_Disclosures.doc>, last visited: 02.12.2005.

TRUSTe, *The TRUSTe White Paper: Building Trust Online: TRUSTe, Privacy and Self Governance*, available at <http://www.truste.org/about/truste%20white%20paperfinal.doc or http://www.truste.org/about/truste/about_whitepaper.html>, last visited: 31/08/2002.

Tunkin, G.I. (1961), *Remarks On the Juridical Nature of Customary Norms of International Law*, California Law Review 49(3): 419-430.

Tunkin, G.I. (1974), *Theory of International Law*, W.E. Buthler (trans.), Cambridge, Massachusetts: Harvard University Press.

UN/CEFACT (May 2000), *Electronic Commerce Agreement; Recommendation No. 31, first edition, adopted by the United Nations Centre for Trade Facilitation and Electronic Business (UN/CEFACT), Geneva, Source: ECE/TRADE/257*, United Nations Centre for Trade Facilitation and Electronic Business, available at <http://www.unece.org/cefact/rec/rec31en.htm>, last visited: 10/09/2002.

UN/CEFACT *The Model Interchange Agreement for the International Commercial use of Electronic Data Interchange*, United Nations Centre for Trade Facilitation and Electronic Business, available at <http://www.unece.org/cefact/rec/rec26en1.htm>, last visited: 10/09/2002.

UNCITRAL (1980), *United Nations Convention on Contracts for the International Sale of Goods*, adopted in Vienna, available at <http://www.uncitral.org/english/texts/sales/CISG.htm>, last visited: 24/08/2002.

UNCITRAL (1996), *General Assembly Resolution 51/162 of 16 December 1996 - UNCITRAL Model Law on Electronic Commerce with Guide to Enactment with additional Art. 5 bis as adopted in 1998*, available at <http://www.uncitral.org/english/texts/electcom/ml-ecomm.htm>, last visited: 23/08/2002.

UNCITRAL (2001), *General Assembly Resolution 56/80 - Model Law on Electronic Signatures with Guide to Enactment*, available at <http://www.uncitral.org/english/texts/electcom/ml-elecsig-e.pdf>, last visited: 23/08/2002.

UNCITRAL (12 August 2004), *ICC eTerms 2004. ICC Guide to electronic contracting. (A/CN.9/WG.IV/WP.113),* available at <http://www.uncitral.org>, last visited: 12/12/2004.

UNCITRAL (11-22 October 2004), *A/CN.9/571 - Report of the Working Group on Electronic Commerce on the work of its forty-fourth session*, Vienna, available at <http://daccessdds.un.org/doc/UNDOC/GEN/V04/589/92/PDF/V0458992.pdf?Open Element>, last visited: 01/02/2006.

UNCITRAL (23 November 2005), *General Assembly adopts new Convention on the Use of Electronic Communications in International Contracting*, available at <http://www.un.org/News/Press/docs/2005/ga10424.doc.htm>, last visited: 03.12.2005.

UNCITRAL Working Group IV (Electronic Commerce), (2005), *A/60/17 - Report of the United Nations Commission on International Trade Law on the work of its thirty-eighth session, 4-15 July 2005*, United Nations, available at <http://daccessdds.un.org/doc/UNDOC/GEN/V05/868/63/PDF/V0586863.pdf?OpenElement>, last visited: 05/11/2005.

UNIDROIT (1994), *UNIDROIT Principles of International Commercial Contracts*, available at <http://www.unidroit.org/english/principles/princ.htm>, last visited: 24/08/2002.

UNIDROIT (2004), *UNIDROIT Principles of International Commercial Contracts 2004*, available at <http://www.unidroit.org/english/principles/contracts/principles2004/blackletter2004.pdf>, last visited: 05/11/2005.

United Nations (23 November 2005), *United Nations Convention on the Use of Electronic Communications in International Contracts*, A/60/515, available at <http://www.uncitral.org/pdf/english/texts/electcom/2005Convention.pdf>, last visited: 03.12.2005.

United Nations Conference on International Organization at San Francisco (26 June 1945), *Charter of the United Nations*, available at <http://www.icj-cij.org/icjwww/ibasicdocuments>, last visited: 01/11/2002.

United Nations Conference on International Organization at San Francisco (26 June 1945), *Statute of the International Court of Justice*, available at <http://www.icj-cij.org/icjwww/ibasicdocuments/ibasictext/ibasicstatute.htm>, last visited: 23/08/2002.

Universal Music Australia Pty Ltd v. *Sharman License Holdings Ltd* [2005] FCA 1242 (5 September 2005).

Valles, C.M. (2003 Supp), *eCommerce in International and Regional Organizations*, in M.S. Shapo and A.N. Weber (eds.), International eCommerce: Business and Legal Issues.

van Caenegem, R.C. (1992), *An historical introduction to private law*, D.E.L. Johnston (trans.), Cambridge [England]; New York: Cambridge University Press.

van der Hoff, S. (5 July 2002), *Digital Signature Law Survey*, available at <http://rechten.uvt.nl/simone/ds-lawsu.htm>, last visited: 14/11/2002.

van Hoof, G.J.H. (1983), *Rethinking the sources of international law*, Deventer: Kluwer.

Vangelowa, L. (19 June 2002), *A Global Audience, a World of Worries? Australian Court's Ruling in Libel Case Could Have a Chilling Effect on Web Publications*, Washingtonpost.com, available at <http://www.washingtonpost.com/ac2/wp-dyn/A5695-2002Jun18?language =printer>, last visited: 10/09/2002.

Veen, J. (2001), *The Art & Science of Web Design*, Indianapolis, Indiana: New Riders.

Verdross, A. (1955), *Völkerrecht*, 3rd edn., Wien: Springer.

Verisign, *128-bit SSL Global Server IDs: Frequently Asked Questions*, available at <http://www.verisign.com/products/site/faq/128-bit.html#qualify3>, last visited: 29/10/2002.

Verisign (18 May 1998), *Lotus Joins With Verisign To Provide Secure Global Communications And Commerce With Strongest Encryption Approved By The U.S. Government*, Verisign Corporate News, available at <http://www.verisign.com/corporate/news/1998/lotus.html>, last visited: 01/05/2003.

Verisign (2002), *Securing Your Website for Business: A step by step guide for secure online commerce*, available at <http://www.verisign.com/resources/gd/secureBusiness/secureBusiness.html>, last visited: 29/10/2002.

Villiger, M.E. (1997), *Customary International Law and Treaties. A Manual on the Theory and Practice of the Interrelation of Sources*, 2nd edn., The Hague, London, Boston: Kluwer Law International.

Virally, M. (1968), *The Sources of International Law*, in M. Sőrensen (ed.), Manual of Public International Law, London: Macmillian 116-174.

von Mehren, A.T. (ed.) (1963), *Law in Japan. The Legal Order in a Changing Society*. Cambridge, Massachusetts, Harvard University Press.

von Savigny, F.K. (1840), *Vom Beruf Unserer Zeit fur Gesetzgebung und Rechtswissenschaft*, 3rd edn.

von Savigny, F.K. (1840-49), *System des Heutigen Romischen Rechts*.

W3C (5 May 1999), *Web Content Accessibility Guidelines 1.0*, available at <http://www.w3.org/TR/WCAG10/>, last visited: 02.12.2005.

W3C (2000), *About the World Wide Web Consortium (W3C)*, available at <http://www.w3c.org/Consortium/>, last visited: 08/08/2002.

Walden, R.M. (1977), *The Subjective Element in the Formation of Customary International Law*, Israel Law Review 12(3): 344-364.

Waldock, H. (1962), *General Course of International Law*, Recueil des Cours de l'Académie de Droit International 106(II): 1-251.

Weber, M. (1967), *Max Weber on Law in Economy and Society*, M. Rheinstein (ed.), E. Shils and M. Rheinstein (trans.), New York: Simon and Schuster.

Weber, R.H. (2001), *Does Intellectual Property Law Become Unimportant in Cyberspace?*, International Journal of Law and Information Technology 9(2): 171-185.

Wei Zhu v. *Merrill Lynch* [2002] HSBC, BCPC 0535.

Weitzenboeck, E.M. (2001), *Electronic Agents and the Formation of Contracts*, International Journal of Law and Information Technology 9(3): 204-234.

Wells Fargo (2002), *Browser Frequently Asked Questions*, available at <http://www.wellsfargo.com/per/wfonline/help/browser_faq.jhtml?_requestid=73348>, last visited: 01/11/2002.

Wells Fargo (2002), *Online Security Guarantee*, available at <http://www.wellsfargo.com/security/security.jhtml>, last visited: 01/11/2002.

Wells Fargo (2002), *Online Security Guarantee: Frequently Asked Questions*, available at <http://www.wellsfargo.com/security/security_qa.jhtml>, last visited: 01/11/2002.

Wellwood, J.W. (1975), *Custom and usage*, in Lord Hailsham of St. Marylebone (ed.), Halsbury's Laws of England, London: Butterworths.

Westlake, J. (1910), *International Law*, 2nd edn., Cambridge: Cambridge University Press.

WGIG (June 2005), *Report of the Working Group on Internet Governance*, Château de Bossey, available at <http://www.wgig.org/docs/WGIGREPORT.doc>, last visited: 16/09/2005.

WGIG (2005), *Tunis Agenda for the Information Society. Second Phase of the WSIS (16-18 November 2005, Tunis),* WSIS-05/TUNIS/DOC/6 (rev. 1), available at <http://www.itu.int/wsis/docs2/tunis/off/6rev1.doc>, last visited: 30/12/2005.

Whitcomb, D. (3 November 2005), *US charges 'Botmaster' in unique computer crime*, Reuters, available at <http://today.reuters.com/news/newsArticle.aspx?type=domesticNews&storyID=2005-11-03T235148Z_01_MOL385869_RTRUKOC_0_US-CRIME-BOTMASTER.xml&archived=False>, last visited: 08.11.2005.

White House (1 July 1997), *A Framework for Global Electronic Commerce: Policy statement issued by President Clinton and Vice-President Al Gore*, White House, available at <http://www.cmcnyls.edu/Papers/WHGIIFra.HTM or http://www.w3.org/TR/NOTE-framework-970706.html#Annotated%20Version>, last visited: 23/08/2002.

Wikipedia (2006), *Peer-to-peer*, Wikipedia, available at <http://en.wikipedia.org/wiki/Peer-to-peer>, last visited: 25/02/3005.

Williams, J.F.S. (1939), *Aspects of Modern International Law: An Essay*, London, New York, Toronto: Oxford University Press.

Winn, J.K. (November 1998), *Regulating The Use Of The Internet In Securities Markets*, Business Lawyer(54): 443-458.

WIPO, *Internet Domain Name Disputes: Some Questions and Answers*, available at <http://www.wipo.org/about-ip/en/index.html?wipo_content_frame=/about-ip/en/studies/index.html>, last visited: 10/09/2002.

WIPO (1971), *Paris Act of July 24, 1971, as amended on September 28, 1979 of Berne Convention for the Protection of Literary and Artistic Works of September 9, 1886*, available at <http://www.wipo.int/clea/docs/en/wo/wo001en.htm>, last visited: 14/08/2002.

WIPO (1996), *Copyright Treaty (adopted in Geneva on December 20, 1996),* available at <http://www.wipo.int/clea/docs/en/wo/wo033en.htm>, last visited: 18/08/2002.

WIPO (1996), *Performances and Phonograms Treaty (adopted in Geneva on December 20, 1996),* available at <http://www.wipo.int/clea/docs/en/wo/wo034en.htm>, last visited: 18/08/2002.

WIPO (30 April 1999), *The Management of Internet Names and Addresses: Intellectual Property Issues*, WIPO Internet Domain Name Process, available at <http://ecommerce.wipo.int/domains>, last visited: 01/07/2002.

WIPO (May 2000), *Primer On Electronic Commerce And Intellectual Property Issues*, WIPO, available at <http://ecommerce.wipo.int>, last visited: 10/09/2002.

WIPO (2005), *WIPO Overview of WIPO Panel Views on Selected UDRP Questions*, Arbitration and Mediation Centre, available at <http://arbiter.wipo.int/domains/search/overview/index.html>, last visited: 09/05/2005.

WIPO Arbitration and Mediation Centre (24 May 2005), *Societe Air France* v. *Virtual Dates, Inc. Case No. D2005-0168*, Administrative Panel Decision, available at <http://arbiter.wipo.int/domains/decisions/html/2005/d2005-0168.html>, last visited: 10/06/2005.

Wolfke, K. (1993), *Custom in Present International Law*, 2nd edn., Dordrecht, Boston, London: Martinus Nijhoff Publishers.

Wolfke, K. (1993), *Some Persistent Controversies Regarding Customary International Law*, Netherlands Yearbook of International Law XXIV: 1-16.

Wooldridge, M. and Jennings, N.R. (June 1995), *Intelligent Agents: Theory and Practice*, Knowledge Engineering Review 10(2): 115-152.

WSIS (12 December 2003), *Declaration of Principles. Building the Information Society: a global challenge in the new Millennium*, Document WSIS-03/GENEVA/DOC/4-E, available at <http://www.itu.int/wsis/docs/geneva/official/dop.html>, last visited: 16/09/2005.

WSIS (12 December 2003), *Plan of Action*, Document WSIS-03/GENEVA/DOC/5-E, available at <http://www.itu.int/wsis/docs/geneva/official/poa.html>, last visited: 16/09/2005.

WTO (15 April 1994), *Annex 1c: Agreement On Trade-Related Aspects Of Intellectual Property Rights (TRIPS), to Agreement Establishing World Trade Organisation*, available at <http://www.wto.org/english/docs_e/legal_e/27-trips.pdf>, last visited: 10/09/2002.

Zakon H'obbes', R. *Hobbes' Internet Timeline v5.6*, available at <http://www.zakon.org/robert/internet/timeline/HIT.html>, last visited: 23/07/2002.

Zilberman, I. (1996), *Palestynian customary law in the Jerusalem area*, Catholic University Law Review 45: 795-811.

Zweigert, K. and Kötz, H. (1998), *An Introduction to Comparative Law*, T. Weir (trans.), 3rd edn., Oxford: Clarendon Press.

INDEX

INFORMATION TECHNOLOGY & LAW SERIES

1. E-Government and its Implications for Administrative Law – Regulatory Initiatives in France, Germany, Norway and the United States (The Hague: T·M·C·ASSER PRESS, 2002)
   Editor: J.E.J. Prins / ISBN 90-6704-141-6
2. Digital Anonymity and the Law – Tensions and Dimensions (The Hague: T·M·C·ASSER PRESS, 2003)
   Editors: C. Nicoll, J.E.J. Prins and M.J.M. van Dellen / ISBN 90-6704-156-4
3. Protecting the Virtual Commons – Self-Organizing Open Source and Free Software Communities and Innovative Intellectual Property Regimes (The Hague: T·M·C·ASSER PRESS, 2003)
   Authors: R. van Wendel de Joode, J.A. de Bruijn and M.J.G. van Eeten / ISBN 90-6704-159-9
4. IT Support and the Judiciary – Australia, Singapore, Venezuela, Norway, The Netherlands and Italy (The Hague: T·M·C·ASSER PRESS, 2004)
   Editors: A. Oskamp, A.R. Lodder and M. Apistola / ISBN 90-6704-168-8
5. Electronic Signatures – Authentication Technology from a Legal Perspective (The Hague: T·M·C·ASSER PRESS, 2004)
   Author: M.H.M. Schellekens / ISBN 90-6704-174-2
6. Virtual Arguments – On the Design of Argument Assistants for Lawyers and Other Arguers (The Hague: T·M·C·ASSER PRESS, 2004)
   Author: B. Verheij / ISBN 90-6704-190-4
7. Reasonable Expectations of Privacy? – Eleven Country Reports on Camera Surveillance and Workplace Privacy (The Hague: T·M·C·ASSER PRESS, 2005)
   Editors: S. Nouwt, B.R. de Vries and J.E.J. Prins / ISBN 90-6704-198-X
8. Unravelling the Myth Around Open Source Licences – An Analysis from a Dutch and European Law Perspective (The Hague: T·M·C·ASSER PRESS, 2006)
   Authors: L. Guibault and O. van Daalen / ISBN 90-6704-214-5
9. Starting Points for ICT Regulation – Deconstructing Prevalent Policy One-Liners (The Hague: T·M·C·ASSER PRESS, 2006)
   Editors: B-J. Koops, M. Lips, J.E.J. Prins and M. Schellekens / ISBN 90-6704-216-1
10. Regulating Spam – A European Perspective after the Adoption of the E-Privacy Directive (The Hague: T·M·C·ASSER PRESS, 2006)
    Author: L.F. Asscher / ISBN 90-6704-220-X
11. Cybercrime and Jurisdiction – A Global Survey (The Hague: T·M·C·ASSER PRESS, 2006)
    Editors: B-J. Koops and Susan W. Brenner / ISBN 90-6704-221-8
12. Coding Regulation – Essays on the Normative Role of Information Technology (The Hague: T·M·C·ASSER PRESS, 2006)
    Editors: E.J. Dommering and L.F. Asscher / ISBN 90-6704-229-3
13. Customary Law of the Internet – In the Search for a Supranational Cyberspace Law (The Hague: T·M·C·ASSER PRESS, 2007)
    Author: P.P. Polánski / ISBN 90-6704-230-7